# Report

of the

# Adjutant General

of the

## State of Kentucky

# Mexican War Veterans

Printed by Authority of the
Legislature of Kentucky

Heritage Books
2024

# HERITAGE BOOKS
*AN IMPRINT OF HERITAGE BOOKS, INC.*

### Books, CDs, and more—Worldwide

For our listing of thousands of titles see our website
at
www.HeritageBooks.com

A Facsimile Reprint
Published 2024 by
HERITAGE BOOKS, INC.
Publishing Division
5810 Ruatan Street
Berwyn Heights, MD 20740

Indexed by Jackie Couture

Originally published
Frankfort, Kentucky:
Capital Office, John D. Woods,
Public Printer and Binder
1889

— Publisher's Notice —
In reprints such as this, it is often not possible to remove
blemishes from the original. We feel the contents of this
book warrant its reissue despite these blemishes and
hope you will agree and read it with pleasure.

International Standard Book Number
Paperbound: 978-0-7884-4844-7

# ADJUTANT GENERAL'S OFFICE.

FRANKFORT, KENTUCKY, January 2, 1889.

*To His Excellency, S. B. BUCKNER, Governor of Kentucky:*

SIR: I have the honor to submit the accompanying roster of the officers and soldiers of the Mexican War from Kentucky, prepared in a highly creditable manner, by Col. S. S. ANDERSON, himself a veteran of that war, pursuant to an act of the General Assembly, approved April 27th, 1888. This act of justice to our veterans of the war with Mexico, though tardy and inadequate, will, I am sure, command the hearty approval of our people, as it will place within easy reach the names, together with organizations in which they severally served, of many Kentuckians whose prowess in that conflict shed additional lustre upon the name of our State, and whose valor assisted, in no small degree, in winning for our common country an empire in area of territory and a Golconda in wealth. The subsequent career during our late deplorable civil war of many of Kentucky's sons who distinguished themselves in Mexico was the ripening of the fame of which their gallantry on foreign soil was but the token; for in scanning the pages of this roster, we find the names of many subalterns of the Mexican War, who rose to high command during the late war, and who justified the confidence reposed in their leadership on many a hard fought field. Upon the Confederate side were Breckinridge, Preston, Hanson, Williams, Morgan, Marshall, Moss and others, who exhibited in later life the same fiery courage and disregard of danger which characterized their youthful valor on the plains and heights of Mexico; while arrayed on the side of the Union were Crittenden, Rousseau, Ward, Garrard, Wolford, Fry, Hobson, Shackleford, the Landrums and others, who battled with equal heroism for the cause of their choice, and all proved themselves worthy of their State, which has adopted this method of preserving their names, and in part their fame, for the use of the future historian of the stirring times in which they lived, and the gallant part borne by them therein. As for Clay, McKee, Willis, and their brave comrades who sealed our national victory with their lives, their fame has been perpetuated in immortal verse by their fond companion in arms, and Kentucky's High Priest of song, the brilliant O'Hara, and "Glory guards with solemn round" their silent bivouac, while their renown is the rich heritage of Kentucky.

Very respectfully,

SAM E. HILL, *Adjutant General.*

## MEXICAN WAR VETERANS.

# ROLL OF THE FIELD AND STAFF FIRST REGIMENT

| No. of each grade | Name | Rank | Enrolled | Mustered In When | Mustered In Where | Period | Mustered Out When | Mustered Out Where |
|---|---|---|---|---|---|---|---|---|
| 1 | Humphrey Marshall | Colonel | June 9, 1846 | June 9, '46 | Louisville, Ky | 1 yr | June 8, '47 | New Orleans, La |
| 1 | Ezekiel H. Field | Lieut. Colonel | June 9, 1846 | June 9, '46 | Louisville, Ky | 1 yr | June 8, '47 | New Orleans, La |
| 1 | John P. Gaines | Major | June 9, 1846 | June 9, '46 | Louisville, Ky | 1 yr | June 8, '47 | New Orleans, La |
| 1 | Alexander C. Hensley | Surgeon | June 9, 1846 | June 9, '46 | Louisville, Ky | 1 yr | June 8, '47 | New Orleans, La |
| 1 | Alexander M. Blanton | Ass't Surgeon | June 9, 1846 | June 9, '46 | Louisville, Ky | 1 yr | June 8, '47 | New Orleans, La |
| 1 | Edward W. Vaughn | Adjutant | June 9, 1846 | June 9, '46 | Louisville, Ky | 1 yr | June 8, '47 | New Orleans, La |
| 2 | Thomas T. Hawkins | Adjutant | June 9, 1846 | June 9, '46 | Louisville, Ky | 1 yr | June 8, '47 | New Orleans, La |
| 3 | Thomas H. Barnes | Adjutant | June 9, 1846 | June 9, '46 | Louisville, Ky | 1 yr | June 8, '47 | New Orleans, La |
| 1 | Moses V. Grant | 2d Lt. and A.C.S. | June 9, 1846 | June 9, '46 | Louisville, Ky | 1 yr | June 8, '47 | New Orleans, La |
| 1 | Thomas Turner | Sergeant Major | June 9, 1846 | June 9, '46 | Louisville, Ky | 1 yr | June 8, '47 | New Orleans, La |
| 2 | Charles Gore | Qr. Mr. Serg't | June 9, 1846 | June 9, '46 | Louisville, Ky | 1 yr | June 8, '47 | New Orleans, La |
| 3 | Samuel Barlow | Chief Bugler | June 9, 1846 | June 9, '46 | Louisville, Ky | 1 yr | June 8, '47 | New Orleans, La |
| 4 | George W. Mudd | Chief Bugler | June 9, 1846 | June 9, '46 | Louisville, Ky | 1 yr | June 8, '47 | New Orleans, La |

## ROLL OF COMPANY "A," FIRST REGIMENT KENTUCKY

This Company was enrolled June 2d, 1846 at Lancaster, Ky., by Capt. Johnson Price.

| No. | Name | Rank | Mustered In When | Mustered In Where | Period | Mustered Out When | Mustered Out Where |
|---|---|---|---|---|---|---|---|
| 1 | Johnson Price | Captain | June 9, '46 | Louisville, Ky | 1 yr | June 8, '47 | New Orleans, La |
| 1 | L. F. Dunlap | 1st Lieutenant | June 9, '46 | Louisville, Ky | 1 yr | June 8, '47 | New Orleans, La |
| 1 | George F Sartain | 2d Lieutenant | June 9, '46 | Louisville, Ky | 1 yr | June 8, '47 | New Orleans, La |
| 2 | Thomas K. Conn | Br. 2d Lieut | June 9, '46 | Louisville, Ky | 1 yr | June 8, '47 | New Orleans, La |
| 1 | Landrain, William J | 1st Sergeant | June 9, '46 | Louisville, Ky | 1 yr | June 8, '47 | New Orleans, La |
| 2 | Thornton, James B | Sergeant | June 9, '46 | Louisville, Ky | 1 yr | June 8, '47 | New Orleans, La |
| 3 | Sellers, John | Sergeant | June 9, '46 | Louisville, Ky | 1 yr | June 8, '47 | New Orleans, La |
| 1 | Hamp, Anderson | Corporal | June 9, '46 | Louisville, Ky | 1 yr | June 8, '47 | New Orleans, La |
| 2 | Collier, Robert | Corporal | June 9, '46 | Louisville, Ky | 1 yr | June 8, '47 | New Orleans, La |
| 3 | Jennings, William | Corporal | June 9, '46 | Louisville, Ky | 1 yr | June 8, '47 | New Orleans, La |
| 4 | Grooms, John T | Corporal | June 9, '46 | Louisville, Ky | 1 yr | June 8, '47 | New Orleans, La |
| 1 | Dunn, James G | Musician | June 9, '46 | Louisville, Ky | 1 yr | June 8, '47 | New Orleans, La |
| 1 | Smiley, Grandison | Far. and Blac'th | June 9, '46 | Louisville, Ky | 1 yr | June 8, '47 | New Orleans, La |
| 1 | Arnold, Alexander | Private | June 9, '46 | Louisville, Ky | 1 yr | June 8, '47 | New Orleans, La |
| 2 | Arbuckle, John W | Private | June 9, '46 | Louisville, Ky | 1 yr | June 8, '47 | New Orleans, La |
| 3 | Ball, Thomas | Private | June 9, '46 | Louisville, Ky | 1 yr | June 8, '47 | New Orleans, La |
| 4 | Banton, Oliver O | Private | June 9, '46 | Louisville, Ky | 1 yr | June 8, '47 | New Orleans, La |
| 5 | Banton, Daniel | Private | June 9, '46 | Louisville, Ky | 1 yr | June 8, '47 | New Orleans, La |
| 6 | Bruce, Richard P | Private | June 9, '46 | Louisville, Ky | 1 yr | June 8, '47 | New Orleans, La |
| 7 | Buttner, Jesse | Private | June 9, '46 | Louisville, Ky | 1 yr | June 8, '47 | New Orleans, La |
| 8 | Cleveland, John H | Private | June 9, '46 | Louisville, Ky | 1 yr | June 8, '47 | New Orleans, La |
| 9 | Duggins, Hamilton | Private | June 9, '46 | Louisville, Ky | 1 yr | June 8, '47 | New Orleans, La |
| 10 | Evans, William G | Private | June 9, '46 | Louisville, Ky | 1 yr | June 8, '47 | New Orleans, La |
| 11 | Evans, Samuel G | Private | June 9, '46 | Louisville, Ky | 1 yr | June 8, '47 | New Orleans, La |
| 12 | Ford, James M | Private | June 9, '46 | Louisville, Ky | 1 yr | June 8, '47 | New Orleans, La |
| 13 | Forbes, William | Private | June 9, '46 | Louisville, Ky | 1 yr | June 8, '47 | New Orleans, La |
| 14 | Hall, Sidney | Private | June 9, '46 | Louisville, Ky | 1 yr | June 8, '47 | New Orleans, La |
| 15 | Hanson, Leonidas | Private | June 9, '46 | Louisville, Ky | 1 yr | June 8, '47 | New Orleans, La |
| 16 | Harlon, Andrew J | Private | June 9, '46 | Louisville, Ky | 1 yr | June 8, '47 | New Orleans, La |
| 17 | Herndon, William | Private | June 9, '46 | Louisville, Ky | 1 yr | June 8, '47 | New Orleans, La |
| 18 | Lawless, William O | Private | June 9, '46 | Louisville, Ky | 1 yr | June 8, '47 | New Orleans, La |
| 19 | Lemaster, Warren | Private | June 9, '46 | Louisville, Ky | 1 yr | June 8, '47 | New Orleans, La |
| 20 | Logan, Mason | Private | June 9, '46 | Louisville, Ky | 1 yr | June 8, '47 | New Orleans, La |
| 21 | Mullins, Samuel | Private | June 9, '46 | Louisville, Ky | 1 yr | June 8, '47 | New Orleans, La |
| 22 | Montgomery, Geo. W | Private | June 9, '46 | Louisville, Ky | 1 yr | June 8, '47 | New Orleans, La |
| 23 | McKee, Samuel F | Private | June 9, '46 | Louisville, Ky | 1 yr | June 8, '47 | New Orleans, La |
| 24 | May, Jesse | Private | June 9, '46 | Louisville, Ky | 1 yr | June 8, '47 | New Orleans, La |
| 25 | Miller, George H | Private | June 9, '46 | Louisville, Ky | 1 yr | June 8, '47 | New Orleans, La |
| 26 | Miller, James F | Private | June 9, '46 | Louisville, Ky | 1 yr | June 8, '47 | New Orleans, La |
| 27 | Mershon, Benjamin F | Private | June 9, '46 | Louisville, Ky | 1 yr | June 8, '47 | New Orleans, La |
| 28 | Owens, Horatio | Private | June 9, '46 | Louisville, Ky | 1 yr | June 8, '47 | New Orleans, La |
| 29 | Perkins, William | Private | June 9, '46 | Louisville, Ky | 1 yr | June 8, '47 | New Orleans, La |
| 30 | Robinson, George | Private | June 9, '46 | Louisville, Ky | 1 yr | June 8, '47 | New Orleans, La |
| 31 | Renfro, Samuel H | Private | June 9, '46 | Louisville, Ky | 1 yr | June 8, '47 | New Orleans, La |
| 32 | Robinson, William B | Private | June 9, '46 | Louisville, Ky | 1 yr | June 8, '47 | New Orleans, La |
| 33 | Smiley, James J | Private | June 9, '46 | Louisville, Ky | 1 yr | June 8, '47 | New Orleans, La |
| 34 | Southerland, Charles | Private | June 9, '46 | Louisville, Ky | 1 yr | June 8, '47 | New Orleans, La |
| 35 | Scott, Joseph | Private | June 9, '46 | Louisville, Ky | 1 yr | June 8, '47 | New Orleans, La |
| 36 | Suel, James | Private | June 9, '46 | Louisville, Ky | 1 yr | June 8, '47 | New Orleans, La |
| 37 | Terrill, Henry B | Private | June 9, '46 | Louisville, Ky | 1 yr | June 8, '47 | New Orleans, La |

# MEXICAN WAR VETERANS.

# KENTUCKY MOUNTED VOLUNTEERS—MEXICAN WAR.

**No. of each grade.** | **REMARKS.**

1
1
1 | Prisoner of war in Mexico from January 26.
1 |
1 | On leave of absence since June 5th, by order of Gen. Brooke, on account of sickness.
1 | Killed in battle Buena Vista, Mexico, February 23, 1847.
2 | Appointed Second Lieutenant 16th Infantry and transferred May 8th.
3 | Appointed from Second Lieutenant Company "H," May 8, vice Hawkins transferred.
1 | Was chief musician from enrollment to July 5th; died at Port Lavacca of fever October 5th.
1
2
3
4

# MOUNTED VOLUNTEERS—MEXICAN WAR.

1
1
1 | Absent in New Orleans without leave.
2 | Sick in hospital at Camargo, Mexico, from May 17.
1
2
3

1
2
3
4 | Sick in New Orleans, Louisiana, from June 8.

1 | On furlough from May 17th at Monterey, Mexico, by order of Lieutenant Colonel Field.

1 | On furlough from May 17th, at Monterey, Mexico, by order of Lieutenant Colonel Field.

1 | On furlough from May 17th, at Monterey, Mexico, by order of Lieutenant Colonel Field.
2 | Sick in hospital at New Orleans, Louisiana, from June 3.
3
4 | Sick, absent at Reynosa, Mexico from May 23.
5 | On furlough from May 17th, at Camargo, Mexico, by order of Lieutenant Colonel Field.
6 | On furlough from May 17th, at Camargo, Mexico, by order of Lieutenant Colonel Field.
7
8
9
10
11
12
13 | Sick in New Orleans, Louisiana.
14
15
16 | Left sick in Texas from August 12.
17 | Sick; absent at Reynosa, Mexico, from May 23.
18 | Absent in Louisiana without leave, from December 1.
19
20 | Left sick at Port Lavacca, Texas, from October 13.
21
22
23
24
25 | Left sick in hospital at Memphis, Tenn., from July 16.
26 | Left sick in hospital at Memphis, Tenn., from July 16.
27 | Left sick in Little Rock, Arkansas, from July 29.
28
29
30
31
32
33
34
35 | On furlough from May 17, at Camargo, Mexico, by order of Lieutenant Colonel Field.
36 | Left sick at Port Lavacca, Texas, from October 13.
37

## MEXICAN WAR VETERANS.

### ROLL OF COMPANY "A," FIRST REGIMENT KENTUCKY

| No. of each grade | Name | Rank | Enrolled | Mustered In When | Mustered In Where | Period | Mustered Out When | Mustered Out Where |
|---|---|---|---|---|---|---|---|---|
| 38 | Turner, George | Private | | June 9, '46 | Louisville, Ky | 1 yr | June 8, '47 | New Orleans, La |
| 39 | Vaughn, Thomas | Private | | June 9, '46 | Louisville, Ky | 1 yr | June 8, '47 | New Orleans, La |
| 40 | White, Robert | Private | | June 9, '46 | Louisville, Ky | 1 yr | June 8, '47 | New Orleans, La |
| 41 | Williamson, P. O. J. | Private | | June 9, '46 | Louisville, Ky | 1 yr | June 8, '47 | New Orleans, La |
| 42 | Yates, Oliver | Private | | June 9, '46 | Louisville, Ky | 1 yr | June 8, '47 | New Orleans, La |
| 43 | Yates, Thompson | Private | | June 9, '46 | Louisville, Ky | 1 yr | June 8, '47 | New Orleans, La |
| | **Transferred.** | | | | | | | |
| 1 | Graham, Benjamin F. | Corporal | | June 9, '46 | Louisville, Ky | 1 yr | June 8, '47 | New Orleans, La |
| | **Discharged.** | | | | | | | |
| 1 | Smith, Horace | Sergeant | | June 9, '46 | Louisville, Ky | 1 yr | | |
| 1 | Arnold, Horatio C. | Private | | June 9, '46 | Louisville, Ky | 1 yr | | |
| 2 | Alspaugh, David C. | Private | | June 9, '46 | Louisville, Ky | 1 yr | | |
| 3 | Brown, John | Private | | June 9, '46 | Louisville, Ky | 1 yr | | |
| 4 | Butner, Isaac | Private | | June 9, '46 | Louisville, Ky | 1 yr | | |
| 5 | Huffman, Joel E. | Private | | June 9, '46 | Louisville, Ky | 1 yr | | |
| 6 | Holmes, Jackson | Private | | June 9, '46 | Louisville, Ky | 1 yr | | |
| 7 | Hardin, James | Private | | June 9, '46 | Louisville, Ky | 1 yr | | |
| 8 | Hutchison, James | Private | | June 9, '46 | Louisville, Ky | 1 yr | | |
| 9 | Lawless, James K. | Private | | June 9, '46 | Louisville, Ky | 1 yr | | |
| 10 | Murphy, Joseph | Private | | June 9, '46 | Louisville, Ky | 1 yr | | |
| 11 | Mershon, James | Private | | June 9, '46 | Louisville, Ky | 1 yr | | |
| 12 | Shipley, Thos. W. | Private | | June 9, '46 | Louisville, Ky | 1 yr | | |
| 13 | Smith, V. B. | Private | | June 9, '46 | Louisville, Ky | 1 yr | | |
| | **Killed in Battle** | | | | | | | |
| 1 | Miller, John | Private | | June 9, '46 | Louisville, Ky | 1 yr | | |
| 2 | Warren, Banson | Private | | June 9, '46 | Louisville, Ky | 1 yr | | |
| | **Died.** | | | | | | | |
| 1 | Grant, Moses V. | Adj't 2d Lieut. | | June 9, '46 | Louisville, Ky | 1 yr | | |
| 1 | Huffman, Hamilton | Musician | | June 9, '46 | Louisville, Ky | 1 yr | | |
| 1 | Blackaby, Thomas | Private | | June 9, '46 | Louisville, Ky | 1 yr | | |
| 2 | Brown, James | Private | | June 9, '46 | Louisville, Ky | 1 yr | | |
| 3 | Haum, Joseph | Private | | June 9, '46 | Louisville, Ky | 1 yr | | |
| 4 | Miller, John J. | Private | | June 9, '46 | Louisville, Ky | 1 yr | | |
| 5 | Teater, Stephen F. | Private | | June 9, '46 | Louisville, Ky | 1 yr | | |

*This Company was enrolled June 2d, 1846, at Lancaster, Ky., by Capt. Johnson Price.*

### ROLL OF COMPANY "B," FIRST REGIMENT KENTUCKY

| | Name | Rank | Enrolled | Mustered In When | Mustered In Where | Period | Mustered Out When | Mustered Out Where |
|---|---|---|---|---|---|---|---|---|
| 1 | Jos. S. Lillard | Captain | June 9, 1846 | June 9, '46 | Louisville, Ky | 1 yr | June 7, '47 | New Orleans |
| 1 | John Field | 1st Lieutenant | June 9, 1846 | June 9, '46 | Louisville, Ky | 1 yr | June 7, '47 | New Orleans |
| 1 | Jefferson Peak | 2d Lieutenant | June 9, 1846 | June 9, '46 | Louisville, Ky | 1 yr | June 7, '47 | New Orleans |
| 2 | George W. Keene | 2d Lieutenant | June 9, 1846 | June 9, '46 | Louisville, Ky | 1 yr | June 7, '47 | New Orleans |
| 1 | Landrum, John J. | 1st Sergeant | June 9, 1846 | June 9, '46 | Louisville, Ky | 1 yr | June 7, '47 | New Orleans |
| 2 | Beall, Benj. F. | Sergeant | June 9, 1846 | June 9, '46 | Louisville, Ky | 1 yr | June 7, '47 | New Orleans |
| 1 | Hughes, A. J. | Corporal | June 9, 1846 | June 9, '46 | Louisville, Ky | 1 yr | June 7, '47 | New Orleans |
| 2 | Metcalf, Henry | Corporal | June 9, 1846 | June 9, '46 | Louisville, Ky | 1 yr | June 7, '47 | New Orleans |
| 1 | Braun, A. J. | Private | June 9, 1846 | June 9, '46 | Louisville, Ky | 1 yr | June 7, '47 | New Orleans |
| 2 | Bower, Christian | Private | June 9, 1846 | June 9, '46 | Louisville, Ky | 1 yr | June 7, '47 | New Orleans |
| 3 | Berkley, Henry | Private | June 9, 1846 | June 9, '46 | Louisville, Ky | 1 yr | June 7, '47 | New Orleans |
| 4 | Brown, Isaac | Private | June 9, 1846 | June 9, '46 | Louisville, Ky | 1 yr | June 7, '47 | New Orleans |
| 5 | Bailes, Thompson | Private | June 9, 1846 | June 9, '46 | Louisville, Ky | 1 yr | June 7, '47 | New Orleans |
| 6 | Catterson, Hiram | Private | June 9, 1846 | June 9, '46 | Louisville, Ky | 1 yr | June 7, '47 | New Orleans |
| 7 | Catterson, William | Private | June 9, 1846 | June 9, '46 | Louisville, Ky | 1 yr | June 7, '47 | New Orleans |
| 8 | Crawford, H. H. | Private | June 9, 1846 | June 9, '46 | Louisville, Ky | 1 yr | June 7, '47 | New Orleans |
| 9 | Dorman, Matthew | Private | June 9, 1846 | June 9, '46 | Louisville, Ky | 1 yr | June 7, '47 | New Orleans |
| 10 | Duncan, Jos. S. | Private | June 9, 1846 | June 9, '46 | Louisville, Ky | 1 yr | June 7, '47 | New Orleans |
| 11 | Ennis, William R. | Private | June 9, 1846 | June 9, '46 | Louisville, Ky | 1 yr | June 7, '47 | New Orleans |
| 12 | Ewalt, Richard | Private | June 9, 1846 | June 9, '46 | Louisville, Ky | 1 yr | June 7, '47 | New Orleans |
| 13 | Graham, Franklin | Private | June 9, 1846 | June 9, '46 | Louisville, Ky | 1 yr | June 7, '47 | New Orleans |
| 14 | Hall, Elijah | Private | June 9, 1846 | June 9, '46 | Louisville, Ky | 1 yr | June 7, '47 | New Orleans |
| 15 | Lindsey, William J. | Private | June 9, 1846 | June 9, '46 | Louisville, Ky | 1 yr | June 7, '47 | New Orleans |
| 16 | Lillard, William C. (a) | Private | July 3, 1846 | July 3, '46 | Louisville, Ky | 1 yr | June 7, '47 | New Orleans |
| 17 | Marsh, A. A. | Private | June 9, 1846 | June 9, '46 | Louisville, Ky | 1 yr | June 7, '47 | New Orleans |
| 18 | Miner, M. F. | Private | June 9, 1846 | June 9, '46 | Louisville, Ky | 1 yr | June 7, '47 | New Orleans |
| 19 | Parker, William | Private | June 9, 1846 | June 9, '46 | Louisville, Ky | 1 yr | June 7, '47 | New Orleans |
| 20 | Payne, Hiram (a) | Private | June 30, 1846 | June 30, '46 | Louisville, Ky | 1 yr | June 7, '47 | New Orleans |
| 21 | Ramey, J. H. | Private | June 9, 1846 | June 9, '46 | Louisville, Ky | 1 yr | June 7, '47 | New Orleans |
| 22 | Rosenburg, Henry | Private | June 9, 1846 | June 9, '46 | Louisville, Ky | 1 yr | June 7, '47 | New Orleans |

## MOUNTED VOLUNTEERS—MEXICAN WAR—Continued.

| No. of each grade. | REMARKS. |
|---|---|
| 38 | |
| 39 | |
| 40 | Prisoner of war in Mexico from January 26. |
| 41 | |
| 42 | Left at Reynosa, Mexico, as attendant in hospital, from May 23. |
| 43 | |
| 1 | Appointed Assistant Quartermaster by the President. |
| 1 | Discharged on Surgeon's certificate of disability at New Orleans, La., May 30, by order of General Brooke. |
| 1 | Discharged on Surgeon's certificate of disability at Port Lavacca, Texas, October 12, by order of Colonel Marshall. |
| 2 | Discharged on Surgeon's certificate of disability at Port Lavacca, Texas, October 12. Order of Colonel Marshall. |
| 3 | Discharged on Surgeon's certificate of disability at Port Lavacca, Texas, October 12. Order of Colonel Marshall. |
| 4 | Discharged on Surgeon's certificate of disability at Port Lavacca, Texas, October 12. Order of Colonel Marshall. |
| 5 | Discharged on Surgeon's certificate of disability at Port Lavacca, Texas, October 12. Order of Colonel Marshall. |
| 6 | Discharged on Surgeon's certificate of disability at Port Lavacca, Texas, October 12. Order of Colonel Marshall. |
| 7 | Discharged on Surgeon's certificate of disability at Port Lavacca, Texas, October 12th. Order of Col. Marshall. |
| 8 | Discharged on Surgeon's certificate of disability at Camargo, Mexico, December 13th. Order of Col. Marshall. |
| 9 | Discharged on Surgeon's certificate of disability at New Orleans, May 30th. Order of Gen. Brooke. |
| 10 | Discharged on Surgeon's certificate of disability at New Orleans, Louisiana, May 30th. Order of Gen. Brooke. |
| 11 | Discharged on Surgeon's certificate of disability at Port Lavacca, Texas, October 12th. Order of Col. Marshall. |
| 12 | Discharged on Surgeon's certificate of disability at Camargo, Mexico, December 13th. Order of Gen. Marshall. |
| 13 | Discharged on Surgeon's certificate of disability at Port Lavacca, Texas, October 12th. Order of Col. Marshall. |
| 1 | Killed in battle at Buena Vista, February 23d. |
| 2 | Killed in battle at Buena Vista, February 23d. |
| 1 | Died at Port Lavacca, Texas, October 6th. |
| 1 | Died at Port Lavacca, Texas, October 7th. |
| 1 | Died at Carmargo, Mexico, May 21st. |
| 2 | Died at Carmargo, Mexico, December 21st. |
| 3 | Died at Little Rock, Arkansas, August 1st. |
| 4 | Died at Caddo River, Arkansas, August 3d. |
| 5 | Died at Ceralvo, Mexico, May 1st. |

## MOUNTED VOLUNTEERS—MEXICAN WAR.

| No. | REMARKS. |
|---|---|
| 1 | Discharged by resignation November 11th, at Camargo, by order of Gen. Marshall. |
| 1 | |
| 1 | |
| 2 | Was private from enrollment to July 23d. Sick; absent with leave from February 19th. Surgeon's certificate. |
| 1 | |
| 2 | |
| 1 | |
| 2 | |
| 1 | |
| 2 | On detached service. Hospital attendant from May 19, by order of Lieut. Col. Field. |
| 3 | |
| 4 | |
| 5 | |
| 6 | |
| 7 | |
| 8 | |
| 9 | |
| 10 | |
| 11 | |
| 12 | |
| 13 | |
| 14 | |
| 15 | |
| 16 | Joined at Louisville July 3d, as substitute for Jonas Jones, by order of Col. Marshall. On detached service as hospital attendant at Camargo November 11th. Order of Col. Marshall. |
| 17 | |
| 18 | |
| 19 | Absent sick at Little Rock from July 28th, by order of Col. Marshall. |
| 20 | Joined at Louisville June 30th as substitute for G. W. Wolf, by order of Col. Marshall. |
| 21 | |
| 22 | |

## MEXICAN WAR VETERANS.

### ROLL OF COMPANY "B," FIRST REGIMENT KENTUCKY

| No. of each grade. | Name. | Rank. | Enrolled. | Mustered In. When. | Mustered In. Where. | Period. | Mustered Out. When. | Mustered Out. Where. |
|---|---|---|---|---|---|---|---|---|
| 23 | Scandrett, Thos. B. | Private | June 9, 1846 | June 9, '46 | Louisville, Ky. | 1 yr. | June 7, '47 | New Orleans |
| 24 | Vories, A. H. | Private | June 9, 1846 | June 9, '46 | Louisville, Ky. | 1 yr. | June 7, '47 | New Orleans |
| 25 | Van Every, Martin | Private | June 9, 1846 | June 9, '46 | Louisville, Ky. | 1 yr. | June 7, '47 | New Orleans |
| 26 | Violett, F. T. | Private | June 9, 1846 | June 9, '46 | Louisville, Ky. | 1 yr. | June 7, '47 | New Orleans |
| 27 | Walker, John I. | Private | June 9, 1846 | June 9, '46 | Louisville, Ky. | 1 yr. | June 7, '47 | New Orleans |
| 28 | Young, John J. | Private | June 9, 1846 | June 9, '46 | Louisville, Ky. | 1 yr. | June 7, '47 | New Orleans |
| | **KILLED IN BATTLE.** | | | | | | | |
| 1 | Lillard, David I. | Sergeant | June 9, 1846 | June 9, '46 | Louisville, Ky. | 1 yr. | | |
| 2 | Martin, A. J. | Private | June 9, 1846 | June 9, '46 | Louisville, Ky. | 1 yr | | |
| 3 | Quigley, Patrick | Private | June 9, 1846 | June 9, '46 | Louisville, Ky. | 1 yr. | | |
| 4 | Sanders, Lewis | Private | June 9, 1846 | June 9, '46 | Louisville, Ky. | 1 yr. | | |
| | **DIED** | | | | | | | |
| 1 | Jones, Juba M. | Private | June 9, 1846 | June 9, '46 | Louisville, Ky. | 1 yr. | | |
| 2 | Lee, George W. | Private | June 9, 1846 | June 9, '46 | Louisville, Ky. | 1 yr. | | |
| 3 | Moore, James | Private | June 9, 1846 | June 9, '46 | Louisville, Ky. | 1 yr. | | |
| 4 | Morton, E. J. H. | Private | June 9, 1846 | June 9, '46 | Louisville, Ky. | 1 yr. | | |
| 5 | Nouse, Michael | Private | June 9, 1846 | June 9, '46 | Louisville, Ky. | 1 yr. | | |
| | **DISCHARGED.** | | | | | | | |
| 1 | Hughes, C. D. | Sergeant | June 9, 1846 | June 9, '46 | Louisville, Ky. | 1 yr. | | |
| 2 | Sayre, Adolphus | Sergeant | June 9, 1846 | June 9, '46 | Louisville, Ky. | 1 yr. | | |
| 3 | Sanford, M. H. | Corporal | June 9, 1846 | June 9, '46 | Louisville, Ky. | 1 yr. | | |
| 4 | Edwards, W. M. W. | Corporal | June 9, 1846 | June 9, '46 | Louisville, Ky. | 1 yr. | | |
| 5 | Kirtly, Cane | Corporal | June 9, 1846 | June 9, '46 | Louisville, Ky. | 1 yr. | | |
| 6 | Gregg, James C. | Musician | June 9, 1846 | June 9, '46 | Louisville, Ky. | 1 yr. | | |
| 7 | Sanders, Nathaniel L. | Musician | June 9, 1846 | June 9, '46 | Louisville, Ky. | 1 yr | | |
| 8 | Wolf, Geo. W. | Blac'th and Far. | June 9, 1846 | June 9, '46 | Louisville, Ky. | 1 yr. | | |
| 9 | Wolf, William H. | Blac'th and Far. | June 9, 1846 | June 9, '46 | Louisville, Ky. | 1 yr. | | |
| 10 | Braun, Joseph S. | Private | June 9, 1846 | June 9, '46 | Louisville, Ky. | 1 yr. | | |
| 11 | Chambers, James C. | Private | June 9, 1846 | June 9, '46 | Louisville, Ky. | 1 yr. | | |
| 12 | Furnish, Garritt | Private | June 9, 1846 | June 9, '46 | Louisville, Ky. | 1 yr. | | |
| 13 | Gilbert, John | Private | June 9, 1846 | June 9, '46 | Louisville, Ky. | 1 yr. | | |
| 14 | Hays, Thomas | Private | June 9, 1846 | June 9, '46 | Louisville, Ky. | 1 yr. | | |
| 15 | Helton, William | Private | June 9, 1846 | June 9, '46 | Louisville, Ky. | 1 yr. | | |
| 16 | Jones, Jonas | Private | June 9, 1846 | June 9, '46 | Louisville, Ky. | 1 yr. | | |
| 17 | Keene, Van W. | Private | June 9, 1846 | June 9, '46 | Louisville, Ky. | 1 yr. | | |
| 18 | Kyle, Samuel H. | Private | June 9, 1846 | June 9, '46 | Louisville, Ky. | 1 yr. | | |
| 19 | Lynn, William N. | Private | June 9, 1846 | June 9, '46 | Louisville, Ky. | 1 yr. | | |
| 20 | McMillan, Joseph | Private | June 9, 1846 | June 9, '46 | Louisville, Ky. | 1 yr. | | |
| 21 | McGuire, Nathaniel | Private | June 9, 1846 | June 9, '46 | Louisville, Ky. | 1 yr. | | |
| 22 | Myrick, Joseph A. | Private | June 9, 1846 | June 9, '46 | Louisville, Ky. | 1 yr. | | |
| 23 | Miner, L. D. | Private | June 9, 1846 | June 9, '46 | Louisville, Ky. | 1 yr. | | |
| 24 | Netherland, Jos. H. | Private | June 9, 1846 | June 9, '46 | Louisville, Ky. | 1 yr. | | |
| 25 | North, Henry B. | Private | June 9, 1846 | June 9, '46 | Louisville, Ky. | 1 yr. | | |
| 26 | Patton, Reason | Private | June 9, 1846 | June 9, '46 | Louisville, Ky. | 1 yr. | | |
| 27 | Peak, Joseph | Private | June 9, 1846 | June 9, '46 | Louisville, Ky. | 1 yr. | | |
| 28 | Resor, N. B. | Private | June 9, 1846 | June 9, '46 | Louisville, Ky. | 1 yr. | | |
| 29 | Resor, Charles W. | Private | June 9, 1846 | June 9, '46 | Louisville, Ky. | 1 yr. | | |
| 30 | Sanford, Robert (a) | Private | June 30, 1846 | June 9, '46 | Louisville, Ky. | 1 yr. | | |
| 31 | Spencer, B. M. | Private | June 9, 1846 | June 9, '46 | Louisville, Ky. | 1 yr. | | |
| 32 | Sanders, Taliaferro | Private | June 9, 1846 | June 9, '46 | Louisville, Ky. | 1 yr. | | |
| 33 | Scandreth, R. M. | Private | June 9, 1846 | June 9, '46 | Louisville, Ky. | 1 yr. | | |
| 34 | Thorn, John | Private | June 9, 1846 | June 9, '46 | Louisville, Ky. | 1 yr. | | |
| 35 | Work, David P. | Private | June 9, 1846 | June 9, '46 | Louisville, Ky. | 1 yr. | | |
| 36 | Wright, Thomas | Private | June 9, 1846 | June 9, '46 | Louisville, Ky. | 1 yr. | | |

This Company was enrolled at Warsaw, Kentucky, June 9, 1846, by Captain Joseph S. Lillard.
(a) Enrolled at Louisville.

### ROLL OF COMPANY "C," FIRST REGIMENT KENTUCKY

| | | | | | | | | |
|---|---|---|---|---|---|---|---|---|
| 1 | Ben. C. Milam | Captain | May 25, 1846 | June 9, '46 | Louisville, Ky. | 1 yr. | June 8, '47 | New Orleans, La. |
| 1 | James H. D. McKee | 1st Lieutenant | May 25, 1846 | June 9, '46 | Louisville, Ky. | 1 yr. | June 8, '47 | New Orleans, La. |
| 1 | Richard D. Harlan | 2d Lieutenant | May 25, 1846 | June 9, '46 | Louisville, Ky. | 1 yr. | June 8, '47 | New Orleans, La. |
| 2 | George R. Davidson | 2d Lieutenant | May 25, 1846 | June 9, '46 | Louisville, Ky. | 1 yr. | June 8, '47 | New Orleans, La. |
| 1 | John T. Roberts | 1st Sergeant | May 25, 1846 | June 9, '46 | Louisville, Ky. | 1 yr. | June 8, '47 | New Orleans, La. |
| 2 | Ben B. Bennett | Sergeant | May 25, 1846 | June 9, '46 | Louisville, Ky. | 1 yr. | June 8, '47 | New Orleans, La. |
| 3 | Humphrey Evans | Sergeant | May 25, 1846 | June 9, '46 | Louisville, Ky. | 1 yr. | June 8, '47 | New Orleans, La. |
| 1 | John Swigert | Corporal | May 25, 1846 | June 9, '46 | Louisville, Ky. | 1 yr. | June 8, '47 | New Orleans, La. |
| 2 | Lewis J. Foster | Corporal | May 25, 1846 | June 9, '46 | Louisville, Ky. | 1 yr. | June 8, '47 | New Orleans, La. |

## MOUNTED VOLUNTEERS—MEXICAN WAR—Continued.

### REMARKS.

| No. of each grade | Remarks |
|---|---|
| 23 | |
| 24 | Sick in the city of New Orleans. |
| 25 | |
| 26 | |
| 27 | |
| 28 | |
| 1 | Killed in battle of Buena Vista, February 23d. |
| 2 | Killed in battle of Buena Vista, February 23d. |
| 3 | Killed in battle of Buena Vista, February 23d. |
| 4 | Killed in battle of Buena Vista, February 23d. |
| 1 | Died October 11th, at Lavacca. |
| 2 | Died October 26th, on the Rio Grande. |
| 3 | Died July 18th, in Arkansas. |
| 4 | Died August 17th, in Arkansas. |
| 5 | Died December 10th, at Camargo, in hospital. |
| 1 | Discharged on Surgeon's certificate of disability October 5th, at Lavacca, by order of Col. Marshall. |
| 2 | Discharged on Surgeon's certificate of disability May 29th, at New Orleans. Order of Gen. Brooke. |
| 3 | Discharged on Surgeon's certificate of disability October 15th, at Victoria, by order of Col. Marshall. |
| 4 | Discharged on Surgeon's certificate of disability May 29th, at New Orleans. Order of Gen. Brooke. |
| 5 | Discharged on Surgeon's certificate of disability February 14th, at Monterey. Order of Gen. Marshall. |
| 6 | Discharged on Surgeon's certificate of disability May 28th, at New Orleans. Order of Gen. Brooke. |
| 7 | Discharged on Surgeon's certificate of disability May 28th, at New Orleans. Order of Gen Brooke. |
| 8 | Discharged at Louisville June 30th, by procuring a substitute, H. Payne. Order of Col. Marshall. |
| 9 | Discharged on Surgeon's certificate of disability May 28th, at New Orleans. Order of Gen. Brooke. |
| 10 | Discharged on Surgeon's certificate of disability November 15th, at Camargo. Order of Gen. Marshall. |
| 11 | Discharged on Surgeon's certificate of disability October 15th, at Victoria. Order of Col. Marshall. |
| 12 | Discharged on Surgeon's certificate of disability May 28th, at New Orleans. Order of Gen. Brooke. |
| 13 | Discharged on Surgeon's certificate of disability May 28th, at New Orleans. Order of Gen. Brooke. |
| 14 | Discharged on Surgeon's certificate of disability May 28th, at New Orleans. Order of Gen. Brooke. |
| 15 | Discharged on Surgeon's certificate of disability May 28th, at New Orleans. Order of Gen. Brooke. |
| 16 | Discharged on Surgeon's certificate of disability July 3d, at Louisville, by procuring substitute, W. C. Lillard. Order of Col. Marshall |
| 17 | Discharged on Surgeon's certificate of disability October 5th, at Lavacca. Order of Col. Marshall. [shall. |
| 18 | Discharged on Surgeon's certificate of disability at Louisville, June 30th, by procuring a substitute, Rob't Sanford. Order of Col. Mar- |
| 19 | Discharged on Surgeon's certificate of disability May 28th, at New Orleans. Order of Gen. Brooke. |
| 20 | Discharged on Surgeon's certificate of disability December 16th, at Monterey. Order of Gen. Butler. |
| 21 | Discharged on Surgeon's certificate of disability May 28th, at New Orleans. Order of Gen. Brooke. |
| 22 | Discharged on Surgeon's certificate of disability October 26th, at Camargo. Order of Gen. Marshall. |
| 23 | Discharged on Surgeon's certificate of disability October 29th, at Camargo. Order of Gen. Marshall. |
| 24 | Discharged on Surgeon's certificate of disability December 16th, at Monterey. Order of Gen. Butler. |
| 25 | Discharged on Surgeon's certificate of disability May 28th, at New Orleans. Order of Gen. Brooke. |
| 26 | Discharged on Surgeon's certificate of disability May 28th, at New Orleans. Order of Gen. Brooke. |
| 27 | Discharged on Surgeon's certificate of disability May 28th, at New Orleans. Order of Gen. Brooke. |
| 28 | Discharged on Surgeon's certificate of disability May 28th, at New Orleans. Order of Gen. Brooke. |
| 29 | Discharged on Surgeon's certificate of disability May 28th, at New Orleans. Order of Gen. Brooke. [27th, at N. Orleans. Order Gen. Brooke. |
| 30 | Joined at Louisville June 30th, as a substitute for Sam'l Kytely, order Col. Marshall. Discharged on Surgeon' scertificate of disability May |
| 31 | Discharged on Surgeon's certificate of disability May 28th, at New Orleans. Order of Gen. Brooke. |
| 32 | Discharged on Surgeon's certificate of disability October 17th, at Goliah. Order of Col. Marshall. |
| 33 | Discharged on Surgeon's certificate of disability March 14th, at Monterey. Order of Gen. Taylor. |
| 34 | Discharged on Surgeon's certificate of disability October 5th, at Lavacca. Order of Col. Marshall. |
| 35 | Discharged on Surgeon's certificate of disability May 28th, at New Orleans. Order of Gen. Brooke. |
| 36 | Discharged on Surgeon's certificate of disability May 28th, at New Orleans. Order of Gen. Brooke. |

## MOUNTED VOLUNTEERS—MEXICAN WAR.

| No. of each grade | Remarks |
|---|---|
| 1 | |
| 1 | |
| 1 | |
| 2 | 1st Sergeant from enrollment until July 15. Prisoner of war in Mexico since January 22. |
| 1 | |
| 2 | |
| 3 | Appointed Sergeant from private, March. Order Col. Marshall. |
| 1 | Prisoner of war in Mexico since January 22. |
| 2 | |

## MEXICAN WAR VETERANS.

### ROLL OF COMPANY "C," FIRST REGIMENT KENTUCKY

| No. of each grade | Name | Rank | Enrolled | Mustered In. When | Mustered In. Where | Period | Mustered Out. When | Mustered Out. Where |
|---|---|---|---|---|---|---|---|---|
| 1 | James Herring | Bugler | May 25, 1846 | June 9, '46 | Louisville, Ky. | 1 yr | June 8, '47 | New Orleans, La. |
| 2 | B. S. Gayle | Bugler | May 25, 1846 | June 9, '46 | Louisville, Ky. | 1 yr | June 8, '47 | New Orleans, La. |
| 1 | Joseph Robb | Far. and Blac'th. | May 25, 1846 | June 9, '46 | Louisville, Ky. | 1 yr | June 8, '47 | New Orleans, La. |
| 1 | Bates, James | Private | May 25, 1846 | June 9, '46 | Louisville, Ky. | 1 yr | June 8, '47 | New Orleans, La. |
| 2 | Cavender, Johnty | Private | May 25, 1846 | June 9, '46 | Louisville, Ky. | 1 yr | June 8, '47 | New Orleans, La. |
| 3 | Calvert, Cyrus | Private | May 25, 1846 | June 9, '46 | Louisville, Ky. | 1 yr | June 8, '47 | New Orleans, La. |
| 4 | Cochran, Robert | Private | May 25, 1846 | June 9, '46 | Louisville, Ky. | 1 yr | June 8, '47 | New Orleans, La. |
| 5 | Cook, Nathanel C. | Private | May 25, 1846 | June 9, '46 | Louisville, Ky. | 1 yr | June 8, '47 | New Orleans, La. |
| 6 | Cook, Clinton D. W. | Private | May 25, 1846 | June 9, '46 | Louisville, Ky. | 1 yr | June 8, '47 | New Orleans, La. |
| 7 | Church, Benjamin | Private | May 25, 1846 | June 9, '46 | Louisville, Ky. | 1 yr | June 8, '47 | New Orleans, La. |
| 8 | Davenport, Richard | Private | May 25, 1846 | June 9, '46 | Louisville, Ky. | 1 yr | June 8, '47 | New Orleans, La. |
| 9 | Dougherty, Zachariah | Private | May 25, 1846 | June 9, '46 | Louisville, Ky. | 1 yr | June 8, '47 | New Orleans, La. |
| 10 | Evans, James S. | Private | May 25, 1846 | June 9, '46 | Louisville, Ky. | 1 yr | June 8, '47 | New Orleans, La. |
| 11 | Edwards, Bennett | Private | May 25, 1846 | June 9, '46 | Louisville, Ky. | 1 yr | June 8, '47 | New Orleans, La. |
| 12 | Field, B. S. | Private | May 25, 1846 | June 9, '46 | Louisville, Ky. | 1 yr | June 8, '47 | New Orleans, La. |
| 13 | Holeman, A. W. | Private | May 25, 1846 | June 9, '46 | Louisville, Ky. | 1 yr | June 8, '47 | New Orleans, La. |
| 14 | Harrison, Jeremiah | Private | May 25, 1846 | June 9, '46 | Louisville, Ky. | 1 yr | June 8, '47 | New Orleans, La. |
| 15 | Hassett, William | Private | May 25, 1846 | June 9, '46 | Louisville, Ky. | 1 yr | June 8, '47 | New Orleans, La. |
| 16 | Hawkins, Fielding S. | Private | May 25, 1846 | June 9, '46 | Louisville, Ky. | 1 yr | June 8, '47 | New Orleans, La. |
| 17 | Lee, James F. | Private | May 25, 1846 | June 9, '46 | Louisville, Ky. | 1 yr | June 8, '47 | New Orleans, La. |
| 18 | Leonard, Samuel C. | Private | May 25, 1846 | June 9, '46 | Louisville, Ky. | 1 yr | June 8, '47 | New Orleans, La. |
| 19 | Lafon, John W. (a) | Private | July 4, 1846 | Not known | Camargo, Mexico | 1 yr | June 8, '47 | New Orleans, La. |
| 20 | Macey, T. J. | Private | May 25, 1846 | June 9, '46 | Louisville, Ky. | 1 yr | June 8, '47 | New Orleans, La. |
| 21 | Martin, L. | Private | May 25, 1846 | June 9, '47 | Louisville, Ky. | 1 yr | June 8, '47 | New Orleans, La. |
| 22 | Mitchell, A. J. | Private | May 25, 1846 | June 9, '46 | Louisville, Ky. | 1 yr | June 8, '47 | New Orleans, La. |
| 23 | McDonald, A. J. | Private | May 25, 1846 | June 9, '46 | Louisville, Ky. | 1 yr | June 8, '47 | New Orleans, La. |
| 24 | McLain, William | Private | May 25, 1846 | June 9, '46 | Louisville, Ky. | 1 yr | June 8, '47 | New Orleans, La. |
| 25 | Pearce, Ben Franklin | Private | May 25, 1846 | June 9, '46 | Louisville, Ky. | 1 yr | June 8, '47 | New Orleans, La. |
| 26 | Reddish, John H. | Private | May 25, 1846 | June 9, '46 | Louisville, Ky. | 1 yr | June 8, '47 | New Orleans, La. |
| 27 | Shannon, Geo. M. | Private | May 25, 1846 | June 9, '46 | Louisville, Ky. | 1 yr | June 8, '47 | New Orleans, La. |
| 28 | Snelling, John A. | Private | May 25, 1846 | June 9, '46 | Louisville, Ky. | 1 yr | June 8, '47 | New Orleans, La. |
| 29 | Soward, J. J. | Private | May 25, 1846 | June 9, '46 | Louisville, Ky. | 1 yr | June 8, '47 | New Orleans, La. |
| 30 | Scott, John A. | Private | May 25, 1846 | June 9, '46 | Louisville, Ky. | 1 yr | June 8, '47 | New Orleans, La. |
| 31 | Stapp, W. W. | Private | May 25, 1846 | June 9, '46 | Louisville, Ky. | 1 yr | June 8, '47 | New Orleans, La. |
| 32 | Stockton, W. C. | Private | May 25, 1846 | June 9, '46 | Louisville, Ky. | 1 yr | June 8, '47 | New Orleans, La. |
| 33 | Wilkerson, A. | Private | May 25, 1846 | June 9, '46 | Louisville, Ky. | 1 yr | June 8, '47 | New Orleans, La. |
| 34 | Whitehead, William | Private | May 25, 1846 | June 9, '46 | Louisville, Ky. | 1 yr | June 8, '47 | New Orleans, La. |
| 35 | Wood, W. S. | Private | May 25, 1846 | June 9, '46 | Louisville, Ky. | 1 yr | June 8, '47 | New Orleans, La. |
| 36 | Sammis, Jno. S. | Private | May 25, 1846 | June 9, '46 | Louisville, Ky. | 1 yr | June 8, '47 | New Orleans, La. |

**DIED.**

| | | | | | | | | |
|---|---|---|---|---|---|---|---|---|
| 1 | Bailey, James | Private | May 25, 1846 | June 9, '46 | Louisville, Ky. | 1 yr | | |
| 2 | Hall, W. J. | Private | May 25, 1846 | June 9, '46 | Louisville, Ky. | 1 yr | | |
| 3 | Latta, Robert | Private | May 25, 1846 | June 9, '46 | Louisville, Ky. | 1 yr | | |
| 4 | Newton, W. | Private | May 25, 1846 | June 9, '46 | Louisville, Ky. | 1 yr | | |
| 5 | Williamson, W. | Private | May 25, 1846 | June 9, '46 | Louisville, Ky. | 1 yr | | |

**KILLED IN ACTION.**

| | | | | | | | | |
|---|---|---|---|---|---|---|---|---|
| 1 | Ellingwood, J. F. | Private | May 25, 1846 | June 9, '46 | Louisville, Ky. | 1 yr | | |
| 2 | Leston, James | Private | May 25, 1846 | June 9, '46 | Louisville, Ky. | 1 yr | | |
| 3 | Sanders, John | Private | May 25, 1846 | June 9, '46 | Louisville, Ky. | 1 yr | | |

**DISCHARGED.**

| | | | | | | | | |
|---|---|---|---|---|---|---|---|---|
| 1 | Robb, W. N. | Sergeant | May 25, 1846 | June 9, '46 | Louisville, Ky. | 1 yr | | |
| 1 | Utterback, B. | Corporal | May 25, 1846 | June 9, '46 | Louisville, Ky. | 1 yr | | |
| 2 | Parent, E. T. | Corporal | May 25, 1846 | June 9, '46 | Louisville, Ky. | 1 yr | | |
| 1 | Bailey, G. W. | Private | May 25, 1846 | June 9, '46 | Louisville, Ky. | 1 yr | | |
| 2 | Howard, R. B. | Private | May 25, 1846 | June 9, '46 | Louisville, Ky. | 1 yr | | |
| 3 | Hancock, D. | Private | May 25, 1846 | June 9, '46 | Louisville, Ky. | 1 yr | | |
| 4 | Harper, Thomas | Private | May 25, 1846 | June 9, '46 | Louisville, Ky. | 1 yr | | |
| 5 | Ashley, Joel | Private | May 25, 1846 | June 9, '46 | Louisville, Ky. | 1 yr | | |
| 6 | Jones, W. P. | Private | May 25, 1846 | June 9, '46 | Louisville, Ky. | 1 yr | | |
| 7 | Kendall, J. J. | Private | May 25, 1846 | June 9, '46 | Louisville, Ky. | 1 yr | | |
| 8 | McKee, J. D. | Private | May 25, 1846 | June 9, '46 | Louisville, Ky. | 1 yr | | |
| 9 | Montague, S. | Private | May 25, 1846 | June 9, '46 | Louisville, Ky. | 1 yr | | |
| 10 | Miles, J. G. | Private | May 25, 1846 | June 9, '46 | Louisville, Ky. | 1 yr | | |
| 11 | Milam, F. M. | Private | May 25, 1846 | June 9, '46 | Louisville, Ky. | 1 yr | | |
| 12 | McQueen, S. | Private | May 25, 1846 | June 9, '46 | Louisville, Ky. | 1 yr | | |
| 13 | Mars, Samuel | Private | May 25, 1846 | June 9, '46 | Louisville, Ky. | 1 yr | | |
| 14 | Noel R. P. W. | Private | May 25, 1846 | June 9, '46 | Louisville, Ky. | 1 yr | | |
| 15 | Price, W. H. | Private | May 25, 1846 | June 9, '46 | Louisville, Ky. | 1 yr | | |
| 16 | Reed, A. B. | Private | May 25, 1846 | June 9, '46 | Louisville, Ky. | 1 yr | | |
| 17 | Suddith, W. H. | Private | May 25, 1846 | June 9, '46 | Louisville, Ky. | 1 yr | | |
| 18 | Wilson, J. | Private | May 25, 1846 | June 9, '46 | Louisville, Ky. | 1 yr | | |

# MOUNTED VOLUNTEERS—MEXICAN WAR.—Continued.

| No. of each grade | REMARKS. |
|---|---|
| 1 | Prisoner of war in Mexico since January 22. |
| 2 | |
| 1 | |
| 1 | Prisoner of war in Mexico from January 22. |
| 2 | |
| 3 | Prisoner of war in Mexico from January 22. |
| 4 | Prisoner of war in Mexico from January 22. |
| 5 | |
| 6 | |
| 7 | |
| 8 | |
| 9 | Prisoner of war in Mexico from January 22. |
| 10 | |
| 11 | |
| 12 | Left sick at Monterey, Mexico, December 17. |
| 13 | Prisoner of war in Mexico from January 22. |
| 14 | |
| 15 | |
| 16 | Left sick at Washington, Ark., August 9; returned home by leave of Lieutenant Davidson about 15th September. |
| 17 | |
| 18 | |
| 19 | Joined as a substitute for Geo. W. Bailey, July 4. By permission of Col. Marshall. |
| 20 | |
| 21 | Left sick at Lavacca, Texas, October 12. |
| 22 | |
| 23 | |
| 24 | |
| 25 | |
| 26 | |
| 27 | |
| 28 | |
| 29 | |
| 30 | Prisoner of war in Mexico from January 22. |
| 31 | Left sick at Goliad, Texas, October 7. Returned and put on extra duty January 25 Order of Gen. Patterson. |
| 32 | Left sick at Levacca, Texas, October 14. |
| 33 | Prisoner of war in Mexico from January 22. |
| 34 | Prisoner of war in Mexico from January 22. |
| 35 | Prisoner of war in Mexico from January 22. |
| 36 | |
| 1 | Died at Levacca, Texas, of fever, September 26. |
| 2 | Died at Saltillo, Mexico, of pleurisy, February 3. |
| 3 | Died at Carmargo, Mexico, fever, May 10. |
| 4 | Died at Carmargo, Mexico, fever, December 4. |
| 5 | Died at Lavacca, Texas, of fever October 11, '46. |
| 1 | Killed at Battle of Buena-Vista, February 23. |
| 2 | Killed at battle of Buena Vista, February 23. |
| 3 | Killed at battle of Buena Vista, February 23. |
| 1 | Discharged at New Orleans, May 31. Surgeon's certificate of disability. Order of General Brooke. |
| 1 | Discharged at New Orleans, May 31. Surgeon's certificate of disability. Order of General Brooke. |
| 2 | Discharged at Lavacca, October 12. Surgeon's certificate of disability. Order of Colonel Marshall. |
| 1 | Discharged at Louisville, Ky., July 4. Surgeon's certificate of disability. Order of Colonel Marshall. |
| 2 | Discharged at New Orleans, May 31. Surgeon's certificate of disability. Order of General Brooke. |
| 3 | Discharged at New Orleans, May 29. Surgeon's certificate of disability. Order of General Brooke. |
| 4 | Discharged at New Orleans, May 29. Surgeon's certificate of disability. Order of General Brooke. |
| 5 | Discharged at Camargo, Mexico, December 19. Surgeon's certificate of disability. Order of Lieutenant Davidson. |
| 6 | Discharged at New Orleans, October 20. Surgeon's certificate of disability. Order (of whom) unknown. |
| 7 | Discharged at Goliad, Texas, October 12. Surgeon's certificate of disability. Order of Colonel Marshall. |
| 8 | Discharged at Lavacca, Texas, October 14. Surgeon's certificate of disability. Order of Colonel Marshall. |
| 9 | Discharged at Lavacca, Texas, September 27. Surgeon's certificate of disability. Order of Col. Marshall. |
| 10 | Discharged at Lavacca, Texas, October 14. Surgeon's certificate of disability. Order of Col. Marshall. |
| 11 | Discharged at Lavacca, Texas, September 27. Surgeon's certificate of disability. Order of Col. Marshall. |
| 12 | Discharged at New Orleans, May 29. Surgeon's certificate of disability. Order of Gen'l Brooke. |
| 13 | Discharged at New Orleans, May 30. Surgeon's certificate of disability. Order of Gen'l Brooke. |
| 14 | Discharged at New Orleans, May 31. Surgeon's certificate of disability. Order of Gen'l Brooke. |
| 15 | Discharged at New Orleans, May 31. Surgeon's certificate of disability. Order of Gen'l Brooke. |
| 16 | Discharged at New Orleans, October 14. Surgeon's certificate of disability. Order of Gen'l Brooke. |
| 17 | Discharged at Lavacca, Texas, October 14. Surgeon's certificate of disability. Order of Col. Marshall. |
| 18 | Discharged at Camargo, Mexico, November 10. Surgeon's certificate of disability. Order of Col. Marshall. |

## MEXICAN WAR VETERANS.

### ROLL OF COMPANY "C," FIRST REGIMENT KENTUCKY

| No. of each grade. | Name. | Rank. | Enrolled. | Mustered In. When. | Mustered In. Where. | Period. | Mustered Out. When. | Mustered Out. Where. |
|---|---|---|---|---|---|---|---|---|
| 19 | Theobald, G. P. | Private | May 25, 1846 | June 9, '46 | Louisville, Ky. | 1 yr. | | |
| | DESERTED. | | | | | | | |
| 1 | Gibbs, D. G. | Private | May 25, 1846 | June 9, '46 | Louisville, Ky. | 1 yr. | | |

This company was enrolled at Frankfort, with the exception of (a); enrolled at Louisville.

### ROLL OF COMPANY "D," FIRST REGIMENT KENTUCKY

| | Name | Rank | Enrolled | Mustered In When | Mustered In Where | Period | Mustered Out When | Mustered Out Where |
|---|---|---|---|---|---|---|---|---|
| 1 | John Shawhan | Captain | May 27, 1846 | June 9, '46 | Louisville, Ky. | 1 yr. | June 7, '47 | New Orleans, La. |
| 1 | William H. Vanhook | 1st Lieutenant | May 27, 1846 | June 9, '46 | Louisville, Ly. | 1 yr. | June 7, '47 | New Orleans, La. |
| 1 | George P. Levinford | 2d Lieutenant | May 27, 1846 | June 9, '46 | Louisville, Ky. | 1 yr. | June 7, '47 | New Orleans, La. |
| 2 | John W. Kimbrough | 2d Lieutenant | May 27, 1846 | June 9, '46 | Louisville, Ky. | 1 yr. | June 7, '47 | New Orleans, La. |
| 1 | Noah S. Patterson | 1st Sergeant | May 27 1846 | June 9 '46 | Louisville, Ky. | 1 yr. | June 7, '47 | New Orleans, La. |
| 2 | Henry Williams | Sergeant | May 27, 1846 | June 9, '46 | Louisville, Ky. | 1 yr. | June 7, '47 | New Orleans, La. |
| 3 | Joseph Harden | Sergeant | May 27, 1846 | June 9, '46 | Louisville, Ky. | 1 yr. | June 7, '47 | New Orleans, La. |
| 4 | John B. Fowler | Sergeant | May 27, 1846 | June 9, '46 | Louisville, Ky. | 1 yr. | June 7, '47 | New Orleans, La. |
| 1 | Levi F. Boyd | Corporal | May 27, 1846 | June 9, '46 | Louisville, Ly. | 1 yr. | June 7, '47 | New Orleans, La. |
| 2 | Francis E. Walter | Corporal | May 27, 1846 | June 9, '46 | Louisville, Ky. | 1 yr. | June 7, '47 | New Orleans, La. |
| 1 | Alexander Douglass | Bugler | May 27, 1846 | June 9, '46 | Louisville, Ky. | 1 yr. | June 7, '47 | New Orleans, La. |
| 1 | Brown, Silas F. | Private | May 27, 1846 | June 9, '46 | Louisville, Ky. | 1 yr | June 7, '47 | New Orleans, La. |
| 2 | Byram, Jacob S. | Private | May 27, 1846 | June 9, '46 | Louisville, Ky. | 1 yr. | June 7, '47 | New Orleans, La. |
| 3 | Boyd, Jesse T. | Private | May 27, 1846 | June 9, '46 | Louisville, Ky. | 1 yr. | June 7, '47 | New Orleans, La. |
| 4 | Burton, Charles (a) | Private | June 15, 1846 | Oct. 31, '46 | Camargo, Mexico | 1 yr. | June 7, '47 | New Orleans, La. |
| 5 | Boneville, Charles | Private | June 15, 1846 | Oct. 31, '46 | Camargo, Mexico | 1 yr. | June 7, '47 | New Orleans, La. |
| 6 | Curry, William | Private | May 27, 1846 | June 9, '46 | Louisville, Ky. | 1 yr. | June 7, '47 | New Orleans, La. |
| 7 | Duncan, Joseph J. | Private | May 27, 1846 | June 9, '46 | Louisville, Ky. | 1 yr. | June 7, '47 | New Orleans, La. |
| 8 | Dennis, Thomas | Private | May 27, 1846 | June 9, '46 | Louisville, Ky. | 1 yr. | June 7, '47 | New Orleans, La. |
| 9 | Fowler, Charles H. | Private | May 27, 1846 | June 9, '46 | Louisville, Ky. | 1 yr. | June 7, '47 | New Orleans, La. |
| 10 | Funkhouser, Job | Private | May 27, 1846 | June 9, '46 | Louisville, Ky. | 1 yr. | June 7, '47 | New Orleans, La. |
| 11 | Fishwater, Edward J. | Private | May 27, 1846 | June 9, '46 | Louisville, Ky. | 1 yr. | June 7, '47 | New Orleans, La. |
| 12 | Foxworthy, William S. | Private | May 27, 1846 | June 9, '46 | Louisville, Ky. | 1 yr. | June 7, '47 | New Orleans, La. |
| 13 | Glane, Edward R. M. | Private | May 27, 1846 | June 9, '46 | Louisville, Ky. | 1 yr. | June 7, '47 | New Orleans, La. |
| 14 | Givens, George H. | Private | May 27, 1846 | June 9, '46 | Louisville, Ky. | 1 yr. | June 7, '47 | New Orleans, La. |
| 15 | Jeter, Benjamin (a) | Private | June 15, 1846 | June 9, '46 | Louisville, Ky. | 1 yr. | June 7, '47 | New Orleans, La. |
| 16 | Levi, Andrew J. | Private | May 27, 1846 | June 9, '46 | Louisville, Ky. | 1 yr. | June 7, '47 | New Orleans, La. |
| 17 | Logan, James E. (a) | Private | June 15, 1846 | Oct. 31, '46 | Camargo, Mexico | 1 yr. | June 7, '47 | New Orleans, La. |
| 18 | Murphy, Cornelius | Private | May 27, 1846 | June 9, '46 | Louisville, Ky. | 1 yr. | June 7, '47 | New Orleans, La. |
| 19 | Miller, Thomas | Private | May 27, 1846 | June 9, '46 | Louisville, Ky. | 1 yr. | June 7, '47 | New Orleans, La. |
| 20 | Oder, Thomas W. | Private | May 27, 1846 | June 9, '46 | Louisville, Ky. | 1 yr. | June 7, '47 | New Orleans, La. |
| 21 | Overly, Jacob C. | Private | May 27, 1846 | June 9, '46 | Louisville, Ky. | 1 yr. | June 7, '47 | New Orleans, La. |
| 22 | Painter, Daniel | Private | May 27, 1846 | June 9, '46 | Louisville, Ky. | 1 yr. | June 7, '47 | New Orleans, La. |
| 23 | Pope, John M. | Private | May 27, 1846 | June 9, '46 | Louisville, Ky. | 1 yr. | June 7, '47 | New Orleans, La. |
| 24 | Parker, William C. | Private | May 27, 1846 | June 9, '46 | Louisville, Ky. | 1 yr. | June 7, '47 | New Orleans, La. |
| 25 | Richey, Joseph M. | Private | May 27, 1846 | June 9, '46 | Louisville, Ky. | 1 yr. | June 7, '47 | New Orleans, La. |
| 26 | Richey, William B. | Private | May 27, 1846 | June 9, '46 | Louisville, Ky. | 1 yr. | June 7, '47 | New Orleans, La. |
| 27 | Ross, David | Private | May 27, 1846 | June 9, '46 | Louisville, Ky. | 1 yr. | June 7, '47 | New Orleans, La. |
| 28 | Rout, Isham T. | Private | May 27, 1846 | June 9, '46 | Louisville, Ky. | 1 yr. | June 7, '47 | New Orleans, La. |
| 29 | Stilly, Samuel | Private | May 27, 1846 | June 9, '46 | Louisville, Ky. | 1 yr. | June 7, '47 | New Orleans, La. |
| 30 | Thompson, McCalla | Private | May 27, 1846 | June 9, '46 | Louisville, Ky. | 1 yr. | June 7, '47 | New Orleans, La. |
| 31 | Vanhook, John M. | Private | May 27, 1846 | June 9, '46 | Louisville, Ky. | 1 yr. | June 7, '47 | New Orleans, La. |
| 32 | Waller, James H. | Private | May 27, 1846 | June 9, '46 | Louisville, Ky. | 1 yr. | June 7, '47 | New Orleans, La. |
| 33 | Wilson, George H. | Private | May 27, 1846 | June 9, '46 | Louisville, Ky. | 1 yr. | June 7, '47 | New Orleans, La. |
| 34 | Wilson, Michael C. | Private | May 27, 1846 | June 9, '46 | Louisville, Ky. | 1 yr. | June 7, '47 | New Orleans, La. |
| 35 | White, John H. | Private | May 27, 1846 | June 9, '46 | Louisville, Ky. | 1 yr. | June 7, '47 | New Orleans, La. |
| 36 | Woodyard, Henry W. | Private | May 27, 1846 | June 9, '46 | Louisville, Ky. | 1 yr. | June 7, '47 | New Orleans, La. |
| 37 | Warford, James H. | Private | May 27, 1846 | June 9, '46 | Louisville, Ky. | 1 yr. | June 7, '47 | New Orleans, La. |
| 38 | Wall, John T. | Private | May 27, 1846 | June 9, '46 | Louisville, Ky. | 1 yr. | June 7, '47 | New Orleans, La. |
| 39 | Williams, James C. (a) | Private | June 9, 1846 | June 9, '46 | Louisville, Ky. | 1 yr. | June 7, '47 | New Orleans, La. |
| 40 | Snodgrass, William | Private | May 27, 1846 | June 9, '46 | Louisville, Ky. | 1 yr. | June 7, '47 | New Orleans, La. |
| | KILLED IN BATTLE. | | | | | | | |
| 1 | John A. Jones | Corporal | May 27, 1846 | June 9, '46 | Louisville, Ky. | 1 yr. | | |
| 1 | McClintock, Wm. A. | Private | May 27, 1846 | June 9, '46 | Louisville, Ky. | 1 yr. | | |
| 2 | Pomeroy, James | Private | May 27, 1846 | June 9, '46 | Louisville, Ky. | 1 yr. | | |
| 3 | Rodgers, David P. | Private | May 27, 1846 | June 9, '46 | Louisville, Ky. | 1 yr. | | |
| | DIED. | | | | | | | |
| 1 | Brawner, William (a) | Blacksmith | June 15, 1846 | Never mus. | | | | |
| 1 | Cummins, Worthen | Private | May 27, 1846 | June 9, '46 | Louisville, Ky. | 1 yr. | | |
| 2 | Duncan, Wm. O. | Private | May 27, 1846 | June 9, '46 | Louisville, Ky. | 1 yr. | | |
| 3 | Fisher, James H. | Private | May 27, 1846 | June 9, '46 | Louisville, Ky. | 1 yr. | | |

MEXICAN WAR VETERANS.

## MOUNTED VOLUNTEERS—MEXICAN WAR—Continued.

| No. of each grade | REMARKS. |
|---|---|
| 19 | Discharged at New Orleans (no date). Surgeon's certificate of disability. Order of Gen. Brooke. |
| 1 | Deserted at Camargo, Mexico, April 5th. |

## MOUNTED VOLUNTEERS—MEXICAN WAR.

| No. | REMARKS. |
|---|---|
| 1 | Wounded in battle of Buena Vista, Februaray 23d; slightly. |
| 1 | |
| 1 | |
| 2 | Elected from private July 13th. Slightly wounded in battle of Buena Vista, February 23d. |
| 1 | |
| 2 | |
| 3 | |
| 4 | Appointed from private September 12th. Order of Col. Marshall. |
| 1 | |
| 2 | |
| 1 | |
| 1 | |
| 2 | Wounded severely in battle of Buena Vista, February 23d. |
| 3 | |
| 4 | Joined as substitute for private Trimble at Louisville, Ky., June 15th. Order of Col. Marshall. |
| 5 | Joined as substitute for private Snodgrass at Louisville, Ky., June 15th. Order of Col. Marshall. |
| 6 | |
| 7 | |
| 8 | |
| 9 | Wounded slightly in battle of Buena Vista, February 23d. |
| 10 | |
| 11 | |
| 12 | |
| 13 | |
| 14 | |
| 15 | |
| 16 | |
| 17 | Joined as substituted for private J. Price at Louisville, June 15th. Order of Col. Marshall. |
| 18 | |
| 19 | |
| 20 | |
| 21 | |
| 22 | |
| 23 | |
| 24 | Wounded severely at battle of Buena Vista, February 23d. |
| 25 | Left sick in hospital at Little Rock, Arkansas, July 26th. Not reported since. |
| 26 | Reduced from Corporal December 1st, by sentence regimental court-martial. |
| 27 | |
| 28 | |
| 29 | |
| 30 | |
| 31 | Severely wounded in battle of Buena Vista, February 23d. |
| 32 | |
| 33 | Severely wounded in battle of Buena Vista, February 23d. |
| 34 | |
| 35 | |
| 36 | |
| 37 | Severely wounded at battle of Buena Vista, February 23d. |
| 38 | |
| 39 | |
| 40 | Severely wounded at battle of Buena Vista, February 23d. |
| 1 | Killed in battle of Buena Vista, February 23d. |
| 1 | Killed in battle of Buena Vista, February 23d. |
| 2 | Killed in battle of Buena Vista, February 23d. |
| 3 | Killed in battle of Buena Vista, February 23d. |
| 1 | Joined as substitute for private Hall, June 15th. Order of Col. Marshall; died August 18th, on the march through Arkansas. |
| 1 | Died at Memphis, Tenn., July 28th. |
| 2 | Died at Captain Friar's, Texas, September 25th. |
| 3 | Died at Matamoras, March 1, 1847. |

MEXICAN WAR VETERANS.

## ROLL OF COMPANY "D," FIRST REGIMENT KENTUCKY

| No. of each grade | Name. | Rank. | Enrolled. | Mustered In. When. | Mustered In. Where. | Period. | Mustered Out. When. | Mustered Out. Where. |
|---|---|---|---|---|---|---|---|---|
| 4 | Overby, Jno. C. | Private | May 27, 1846 | June 9, '46 | Louisville, Ky. | 1 yr. | | |
| | DISCHARGED. | | | | | | | |
| 1 | J. N. Anderson | Sergeant | May 27, 1846 | June 9, '46 | Louisville, Ky. | 1 yr. | | |
| 1 | James Johnson (a) | Corporal | June 9, 1846 | June 9, '46 | Louisville, Ky. | 1 yr. | | |
| 1 | William Marshall | Bugler | May 27, 1846 | June 9, '46 | Louisville, Ky. | 1 yr. | | |
| 1 | Bean, John | Private | May 27, 1846 | June 9, '46 | Louisville, Ky. | 1 yr. | | |
| 2 | Conner, George W. | Private | May 27, 1846 | June 9, '46 | Louisville, Ky. | 1 yr. | | |
| 3 | Renney, George M. | Private | May 27, 1846 | June 9, '46 | Louisville, Ky. | 1 yr. | | |
| 4 | Moore, Richard G. R. | Private | May 27, 1846 | June 9, '46 | Louisville, Ky. | 1 yr. | | |
| 5 | Perrin, William J. | Private | May 27, 1846 | June 9, '46 | Louisville, Ky. | 1 yr. | | |
| 6 | Smith, Wesley | Private | May 27, 1846 | June 9, '46 | Louisville, Ky. | 1 yr. | | |
| 7 | Smith, Francis | Private | May 27, 1846 | June 9, '46 | Louisville, Ky. | 1 yr. | | |
| 8 | Wilson, Jonathan C. | Private | May 27, 1846 | June 9, '46 | Louisville, Ky. | 1 yr. | | |
| 9 | Worthen, Osker B. | Private | May 27, 1846 | June 9, '46 | Louisville, Ky. | 1 yr. | | |
| 10 | Hall, Squire | Private | May 27, 1846 | June 9, '46 | Louisville, Ky. | 1 yr. | | |
| 11 | Makee (or Magee) T. T. | Private | May 27, 1846 | June 9, '46 | Louisville, Ky. | 1 yr. | | |
| 12 | McChesney, Wm. | Private | May 27, 1846 | June 9, '46 | Louisville, Ky. | 1 yr. | | |
| 13 | Murphy, Philip | Private | May 27, 1846 | June 9, '46 | Louisville, Ky. | 1 yr. | | |
| 14 | McCarthy, Wm. P. | Private | May 27, 1846 | June 9, '46 | Louisville, Ky. | 1 yr. | | |
| 15 | Price, James | Private | May 27, 1846 | June 9, '46 | Louisville, Ky. | 1 yr. | | |
| 16 | Pope, Wm. A. | Private | May 27, 1846 | June 9, '46 | Louisville, Ky. | 1 yr. | | |
| 17 | Snodgrass, Jasper | Private | May 27, 1846 | June 9, '46 | Louisville, Ky. | 1 yr. | | |
| 18 | Trimble, John | Private | May 27, 1846 | June 9, '46 | Louisville, Ky. | 1 yr. | | |
| 19 | Stowers, David L. | Private | May 27, 1846 | June 9, '46 | Louisville, Ky. | 1 yr. | | |
| | DESERTED. | | | | | | | |
| 1 | Dudley, T. Calvert (a) | Private | June 15, 1846 | | | | | |

(*a*.) Enrolled at Louisville.
All others at Cynthiana.

## ROLL OF COMPANY "E," FIRST REGIMENT KENTUCKY

| | Name | Rank | Enrolled | Mustered In When | Mustered In Where | Period | Mustered Out When | Mustered Out Where |
|---|---|---|---|---|---|---|---|---|
| 1 | William J. Heady | Captain | June 9, 1846 | June 9, '46 | Louisville, Ky. | 1 yr. | June 7, '47 | New Orleans, La. |
| 1 | J. J. Churchill | 1st Lieutenant | June 9, 1846 | June 9, '46 | Louisville, Ky. | 1 yr. | June 7, '47 | New Orleans, La. |
| 1 | J. A. Merrifield | 2d Lieutenant | June 9, 1846 | June 9, '46 | Louisville, Ky. | 1 yr. | June 7, '47 | New Orleans, La. |
| 1 | J. W. Owings | 1st Sergeant | June 9, 1846 | June 9, '46 | Louisville, Ky. | 1 yr. | June 7, '47 | New Orleans, La. |
| 2 | Joseph White | Sergeant | June 9, 1846 | June 9, '46 | Louisville, Ky. | 1 yr. | June 7, '47 | New Orleans, La. |
| 3 | John A. Shrader | Sergeant | June 9, 1846 | June 9, '46 | Louisville, Ky. | 1 yr. | June 7, '47 | New Orleans, La. |
| 4 | Sylvester Maratea | Sergeant | June 9, 1846 | June 9, '46 | Louisville, Ky. | 1 yr. | June 7, '47 | New Orleans, La. |
| 1 | D. G. O'Riley | Corporal | June 9, 1846 | June 9, '46 | Louisville, Ky. | 1 yr. | June 7, '47 | New Orleans, La. |
| 2 | S. (or T.) J. Springer | Corporal | June 9, 1846 | June 9, '46 | Louisville, Ky. | 1 yr. | June 7, '47 | New Orleans, La. |
| 3 | George Sharp | Corporal | June 9, 1846 | June 9, '46 | Louisville, Ky. | 1 yr. | June 7, '47 | New Orleans, La. |
| 4 | James Kemp | Corporal | June 9, 1846 | June 9, '46 | Louisville, Ky. | 1 yr. | June 7, '47 | New Orleans, La. |
| 1 | W. M. Williams | Bugler | June 9, 1846 | June 9, '46 | Louisville, Ky. | 1 yr. | June 7, '47 | New Orleans, La. |
| 1 | Wm. H. Thomas | Farrier | June 9, 1846 | June 9, '46 | Louisville, Ky. | 1 yr. | June 7, '47 | New Orleans, La. |
| 1 | Alexander, Abram S. | Private | June 9, 1846 | June 9, '46 | Louisville, Ky. | 1 yr. | June 7, '47 | New Orleans, La. |
| 2 | Burnett, G. W. | Private | June 9, 1846 | June 9, '46 | Louisville, Ky. | 1 yr. | June 7, '47 | New Orleans, La. |
| 3 | Burnett, Wesley | Private | June 9, 1846 | June 9, '46 | Louisville, Ky. | 1 yr | June 7, '47 | New Orleans, La. |
| 4 | Bell, James F. | Private | June 9, 1846 | June 9, '46 | Louisville, Ky. | 1 yr. | June 7, '47 | New Orleans, La. |
| 5 | Clark, Wm. A. | Private | June 9, 1846 | June 9, '46 | Louisville, Ky. | 1 yr. | June 7, '47 | New Orleans, La. |
| 6 | Coleman, John C. | Private | June 9, 1846 | June 9, '46 | Louisville, Ky. | 1 yr. | June 7, '47 | New Orleans, La. |
| 7 | Cox, James G. | Private | June 9, 1846 | June 9, '46 | Louisville, Ky. | 1 yr. | June 7, '47 | New Orleans, La. |
| 8 | Doyle, (similar to it) | Private | June 9, 1846 | June 9, '46 | Louisville, Ky. | 1 yr. | June 7, '47 | New Orleans, La. |
| 9 | Denormanie, W. P. | Private | June 9, 1846 | June 9, '46 | Louisville, Ky. | 1 yr. | June 7, '47 | New Orleans, La. |
| 10 | Fleming, David | Private | June 9, 1846 | June 9, '46 | Louisville, Ky. | 1 yr. | June 7, '47 | New Orleans, La. |
| 11 | Florence, M. D. | Private | June 9, 1846 | June 9, '46 | Louisville, Ky. | 1 yr. | June 7, '47 | New Orleans, La. |
| 12 | Finnes, J. | Private | June 9, 1846 | June 9, '46 | Louisville, Ky. | 1 yr. | June 7, '47 | New Orleans, La. |
| 13 | Havenhill, George | Private | June 9, 1846 | June 9, '46 | Louisville, Ky. | 1 yr. | June 7, '47 | New Orleans, La. |
| 14 | Hart, James | Private | June 9, 1846 | June 9, '46 | Louisville, Ky. | 1 yr. | June 7, '47 | New Orleans, La. |
| 15 | Humphries, W. H. (a) | Private | July 15, 1846 | June 9, '46 | Louisville, Ky. | 1 yr. | June 7, '47 | New Orleans, La. |
| 16 | Koons, R. | Private | June 9, 1846 | June 9, '46 | Louisville, Ky. | 1 yr. | June 7, '47 | New Orleans, La. |
| 17 | Levan, D. W. | Private | June 9, 1846 | June 9, '46 | Louisville, Ky. | 1 yr. | June 7, '47 | New Orleans, La. |
| 18 | McDonough, Michael | Private | June 9, 1846 | June 9, '46 | Louisville, Ky. | 1 yr. | June 7, '47 | New Orleans, La. |
| 19 | May, Stephen | Private | June 9, 1846 | June 9, '46 | Louisville, Ky. | 1 yr. | June 7, '47 | New Orleans, La. |
| 20 | McCarty, Thomas | Private | June 9, 1846 | June 9, '46 | Louisville, Ky. | 1 yr. | June 7, '47 | New Orleans, La. |
| 21 | Marshall, Ben | Private | June 9, 1846 | June 9, '46 | Louisville, Ky. | 1 yr. | June 7, '47 | New Orleans, La. |
| 22 | McKegg, James (f) | Private | June 9, 1846 | June 9, '46 | Louisville, Ky. | 1 yr. | June 7, '47 | New Orleans, La. |
| 23 | Marshall, A. G. | Private | June 9, 1846 | June 9, '46 | Louisville, Ky. | 1 yr. | June 7, '47 | New Orleans, La. |
| 24 | Pennabaker, C. D. | Private | June 9, 1846 | June 9, '46 | Louisville, Ky. | 1 yr. | June 7, '47 | New Orleans, La. |
| 25 | Rose, William S. | Private | June 9, 1846 | June 9, '46 | Louisville, Ky. | 1 yr. | June 7, '47 | New Orleans, La. |

# MOUNTED VOLUNTEERS—MEXICAN WAR—Continued.

| No. of each grade | REMARKS. |
|---|---|
| 4 | Died at Matamoras, February 1st. |
| | |
| 1 | Discharged at Port Lavacca, Texas, October 12th; Surgeon's certificate of disability. Order of Col. Marshall. |
| 1 | Discharged at New Orleans, La., June —; Surgeon's certificate of disability. Order of Gen. Brooke. |
| 1 | Discharged at Camargo, Mex., November 12th; Surgeon's certificate of disability. Order of Gen. Patterson. |
| 1 | Discharged at Port Lavacca, Texas, October 9th; Surgeon's certificate of disability. Order of Col. Marshall. |
| 2 | Discharged at Port Lavacca, Texas, October 12th; Surgeon's certificate of disability. Order of Col. Marshall. |
| 3 | Discharged at Port Lavacca, Texas, October 12th; Surgeon's certificate of disability. Order of Col. Marshall. |
| 4 | Discharged at Port Lavacca, Texas, October 9th; Surgeon's certificate of disability. Order of Col. Marshall. |
| 5 | Discharged at Victoria, Texas, October 14th; Surgeon's certificate of disability. Order of Col. Marshall. |
| 6 | Discharged at Memphis, Tenn., July 26th; Surgeon's certificate of disability. Order of Col. Marshall. |
| 7 | Discharged at Port Lavacca, Texas, October 12th; Surgeon's certificate of disability. Order of Col. Marshall. |
| 8 | Discharged at Port Lavacca, Texas, October 12th; Surgeon's certificate of disability. Order of Col. Marshall. |
| 9 | Discharged at Port Lavacca, Texas, October 12th; Surgeon's certificate of disability. Order of Col. Marshall. |
| 10 | Discharged at Louisville, Ky., June 15th, by procuring substitute, private Brawner. Order of Col. Marshall. |
| 11 | Discharged at New Orleans, June 1st. Order of Gen. Brooke. |
| 12 | Discharged at New Orleans, June 1st; Surgeon's certificate of disability. Order of Gen. Brooke. |
| 13 | Discharged at New Orleans, June 1st; Surgeon's certificate of disability. Order of Gen. Brooke. |
| 14 | Discharged at Monterey, Mex., April 1st; Surgeon's certificate of disability. Order of Col. Ormsby. |
| 15 | Discharged at Louisville, Ky., June 15th, by procuring substitute, private Logan. Permission of Col. Marshall. |
| 16 | Discharged at Louisville, Ky., June 15th, by procuring substitute, private Calvert. Permission of Col. Marshall. |
| 17 | Discharged at Louisville, Ky., June 15th, by procuring substitute, private Bonneville. Permission of Col. Marshall. |
| 18 | Discharged at Louisville, Ky., June 15th, by procuring substitute, private Burton. Permission of Col. Marshall. |
| 19 | Discharged at New Orleans, June 1st; Surgeon's certificate of disability. Order of Gen. Brooke. |
| | |
| 1 | Deserted on the march through Arkansas, August 5th. |

# MOUNTED VOLUNTEERS MEXICAN WAR.

| No. of each grade | REMARKS. |
|---|---|
| 1 | Prisoner of war in Mexico from January 28th. |
| 1 | Prisoner of war in Mexico from January 28th. |
| 1 | Was private from enrollment to July 13th. |
| 1 | Was Sergeant from enrollment to October 9th. Prisoner of war in Mexico from January 28th. |
| 2 | Prisoner of war in Mexico from January 28th. |
| 3 | Performed duty as 1st Sergeant from January 28th. |
| 4 | Private from enrollment to October 9th. |
| 1 | |
| 2 | Prisoner of war in Mexico from January 28th. |
| 3 | Prisoner of war in Mexico from January 28th. |
| 4 | Prisoner of war in Mexico from January 28th; was private from enrollment until July 13th. |
| 1 | |
| 1 | Joined as substitute, Carmago, November 18th, for J. S. Lindenberger. Order of Col. Marshall. Prisoner of war in Mexico, Jan. 28th. |
| 1 | Prisoner of war in Mexico from January 28th. |
| 2 | Prisoner of war in Mexico from January 28th. |
| 3 | Absent on furlough in Mexico from May 12th. Order of Lieut. Col. Fields. |
| 4 | Prisoner of war in Mexico from January 28th. |
| 5 | Prisoner of war in Mexico from January 28th. |
| 6 | |
| 7 | |
| 8 | Prisoner of war in Mexico from January 28th. |
| 9 | |
| 10 | |
| 11 | Sick; absent in Kentucky from July 4th. |
| 12 | |
| 13 | |
| 14 | |
| 15 | Joined as substitute at Camargo, November 18th, for J. C. Smith. Order of Col. Marshall. |
| 16 | Prisoner of war in Mexico from January 28th. |
| 17 | Prisoner of war in Mexico from January 28th. |
| 18 | |
| 19 | |
| 20 | |
| 21 | Absent on furlough in Mexico from May 12th. Order Lieut. Col. Field. |
| 22 | Sick; absent in Kentucky from July 9th. |
| 23 | Prisoner of war in Mexico from January 28th. |
| 24 | Absent in Mexico from April 30th. Order of Col. Fields. |
| 25 | |

## ROLL OF COMPANY "E," FIRST REGIMENT KENTUCKY

| No. of each grade | Name | Rank | Enrolled | Mustered In. When | Mustered In. Where | Period | Mustered Out. When | Mustered Out. Where |
|---|---|---|---|---|---|---|---|---|
| 26 | Russell, Robert | Private | June 9, 1846 | June 9, '46 | Louisville, Ky. | 1 yr. | June 7, '47 | New Orleans |
| 27 | Rue, Charles H. | Private | June 9, 1846 | June 9, '46 | Louisville, Ky. | 1 yr. | June 7, '47 | New Orleans |
| 28 | Staltman, J. A. | Private | June 9, 1846 | June 9, '46 | Louisville, Ky. | 1 yr. | June 7, '47 | New Orleans |
| 29 | Tilford, Joseph | Private | June 9, 1846 | June 9, '46 | Louisville, Ky. | 1 yr. | June 7, '47 | New Orleans |
| 30 | Freeranel, Joseph | Private | June 9, 1846 | June 9, '46 | Louisville, Ky. | 1 yr. | June 7, '47 | New Orleans |
| 31 | Woods, W. H. | Private | June 9, 1846 | June 9, '46 | Louisville, Ky. | 1 yr. | June 7, '47 | New Orleans |
| 32 | Woods, R. E. | Private | June 9, 1846 | June 9, '46 | Louisville, Ky. | 1 yr. | June 7, '47 | New Orleans |
| 33 | White, Albert | Private | June 9, 1846 | June 9, '46 | Louisville, Ky. | 1 yr. | June 7, '47 | New Orleans |
| 34 | Vettitoe, James | Private | June 9, 1846 | June 9, '46 | Louisville, Ky. | 1 yr. | June 7, '47 | New Orleans |
|  | **KILLED IN BATTLE.** |  |  |  |  |  |  |  |
| 1 | Thompson, C. B. | Private | June 9, 1846 | June 9, '46 | Louisville, Ky. | 1 yr. |  |  |
|  | **DIED.** |  |  |  |  |  |  |  |
| 1 | Ford, W. M. | Private | June 9, 1846 | June 9, '46 | Louisville, Ky. | 1 yr. |  |  |
| 2 | Fowler, J. D. | Private | June 9, 1846 | June 9, '46 | Louisville, Ky. | 1 yr. |  |  |
| 3 | Leghton, William | Private | June 9, 1846 | June 9, '46 | Louisville, Ky. | 1 yr. |  |  |
| 4 | Milligan, A. M. | Private | June 9, 1846 | June 9, '46 | Louisville, Ky. | 1 yr. |  |  |
|  | **DISCHARGED.** |  |  |  |  |  |  |  |
| 1 | Lawrence, B. H. | 2d Lieutenant | June 9, 1846 | June 9, '46 | Louisville, Ky. | 1 yr. |  |  |
| 1 | Sherley, W. M. | Sergeant | June 9, 1846 | June 9, '46 | Louisville, Ky. | 1 yr. |  |  |
| 1 | Conklin, H. C. | Bugler | June 9, 1846 | June 9, '46 | Louisville, Ky. | 1 yr. |  |  |
| 1 | Leadenburg, J. S. | Farrier | June 9, 1846 | June 9, '46 | Louisville, Ky. | 1 yr. |  |  |
| 1 | Able, Monroe | Private | June 9, 1846 | June 9, '46 | Louisville, Ky. | 1 yr. |  |  |
| 2 | Andrews, A. M. | Private | June 9, 1846 | June 9, '46 | Louisville, Ky. | 1 yr. |  |  |
| 3 | Barnet, Theodore | Private | June 9, 1846 | June 9, '46 | Louisville, Ky. | 1 yr. |  |  |
| 4 | Brown, Thomas | Private | June 9, 1846 | June 9, '46 | Louisville, Ky. | 1 yr. |  |  |
| 5 | Babe, George | Private | June 9, 1846 | June 9, '46 | Louisville, Ky. | 1 yr. |  |  |
| 6 | Coleman, Samuel | Private | June 9, 1846 | June 9, '46 | Louisville, Ky. | 1 yr. |  |  |
| 7 | Clements, T. J. | Private | June 9, 1846 | June 9, '46 | Louisville, Ky. | 1 yr. |  |  |
| 8 | Cook, G. | Private | June 9, 1846 | June 9, '46 | Louisville, Ky. | 1 yr. |  |  |
| 9 | Duncan, W. H. | Private | June 9, 1846 | June 9, '46 | Louisville, Ky. | 1 yr. |  |  |
| 10 | Trigg, Ben | Private | June 9, 1846 | June 9, '46 | Louisville, Ky. | 1 yr. |  |  |
| 11 | Hite, A. H. | Private | June 9, 1846 | June 9, '46 | Louisville, Ky. | 1 yr. |  |  |
| 12 | Hunt, R. | Private | June 9, 1846 | June 9, '46 | Louisville, Ky. | 1 yr. |  |  |
| 13 | Malcom, Greenburg | Private | June 9, 1846 | June 9, '46 | Louisville, Ky. | 1 yr. |  |  |
| 14 | McHenry, James | Private | June 9, 1846 | June 9, '46 | Louisville, Ky. | 1 yr. |  |  |
| 15 | Manson, William | Private | June 9, 1846 | June 9, '46 | Louisville, Ky. | 1 yr. |  |  |
| 16 | Maddox, Edward | Private | June 9, 1846 | June 9, '46 | Louisville, Ky. | 1 yr. |  |  |
| 17 | Monroe, C. E. | Private | June 9, 1846 | June 9, '46 | Louisville, Ky. | 1 yr. |  |  |
| 18 | Newland, W. B. | Private | June 9, 1846 | June 9, '46 | Louisville, Ky. | 1 yr. |  |  |
| 19 | Pennabaker, Thomas | Private | June 9, 1846 | June 9, '46 | Louisville, Ky. | 1 yr. |  |  |
| 20 | Roan, F. A. | Private | June 9, 1846 | June 9, '46 | Louisville, Ky. | 1 yr. |  |  |
| 21 | Ridgway, William | Private | June 9, 1846 | June 9, '46 | Louisville, Ky. | 1 yr. |  |  |
| 22 | Slaughter, P. J. | Private | June 9, 1846 | June 9, '46 | Louisville, Ky. | 1 yr. |  |  |
| 23 | Sims, G. W. | Private | June 9, 1846 | June 9, '46 | Louisville, Ky. | 1 yr. |  |  |
| 24 | Smith, J. C. P. | Private | June 9, 1846 | June 9, '46 | Louisville, Ky. | 1 yr. |  |  |
| 25 | Wakeman, W. H. | Private | June 9, 1846 | June 9, '46 | Louisville, Ky. | 1 yr. |  |  |
| 26 | White, Zachariah | Private | June 9, 1846 | June 9, '46 | Louisville, Ky. | 1 yr. |  |  |

This company was enrolled at Louisville, with the exception of (a), this man being enrolled at Memphis, Tenn.
(f) Muster rolls say this name should have been among those discharged.

## ROLL OF COMPANY "F," FIRST REGIMENT KENTUCKY

| No. | Name | Rank | Enrolled | Mustered In. When | Mustered In. Where | Period | Mustered Out. When | Mustered Out. Where |
|---|---|---|---|---|---|---|---|---|
| 1 | Thomas F. Marshall | Captain | June 9, 1846 | June 9, '46 | Louisville, Ky. | 1 yr. | June 10, '47 | New Orleans, La. |
| 1 | Samuel F. Patterson | 1st Lieutenant | June 9, 1846 | June 9, '46 | Louisville, Ky. | 1 yr. | June 10, '47 | New Orlerns, La. |
| 1 | John Brown | 2d Lieutenant | June 9, 1846 | June 9, '46 | Louisville, Ky. | 1 yr. | June 10, '47 | New Orleans, La. |
| 2 | Randolph Braisfield | Lieutenant | June 9, 1846 | June 9, '46 | Louisville, Ky. | 1 yr. | June 10, '47 | New Orleans, La. |
| 1 | William L. Moseby | 1st Sergeant | June 9, 1846 | June 9, '46 | Louisville, Ky. | 1 yr. | June 10, '47 | New Orleans, La. |
| 2 | Walter L. Peters | Sergeant | June 9, 1846 | June 9, '46 | Louisville, Ky. | 1 yr. | June 10, '47 | New Orleans, La. |
| 3 | James Lockite | Sergeant | June 9, 1846 | June 9, '46 | Louisville, Ky. | 1 yr. | June 10, '47 | New Orleans, La. |
| 1 | Samuel H. Bradley | Corporal | June 9, 1846 | June 9, '46 | Louisville, Ky. | 1 yr. | June 10, '47 | New Orleans, La. |
| 2 | Thomas Lister | Corporal | June 9, 1846 | June 9, '46 | Louisville, Ky. | 1 yr. | June 10, '47 | New Orleans, La. |
| 3 | William C. Gillespie | Corporal | June 9, 1846 | June 9, '46 | Louisville, Ky. | 1 yr. | June 10, '47 | New Orleans, La. |
| 4 | James M. Kinkead | Corporal | June 9, 1846 | June 9, '46 | Louisville, Ky. | 1 yr. | June 10, '47 | New Orleans, La. |
| 1 | Boon Maja | Musician | June 9, 1846 | June 9, '46 | Louisville, Ky. | 1 yr. | June 10, '47 | New Orleans, La. |
| 1 | Henry C. Brady | Farrier | June 9, 1846 | June 9, '46 | Louisville, Ky. | 1 yr. | June 10, '47 | New Orleans, La. |
| 1 | Ashmore, John I. | Private | June 9, 1846 | June 9, '46 | Louisville, Ky. | 1 yr. | June 10, '47 | New Orleans, La. |
| 2 | Ashford, Franklin P. | Private | June 9, 1846 | June 9, '46 | Louisville, Ky. | 1 yr. | June 10, '47 | New Orleans, La. |
| 3 | Booth, Thomas A. | Private | June 9, 1846 | June 9, '46 | Louisville, Ky. | 1 yr. | June 10, '47 | New Orleans, La. |
| 4 | Brown, Andrew | Private | June 9, 1846 | June 9, '46 | Louisville, Ky. | 1 yr. | June 10, '47 | New Orleans, La. |

## MOUNTED VOLUNTEERS—MEXICAN WAR—Continued.

| No. of each grade | REMARKS. |
|---|---|
| 26 | |
| 27 | Prisoner of war in Mexico from January 28th. |
| 28 | |
| 29 | Sick; absent in Kentucky from October 13th. |
| 30 | After this roll was made out it was found that this man was discharged at New Orleans; Surgeon's certificate of disability. Order of [Gen. Brooke. |
| 31 | Absent on furlough in Mexico from May 12th. Order of Lieut. Col. Fields. |
| 32 | Joined as substitute, Camargo, Mex., November 18th, for A. Andrews. Order of Col. Marshall. |
| 33 | Prisoner of war in Mexico from January 28th. |
| 34 | |
| 1 | Killed in battle of Buena Visita, February 23d. |
| 1 | Died of fever at Memphis, Tenn., July 30th. |
| 2 | Died of abscess at Polomas, Mex., in camp, January 19th. |
| 3 | Died of fever at Memphis, Tenn., July 30th. |
| 4 | Died of fever at Washington, Texas, September 19th. |
| 1 | Discharged by reorganization at Louisville, November 18th. Order not known. |
| 1 | Discharged at Port Lavacca, October 9th; Surgeon's certificate of disability. Order of Col. Marshall. |
| 1 | Discharged at New Orleans, La., about May 28th; Surgeon's certificate of disability. Order of Gen. Brooke. |
| 1 | Discharged at Louisville, July 4th; procuring substitute, W. H. Thomas. Order of Col. Marshall. |
| 1 | Discharged at Port Lavacca, October 14th; Surgeon's certificate of disability. Order of Col. Marshall. |
| 2 | Discharged at Louisville, June 23d, procuring substitute, A. White. Order of Col. Marshall. |
| 3 | Discharged at Port Lavacca, October 14th; Surgeon's certificate of disability. Order of Col. Marshall |
| 4 | Discharged at New Orleans about October 28th, by whose order not known. |
| 5 | Discharged at Port Lavacca, September 25th; Surgeon's certificate of disability. Order of Col. Marshall. |
| 6 | Discharged at New Orleans about May 28th; Surgeon's certificate of disability Order of Gen. Brooke. |
| 7 | Discharged at New Orleans about May 28th; Surgeon's certificate of disability. Order of Gen. Brooke. |
| 8 | Discharged at Matamoras, January 8th; Surgeon's certificate of disability. Whose order not known. |
| 9 | Discharged at Camargo about March 25th; Surgeon's certificate of disability. Order of Col Marshall. |
| 10 | Discharged at New Orleans about May 28th; Surgeon's certificate of disability. Order of Gen. Brooke. |
| 11 | Discharged at Little Rock, Ark., July 30th; Surgeon's certificate of disability. Order of Col. Marshall. |
| 12 | Discharged at Louisville, June 23d, procured substitute, J. McHenry. Order of Col. Marshall. |
| 13 | Discharged at New Orleans, January 1st. Order of Gen. Brooke. [at New Orleans. Order of Gen. Brooke. |
| 14 | Joined at Camargo, November 18th, substitute for R. Hartley. Order of Col. Marshall. Discharged on Surgeon's certificate of disability. |
| 15 | Discharged at Matamoras; Surgeon's certificate of disability. Time not known. |
| 16 | Discharged at Louisville, June 25th; Surgeon's certificate of disability. Order of Gen. Brooke. |
| 17 | Discharged at Port Lavacca, October 1st; Surgeon's certificate of disability. Order of Col. Marshall. |
| 18 | Discharged at Washington, Ark., January 5th; Surgeon's certificate of disability. Order of Col. Marshall. |
| 19 | Discharged at New Orleans about October 28th. Not known. |
| 20 | Discharged at New Orleans about October 28th; Surgeon's certificate of disability. Order of Gen. Brooke. |
| 21 | Discharged at New Orleans about October 28th; Surgeon's certificate of disability. Order of Gen. Brooke. |
| 22 | Discharged at New Orleans about October 28th. Manner and by whom unknown. |
| 23 | Discharged at New Orleans about October 28th; Surgeon's certificate of disability. Order of Gen. Brooke. |
| 24 | Discharged at Memphis, Tenn., July 15th, procuring substitute, W. H. Humphries. Order of Col. Marshall. |
| 25 | Discharged at Little Rock, Ark., July 30th; Surgeon's certificate of disability. Order of Col. Marshall. |
| 26 | Discharged at New Orleans about May 28th; Surgeon's certificate of disability. Order of Gen. Brooke. |

## MOUNTED VOLUNTEERS—MEXICAN WAR.

| | |
|---|---|
| 1 | |
| 1 | |
| 1 | |
| 2 | Sergeant from enrollment to July 14th. |
| 1 | Sergeant from enrollment to November 9th. |
| 2 | Corporal from enrollment to July 14th. |
| 3 | |
| 1 | Private from enrollment to August 1st. |
| 2 | Corporal (4th) from enrollment to November 9th. |
| 3 | Private from enrollment to November 9th. |
| 4 | Private from enrollment to June 8th. |
| 1 | |
| 1 | |
| 1 | |
| 2 | [turned from Kentucky, and rejoined his Company February 9th, at Monterey, Mexico. |
| 3 | Discharged on Surgeon's certificate of disability at Port Lavacca, September 26th Order of Col Marshall. Regained his health, re- |
| 4 | |

## MEXICAN WAR VETERANS.

### ROLL OF COMPANY "F," FIRST REGIMENT KENTUCKY

| No. of each grade | Name. | Rank. | Enrolled. | Mustered In. When. | Mustered In. Where. | Period. | Mustered Out. When. | Mustered Out. Where. |
|---|---|---|---|---|---|---|---|---|
| 5 | Boyce, William | Private | June 9, 1846 | June 9, '46 | Louisville, Ky. | 1 yr. | June 10,'47 | New Orleans, La. |
| 6 | Barclay, Hugh A. | Private | June 9, 1846 | June 9, '46 | Louisville, Ky. | 1 yr. | June 10,'47 | New Orleans, La. |
| 7 | Cox, Alexander | Private | June 9, 1846 | June 9, '46 | Louisville, Ky. | 1 yr. | June 10,'47 | New Orleans, La. |
| 8 | Darneal, John S. | Private | June 9, 1846 | June 9, '46 | Louisville, Ky. | 1 yr. | June 10,'47 | New Orleans, La. |
| 9 | Donaldson, John (a) | Private | Mar. 7, 1847 | | | 1 yr. | June 10,'47 | New Orleans, La. |
| 10 | Ellis, Benjamin E. | Private | June 9, 1846 | June 9, '46 | Louisville, Ky. | 1 yr. | June 10,'47 | New Orleans, La. |
| 11 | Eddings, James W. | Private | June 9, 1846 | June 9, '46 | Louisville, Ky. | 1 yr. | June 10,'47 | New Orleans, La. |
| 12 | Ellis, John M. | Private | June 9, 1846 | June 9, '46 | Louisville, Ky. | 1 yr. | June 10,'47 | New Orleans, La. |
| 13 | Goodloe, John Kemp | Private | June 9, 1846 | June 9, '46 | Louisville, Ky. | 1 yr. | June 10,'47 | New Orleans, La. |
| 14 | Grubbs, William | Private | June 9, 1846 | June 9, '46 | Louisville, Ky. | 1 yr. | June 10,'47 | New Orleans, La. |
| 15 | Gillner, Henry | Private | June 9, 1846 | June 9, '46 | Louisville, Ky. | 1 yr. | June 10,'47 | New Orleans, La. |
| 16 | Gordon, Burgiss P. | Private | June 9, 1846 | June 9, '46 | Louisville, Ky. | 1 yr. | June 10,'47 | New Orleans, La. |
| 17 | Hearn, Fleming G. | Private | June 9, 1846 | June 9, '46 | Louisville, Ky. | 1 yr. | June 10,'47 | New Orleans, La. |
| 18 | Hale William | Private | June 9, 1846 | June 9, '46 | Louisville, Ky. | 1 yr. | June 10,'47 | New Orleans, La. |
| 19 | Hensley, Lucien | Private | June 9, 1846 | June 9, '46 | Louisville, Ky. | 1 yr. | June 10,'47 | New Orleans, La. |
| 20 | Isbel, Thomas H. | Private | June 9, 1846 | June 9, '46 | Louisville, Ky. | 1 yr. | June 10,'47 | New Orleans, La. |
| 21 | Jeter, James | Private | June 9, 1846 | June 9, '46 | Louisville, Ky. | 1 yr. | June 10,'47 | New Orleans, La. |
| 22 | Jacobs, Herod K. | Private | June 9, 1846 | June 9, '46 | Louisville, Ky. | 1 yr. | June 10,'47 | New Orleans, La. |
| 23 | Johnson, Nathaniel | Private | June 9, 1846 | June 9, '46 | Louisville, Ky. | 1 yr. | June 10,'47 | New Orleans, La. |
| 24 | Miles, John | Private | June 9, 1846 | June 9, '46 | Louisville, Ky. | 1 yr. | June 10,'47 | New Orleans, La. |
| 25 | Morrison, Joseph | Private | June 9, 1846 | June 9, '46 | Louisville, Ky. | 1 yr. | June 10,'47 | New Orleans, La. |
| 26 | Petty, Jefferson | Private | June 9, 1846 | June 9, '46 | Louisville, Ky. | 1 yr. | June 10,'47 | New Orleans, La. |
| 27 | Rollins, Johnson | Private | June 9, 1846 | June 9, '46 | Louisville, Ky. | 1 yr. | June 10,'47 | New Orleans, La. |
| 28 | Rogers, David | Private | June 9, 1846 | June 9, '46 | Louisville, Ky. | 1 yr. | June 10,'47 | New Orleans, La. |
| 29 | Skelton, Hiram W. | Private | June 9, 1846 | June 9, '46 | Louisville, Ky. | 1 yr. | June 10,'47 | New Orleans, La. |
| 30 | Sumner, George | Private | June 9, 1846 | June 9, '46 | Louisville, Ky. | 1 yr. | June 10,'47 | New Orleans, La. |
| 31 | Scearce, Simeon | Private | June 9, 1846 | June 9, '46 | Louisville, Ky. | 1 yr. | June 10,'47 | New Orleans, La. |
| 32 | Spencer, Wm. H. | Private | June 9, 1846 | June 9, '46 | Louisville, Ky. | 1 yr. | June 10,'47 | New Orleans, La. |
| 33 | Scearce, Albert | Private | June 9, 1846 | June 9, '46 | Louisville, Ky. | 1 yr. | June 10,'47 | New Orleans, La. |
| 34 | Searcy, John | Private | June 9, 1846 | June 9, '46 | Louisville, Ky. | 1 yr. | June 10,'47 | New Orleans, La. |
| 35 | Somers, John | Private | June 9, 1846 | June 9, '46 | Louisville, Ky. | 1 yr. | June 10,'47 | New Orleans, La. |
| 36 | Spratt, John | Private | June 9, 1846 | June 9, '46 | Louisville, Ky. | 1 yr. | June 10,'47 | New Orleans, La. |
| 37 | Stevenson, Andrew M. | Private | June 9, 1846 | June 9, '46 | Louisville, Ky. | 1 yr. | June 10,'47 | New Orleans, La. |
| 38 | Sullivan, Patrick | Private | June 9, 1846 | June 9, '46 | Louisville, Ky. | 1 yr. | June 10,'47 | New Orleans, La. |
| 39 | Thornton, James | Private | June 9, 1846 | June 9, '46 | Louisville, Ky. | 1 yr. | June 10,'47 | New Orleans, La. |
| 40 | Thornton, George | Private | June 9, 1846 | June 9, '46 | Louisville, Ky. | 1 yr. | June 10,'47 | New Orleans, La. |
| 41 | Wood, Archibald | Private | June 9, 1846 | June 9, '46 | Louisville, Ky. | 1 yr. | June 10,'47 | New Orleans, La. |
| 42 | Wallace, Samuel | Private | June 9, 1846 | June 9, '46 | Louisville, Ky. | 1 yr. | June 10,'47 | New Orleans, La. |
| | **KILLED IN BATTLE.** | | | | | | | |
| 1 | Dement, Charles B. | Private | June 9, 1846 | June 9, '46 | Louisville, Ky. | 1 yr. | | |
| | **DIED.** | | | | | | | |
| 1 | Rumsey, Thomas | Blacksmith | June 9, 1846 | June 9, '46 | Louisville, Ky. | 1 yr. | | |
| 1 | Elliston, Loudon | Private | June 9, 1846 | June 9, '46 | Louisville, Ky. | 1 yr. | | |
| 2 | Haydon, LaFayette | Private | June 9, 1846 | June 9, '46 | Louisville, Ky. | 1 yr. | | |
| 3 | Haydon, Jessee | | | | | | | |
| 4 | Lewis, Johnson | | | | | | | |
| 5 | Morton, John | | | | | | | |
| | **DESERTED.** | | | | | | | |
| 1 | George Dougherty | Private | June 9, 1846 | June 9, '46 | Louisville, Ky. | 1 yr. | | |
| 2 | White, Nathan | Private | June 9, 1846 | June 9, '46 | Louisville Ky. | 1 yr. | | |
| | **DISCHARGED.** | | | | | | | |
| 1 | Robert Brown | 1st Sergeant | June 9, 1846 | June 9, '46 | Louisville, Ky. | 1 yr. | | |
| 2 | Hawkins, Wm. A. | Sergeant | June 9, 1846 | June 9, '46 | Louisville, Ky. | 1 yr. | | |
| 1 | Hunter, Abner | Corporal | June 9, 1846 | June 9, '46 | Louisville, Ky. | 1 yr. | | |
| 1 | Alvin, Bates | Private | June 9, 1846 | June 9, '46 | Louisville, Ky. | 1 yr. | | |
| 2 | Burchill, Owen | Private | June 9, 1846 | June 9, '46 | Louisville, Ky. | 1 yr. | | |
| 3 | Baker, Benjamin | Private | June 9, 1846 | June 9, '46 | Louisville, Ky. | 1 yr. | | |
| 4 | Crammer, Washington | Private | June 9, 1846 | June 9, '46 | Louisville, Ky. | 1 yr. | | |
| 5 | Frast, John | Private | June 9, 1846 | June 9, '46 | Louisville, Ky. | 1 yr. | | |
| 6 | Graves, Wm. H. | Private | June 9, 1846 | June 9, '46 | Louisville, Ky. | 1 yr. | | |
| 7 | Helm, Samuel | Private | June 9, 1846 | June 9, '46 | Louisville, Ky. | 1 yr. | | |
| 8 | Hawkins, Wm S. | Private | June 9, 1846 | June 9, '46 | Louisville, Ky. | 1 yr. | | |
| 9 | Hawkins, Benjamin | Private | June 9, 1846 | June 9, '46 | Louisville, Ky. | 1 yr. | | |
| 10 | Hazel, William | Private | June 9, 1846 | June 9, '46 | Louisville, Ky. | 1 yr. | | |
| 11 | McCallister, Enoch | Private | June 9, 1846 | June 9, '46 | Louisville, Ky. | 1 yr. | | |
| 12 | McCalla, James P. | Private | June 9, 1846 | June 9, '46 | Louisville, Ky. | 1 yr. | | |
| 13 | Meredith, John | Private | June 9, 1846 | June 9, '46 | Louisville, Ky. | 1 yr. | | |
| 14 | Porter, Joseph | Private | June 9, 1846 | June 9, '46 | Louisville, Ky. | 1 yr. | | |
| 15 | Poindexter, L. | Private | June 9, 1846 | June 9, '46 | Louisville, Ky. | 1 yr. | | |
| 16 | Powell, Geo. M. | Private | June 9, 1846 | June 9, '46 | Louisville, Ky. | 1 yr. | | |
| 17 | Rossiter, P. P. | Private | June 9, 1846 | June 9, '46 | Louisville, Ky. | 1 yr. | | |

## MOUNTED VOLUNTEERS—MEXICAN WAR—Continued.

| No. of each | REMARKS. |
|---|---|
| 5 | |
| 6 | |
| 7 | |
| 8 | Left sick at Louisville, July 4th; rejoined his company at Port Lavacca September 20th. [Mexico to New Orleans. |
| 9 | Not regularly mustered in (enrolled) by assent of Lieut. Col. Field, on duty regularly with equipment of horse, etc., till ordered from |
| 10 | |
| 11 | |
| 12 | |
| 13 | |
| 14 | |
| 15 | |
| 16 | |
| 17 | |
| 18 | |
| 19 | Corporal until July 8th, when he was detailed at Memphis for hospital service, and has not since rejoined his company. |
| 20 | |
| 21 | |
| 22 | |
| 23 | Left at Louisville July 4th; crippled by fall from his horse; rejoined his company at Matamoras, January 8th. |
| 24 | |
| 25 | |
| 26 | Was discharged on Surgeon's certificate of disability; recovered his health and rejoined his company April 7th. |
| 27 | |
| 28 | |
| 29 | Reduced from Corporal November 28th. [Gen. Wool's column to Satillo; rejoined his company February 1st. |
| 30 | Left sick in Washington early in August; went to San Antonio where he expected to join, but failed to meet his regiment; marched with |
| 31 | |
| 32 | |
| 33 | |
| 34 | |
| 35 | |
| 36 | |
| 37 | Was detailed at Port Lavacca, October 1st, for commissary service, in which he has remained to this date. |
| 38 | |
| 39 | Left sick at Memphis July 17th; has never come up; fate unknown. |
| 40 | |
| 41 | |
| 42 | |
| | |
| 1 | Killed in battle of Buena Vista, February 23d. |
| | |
| 1 | Died in hospital at New Orleans. Time unknown. |
| 1 | Left sick in Little Rock, and there died. Time unknown. |
| 2 | Died near Camargo, November 14th. |
| 3 | Died near Camargo, November 12th. |
| 4 | Died near Camargo, November 17th. |
| 5 | Died near Camargo, November 27th. |
| | |
| 1 | Deserted from Washington, Ark., August 5th. |
| 2 | Deserted from Memphis, where he had been left sick in July. Time unknown. |
| | |
| 1 | Discharged at Camargo; Surgeon's certificate of disability, November 9th. Order of Col. Marshall. |
| 2 | Private till November 9th. Discharged at New Orleans; Surgeon's certificate of disability, May 13th. Order of Gen. Brooke. |
| 1 | Private until July 14th. Discharged at Camargo; Surgeon's certificate of disability, December 15th. Order of Col. Marshall. |
| 1 | Discharged at New Orleans, May 13th.; Surgeon's certificate of disability. Order of Gen. Brooke. |
| 2 | Discharged at Port Lavacca; Surgeon's certificate of disability, October 12th. Order of Col. Marshall. |
| 3 | Discharged at Camargo; Surgeon's certificate of disability, December 13th. Order of Col. Marshall. |
| 4 | Discharged at Port Lavacca; Surgeon's certificate of disability, October 12th. Order of Col. Marshall. |
| 5 | Discharged at New Orleans; Surgeon's certificate of disability, May 31st. Order of Gen. Brooke. |
| 6 | Discharged at New Orleans; Surgeon's certificate of disability, May 31st. Order of Gen. Brooke. |
| 7 | Discharged at New Orleans; Surgeon's certificate of disability, May 31st. Order of Gen. Brooke. |
| 8 | Discharged at Washington, Ark.; Surgeon's certificate of disability. Date and by whose order unknown. |
| 9 | Discharged at New Orleans; Surgeon's certificate of disability, May 31st. Order of Gen. Brooke. |
| 10 | Discharged at Memphis, Tenn.; Surgeon's certificate of disability, July 23d. Order of Major General Butler. |
| 11 | Discharged at Camargo; Surgeon's certificate of disability, December 15th. Order of Col. Marshall. |
| 12 | Discharged at Camargo; Surgeon's certificate of disability, December 15th. Order of Col. Marshall. |
| 13 | Discharged at Port Lavacca; Surgeon's certificate of disability, October 12th. Order of Col. Marshall. |
| 14 | Discharged at New Orleans; Surgeon's certificate of disability, May 31st. Order of Gen. Brooke. |
| 15 | His name was stricken from the rolls with the approbation of Gen. Wool; he was found to be insane a few days after the muster. |
| 16 | Discharged at Camargo; Surgeon's certificate of disability, December 15th. Order of Col. Marshall. |
| 17 | Discharged at New Orleans, whither he was sent sick from Memphis. Date unknown. |

## ROLL OF COMPANY "F," FIRST REGIMENT KENTUCKY

| No. of each grade | Name | Rank | Enrolled | Mustered In When | Mustered In Where | Period | Mustered Out When | Mustered Out Where |
|---|---|---|---|---|---|---|---|---|
| 18 | Raily, John C. | Private | June 9, 1846 | June 9, '46 | Louisville, Ky. | 1 yr | | |
| 19 | Reading, John B. | Private | June 9, 1846 | June 9, '46 | Louisville, Ky. | 1 yr | | |
| 20 | Smith, Wm. H. | Private | June 9, 1846 | June 9, '46 | Louisville, Ky. | 1 yr | | |
| 21 | Taylor, Robert | Private | June 9, 1846 | June 9, '46 | Louisville, Ky. | 1 yr | | |
| 22 | Toppass, James | Private | June 9, 1846 | June 9, '46 | Louisville, Ky. | 1 yr | | |
| 23 | Woods, William | Private | June 9, 1846 | June 9, '46 | Louisville, Ky. | 1 yr | | |
| 24 | Wallace, G. W. | Private | June 9, 1846 | June 9, '46 | Louisville, Ky. | 1 yr | | |
| 25 | Watkins, John W. | Private | June 9, 1846 | June 9, '46 | Louisville, Ky. | 1 yr | | |
| 26 | White, Nicholas A. | Private | June 9, 1846 | June 9, '46 | Louisville, Ky. | 1 yr | | |
| | TRANSFERRED. | | | | | | | |
| 1 | Harman, Bledsoe D. | Musician | June 9, 1846 | June 9, '46 | Louisville, Ky. | 1 yr | | |

This Company was enrolled at Louisville, with the exception of (a), who was enrolled at Camargo.

## ROLL OF COMPANY "G," FIRST REGIMENT KENTUCKY

| No. of each grade | Name | Rank | Enrolled | Mustered In When | Mustered In Where | Period | Mustered Out When | Mustered Out Where |
|---|---|---|---|---|---|---|---|---|
| 1 | A. Pennington | Captain | June 9, 1846 | June 9, '46 | Louisville, Ky. | 1 yr | June 7, '47 | New Orleans, La. |
| 1 | W. M. G. Torrence | 1st Lieutenant | June 9, 1846 | June 9, '46 | Louisville, Ky. | 1 yr | June 7, '47 | New Orleans, La. |
| 1 | John Allen | 2d Lieutenant | June 9, 1846 | June 9, '46 | Louisville, Ky. | 1 yr | June 7, '47 | New Orleans, La. |
| 1 | Griffith Jacob Werk | 1st Sergeant | June 9, 1846 | June 9, '46 | Louisville, Ky. | 1 yr | June 7, '47 | New Orleans, La. |
| 2 | Payne, William L. | Sergeant | June 9, 1846 | June 9, '46 | Louisville, Ky. | 1 yr | June 7, '47 | New Orleans, La. |
| 3 | Goodson, James | Sergeant | June 9, 1846 | June 9, '46 | Louisville, Ky. | 1 yr | June 7, '47 | New Orleans, La. |
| 4 | Scott, David K. | Sergeant | June 9, 1846 | June 9, '46 | Louisville, Ky. | 1 yr | June 7, '47 | New Orleans, La. |
| 1 | Razor, Henry | Corporal | June 9, 1846 | June 9, '46 | Louisville, Ky. | 1 yr | June 7, '47 | New Orleans, La. |
| 2 | James, Wil | Corporal | June 9, 1846 | June 9, '46 | Louisville, Ky. | 1 yr | June 7, '47 | New Orleans, La. |
| 1 | Miner, Williams | 1st Musician | June 9, 1846 | June 9, '46 | Louisville, Ky. | 1 yr | June 7, '47 | New Orleans, La. |
| 2 | Buck, Harry | Musician | June 9, 1846 | June 9, '46 | Louisville, Ky. | 1 yr | June 7, '47 | New Orleans, La. |
| 1 | Bullock, Hardin | Blacksmith | June 9, 1846 | June 9, '46 | Louisville, Ky. | 1 yr | June 7, '47 | New Orleans, La. |
| 1 | Baldwin, Annis | Private | June 9, 1846 | June 9, '46 | Louisville, Ky. | 1 yr | June 7, '47 | New Orleans, La. |
| 2 | Brown, Tho | Private | June 9, 1846 | June 9, '46 | Louisville, Ky. | 1 yr | June 7, '47 | New Orleans, La. |
| 3 | Bonham, Archibald D. | Private | June 9, 1846 | June 9, '46 | Louisville, Ky. | 1 yr | June 7, '47 | New Orleans, La. |
| 4 | Coffman, Peter | Private | June 9, 1846 | June 9, '46 | Louisville, Ky. | 1 yr | June 7, '47 | New Orleans, La. |
| 5 | Curtis, Geo. | Private | June 9, 1846 | June 9, '46 | Louisville, Ky. | 1 yr | June 7, '47 | New Orleans, La. |
| 6 | Cregg, Joseph | Private | June 9, 1846 | June 9, '46 | Louisville, Ky. | 1 yr | June 7, '47 | New Orleans, La. |
| 7 | Dowell, Benj. S. | Private | June 9, 1846 | June 9, '46 | Louisville, Ky. | 1 yr | June 7, '47 | New Orleans, La. |
| 8 | Fenton, David | Private | June 9, 1846 | June 9, '46 | Louisville, Ky. | 1 yr | June 7, '47 | New Orleans, La. |
| 9 | Forsyth, Wm. | Private | June 9, 1846 | June 9, '46 | Louisville, Ky. | 1 yr | June 7, '47 | New Orleans, La. |
| 10 | Funk, Wm. | Private | June 9, 1846 | June 9, '46 | Louisville, Ky. | 1 yr | June 7, '47 | New Orleans, La. |
| 11 | Hanson, Thos. J. | Private | June 9, 1846 | June 9, '46 | Louisville, Ky. | 1 yr | June 7, '47 | New Orleans, La. |
| 12 | Hamilton, G. R. | Private | June 9, 1846 | June 9, '46 | Louisville, Ky. | 1 yr | June 7, '47 | New Orleans, La. |
| 13 | Hurley, Wm. | Private | June 9, 1846 | June 9, '46 | Louisville, Ky. | 1 yr | June 7, '47 | New Orleans, La. |
| 14 | Johnson, Henry | Private | June 9, 1846 | June 9, '46 | Louisville, Ky. | 1 yr | June 7, '47 | New Orleans, La. |
| 15 | Johnson, J. W. | Private | June 9, 1846 | June 9, '46 | Louisville, Ky. | 1 yr | June 7, '47 | New Orleans, La. |
| 16 | Kenedy, James | Private | June 9, 1846 | June 9, '46 | Louisville, Ky. | 1 yr | June 7, '47 | New Orleans, La. |
| 17 | Kendall, Wm. | Private | June 9, 1846 | June 9, '46 | Louisville, Ky. | 1 yr | June 7, '47 | New Orleans, La. |
| 18 | Kelly, Wm. | Private | June 9, 1846 | June 9, '46 | Louisville, Ky. | 1 yr | June 7, '47 | New Orleans, La. |
| 19 | Minter, Wm. H. | Private | June 9, 1846 | June 9, '46 | Louisville, Ky. | 1 yr | June 7, '47 | New Orleans, La. |
| 20 | Myers, D. R. | Private | June 9, 1846 | June 9, '46 | Louisville, Ky. | 1 yr | June 7, '47 | New Orleans, La. |
| 21 | Mitchell, W. J. | Private | June 9, 1846 | June 9, '46 | Louisville, Ky. | 1 yr | June 7, '47 | New Orleans, La. |
| 22 | Magner, John | Private | June 9, 1846 | June 9, '46 | Louisville, Ky. | 1 yr | June 7, '47 | New Orleans, La. |
| 23 | Murphy, James C. | Private | June 9, 1846 | June 9, '46 | Louisville, Ky. | 1 yr | June 7, '47 | New Orleans, La. |
| 24 | Newkirk, J. Y. | Private | June 9, 1846 | June 9, '46 | Louisville, Ky. | 1 yr | June 7, '47 | New Orleans, La. |
| 25 | Owens, Wm. H. | Private | June 9, 1846 | June 9, '46 | Louisville, Ky. | 1 yr | June 7, '47 | New Orleans, La. |
| 26 | Rodgers, Isaac | Private | June 9, 1846 | June 9, '46 | Louisville, Ky. | 1 yr | June 7, '47 | New Orleans, La. |
| 27 | Ruckstool, John | Private | June 9, 1846 | June 9, '46 | Louisville, Ky. | 1 yr | June 7, '47 | New Orleans, La. |
| 28 | Ross, James | Private | June 9, 1846 | June 9, '46 | Louisville, Ky. | 1 yr | June 7, '47 | New Orleans, La. |
| 29 | Rice, Wm. B. | Private | June 9, 1846 | June 9, '46 | Louisville, Ky. | 1 yr | June 7, '47 | New Orleans, La. |
| 30 | Scott, John | Private | June 9, 1846 | June 9, '46 | Louisville, Ky. | 1 yr | June 7, '47 | New Orleans, La. |
| 31 | Wood, Peter | Private | June 9, 1846 | June 9, '46 | Louisville, Ky. | 1 yr | June 7, '47 | New Orleans, La. |
| 32 | Wright, R. R. | Private | June 9, 1846 | June 9, '46 | Louisville, Ky. | 1 yr | June 7, '47 | New Orleans, La. |
| 33 | Welch, James C. | Private | June 9, 1846 | June 9, '46 | Louisville, Ky. | 1 yr | June 7, '47 | New Orleans, La. |
| 34 | Ware, Nicholas | Private | June 9, 1846 | June 9, '46 | Louisville, Ky. | 1 yr | June 7, '47 | New Orleans, La. |
| 35 | Williams, Franklin | Private | June 9, 1846 | June 9, '46 | Louisville, Ky. | 1 yr | June 7, '47 | New Orleans, La. |
| 36 | Yilhart, George | Private | June 9, 1846 | June 9, '46 | Louisville, Ky. | 1 yr | June 7, '47 | New Orleans, La. |
| | KILLED IN BATTLE. | | | | | | | |
| 1 | Danforth, Henry | Private | June 9, 1846 | June 9, '46 | Louisville, Ky. | 1 yr | | |
| 2 | Ross, John | Private | June 9, 1846 | June 9, '46 | Louisville, Ky. | 1 yr | | |
| 3 | Rowlin, J. M. | Private | June 9, 1846 | June 9, '46 | Louisville, Ky. | 1 yr | | |
| 4 | Martin, Jesse G. | Private | June 9, 1846 | June 9, '46 | Louisville, Ky. | 1 yr | | |
| 5 | Lilley, E. F. | Private | June 9, 1846 | June 9, '46 | Louisville, Ky. | 1 yr | | |

MEXICAN WAR VETERANS.                                                                 19

## MOUNTED VOLUNTEERS—MEXICAN WAR—Continued.

| No. of each grade | REMARKS. |
|---|---|
| 18 | Discharged at New Orleans; Surgeon's certificate of disability. Order of General Brooke. (See manuscript muster roll.) |
| 19 | Discharged at Louisville without being regularly mustered, being, in the judgment of the Captain, the Surgeon and General Wool, too feeble, by reason of injury received from falling from his horse; for service he was not paid any thing. |
| 20 | Discharged at New Orleans; Surgeon's certificate of disability, November 18  Order of General Brooke. |
| 21 | Discharged at Camargo; Surgeon's certificate of disability, December 15.  Order of Colonel Marshall. |
| 22 | Discharged at Port Lavacca; Surgeon's certificate of disability, October 1.  Order of Colonel Marshall. |
| 23 | Discharged at Port Lavacca; Surgeon's certificate of disability, October 12.  Order of Colonel Marshall. |
| 24 | No advance was made to this man, but his name was stricken from the roll for outrageous bad conduct, with the approbation of General Wool. |
| 25 | Discharged at Little Rock; Surgeon's certificate of disability, August 21st.  By whose order unknown. |
| 26 | Discharged at Little Rock; Surgeon's certificate of disability, August 8.  By whose order unknown. |
| 1 | Transferred to Captain Clay's Company by his own request, and with the assent of Captains Clay and Marshall, August 28. |

## MOUNTED VOLUNTEERS—MEXICAN WAR.

| No. | REMARKS. |
|---|---|
| 1 | |
| 1 | Was 2d Lieutenant from enrollment to October 22d. |
| 1 | Was 1st Sergeant from enrollment to July 12th. |
| 1 | Was private from enrollment to July 12th. |
| 2 | Was private from enrollment to September 1st.   Prisoner of war in Mexico from January 22d. |
| 3 | Was private from enrollment to November 3d. |
| 4 | Was private from enrollment to November 3d. |
| 1 | |
| 2 | |
| 1 | |
| 2 | |
| 1 | Was private from enrollment to November 3d. |
| 1 | |
| 2 | |
| 3 | |
| 4 | |
| 5 | |
| 6 | |
| 7 | Prisoner of war in Mexico from January 22d. |
| 8 | |
| 9 | |
| 10 | Prisoner of war in Mexico from January 22d. |
| 11 | |
| 12 | Absent without leave from January 6th. |
| 13 | |
| 14 | |
| 15 | Prisoner of war in Mexico from January 22d. |
| 16 | Prisoner of war in Mexico from January 22d. |
| 17 | |
| 18 | Prisoner of war in Mexico from January 22d. |
| 19 | Absent without leave from May 8th. |
| 20 | Prisoner of war in Mexico from January 22d. |
| 21 | |
| 22 | Prisoner of war in Mexico from January 22d. |
| 23 | Absent with leave from Col. Marshall from May 8th. |
| 24 | |
| 25 | |
| 26 | Prisoner of war in Mexico from January 22d. |
| 27 | |
| 28 | |
| 29 | |
| 30 | Prisoner of war in Mexico from January 22d. |
| 31 | |
| 32 | |
| 33 | |
| 34 | Prisoner of war in Mexico from January 22d. |
| 35 | |
| 36 | |
| 1 | Killed in battle of Buena Vista, February 23d. |
| 2 | Killed in battle of Buena Vista, February 23d. |
| 3 | Killed in battle of Buena Vista, February 23d. |
| 4 | Killed in battle of Buena Vista, February 23d. |
| 5 | Killed in battle of Buena Vista, February 23d. |

## ROLL OF COMPANY "G," FIRST REGIMENT KENTUCKY

| No. of each grade | Name | Rank | Enrolled | Mustered In When | Mustered In Where | Period | Mustered Out When | Mustered Out Where |
|---|---|---|---|---|---|---|---|---|
| 6 | Rouston, Ephraim | Private | June 9, 1846 | June 9, '46 | Louisville, Ky | 1 yr | | |
| | **Died.** | | | | | | | |
| 1 | Help, Lypold | Private | June 9, 1846 | June 9, '46 | Louisville, Ky | 1 yr | | |
| 2 | Green, T. W. | Private | June 9, 1846 | June 9, '46 | Louisville, Ky | 1 yr | | |
| 3 | Jackson, Feries | Private | June 9, 1846 | June 9, '46 | Louisville, Ky | 1 yr | | |
| 4 | Bird, W. C. | Corporal | June 9, 1846 | June 9, '46 | Louisville, Ky | 1 yr | | |
| 5 | Killer, George | Corporal | June 9, 1846 | June 9, '46 | Louisville, Ky | 1 yr | | |
| 6 | McBride, Isaac | Private | June 9, 1846 | June 9, '46 | Louisville, Ky | 1 yr | | |
| 7 | Applegate, George | Private | June 9, 1846 | June 9, '46 | Louisville, Ky | 1 yr | | |
| 8 | Womack, John | Corporal | June 9, 1846 | June 9, '46 | Louisville, Ky | 1 yr | | |
| | **Discharged.** | | | | | | | |
| 1 | Bullitt, Cutt | Private | June 9, 1846 | June 9, '46 | Louisville, Ky | 1 yr | | |
| 2 | Murphy, J. | Private | June 9, 1846 | June 9, '46 | Louisville, Ky | 1 yr | | |
| 3 | Hurst, William | Private | June 9, 1846 | June 9, '46 | Louisville, Ky | 1 yr | | |
| 4 | Gaar, B. F. | Private | June 9, 1846 | June 9, '46 | Louisville, Ky | 1 yr | | |
| 5 | Gaar, N. H. | Private | June 9, 1846 | June 9, '46 | Louisville, Ky | 1 yr | | |
| 6 | Morrison, W. | Private | June 9, 1846 | June 9, '46 | Louisville, Ky | 1 yr | | |
| 7 | Stivers, Jeremiah | Private | June 9, 1846 | June 9, '46 | Louisville, Ky | 1 yr | | |
| 8 | Smith, R. D. | Private | June 9, 1846 | June 9, '46 | Louisville, Ky | 1 yr | | |
| | **Deserted.** | | | | | | | |
| 1 | Bruce, J. C. | Private | June 9, 1846 | June 9, '46 | Louisville, Ky | 1 yr | | |
| 2 | Dramos, A. | Private | June 9, 1846 | June 9, '46 | Louisville, Ky | 1 yr | | |
| 3 | Eckfeldt, G. M. | Private | June 9, 1846 | June 9, '46 | Louisville, Ky | 1 yr | | |
| 4 | Neff, John | Private | June 9, 1846 | June 9, '46 | Louisville, Ky | 1 yr | | |
| 5 | Grinstead, E. F. | Private | June 9, 1846 | June 9, '46 | Louisville, Ky | 1 yr | | |
| 6 | But'er, A. A. | Private | June 9, 1846 | June 9, '46 | Louisville, Ky | 1 yr | | |
| | **Transferred** | | | | | | | |
| 1 | H. B. Hornsby | 1st Lieutenant | June 9, 1846 | June 9, '46 | Louisville, Ky | 1 yr | | |
| 1 | G. Holland | Sergeant | June 9, 1846 | June 9, '46 | Louisville, Ky | 1 yr | | |

This Company was enrolled at Louisville, Kentucky, June 9, 1846.

## ROLL OF COMPANY "H," FIRST REGIMENT KENTUCKY

| No. | Name | Rank | Enrolled | Mustered In When | Mustered In Where | Period | Mustered Out When | Mustered Out Where |
|---|---|---|---|---|---|---|---|---|
| 1 | James C. Stone | Captain | June 8, 1846 | June 9, '46 | Louisville, Ky | 1 yr | June 8, '47 | New Orleans, La |
| 1 | G. B. F. Broaddus | 1st Lieutenant | June 8, 1846 | June 9, '46 | Louisville, Ky | 1 yr | June 8, '47 | New Orleans, La |
| 1 | G. Clay Smith | 2d Lieutenant | June 8, 1846 | June 9, '46 | Louisville, Ky | 1 yr | June 8, '47 | New Orleans, La |
| 2 | Thomas H. Barnes | Adj't 2d Lieut. | June 8, 1846 | June 9, '46 | Louisville, Ky | 1 yr | June 8, '47 | New Orleans, La |
| 1 | John Lawrence | 1st Sergeant | June 8, 1846 | June 9, '46 | Louisville, Ky | 1 yr | June 8, '47 | New Orleans, La |
| 2 | C. J. Dejarnatt | Sergeant | June 8, 1846 | June 9, '46 | Louisville, Ky | 1 yr | June 8, '47 | New Orleans, La |
| 3 | William Guess | Sergeant | June 8, 1846 | June 9, '46 | Louisville, Ky | 1 yr | June 8, '47 | New Orleans, La |
| 4 | James Barnes | Sergeant | June 8, 1846 | June 9, '46 | Louisville, Ky | 1 yr | June 8, '47 | New Orleans, La |
| 1 | James Mohan | Corporal | June 8, 1846 | June 9, '46 | Louisville, Ky | 1 yr | June 8, '47 | New Orleans, La |
| 2 | Oscar F. Watts | Corporal | June 8, 1846 | June 9, '46 | Louisville, Ky | 1 yr | June 8, '47 | New Orleans, La |
| 3 | William Pravitt | Corporal | June 8, 1846 | June 9, '46 | Louisville, Ky | 1 yr | June 8, '47 | New Orleans, La |
| 1 | Barnes, George O. | Musician | June 8, 1846 | June 9, '46 | Louisville, Ky | 1 yr | June 8, '47 | New Orleans, La |
| 1 | Burriss, Nelson | Blac'th and Far. | June 8, 1846 | June 9, '46 | Louisville, Ky | 1 yr | June 8, '47 | New Orleans, La |
| 1 | Alexander, George | Private | June 8, 1846 | June 9, '46 | Louisville, Ky | 1 yr | June 8, '47 | New Orleans, La |
| 2 | Amerine, David | Private | June 8, 1846 | June 9, '46 | Louisville, Ky | 1 yr | June 8, '47 | New Orleans, La |
| 3 | Armstrong, J. Wesley | Private | June 8, 1846 | June 9, '46 | Louisville, Ky | 1 yr | June 8, '47 | New Orleans, La |
| 4 | Brakebill, Philip | Private | June 8, 1846 | June 9, '46 | Louisville, Ky | 1 yr | June 8, '47 | New Orleans, La |
| 5 | Berkley, Benjamin | Private | June 8, 1846 | June 9, '46 | Louisville, Ky | 1 yr | June 8, '47 | New Orleans, La |
| 6 | Barnes, Hudson M. | Private | June 8, 1846 | June 9, '46 | Louisville, Ky | 1 yr | June 8, '47 | New Orleans, La |
| 7 | Bradford, Dozier | Private | June 8, 1846 | June 9, '46 | Louisville, Ky | 1 yr | June 8, '47 | New Orleans, La |
| 8 | Denham, Bowen | Private | June 8, 1846 | June 9, '46 | Louisville, Ky | 1 yr | June 8, '47 | New Orleans, La |
| 9 | Field, Edmund I. | Private | June 8, 1846 | June 9, '46 | Louisville, Ky | 1 yr | June 8, '47 | New Orleans, La |
| 10 | Freeman, Wm. | Private | June 8, 1846 | June 9, '46 | Louisville, Ky | 1 yr | June 8, '47 | New Orleans, La |
| 11 | Hart, Wm. | Private | June 8, 1846 | June 9, '46 | Louisville, Ky | 1 yr | June 8, '47 | New Orleans, La |
| 12 | Holeman, John | Private | June 8, 1846 | June 9, '46 | Louisville, Ky | 1 yr | June 8, '47 | New Orleans, La |
| 13 | Harvey, Jonathan | Private | June 8, 1846 | June 9, '46 | Louisville, Ky | 1 yr | June 8, '47 | New Orleans, La |
| 14 | James, Decatur | Private | June 8, 1846 | June 9, '46 | Louisville, Ky | 1 yr | June 8, '47 | New Orleans, La |
| 15 | Land, Hiram | Private | June 8, 1846 | June 9, '46 | Louisville, Ky | 1 yr | June 8, '47 | New Orleans, La |
| 16 | Magee, Irwin | Private | June 8, 1846 | June 9, '46 | Louisville, Ky | 1 yr | June 8, '47 | New Orleans, La |
| 17 | Orchard, James | Private | June 8, 1846 | June 9, '46 | Louisville, Ky | 1 yr | June 8, '47 | New Orleans, La |
| 18 | Perkins, Joseph | Private | June 8, 1846 | June 9, '46 | Louisville, Ky | 1 yr | June 8, '47 | New Orleans, La |
| 19 | Rhea, Horace P. | Private | June 8, 1846 | June 9, '46 | Louisville, Ky | 1 yr | June 8, '47 | New Orleans, La |
| 20 | Roberts, Merrill | Private | June 8, 1846 | June 9, '46 | Louisville, Ky | 1 yr | June 8, '47 | New Orleans, La |
| 21 | Searcy, Francis M. | Private | June 8, 1846 | June 9, '46 | Louisville, Ky | 1 yr | June 8, '47 | New Orleans, La |

## MOUNTED VOLUNTEERS—MEXICAN WAR.—Continued.

| No. of each grade | REMARKS. |
|---|---|
| 6 | Killed in battle of Buena Vista, February 23d. |
| | |
| 1 | Died in hospital at Saltillo, March 1st. |
| 2 | Assassinated at Saltillo by Mexicans, March 2d. |
| 3 | Died in hospital at Saltillo, March 12th. |
| 4 | Died in Camp at Camargo, April 30th.  Was private from enlistment to August 10th. |
| 5 | Died in hospital at Monterey, May 1st.  Private from enrollment to August 10th. |
| 6 | Died in Texas near Sabine river, September 1st. |
| 7 | Died in Texas near Sabine river, September 9th. |
| 8 | Died in Arkansas, July 20th.  Corporal from enrollment to July 20th. |
| | |
| 1 | Discharged on Surgeon's certificate of disability at Memphis, Tenn., July 20th.  Order of Col. Marshall. |
| 2 | Discharged dishonorably at Little Rock, August 1st.  Order of Col. Marshall. |
| 3 | Discharged on Surgeon's certificate of disability, at Camargo, November 16th.  Order of Col. Marshall. |
| 4 | Discharged on Surgeon's certificate of disability, at New Orleans, May 28th.  Order of Gen. Brooke. |
| 5 | Discharged on Surgeon's certificate of disability, at New Orleans, May 28th.  Order of Gen. Brooke. |
| 6 | Discharged on Surgeon's certificate of disability, at New Orleans, May 28th.  Order of Gen. Brooke. |
| 7 | Discharged on Surgeon's certificate of disability, at New Orleans, May 28th.  Order of Gen. Brooke. |
| 8 | Discharged on Surgeon's certificate of disability, at Camargo, April 1st.  Order of Col. Marshall. |
| | |
| 1 | Deserted at Laredo, September 20th. |
| 2 | Deserted at Laredo, September 20th. |
| 3 | Deserted at Laredo, September 20th. |
| 4 | Deserted at Laredo, September 20th. |
| 5 | Deserted at Washington, Texas, September 13th. |
| 6 | Deserted at Independence, Texas, September 12th. |
| | |
| 1 | Resigned October 21st.  Was 1st Lieutenant from enlistment to October 21. |
| 1 | Transferred to First Illinois Regiment, at Lavacca, October 4th.  Order of Col. Marshall. |

## MOUNTED VOLUNTEERS—MEXICAN WAR.

| No. of each grade | REMARKS. |
|---|---|
| 1 | |
| 1 | |
| 1 | |
| 2 | Private from enrollment to July 15th.  Absent. |
| 1 | |
| 2 | |
| 3 | |
| 4 | |
| 1 | Private from enrollment to November 21st. |
| 2 | Private from enrollment to November 21st. |
| 3 | Private from enrollment to November 21st. |
| 1 | Private from enrollment to September 9th. |
| 1 | |
| 1 | |
| 2 | |
| 3 | Detached service; hospital attendant at Sabine, Texas.  Order of Col. Marshall. |
| 4 | |
| 5 | |
| 6 | |
| 7 | |
| 8 | |
| 9 | |
| 10 | |
| 11 | |
| 12 | |
| 13 | Left sick at Louisville, July 4th, and ordered to be discharged January 1st, but rejoined for duty March 1st. |
| 14 | Left sick at Louisville, July 4th, and ordered to be discharged January 1st, but rejoined for duty March 1st. |
| 15 | |
| 16 | |
| 17 | |
| 18 | |
| 19 | |
| 20 | |
| 21 | |

## ROLL OF COMPANY "H," FIRST REGIMENT KENTUCKY

| No. of each grade. | Name. | Rank. | Enrolled. | Mustered In. When. | Mustered In. Where. | Period. | Mustered Out. When. | Mustered Out. Where. |
|---|---|---|---|---|---|---|---|---|
| 22 | Shearer, Zachariah | Private | June 8, 1846 | June 9, '46 | Louisville, Ky. | 1 yr. | June 8, '47 | New Orleans, La. |
| 23 | Simpson, Jas. | Private | June 8, 1846 | June 9, '46 | Louisville, Ky. | 1 yr. | June 8, '47 | New Orleans, La. |
| 24 | Simpson, Richard B. | Private | June 8, 1846 | June 9, '46 | Louisville, Ky. | 1 yr. | June 8, '47 | New Orleans, La. |
| 25 | Shifflett, John | Private | June 8, 1846 | June 9, '46 | Louisville, Ky. | 1 yr. | June 8, '47 | New Orleans, La. |
| 26 | Shifflett, Clifton | Private | June 8, 1846 | June 9, '46 | Louisville, Ky. | 1 yr. | June 8, '47 | New Orleans, La. |
| 27 | Storms, James A. B. | Private | June 8, 1846 | June 9, '46 | Louisville, Ky. | 1 yr. | June 8, '47 | New Orleans, La. |
| 28 | Tuder, Thomas H. | Private | June 8, 1846 | June 9, '46 | Louisville, Ky. | 1 yr. | June 8, '47 | New Orleans, La. |
| 29 | Williams, Shadrack | Private | June 8, 1846 | June 9, '46 | Louisville, Ky. | 1 yr. | June 8, '47 | New Orleans, La. |
| 30 | Wright, Henry W. | Private | June 8, 1846 | June 9, '46 | Louisville, Ky. | 1 yr. | June 8, '47 | New Orleans, La. |
| 31 | White, Franklin J. | Private | June 8, 1846 | June 9, '46 | Louisville, Ky. | 1 yr. | June 8, '47 | New Orleans, La. |
| 32 | Wilkerson, Thomas J. | Private | June 8, 1846 | June 9, '46 | Louisville, Ky. | 1 yr. | June 8, '47 | New Orleans, La. |
| 33 | Williams, Alford | Private | June 8, 1846 | June 9, '46 | Louisville, Ky. | 1 yr. | June 8, '47 | New Orleans, La. |
| | **Discharged.** | | | | | | | |
| 1 | Chenault, David W. | Sergeant | June 8, 1846 | June 9, '46 | Louisville, Ky. | 1 yr. | | |
| 2 | Garrison, Willis H. | Corporal | June 8, 1846 | June 9, '46 | Louisville, Ky. | 1 yr. | | |
| 3 | Howell, Wm. H. | Corporal | June 8, 1846 | June 9, '46 | Louisville, Ky. | 1 yr. | | |
| 4 | Davis, John | Corporal | June 8, 1846 | June 9, '46 | Louisville, Ky. | 1 yr. | | |
| 5 | Neale, Jas. W. | Musician | June 8, 1846 | June 9, '46 | Louisville, Ky. | 1 yr. | | |
| 6 | Barnes, Jackson | Private | June 8, 1846 | June 9, '46 | Louisville, Ky. | 1 yr. | | |
| 7 | Corey, John A. | Private | June 8, 1846 | June 9, '46 | Louisville, Ky. | 1 yr. | | |
| 8 | Cox, John N. | Private | June 8, 1846 | June 9, '46 | Louisville, Ky. | 1 yr. | | |
| 9 | Denham, James | Private | June 8, 1846 | June 9, '46 | Louisville, Ky. | 1 yr. | | |
| 10 | Harris, Benjamin F. | Private | June 8, 1846 | June 9, '46 | Louisville, Ky. | 1 yr. | | |
| 11 | Halsey, John J. | Private | June 8, 1846 | June 9, '46 | Louisville, Ky. | 1 yr. | | |
| 12 | Kavanaugh, H. W. | Private | June 8, 1846 | June 9, '46 | Louisville, Ky. | 1 yr. | | |
| 13 | Kelly, John H. | Private | June 8, 1846 | June 9, '46 | Louisville, Ky. | 1 yr. | | |
| 14 | Land, Thos. H. | Private | June 8, 1846 | June 9, '46 | Louisville, Ky. | 1 yr. | | |
| 15 | Lowry, Simpson | Private | June 8, 1846 | June 9, '46 | Louisville, Ky. | 1 yr. | | |
| 16 | Magee, Thos. J. | Private | June 8, 1846 | June 9, '46 | Louisville, Ky. | 1 yr. | | |
| 17 | Million, Squire | Private | June 8, 1846 | June 9, '46 | Louisville, Ky. | 1 yr. | | |
| 18 | McMillon, John C. | Private | June 8, 1846 | June 9, '46 | Louisville, Ky. | 1 yr. | | |
| 19 | Miller, Milton J. | Private | June 8, 1846 | June 9, '46 | Louisville, Ky. | 1 yr. | | |
| 20 | Stagner, Jas. C. | Private | June 8, 1846 | June 9, '46 | Louisville, Ky. | 1 yr. | | |
| 21 | Taylor, Harrison M. | Private | June 8, 1846 | June 9, '46 | Louisville, Ky. | 1 yr. | | |
| 22 | Wilkerson, Wyatt | Private | June 8, 1846 | June 9, '46 | Louisville, Ky. | 1 yr. | | |
| 23 | Wilson, Jas. | Private | June 8, 1846 | June 9, '46 | Louisville, Ky. | 1 yr. | | |
| 24 | Wilson, Franklin B. | Private | June 8, 1846 | June 9, '46 | Louisville, Ky. | 1 yr. | | |
| 25 | Warren, C. Greenhalch | Private | June 8, 1846 | June 9, '46 | Louisville, Ky. | 1 yr. | | |
| | **Died.** | | | | | | | |
| 1 | Chenault, Wm. J. | Corporal | June 8, 1846 | June 9, '46 | Louisville, Ky. | 1 yr. | | |
| 2 | Baker, Peter | Private | June 8, 1846 | June 9, '46 | Louisville, Ky. | 1 yr. | | |
| 3 | Barden, Louis M. | Private | June 8, 1846 | June 9, '46 | Louisville, Ky. | 1 yr. | | |
| 4 | Coyle, McKenzie | Private | June 8, 1846 | June 9, '46 | Louisville, Ky. | 1 yr. | | |
| 5 | DeCoursey, Samuel B. | Private | June 8, 1846 | June 9, '46 | Louisville, Ky. | 1 yr. | | |
| 6 | Hendron, Lorenzo D. | Private | June 8, 1846 | June 9, '46 | Louisville, Ky. | 1 yr. | | |
| 7 | Redfield, Lyman | Private | June 8, 1846 | June 9, '46 | Louisville, Ky. | 1 yr. | | |

This Company was enrolled in Richmond, Madison county.

## ROLL OF COMPANY "I," FIRST REGIMENT KENTUCKY

| No. | Name | Rank | Enrolled | Mustered In When | Mustered In Where | Period | Mustered Out When | Mustered Out Where |
|---|---|---|---|---|---|---|---|---|
| 1 | C. M. Clay | Captain | May 25, 1846 | June 9, '46 | Louisville, Ky. | 1 yr. | June 7, '47 | New Orleans, La. |
| 1 | Jessee Woodruff | 1st Lieutenant | May 25, 1846 | June 9, '46 | Louisville, Ky. | 1 yr. | June 7, '47 | New Orleans, La. |
| 1 | Geo. Mason Brown | 2d Lieutenant | May 25, 1846 | June 9, '46 | Louisville, Ky. | 1 yr. | June 7, '47 | New Orleans, La. |
| 1 | Dempsey Carroll | 1st Sergeant | May 25, 1846 | June 9, '46 | Louisville, Ky. | 1 yr. | June 7, '47 | New Orleans, La. |
| 2 | John McMain | 2d Sergeant | May 25, 1846 | June 9, '46 | Louisville, Ky. | 1 yr. | June 7, '47 | New Orleans, La. |
| 3 | James H. Miller | 3d Sergeant | May 25, 1846 | June 9, '46 | Louisville, Ky. | 1 yr. | June 7, '47 | New Orleans, La. |
| 4 | Francis M. Brennan (a) | 4th Sergeant | June 10, 1846 | Nov. 1, '46 | Camargo Mex. | 1 yr. | June 7, '47 | New Orleans, La. |
| 1 | James McGuire | Corporal | May 25, 1846 | June 9, '46 | Louisville, Ky. | 1 yr. | June 7, '47 | New Orleans, La. |
| 2 | John C. Falkner | Corporal | May 25, 1846 | June 9, '46 | Louisville, Ky. | 1 yr. | June 7, '47 | New Orleans, La. |
| 3 | James Schooley | Corporal | May 25, 1846 | June 9, '46 | Louisville, Ky. | 1 yr. | June 7, '47 | New Orleans, La. |
| 4 | George Sraikart | Corporal | May 25, 1846 | June 9, '46 | Louisville, Ky. | 1 yr. | June 7, '47 | New Orleans, La. |
| 1 | Harry H. Hellox | Blacksmith | May 25, 1846 | June 9, '46 | Louisville, Ky. | 1 yr. | June 7, '47 | New Orleans, La. |
| 1 | Argerbright, Alfred | Private | May 25, 1846 | June 9, '46 | Louisville, Ky. | 1 yr. | June 7, '47 | New Orleans, La. |
| 2 | Burton, Ambrose | Private | May 25, 1846 | June 9, '46 | Louisville, Ky. | 1 yr. | June 7, '47 | New Orleans, La. |
| 3 | Beaver, Henry C. | Private | May 25, 1846 | June 9, '46 | Louisville, Ky. | 1 yr. | June 7, '47 | New Orleans, La. |
| 4 | Barry, David | Private | May 25, 1846 | June 9, '46 | Louisville, Ky. | 1 yr. | June 7, '47 | New Orleans, La. |
| 5 | Bryan, Abram C. | Private | May 25, 1846 | June 9, '46 | Louisville, Ky. | 1 yr. | June 7, '47 | New Orleans, La. |
| 6 | Barkley, Samuel S. | Private | May 25, 1846 | June 9, '46 | Louisville, Ky. | 1 yr. | June 7, '47 | New Orleans, La. |
| 7 | Barlay, James | Private | May 25, 1846 | June 9, '46 | Louisville, Ky. | 1 yr. | June 7, '47 | New Orleans, La. |

MEXICAN WAR VETERANS.

23

## MOUNTED VOLUNTEERS—MEXICAN WAR—Continued.

| No. of each grade. | REMARKS. |
|---|---|
| 22 | |
| 23 | Left sick at Washington, Ark., August 23d; rejoined for duty January 25th. Absent on leave in hospital New Orleans. |
| 24 | Left sick at Washington, Ark., August 23d; rejoined for duty January 25th. Absent sick in New Orleans. |
| 25 | |
| 26 | |
| 27 | |
| 28 | |
| 29 | |
| 30 | |
| 31 | |
| 32 | |
| 33 | Left sick at Washington, Ark., August 10th; ordered to be discharged January 1st; rejoined for duty March 1st. |
| | |
| 1 | Discharged on Surgeon's certificate of disability at New Orleans, October 29th. Order of Col Hunt. |
| 2 | Discharged on Surgeon's certificate of disability at Victoria, Texas, October 15th. Order of Col. Marshall. |
| 3 | Discharged on Surgeon's certificate of disability at Lavacca, Texas, October 11th. Order of Col. Marshall. |
| 4 | Discharged on Surgeon's certificate of disability at New Orleans, May 31st. Order of Gen. Brooke. |
| 5 | Discharged on Surgeon's certificate of disability at Victoria, Texas, October 15th. Order of Col. Marshall. |
| 6 | Discharged on Surgeon's certificate of disability at Camargo, Mex., December 15th. Order of Col. Marshall. |
| 7 | Discharged on Surgeon's certificate of disability at Victoria, Texas, October 15th. Order of Col. Marshall. |
| 8 | Discharged on Surgeon's certificate of disability at Louisville, Ky., January 1st. Order of Col. Marshall. |
| 9 | Discharged on Surgeon's certificate of disability at Victoria, Texas, October 15th. Order of Col. Marshall. |
| 10 | Discharged on Surgeon's certificate of disability at Victoria, Texas, October 15th. Order of Col. Marshall. |
| 11 | Discharged on Surgeon's certificate of disability at New Orleans, May 31st. Order of Gen. Brooke. |
| 12 | Discharged on Surgeon's certificate of disability at New Orleans, October 29th. Order of Col. Hunt. |
| 13 | Discharged on Surgeon's certificate of disability at New Orleans, May 31st. Order of Gen Brooke. |
| 14 | Discharged on Surgeon's certificate of disability at Port Lavacca, Texas, October 11th. Order of Col. Marshall. |
| 15 | Discharged on Surgeon's certificate of disability at Victoria, Texas, October 15th. Order of Col. Marshall. |
| 16 | Discharged on Surgeon's certificate of disability at Port Lavacca, Texas, October 11th. Order of Col. Marshall. |
| 17 | Discharged on Surgeon's certificate of disability at New Orleans, October 29th. Order of Col. Hunt. |
| 18 | Discharged on Surgeon's certificate of disability at New Orleans, October 31st. Order of Col. Hunt. |
| 19 | Discharged on Surgeon's certificate of disability at New Orleans, May 31st. Order of Gen. Brooke. |
| 20 | Discharged on Surgeon's certificate of disability at Victoria, Texas, October 15th. Order of Col. Marshall. |
| 21 | Discharged on Surgeon's certificate of disability at New Orleans, October 29th. Order of Col. Hunt. |
| 22 | Discharged on Surgeon's certificate of disability at Port Lavacca, Texas, October 11th. Order of Col. Marshall. |
| 23 | Discharged on Surgeon's certificate of disability at Louisville, Ky., October 11th. Order of Col. Marshall. |
| 24 | Discharged on Surgeon's certificate of disability at Victoria, Texas, October 15th. Order of Col. Marshall. |
| 25 | Discharged on Surgeon's certificate of disability at Louisville, Ky., January 1st. Order of Col. Marshall. |
| | |
| 1 | Died at Port Lavacca, Texas, September 15th. |
| 2 | Died at Louisville, Kentucky, July 23d. |
| 3 | Died at Louisville, Kentucky, July 4th. |
| 4 | Died at Camargo, Mexico, December 15th. |
| 5 | Died at Bazos, Santiago, November 5th. |
| 6 | Died at Victoria, Texas, October 5th. |
| 7 | Died at Matamoras, Mexico, January 16th. |

## MOUNTED VOLUNTEERS—MEXICAN WAR.

| | |
|---|---|
| 1 | Prisoner of war since January 22d. |
| 1 | |
| 1 | Slightly wounded in battle February 23d. Absent in the city. |
| 1 | Promoted 1st Sergeant from private by order of Capt. Clay, December 16th. |
| 2 | Horse killed in battle February 23; remounted next day. |
| 3 | |
| 4 | Promoted from Corporal December 16th. Order of Capt. Clay. |
| 1 | Promoted from private December 16th. Order of Capt. Clay. |
| 2 | Promoted from private December 16th. Order of Capt Clay. |
| 3 | Slightly wounded in battle February 23d. |
| 4 | |
| 1 | |
| 1 | Taken prisoner by the enemy at Incarnation, Mex., January 22d. |
| 2 | |
| 3 | |
| 4 | Taken prisoner by the enemy at Incarnation, Mex., January 22d. |
| 5 | Taken prisoner by the enemy at Incarnation, Mex., January 22d. |
| 6 | |
| 7 | |

## ROLL OF COMPANY "I," FIRST REGIMENT KENTUCKY

| No. of each grade | Name | Rank | Enrolled | Mustered In When | Mustered In Where | Period | Mustered Out When | Mustered Out Where |
|---|---|---|---|---|---|---|---|---|
| 8 | Curtis, David N. | Private | May 25, 1846 | June 9, '46 | Louisville, Ky. | 1 yr. | June 7, '47 | New Orleans, La. |
| 9 | Crouch, Nathaniel | Private | May 25, 1846 | June 9, '46 | Louisville, Ky. | 1 yr. | June 7, '47 | New Orleans, La. |
| 10 | Chapman, Benj. A. | Private | May 25, 1846 | June 9, '46 | Louisville, Ky. | 1 yr. | June 7, '47 | New Orleans, La. |
| 11 | Ellis, Charles C. | Private | May 25, 1846 | June 9, '46 | Louisville, Ky. | 1 yr. | June 7, '47 | New Orleans, La. |
| 12 | Ellis, Richard L. | Private | May 25, 1846 | June 9, '46 | Louisville, Ky. | 1 yr. | June 7, '47 | New Orleans, La. |
| 13 | Finch, John I. | Private | May 25, 1846 | June 9, '46 | Louisville, Ky. | 1 yr. | June 7, '47 | New Orleans, La. |
| 14 | Gaylord, Henry M. | Private | May 25, 1846 | June 9, '46 | Louisville, Ky. | 1 yr. | June 7, '47 | New Orleans, La. |
| 15 | Gallager, John | Private | May 25, 1846 | June 9, '46 | Louisville, Ky. | 1 yr. | June 7, '47 | New Orleans, La. |
| 16 | Harman, Blidso | Private | May 25, 1846 | June 9, '46 | Louisville, Ky. | 1 yr. | June 7, '47 | New Orleans, La. |
| 17 | Igo, Harison | Private | May 25, 1846 | June 9, '46 | Louisville, Ky. | 1 yr. | June 7, '47 | New Orleans, La. |
| 18 | Jackson, Henry C. | Private | May 25, 1846 | June 9, '46 | Louisville, Ky. | 1 yr. | June 7, '47 | New Orleans, La. |
| 19 | Jones, David C. | Private | May 25, 1846 | June 9, '46 | Louisville, Ky. | 1 yr. | June 7, '47 | New Orleans, La. |
| 20 | Letcher, John W. | Private | May 25, 1846 | June 9, '46 | Louisville, Ky. | 1 yr. | June 7, '47 | New Orleans, La. |
| 21 | Moppin, Thomas | Private | May 25, 1846 | June 9, '46 | Louisville, Ky. | 1 yr. | June 7, '47 | New Orleans, La. |
| 22 | Mooney, Charles E. | Private | May 25, 1846 | June 9, '46 | Louisville, Ky. | 1 yr. | June 7, '47 | New Orleans, La. |
| 23 | Merchant, John L. | Private | May 25, 1846 | June 9, '46 | Louisville, Ky. | 1 yr. | June 7, '47 | New Orleans, La. |
| 24 | Nicholson, Lewis H. | Private | May 25, 1846 | June 9, '46 | Louisville, Ky. | 1 yr. | June 7, '47 | New Orleans, La. |
| 25 | Prentis, Nath. S. | Private | May 25, 1846 | June 9, '46 | Louisville, Ky. | 1 yr. | June 7, '47 | New Orleans, La. |
| 26 | Poindexter, James M. | Private | May 25, 1846 | June 9, '46 | Louisville, Ky. | 1 yr. | June 7, '47 | New Orleans, La. |
| 27 | Radcliff, William | Private | May 25, 1846 | June 9, '46 | Louisville, Ky. | 1 yr. | June 7, '47 | New Orleans, La. |
| 28 | Richardson, Robert C. | Private | May 25, 1846 | June 9, '46 | Louisville, Ky. | 1 yr. | June 7, '47 | New Orleans, La. |
| 29 | Rogers, Samuel E. | Private | May 25, 1846 | June 9, '46 | Louisville, Ky. | 1 yr. | June 7, '47 | New Orleans, La. |
| 30 | Richardson, John | Private | May 25, 1846 | June 9, '46 | Louisville, Ky. | 1 yr. | June 7, '47 | New Orleans, La. |
| 31 | Redman, Loyd H. | Private | May 25, 1846 | June 9, '46 | Louisville, Ky. | 1 yr. | June 7, '47 | New Orleans, La. |
| 32 | Smith, William | Private | May 25, 1846 | June 9, '46 | Louisville, Ky. | 1 yr. | June 7, '47 | New Orleans, La. |
| 33 | Snider, Geo. W. | Private | May 25, 1846 | June 9, '46 | Louisville, Ky. | 1 yr. | June 7, '47 | New Orleans, La. |
| 34 | Sessel, Henry | Private | May 25, 1846 | June 9, '46 | Louisville, Ky. | 1 yr. | June 7, '47 | New Orleans, La. |
| 35 | Shaw, William | Private | May 25, 1846 | June 9, '46 | Louisville, Ky. | 1 yr. | June 7, '47 | New Orleans, La. |
| 36 | Simpson, John H. | Private | May 25, 1846 | June 9, '46 | Louisville, Ky. | 1 yr. | June 7, '47 | New Orleans, La. |
| 37 | Thornton, Joseph | Private | May 25, 1846 | June 9, '46 | Louisville, Ky. | 1 yr. | June 7, '47 | New Orleans, La. |
| 38 | Taylor, Jackson M. | Private | May 25, 1846 | June 9, '46 | Louisville, Ky. | 1 yr. | June 7, '47 | New Orleans, La. |
| 39 | Taylor, James M. | Private | May 25, 1846 | June 9, '46 | Louisville, Ky. | 1 yr. | June 7, '47 | New Orleans, La. |
| 40 | White, Thomas | Private | May 25, 1846 | June 9, '46 | Louisville, Ky. | 1 yr. | June 7, '47 | New Orleans, La. |
| 41 | Young, Alfred | Private | May 25, 1846 | June 9, '46 | Louisville, Ky. | 1 yr. | June 7, '47 | New Orleans, La. |
| 42 | Yarbor, Jackson | Private | May 25, 1846 | June 9, '46 | Louisville, Ky. | 1 yr. | June 7, '47 | New Orleans, La. |
| | **Died.** | | | | | | | |
| 1 | Mulay, William H. | 1st Sergeant | May 25, 1846 | June 9, '46 | Louisville, Ky. | 1 yr. | | |
| 2 | Bryan, Albert G. | Private | May 25, 1846 | June 9, '46 | Louisville, Ky. | 1 yr. | | |
| 3 | Beaver, William | Private | May 25, 1846 | June 9, '46 | Louisville, Ky. | 1 yr. | | |
| | **Killed in Battle.** | | | | | | | |
| 1 | Weigart, Thomas | Private | May 25, 1846 | June 9, '46 | Louisville, Ky. | 1 yr. | | |
| | **Discharged.** | | | | | | | |
| 1 | Woodruff, James | 1st Sergeant | May 25, 1846 | June 9, '46 | Louisville, Ky. | 1 yr. | | |
| 2 | Bryan, Enoch | 2d Sergeant | May 25, 1846 | June 9, '46 | Louisville, Ky. | 1 yr. | | |
| 3 | Wilmot, Samuel T. | 3d Sergeant | May 25, 1846 | June 9, '46 | Louisville, Ky. | 1 yr. | | |
| 4 | Lanckart, Sylvester | Corporal | May 25, 1846 | June 9, '46 | Louisville, Ky. | 1 yr. | | |
| 5 | Frily, James C. | Corporal | May 25, 1846 | June 9, '46 | Louisville, Ky. | 1 yr. | | |
| 1 | Stafford, John | Private | May 25, 1846 | June 9, '46 | Louisville, Ky. | 1 yr. | | |
| 2 | Currie, James | Private | May 25, 1846 | June 9, '46 | Louisville, Ky. | 1 yr. | | |
| 3 | Ragen, Wm. | Private | May 25, 1846 | June 9, '46 | Louisville, Ky. | 1 yr. | | |
| 4 | Glass, Wm. | Private | May 25, 1846 | June 9, '46 | Louisville, Ky. | 1 yr. | | |
| 5 | Swenk, Alexander | Private | May 25, 1846 | June 9, '46 | Louisville, Ky. | 1 yr. | | |
| 6 | Bell, John W. | Private | May 25, 1846 | June 9, '46 | Louisville, Ky. | 1 yr. | | |
| 7 | Benjamin, George | Private | May 25, 1846 | June 9, '46 | Louisville, Ky. | 1 yr. | | |
| 8 | Slepp, George | Private | May 25, 1846 | June 9, '46 | Louisville, Ky. | 1 yr. | | |
| 9 | Gaines, R. W. | Private | May 25, 1846 | June 9, '46 | Louisville, Ky. | 1 yr. | | |
| 10 | Buckner, Hubard | Private | May 25, 1846 | June 9, '46 | Louisville, Ky. | 1 yr. | | |
| 11 | Powell, Thomas R. | Private | May 25, 1846 | June 9, '46 | Louisville, Ky. | 1 yr. | | |
| 12 | Mason, George | Private | May 25, 1846 | June 9, '46 | Louisville, Ky. | 1 yr. | | |
| 13 | Phillips, Isaac J. | Bugler | May 25, 1846 | June 9, '46 | Louisville, Ky. | 1 yr. | | |
| | **Deserted.** | | | | | | | |
| 1 | Holley, Wesley | Private | May 25, 1846 | June 9, '46 | Louisville, Ky. | 1 yr. | | |
| 2 | Duke, Wm. | Private | May 25, 1846 | June 9, '46 | Louisville, Ky. | 1 yr. | | |
| | **Resigned.** | | | | | | | |
| 1 | James Jackson | 2d Lieutenant | May 25, 1846 | June 9, '46 | Louisville, Ky. | 1 yr. | | |

This Company was enrolled in Lexington, Ky.; (a) enrolled in Louisville

## MOUNTED VOLUNTEERS—MEXICAN WAR—Continued.

| No. of each grade | REMARKS. |
|---|---|
| 8 | Detached service Quartermaster Department from May 18th. By order of Lieutenant Colonel Field. |
| 9 | |
| 10 | |
| 11 | |
| 12 | Sick. Present. |
| 13 | Taken prisoner by the enemy at Incarnation. |
| 14 | |
| 15 | |
| 16 | Sick. Present. |
| 17 | Taken prisoner by the enemy at Incarnation, Mexico, January 22d. |
| 18 | Reported by Captain on December roll as discharged by mistake, his name again put on the roll by order of the Colonel commanding. |
| 19 | Taken prisoner by the enemy at Incarnation, Mex., January 22d. |
| 20 | |
| 21 | |
| 22 | Taken prisoner by the enemy at Incarnation, Mex., January 22d. |
| 23 | |
| 24 | |
| 25 | |
| 26 | |
| 27 | Taken prisoner by the enemy at Incarnation, Mex., January 22d. |
| 28 | Sick. Present. Pay due as Sergeant from enlistment June 9th to October 31st. |
| 29 | |
| 30 | Taken prisoner by the enemy at Incarnation, Mex., January 22d. |
| 31 | |
| 32 | |
| 33 | |
| 34 | Horse killed in battle February 23d; remounted next day. |
| 35 | |
| 36 | |
| 37 | |
| 38 | |
| 39 | Detached service Quartermaster Department May 17th. Order of Lieutenant Colonel Field. |
| 40 | |
| 41 | [commanding. |
| 42 | Reported on the December roll as discharged by Captain Clay. By mistake, his name again put on the roll by order of the Colonel |
| 1 | Missing since December 16th. Supposed to be killed. |
| 2 | Died in hospital at New Orleans. Time not known. |
| 3 | Died at Ceralvo about March 1st. |
| 1 | Killed in battle February 23d. |
| 1 | Honorably discharged on Surgeon's certificate of disability. Order of Gen. T. Marshall at Camargo. Date not known. |
| 2 | Honorably discharged on Surgeon's certificate of disability. Order of Gen. T. Marshall at Camargo. Date not known. |
| 3 | Honorably discharged on Surgeon's certificate of disability. Order of Col. Marshall. Place and date not known. |
| 4 | Honorably discharged on Surgeon's certificate of disability. Order of Col. Marshall at Lavacca. Date not known. |
| 5 | Honorably discharged on Surgeon's certificate of disability. Order of Gen. T. Marshall at Camargo. Date not known. |
| 1 | Honorably discharged on Surgeon's certificate of disability. Order of Col. H Marshall at Lavacca. Date not known. |
| 2 | Honorably discharged on Surgeon's certificate of disability. Order of Col. H. Marshall at Lavacca. Date not known. |
| 3 | Honorably discharged on Surgeon's certificate of disability. Order of Col. H. Marshall at Lavacca. Date not known. |
| 4 | Honorably discharged on Surgeon's certificate of disability. Order of Col. H. Marshall at Lavacca. Date not known. |
| 5 | Honorably discharged on Surgeon's certificate of disability. Order of Col. H. Marshall at Lavacca. Date not known. |
| 6 | Honorably discharged on Surgeon's certificate of disability. Order of Col. H. Marshall at Camargo. Date not known. |
| 7 | Honorably discharged on Surgeon's certificate of disability. Order of Gen. T. Marshall at Camargo. Date not known. |
| 8 | Honorably discharged on Surgeon's certificate of disability. Order of Col. H. Marshall at Lavacca. Date not known. |
| 9 | Honorably discharged on Surgeon's certificate of disability. Order of Col. Marshall, Lavacca. March 22d. |
| 10 | Honorably discharged on Surgeon's certificate of disability. Order of Gen. Brooke at New Orleans. May 27th. |
| 11 | Honorably discharged on Surgeon's certificate of disability. Order of Gen. Brooke at New Orleans. May 27th. |
| 12 | Honorably discharged on Surgeon's certificate of disability. Order of Gen. Brooke at New Orleans. May 27th. |
| 13 | (Muster out roll fails to state cause, place and date.)—S. S. A., *A. A. G.* |
| 1 | Left at Arkansas, said to be sick; not since heard from. |
| 2 | Reported on the December roll as a deserter by Captain Clay; went home from Lavacca, Texas sick, without leave of absence; subsequently joined his company March 18th, but was not mustered. Discharged on Surgeon's certificate of disability at New Orleans, May 25. Order of Gen. Brooke. |
| 1 | Resigned at Lavacca October 10th. |

## MEXICAN WAR VETERANS.

### ROLL OF COMPANY "K," FIRST REGIMENT KENTUCKY

| No. of each grade | Name. | Rank. | Enrolled. | Mustered In. When. | Mustered In. Where. | Period. | Mustered Out. When. | Mustered Out. Where. |
|---|---|---|---|---|---|---|---|---|
| 1 | Oliver P. Beard | Captain | June 4, 1846 | June 9, '46 | Louisville, Ky. | 1 yr. | June 7, '47 | New Orleans, La. |
| 1 | John H. Morgan | 1st Lieutenant | June 4, 1846 | June 9, '46 | Louisville, Ky. | 1 yr. | June 7, '47 | New Orleans, La. |
| 1 | Lowry J. Beard | 2d Lieutenant | June 4, 1846 | June 9, '46 | Louisville, Ky. | 1 yr. | June 7, '47 | New Orleans, La. |
| 2 | Norbourn B. Scott | 2d Lieutenant | June 4, 1846 | June 9, '46 | Louisville, Ky. | 1 yr. | June 7, '47 | New Orleans, La. |
| 1 | Thomas L. Campbell | 1st Sergeant | June 4, 1846 | June 9, '46 | Louisville, Ky. | 1 yr. | June 7, '47 | New Orleans, La. |
| 2 | A. S. Jouett | Sergeant | June 4, 1846 | June 9, '46 | Louisville, Ky. | 1 yr. | June 7, '47 | New Orleans, La. |
| 3 | E. Prolzman | Sergeant | June 4, 1846 | June 9, '46 | Louisville, Ky. | 1 yr. | June 7, '47 | New Orleans, La. |
| 4 | Richard M. Adams | Sergeant | June 4, 1846 | June 9, '46 | Louisville, Ky. | 1 yr. | June 7, '47 | New Orleans, La. |
| 1 | Isaac Smith | Corporal | June 4, 1846 | June 9, '46 | Louisville, Ky. | 1 yr. | June 7, '47 | New Orleans, La. |
| 2 | Samuel Rigg | Corporal | June 4, 1846 | June 9, '46 | Louisville, Ky. | 1 yr. | June 7, '47 | New Orleans, La. |
| 3 | Henry Bitterman | Corporal | June 4, 1846 | June 9, '46 | Louisville, Ky. | 1 yr. | June 7, '47 | New Orleans, La. |
| 4 | James Mahoney | Corporal | June 4, 1846 | June 9, '46 | Louisville, Ky. | 1 yr. | June 7, '47 | New Orleans, La. |
| 1 | Isaac Sheppard | Blacksmith | June 4, 1846 | June 9, '46 | Louisville, Ky. | 1 yr. | June 7, '47 | New Orleans, La. |
| 1 | James W. Farse | Bugler | June 4, 1846 | June 9, '46 | Louisville, Ky. | 1 yr. | June 7, '47 | New Orleans, La. |
| 1 | Anderson, Robert | Private | June 4, 1846 | June 9, '46 | Louisville, Ky. | 1 yr. | June 7, '47 | New Orleans, La. |
| 2 | Bryan, Thomas | Private | June 4, 1846 | June 9, '46 | Louisville, Ky. | 1 yr. | June 7, '47 | New Orleans, La. |
| 3 | Biles, Samuel | Private | June 4, 1846 | June 9, '46 | Louisville, Ky. | 1 yr. | June 7, '47 | New Orleans, La. |
| 4 | Carter, George W. | Private | June 4, 1846 | June 9, '46 | Louisville, Ky. | 1 yr. | June 7, '47 | New Orleans, La. |
| 5 | Castleman, Bushrod | Private | June 4, 1846 | June 9, '46 | Louisville, Ky. | 1 yr. | June 7, '47 | New Orleans, La. |
| 6 | Conover, Sylvester | Private | June 4, 1846 | June 9, '46 | Louisville, Ky. | 1 yr. | June 7, '47 | New Orleans, La. |
| 7 | Daly, Lawrence | Private | June 4, 1846 | June 9, '46 | Louisville, Ky. | 1 yr. | June 7, '47 | New Orleans, La. |
| 8 | Estelle, Eli | Private | June 4, 1846 | June 9, '46 | Louisville, Ky. | 1 yr. | June 7, '47 | New Orleans, La. |
| 9 | Fox, Henry | Private | June 4, 1846 | June 9, '46 | Louisville, Ky. | 1 yr. | June 7, '47 | New Orleans, La. |
| 10 | Fitzpatrick, William | Private | June 4, 1846 | June 9, '46 | Louisville, Ky. | 1 yr. | June 7, '47 | New Orleans, La. |
| 11 | Gharam, George W.? | Private | June 4, 1846 | June 9, '46 | Louisville, Ky. | 1 yr. | June 7, '47 | New Orleans, La. |
| 12 | Hampton, George | Private | June 4, 1846 | June 9, '46 | Louisville, Ky. | 1 yr. | June 7, '47 | New Orleans, La. |
| 13 | Lowe, John M. | Private | June 4, 1846 | June 9, '46 | Louisville, Ky. | 1 yr. | June 7, '47 | New Orleans, La. |
| 14 | Leonard, William | Private | June 4, 1846 | June 9, '46 | Louisville, Ky. | 1 yr. | June 7, '47 | New Orleans, La. |
| 15 | Megowan, James F. | Private | June 4, 1846 | June 9, '46 | Louisville, Ky. | 1 yr. | June 7, '47 | New Orleans, La. |
| 16 | Morgan, Calvin C. | Private | June 4, 1846 | June 9, '46 | Louisville, Ky. | 1 yr. | June 7, '47 | New Orleans, La. |
| 17 | McIntyre, Hezekiah | Private | June 4, 1846 | June 9, '46 | Louisville, Ky. | 1 yr. | June 7, '47 | New Orleans, La. |
| 18 | Moore, James | Private | June 4, 1846 | June 9, '46 | Louisville, Ky. | 1 yr. | June 7, '47 | New Orleans, La. |
| 19 | Ohaver, Thomas | Private | June 4, 1846 | June 9, '46 | Louisville, Ky. | 1 yr. | June 7, '47 | New Orleans, La. |
| 20 | Runyon, George W. | Private | June 4, 1846 | June 9, '46 | Louisville, Ky. | 1 yr. | June 7, '47 | New Orleans, La. |
| 21 | Sheppard, David | Private | June 4, 1846 | June 9, '46 | Louisville, Ky. | 1 yr. | June 7, '47 | New Orleans, La. |
| 22 | Sheppard, Charles J. | Private | June 4, 1846 | June 9, '46 | Louisville, Ky. | 1 yr. | June 7, '47 | New Orleans, La. |
| 23 | Thwaits, Ezekiel | Private | June 4, 1846 | June 9, '46 | Louisville, Ky. | 1 yr. | June 7, '47 | New Orleans, La. |
| 24 | Tempy, Christopher | Private | June 4, 1846 | June 9, '46 | Louisville, Ky. | 1 yr. | June 7, '47 | New Orleans, La. |
| 25 | Thomas, William | Private | June 4, 1846 | June 9, '46 | Louisville, Ky. | 1 yr. | June 7, '47 | New Orleans, La. |
| 26 | Weigart, William | Private | June 4, 1846 | June 9, '46 | Louisville, Ky. | 1 yr. | June 7, '47 | New Orleans, La. |
| 27 | Whitney, Richard P. | Private | June 4, 1846 | June 9, '46 | Louisville, Ky. | 1 yr. | June 7, '47 | New Orleans, La. |
| 28 | Wisecarver, John | Private | June 4, 1846 | June 9, '46 | Louisville, Ky. | 1 yr. | June 7, '47 | New Orleans, La. |
| 29 | McCarty, Edward | Private | June 4, 1846 | June 9, '46 | Louisville, Ky. | 1 yr. | June 7, '47 | New Orleans, La. |
| 30 | McCracken, Marcus W. | Private | June 4, 1846 | June 9, '46 | Louisville, Ky. | 1 yr. | June 7, '47 | New Orleans, La. |
| | DIED. | | | | | | | |
| 1 | Cummings, Hervey | Private | June 4, 1846 | June 9, '46 | Louisville, Ky. | 1 yr. | | |
| 2 | Jackson, Columbus | Private | June 4, 1846 | June 9, '46 | Louisville, Ky. | 1 yr. | | |
| 3 | Weigart, A. B. | Private | June 4, 1846 | June 9, '46 | Louisville, Ky. | 1 yr | | |
| | KILLED. | | | | | | | |
| 1 | Bayless, William W. | Corporal | June 4, 1846 | June 9, '46 | Louisville, Ky. | 1 yr. | | |
| 2 | Carty, Henry | Private | June 4, 1846 | June 9, '46 | Louisville, Ky. | 1 yr. | | |
| 3 | Jones, Clement | Private | June 4, 1846 | June 9, '46 | Louisville, Ky. | 1 yr. | | |
| 4 | Morgan, A. G. | Private | June 4, 1846 | June 9, '46 | Louisville, Ky. | 1 yr. | | |
| 5 | Thwaits, William | Private | June 4, 1846 | June 9, '46 | Louisville, Ky. | 1 yr. | | |
| 6 | Ramey, N. | Private | June 4, 1846 | June 9, '46 | Louisville, Ky. | 1 yr. | | |
| 7 | Patterson, Joseph R. | Private | June 4, 1846 | June 9, '46 | Louisville, Ky. | 1 yr. | | |
| | DISCHARGED. | | | | | | | |
| 1 | Bacon, Samuel P. | Private | June 4, 1846 | June 9, '46 | Louisville, Ky. | 1 yr. | | |
| 2 | Berrone, M. | Private | June 4, 1846 | June 9, '46 | Louisville, Ky. | 1 yr. | | |
| 3 | Berry, S. O. | Corporal | June 4, 1846 | June 9, '46 | Louisville, Ky. | 1 yr. | | |
| 4 | Bowman, William | Private | June 4, 1846 | June 9, '46 | Louisville, Ky. | 1 yr. | | |
| 5 | Coppage, Charles | Corporal | June 4, 1846 | June 9, '46 | Louisville, Ky. | 1 yr. | | |
| 6 | Callaghan, M. B. | Private | June 4, 1846 | June 9, '46 | Louisville, Ky. | 1 yr. | | |
| 7 | Delph, Geo. W. M. | Private | June 4, 1846 | June 9, '46 | Louisville, Ky. | 1 yr. | | |
| 8 | Gallagher, John | Private | June 4, 1846 | June 9, '46 | Louisville, Ky. | 1 yr. | | |
| 9 | Hutchens, Abner | Private | June 4, 1846 | June 9, '46 | Louisville, Ky. | 1 yr. | | |
| 10 | Dishman, John | Private | June 4, 1846 | June 9, '46 | Louisville, Ky. | 1 yr. | | |
| 11 | Harris, Joseph B. | Private | June 4, 1846 | June 9, '46 | Louisville, Ky. | 1 yr. | | |
| 12 | Jeter, Henry | Private | June 4, 1846 | June 9, '46 | Louisville, Ky. | 1 yr. | | |
| 13 | Levasay, James A. | Private | June 4, 1846 | June 9, '46 | Louisville, Ky. | 1 yr. | | |

# MEXICAN WAR VETERANS.

## MOUNTED VOLUNTEERS—MEXICAN WAR.

| No. of each grade | REMARKS. |
|---|---|
| 1 | |
| 1 | Promoted from 2d Lieutenant June 9th, vice Vaughn appointed Adjutant. |
| 1 | Promoted from Sergeant June 9th, vice Morgan promoted. |
| 2 | Was Sergeant from enrollment to July 13th. Pay due as Sergeant from muster to July 12th. Absent in New Orleans. |
| 1 | Absent with leave from May 17th. Order of Lieut. Col. Field. |
| 2 | |
| 3 | Promoted from Corporal March 22d. |
| 4 | |
| 1 | |
| 2 | |
| 3 | Appointed from private March 1st. |
| 4 | Appointed from private March 22d. |
| 1 | Slightly wounded in the battle of Buena Vista, February 23d. |
| 1 | |
| 1 | |
| 2 | Absent with leave from May 17th. Order of Lieut. Col. Field. |
| 3 | |
| 4 | |
| 5 | Absent with leave from May 18th. Order of Lieut. Col. Field. |
| 6 | |
| 7 | |
| 8 | |
| 9 | |
| 10 | Sick in New Orleans. |
| 11 | |
| 12 | |
| 13 | |
| 14 | Absent. Sick in Arkansas since August 20th. |
| 15 | |
| 16 | |
| 17 | |
| 18 | |
| 19 | |
| 20 | |
| 21 | |
| 22 | Wounded severely in the battle of Buena Vista, February 23d. |
| 23 | |
| 24 | |
| 25 | |
| 26 | |
| 27 | |
| 28 | |
| 29 | |
| 30 | |
| 1 | Died in Texas, September 14th. |
| 2 | Died in Texas, September 25th. |
| 3 | Died in Matamoras, Mexico, time not known. |
| 1 | Killed in battle of Buena Vista, February 23d. |
| 2 | Killed in battle of Buena Vista, February 23d. |
| 3 | Killed in battle of Buena Vista, February 23d. |
| 4 | Killed in battle of Buena Vista, February 23d. |
| 5 | Killed in battle of Buena Vista, February 23d. |
| 6 | Killed in battle of Buena Vista, February 23d. |
| 7 | Missing since December 16th, and supposed to be killed by the enemy. |
| 1 | Honorably discharged on Surgeon's certificate of disability. Order of Col. Marshall, August 19th. Arkansas. |
| 2 | Honorably discharged on Surgeon's certificate of disability. Order of Capt. Irvine. Lavacca. |
| 3 | Honorably discharged on Surgeon's certificate of disability. Order of Gen. Marshall. Camargo, November 5th. |
| 4 | Honorably discharged on Surgeon's certificate of disability. Order of Col. Marshall, at Lavacca, October 6th. |
| 5 | Honorably discharged on Surgeon's certificate of disability. Order of Gen. Brooke, at New Orleans, October 6th. |
| 6 | Honorably discharged on Surgeon's certificate of disability. Order of Gen. Brooke, at New Orleans, May 31st; wounded severely in the battle of Buena Vista, February 23d. |
| 7 | Honorably discharged on Surgeon's certificate of disability. Order of Col. Marshall, at Lavacca, October 6th. |
| 8 | Honorably discharged on Surgeon's certificate of disability. Order of Col. Marshall, at Lavacca, October 6th. |
| 9 | Honorably discharged on Surgeon's certificate of disability. Order of Col. Marshall, at Camargo, December 12th. |
| 10 | Honorably discharged on Surgeon's certificate of disability. Order of Gen. Brooke, at New Orleans, May 31st. |
| 11 | Honorably discharged on Surgeon's certificate of disability. Order of Col. Marshall, at Victoria, October 15th. |
| 12 | Honorably discharged on Surgeon's certificate of disability. Order of Col. Marshall, at Lavacca, October 12th. |
| 13 | Honorably discharged on Surgeon's certificate of disability. Order of Gen. Brooke, at New Orleans, May 31st; wounded severely in the battle of Buena Vista, February 28d. |

## MEXICAN WAR VETERANS.

### ROLL OF COMPANY "K," FIRST REGIMENT KENTUCKY

| No. of each grade | Name. | Rank. | Enrolled. | Mustered In. When. | Mustered In. Where. | Period. | Mustered Out. When. | Mustered Out. Where. |
|---|---|---|---|---|---|---|---|---|
| 14 | Levasay, John | Private | June 4, 1846 | June 9, '46 | Louisville, Ky. | 1 yr. | | |
| 15 | Martin, James G. | Private | June 4, 1846 | June 9, '46 | Louisville, Ky. | 1 yr. | | |
| 16 | Patterson, Samuel R. | Private | June 4, 1846 | June 9, '46 | Louisville, Ky. | 1 yr. | | |
| 17 | Parott, Henry | Private | June 4, 1846 | June 9, '46 | Louisville, Ky. | 1 yr. | | |
| 18 | Roberts, Samuel E. | Private | June 4, 1846 | June 9, '46 | Louisville, Ky. | 1 yr. | | |
| 19 | Skelton, John | Private | June 4, 1846 | June 9, '46 | Louisville, Ky. | 1 yr. | | |
| 20 | Taylor, James M. | Sergeant | June 4, 1846 | June 9, '46 | Louisville, Ky. | 1 yr. | | |
| 21 | Wait, John | Private | June 4, 1846 | June 9, '46 | Louisville, Ky. | 1 yr. | | |
| 22 | Williams, E. B. | Private | June 4, 1846 | June 9, '46 | Louisville, Ky. | 1 yr. | | |
|   | TRANSFERRED. | | | | | | | |
| 1 | Edward M. Vaughn | 1st Lieutenant | June 4, 1846 | June 9, '46 | Louisville, Ky. | 1 yr. | | |
| 1 | Hawkins, Thomas T. | Private | June 4, 1846 | June 9, '46 | Louisville, Ky. | 1 yr. | | |

### ROLL OF THE FIELD AND STAFF SECOND REGIMENT

| No. | Name. | Rank. | Enrolled. | Mustered In. When. | Mustered In. Where. | Period. | Mustered Out. When. | Mustered Out. Where. |
|---|---|---|---|---|---|---|---|---|
| 1 | William R. McKee | Colonel | June 9, 1846 | June 9, '46 | Louisville, Ky. | 1 yr. | | |
| 1 | Henry Clay, Jr. | Lieut. Colonel | June 9, 1846 | June 9, '46 | Louisville, Ky. | 1 yr. | | |
| 1 | Carey H. Fry | Major | June 9, 1846 | June 9, '46 | Louisville, Ky. | 1 yr. | June 9, '47 | New Orleans, La. |
| 1 | Robert P. Hunt | Surgeon | June 9, 1846 | June 9, '46 | Louisville, Ky. | 1 yr. | | |
| 1 | James B. Snail | Ass't Surgeon | June 9, 1846 | June 9, '46 | Louisville, Ky. | 1 yr. | June 9, '47 | New Orleans, La. |
| 1 | Thomas J. Todd | Adjutant | June 9, 1846 | June 9, '46 | Louisville, Ky. | 1 yr. | | |
| 2 | George N. Cardwell | Adjutant | June 9, 1846 | June 9, '46 | Louisville, Ky. | 1 yr. | June 9, '47 | New Orleans, La. |
| 1 | Edward A. Tilford | Sergeant Major | June 9, 1846 | June 9, '46 | Louisville, Ky. | 1 yr. | June 9, '47 | New Orleans, La. |
| 2 | Harry Helm | Qr. M. Serg't | June 9, 1846 | June 9, '46 | Louisville, Ky. | 1 yr. | | |
| 3 | William McCrorty | Qr. M. Serg't | June 9, 1846 | June 9, '46 | Louisville, Ky. | 1 yr. | June 9, '47 | New Orleans, La. |
| 4 | John Wheatley | Qr. M. Serg't | May, 1846 | June 9, '46 | Louisville, Ky. | 1 yr. | June 9, '47 | New Orleans, La. |
| 1 | John Littell | Fife Major | June 9, 1846 | June 9, '46 | Louisville, Ky. | 1 yr. | June 9, '47 | New Orleans, La. |
| 2 | E. Wickersham | Drum Major | June 9, 1846 | June 9, '46 | Louisville, Ky. | 1 yr. | June 9, '47 | New Orleans, La. |

### ROLL OF COMPANY "A," SECOND REGIMENT KENTUCKY

| No. | Name. | Rank. | Enrolled. | Mustered In. When. | Mustered In. Where. | Period. | Mustered Out. When. | Mustered Out. Where. |
|---|---|---|---|---|---|---|---|---|
| 1 | James W. Moss | Captain | June 4, 1846 | June 9, '46 | Louisville, Ky. | 1 yr. | June 9, '47 | New Orleans. |
| 1 | Edward H. Hobson | 1st Lieutenant | June 4, 1846 | June 9, '46 | Louisville, Ky. | 1 yr. | June 9, '47 | New Orleans. |
| 1 | Wm. H. Moss | 2d Lieutenant | June 4, 1846 | June 9, '46 | Louisville, Ky. | 1 yr. | June 9, '47 | New Orleans. |
| 2 | E. L. Barbee | 2d Lieutenant | June 4, 1846 | June 9, '46 | Louisville, Ky. | 1 yr. | June 9, '47 | New Orleans. |
| 1 | John H. Cox | 1st Sergeant | June 4, 1846 | June 9, '46 | Louisville, Ky. | 1 yr. | June 9, '47 | New Orleans. |
| 2 | John A. Moss | Sergeant | June 4, 1846 | June 9, '46 | Louisville, Ky. | 1 yr. | June 9, '47 | New Orleans. |
| 3 | John Minton | Sergeant | June 4, 1846 | June 9, '46 | Louisville, Ky. | 1 yr. | June 9, '47 | New Orleans. |
| 4 | Charles D. Moore | Sergeant | June 4, 1846 | June 9, '46 | Louisville, Ky. | 1 yr. | June 9, '47 | New Orleans. |
| 1 | Charles M. Buckner | Corporal | June 4, 1846 | June 9, '46 | Louisville, Ky. | 1 yr. | June 9, '47 | New Orleans. |
| 2 | Samuel H. Wooding | Corporal | June 4, 1846 | June 9, '46 | Louisville, Ky. | 1 yr. | June 9, '47 | New Orleans. |
| 3 | Nathan G. Burton | Corporal | June 4, 1846 | June 9, '46 | Louisville, Ky. | 1 yr. | June 9, '47 | New Orleans. |
| 4 | James M. Johnston | Corporal | June 4, 1846 | June 9, '46 | Louisville, Ky. | 1 yr. | June 9, '47 | New Orleans. |
| 1 | Wm. S. Wilson | Bugler | June 4, 1846 | June 9, '46 | Louisville, Ky. | 1 yr. | June 9, '47 | New Orleans. |
| 1 | Asper, J. M. | Private | June 4, 1846 | June 9, '46 | Louisville, Ky. | 1 yr. | June 9, '47 | New Orleans. |
| 2 | Akin, Willis | Private | June 4, 1846 | June 9, '46 | Louisville, Ky. | 1 yr. | June 9, '47 | New Orleans. |
| 3 | Buckner, Rob't W. | Private | June 4, 1846 | June 9, '46 | Louisville, Ky. | 1 yr. | June 9, '47 | New Orleans. |
| 4 | Bishop, Henry | Private | June 4, 1846 | June 9, '46 | Louisville, Ky. | 1 yr. | June 9, '47 | New Orleans. |
| 6 | Buckner, Richard A. | Private | June 4, 1846 | June 9, '46 | Louisville, Ky. | 1 yr. | June 9, '47 | New Orleans. |
| 7 | Cofer, Owen | Private | June 4, 1846 | June 9, '46 | Louisville, Ky. | 1 yr. | June 9, '47 | New Orleans. |
| 8 | Chadoin, Isaac C. | Private | June 4, 1846 | June 9, '46 | Louisville, Ky. | 1 yr. | June 9, '47 | New Orleans. |
| 9 | Elliott, Abram B. | Private | June 4, 1846 | June 9, '46 | Louisville, Ky. | 1 yr. | June 9, '47 | New Orleans. |
| 10 | Elliott, Whitfield | Private | June 4, 1846 | June 9, '46 | Louisville, Ky. | 1 yr. | June 9, '47 | New Orleans. |
| 11 | Goodman, Ansel | Private | June 4, 1846 | June 9, '46 | Louisville, Ky. | 1 yr. | June 9, '47 | New Orleans. |
| 12 | Hutchason, Oscar F. | Private | June 4, 1846 | June 9, '46 | Louisville, Ky. | 1 yr. | June 9, '47 | New Orleans. |
| 13 | Johnston, Thomas | Private | June 4, 1846 | June 9, '46 | Louisville, Ky. | 1 yr. | June 9, '47 | New Orleans. |
| 14 | Jones, Warner E. | Private | June 4, 1846 | June 9, '46 | Louisville, Ky. | 1 yr. | June 9, '47 | New Orleans. |
| 15 | Johnston, Thomas M. | Private | June 4, 1846 | June 9, '46 | Louisville, Ky. | 1 yr. | June 9, '47 | New Orleans. |
| 16 | Long, John | Private | June 4, 1846 | June 9, '46 | Louisville, Ky. | 1 yr. | June 9, '47 | New Orleans. |
| 17 | Long, James | Private | June 4, 1846 | June 9, '46 | Louisville, Ky. | 1 yr. | June 9, '47 | New Orleans. |
| 18 | Loyall, John | Private | June 4, 1846 | June 9, '46 | Louisville, Ky. | 1 yr. | June 9, '47 | New Orleans. |
| 19 | Larue, John H. | Private | June 4, 1846 | June 9, '46 | Louisville, Ky. | 1 yr. | June 9, '47 | New Orleans. |
| 20 | Martin, John O. | Private | June 4, 1846 | June 9, '46 | Louisville, Ky. | 1 yr. | June 9, '47 | New Orleans. |
| 21 | Mays, Jackson | Private | June 4, 1846 | June 9, '46 | Louisville, Ky. | 1 yr. | June 9, '47 | New Orleans. |

# MOUNTED VOLUNTEERS—MEXICAN WAR—Continued.

| No. of each grade | REMARKS. |
|---|---|
| 14 | Honorably discharged on Surgeon's certificate of disability. Order of Gen Brooke at New Orleans, May 31st. |
| 15 | Honorably discharged on Surgeon's certificate of disability. Order of Col. Marshall at Lavacca, October 6th. |
| 16 | Honorably discharged on Surgeon's certificate of disability. Order of Col. Marshall at Lavacca, October 20th. |
| 17 | Honorably discharged on Surgeon's certificate of disability. Order of Col. Marshall at Lavacca, September 25th. |
| 18 | Honorably discharged on Surgeon's certificate of disability. Order of ——— at Little Rock, August 18th. |
| 19 | Honorably discharged on Surgeon's certificate of disability. Order of Col. Marshall at Lavacca, October 6th. |
| 20 | Honorably discharged on Surgeon's certificate of disability. Order of Col. Marshall at Camargo, March 22d. |
| 21 | Honorably discharged on Surgeon's certificate of disability. Order of Col. Marshall at Lavacca, September 26th. |
| 22 | Honorably discharged on Surgeon's certificate of disability. Order of Gen. Brooke at New Orleans, September 10th. |
| 1 | Appointed Adjutant June 9th; killed in the battle of Buena Vista, February 23d. |
| 1 | Appointed Adjutant February 24th, vice Vaughn; killed in battle and transferred to Regimental Staff. |

# KENTUCKY VOLUNTEERS—MEXICAN WAR.

| | |
|---|---|
| 1 | Killed in battle of Buena Vista, Mexico, February 23d. |
| 1 | Killed in battle of Buena Vista, Mexico, February 23d. |
| 1 | |
| 1 | Discharged at Camargo, Mexico, by resignation   Order Gen. Taylor. |
| 1 | |
| 1 | Discharged at Camargo, Mexico, by resignation, August 17th.   Order Gen. Taylor. |
| 2 | Appointed from 1st Lieutenant Company "C," August 17th, vice Todd, resigned. Left sick at Salerno, May 14th. |
| 1 | |
| 2 | Discharged at Carmago, August 18th. Order Major-General Patterson. |
| 3 | Appointed from Company "D," vice Helm, discharged. Absent on furlough March 11th. Order of Major Long. [from that time. |
| 4 | Appointed from Sergeant Company "D," vice McCrorty, reduced. Pay due as Sergeant from March 11th, and as Quartermaster Sergeant |
| 1 | Appointed from private in Company "H," September 29th, vice Dentton, reduced. Pay due as Musician. Distance to place of enrollment 130 miles. [Drummer. |
| 2 | Appointed from Drummer in Company "B," July 23d, vice Rudslley, reduced. Distance to place of enrollment 130 miles. Pay due as |

# FOOT VOLUNTEERS—MEXICAN WAR.

| | |
|---|---|
| 1 | Was 1st Lieutenant from enrollment to October 1st. |
| 1 | Was 2d 2d Lieutenant from enrollment to October 1st. |
| 1 | Was Corporal from enrollment to September 3d. |
| 2 | Was private from enrollment to September 14th. |
| 1 | |
| 2 | |
| 3 | Was private from enrollment to September 3d. |
| 4 | |
| 1 | Was private from enrollment to September 3d. |
| 2 | |
| 3 | Was private from enrollment to September 3d. |
| 4 | Was private from enrollment to November 1st. |
| 1 | Was private from enrollment to June 26th. |
| 1 | |
| 2 | |
| 3 | |
| 4 | |
| 6 | |
| 7 | |
| 8 | |
| 9 | |
| 10 | |
| 11 | |
| 12 | |
| 13 | |
| 14 | |
| 15 | Absent sick at Monterey, Mexico, May 14th. Order of Gen. Wool. |
| 16 | |
| 17 | |
| 18 | |
| 19 | |
| 20 | |
| 21 | |

MEXICAN WAR VETERANS.

## ROLL OF COMPANY "A," SECOND REGIMENT KENTUCKY

| No. of each grade. | Name. | Rank. | Enrolled. | Mustered In. When. | Mustered In. Where. | Period. | Mustered Out. When. | Mustered Out. Where. |
|---|---|---|---|---|---|---|---|---|
| 22 | Morris, Elzy | Private | June 4, 1846 | June 9, '46 | Louisville, Ky. | 1 yr. | June 9, '47 | New Orleans |
| 23 | McCalla, William | Private | June 4, 1846 | June 9, '46 | Louisville, Ky. | 1 yr. | June 9, '47 | New Orleans |
| 24 | Reynolds, Alexander | Private | June 4, 1846 | June 9, '46 | Louisville, Ky. | 1 yr. | June 9, '47 | New Orleans |
| 25 | Richmon, Howard | Private | June 4, 1846 | June 9, '46 | Louisville, Ky. | 1 yr. | June 9, '47 | New Orleans |
| 26 | Spencer, William H. | Private | June 4, 1846 | June 9, '46 | Louisville, Ky. | 1 yr. | June 9, '47 | New Orleans |
| 27 | Sutton, John | Private | June 4, 1846 | June 9, '46 | Louisville, Ky. | 1 yr. | June 9, '47 | New Orleans |
| 28 | Sydnor, Anthony | Private | June 4, 1846 | June 9, '46 | Louisville, Ky. | 1 yr. | June 9, '47 | New Orleans |
| 29 | Smith, John I. | Private | June 4, 1846 | June 9, '46 | Louisville, Ky. | 1 yr. | June 9, '47 | New Orleans |
| 30 | Slack, John B. | Private | June 4, 1846 | June 9, '46 | Louisville, Ky. | 1 yr. | June 9, '47 | New Orleans |
| 31 | Stanford, Wm. M. | Private | June 4, 1846 | June 9, '46 | Louisville, Ky. | 1 yr. | June 9, '47 | New Orleans |
| 32 | Southern, Simon F. | Private | June 4, 1846 | June 9, '46 | Louisville, Ky. | 1 yr. | June 9, '47 | New Orleans |
| 33 | Turner, Henry T. | Private | June 4, 1846 | June 9, '46 | Louisville, Ky. | 1 yr. | June 9, '47 | New Orleans |
| 34 | Tull, Frederick | Private | June 4, 1846 | June 9, '46 | Louisville, Ky. | 1 yr. | June 9, '47 | New Orleans |
| 35 | Towles, David T. | Private | June 4, 1846 | June 9, '46 | Louisville, Ky. | 1 yr. | June 9, '47 | New Orleans |
| 36 | Tolly, William | Private | June 4, 1846 | June 9, '46 | Louisville, Ky. | 1 yr. | June 9, '47 | New Orleans |
| 37 | Underwood, Eli | Private | June 4, 1846 | June 9, '46 | Louisville, Ky. | 1 yr. | June 9, '47 | New Orleans |
| 38 | Vaughan, Fielding | Private | June 4, 1846 | June 9, '46 | Louisville, Ky. | 1 yr. | June 9, '47 | New Orleans |
| 39 | Wallace, Samuel | Private | June 4, 1846 | June 9, '46 | Louisville, Ky. | 1 yr. | June 9, '47 | New Orleans |
| 40 | Wade, Benjamin | Private | June 4, 1846 | June 9, '46 | Louisville, Ky. | 1 yr. | June 9, '47 | New Orleans |
| 41 | Wills, Peter C. | Private | June 4, 1846 | June 9, '46 | Louisville, Ky. | 1 yr. | June 9, '47 | New Orleans |
| 42 | Willock, John | Private | June 4, 1846 | June 9, '46 | Louisville, Ky. | 1 yr. | June 9, '47 | New Orleans |
| 43 | Winlock, Robert S. | Private | June 4, 1846 | June 9, '46 | Louisville, Ky. | 1 yr. | June 9, '47 | New Orleans |
| 44 | Wilson, William A. | Private | June 4, 1846 | June 9, '46 | Louisville, Ky. | 1 yr. | June 9, '47 | New Orleans |
| 45 | Stith, Abner H. | Private | June 4, 1846 | June 9, '46 | Louisville, Ky. | 1 yr. | June 9, '47 | New Orleans |
| 46 | Morris, Thomas | Private | June 4, 1846 | June 9, '46 | Louisville, Ky. | 1 yr. | June 9, '47 | New Orleans |
| | DISCHARGED. | | | | | | | |
| 1 | W. H. Maxey | Captain | June 4, 1846 | June 9, '46 | Louisville, Ky. | 1 yr. | | |
| 1 | John M. Williams | 2d Lieutenant | June 4, 1846 | June 9, '46 | Louisville, Ky. | 1 yr. | | |
| 1 | Levi Moore | Sergeant | June 4, 1846 | June 9, '46 | Louisville, Ky. | 1 yr. | | |
| 1 | John A. Jeter | Corporal | June 4, 1846 | June 9, '46 | Louisville, Ky. | 1 yr. | | |
| 2 | Henry Embry | Corporal | June 4, 1846 | June 9, '46 | Louisville, Ky. | 1 yr. | | |
| 1 | Henry Allen | Musician | June 4, 1846 | June 9, '46 | Louisville, Ky. | 1 yr. | | |
| 2 | Andrew Crail | Musician | June 4, 1846 | June 9, '46 | Louisville, Ky. | 1 yr. | | |
| 1 | Brown, Shadrack D. | Private | June 4, 1846 | June 9, '46 | Louisville, Ky. | 1 yr. | | |
| 2 | Brownlea, John A. | Private | June 4, 1846 | June 9, '46 | Louisville, Ky. | 1 yr. | | |
| 3 | Cofer, Cyrus W. | Private | June 4, 1846 | June 9, '46 | Louisville, Ky. | 1 yr. | | |
| 4 | Coakley, Edward | Private | June 4, 1846 | June 9, '46 | Louisville, Ky. | 1 yr. | | |
| 5 | Davis, James M. | Private | June 4, 1846 | June 9, '46 | Louisville, Ky. | 1 yr. | | |
| 6 | Durham, Geo. W. | Private | June 4, 1846 | June 9, '46 | Louisville, Ky. | 1 yr. | | |
| 7 | Elmore, Lewis | Private | June 4, 1846 | June 9, '46 | Louisville, Ky. | 1 yr. | | |
| 8 | Lisle, Valentine | Private | June 4, 1846 | June 9, '46 | Louisville, Ky. | 1 yr. | | |
| 9 | McCabbins, James | Private | June 4, 1846 | June 9, '46 | Louisville, Ky. | 1 yr. | | |
| 10 | Owens, George B. | Private | June 4, 1846 | June 9, '46 | Louisville, Ky. | 1 yr. | | |
| 11 | Strader, George W. | Private | June 4, 1846 | June 9, '46 | Louisville, Ky. | 1 yr. | | |
| 12 | Sanders, William C. | Private | June 4, 1846 | June 9, '46 | Louisville, Ky. | 1 yr. | | |
| 13 | Taylor, Levi | Private | June 4, 1846 | June 9, '46 | Louisville, Ky. | 1 yr. | | |
| 14 | Vaughan, John L. | Private | June 4, 1846 | June 9, '46 | Louisville, Ky. | 1 yr. | | |
| 15 | Honsby, William R. | Private | June 4, 1846 | June 9, '46 | Louisville, Ky. | 1 yr. | | |
| 16 | Henry, Thomas | Private | June 4, 1846 | June 9, '46 | Louisville, Ky. | 1 yr. | | |
| 17 | Wheat, John P. | Private | June 4, 1846 | June 9, '46 | Louisville, Ky. | 1 yr. | | |
| 18 | Willock, James | Private | June 4, 1846 | June 9, '46 | Louisville, Ky. | 1 yr. | | |
| 19 | Arnold, Daniel | Private | June 4, 1846 | June 9, '46 | Louisville, Ky. | 1 yr. | | |
| 20 | Simmonds, A. M. C. | Private | June 4, 1846 | June 9, '46 | Louisville, Ky. | 1 yr. | | |
| | DEATHS. | | | | | | | |
| 1 | Buly, John | Private | June 4, 1846 | June 9, '46 | Louisville, Ky. | 1 yr. | | |
| 2 | Elmore, Johnson | Private | June 4, 1846 | June 9, '46 | Louisville, Ky. | 1 yr. | | |
| 3 | Hatcher, Green W. | Private | June 4, 1846 | June 9, '46 | Louisville, Ky. | 1 yr. | | |
| 4 | Sweany, Thomas A. | Private | June 4, 1846 | June 9, '46 | Louisville, Ky. | 1 yr. | | |
| 5 | Summers, Samuel C. | Private | June 4, 1846 | June 9, '46 | Louisville, Ky. | 1 yr. | | |
| | KILLED IN BATTLE. | | | | | | | |
| 1 | Chadoin, Austin M. | Private | June 4, 1846 | June 9, '46 | Louisville, Ky. | 1 yr. | | |
| 2 | Smith, John W. | Private | June 4, 1846 | June 9, '46 | Louisville, Ky. | 1 yr. | | |

This Company was enrolled at Greensburg, Ky.

## ROLL OF COMPANY "B," SECOND REGIMENT KENTUCKY

| 1 | Frank Chambers | Captain | May 20, 1846 | June 9, '46 | Louisville, Ky. | 1 yr. | June 9, '47 | New Orleans, La. |
|---|---|---|---|---|---|---|---|---|
| 1 | James Monroe | 1st Lieutenant | May 20, 1846 | June 9, '46 | Louisville, Ky. | 1 yr. | June 9, '47 | New Orleans, La. |
| 1 | Henry C. Long | Adj't & 2d Lieut. | May 20, 1846 | June 9, '46 | Louisville, Ky. | 1 yr. | June 9, '47 | New Orleans, La. |

MEXICAN WAR VETERANS. 31

# FOOT VOLUNTEERS—MEXICAN WAR—Continued.

| No. of each grade. | REMARKS. |
|---|---|
| 22 | |
| 23 | |
| 24 | |
| 25 | |
| 26 | |
| 27 | |
| 28 | |
| 29 | |
| 30 | |
| 31 | |
| 32 | |
| 33 | |
| 34 | |
| 35 | |
| 36 | |
| 37 | |
| 38 | |
| 39 | |
| 40 | |
| 41 | |
| 42 | |
| 43 | |
| 44 | |
| 45 | |
| 46 | Reduced from Bugler March 7th. |
| | |
| 1 | Discharged at Camargo by resignation. Order of General Taylor. |
| 1 | Discharged at Camargo by resignation, August 27th. Order of Gen. Taylor. |
| 1 | Discharged at Camp Belknap, August 18th; Surgeon's certificate of disability. Order of Col. McKee. |
| 1 | Discharged at Matamoras, September 16th; Surgeon's certificate of disability. Order of Gen. Taylor. |
| 2 | Discharged at Matamoras, October 8th; Surgeon's certificate of disability. Order of Gen. Taylor. |
| 1 | Discharged at Louisville, Ky., June 26th, with disgrace, for drunkenness. Order of Col. McKee. |
| 2 | Discharged at Louisville, Ky., June 26th, with disgrace, for drunkenness. Order of Col. McKee. |
| 1 | Discharged at Matamoras, October 29th, on Surgeon's certificate of disability. Order of Gen. Taylor. |
| 2 | Discharged at Camp Belknap, August 18th, on Surgeon's certificate of disability. Order of Gen. Taylor. |
| 3 | Discharged at Matamoras, September 23d, on Surgeon's certificate of disability. Order of Gen. Taylor. |
| 4 | Discharged at Matamoras, September 28th. Surgeon's certificate of disability. Order of Gen. Taylor. |
| 5 | Discharged at Brazos Santiago, July 28th. Surgeon's certificate of disability. Order of Gen. Taylor. |
| 6 | Discharged at Matamoras, September 24th. Surgeon's certificate of disability. Order of Gen. Taylor. |
| 7 | Discharged at Matamoras, October 2d. Surgeon's certificate of disability. Order of Gen. Taylor. |
| 8 | Discharged at Camp Belknap, August 18th. Surgeon's certificate of disability. Order of Gen. Taylor. |
| 9 | Discharged at Matamoras, September 24th. Surgeon's certificate of disability. Order of Gen. Taylor. |
| 10 | Discharged at Matamoras, September 16th. Surgeon's certificate of disability. Order of Gen. Taylor. |
| 11 | Discharged at Matamoras, October 6th. Surgeon's certificate of disability. Order of Gen. Taylor. |
| 12 | Discharged at Matamoras, September 16th. Surgeon's certificate of disability. Order of Gen. Taylor. |
| 13 | Discharged at Camp Belknap, August 18th. Surgeon's certificate of disability. Order of Gen. Taylor. |
| 14 | Discharged at Saltillo, March 15th. Surgeon's certificate of disability. Order of Gen. Taylor. |
| 15 | Discharged at Monterey, March 1st. Surgeon's certificate of disability. Order of Gen. Taylor. |
| 16 | Discharged at Louisville. Ky., June 28th. Surgeon's certificate of disability. Order of Col. McKee. |
| 17 | Discharged at Camp Belknap, August 18th. Surgeon's certificate of disability. Order of Col. McKee. |
| 18 | Discharged at Matamoras, September 24th. Surgeon's certificate of disability. Order of Gen. Taylor. |
| 19 | Discharged at Matamoras, September 24th. Surgeon's certificate of disability. Order of Gen. Taylor. |
| 20 | Discharged at Louisville, Ky., June 15th. Surgeon's certificate of disability. Order of Col. McKee. |
| | |
| 1 | Died at Camp Belknap, August 5th. |
| 2 | Died at Camargo, December 10th. |
| 3 | Died at Matamoras, September 10th. |
| 4 | Died on Gulf of Mexico, July 15th. |
| 5 | Died at Camp Belknap, August 10th. |
| | |
| 1 | Killed in battle of Buena Vista, February 23d. |
| 2 | Killed in battle of Buena Vista, February 23d. |

# FOOT VOLUNTEERS—MEXICAN WAR.

| | |
|---|---|
| 1 | |
| 1 | Was 2d Lieutenant from enrollment to September 1st. |
| 1 | Was 1st Sergeant from enrollment to July 29th. |

## MEXICAN WAR VETERANS.

### ROLL OF COMPANY "B," SECOND REGIMENT KENTUCKY

| No. of each grade. | Name. | Rank. | Enrolled. | Mustered In. When. | Mustered In. Where. | Period. | Mustered Out. When. | Mustered Out. Where. |
|---|---|---|---|---|---|---|---|---|
| 2 | William D. Robertson | 2d Lieutenant | May 20, 1846. | June 9, '46. | Louisville, Ky. | 1 yr. | June 9, '47. | New Orleans, La. |
| 1 | Samuel P. Barbee | 1st Sergeant | May 20, 1846. | June 9, '46. | Louisville, Ky. | 1 yr. | June 9, '47. | New Orleans, La. |
| 2 | William F. Gaines | Sergeant | May 20, 1846. | June 9, '46. | Louisville, Ky. | 1 yr. | June 9, '47. | New Orleans, La. |
| 3 | William Hardy | Sergeant | May 20, 1846. | June 9, '46. | Louisville, Ky. | 1 yr. | June 9, '47. | New Orleans, La. |
| 4 | Hanson S. Mayhall | Sergeant | May 20, 1846. | June 9, '46. | Louisville, Ky. | 1 yr. | June 9, '47. | New Orleans, La. |
| 1 | Richard P. Evans | Corporal | May 20, 1846. | June 9, '46. | Louisville, Ky. | 1 yr. | June 9, '47. | New Orleans, La. |
| 2 | Clark Knott | Corporal | May 20, 1846. | June 9, '46. | Louisville, Ky. | 1 yr. | June 9, '47. | New Orleans, La. |
| 3 | James B. Davidson | Corporal | May 20, 1846. | June 9, '46. | Louisville, Ly. | 1 yr. | June 9, '47. | New Orleans, La. |
| 4 | Ambrose W. Hampton | Corporal | May 20, 1846. | June 9, '46. | Louisville, Ky. | 1 yr. | June 9, '47. | New Orleans, La. |
| 1 | Thos. B. Heffner | Bugler | May 20, 1846. | June 9, '46. | Louisville, Ky. | 1 yr. | June 9, '47. | New Orleans, La. |
| 2 | Geo. W. Chambers | Bugler | May 20, 1846. | June 9, '46. | Louisville, Ky. | 1 yr. | June 9, '47 | New Orleans, La. |
| 1 | Allen, George | Private | May 20, 1846 | June 9, '46. | Louisville, Ky. | 1 yr. | June 9, '47. | New Orleans, La. |
| 2 | Amer, John | Private | May 20, 1846. | June 9, '46. | Louisville, Ky. | 1 yr. | June 9, '47. | New Orleans, La. |
| 3 | Bartlett, Elisa T. | Private | May 20, 1846. | June 9, '46. | Louisville, Ky. | 1 yr. | June 9, '47 | New Orleans, La. |
| 4 | Bartlett, Willis T. | Private | May 20, 1846. | June 9, '46. | Louisville, Ky. | 1 yr. | June 9, '47. | New Orleans, La. |
| 5 | Bartlett, Saml. S. | Private | May 20, 1846. | June 9, '46. | Louisville, Ky. | 1 yr. | June 9, '47. | New Orleans, La. |
| 6 | Branham, Benjamin O. | Private | May 20, 1846. | June 9, '46. | Louisville, Ky. | 1 yr. | June 9, '47. | New Orleans, La. |
| 7 | Brea, Ameal | Private | May 20, 1846. | June 9, '46. | Louisville Ky. | 1 yr. | June 9, '47 | New Orleans, La. |
| 8 | Christopher, John J. | Private | May 20, 1846. | June 9, '46. | Louisville, Ky. | 1 yr. | June 9, '47. | New Orleans, La. |
| 9 | Chambers, Patrick H. | Private | May 20, 1846. | June 9, '46 | Louisville, Ky. | 1 yr. | June 9, '47 | New Orleans, La. |
| 10 | Collins, John L. | Private | May 20, 1846. | June 9, '46. | Louisville, Ky. | 1 yr. | June 9, '47. | New Orleans, La. |
| 11 | Crane, William L. | Private | May 20, 1846. | June 9, '46. | Louisville, Ky. | 1 yr. | June 9, '47. | New Orleans, La. |
| 12 | Cummings, James W. | Private | May 20, 1846. | June 9, '46. | Louisville, Ky. | 1 yr. | June 9, '47. | New Orleans, La. |
| 13 | Easley, Dan'l | Private | May 20, 1846. | June 9, '46 | Louisville, Ky. | 1 yr. | June 9, '47. | New Orleans, La. |
| 14 | Edward, George W. | Private | May 20, 1846. | June 9, '46. | Louisville, Ky. | 1 yr. | June 9, '47. | New Orleans, La. |
| 15 | Featherston, Charles R. | Private | May 20, 1846. | June 9, '46. | Louisville, Ky. | 1 yr | June 9, '47. | New Orleans, La. |
| 16 | Gayle, Richard A. | Private | May 20, 1846. | June 9, '46. | Louisville, Ky. | 1 yr. | June 9, '47. | New Orleans, La. |
| 17 | Harris, Abel P. | Private | May 20, 1846. | June 9, '46. | Louisville, Ky. | 1 yr. | June 9, '47. | New Orleans, La. |
| 18 | Hawkins, Reuben A. | Private | May 20, 1846. | June 9, '46. | Louisville, Ky. | 1 yr. | June 9, '47. | New Orleans, La. |
| 19 | Hayden, Wm. M. | Private | May 20, 1846 | June 9, '46 | Louisville, Ky. | 1 yr. | June 9, '47. | New Orleans, La. |
| 20 | Hayden, John R. | Private | May 20, 1846 | June 9, '46. | Louisville, Ky. | 1 yr. | June 9, '47. | New Orleans, La |
| 21 | Henderson, William | Private | May 20, 1846. | June 9, '46. | Louisville, Ky. | 1 yr. | June 9, '47. | New Orleans, La. |
| 22 | Herndon, David I. | Private | May 20, 1846. | June 9, '46. | Louisville, Ky. | 1 yr. | June 9, '47. | New Orleans, La. |
| 23 | Jordon, Wilson J. | Private | May 20, 1846. | June 9, '46. | Louisville, Ky. | 1 yr. | June 9, '47. | New Orleans, La. |
| 24 | McGune, James E. | Private | May 20, 1846. | June 9, '46. | Louisville, Ky. | 1 yr. | June 9, '47. | New Orleans, La. |
| 25 | McQueen, David | Private | May 20, 1846. | June 9, '46. | Louisville, Ky. | 1 yr. | June 9, '47. | New Orleans, La. |
| 26 | Milam, Moses S. | Private | May 20, 1846. | June 9, '46. | Louisville, Ky. | 1 yr. | June 9, '47. | New Orleans, La. |
| 27 | Milam, Thos. J. | Private | May 20, 1846. | June 9, '46. | Louisville, Ky. | 1 yr. | June 9, '47. | New Orleans, La. |
| 28 | Morrison, William | Private | May 20, 1846. | June 9, '46. | Louisville, Ky. | 1 yr. | June 9, '47. | New Orleans, La. |
| 29 | Moore, John E. | Private | May 20, 1846. | June 9, '46. | Louisville, Ky. | 1 yr. | June 9, '47. | New Orleans, La. |
| 30 | Perrin, William W. | Private | May 20, 1846. | June 9, '46. | Louisville, Ky. | 1 yr. | June 9, '47. | New Orleans, La. |
| 31 | Polsgrove, Almus W. | Private | May 20, 1846. | June 9, '46. | Louisville, Ky. | 1 yr. | June 9, '47. | New Orleans, La. |
| 32 | Polsgrove, John | Private | May 20, 1846. | June 9, '46. | Louisville, Ky. | 1 yr. | June 9, '47. | New Orleans, La. |
| 33 | Reed, James N. | Private | May 20, 1846. | June 9, '46. | Louisville, Ky. | 1 yr. | June 9, '47. | New Orleans, La. |
| 34 | Satterwhite, William R | Private | May 20, 1846. | June 9, '46 | Louisville, Ky. | 1 yr. | June 9, '47. | New Orleans, La. |
| 35 | Sheets, James W. | Private | May 20, 1846. | June 9, '46 | Louisville, Ky. | 1 yr. | June 9, '47. | New Orleans, La. |
| 36 | Sheets, Saml. | Private | May 20, 1846. | June 9, '46 | Louisville, Ky. | 1 yr. | June 9, '47. | New Orleans, La. |
| 37 | Sidbottom, Norman | Private | May 20, 1846. | June 9, '46. | Louisville, Ky. | 1 yr. | June 9, '47. | New Orleans, La. |
| 38 | Sheriaden, Robert | Private | May 20, 1846. | June 9, '46. | Louisville, Ky. | 1 yr. | June 9, '47. | New Orleans, La. |
| 39 | Sherrin, James | Private | May 20, 1846. | June 9, '46. | Louisville, Ky. | 1 yr. | June 9, '47. | New Orleans, La. |
| 40 | Skyler, William | Private | May 20, 1846. | June 9, '46. | Louisville, Ky. | 1 yr. | June 9, '47. | New Orleans, La. |
| 41 | Stevens, Walker | Private | May 20, 1846. | June 9, '46. | Louisville, Ky. | 1 yr. | June 9, '47. | New Orleans, La. |
| 42 | Taylor, James D. | Private | May 20, 1846. | June 9, '46. | Louisville, Ky. | 1 yr. | June 9, '47. | New Orleans, La. |
| 43 | Tull, Lewis | Private | May 20, 1846. | June 9, '46. | Louisville, Ky. | 1 yr. | June 9, '47. | New Orleans, La. |
| 44 | Webb, Thomas | Private | May 20, 1846. | June 9, '46. | Louisville, Ky. | 1 yr. | June 9, '47. | New Orleans, La. |
| 45 | Williams, James L. | Private | May 20, 1846. | June 9, '46 | Louisville, Ky. | 1 yr | June 9, '47 | New Orleans, La. |
| **DEAD.** | | | | | | | | |
| 1 | Rowland S. Parker | Private | May 20, 1846. | June 9, '46. | Louisville, Ky. | 1 yr. | | |
| 2 | Leander, Ford | Private | May 20, 1846. | June 9, '46. | Louisville, Ky. | 1 yr. | | |
| 3 | Thomas J. Chambers | Lieutenant | May 20, 1846. | June 9, '46. | Louisville, Ky. | 1 yr. | | |
| 4 | Lafayette B. Fredericks | Private | May 20, 1846. | June 9, '46. | Louisville, Ky. | 1 yr. | | |
| 5 | James S. Johnson | Private | May 20, 1846. | June 9, '46. | Louisville, Ky. | 1 yr. | | |
| 6 | Francis C. Lecompt | Private | May 20, 1846. | June 9, '46. | Louisville, Ky. | 1 yr. | | |
| **KILLED.** | | | | | | | | |
| 1 | Henry Wolf | 4th Sergeant | May 20, 1846. | June 9, '46. | Louisville, Ky. | 1 yr. | | |
| 1 | William Blackwell | Private | May 20, 1846. | June 9, '46. | Louisville, Ky. | 1 yr. | | |
| 2 | Samuel Bartlett | Private | May 20, 1846. | June 9, '46. | Louisville, Ky. | 1 yr. | | |
| 3 | Major Updike | Private | May 20, 1846. | June 9, '46. | Louisville, Ky. | 1 yr. | | |
| **DISCHARGED.** | | | | | | | | |
| 1 | William K. Major | Private | May 20, 1846. | June 9, '46. | Louisville, Ky. | 1 yr. | | |

## FOOT VOLUNTEERS—MEXICAN WAR—Continued.

| No. of each grade | REMARKS. |
|---|---|
| 2 | Was Sergeant from enrollment to September 15th, on detached service; Acting Assistant Commissary of Subsistence from February 27th, by order of Major Fry. |
| 1 | Was private from enrollment to September 15th. |
| 2 | Was private from enrollment to September 15th. |
| 3 | Was private from enrollment to September 3d. |
| 4 | Promoted from Corporal, February 24th, vice Wolf, killed. |
| 1 | |
| 2 | |
| 3 | Was private from enrollment to June 29th. |
| 4 | Appointed from private February 28th, vice Mayhall, promoted. |
| 1 | Absent without leave. Left somewhere in the neighborhood of Camargo, Mex.; supposed to be killed. |
| 2 | |
| 1 | |
| 2 | |
| 3 | |
| 4 | |
| 5 | |
| 6 | |
| 7 | |
| 8 | |
| 9 | Left sick at Louisville, Ky., June 29th. |
| 10 | |
| 11 | |
| 12 | |
| 13 | |
| 14 | |
| 15 | |
| 16 | |
| 17 | |
| 18 | |
| 19 | |
| 20 | |
| 21 | This man has been committing depredations since he arrived in New Orleans, which deserves a dishonorable discharge; he has been buying goods and having the same charged to his fellow-soldiers. |
| 22 | |
| 23 | |
| 24 | |
| 25 | |
| 26 | |
| 27 | |
| 28 | |
| 29 | |
| 30 | |
| 31 | |
| 32 | |
| 33 | |
| 34 | |
| 35 | |
| 36 | |
| 37 | |
| 38 | |
| 39 | |
| 40 | |
| 41 | |
| 42 | |
| 43 | |
| 44 | |
| 45 | |
| 1 | Died in Gulf of Mexico July 17th. |
| 2 | Died in general hospital, Matamoras, Mexico, September 9. |
| 3 | Elected from Sergeant to 2d Lieutenant September 3d; died in general hospital, Camargo, Mexico, September 14. |
| 4 | Died at Monterey, Mexico, January 9. |
| 5 | Died in general hospital, Camargo, Mexico, September 12th. |
| 6 | Died at Anga Neuaro, Mexico, February 10th. |
| 1 | Killed in battle Buena Vista, Mexico, February 23d. |
| 1 | Killed in battle Buena Vista, Mexico, February 23d. |
| 2 | Killed in battle Buena Vista, Mexico, February 23d. |
| 3 | Killed in battle Buena Vista, Mexico, February 23d. |
| 1 | Discharged at Brazos Santiago, July 31; Surgeon's certificate of disabiltiy. Order of Col. McKee. |

## ROLL OF COMPANY "B," SECOND REGIMENT KENTUCKY

| No. of each grade. | Name. | Rank. | Enrolled. | Mustered In. When. | Mustered In. Where. | Period. | Mustered Out. When. | Mustered Out. Where. |
|---|---|---|---|---|---|---|---|---|
| 2 | James R. Page | Private | May 20, 1846 | June 9, '46 | Louisville, Ky. | 1 yr. | | |
| 3 | James E. Coleman | Private | May 20, 1846 | June 9, '46 | Louisville, Ky. | 1 yr. | | |
| 4 | Merriat Young | Private | May 20, 1846 | June 9, '46 | Louisville, Ky. | 1 yr. | | |
| 5 | James W. Harris | Private | May 20, 1846 | June 9, '46 | Louisville, Ky. | 1 yr. | | |
| 6 | James Blaesehard | Private | May 20, 1846 | June 9, '46 | Louisville, Ky. | 1 yr. | | |
| 7 | Wesley Christopher | Private | May 20, 1846 | June 9, '46 | Louisville, Ky. | 1 yr. | | |
| 8 | Benjamin Robinson | Private | May 20, 1846 | June 9, '46 | Louisville, Ky. | 1 yr. | | |
| 9 | John Taylor | Private | May 20, 1846 | June 9, '46 | Louisville, Ky. | 1 yr. | | |
| 10 | Matthew L. Hazelett | Private | May 20, 1846 | June 9, '46 | Louisville, Ky. | 1 yr. | | |
| 11 | Stephen Sesfield | Private | May 20, 1846 | June 9, '46 | Louisville, Ky. | 1 yr. | | |
| 12 | Alexander Moss | Private | May 20, 1846 | June 9, '46 | Louisville, Ky. | 1 yr. | | |
| 13 | Enoch Ford | Private | May 20, 1846 | June 9, '46 | Louisville, Ky. | 1 yr. | | |
| 14 | Thos. J. Todd | Lieutenant | May 20, 1846 | June 9, '46 | Louisville, Ky. | 1 yr. | | |
| | **DESERTED.** | | | | | | | |
| 1 | John White | Private | May 20, 1846 | June 9, '46 | Louisville, Ky. | 1 yr. | | |
| 2 | James Crummery | Private | May 20, 1846 | June 9, '46 | Louisville, Ky. | 1 yr. | | |

This Company was enrolled at Frankfort, Ky.

## ROLL OF COMPANY "C," SECOND REGIMENT KENTUCKY

| No. | Name. | Rank. | Enrolled. | Mustered In. When. | Mustered In. Where. | Period. | Mustered Out. When. | Mustered Out. Where. |
|---|---|---|---|---|---|---|---|---|
| 1 | John H. McBrayer | Captain | May 23, 1846 | June 9, '46 | Louisville, Ky. | 1 yr. | June 8, '47 | New Orleans, La. |
| 1 | Andrew J. Galt | 1st Lieutenant | May 23, 1846 | June 9, '46 | Louisville, Ky. | 1 yr. | June 8, '47 | New Orleans, La. |
| 1 | John H. Lillard | 2d Lieutenant | May 23, 1846 | June 9, '46 | Louisville, Ky. | 1 yr. | June 8, '47 | New Orleans, La. |
| 2 | Alvey C. Threldkell | 2d Lieutenant | May 23, 1846 | June 9, '46 | Louisville, Ky. | 1 yr. | June 8, '47 | New Orleans, La. |
| 1 | W. S. Galt | 1st Sergeant | May 23, 1846 | June 9, '46 | Louisville, Ky. | 1 yr. | June 8, '47 | New Orleans, La. |
| 2 | John S. Petty | Sergeant | May 23, 1846 | June 9, '46 | Louisville, Ky. | 1 yr. | June 8, '47 | New Orleans, La. |
| 3 | William W. Lillard | Sergeant | May 23, 1846 | June 9, '46 | Louisville, Ky. | 1 yr. | June 8, '47 | New Orleans, La. |
| 4 | Joseph Warren | Sergeant | May 23, 1846 | June 9, '46 | Louisville, Ky. | 1 yr. | June 8, '47 | New Orleans, La. |
| 1 | John Bettersworth | Corporal | May 23, 1846 | June 9, '46 | Louisville, Ky. | 1 yr. | June 8, '47 | New Orleans, La. |
| 2 | Thomas Monday | Corporal | May 23, 1846 | June 9, '46 | Louisville, Ky. | 1 yr. | June 8, '47 | New Orleans, La. |
| 3 | James B. Oliver | Corporal | May 23, 1846 | June 9, '46 | Louisville, Ky. | 1 yr. | June 8, '47 | New Orleans, La. |
| 4 | William F. Bond | Corporal | May 23, 1846 | June 9, '46 | Louisville, Ky. | 1 yr. | June 8, '47 | New Orleans, La. |
| 1 | Brown, Hugh H. | Private | May 23, 1846 | June 9, '46 | Louisville, Ky. | 1 yr. | June 8, '47 | New Orleans, La. |
| 2 | Brown James | Private | May 23, 1846 | June 9, '46 | Louisville, Ky. | 1 yr. | June 8, '47 | New Orleans, La. |
| 3 | Banfield, John | Private | May 23, 1846 | June 9, '46 | Louisville, Ky. | 1 yr. | June 8, '47 | New Orleans, La. |
| 4 | Catlett, Jackson | Private | May 23, 1846 | June 9, '46 | Louisville, Ky. | 1 yr. | June 8, '47 | New Orleans, La. |
| 5 | Catlett, Francis | Private | May 23, 1846 | June 9, '46 | Louisville, Ky. | 1 yr. | June 8, '47 | New Orleans, La. |
| 6 | Cardwell, John | Private | May 23, 1846 | June 9, '46 | Louisville, Ky. | 1 yr. | June 8, '47 | New Orleans, La. |
| 7 | Cummings, Francis M. | Private | May 23, 1846 | June 9, '46 | Louisville, Ky. | 1 yr. | June 8, '47 | New Orleans, La. |
| 8 | Craig, William | Private | May 23, 1846 | June 9, '46 | Louisville, Ky. | 1 yr. | June 8, '47 | New Orleans, La. |
| 9 | Craig, John R. | Private | May 23, 1846 | June 9, '46 | Louisville, Ky. | 1 yr | June 8, '47 | New Orleans, La. |
| 10 | Davis, Thomas R. | Private | May 23, 1846 | June 9, '46 | Louisville, Ky. | 1 yr. | June 8, '47 | New Orleans, La. |
| 11 | Davis, Travis H. | Private | May 23, 1846 | June 9, '46 | Louisville, Ky. | 1 yr. | June 8, '47 | New Orleans, La. |
| 12 | Davis, John G. | Private | May 23, 1846 | June 9, '46 | Louisville, Ky. | 1 yr. | June 8, '47 | New Orleans, La. |
| 13 | Gilpin, George W. | Private | May 23, 1846 | June 9, '46 | Louisville, Ky. | 1 yr | June 8, '47 | New Orleans, La. |
| 14 | Howard, William | Private | May 23, 1846 | June 9, '46 | Louisville, Ky. | 1 yr. | June 8, '47 | New Orleans, La. |
| 15 | Howard, Samuel | Private | May 23, 1846 | June 9, '46 | Louisville, Ky. | 1 yr. | June 8, '47 | New Orleans, La. |
| 16 | Hanks, Joseph | Private | May 23, 1846 | June 9, '46 | Louisville, Ky. | 1 yr. | June 8, '47 | New Orleans, La. |
| 17 | Hewlett, James | Private | May 23, 1846 | June 9, '46 | Louisville, Ky. | 1 yr. | June 8, '47 | New Orleans, La. |
| 18 | Haslett, William F. | Private | May 23, 1846 | June 9, '46 | Louisville, Ky. | 1 yr. | June 8, '47 | New Orleans, La. |
| 19 | Hoffman, Fredrick | Private | May 23, 1846 | June 9, '46 | Louisville, Ky. | 1 yr. | June 8, '47 | New Orleans, La. |
| 20 | Leathers, Jefferson | Private | May 23, 1846 | June 9, '46 | Louisville, Ky. | 1 yr. | June 8, '47 | New Orleans, La. |
| 21 | Leathers, Larkin | Private | May 23, 1846 | June 9, '46 | Louisville, Ky. | 1 yr. | June 8, '47 | New Orleans, La. |
| 22 | McGaughery, James | Private | May 23, 1846 | June 9, '46 | Louisville, Ky. | 1 yr. | June 8, '47 | New Orleans, La. |
| 23 | Morgan, George | Private | May 23, 1846 | June 9, '46 | Louisville, Ky. | 1 yr. | June 8, '47 | New Orleans, La. |
| 24 | Moore, Hamilton G. | Private | May 23, 1846 | June 9, '46 | Louisville, Ky. | 1 yr. | June 8, '47 | New Orleans, La. |
| 25 | Martin, Samuel | Private | May 23, 1846 | June 9, '46 | Louisville, Ky. | 1 yr. | June 8, '47 | New Orleans, La. |
| 26 | Montgomery, Jos. | Private | May 23, 1846 | June 9, '46 | Louisville, Ky. | 1 yr. | June 8, '47 | New Orleans, La. |
| 27 | Neeley, Hezekiah F. | Private | May 23, 1846 | June 9, '46 | Louisville, Ky. | 1 yr. | June 8, '47 | New Orleans, La. |
| 28 | Perry, Berry | Private | May 23, 1846 | June 9, '46 | Louisville, Ky. | 1 yr. | June 8, '47 | New Orleans, La. |
| 29 | Reed, George W. | Private | May 23, 1846 | June 9, '46 | Louisville, Ky. | 1 yr. | June 8, '47 | New Orleans, La. |
| 30 | Searsey, Thos. | Private | May 23, 1846 | June 9, '46 | Louisville, Ky. | 1 yr. | June 8, '47 | New Orleans, La. |
| 31 | Searsey, George | Private | May 23, 1846 | June 9, '46 | Louisville, Ky. | 1 yr. | June 8, '47 | New Orleans, La. |
| 32 | Searsey, Beverly | Private | May 23, 1846 | June 9, '46 | Louisville, Ky. | 1 yr. | June 8, '47 | New Orleans, La. |
| 33 | Shouse, Leonard | Private | May 23, 1846 | June 9, '46 | Louisville, Ky. | 1 yr. | June 8, '47 | New Orleans, La. |
| 34 | Syres, Joseph | Private | May 23, 1846 | June 9, '46 | Louisville, Ky. | 1 yr. | June 8, '47 | New Orleans, La. |
| 35 | Syres, Thomas | Private | May 23, 1846 | June 9, '46 | Louisville, Ky. | 1 yr. | June 8, '47 | New Orleans, La. |
| 36 | Syres, John | Private | May 23, 1846 | June 9, '46 | Louisville, Ky. | 1 yr. | June 8, '47 | New Orleans, La. |
| 37 | Tindle, John | Private | May 23, 1846 | June 9, '46 | Louisville, Ky. | 1 yr. | June 8, '47 | New Orleans, La. |
| 38 | Taylor, Henry | Private | May 23, 1846 | June 9, '46 | Louisville, Ky. | 1 yr. | June 8, '47 | New Orleans, La. |

## FOOT VOLUNTEERS—MEXICAN WAR—Continued.

| No. of each grade | REMARKS. |
|---|---|
| 2 | Discharged at Brazos Santiago, July 31; Surgeon's certificate of disability. Order of Col. McKee. |
| 3 | Discharged at Camp Belknap, Texas, August 6th; Surgeon's certificate of disability. Order of Col. McKee. |
| 4 | Discharged at Camp Belknap, Texas, August 6th; Surgeon's certificate of disability. Order of Col. KcKee. |
| 5 | Discharged at Camp Belknap, Texas, August 6th; Surgeon's certificate of disability. Order of Col. McKee. |
| 6 | Discharged at Camp Belknap, Texas, August 18th; Surgeon's certificate of disability. Order of Col. McKee. |
| 7 | Discharged at Camp Belknap, Texas, August 18th; Surgeon's certificate of disability. Order of Col. McKee. |
| 8 | Discharged at Camp Belknap, Texas, August 18th; Surgeon's certificate of disability. Order of Col. McKee. |
| 9 | Discharged at Camargo, Mexico, September 13th; Surgeon's certificate of disability. Order of Col. McKee. |
| 10 | Discharged at Camargo, Mexico, September 13th; Surgeon's certificate of disability. Order of Col. McKee. |
| 11 | Discharged at Camargo, Mexico, October 24th; Surgeon's certificate of disability. Order of Gen. Marshall. |
| 12 | Discharged at Matamoras, Mexico, on or about October 19th; Surgeon's certificate of disability. Order not known. |
| 13 | Discharged at Monterey, Mexico, January 5th; Surgeon's certificate of disability. Order of Gen. Marshall. |
| 14 | Discharged by resignation on or about September 15th. Order of Gen. Taylor. |
| 1 | Deserted at Louisville, Ky., June 13th. |
| 2 | Deserted at Matamoras, Mexico, August 22d. |

## FOOT VOLUNTEERS—MEXICAN WAR.

## ROLL OF COMPANY "C," SECOND REGIMENT KENTUCKY

| No. of each grade | Name | Rank | Enrolled | Mustered In When | Mustered In Where | Period | Mustered Out When | Mustered Out Where |
|---|---|---|---|---|---|---|---|---|
| 39 | Vaughn, Edmond | Private | May 23, 1846 | June 9, '46 | Louisville, Ky. | 1 yr. | June 8, '47 | New Orleans, La. |
| 40 | Warford, Wm. | Private | May 23, 1846 | June 9, '46 | Louisville, Ky. | 1 yr. | June 8, '47 | New Orleans, La. |
| 41 | Warford, George | Private | May 23, 1846 | June 9, '46 | Louisville, Ky. | 1 yr. | June 8, '47 | New Orleans, La. |
| 42 | Warford, Nathaniel | Private | May 23, 1846 | June 9, '46 | Louisville, Ky. | 1 yr. | June 8, '47 | New Orleans, La. |
| 43 | Whip, John W. | Private | May 23, 1846 | June 9, '46 | Louisville, Ky. | 1 yr. | June 8, '47 | New Orleans, La. |
| 44 | Zimmerman, —— | Private | May 23, 1846 | June 9, '46 | Louisville, Ky. | 1 yr. | June 8, '47 | New Orleans, La. |
|  | DEATHS. |  |  |  |  |  |  |  |
| 1 | Brown, Peyton | Private | May 23, 1846 | June 9, '46 | Louisville, Ky. | 1 yr. |  |  |
| 2 | Bryant, Carter | Private | May 23, 1846 | June 9, '46 | Louisville, Ky. | 1 yr |  |  |
| 3 | Driskell, Thos. L. | Private | May 23, 1846 | June 9, '46 | Louisville, Ky. | 1 yr. |  |  |
| 4 | Gudgell, Thos. | Private | May 23, 1846 | June 9, '46 | Louisville, Ky. | 1 yr. |  |  |
| 5 | Huffman, John | Private | May 23, 1846 | June 9, '46 | Louisville, Ky. | 1 yr. |  |  |
| 6 | Leathers, Mark | Private | May 23, 1846 | June 9, '46 | Louisville, Ky. | 1 yr. |  |  |
| 7 | Wise, Henderson | Private | May 23, 1846 | June 9, '46 | Louisville, Ky. | 1 yr. |  |  |
|  | KILLED IN BATTLE. |  |  |  |  |  |  |  |
| 1 | Davis, David | Private | May 23, 1846 | June 9, '46 | Louisville, Ky. | 1 yr. |  |  |
| 2 | Johnson, James | Private | May 23, 1846 | June 9, '46 | Louisville, Ky. | 1 yr. |  |  |
| 3 | Layten, James | Private | May 23, 1846 | June 9, '46 | Louisville, Ky. | 1 yr. |  |  |
| 4 | Reynolds, William P. | Private | May 23, 1846 | June 9, '46 | Louisville, Ky. | 1 yr. |  |  |
| 5 | Thacker, Arthur | Private | May 23, 1846 | June 9, '46 | Louisville, Ky. | 1 yr. |  |  |
| 6 | Watson, John W. | Private | May 23, 1846 | June 9, '46 | Louisville, Ky. | 1 yr. |  |  |
| 7 | Board, William | Private | May 23, 1846 | June 9, '46 | Louisville, Ky. | 1 yr. |  |  |
|  | DISCHARGED. |  |  |  |  |  |  |  |
| 1 | Geo. W. Ravanaugh | Captain | May 23, 1846 | June 9, '46 | Louisville, Ky. | 1 yr. |  |  |
| 1 | John M. McBrayer | 2d Lieutenant | May 23, 1846 | June 9, '46 | Louisville, Ky. | 1 yr. |  |  |
| 1 | Bradshaw, Peter G. | Private | May 23, 1846 | June 9, '46 | Louisville, Ky. | 1 yr. |  |  |
| 2 | Brown, Sanford | Private | May 23, 1846 | June 9, '46 | Louisville, Ky. | 1 yr. |  |  |
| 3 | Breckinridge, Larkin | Private | May 23, 1846 | June 9, '46 | Louisville, Ky. | 1 yr. |  |  |
| 4 | Driskell, Henry | Private | May 23, 1846 | June 9, '46 | Louisville, Ky. | 1 yr. |  |  |
| 5 | Frazier, Jordan | Private | May 23, 1846 | June 9, '46 | Louisville, Ky. | 1 yr. |  |  |
| 6 | McGaughey, William | Private | May 23, 1846 | June 9, '46 | Louisville, Ky. | 1 yr |  |  |
| 7 | Maischel, Neuman | Private | May 23, 1846 | June 9, '46 | Louisville, Ky. | 1 yr. |  |  |
| 8 | Montgomery, John | Private | May 23, 1846 | June 9, '46 | Louisville, Ky. | 1 yr. |  |  |
| 9 | Palmer, Wilkerson | Private | May 23, 1846 | June 9, '46 | Louisville, Ky. | 1 yr. |  |  |
| 10 | Petty, James | Private | May 23, 1846 | June 9, '46 | Louisville, Ky. | 1 yr. |  |  |
| 11 | Patterson, A. D. | Private | May 23, 1846 | June 9, '46 | Louisville, Ky. | 1 yr. |  |  |
| 12 | Roach, Frederick | Private | May 23, 1846 | June 9, '46 | Louisville, Ky. | 1 yr. |  |  |
| 13 | Fitzgerald, Smith | Private | May 23, 1846 | June 9, '46 | Louisville, Ky. | 1 yr. |  |  |
| 14 | Silvy, Samuel | Private | May 23, 1846 | June 9, '46 | Louisville, Ky. | 1 yr. |  |  |
| 15 | Paxton, James | Private | May 23, 1846 | June 9, '46 | Louisville, Ky. | 1 yr. |  |  |
| 16 | Garvey, Robert | Private | May 23, 1846 | June 9, '46 | Louisville, Ky. | 1 yr. |  |  |
| 17 | Norton, James | Private | May 23, 1846 | June 9, '46 | Louisville, Ky. | 1 yr. |  |  |
| 18 | McComack, George | Private | May 23, 1846 | June 9, '46 | Louisville, Ky. | 1 yr. |  |  |
|  | DESERTED. |  |  |  |  |  |  |  |
| 1 | Morgan, Daniel | Private | May 23, 1846 | June 9, '46 | Louisville, Ky. | 1 yr. |  |  |

This Company was enrolled at Lawrenceburg, Ky.

## ROLL OF COMPANY "D," SECOND REGIMENT KENTUCKY

| No. | Name | Rank | Enrolled | Mustered In When | Mustered In Where | Period | Mustered Out When | Mustered Out Where |
|---|---|---|---|---|---|---|---|---|
| 1 | Speed S. Fry | Captain | May 20, 1846 | June 9, '46 | Louisville, Ky. | 1 yr. | June, 9 '47 | New Orleans |
| 1 | John M. Cowan | 1st Lieutenant | May 20, 1846 | June 9, '46 | Louisville, Ky. | 1 yr. | June 9, '47 | New Orleans |
| 1 | William E. Akin | 2d Lieutenant | May 20, 1846 | June 9, '46 | Louisville, Ky. | 1 yr. | June 9, '47 | New Orleans |
| 2 | Richard A. Clark | 2d Lieutenant | May 20, 1846 | June 9, '46 | Louisville, Ky. | 1 yr. | June 9, '47 | New Orleans |
| 1 | George Perkins | 1st Sergeant | May 20, 1846 | June 9, '46 | Louisville, Ky. | 1 yr. | June 9, '47 | New Orleans |
| 2 | John C. Dunn | Sergeant | May 20, 1846 | June 9, '46 | Louisville, Ky. | 1 yr. | June 9, '47 | New Orleans |
| 3 | Samuel M. Long | Sergeant | May 20, 1846 | June 9, '46 | Louisville, Ky. | 1 yr. | June 9, '47 | New Orleans |
| 4 | Wm. H. Harrison | Sergeant | May 20, 1846 | June 9, '46 | Louisville, Ky. | 1 yr. | June 9, '47 | New Orleans |
| 1 | James E. Conan | Corporal | May 20, 1846 | June 9, '46 | Louisville, Ky. | 1 yr. | June 9, '47 | New Orleans |
| 2 | John Craig | Corporal | May 20, 1846 | June 9, '46 | Louisville, Ky. | 1 yr. | June 9, '47 | New Orleans |
| 3 | John W. Tompkins | Corporal | May 20, 1846 | June 9, '46 | Louisville, Ky. | 1 yr. | June 9, '47 | New Orleans |
| 4 | Thomas J. Armstrong | Corporal | May 20, 1846 | June 9, '46 | Louisville, Ky. | 1 yr. | June 9, '47 | New Orleans |
| 1 | Miles Calvert | Fifer | May 20, 1846 | June 9, '46 | Louisville, Ky. | 1 yr. | June 9, '47 | New Orleans |
| 1 | John Richards | Drummer | May 20, 1846 | June 9, '46 | Louisville, Ky. | 1 yr. | June 9, '47 | New Orleans |
| 1 | Burgess, Timothy | Private | May 20, 1846 | June 9, '46 | Louisville, Ky. | 1 yr. | June 9, '47 | New Orleans |
| 2 | Bowman, John L. | Private | May 20, 1846 | June 9, '46 | Louisville, Ky. | 1 yr. | June 9, '47 | New Orleans |
| 3 | Becket, Elza | Private | May 20, 1846 | June 9, '46 | Louisville, Ky. | 1 yr. | June 9, '47 | New Orleans |
| 4 | Blackster, Jerry | Private | May 20, 1846 | June 9, '46 | Louisville, Ky. | 1 yr. | June 9, '47 | New Orleans |

## FOOT VOLUNTEERS—MEXICAN WAR—Continued.

| No. of each grade | REMARKS. |
|---|---|
| 39 | |
| 40 | |
| 41 | |
| 42 | |
| 43 | |
| 44 | |
| | |
| 1 | Died at Camp Belknap, August 10th. |
| 2 | Died at Buena Vista, Mexico, May 8th. |
| 3 | Died at Camp Belknap, Texas, August 13th. |
| 4 | Died in general hospital, Saltillo, Mexico, April 4th. |
| 5 | Died at camp opposite Camargo, Mexico, September 28th. |
| 6 | Died in hospital, Matamoras, Mexico, September 3d. |
| 7 | Died at camp opposite Camargo, Mexico, November 19th. |
| | |
| 1 | Killed in battle of Buena Vista, February 23d. |
| 2 | Killed in battle of Buena Vista, February 23d. |
| 3 | Killed in battle of Buena Vista, February 23d. |
| 4 | Killed in battle of Buena Vista, February 23d. |
| 5 | Killed in battle of Buena Vista, February 23d. |
| 6 | Killed in battle of Buena Vista, February 23d. |
| 7 | Killed in battle of Buena Vista, February 23d. |
| | |
| 1 | Discharged by resignation at Camargo, Mexico, September 9th. |
| 1 | Discharged by resignation at Camargo, Mexico, September 9th. |
| 1 | Discharged on Surgeon's certificate at Camargo, Mexico, September 28th. Certificate of pay furnished. |
| 2 | Discharged on Surgeon's certificate at Camargo, Mexico, September 30th. Certificate of pay furnished. |
| 3 | Discharged on Surgeon's certificate at Camargo, Mexico, September 30th. Certificate of pay furnished. |
| 4 | Discharged on Surgeon's certificate at Matamoras, Mexico, September 28th. Certificate of pay furnished. |
| 5 | Discharged on Surgeon's certificate at Camargo, Mexico, September 30th. Certificate of pay furnished. |
| 6 | Discharged on Surgeon's certificate at Matamoras, Mexico, September 28th. Certificate of pay furnished. |
| 7 | Discharged on Surgeon's certificate at Matamoras, Mexico, September 28th. Certificate of pay furnished. |
| 8 | Discharged on Surgeon's certificate at Matomoras, Mexico, September 28th. Certificate of pay furnished. |
| 9 | Discharged on Surgeon's certificate at Matamoras, Mexico, September 28th. Certificate of pay furnished. |
| 10 | Discharged on Surgeon's certificate at Camargo, Mexico, September 30th. Certificate of pay furnished. |
| 11 | Discharged on Surgeon's certificate at Camargo, Mexico, September 30th. Certificate of pay furnished. |
| 12 | Discharged on Surgeon's certificate at Camargo, Mexico, September 30th. Certificate of pay furnished. |
| 13 | Discharged on Surgeon's certificate at Camp Belknap, Texas, August 10th. Certificate of pay furnished. |
| 14 | Discharged on Surgeon's certificate at Camp Belknap, Texas, August 10th. Certificate of pay furnished. |
| 15 | Discharged on Surgeon's certificate at Camp Belknap, Texas, August 15th. Certificate of pay furnished. |
| 16 | Discharged on Surgeon's certificate at Camp Belknap, Texas, August 15th. Certificate of pay furnished. |
| 17 | Discharged on Surgeon's certificate at Camp Belknap, Texas, August 15th. Certificate of pay furnished. |
| 18 | Discharged on Surgeon's certificate at Ceralvo, Mexico, December 18th. Certificate of pay furnished. |
| | |
| 1 | Deserted at Louisville, Kentucky, June 30th. |

## FOOT VOLUNTEERS—MEXICAN WAR.

| No. of each grade |
|---|
| 1 |
| 1 |
| 1 |
| 2 |
| 1 |
| 2 |
| 3 |
| 4 |
| 1 |
| 2 |
| 3 |
| 4 |
| 1 |
| 2 |
| 1 |
| 2 |
| 3 |
| 4 |

## MEXICAN WAR VETERANS.

### ROLL OF COMPANY "D," SECOND REGIMENT KENTUCKY

| No. of each grade | Name. | Rank. | Enrolled. | Mustered In. When. | Mustered In. Where. | Period. | Mustered Out. When. | Mustered Out. Where. |
|---|---|---|---|---|---|---|---|---|
| 5 | Barker, Abram | Private | May 20, 1846 | June 9, '46 | Louisville, Ky. | 1 yr. | June 9, '47 | New Orleans |
| 6 | Benmie, William H. | Private | May 20, 1846 | June 9, '46 | Louisville, Ky. | 1 yr. | June 9, '47 | New Orleans |
| 7 | Bridgewater, Rich'd F. | Private | May 20, 1846 | June 9, '46 | Louisville, Ky. | 1 yr. | June 9, '47 | New Orleans |
| 8 | Cox, George | Private | May 20, 1846 | June 9, '46 | Louisville, Ky. | 1 yr. | June 9, '47 | New Orleans |
| 9 | Crane, James | Private | May 20, 1846 | June 9, '46 | Louisville, Ky. | 1 yr. | June 9, '47 | New Orleans |
| 10 | Cob, James | Private | May 20, 1846 | June 9, '46 | Louisville, Ky. | 1 yr. | June 9, '47 | New Orleans |
| 11 | Cochran, Thos. I. | Private | May 20, 1846 | June 9, '46 | Louisville, Ky. | 1 yr. | June 9, '47 | New Orleans |
| 12 | Curtis, Peter | Private | May 20, 1846 | June 9, '46 | Louisville, Ky. | 1 yr. | June 9, '47 | New Orleans |
| 13 | Cohen, John | Private | May 20, 1846 | June 9, '46 | Louisville, Ky. | 1 yr. | June 9, '47 | New Orleans |
| 14 | Daviess, Thos. D. | Private | May 20, 1846 | June 9, '46 | Louisville, Ky. | 1 yr. | June 9, '47 | New Orleans |
| 15 | Dotson, James | Private | May 20, 1846 | June 9, '46 | Louisville, Ky. | 1 yr. | June 9, '47 | New Orleans |
| 16 | Gibson, Harvey | Private | May 20, 1846 | June 9, '46 | Louisville, Ky. | 1 yr. | June 9, '47 | New Orleans |
| 17 | Garrett, William | Private | May 20, 1846 | June 9, '46 | Louisville, Ky. | 1 yr. | June 9, '47 | New Orleans |
| 18 | Guthrie, John P. | Private | May 20, 1846 | June 9, '46 | Louisville, Ky. | 1 yr. | June 9, '47 | New Orleans |
| 19 | Harlan, James | Private | May 20, 1846 | June 9, '46 | Louisville, Ky. | 1 yr. | June 9, '47 | New Orleans |
| 20 | Hamilton, Peter | Private | May 20, 1846 | June 9, '46 | Louisville, Ky. | 1 yr. | June 9, '47 | New Orleans |
| 21 | Harness, Anderson | Private | May 20, 1846 | June 9, '46 | Louisville, Ky. | 1 yr. | June 9, '47 | New Orleans |
| 22 | Horne, William | Private | May 20, 1846 | June 9, '46 | Louisville, Ky. | 1 yr. | June 9, '47 | New Orleans |
| 23 | Hocker, Rich'd W. | Private | May 20, 1846 | June 9, '46 | Louisville, Ky. | 1 yr. | June 9, '47 | New Orleans |
| 24 | Hauser, William | Private | May 20, 1846 | June 9, '46 | Louisville, Ky. | 1 yr. | June 9, '47 | New Orleans |
| 25 | Kimball, Thomas | Private | May 20, 1846 | June 9, '46 | Louisville, Ky. | 1 yr. | June 9, '47 | New Orleans |
| 26 | Maury, Reuben E. | Private | May 20, 1846 | June 9, '46 | Louisville, Ky. | 1 yr. | June 9, '47 | New Orleans |
| 27 | Montgomery, John L. | Private | May 20, 1846 | June 9, '46 | Louisville, Ky. | 1 yr. | June 9, '47 | New Orleans |
| 28 | Montgomery, Allen S. | Private | May 20, 1846 | June 9, '46 | Louisville, Ky. | 1 yr. | June 9, '47 | New Orleans |
| 29 | McGinnis, Thomas | Private | May 20, 1846 | June 9, '46 | Louisville, Ky. | 1 yr. | June 9, '47 | New Orleans |
| 30 | McChesney, Sam'l D. | Private | May 20, 1846 | June 9, '46 | Louisville, Ky. | 1 yr. | June 9, '47 | New Orleans |
| 31 | McGrorty, William | Private | May 20, 1846 | June 9, '46 | Louisville, Ky. | 1 yr. | June 9, '47 | New Orleans |
| 32 | Overstreet, Archibald | Private | May 20, 1846 | June 9, '46 | Louisville, Ky. | 1 yr. | June 9, '47 | New Orleans |
| 33 | Prewitt, John N. | Private | May 20, 1846 | June 9, '46 | Louisville, Ky. | 1 yr. | June 9, '47 | New Orleans |
| 34 | Prewitt, Wm. H. | Private | May 20, 1846 | June 9, '46 | Louisville, Ky. | 1 yr. | June 9, '47 | New Orleans |
| 35 | Rains, Jerry D. | Private | May 20, 1846 | June 9, '46 | Louisville, Ky. | 1 yr. | June 9, '47 | New Orleans |
| 36 | Russell, George | Private | May 20, 1846 | June 9, '46 | Louisville, Ky. | 1 yr. | June 9, '47 | New Orleans |
| 37 | Randall, Alexander | Private | May 20, 1846 | June 9, '46 | Louisville, Ky. | 1 yr. | June 9, '47 | New Orleans |
| 38 | Stroud, Sam'l M. D. | Private | May 20, 1846 | June 9, '46 | Louisville, Ky. | 1 yr. | June 9, '47 | New Orleans |
| 39 | Suddeth, James W. | Private | May 20, 1846 | June 9, '46 | Louisville, Ky. | 1 yr. | June 9, '47 | New Orleans |
| 40 | Short, William | Private | May 20, 1846 | June 9, '46 | Louisville, Ky. | 1 yr. | June 9, '47 | New Orleans |
| 41 | Stuck, Matthias | Private | May 20, 1846 | June 9, '46 | Louisville, Ky. | 1 yr. | June 9, '47 | New Orleans |
| 42 | Sneed, Benjamin | Private | May 20, 1846 | June 9, '46 | Louisville, Ky. | 1 yr. | June 9, '47 | New Orleans |
| 43 | Servant, Richard | Private | May 20, 1846 | June 9, '46 | Louisville, Ky. | 1 yr. | June 9, '47 | New Orleans |
| 44 | Swan, Thomas | Private | May 20, 1846 | June 9, '46 | Louisville, Ky. | 1 yr. | June 9, '47 | New Orleans |
| 45 | Varmoy, William | Private | May 20, 1846 | June 9, '46 | Louisville, Ky. | 1 yr. | June 9, '47 | New Orleans |
| 46 | Vanflute, Henry | Private | May 20, 1846 | June 9, '46 | Louisville, Ky. | 1 yr. | June 9, '47 | New Orleans |
| 47 | Withers, Horace | Private | May 20, 1846 | June 9, '46 | Louisville, Ky. | 1 yr. | June 9, '47 | New Orleans |
| 48 | Wade, Wm. P. | Private | May 20, 1846 | June 9, '46 | Louisville, Ky. | 1 yr. | June 9, '47 | New Orleans |
| 49 | Webb, James L. | Private | May 20, 1846 | June 9, '46 | Louisville, Ky. | 1 yr. | June 9, '47 | New Orleans |
| 50 | White, James | Private | May 20, 1846 | June 9, '46 | Louisville, Ky. | 1 yr. | June 9, '47 | New Orleans |
| | **DISCHARGED.** | | | | | | | |
| 1 | Paul J. Doneghy | 1st Sergeant | May 20, 1846 | June 9, '46 | Louisville, Ky. | 1 yr. | | |
| 2 | Samuel D. Lapsley | Sergeant | May 20, 1846 | June 9, '46 | Louisville, Ky. | 1 yr. | | |
| 3 | James G. Yeiser | Sergeant | May 20, 1846 | June 9, '46 | Louisville, Ky. | 1 yr. | | |
| 1 | James B. Foster | Corporal | May 20, 1846 | June 9, '46 | Louisville, Ky. | 1 yr. | | |
| 1 | Brumfield, James P | Private | May 20, 1846 | June 9, '46 | Louisville, Ky. | 1 yr. | | |
| 2 | Brown, William | Private | May 20, 1846 | June 9, '46 | Louisville, Ky. | 1 yr. | | |
| 3 | Brown, George | Private | May 20, 1846 | June 9, '46 | Louisville, Ky. | 1 yr. | | |
| 4 | Conley, Patrick | Private | May 20, 1846 | June 9, '46 | Louisville, Ky. | 1 yr. | | |
| 5 | Edgerton, John J. | Private | May 20, 1846 | June 9, '46 | Louisville, Ky. | 1 yr. | | |
| 6 | Griswold, Wiley P. | Private | May 20, 1846 | June 9, '46 | Louisville, Ky. | 1 yr. | | |
| 7 | Hughes, Crawford | Private | May 20, 1846 | June 9, '46 | Louisville, Ky. | 1 yr. | | |
| 8 | McCormac, William | Private | May 20, 1846 | June 9, '46 | Louisville, Ky. | 1 yr. | | |
| 9 | Merritt, Richard | Private | May 20, 1846 | June 9, '46 | Louisville, Ky. | 1 yr. | | |
| 10 | Overstreet, Cabel | Private | May 20, 1846 | June 9, '46 | Louisville, Ky. | 1 yr. | | |
| 11 | Rains, William | Private | May 20, 1846 | June 9, '46 | Louisville, Ky. | 1 yr. | | |
| 12 | Wallace, Edward | Private | May 20, 1846 | June 9, '46 | Louisville, Ky. | 1 yr. | | |
| | **DIED.** | | | | | | | |
| 1 | Burdett, Henry | Private | May 20, 1846 | June 9, '46 | Louisville, Ky. | 1 yr. | | |
| 2 | Crane, Nelson | Private | May 20, 1846 | June 9, '46 | Louisville, Ky. | 1 yr. | | |
| 3 | Sandifer, James | Private | May 20, 1846 | June 9, '46 | Louisville, Ky. | 1 yr. | | |
| | **KILLED IN BATTLE.** | | | | | | | |
| 1 | Trough, Peter | Corporal | May 20, 1846 | June 9, '46 | Louisville, Ky. | 1 yr. | | |
| 1 | Hammond, William | Private | May 20, 1846 | June 9, '46 | Louisville, Ky. | 1 yr. | | |
| 2 | Jones, Harvey | Private | May 20, 1846 | June 9, '46 | Louisville, Ky. | 1 yr. | | |

## FOOT VOLUNTEERS—MEXICAN WAR—Continued.

| No. of each grade | REMARKS |
|---|---|
| 5 | |
| 6 | |
| 7 | |
| 8 | |
| 9 | |
| 10 | |
| 11 | |
| 12 | |
| 13 | |
| 14 | |
| 15 | |
| 16 | |
| 17 | |
| 18 | |
| 19 | |
| 20 | |
| 21 | |
| 22 | |
| 23 | |
| 24 | |
| 25 | |
| 26 | |
| 27 | |
| 28 | |
| 29 | |
| 30 | |
| 31 | |
| 32 | |
| 33 | |
| 34 | |
| 35 | |
| 36 | |
| 37 | |
| 38 | |
| 39 | |
| 40 | |
| 41 | |
| 42 | |
| 43 | |
| 44 | |
| 45 | |
| 46 | |
| 47 | |
| 48 | |
| 49 | |
| 50 | |
| 1 | Discharged at Brazos, Santiago, Texas, on Surgeon's certificate of disability, July 27th. Order of Col. McKee. |
| 2 | Discharged at Camp Rio Grande, Texas, on Surgeon's certificate of disability, August 14th. Order of Col. McKee. |
| 3 | Discharged at Camp Rio Grande, Texas, on Surgeon's certificate of disability, August 14th. Order of Col. McKee. |
| 1 | Discharged at Camp Rio Grande, Texas, on Surgeon's certificate of disability, August 14th. Order of Col. McKee. |
| 1 | Discharged at Brazos Santiago, Texas, on Surgeon's certificate of disability, July 27th. Order of Col. McKee. |
| 2 | Discharged at Camp Rio Grande, Texas, on Surgeon's certificate of disability, August 13th. Order of Col. McKee. |
| 3 | Discharged at Camargo, Mexico, on Surgeon's certificate of disability, September 28th. Order of Gen. Marshall. |
| 4 | Discharged at Camp Rio Grande, Texas, on Surgeon's certificate of disability, August 14th. Order of Col. McKee. |
| 5 | Discharged at Camargo, Mexico, on Surgeon's certificate of disability, September 16th. Order of Gen. Marshall. |
| 6 | Discharged at Camp Rio Grande, Texas, on Surgeon's certificate of disability, August 14th. Order of Col. McKee. |
| 7 | Discharged at Camp Rio Grande, Texas, on Surgeon's certificate of disability, August 6th. Order of Col. McKee. |
| 8 | Discharged at Camp Rio Grande, Texas, on Surgeon's certificate of disability, August 14th. Order of Col. McKee. |
| 9 | Discharged at Camargo, Mexico, on Surgeon's certificate of disability, September 16th. Order of Gen. Marshall. |
| 10 | Discharged at Camargo, Mexico, on Surgeon's certificate of disability, September 16th. Order of Gen. Marshall. |
| 11 | Discharged at Camargo, Mexico, on Surgeon's certificate of disability, September 28th. Order of Gen. Marshall. |
| 12 | Discharged at Camargo, Mexico, on Surgeon's certificate of disability, September 7th. Order of Gen. Marshall. |
| 1 | Died in Saltillo, Mexico, February 27th, of wounds received in battle of Buena Vista, February 23d. |
| 2 | Died in Mier, Mexico, December 15th. |
| 3 | Died in Camargo, Mexico, September 29th. |
| 1 | Killed in battle of Buena Vista, February 23d. |
| 1 | Killed in battle of Buena Vista, February 23d. |
| 2 | Killed in battle of Buena Vista, February 23d. |

MEXICAN WAR VETERANS.

## ROLL OF COMPANY "D," SECOND REGIMENT KENTUCKY

| No. of each grade. | Name. | Rank. | Enrolled. | Mustered In. When. | Mustered In. Where. | Period. | Mustered Out. When. | Mustered Out. Where. |
|---|---|---|---|---|---|---|---|---|
| 3 | Walden, Joseph | Private | May 20, 1846. | June 9, '46. | Louisville, Ky. | 1 yr. | | |
|   | DESERTED. | | | | | | | |
| 1 | Cox, Chapman | Private | May 20, 1846. | June 9, '46. | Louisville, Ky. | 1 yr. | | |

This Company was enrolled in Danville, Ky.

## ROLL OF COMPANY "E," SECOND REGIMENT KENTUCKY

| | Name. | Rank. | Enrolled. | When. | Where. | Period. | When. | Where. |
|---|---|---|---|---|---|---|---|---|
| 1 | Geo. W. Cutter | Captain | May 23, 1846. | June 9, '46. | Louisville, Ky. | 1 yr. | June 10,'47. | New Orleans, La. |
| 1 | Littleton T. Lacy | 1st Lieutenant | May 23, 1846. | June 9, '46. | Louisville, Ky. | 1 yr. | June 10,'47. | New Orleans, La. |
| 1 | Wm. McDougal | 1st Sergeant | May 23, 1846. | June 9, '46. | Louisville, Ky. | 1 yr. | June 10,'47. | New Orleans, La. |
| 2 | Robert L. Morehead | Sergeant | May 23, 1846. | June 9, '46. | Louisville, Ky. | 1 yr. | June 10,'47. | New Orleans, La. |
| 3 | Thos. C. Flournoy | Sergeant | May 23, 1846. | June 9, '46. | Louisville, Ky. | 1 yr. | June 10,'47. | New Orleans, La. |
| 4 | James Hardin | Sergeant | May 23, 1846. | June 9, '46. | Louisville, Ky. | 1 yr. | June 10,'47. | New Orleans, La. |
| 1 | John S. Jennison | 1st Corporal | May 23, 1846. | June 9, '46. | Louisville, Ky. | 1 yr. | June 10,'47. | New Orleans, La. |
| 2 | James S. Jennison | 2d Corporal | May 23, 1846. | June 9, '46. | Louisville, Ky. | 1 yr. | June 10,'47. | New Orleans, La. |
| 3 | Charles Shannon | Corporal | May 23, 1846. | June 9, '46. | Louisville, Ky. | 1 yr. | June 10,'47. | New Orleans, La. |
| 4 | Richard McDonough | Corporal | May 23, 1846. | June 9, '46. | Louisville, Ky. | 1 yr. | June 10,'47. | New Orleans, La. |
| 1 | Ammerman, Peter | Private | May 23, 1846. | June 9, '46. | Louisville, Ky. | 1 yr. | June 10,'47. | New Orleans, La. |
| 2 | Atkinson, Thomas | Private | May 23, 1846. | June 9, '46. | Louisville, Ky. | 1 yr. | June 10,'47. | New Orleans, La. |
| 3 | Beasman, Wm. | Private | May 23, 1846. | June 9, '46. | Louisville, Ky. | 1 yr. | June 10,'47. | New Orleans, La. |
| 4 | Booth, Wm. | Private | May 23, 1846. | June 9, '46. | Louisville, Ky. | 1 yr. | June 10,'47. | New Orleans, La. |
| 5 | Boggs, Edward | Private | May 23, 1846. | June 9, '46. | Louisville, Ky. | 1 yr. | June 10,'47. | New Orleans, La. |
| 6 | Bonnewell, Elijah | Private | May 23, 1846. | June 9, '46. | Louisville, Ky. | 1 yr. | June 10,'47. | New Orleans, La. |
| 7 | Campbell, John | Private | May 23, 1846. | June 9, '46. | Louisville, Ky. | 1 yr. | June 10,'47. | New Orleans, La. |
| 8 | Clark, Thomas | Private | May 23, 1846 | June 9, '46. | Louisville, Ky. | 1 yr. | June 10,'47. | New Orleans, La. |
| 9 | Cook, William | Private | May 23, 1846. | June 9, '46. | Louisville, Ky. | 1 yr. | June 10,'47 | New Orleans, La. |
| 10 | Doolittle, Charles | Private | May 23, 1846. | June 9, '46. | Louisville, Ky. | 1 yr. | June 10,'47. | New Orleans, La. |
| 11 | Dunham, Edward | Private | May 23, 1846. | June 9, '46. | Louisville, Ky. | 1 yr. | June 10,'47. | New Orleans, La. |
| 12 | Easley, John | Private | May 23, 1846. | June 9, '46. | Louisville, Ky. | 1 yr. | June 10,'47. | New Orleans, La. |
| 13 | Farmer, John | Private | May 28, 1846. | June 9, '46. | Louisville, Ky. | 1 yr. | June 10,'47. | New Orleans, La. |
| 14 | Gosney, Benjamin | Private | May 23, 1846. | June 9, '46. | Louisville, Ky. | 1 yr. | June 10,'47. | New Orleans, La. |
| 15 | Guy, Samuel | Private | May 23, 1846. | June 9, '46. | Louisville, Ky. | 1 yr. | June 10,'47. | New Orleans, La. |
| 16 | Green, Abraham | Private | May 23, 1846. | June 9, '46. | Louisville, Ky. | 1 yr. | June 10,'47. | New Orleans, La. |
| 17 | Gregg, Joseph | Private | May 23, 1846. | June 9, '46. | Louisville, Ky. | 1 yr. | June 10,'47. | New Orleans, La. |
| 18 | Gray, Andrew | Private | May 23, 1846. | June 9, '46. | Louisville, Ky. | 1 yr. | June 10,'47. | New Orleans, La. |
| 19 | Gardner, Stephen | Private | May 23, 1846. | June 9, '46. | Louisville, Ky. | 1 yr. | June 10,'47. | New Orleans, La. |
| 20 | Houk, Jasper | Private | May 23, 1846. | June 9, '46. | Louisville, Ky. | 1 yr. | June 10,'47. | New Orleans, La. |
| 21 | Hubert, John | Private | May 23, 1846. | June 9, '46. | Louisville, Ky. | 1 yr. | June 10,'47. | New Orleans, La. |
| 22 | Krautz, John | Private | May 23, 1846 | June 9, '46. | Louisville, Ky. | 1 yr. | June 10,'47. | New Orleans, La. |
| 23 | Morgan, Milton | Private | May 23, 1846. | June 9, '46. | Louisville, Ky. | 1 yr. | June 10,'47. | New Orleans, La. |
| 24 | McBride, James | Private | May 23, 1846. | June 9, '46. | Louisville, Ky. | 1 yr. | June 10,'47. | New Orleans, La. |
| 25 | McLaughlin, John | Private | May 23, 1848. | June 9, '46. | Louisville, Ky. | 1 yr. | June 10,'47. | New Orleans, La. |
| 26 | Mitchell, James W. | Private | May 23, 1846. | June 9, '46. | Louisville, Ky. | 1 yr. | June 10,'47. | New Orleans, La. |
| 27 | Park, Wm. | Private | May 23, 1846. | June 9, '46. | Louisville, Ky. | 1 yr. | June 10,'47. | New Orleans, La. |
| 28 | Rhineland, John | Private | May 23, 1846. | June 9, '46. | Louisville, Ky. | 1 yr. | June 10,'47. | New Orleans, La. |
| 29 | Stanley, Wm. | Private | May 23, 1846. | June 9, '46. | Louisville, Ky. | 1 yr. | June 10,'47 | New Orleans, La. |
| 30 | Stanley, Robert | Private | May 23, 1846. | June 9, '46. | Louisville, Ky. | 1 yr. | June 10,'47. | New Orleans, La. |
| 31 | Sandbatch, Isaac | Private | May 23, 1846. | June 9, '46. | Louisville, Ky. | 1 yr. | June 10,'47. | New Orleans, La. |
| 32 | Tuthill, Charles | Private | May 23, 1846. | June 9, '46. | Louisville, Ky. | 1 yr. | June 10 '47. | New Orleans, La. |
| 33 | Thomas, Alexander | Private | May 23, 1846. | June 9, '46. | Louisville, Ky. | 1 yr. | June 10,'47. | New Orleans, La. |
| 34 | Walker, David | Private | May 23, 1846 | June 9, '46. | Louisville, Ky. | 1 yr. | June 10,'47 | New Orleans, La. |
| 35 | Wood, Isaiah | Private | May 23, 1846. | June 9, '46. | Louisville, Ky. | 1 yr. | June 10,'47. | New Orleans, La. |
| 36 | Welsh, Thomas | Private | May 23, 1846. | June 9, '46. | Louisville, Ky. | 1 yr. | June 10,'47. | New Orleans, La. |
| 37 | Whitehead, Wm. | Private | May 23, 1846. | June 9, '46. | Louisville, Ky. | 1 yr. | June 10,'47. | New Orleans, La. |
| 38 | Wegnell, Samuel | Private | May 23, 1846. | June 9, '46. | Louisville, Ky. | 1 yr. | June 10,'47. | New Orleans, La. |
| 39 | Yelton, Isaac | Private | May 23, 1846. | June 9, '46. | Louisville, Ky. | 1 yr. | June 10,'47. | New Orleans, La. |
| | TRANSFERRED. | | | | | | | |
| 1 | Harris, John C. | Private | May 23, 1846. | June 9, '46. | Louisville, Ky. | 1 yr. | | |
| 2 | Rodebaugh, Martin | Musician | May 23, 1846. | June 9, '46. | Louisville, Ky. | 1 yr. | | |
| | DISCHARGED. | | | | | | | |
| 1 | Littleton E. Bennett | 1st Lieutenant | May 23, 1846. | June 9, '46. | Louisville, Ky. | 1 yr. | | |
| 1 | Henry Robinson | 2d Lieutenant | May 23, 1846 | June 9, '46. | Louisville, Ky. | 1 yr. | | |
| 1 | James Wilson | 3d Lieutenant | May 23, 1846. | June 9, '46. | Louisville, Ky. | 1 yr. | | |
| 1 | Baker, John B. | Private | May 23, 1846. | June 9, '46. | Louisville, Ky. | 1 yr. | | |
| 2 | Cosgrove, Geo. C. | Private | May 23, 1846. | June 9, '46. | Louisville, Ky. | 1 yr. | | |
| 3 | Duskey, Wm. | Private | May 23, 1846. | June 9, '46. | Louisville, Ky. | 1 yr. | | |
| 4 | Griffery, Thos. L. | Private | May 23, 1846. | June 9, '46. | Louisville, Ky. | 1 yr. | | |
| 5 | Gregg, George | Private | May 23, 1846. | June 9, '46. | Louisville, Ky. | 1 yr. | | |

## FOOT VOLUNTEERS—MEXICAN WAR—Continued.

| No. of each | REMARKS. |
|---|---|
| 3 | Killed in battle of Buena Vista, February 23d. |
| 1 | Deserted at Monterey, Mexico, January 10th. |

## FOOT VOLUNTEERS—MEXICAN WAR.

| | |
|---|---|
| 1 | |
| 1 | Was private from enrollment to June 29th; promoted from 2d, March 4th, vice L. E. Bennett, resigned. |
| 1 | Was private from enrollment to August 14th. |
| 2 | |
| 3 | Was Corporal from enrollment to October 20th. |
| 4 | Promoted from private February 20th, vice Carlin, killed. |
| 1 | Was private from enrollment to September 3d. |
| 2 | Was private from enrollment to October 20th. |
| 3 | Was private from enrollment to February 17th. |
| 4 | Was private from enrollment to February 28th. |
| 1 | |
| 2 | |
| 3 | |
| 4 | |
| 5 | |
| 6 | |
| 7 | |
| 8 | |
| 9 | |
| 10 | |
| 11 | |
| 12 | |
| 13 | |
| 14 | |
| 15 | |
| 16 | |
| 17 | |
| 18 | |
| 19 | |
| 20 | |
| 21 | |
| 22 | |
| 23 | |
| 24 | |
| 25 | |
| 26 | Reduced from Sergeant October 20th, by order of Col. McKee. |
| 27 | |
| 28 | |
| 29 | |
| 30 | |
| 31 | |
| 32 | |
| 33 | |
| 34 | |
| 35 | |
| 36 | Reduced from Sergeant September 5th, by order of Col. McKee. |
| 37 | |
| 38 | |
| 39 | |
| 1 | Transferred to 1st Regiment Kentucky Volunteers. Order of Col. McKee, August 30th. |
| 2 | Transferred to non-commissioned staff as principal musician, July 7th. Order of Col. McKee. |
| 1 | Discharged by resignation at Saltillo, Mexico, March, 31st. Order of Gen. Taylor. |
| 1 | Discharged by resignation at Monterey, Mexico, February 1st. Order of Gen. Taylor. |
| 1 | Discharged by resignation at Monterey, Mexico, April 10th. Order of Gen. Taylor. |
| 1 | Discharged on Surgeon's certificate of disability, August 10, 1846, at camp opposite Burieta, Mexico. Order of Col. McKee. |
| 2 | Discharged on Surgeon's certificate of disability, August 10, 1846, at camp opposite Burieta, Mexico. Order of Col. McKee. |
| 3 | Discharged on Surgeon's certificate of disability, August 15, 1846, at camp opposite Burieta, Mexico. Order of Col. McKee. |
| 4 | Discharged on Surgeon's certificate of disability, August 15, 1846, at camp opposite Burieta, Mexico. Order of Col. McKee. |
| 5 | Discharged on Surgeon's certificate of disability, August 15, 1846, at camp opposite Burieta, Mexico. Order of Col. McKee. |

## ROLL OF COMPANY "E," SECOND REGIMENT KENTUCKY

| No. of each grade. | Name. | Rank. | Enrolled. | Mustered in. When. | Mustered in. Where. | Period. | Mustered Out. When. | Mustered Out. Where. |
|---|---|---|---|---|---|---|---|---|
| 6 | Hogan, Zachariah J. | Private | May 23, 1846 | June 9, '46 | Louisville, Ky. | 1 yr. | | |
| 7 | Hunt, W. H. H. | Private | May 23, 1846 | June 9, '46 | Louisville, Ky. | 1 yr. | | |
| 8 | Norman, Henry | Private | May 23, 1846 | June 9, '46 | Louisville, Ky. | 1 yr. | | |
| 9 | Schaefer, Thos. | Private | May 23, 1846 | June 9, '46 | Louisville, Ky. | 1 yr. | | |
| 10 | Smith, Wm. A. | Private | May 23, 1846 | June 9, '46 | Louisville, Ky. | 1 yr. | | |
| 11 | Thomas, Wm. M. | Private | May 23, 1846 | June 9, '46 | Louisville, Ky. | 1 yr. | | |
| 12 | Temple, Philip G. | Private | May 23, 1846 | June 9, '46 | Louisville, Ky. | 1 yr. | | |
| 13 | Hargraves, Hannibal | Private | May 23, 1846 | June 9, '46 | Louisville, Ky. | 1 yr. | | |
| 14 | Warrington, Urich | Private | May 23, 1846 | June 9, '46 | Louisville, Ky. | 1 yr. | | |
| 15 | Werst, George W. | Private | May 23, 1846 | June 9, '46 | Louisville, Ky. | 1 yr. | | |
| 16 | Ward, Lafayette | Private | May 23, 1846 | June 9, '46 | Louisville, Ky. | 1 yr. | | |
| 17 | Zane, Richard | Private | May 23, 1846 | June 9, '46 | Louisville, Ky. | 1 yr. | | |
| 18 | Werk, David | Private | May 23, 1846 | June 9, '46 | Louisville, Ky. | 1 yr. | | |
| 19 | Spalding, James O. | Private | May 23, 1846 | June 9, '46 | Louisville, Ky. | 1 yr. | | |
| 20 | Pense, Isaac M. | Private | May 23, 1846 | June 9, '46 | Louisville, Ky. | 1 yr. | | |
| 21 | Weeks, Jerome | Private | May 23, 1846 | June 9, '46 | Louisville, Ky. | 1 yr. | | |
| | **DIED.** | | | | | | | |
| 1 | Stattman, William | Private | May 23, 1846 | June 9, '46 | Louisville, Ky. | 1 yr. | | |
| 2 | Lockwood, Turman | Private | May 23, 1846 | June 9, '46 | Louisville, Ky. | 1 yr. | | |
| 3 | Taylor, John R. | Private | May 23, 1846 | June 9, '46 | Louisville, Ky. | 1 yr. | | |
| 4 | Vandiver, John S. | Private | May 23, 1846 | June 9, '46 | Louisville, Ky. | 1 yr. | | |
| | **KILLED IN BATTLE.** | | | | | | | |
| 1 | Carlin, Quincy | Sergeant | May 23, 1846 | June 9, '46 | Louisville, Ky. | 1 yr. | | |
| 2 | Rodabaugh, Martin | Drummer | May 23, 1846 | June 9, '46 | Louisville, Ky. | 1 yr. | | |
| 3 | Frazier, Hiram | Private | May 23, 1846 | June 9, '46 | Louisville, Ky. | 1 yr. | | |
| 4 | Harkins, John | Private | May 23, 1846 | June 9, '46 | Louisville, Ky. | 1 yr. | | |
| 5 | McCurdy, Robert | Private | May 23, 1846 | June 9, '46 | Louisville, Ky. | 1 yr. | | |
| 6 | Snow, Hercules | Private | May 23, 1846 | June 9, '46 | Louisville, Ky. | 1 yr. | | |
| | **DESERTED.** | | | | | | | |
| 1 | Chalfart, John S. | Sergeant | May 23, 1846 | June 9, '46 | Louisville, Ky. | 1 yr. | | |
| 2 | Grant, Geo. W. | Corporal | May 23, 1846 | June 9, '46 | Louisville, Ky. | 1 yr. | | |
| 3 | Hill, Richard | Private | May 23, 1846 | June 9, '46 | Louisville, Ky. | 1 yr. | | |
| 4 | Kimball, Amos | Private | May 23, 1846 | June 9, '46 | Louisville, Ky. | 1 yr. | | |
| 5 | Wickham, Robert | Private | May 23, 1846 | June 9, '46 | Louisville, Ky. | 1 yr. | | |
| 6 | Weeks, Jerome | Private | May 23, 1846 | June 9, '46 | Louisville, Ky. | 1 yr. | | |
| 7 | White, Alpheus | Private | May 23, 1846 | June 9, '46 | Louisville, Ky. | 1 yr. | | |
| 8 | Potter, Wm. H. | Private | May 23, 1846 | June 9, '46 | Louisville, Ky. | 1 yr. | | |
| 9 | Dunn, Joseph | Private | May 23, 1846 | June 9, '46 | Louisville, Ky. | 1 yr. | | |
| 10 | Brown, Wm. D. | Private | May 23, 1846 | June 9, '46 | Louisville, Ky. | 1 yr. | | |

This Company was enrolled at Covington, Kentucky.

## ROLL OF COMPANY "F," SECOND REGIMENT KENTUCKY

| | Name | Rank | Enrolled | Mustered in When | Mustered in Where | Period | Mustered Out When | Mustered Out Where |
|---|---|---|---|---|---|---|---|---|
| 1 | James O. Hervey | Captain | May 21, 1846 | June 9, '46 | Louisville, Ky. | 1 yr. | June 9, '47 | New Orleans, La. |
| 1 | William R. Keene | 1st Lieutenant | May 21, 1846 | June 9, '46 | Louisville, Ky. | 1 yr. | June 9, '47 | New Orleans, La. |
| 1 | Thomas J. Proctor | 2d Lieutenant | May 21, 1846 | June 9, '46 | Louisville, Ky. | 1 yr. | June 9, '47 | New Orleans, La. |
| 2 | William C. Lowry | 2d Lieutenant | May 21, 1846 | June 9, '46 | Louisville, Ky. | 1 yr. | June 9, '47 | New Orleans, La. |
| 1 | William L. Smith | 1st Sergeant | May 21, 1846 | June 9, '46 | Louisville, Ky. | 1 yr. | June 9, '47 | New Orleans, La. |
| 2 | Andrew J. Nave | Sergeant | May 21, 1846 | June 9, '46 | Louisville, Ky. | 1 yr. | June 9, '47 | New Orleans, La. |
| 3 | John C. Winter | Sergeant | May 21, 1846 | June 9, '46 | Louisville, Ky. | 1 yr. | June 9, '47 | New Orleans, La. |
| 4 | William Cox | Sergeant | May 21, 1846 | June 9, '46 | Louisville, Ky. | 1 yr. | June 9, '47 | New Orleans, La. |
| 1 | Edward P. Green | Corporal | May 21, 1846 | June 9, '46 | Louisville, Ky. | 1 yr. | June 9, '47 | New Orleans, La. |
| 2 | Dudley Postwood | Corporal | May 21, 1846 | June 9, '46 | Louisville, Ky. | 1 yr. | June 9, '47 | New Orleans, La. |
| 3 | John A. Willis | Corporal | May 21, 1846 | June 9, '46 | Louisville, Ky. | 1 yr. | June 9, '47 | New Orleans, La. |
| 4 | Charles C. Hagan | Corporal | May 21, 1846 | June 9, '46 | Louisville, Ky. | 1 yr. | June 9, '47 | New Orleans, La. |
| 1 | Cortney L. Bunch | Drummer | May 21, 1846 | June 9, '46 | Louisville, Ky. | 1 yr. | June 9, '47 | New Orleans, La. |
| 1 | Brown, George W. | Private | May 21, 1846 | June 9, '46 | Louisville, Ky. | 1 yr. | June 9, '47 | New Orleans, La. |
| 2 | Burchell, Daniel | Private | May 21, 1846 | June 9, '46 | Louisville, Ky. | 1 yr. | June 9, '47 | New Orleans, La. |
| 3 | Burton, Theodoric | Private | May 21, 1846 | June 9, '46 | Louisville, Ky. | 1 yr. | June 9, '47 | New Orleans, La. |
| 4 | Bruner, Thomas J. | Private | May 21, 1846 | June 9, '46 | Louisville, Ky. | 1 yr. | June 9, '47 | New Orleans, La. |
| 5 | Beymer, Samuel | Private | May 21, 1846 | June 9, '46 | Louisville, Ky. | 1 yr. | June 9, '47 | New Orleans, La. |
| 6 | Castle, Augustus B. | Private | May 21, 1846 | June 9, '46 | Louisville, Ky. | 1 yr. | June 9, '47 | New Orleans, La. |
| 7 | Crane, Aca C. | Private | May 21, 1846 | June 9, '46 | Louisville, Ky. | 1 yr. | June 9, '47 | New Orleans, La. |
| 8 | Crane, John P. | Private | May 21, 1846 | June 9, '46 | Louisville, Ky. | 1 yr. | June 9, '47 | New Orleans, La. |
| 9 | Daniel, William H. | Private | May 21, 1846 | June 9, '46 | Louisville, Ky. | 1 yr. | June 9, '47 | New Orleans, La. |
| 10 | Dickerson, Woodson | Private | May 21, 1846 | June 9, '46 | Louisville, Ky. | 1 yr. | June 9, '47 | New Orleans, La. |
| 11 | Day, William | Private | May 21, 1846 | June 9, '46 | Louisville, Ky. | 1 yr. | June 9, '47 | New Orleans, La. |
| 12 | Duman, James | Private | May 21, 1846 | June 9, '46 | Louisville, Ky. | 1 yr. | June 9, '47 | New Orleans, La. |

# MEXICAN WAR VETERANS.

## FOOT VOLUNTEERS—MEXICAN WAR—Continued.

| No. of each grade | REMARKS. |
|---|---|
| 6 | Discharged on Surgeon's certificate of disability, August 15, 1846, at camp opposite Burieta, Mexico. Order of Col. McKee. |
| 7 | Discharged on Surgeon's certificate of disability, August 15, 1846, at camp opposite Burieta, Mexico. Order of Col. McKee. |
| 8 | Discharged on Surgeon's certificate of disability, August 15, 1846, at camp opposite Burieta, Mexico. Order of Col. McKee. |
| 9 | Discharged on Surgeon's certificate of disability, August 15, 1846, at camp opposite Burieta, Mexico. Order of Col. McKee. |
| 10 | Discharged on Surgeon's certificate of disability, August 10, 1846, at camp opposite Burieta, Mexico. Order of Col. McKee. |
| 11 | Discharged on Surgeon's certificate of disability, August 15, 1846, at camp opposite Burieta, Mexico. Order of Col. McKee. |
| 12 | Discharged on Surgeon's certificate of disability, August 15, 1846, at camp opposite Burieta, Mexico. Order of Col. McKee. |
| 13 | Discharged on Surgeon's certificate of disability. Not known. Monterey, Mexico. Order of Col. McKee. |
| 14 | Discharged on Surgeon's certificate of disability, August 15, 1846. at camp opposite Burieta. Order of Col. McKee. |
| 15 | Discharged on Surgeon's certificate of disability, August 10, 1846, at Camp opposite Burieta. Order of Col. McKee. |
| 16 | Discharged on Surgeon's certificate of disability, August 10, 1846, at Camp opposite Burieta. Order of Col. McKee. |
| 17 | Discharged by order of Col. McKee, June 27, 1846, at Louisville, Ky. |
| 18 | Discharged on Surgeon's certificate of disability, October 1, 1846, at Camargo, Mexico, by order of Col. McKee. |
| 19 | Discharged on Surgeon's certificate of disability, September 15, 1846, at Camargo, Mexico, by order of Col. McKee. |
| 20 | Discharged by order of Gen. Wool, at Camp near Saltillo, Mexico, January 26. |
| 21 | Discharged, order of court-martial, October 27, 1846, for desertion at Camargo. |
| 1 | Drowned in the Rio Grande, August 23, 1846, near Reynosa, Mexico. |
| 2 | Died in the general hospital, August 23, 1846, at Matamoras, Mexico. |
| 3 | Died October 18, at Camargo, Mexico. |
| 4 | Died March 24 of wounds received at Buena Vista, in an action with the enemy. |
| 1 | Killed in action with the enemy at the battle of Buena Vista, February 23d. |
| 2 | Killed in action with the enemy at the battle of Buena Vista, February 23d. |
| 3 | Killed in action with the enemy at the battle of Buena Vista, February 23d. |
| 4 | Killed in action with the enemy at the battle of Buena Vista, February 23d. |
| 5 | Killed in action with the enemy at the battle of Buena Vista, February 23d. |
| 6 | Killed in action with the enemy at the battle of Buena Vista, February 23d. |
| 1 | Deserted from steamboat T. E. Roberts, on her passage from Camp opposite Burieta to Camargo, Mexico. August 19. |
| 2 | Deserted from steamboat T. E. Roberts, on her passage from Camp opposite Burieta to Camargo, Mexico, August 19. |
| 3 | Deserted from Camp opposite Burieta, Mexico, August 15. |
| 4 | Deserted; left sick at Louisville, Ky, June 30th; supposed to have deserted. |
| 5 | Deserted from steamboat T. E. Roberts, on her passage from Camp opposite Burieta to Camargo, Mexico, August 19th. |
| 6 | Deserted from Camp opposite Burieta, Mexico, August 11th; apprehended at Camargo, Mexico, September 6th. |
| 7 | Deserted from New Orleans July 6th. |
| 8 | Deserted from Camargo, Mexico, September 5th. |
| 9 | Deserted from Camargo, Mexico, October 18th. |
| 10 | Deserted from Camargo, Mexico, September 5th. |

## FOOT VOLUNTEERS—MEXICAN WAR.

| No. of each grade | REMARKS. |
|---|---|
| 1 | Promoted. Was 1st Lieutenant from February 24th. |
| 1 | Was 1st Sergeant from enrollment to June 29. Promoted February 24th, vice Hervey, promoted. |
| 1 | Was private from enrollment to September 11th. |
| 2 | Was 1st Sergeant from June 30th. Promoted February 24th. |
| 1 | Was private from enrollment to February 24th. |
| 2 | |
| 3 | |
| 4 | |
| 1 | |
| 2 | Absent by permission. |
| 3 | Absent by permission. |
| 4 | |
| 1 | |
| 1 | |
| 2 | |
| 3 | |
| 4 | |
| 5 | |
| 6 | Detached service in Quartermaster Department, Mexico, April 2d. By order of Major C. H. Fry. |
| 7 | |
| 8 | |
| 9 | |
| 10 | |
| 11 | |
| 12 | |

44

MEXICAN WAR VETERANS.

## ROLL OF COMPANY "F," SECOND REGIMENT KENTUCKY

| No. of each grade | Name. | Rank. | Enrolled. | Mustered In. When. | Mustered In. Where. | Period | Mustered Out. When. | Mustered Out. Where. |
|---|---|---|---|---|---|---|---|---|
| 13 | Easby, Andrew L. | Private | May 21, 1846. | June 9, '46. | Louisville, Ky. | 1 yr. | June 9, '47. | New Orleans, La. |
| 14 | Fain, John | Private | May 21, 1846. | June 9, '46. | Louisville, Ky. | 1 yr. | June 9, '47. | New Orleans, La. |
| 15 | Ford, Joshua G. | Private | May 21, 1846. | June 9, '46. | Louisville, Ky. | 1 yr. | June 9, '47. | New Orleans, La. |
| 16 | Ford, Edward D. | Private | May 21, 1846. | June 9, '46. | Louisville, Ky. | 1 yr. | June 9, '47. | New Orleans, La. |
| 17 | Garison, John A. | Private | May 21, 1846. | June 9, '46. | Louisville, Ky. | 1 yr. | June 9, '47. | New Orleans, La. |
| 18 | Graves, Living | Private | May 21, 1846. | June 9, '46. | Louisville, Ky. | 1 yr. | June 9, '47. | New Orleans, La. |
| 19 | Gibony, William | Private | May 21, 1846. | June 9, '46. | Louisville, Ky. | 1 yr. | June 9, '47. | New Orleans, La. |
| 20 | Howard, Robert S. | Private | May 21, 1846. | June 9, '46. | Louisville, Ky. | 1 yr | June 9, '47. | New Orleans, La. |
| 21 | Hamilton, William | Private | May 21, 1846. | June 9, '46. | Louisville, Ky. | 1 yr. | June 9, '47. | New Orleans, La. |
| 22 | Hunter, John | Private | May 21, 1846. | June 9, '46. | Louisville, Ky. | 1 yr. | June 9, '47. | New Orleans, La. |
| 23 | Hayden, Isah P. | Private | May 21, 1846. | June 9, '46. | Louisville, Ky. | 1 yr | June 9, '47. | New Orleans, La. |
| 24 | Hill, Greenbury | Private | May 21, 1846. | June 9, '46. | Louisville, Ky. | 1 yr. | June 9, '47. | New Orleans, La. |
| 25 | Jackman, Joseph | Private | May 21, 1846. | June 9, '46. | Louisville, Ky. | 1 yr. | June 9, '47. | New Orleans, La. |
| 26 | Masters, Irvine | Private | May 21, 1846. | June 9, '46. | Louisville, Ky. | 1 yr. | June 9, '47. | New Orleans, La. |
| 27 | Masters Jackson | Private | May 21, 1846. | June 9, '46. | Louisville, Ky. | 1 yr. | June 9, '47. | New Orleans, La. |
| 28 | Marks, George I. | Private | May 21, 1846. | June 9, '46. | Louisville, Ky. | 1 yr. | June 9, '47. | New Orleans, La. |
| 29 | McCampbell, John G. | Private | May 21, 1846. | June 9, '46. | Louisville, Ky. | 1 yr. | June 9, '47. | New Orleans, La. |
| 30 | McConnel, James A. | Private | May 21, 1846. | June 9, '46. | Louisville, Ky. | 1 yr. | June 9, '47. | New Orleans, La. |
| 31 | Martin, Robert | Private | May 21, 1846. | June 9, '46. | Louisville, Ky. | 1 yr. | June 9, '47. | New Orleans, La. |
| 32 | Moore, Andrew B. | Private | May 21, 1846. | June 9, '46. | Louisville, Ky. | 1 yr. | June 9, '47. | New Orleans, La. |
| 33 | Nooe, Albert K. | Private | May 21, 1846. | June 9, '46. | Louisville, Ky. | 1 yr. | June 9, '47. | New Orleans, La. |
| 34 | O'Brien, William | Private | May 21, 1846. | June 9, '46. | Louisville, Ky. | 1 yr. | June 9, '47. | New Orleans, La. |
| 35 | Overstreet, Samuel R. | Private | May 21, 1846. | June 9, '46. | Louisville, Ky. | 1 yr. | June 9, '47. | New Orleans, La. |
| 36 | Page, Thomas C. | Private | May 21, 1846. | June 9, '46. | Louisville, Ky. | 1 yr. | June 9, '47. | New Orleans, La. |
| 37 | Patterson, William | Private | May 21, 1846 | June 9, '46. | Louisville, Ky. | 1 yr. | June 9, '47. | New Orleans, La. |
| 38 | Roberson, Jacob C. | Private | May 21, 1846. | June 9, '46. | Louisville, Ky. | 1 yr. | June 9, '47. | New Orleans, La. |
| 39 | Roberts, Andrew J. | Private | May 21, 1846 | June 9, '46. | Louisville, Ky. | 1 yr. | June 9, '47. | New Orleans, La. |
| 40 | Rash, John | Private | May 21, 1846. | June 9, '46. | Louisville, Ky. | 1 yr. | June 9, '47. | New Orleans, La. |
| 41 | Saunders, John A. | Private | May 21, 1846. | June 9, '46. | Louisville, Ky. | 1 yr. | June 9, '47. | New Orleans, La. |
| 42 | Saunders, George W. | Private | May 21, 1846. | June 9, '46. | Louisville, Ky. | 1 yr. | June 9, '47. | New Orleans, La. |
| 43 | Switser, John | Private | May 21, 1846 | June 9, '46. | Louisville, Ky. | 1 yr. | June 9, '47. | New Orleans, La. |
| 44 | Tutt, William | Private | May 21, 1846. | June 9, '46 | Louisville, Ky. | 1 yr. | June 9, '47 | New Orleans, La. |
| 45 | White, James N. | Private | May 21, 1846. | June 9, '46. | Louisville, Ky. | 1 yr. | June 9, '47. | New Orleans, La. |
| 46 | Wilson, John | Private | May 21, 1846. | June 9, '46. | Louisville, Ky. | 1 yr. | June 9, '47. | New Orleans, La. |
| 47 | Willis, Edmond C. | Private | May 21, 1846. | June 9, '46. | Louisville, Ky. | 1 yr. | June 9, '47. | New Orleans, La. |
| 48 | Willis, James H. | Private | May 21, 1846. | June 9, '46 | Louisville, Ky. | 1 yr. | June 9, '47. | New Orleans, La. |
|  | **Killed in Battle.** |  |  |  |  |  |  |  |
| 1 | William T. Willis | Captain | May 21, 1846. | June 9, '46. | Louisville, Ky. | 1 yr. |  |  |
| 2 | Harvey, Trotter | Private | May 21, 1846. | June 9, '46. | Louisville, Ky. | 1 yr. |  |  |
|  | **Died.** |  |  |  |  |  |  |  |
| 1 | John H. Allen | Private | May 21, 1846. | June 9, '46. | Louisville, Ky. | 1 yr. |  |  |
|  | **Discharged.** |  |  |  |  |  |  |  |
| 1 | Collins, William | Private | May 21, 1846. | June 9, '46. | Louisville, Ky. | 1 yr. |  |  |
| 2 | Easby, Josiah | Private | May 21, 1846 | June 9, '46. | Louisville, Ky. | 1 yr. |  |  |
| 3 | Grant, George W. | Private | May 21, 1846. | June 9, '46. | Louisville, Ky. | 1 yr. |  |  |
| 4 | Hawkins, James | Private | May 21, 1846. | June 9, '46. | Louisville, Ky. | 1 yr. |  |  |
| 5 | McMurtry, John | Private | May 21, 1846. | June 9, '46. | Louisville, Ky. | 1 yr. |  |  |
| 6 | Sharpe, Ezekiel K. | Private | May 21, 1846 | June 9, '46. | Louisville, Ky. | 1 yr. |  |  |
| 7 | Sacre, John | Private | May 21, 1846. | June 9, '46. | Louisville, Ky. | 1 yr. |  |  |
| 8 | Thompson, John T. | Private | May 21, 1846. | June 9, '46. | Louisville, Ky. | 1 yr. |  |  |
| 9 | James S. England | 2d Lieutenant | May 21, 1846. | June 9, '46. | Louisville, Ky. | 1 yr. |  |  |
|  | **Deserted.** |  |  |  |  |  |  |  |
| 1 | Williams, George | Private | May 21, 1846. | June 9, '46. | Louisville, Ky. | 1 yr. |  |  |
| 2 | Ballard, James L. | Private | May 21, 1846. | June 9, '46. | Louisville, Ky. | 1 yr. |  |  |
| 3 | Baker, Benedict | Private | May 21, 1846. | June 9, '46. | Louisville, Ky. | 1 yr. |  |  |
| 4 | Duncan, Hankes | Private | May 21, 1846. | June 9, '46. | Louisville, Ky. | 1 yr. |  |  |
| 5 | Wallace, David | Private | May 21, 1846. | June 9, '46. | Louisville, Ky. | 1 yr. |  |  |
|  | **Transferred.** |  |  |  |  |  |  |  |
| 1 | Marvin, William F. | Private | May 21, 1846. | June 9, '46. | Louisville, Ky. | 1 yr. |  |  |

This Company was enrolled at Nicholasville, Jessamine county, Ky.

## ROLL OF COMPANY "G," SECOND REGIMENT KENTUCKY

| 1 | William Dougherty | Captain | May 21, 1846 | June 9, '46. | Louisville, Ky. | 1 yr. | June 10, '47. | New Orleans, La. |
|---|---|---|---|---|---|---|---|---|
| 1 | William G. Kincaid | 1st Lieutenant | May 21, 1846. | June 9, '46. | Louisville, Ky. | 1 yr | June 10 '47. | New Orleans, La. |
| 1 | George W. Ball | 2d Lieutenant | May 21, 1846. | June 9, '46. | Louisville, Ky. | 1 yr. | June 10, '47. | New Orleans, La. |

## FOOT VOLUNTEERS—MEXICAN WAR—Continued.

| No. of each grade | REMARKS. |
|---|---|
| 13 | |
| 14 | |
| 15 | |
| 16 | |
| 17 | |
| 18 | |
| 19 | |
| 20 | |
| 21 | |
| 22 | |
| 23 | |
| 24 | |
| 25 | |
| 26 | |
| 27 | |
| 28 | |
| 29 | |
| 30 | |
| 31 | |
| 32 | |
| 33 | |
| 34 | |
| 35 | |
| 36 | |
| 37 | |
| 38 | |
| 39 | |
| 40 | |
| 41 | |
| 42 | |
| 43 | |
| 44 | |
| 45 | |
| 46 | |
| 47 | |
| 48 | |
| 1 | Killed in battle of Buena Vista, February 23. |
| 2 | Killed in battle of Buena Vista, February 23. |
| 1 | Died on the Rio Grande August 29. |
| 1 | Discharged at Camargo, September 5th; Surgeon's certificate of disability. Order of Col. McKee. |
| 2 | Discharged at Camargo, September 10th; Surgeon's certificate of disability. Order of Col. McKee. |
| 3 | Discharged at Camargo, September 5th; Surgeon's certificate of disability. Order of Col. McKee. |
| 4 | Discharged at Matamoras, February 19th; Surgeon's certificate of disability. Order of Col. McKee. |
| 5 | Discharged at Camp Belknap (date not known); Surgeon's certificate of disability. Order of Col. McKee. |
| 6 | Discharged at Camargo (date not known); Surgeon's certificate of disability. Order of Col. McKee. |
| 7 | Discharged at Camp Belknap (date not known); Surgeon's certificate of disability. Order of Col. McKee. |
| 8 | Discharged at Camargo, September 10th; Surgeon's certificate of disability. Order of Col. McKee. |
| 9 | Discharged at Camargo, by resignation, September 11th. Order of Gen. Taylor. |
| 1 | Deserted at Louisville, June 27th. |
| 2 | Deserted at New Orleans, July 7th. |
| 3 | Deserted at New Orleans, July 7th. |
| 4 | Deserted at New Orleans, July 7th. |
| 5 | Deserted on the Rio Grande, August 24th. |
| 1 | Transferred to First Regiment Kentucky Foot (day not known). Order of Gen. Taylor. |

## FOOT VOLUNTEERS—MEXICAN WAR.

| | |
|---|---|
| 1 | |
| 1 | Was 2d Lieutenant from enlistment to November 1st. |
| 1 | Was private from enlistment to June 27th. |

12

46                                   MEXICAN WAR VETERANS.

## ROLL OF COMPANY "G," SECOND REGIMENT KENTUCKY

| No. of each grade | Name | Rank | Enrolled | Mustered In When | Mustered In Where | Period | Mustered Out When | Mustered Out Where |
|---|---|---|---|---|---|---|---|---|
| 2 | Thomas W. Napier | 2d Lieutenant | May 21, 1846 | June 9, '46 | Louisville, Ky. | 1 yr. | June 10, '47 | New Orleans, La. |
| 1 | Charles F. Davenport | 1st Sergeant | May 21, 1846 | June 9, '46 | Louisville, Ky. | 1 yr. | June 10, '47 | New Orleans, La. |
| 2 | John F. Higgins | Sergeant | May 21, 1846 | June 9, '46 | Louisville, Ky. | 1 yr. | June 10, '47 | New Orleans, La. |
| 3 | John H. Farris | Sergeant | May 21, 1846 | June 9, '46 | Louisville, Ky. | 1 yr. | June 10, '47 | New Orleans, La. |
| 4 | Jonathan Kirkpatrick | Sergeant | May 21, 1846 | June 9, '46 | Louisville, Ky. | 1 yr. | June 10, '47 | New Orleans, La. |
| 1 | George B. Cooper | Corporal | May 21, 1846 | June 9, '46 | Louisville, Ky. | 1 yr. | June 10, '47 | New Orleans, La. |
| 2 | Thomas Shanks | Corporal | May 21, 1846 | June 9, '46 | Louisville, Ky. | 1 yr. | June 10, '47 | New Orleans, La. |
| 3 | Alexander Paxton | Corporal | May 21, 1846 | June 9, '46 | Louisville, Ky. | 1 yr. | June 10, '47 | New Orleans, La. |
| 4 | John S. Bosley | Corporal | May 21, 1846 | June 9, '46 | Louisville, Ky. | 1 yr. | June 10, '47 | New Orleans, La. |
| 1 | Adams, Smith | Private | May 21, 1846 | June 9, '46 | Louisville, Ky. | 1 yr. | June 10, '47 | New Orleans, La. |
| 2 | Berry, George W. | Private | May 21, 1846 | June 9, '46 | Louisville, Ky. | 1 yr. | June 10, '47 | New Orleans, La. |
| 3 | Bedou, Rob't A. | Private | May 21, 1846 | June 9, '46 | Louisville, Ky. | 1 yr. | June 10, '47 | New Orleans, La. |
| 4 | Bastian, John | Private | May 21, 1846 | June 9, '46 | Louisville, Ky. | 1 yr. | June 10, '47 | New Orleans, La. |
| 5 | Brown, Willis | Private | May 21, 1846 | June 9, '46 | Louisville, Ky. | 1 yr. | June 10, '47 | New Orleans, La. |
| 6 | Cavel, William H. | Private | May 21, 1846 | June 9, '46 | Louisville, Ky. | 1 yr. | June 10, '47 | New Orleans, La. |
| 7 | Davenport, Michael A. | Private | May 21, 1846 | June 9, '46 | Louisville, Ky. | 1 yr. | June 10, '47 | New Orleans, La. |
| 8 | Dickenson, James | Private | May 21, 1846 | June 9, '46 | Louisville, Ky. | 1 yr. | June 10, '47 | New Orleans, La. |
| 9 | Dickenson, John | Private | May 21, 1846 | June 9, '46 | Louisville, Ky. | 1 yr. | June 10, '47 | New Orleans, La. |
| 10 | Denweddie, Jesse | Private | May 21, 1846 | June 9, '46 | Louisville, Ky. | 1 yr. | June 10, '47 | New Orleans, La. |
| 11 | Edwards, James F. | Private | May 21, 1846 | June 9, '46 | Louisville, Ky. | 1 yr. | June 10, '47 | New Orleans, La. |
| 12 | Edward, Josephus | Private | May 21, 1846 | June 9, '46 | Louisville, Ky. | 1 yr. | June 10, '47 | New Orleans, La. |
| 13 | Edwards, Josiah | Private | May 21, 1846 | June 9, '46 | Louisville, Ky. | 1 yr. | June 10, '47 | New Orleans, La. |
| 14 | Emerson, Franklin W. | Private | May 21, 1846 | June 9, '46 | Louisville, Ky. | 1 yr. | June 10, '47 | New Orleans, La. |
| 15 | Frost, Alexander | Private | May 21, 1846 | June 9, '46 | Louisville, Ky. | 1 yr. | June 10, '47 | New Orleans, La. |
| 16 | Falden, James R. | Private | May 21, 1846 | June 9, '46 | Louisville, Ky. | 1 yr. | June 10, '47 | New Orleans, La. |
| 17 | Hays, Patrick F. | Private | May 21, 1846 | June 9, '46 | Louisville, Ky. | 1 yr. | June 10, '47 | New Orleans, La. |
| 18 | Hall, William | Private | May 21, 1846 | June 9, '46 | Louisville, Ky. | 1 yr. | June 10, '47 | New Orleans, La. |
| 19 | Helm, Willis | Private | May 21, 1846 | June 9, '46 | Louisville, Ky. | 1 yr. | June 10, '47 | New Orleans, La. |
| 20 | Hinds, John W. J. | Private | May 21, 1846 | June 9, '46 | Louisville, Ky. | 1 yr. | June 10, '47 | New Orleans, La. |
| 21 | Hicks, Erastus B. | Private | May 21, 1846 | June 9, '46 | Louisville, Ky. | 1 yr. | June 10, '47 | New Orleans, La. |
| 22 | Hogan, Green M. | Private | May 21, 1846 | June 9, '46 | Louisville, Ky. | 1 yr. | June 10, '47 | New Orleans, La. |
| 23 | Howard, David | Private | May 21, 1846 | June 9, '46 | Louisville, Ky. | 1 yr. | June 10, '47 | New Orleans, La. |
| 24 | Hughes, Thomas | Private | May 21, 1846 | June 9, '46 | Louisville, Ky. | 1 yr. | June 10, '47 | New Orleans, La. |
| 25 | Leeper, George | Private | May 21, 1846 | June 9, '46 | Louisville, Ky. | 1 yr. | June 10, '47 | New Orleans, La. |
| 26 | Logan, Hugh | Private | May 21, 1846 | June 9, '46 | Louisville, Ky. | 1 yr. | June 10, '47 | New Orleans, La. |
| 27 | Manuel, Thomas | Private | May 21, 1846 | June 9, '46 | Louisville, Ky. | 1 yr. | June 10, '47 | New Orleans, La. |
| 28 | Montgomery, Clifton A. | Private | May 21, 1846 | June 9, '46 | Louisville, Ky. | 1 yr. | June 10, '47 | New Orleans, La. |
| 29 | Montgomery, Claytor S. | Private | May 21, 1846 | June 9, '46 | Louisville, Ky. | 1 yr. | June 10, '47 | New Orleans, La. |
| 30 | Orr, Charles C. | Private | May 21, 1846 | June 9, '46 | Louisville, Ky. | 1 yr. | June 10, '47 | New Orleans, La. |
| 31 | Patrick, Jordan J. | Private | May 21, 1846 | June 9, '46 | Louisville, Ky. | 1 yr. | June 10, '47 | New Orleans, La. |
| 32 | Perkins, Green | Private | May 21, 1846 | June 9, '46 | Louisville, Ky. | 1 yr. | June 10, '47 | New Orleans, La. |
| 33 | Powell, William R. | Private | May 21, 1846 | June 9, '46 | Louisville, Ky. | 1 yr. | June 10, '47 | New Orleans, La. |
| 34 | Patrick, Hiram | Private | May 21, 1846 | June 9, '46 | Louisville, Ky. | 1 yr. | June 10, '47 | New Orleans, La. |
| 35 | Renfro, Moses J. | Private | May 21, 1846 | June 9, '46 | Louisville, Ky. | 1 yr. | June 10, '47 | New Orleans, La. |
| 36 | Reynolds, Nicholas S. | Private | May 21, 1846 | June 9, '46 | Louisville, Ky. | 1 yr. | June 10, '47 | New Orleans, La. |
| 37 | Sandifer, Robert S. | Private | May 21, 1846 | June 9, '46 | Louisville, Ky. | 1 yr. | June 10, '47 | New Orleans, La. |
| 38 | Spratt, Andrew G. | Private | May 21, 1846 | June 9, '46 | Louisville, Ky. | 1 yr. | June 10, '47 | New Orleans, La. |
| 39 | Starbuck, Thaddeus B. | Private | May 21, 1846 | June 9, '46 | Louisville, Ky. | 1 yr. | June 10, '47 | New Orleans, La. |
| 40 | Stringer, William | Private | May 21, 1846 | June 9, '46 | Louisville, Ky. | 1 yr. | June 10, '47 | New Orleans, La. |
| 41 | Thompson, John | Private | May 21, 1846 | June 9, '46 | Louisville, Ky. | 1 yr. | June 10, '47 | New Orleans, La. |
| 42 | Walls, John | Private | May 21, 1846 | June 9, '46 | Louisville, Ky. | 1 yr. | June 10, '47 | New Orleans, La. |
| 43 | Worford, John | Private | May 21, 1846 | June 9, '46 | Louisville, Ky. | 1 yr. | June 10, '47 | New Orleans, La. |
| 44 | Woodall, William | Private | May 21, 1846 | June 9, '46 | Louisville, Ky. | 1 yr. | June 10, '47 | New Orleans, La. |
| 45 | Woods, William | Private | May 21, 1846 | June 9, '46 | Louisville, Ky. | 1 yr. | June 10, '47 | New Orleans, La. |
| 46 | Williams, Reuben | Private | May 21, 1846 | June 9, '46 | Louisville, Ky. | 1 yr. | June 10, '47 | New Orleans, La. |
| 47 | Woolford, Franklin L. | Private | May 21, 1846 | June 9, '46 | Louisville, Ky. | 1 yr. | June 10, '47 | New Orleans, La. |
|  | **Transferred.** |  |  |  |  |  |  |  |
| 1 | Dickersham, E. | Private | May 21, 1846 | June 9, '46 | Louisville, Ky. | 1 yr. |  |  |
|  | **Killed in Battle.** |  |  |  |  |  |  |  |
| 1 | Ballard, James R. | Private | May 21, 1846 | June 9, '46 | Louisville, Ky. | 1 yr. |  |  |
| 2 | Gregory, John A. | Private | May 21, 1846 | June 9, '46 | Louisville, Ky. | 1 yr. |  |  |
| 3 | Vest, Willis | Private | May 21, 1846 | June 9, '46 | Louisville, Ky. | 1 yr. |  |  |
| 4 | Waller, Jesse J. | Private | May 21, 1846 | June 9, '46 | Louisville, Ky. | 1 yr. |  |  |
|  | **Deaths.** |  |  |  |  |  |  |  |
| 1 | Lineberry, B. M. | Sergeant | May 21, 1846 | June 9, '46 | Louisville, Ky. | 1 yr. |  |  |
| 2 | Craig, Samuel | Corporal | May 21, 1846 | June 9, '46 | Louisville, Ky. | 1 yr. |  |  |
| 3 | Cummings, Thomas | Private | May 21, 1846 | June 9, '46 | Louisville, Ky. | 1 yr. |  |  |
| 4 | Greenlee, James H. | Private | May 21, 1846 | June 9, '46 | Louisville, Ky. | 1 yr. |  |  |
| 5 | Moreland, Daniel M. | Private | May 21, 1846 | June 9, '46 | Louisville, Ky. | 1 yr. |  |  |
| 6 | Napier, John | Private | May 21, 1846 | June 9, '46 | Louisville, Ky. | 1 yr. |  |  |
| 7 | Barton, John | Private | May 21, 1846 | June 9, '46 | Louisville, Ky. | 1 yr. |  |  |

## FOOT VOLUNTEERS—MEXICAN WAR—Continued.

| No. of each grade. | REMARKS. |
|---|---|
| 2 | Was Corporal from enlistment to November 1st. |
| 1 | |
| 2 | |
| 3 | |
| 4 | Was private from enrollment to October 19th. |
| 1 | |
| 2 | |
| 3 | Was private from enrollment to October 12th. |
| 4 | Was private from enrollment to October 31st. |
| 1 | |
| 2 | |
| 3 | |
| 4 | |
| 5 | |
| 6 | Joined November 26th, a recruit by order of Col. McKee. |
| 7 | |
| 8 | |
| 9 | |
| 10 | |
| 11 | |
| 12 | |
| 13 | |
| 14 | |
| 15 | |
| 16 | |
| 17 | |
| 18 | |
| 19 | |
| 20 | |
| 21 | |
| 22 | |
| 23 | |
| 24 | |
| 25 | |
| 26 | |
| 27 | |
| 28 | |
| 29 | |
| 30 | |
| 31 | |
| 32 | |
| 33 | |
| 34 | Left sick at Louisville, Ky., June 9th. (Absent.) |
| 35 | |
| 36 | |
| 37 | |
| 38 | Absent; left sick at Louisville, Ky., June 9th. |
| 39 | |
| 40 | |
| 41 | |
| 42 | |
| 43 | |
| 44 | |
| 45 | Absent; left sick at Louisville, Ky., June 9th. |
| 46 | |
| 47 | |
| 1 | Transferred to staff as Chief Musician, July 23d. |
| 1 | Killed in battle of Buena Vista, February 23d. |
| 2 | Killed in battle of Buena Vista, February 23d. |
| 3 | Killed in battle of Buena Vista, February 23d. |
| 4 | Killed in battle of Buena Vista, February 23d. |
| 1 | Died October 19th, at Camargo, Mexico. |
| 2 | Died September 12th, at Camargo, Mexico. |
| 3 | Died September 26th, at Camargo, Mexico. |
| 4 | Died September 12th, at Camargo, Mexico. |
| 5 | Died August 11th, at camp on Rio Grande, near Burita. |
| 6 | Died September 27th, at Camargo, Mexico. |
| 7 | Died December 6th, at Ceralvo, Mexico. |

MEXICAN WAR VETERANS.

## ROLL OF COMPANY "G," SECOND REGIMENT KENTUCKY

| No. of each grade. | Name. | Rank. | Enrolled. | Mustered In. When. | Mustered In. Where. | Period. | Mustered Out. When. | Mustered Out. Where. |
|---|---|---|---|---|---|---|---|---|
|  | RESIGNED. |  |  |  |  |  |  |  |
| 1 | Purdom, Benjamin F. | 1st Lieutenant | May 21, 1846. | June 9, '46. | Louisville, Ky. | 1 yr. |  |  |
|  | DISCHARGED. |  |  |  |  |  |  |  |
| 1 | Paxton, James | Corporal | May 21, 1846. | June 9, '46. | Louisville, Ky. | 1 yr. |  |  |
| 2 | Jenkins, James | Fifer | May 21, 1846. | June 9, '46. | Louisville, Ky. | 1 yr. |  |  |
| 3 | Burton, William | Private | May 21, 1846. | June 9, '46. | Louisville, Ky. | 1 yr. |  |  |
| 4 | Dougherty, John | Private | May 21, 1846. | June 9, '46. | Louisville, Ky. | 1 yr. |  |  |
| 5 | Griffin, Andrew J. | Private | May 21, 1846. | June 9, '46. | Louisville, Ky. | 1 yr. |  |  |
| 6 | Gooch, Thomas | Private | May 21, 1846. | June 9, '46. | Louisville, Ky. | 1 yr. |  |  |
| 7 | Hansford, Benjamin F. | Private | May 21, 1846. | June 9, '46. | Louisville, Ky. | 1 yr. |  |  |
| 8 | Hansford, John Q. | Private | May 21, 1846. | June 9, '46. | Louisville, Ky. | 1 yr. |  |  |
| 9 | Harvey, Edward | Private | May 21, 1846. | June 9, '46. | Louisville, Ky. | 1 yr. |  |  |
| 10 | Howard, Aaron | Private | May 21, 1846. | June 9, '46. | Louisville, Ky. | 1 yr |  |  |
| 11 | Logan, David M. | Private | May 21, 1846. | June 9, '46. | Louisville, Ky. | 1 yr. |  |  |
| 12 | Morrison, Hugh E. | Private | May 21, 1846. | June 9, '46. | Louisville, Ky. | 1 yr. |  |  |
| 13 | Parker, William C. | Private | May 21, 1846. | June 9, '46. | Louisville, Ky. | 1 yr. |  |  |
| 14 | Shackleford, James | Private | May 21, 1846. | June 9, '46. | Louisville, Ky. | 1 yr. |  |  |
| 15 | Turner, William | Private | May 21, 1846. | June 9, '46. | Louisville, Ky. | 1 yr. |  |  |
| 16 | Vardemon, William | Private | May 21, 1846. | June 9, '46. | Louisville, Ky. | 1 yr. |  |  |
| 17 | Walls, Jesse | Private | May 21, 1846. | June 9, '46. | Louisville, Ky. | 1 yr. |  |  |
| 18 | Shackleford, John G. | Private | May 21, 1846. | June 9, '46. | Louisville, Ky. | 1 yr. |  |  |
| 19 | Arnold, Elijah C. | Private | May 21, 1846. | June 9, '46. | Louisville, Ky. | 1 yr. |  |  |
| 20 | Hall, Nathaniel G. | Private | May 21, 1846. | June 9, '46. | Louisville, Ky. | 1 yr. |  |  |
| 21 | Jones, Evan | Private | May 21, 1846. | June 9, '46. | Louisville, Ky. | 1 yr. |  |  |

This Company was enrolled at Stanford, Lincoln county, Kentucky.

## ROLL OF COMPANY "H," SECOND REGIMENT KENTUCKY

| | Name. | Rank. | Enrolled. | When. | Where. | Period | When. | Where. |
|---|---|---|---|---|---|---|---|---|
| 1 | William M. Joyner | Captain | June 9, 1846 | June 9, '46. | Louisville, Ky. | 1 yr. | June 10, '47. | New Orleans, La. |
| 1 | David P. Wade | 1st Lieutenant | June 9, 1846 | June 9, '46. | Louisville, Ky. | 1 yr. | June 10, '47. | New Orleans, La. |
| 1 | William O'Brien | 2d Lieutenant | June 9, 1846 | June 9, '46. | Louisville, Ky. | 1 yr. | June 10, '47. | New Orleans, La. |
| 2 | Lewis M. Rees | 2d Lieutenant | June 9, 1846 | June 9, '46. | Louisville, Ky. | 1 yr. | June 10, '47. | New Orleans, La. |
| 1 | Cyrus G. Morrell | 1st Sergeant | June 9, 1846 | June 9, '46. | Louisville, Ky. | 1 yr. | June 10, '47. | New Orleans, La. |
| 2 | Joseph D. Ward | Sergeant | June 9, 1846 | June 9, '46. | Louisville, Ky. | 1 yr. | June 10, '47. | New Orleans, La. |
| 3 | Jas. O. Woodworth | Sergeant | June 9, 1846 | June 9, '46. | Louisville, Ky. | 1 yr. | June 10, '47. | New Orleans, La. |
| 4 | Thomas Stewart | Sergeant | June 9, 1846 | June 9, '46. | Louisville, Ky. | 1 yr. | June 10, '47. | New Orleans, La. |
| 1 | Thomas Fox | Corporal | June 9, 1846 | June 9, '46. | Louisville, Ky. | 1 yr. | June 10, '47. | New Orleans, La. |
| 2 | Hugh Craig | Corporal | June 9, 1846 | June 9, '46. | Louisville, Ky. | 1 yr. | June 10, '47. | New Orleans, La. |
| 3 | John Lee | Corporal | June 9, 1846 | June 9, '46. | Louisville, Ky. | 1 yr. | June 10, '47. | New Orleans, La. |
| 4 | George W. Harris | Corporal | June 9, 1846 | June 9, '46. | Louisville, Ky. | 1 yr. | June 10, '47. | New Orleans, La. |
| 1 | Thomas McGrath | Fifer | June 9, 1846 | June 9, '46. | Louisville, Ky. | 1 yr. | June 10, '47. | New Orleans, La. |
| 1 | Butts, John | Private | June 9, 1846 | June 9, '46. | Louisville, Ky. | 1 yr. | June 10, '47. | New Orleans, La. |
| 2 | Branden, Booth | Private | June 9, 1846 | June 9, '46. | Louisville, Ky. | 1 yr. | June 10, '47. | New Orleans, La. |
| 3 | Bossart, Geo. W. | Private | June 9, 1846 | June 9, '46. | Louisville, Ky. | 1 yr. | June 10, '47. | New Orleans, La. |
| 4 | Clark, John A. | Private | June 9, 1846 | June 9, '46. | Louisville, Ky. | 1 yr. | June 10, '47. | New Orleans, La. |
| 5 | Doane, Jesse | Private | June 9, 1846 | June 9, '46. | Louisville, Ky. | 1 yr. | June 10, '47. | New Orleans, La. |
| 6 | Dively, James | Private | June 9, 1846 | June 9, '46. | Louisville, Ky. | 1 yr. | June 10, '47. | New Orleans, La. |
| 7 | Dailey, Wm. | Private | June 9, 1846 | June 9, '46. | Louisville, Ky. | 1 yr. | June 10, '47. | New Orleans, La. |
| 8 | Dunlap, Jas. | Private | June 9, 1846 | June 9, '46. | Louisville, Ky. | 1 yr. | June 10, '47. | New Orleans, La. |
| 9 | Durrett, John W. | Private | June 9, 1846 | June 9, '46. | Louisville, Ky. | 1 yr. | June 10, '47. | New Orleans, La. |
| 10 | Evans, Amos | Private | June 9, 1846 | June 9, '46. | Louisville, Ky. | 1 yr. | June 10, '47. | New Orleans, La. |
| 11 | Fread, Henry | Private | June 9, 1846 | June 9, '46. | Louisville, Ky. | 1 yr. | June 10, '47. | New Orleans, La. |
| 12 | Gracie, Wm. | Private | June 9, 1846 | June 9, '46. | Louisville, Ky. | 1 yr. | June 10, '47. | New Orleans, La. |
| 13 | Hurd, Joseph | Private | June 9, 1846 | June 9, '46. | Louisville, Ky. | 1 yr. | June 10, '47. | New Orleans, La. |
| 14 | Hughey, Robert | Private | June 9, 1846 | June 9, '46. | Louisville, Ky. | 1 yr. | June 10, '47. | New Orleans, La. |
| 15 | McLilley, John H. | Private | June 9, 1846 | June 9, '46. | Louisville, Ky. | 1 yr. | June 10, '47. | New Orleans, La. |
| 16 | Markham, Jas. | Private | June 9, 1846 | June 9, '46. | Louisville, Ky. | 1 yr. | June 10, '47. | New Orleans, La. |
| 17 | Purnell, Joshua | Private | June 9, 1846 | June 9, '46. | Louisville, Ky. | 1 yr. | June 10, '47. | New Orleans, La. |
| 18 | Riley, Thomas | Private | June 9, 1846 | June 9, '46. | Louisville, Ky. | 1 yr. | June 10, '47. | New Orleans, La. |
| 19 | Riley, Jacob | Private | June 9, 1846 | June 9, '46. | Louisville, Ky. | 1 yr. | June 10, '47. | New Orleans, La. |
| 20 | Sutton, Wm. | Private | June 9, 1846 | June 9, '46. | Louisville, Ky. | 1 yr. | June 10, '47. | New Orleans, La. |
| 21 | Stroph, Jos. | Private | June 9, 1846 | June 9, '46. | Louisville, Ky. | 1 yr. | June 10, '47. | New Orleans, La. |
| 22 | Shields, Jas. L. | Private | June 9, 1846 | June 9, '46. | Louisville, Ky. | 1 yr. | June 10, '47. | New Orleans, La. |
| 23 | Simons, Geo. | Private | June 9, 1846 | June 9, '46. | Louisville, Ky. | 1 yr. | June 10, '47. | New Orleans, La. |
| 24 | Smith, Wm. | Private | June 9, 1846 | June 9, '46. | Louisville, Ky. | 1 yr. | June 10, '47. | New Orleans, La. |
| 25 | Stewart, Michael | Private | June 9, 1846 | June 9, '46. | Louisville, Ky. | 1 yr. | June 10, '47. | New Orleans, La. |
| 26 | Titman, Henry | Private | June 9, 1846 | June 9, '46. | Louisville, Ky. | 1 yr. | June 10, '47. | New Orleans, La. |
| 27 | Thomas, Joseph | Private | June 9, 1846 | June 9, '46. | Louisville, Ky. | 1 yr. | June 10, '47. | New Orleans, La. |
| 28 | Wilson, Edward | Private | June 9, 1846 | June 9, '46. | Louisville, Ky. | 1 yr. | June 10, '47. | New Orleans, La. |
| 29 | Ware, Jas. M. | Private | June 9, 1846 | June 9, '46. | Louisville, Ky. | 1 yr | June 10, '47. | New Orleans, La. |
| 30 | Wellington, John | Private | June 9, 1846 | June 9, '46. | Louisville, Ky. | 1 yr. | June 10, '47. | New Orleans, La. |

MEXICAN WAR VETERANS.

## FOOT VOLUNTEERS—MEXICAN WAR—Continued.

| No. of each grade | REMARKS. |
|---|---|
| 1 | Discharged by resignation at Camargo, Mexico, September 16th. Order of Gen. Marshall. |
| 1 | Discharged June 28th; cause unknown; at Louisville. Order of Col. W. R. McKee. |
| 2 | Discharged August 15th, at Camp Rio Grande, Mexico; Surgeon's certificate of disability. Order of Col. McKee. |
| 3 | Discharged at Camargo, Mexico, September 16th; Surgeon's certificate of disability. Order of Gen. Marshall. |
| 4 | Discharged at Camargo, Mexico, September 16th; Surgeon's certificate of disability. Order of Gen. Marshall. |
| 5 | Discharged August 9th, at Camp Rio Grande; Surgeon's certificate of disability. Order of Gen. Marshall. |
| 6 | Discharged August 15th, at Camp Rio Grande; Surgeon's certificate of disability. Order of Gen. Marshall. |
| 7 | Discharged September 16th, at Camargo, Mexico; Surgeon's certificate of disability. Order of Gen. Marshall. |
| 8 | Discharged September 20th, at Camargo, Mexico. Surgeon's certificate of disability. Order of Gen. Marshall. |
| 9 | Dishonorably discharged for theft, June 27th, at Louisville, Ky. Order of Gen. Marshall. |
| 10 | Discharged September 16th, at Camargo, Mexico; Surgeon's certificate of disability. Order of Gen. Marshall. |
| 11 | Discharged September 16th, at Camargo, Mexico; Surgeon's certificate of disability. Order of Gen. Marshall. |
| 12 | Discharged September 16th, at Camargo, Mexico; Surgeon's certificate of disability. Order of Gen. Marshall. |
| 13 | Discharged September 16th, at Camargo, Mexico; Surgeon's certificate of disability. Order of Gen. Marshall. |
| 14 | Discharged September 16th, at Camargo, Mexico; Surgeon's certificate of disability. Order of Gen. Marshall. |
| 15 | Discharged September 20th, at Camargo, Mexico; Surgeon's certificate of disability. Order of Gen. Marshall. |
| 16 | Discharged June 28th, at Louisville, Ky.; Surgeon's certificate of disability. Order of Col. McKee. |
| 17 | Discharged September 10th, at Camargo, Mexico; Surgeon's certificate of disability. Order of Gen. Marshall. |
| 18 | Discharged about November, at Camargo, Mexico; Surgeon's certificate of disability. Order of Gen. Marshall. |
| 19 | Discharged about November, at Camargo, Mexico; Surgeon's certificate of disability. Order of Gen. Marshall. |
| 20 | Discharged March 2d, at Monterey, Mexico; Surgeon's certificate of disability. Order of Gen. Taylor. |
| 21 | Discharged March 2d, at Monterey, Mexico; Surgeon's certificate of disability. Order of Gen. Taylor. |

## FOOT VOLUNTEERS—MEXICAN WAR.

| | |
|---|---|
| 1 | |
| 1 | Promoted from 2d Lieutenant, January 2d, vice Powell, deceased; pay due from June 9th to 30th, inclusive. |
| 1 | Absent without leave from January 31st. |
| 2 | Appointed from 1st Sergeant, January 2d, vice Wade, promoted. |
| 1 | Appointed from Sergeant, January 2d, vice Rees, promoted. |
| 2 | Wounded in battle of Buena Vista, February 23d, and in camp; promoted from Corporal, January 2d. |
| 3 | Promoted from Corporal, March 1st. vice Kring, killed. |
| 4 | Promoted from Corporal, March 1st, vice Dunlop, killed. |
| 1 | Wounded in battle of Buena Vista, February 23d; was Private from enrollment to December 28th. |
| 2 | Wounded in battle of Buena Vista, February 23; appointed from Private, January 2d, vice Stewart, promoted. |
| 3 | Appointed from Private, March 1st. vice Stewart, promoted. |
| 4 | Appointed from Private, March 1st, vice Woodworth, promoted. |
| 1 | |
| 1 | |
| 2 | |
| 3 | |
| 4 | |
| 5 | |
| 6 | |
| 7 | |
| 8 | |
| 9 | |
| 10 | |
| 11 | |
| 12 | |
| 13 | |
| 14 | |
| 15 | |
| 16 | |
| 17 | |
| 18 | Absent on detached service Quartermaster department, from December 27th. Order of General Marshall. |
| 19 | |
| 20 | |
| 21 | |
| 22 | |
| 23 | |
| 24 | |
| 25 | |
| 26 | |
| 27 | |
| 28 | |
| 29 | |
| 30 | |

## MEXICAN WAR VETERANS.

### ROLL OF COMPANY "H," SECOND REGIMENT KENTUCKY

| No. of each grade. | Name. | Rank. | Enrolled. | Mustered In. When. | Mustered In. Where. | Period. | Mustered Out. When. | Mustered Out. Where. |
|---|---|---|---|---|---|---|---|---|
| 31 | Williamson, Alexander. | Private | June 9, 1846 | June 9, '46 | Louisville, Ky. | 1 yr. | June 10,'47 | New Orleans |
| 32 | Wilson, Wm. W. | Private | June 9, 1846 | June 9, '46 | Louisville, Ky. | 1 yr. | June 10,'47 | New Orleans |
|  | DISCHARGED. |  |  |  |  |  |  |  |
| 1 | Brevard, James | Musician | June 9, 1846 | June 9, '46 | Louisville, Ky. | 1 yr. |  |  |
| 1 | Andrich, Joseph | Private | June 9, 1846 | June 9, '46 | Louisville, Ky. | 1 yr. |  |  |
| 2 | Burns, James | Private | June 9, 1846 | June 9, '46 | Louisville, Ky. | 1 yr. |  |  |
| 3 | Cook, Israel B. | Private | June 9, 1846 | June 9, '46 | Louisville, Ky. | 1 yr. |  |  |
| 4 | Cook, John L. | Private | June 9, 1846 | June 9, '46 | Louisville, Ky. | 1 yr. |  |  |
| 5 | Cole, Daniel | Private | June 9, 1846 | June 9, '46 | Louisville, Ky. | 1 yr. |  |  |
| 6 | Corbin, John | Private | June 9, 1846 | June 9, '46 | Louisville, Ky. | 1 yr. |  |  |
| 7 | Drinkard, H. M. | Private | June 9, 1846 | June 9, '46 | Louisville, Ky. | 1 yr. |  |  |
| 8 | Drinkard, G. W. | Private | June 9, 1846 | June 9, '46 | Louisville, Ky. | 1 yr. |  |  |
| 9 | Drinkard, J. G. | Private | June 9, 1846 | June 9, '46 | Louisville, Ky. | 1 yr. |  |  |
| 10 | Finley, Wm. | Private | June 9, 1846 | June 9, '46 | Louisville, Ky. | 1 yr. |  |  |
| 11 | Himer, Alfred | Private | June 9, 1846 | June 9, '46 | Louisville, Ky. | 1 yr. |  |  |
| 12 | Luke, Wm. S. | Private | June 9, 1846 | June 9, '46 | Louisville, Ky. | 1 yr. |  |  |
| 13 | Lee, Robert S. | Private | June 9, 1846 | June 9, '46 | Louisville, Ky. | 1 yr. |  |  |
| 14 | Maddy, Michael | Private | June 9, 1846 | June 9, '46 | Louisville, Ky. | 1 yr. |  |  |
| 15 | McLain, Wm. | Private | June 9, 1846 | June 9, '46 | Louisville, Ky. | 1 yr. |  |  |
| 16 | Rugg, Charles | Private | June 9, 1846 | June 9, '46 | Louisville, Ky. | 1 yr. |  |  |
| 17 | Silver, Amos | Private | June 9, 1846 | June 9, '46 | Louisville, Ky. | 1 yr. |  |  |
| 18 | St. Clair, Martin | Private | June 9, 1846 | June 9, '46 | Louisville, Ky. | 1 yr. |  |  |
| 19 | Williams, Peter | Private | June 9, 1846 | June 9, '46 | Louisville, Ky. | 1 yr. |  |  |
| 20 | Woods, Peyton | Private | June 9, 1846 | June 9, '46 | Louisville, Ky. | 1 yr. |  |  |
|  | DEATHS. |  |  |  |  |  |  |  |
| 1 | Jos. W. Powell | 1st Lieutenant | June 9, 1846 | June 9, '46 | Louisville, Ky. | 1 yr. |  |  |
| 1 | Hardin, Harrison | Private | June 9, 1846 | June 9, '46 | Louisville, Ky. | 1 yr. |  |  |
| 2 | McLain, Theodore | Private | June 9, 1846 | June 9, '46 | Louisville, Ky. | 1 yr. |  |  |
| 3 | Morgan, Joshua | Private | June 9, 1846 | June 9, '46 | Louisville, Ky. | 1 yr. |  |  |
| 4 | Oliver, Wm. | Private | June 9, 1846 | June 9, '46 | Louisville, Ky. | 1 yr. |  |  |
| 5 | Williamson, Wm. | Private | June 9, 1846 | June 9, '46 | Louisville, Ky. | 1 yr. |  |  |
| 6 | Oak, Frederick | Private | June 9, 1846 | June 9, '46 | Louisville, Ky. | 1 yr. |  |  |
| 7 | Holder, Robert | Private | June 9, 1846 | June 9, '46 | Louisville, Ky. | 1 yr. |  |  |
|  | KILLED IN BATTLE. |  |  |  |  |  |  |  |
| 1 | Kring, Jos. | 2d Sergeant | June 9, 1846 | June 9, '46 | Louisville, Ky. | 1 yr. |  |  |
| 2 | Dunlop, John M. | Sergeant | June 9, 1846 | June 9, '46 | Louisville, Ky. | 1 yr. |  |  |
| 1 | Gilbert, Wm. | Private | June 9, 1846 | June 9, '46 | Louisville, Ky. | 1 yr. |  |  |
| 2 | Rham, Wm. | Private | June 9, 1846 | June 9, '46 | Louisville, Ky. | 1 yr. |  |  |
| 3 | Williams, John | Private | June 9, 1846 | June 9, '46 | Louisville, Ky. | 1 yr. |  |  |
|  | DESERTED. |  |  |  |  |  |  |  |
| 1 | Greenhouse, Andrew J. | Private | June 9, 1846 | June 9, '46 | Louisville, Ky. | 1 yr. |  |  |
| 2 | McGinley, Barney | Private | June 9, 1846 | June 9, '46 | Louisville, Ky. | 1 yr. |  |  |
| 3 | Pollock, Robert | Private | June 9, 1846 | June 9, '46 | Louisville, Ky. | 1 yr. |  |  |
| 4 | Philpot, William H. | Private | June 9, 1846 | June 9, '46 | Louisville, Ky. | 1 yr. |  |  |
| 5 | Lewis, Edward | Private | June 9, 1846 | June 9, '46 | Louisville, Ky. | 1 yr. |  |  |
| 6 | Taylor, John H. | Private | June 9, 1846 | June 9, '46 | Louisville, Ky. | 1 yr. |  |  |
| 7 | Witt, John D. | Private | June 9, 1846 | June 9, '46 | Louisville, Ky. | 1 yr. |  |  |
| 8 | Young, Nathan | Private | June 9, 1846 | June 9, '46 | Louisville, Ky. | 1 yr. |  |  |
|  | TRANSFERRED. |  |  |  |  |  |  |  |
| 1 | Lightell, John | Private | June 9, 1846 | June 9, '46 | Louisville, Ky. | 1 yr. |  |  |

This Company was enrolled at Louisville, Kentucky.

### ROLL OF COMPANY "I," SECOND REGIMENT KENTUCKY

| | Name. | Rank. | Enrolled. | When. | Where. | Period. | When. | Where. |
|---|---|---|---|---|---|---|---|---|
| 1 | Wilkerson, Turpin | Captain | June 6, 1846 | June 9, '46 | Louisville, Ky. | 1 yr. | June 9, '47 | New Orleans, La. |
| 1 | James E. Kelso | 1st Lieutenant | June 6, 1846 | June 9, '46 | Louisville, Ky. | 1 yr. | June 9, '47 | New Orleans, La. |
| 1 | Peter G. Flood | 2d Lieutenant | June 6, 1846 | June 9, '46 | Louisville, Ky. | 1 yr. | June 9, '47 | New Orleans, La. |
| 2 | George M. Coleman | 2d Lieutenant | June 6, 1846 | June 9, '46 | Louisville, Ky. | 1 yr. | June 9, '47 | New Orleans, La. |
| 1 | Albert G. Anderson | 1st Sergeant | June 6, 1846 | June 9, '46 | Louisville, Ky. | 1 yr | June 9, '47 | New Orleans, La. |
| 2 | Roy S. Clarke | Sergeant | June 6, 1846 | June 9, '46 | Louisville, Ky. | 1 yr. | June 9, '47 | New Orleans, La. |
| 3 | Warren Mitchell | Sergeant | June 6, 1846 | June 9, '46 | Louisville, Ky. | 1 yr. | June 9, '47 | New Orleans, La. |
| 4 | William P. Hurt | Sergeant | June 6, 1846 | June 9, '46 | Louisville, Ky. | 1 yr. | June 9, '47 | New Orleans, La. |
| 1 | David McCullough | Corporal | June 6, 1846 | June 9, '46 | Louisville, Ky. | 1 yr. | June 9, '47 | New Orleans, La. |
| 2 | William A. Blard | Corporal | June 6, 1846 | June 9, '46 | Louisville, Ky. | 1 yr. | June 9, '47 | New Orleans, La. |
| 3 | Richard Apperson | Corporal | June 6, 1846 | June 9, '46 | Louisville, Ky. | 1 yr | June 9, '47 | New Orleans, La. |
| 4 | James W. Clarke | Corporal | June 6, 1846 | June 9, '46 | Louisville, Ky. | 1 yr. | June 9, '47 | New Orleans, La. |

# FOOT VOLUNTEERS—MEXICAN WAR—Continued.

REMARKS.

| No. of each grade | Remarks |
|---|---|
| 31 | |
| 32 | |
| | |
| 1 | On Surgeon's certificate, September 12th. Order of Col. McKee. |
| 1 | On Surgeon's certificate, August 15th. Order of Col. McKee. |
| 2 | On Surgeon's certificate, September 12th. Order of Col. McKee. |
| 3 | On Surgeon's certificate, December 15th. Order of Col. McKee. |
| 4 | On Surgeon's certificate, December 25th. Order of Col. McKee. |
| 5 | On Surgeon's certificate, September 15th. Order of Col. McKee. |
| 6 | On Surgeon's certificate, September 25th. Order of Col. McKee. |
| 7 | On Surgeon's certificate, September 25th. Order of Col. McKee. |
| 8 | On Surgeon's certificate, September 25th. Order of Col. McKee. |
| 9 | On Surgeon's certificate, September 25th. Order of Col. McKee. |
| 10 | On Surgeon's certificate, September 29th. Order of Col. McKee. |
| 11 | On Surgeon's certificate, August 15th. Order of Col. McKee. |
| 12 | On Surgeon's certificate, October 14th. Order of Col. McKee. |
| 13 | On Surgeon's certificate, December 15. Order of Col. McKee. |
| 14 | Order of Col. McKee June 28th, for worthlessness. |
| 15 | On Surgeon's certificate, October 30th. Order of Col. McKee. |
| 16 | On Surgeon's certificate, June 28th. Order of Col. McKee. |
| 17 | On Surgeon's certificate, September 12th. Order of Col. McKee. |
| 18 | On Surgeon's certificate, October 30th. Order of Col. McKee. |
| 19 | On Surgeon's certificate, August 15th. Order of Col. McKee. |
| 20 | On Surgeon's certificate, August 15th. Order of Col. McKee. |
| | |
| 1 | Died at Monterey, January 23d, of fever. |
| 1 | Died at Camargo, September 11th, of fever. |
| 2 | Died at Ceralvo, December 3d, of fever. |
| 3 | Died at Ceralvo, January 27th, of fever. |
| 4 | Died at Camargo, October 15th, of fever. |
| 5 | Died at Camargo, October 26th. |
| 6 | Died at Saltillo, March 3d, of wounds received in battle at Buena Vista. |
| 7 | Died at Saltillo, March 20th, of wounds received in battle at Buena Vista. |
| | |
| 1 | Killed in battle Buena Vista, February 23d. |
| 2 | Killed in battle Buena Vista, February 23d. |
| 1 | Killed in battle Buena Vista, February 23d. |
| 2 | Killed in battle Buena Vista, February 23d. |
| 3 | Killed in battle Buena Vista, February 23d. |
| | |
| 1 | Deserted from camp, Monterey, January 5th. |
| 2 | Deserted June 18th from Camp Oakland, near Louisville, Ky. |
| 3 | Deserted from camp near Monterey, March 1st. |
| 4 | Deserted from Ceralvo, November 11th. |
| 5 | Deserted from Monterey, March 5th. |
| 6 | Deserted from hospital, Matamoras, March —. |
| 7 | Deserted from hospital, Camargo, March —. |
| 8 | Deserted from camp Oakland, near Louisville, Ky., June 10th. |
| | |
| 1 | Transferred to non-commissioned staff as principal Musician, September 29th. |

# FOOT VOLUNTEERS—MEXICAN WAR.

| No. of each grade | Remarks |
|---|---|
| 1 | |
| 1 | |
| 1 | Corporal from enrol'ment to September 25th; reduced to ranks on that day. Order of Col. McKee. Promoted October 31st. |
| 2 | Corporal from enrollment to June 28th. |
| 1 | |
| 2 | |
| 3 | |
| 4 | Was private from enrollment to September 25th. |
| 1 | Private from enrollment to September 4th; reduced to ranks January 21st; reappointed February 27th. |
| 2 | |
| 3 | Was private from enrollment to August 15th. |
| 4 | Was private from enrollment to October 25th. |

## MEXICAN WAR VETERANS.
## ROLL OF COMPANY "I," SECOND REGIMENT KENTUCKY

| No. of each grade. | Name. | Rank. | Enrolled. | Mustered in. When. | Mustered in. Where. | Period. | Mustered Out When. | Mustered Out Where. |
|---|---|---|---|---|---|---|---|---|
| 1 | Lewis Dalton | Fifer | June 6, 1846 | June 9, '46 | Louisville, Ky. | 1 yr. | June 9, '47 | New Orleans, La. |
| 1 | Ashley, James P. | Private | June 6, 1846 | June 9, '46 | Louisville, Ky. | 1 yr. | June 9, '47 | New Orleans, La. |
| 2 | Butler, David H. | Private | June 6, 1846 | June 9, '46 | Louisville, Ky. | 1 yr. | June 9, '47 | New Orleans, La. |
| 3 | Beckner, Sampson C. | Private | June 6, 1846 | June 9, '46 | Louisville, Ky. | 1 yr. | June 9, '47 | New Orleans, La. |
| 4 | Brooking, Roger K. | Private | June 6, 1846 | June 9, '46 | Louisville, Ky. | 1 yr. | June 9, '47 | New Orleans, La. |
| 5 | Ball, Richard L. | Private | June 6, 1846 | June 9, '46 | Louisville, Ky. | 1 yr. | June 9, '47 | New Orleans, La. |
| 6 | Brush, Jacob | Private | June 6, 1846 | June 9, '46 | Louisville, Ky. | 1 yr. | June 9, '47 | New Orleans, La. |
| 7 | Blunt, William | Private | June 6, 1846 | June 9, '46 | Louisville, Ky. | 1 yr. | June 9, '47 | New Orleans, La. |
| 8 | Casity, Alvin | Private | June 6, 1846 | June 9, '46 | Louisville, Ky. | 1 yr. | June 9, '47 | New Orleans, La. |
| 9 | Cox, James A. | Private | June 6, 1846 | June 9, '46 | Louisville, Ky. | 1 yr. | June 9, '47 | New Orleans, La. |
| 10 | Cook, John | Private | June 6, 1846 | June 9, '46 | Louisville, Ky. | 1 yr. | June 9, '47 | New Orleans, La. |
| 11 | Corbin, Randolph B. | Private | June 6, 1846 | June 9, '46 | Louisville, Ky. | 1 yr. | June 9, '47 | New Orleans, La. |
| 12 | Cartright, John F. | Private | June 6, 1846 | June 9, '46 | Louisville, Ky. | 1 yr. | June 9, '47 | New Orleans, La. |
| 13 | Devin, James W. | Private | June 6, 1846 | June 9, '46 | Louisville, Ky. | 1 yr. | June 9, '47 | New Orleans, La. |
| 14 | Ficklin, John | Private | June 6, 1846 | June 9, '46 | Louisville, Ky. | 1 yr. | June 9, '47 | New Orleans, La. |
| 15 | Frisby, James | Private | June 6, 1846 | June 9, '46 | Louisville, Ky. | 1 yr. | June 9, '47 | New Orleans, La. |
| 16 | Gentry, Albert C. | Private | June 6, 1846 | June 9, '46 | Louisville, Ky. | 1 yr. | June 9, '47 | New Orleans, La. |
| 17 | Glover, Dewitt C. | Private | June 6, 1846 | June 9, '46 | Louisville, Ky. | 1 yr. | June 9, '47 | New Orleans, La. |
| 18 | Green, James | Private | June 6, 1846 | June 9, '46 | Louisville, Ky. | 1 yr. | June 9, '47 | New Orleans, La. |
| 19 | Herndon, Henry | Private | June 6, 1846 | June 9, '46 | Louisville, Ky. | 1 yr. | June 9, '47 | New Orleans, La. |
| 20 | Hurt, John S. | Private | June 6, 1846 | June 9, '46 | Louisville, Ky. | 1 yr. | June 9, '47 | New Orleans, La. |
| 21 | Howard, James | Private | June 6, 1846 | June 9, '46 | Louisville, Ky. | 1 yr. | June 9, '47 | New Orleans, La. |
| 22 | Jeans, Beal | Private | June 6, 1846 | June 9, '46 | Louisville, Ky. | 1 yr. | June 9, '47 | New Orleans, La. |
| 23 | Kelly, James | Private | June 6, 1846 | June 9, '46 | Louisville, Ky. | 1 yr. | June 9, '47 | New Orleans, La. |
| 24 | Kirk, John | Private | June 6, 1846 | June 9, '46 | Louisville, Ky. | 1 yr. | June 9, '47 | New Orleans, La. |
| 25 | Kirk, William G. | Private | June 6, 1846 | June 9, '46 | Louisville, Ky. | 1 yr. | June 9, '47 | New Orleans, La. |
| 26 | Kahill, Edward S. | Private | June 6, 1846 | June 9, '46 | Louisville, Ky. | 1 yr. | June 9, '47 | New Orleans, La. |
| 27 | Kennedy, Robert | Private | June 6, 1846 | June 9, '46 | Louisville, Ky. | 1 yr. | June 9, '47 | New Orleans, La. |
| 28 | Langley, William S. | Private | June 6, 1846 | June 9, '46 | Louisville, Ky. | 1 yr. | June 9, '47 | New Orleans, La. |
| 29 | Mappin, Caleb | Private | June 6, 1846 | June 9, '46 | Louisville, Ky. | 1 yr. | June 9, '47 | New Orleans, La. |
| 30 | Megowan, John B. | Private | June 6, 1846 | June 9, '46 | Louisville, Ky. | 1 yr. | June 9, '47 | New Orleans, La. |
| 31 | McIlvain, William | Private | June 6, 1846 | June 9, '46 | Louisville, Ky. | 1 yr. | June 9, '47 | New Orleans, La. |
| 32 | Owsley, Benjamin F. | Private | June 6, 1846 | June 9, '46 | Louisville, Ky. | 1 yr. | June 9, '47 | New Orleans, La. |
| 33 | Piersall, Hezekiah | Private | June 6, 1846 | June 9, '46 | Louisville, Ky. | 1 yr. | June 9, '47 | New Orleans, La. |
| 34 | Richardson, Mathew | Private | June 6, 1846 | June 9, '46 | Louisville, Ky. | 1 yr. | June 9, '47 | New Orleans, La. |
| 35 | Piersall, Washington | Private | June 6, 1846 | June 9, '46 | Louisville, Ky. | 1 yr. | June 9, '47 | New Orleans, La. |
| 36 | Redman, John | Private | June 6, 1846 | June 9, '46 | Louisville, Ky. | 1 yr. | June 9, '47 | New Orleans, La. |
| 37 | Reid, William T. | Private | June 6, 1846 | June 9, '46 | Louisville, Ky. | 1 yr. | June 9, '47 | New Orleans, La. |
| 38 | Scott, David | Private | June 6, 1846 | June 9, '46 | Louisville, Ky. | 1 yr. | June 9, '47 | New Orleans, La. |
| 39 | Tomlinson, John A. | Private | June 6, 1846 | June 9, '46 | Louisville, Ky. | 1 yr. | June 9, '47 | New Orleans, La. |
| 40 | Tredway, Moses X. | Private | June 6, 1846 | June 9, '46 | Louisville, Ky. | 1 yr. | June 9, '47 | New Orleans, La. |
| 41 | Tredway, Edward E. | Private | June 6, 1846 | June 9, '46 | Louisville, Ky. | 1 yr. | June 9, '47 | New Orleans, La. |
| 42 | Walker, George H. | Private | June 6, 1846 | June 9, '46 | Louisville, Ky. | 1 yr. | June 9, '47 | New Orleans, La. |
| 43 | Walker, John | Private | June 6, 1846 | June 9, '46 | Louisville, Ky. | 1 yr. | June 9, '47 | New Orleans, La. |
| 44 | Wallace, William | Private | June 6, 1846 | June 9, '46 | Louisville, Ky. | 1 yr. | June 9, '47 | New Orleans, La. |
| 45 | Williams, Zedekiah H. | Private | June 6, 1846 | June 9, '46 | Louisville, Ky. | 1 yr. | June 9, '47 | New Orleans, La. |
| 46 | Wilkerson, James | Private | June 6, 1846 | June 9, '46 | Louisville, Ky. | 1 yr. | June 9, '47 | New Orleans, La. |
| 47 | Weiner, Peter | Private | June 6, 1846 | June 9, '46 | Louisville, Ky. | 1 yr. | June 9, '47 | New Orleans, La. |
| 48 | White, Edward P. | Private | June 6, 1846 | June 9, '46 | Louisville, Ky. | 1 yr. | June 9, '47 | New Orleans, La. |

TRANSFERRED.

| 1 | George Snider | Private | June 6, 1846 | June 9, '46 | Louisville, Ky. | 1 yr. | | |

DISCHARGED.

| 1 | B. H. Shurgin | Sergeant | June 6, 1846 | June 9, '46 | Louisville, Ky. | 1 yr. | | |
| 1 | Samuel Brockway | Musician | June 6, 1846 | June 9, '46 | Louisville, Ky. | 1 yr. | | |
| 1 | William W. Apperson | Private | June 6, 1846 | June 9, '46 | Louisville, Ky. | 1 yr. | | |
| 2 | Joseph Botts | Private | June 6, 1846 | June 9, '46 | Louisville, Ky. | 1 yr. | | |
| 3 | George W. Case | Private | June 6, 1846 | June 9, '46 | Louisville, Ky. | 1 yr. | | |
| 4 | Moses Connor | Private | June 6, 1846 | June 9, '46 | Louisville, Ky. | 1 yr. | | |
| 5 | Benjamin Coleman | Private | June 6, 1846 | June 9, '46 | Louisville, Ky. | 1 yr. | | |
| 6 | John M. Davis | Private | June 6, 1846 | June 9, '46 | Louisville, Ky. | 1 yr. | | |
| 7 | John Dobyns | Private | June 6, 1846 | June 9, '46 | Louisville, Ky. | 1 yr. | | |
| 8 | Charles D. Echols | Private | June 6, 1846 | June 9, '46 | Louisville, Ky. | 1 yr. | | |
| 9 | Franklin Ferguson | Private | June 6, 1846 | June 9, '46 | Louisville, Ky. | 1 yr. | | |
| 10 | William R. Fletcher | Private | June 6, 1846 | June 9, '46 | Louisville, Ky. | 1 yr. | | |
| 11 | William Green | Private | June 6, 1846 | June 9, '46 | Louisville, Ky. | 1 yr. | | |
| 12 | Daniel G. Gray | Private | June 6, 1846 | June 9, '46 | Louisville, Ky. | 1 yr. | | |
| 13 | George W. Jackson | Private | June 6, 1846 | June 9, '46 | Louisville, Ky. | 1 yr. | | |
| 14 | James Y. Massie | Private | June 6, 1846 | June 9, '46 | Louisville, Ky. | 1 yr. | | |
| 15 | William B. Miller | Private | June 6, 1846 | June 9, '46 | Louisville, Ky. | 1 yr. | | |
| 16 | Strother D. Mitchell | Private | June 6, 1846 | June 9, '46 | Louisville, Ky. | 1 yr. | | |
| 17 | Thomas Oldham | Private | June 6, 1846 | June 9, '46 | Louisville, Ky. | 1 yr. | | |
| 18 | Robert F. Thomas | Private | June 6, 1846 | June 9, '46 | Louisville, Ky. | 1 yr. | | |

MEXICAN WAR VETERANS. 53

FOOT VOLUNTEERS—MEXICAN WAR—Continued.

| No. of each grade | REMARKS. |
|---|---|
| 1 | |
| 1 | |
| 2 | |
| 3 | |
| 4 | |
| 5 | |
| 6 | |
| 7 | |
| 8 | |
| 9 | |
| 10 | |
| 11 | |
| 12 | |
| 13 | |
| 14 | |
| 15 | |
| 16 | |
| 17 | |
| 18 | |
| 19 | |
| 20 | |
| 21 | |
| 22 | |
| 23 | |
| 24 | |
| 25 | |
| 26 | Wounded in battle of Buena Vista, February 23d. |
| 27 | |
| 28 | |
| 29 | |
| 30 | |
| 31 | |
| 32 | |
| 33 | |
| 34 | Wounded in battle of Buena Vista, February 23d. |
| 35 | |
| 36 | |
| 37 | |
| 38 | |
| 39 | |
| 40 | |
| 41 | |
| 42 | |
| 43 | |
| 44 | On furlough in Subsistence Department, Mexico, from May 13th. Order of Major C. H. Fry. |
| 45 | |
| 46 | |
| 47 | |
| 48 | |
| 1 | Transferred at Camp Jackson, La., July 8, to Capt. Williams' Company, Kentucky Foot. Order of Col. W. R. McKee. |
| 1 | Discharged at camp near Camargo, Mexico, September 3d. Surgeon's certificate of disability. Order of Gen. Marshall. |
| 1 | Discharged at Camp Rio Grande, Texas. August 15th, on Surgeon's certificate of disability. Order of Col. McKee. |
| 1 | Discharged at camp near Camargo, September 10th, on Surgeon's certificate of disability. Order of Gen. Marshall. |
| 2 | Discharged at Camp Rio Grande, August 15th, on Surgeon's certificate of disability. Order of Col. McKee. |
| 3 | Discharged at camp near Camargo, September 10th, on Surgeon's certificate of disability. Order of Gen. Marshall. |
| 4 | Discharged at Camp Rio Grande, August 14th, on Surgeon's certificate of disability. Order of Col. McKee. |
| 5 | Discharged at camp near Camargo, September 10th, on Surgeon's certificate of disability. Order Gen. Marshall. |
| 6 | Discharged at Camp Rio Grande, August 14th, on Surgeon's certificate of disability. Order of Col. McKee. |
| 7 | Discharged at Camp Rio Grande, August 14th, on Surgeon's certificate of disability. Order of Col. McKee. |
| 8 | Discharged at camp near Camargo, September 10th, on Surgeon's certificate of disability. Order of Gen. Marshall. |
| 9 | Discharged at camp near Camargo, September 10th, on Surgeon's certificate of disability. Order of Gen. Marshall. |
| 10 | Left sick at Louisville, June 29th. Returned to his home about July 15th. Never rejoined. Discharged. Order of Col. Churchill. |
| 11 | Discharged at camp near Camargo, September 26th. Surgeon's certificate of disability. Order of Gen. Marshall. |
| 12 | Discharged at Camp Rio Grande, August 15th. Surgeon's certificate of disability. Order of Col. McKee. |
| 13 | Discharged at Camp Rio Grande August 14th. Surgeon's certificate of disability. Order of Col. McKee. |
| 14 | Discharged at camp near Camargo, September 4th. Surgeon's certificate of disability. Order of Gen. Marshall. |
| 15 | Discharged at Camp Rio Grande, August 14th. Surgeon's certificate of disability. Order of Col. McKee. |
| 16 | Discharged at Camp Rio Grande, August 14th. Surgeon's certificate of disability. Order of Col. McKee. |
| 17 | Discharged at Camp Rio Grande, August 14th. Surgeon's certificate of disability. Order of Col. McKee. |
| 18 | Discharged at Camp Rio Grande, August 14th. Surgeon's certificate of disability. Order of Col. McKee. |

## ROLL OF COMPANY "I," SECOND REGIMENT KENTUCKY.

| No. of each grade | Name | Rank | Enrolled | Mustered In. When | Mustered In. Where | Period | Mustered Out. When | Mustered Out. Where |
|---|---|---|---|---|---|---|---|---|
| 19 | Malin Willoughby | Private | June 6, 1846 | June 9, '46 | Louisville, Ky | 1 yr | | |
| | DIED. | | | | | | | |
| 1 | Mansfield Banton | Private | June 6, 1846 | June 9, '46 | Louisville, Ky | 1 yr | | |
| 2 | Enoch G. Burton | Private | June 6, 1846 | June 9, '46 | Louisville, Ky | 1 yr | | |
| 3 | Thomas Fecklin | Private | June 6, 1846 | June 9, '46 | Louisville, Ky | 1 yr | | |
| 4 | Henry Holland | Private | June 6, 1846 | June 9, '46 | Louisville, Ky | 1 yr | | |
| 5 | Mason Young | Private | June 6, 1846 | June 9, '46 | Louisville, Ky | 1 yr | | |
| | KILLED IN BATTLE. | | | | | | | |
| 1 | Henry Edward | Corporal | June 6, 1846 | June 9, '46 | Louisville, Ky | 1 yr | | |
| 1 | Abram Goodpaster | Private | June 6, 1846 | June 9, '46 | Louisville, Ky | 1 yr | | |
| 2 | Eva Thoreau | Private | June 6, 1846 | June 9, '46 | Louisville, Ky | 1 yr | | |
| | DESERTED. | | | | | | | |
| 1 | William A. Christy | Private | June 6, 1846 | June 9, '46 | Louisville, Ky | 1 yr | | |

This Company was enrolled at Louisville, Ky.

## ROLL OF CAPTAIN PHILIP B. THOMPSON'S COMPANY [NO LETTER], SECOND

| No. of each grade | Name | Rank | Enrolled | Mustered In. When | Mustered In. Where | Period | Mustered Out. When | Mustered Out. Where |
|---|---|---|---|---|---|---|---|---|
| 1 | Philip B. Thompson | Captain | May 19, 1846 | June 9, '46 | Louisville, Ky | 1 yr | June 8, '47 | New Orleans, La |
| 1 | George N. Cardwell | 1st Lieutenant | May 19, 1846 | June 9, '46 | Louisville, Ky | 1 yr | June 8, '47 | New Orleans, La |
| 1 | Joseph C. Ewing | 2d Lieutenant | May 19, 1846 | June 9, '46 | Louisville, Ky | 1 yr | June 8, '47 | New Orleans, La |
| 2 | William T. Withers | 2d Lieutenant | May 19, 1846 | June 9, '46 | Louisville, Ky | 1 yr | June 8, '47 | New Orleans, La |
| 1 | Edward C. Rogers | 1st Sergeant | May 19, 1846 | June 9, '46 | Louisville, Ky | 1 yr | June 8, '47 | New Orleans, La |
| 2 | William T. Shaw | Sergeant | May 19, 1846 | June 9, '46 | Louisville, Ky | 1 yr | June 8, '47 | New Orleans, La |
| 3 | Josiah Mann | Sergeant | May 19, 1846 | June 9, '46 | Louisville, Ky | 1 yr | June 8, '47 | New Orleans, La |
| 4 | Charles C. Smedley | Sergeant | May 19, 1846 | June 9, '46 | Louisville, Ky | 1 yr | June 8, '47 | New Orleans, La |
| 1 | Stephen W. Cloyd | Corporal | May 19, 1846 | June 9, '46 | Louisville, Ky | 1 yr | June 8, '47 | New Orleans, La |
| 2 | William Percell | Corporal | May 19, 1846 | June 9, '46 | Louisville, Ky | 1 yr | June 8, '47 | New Orleans, La |
| 3 | James Cahill | Corporal | May 19, 1846 | June 9, '46 | Louisville, Ky | 1 yr | June 8, '47 | New Orleans, La |
| 4 | Edward Burton | Corporal | May 19, 1846 | June 9, '46 | Louisville, Ky | 1 yr | June 8, '47 | New Orleans, La |
| 1 | Adair, David T. | Private | May 19, 1846 | June 9, '46 | Louisville, Ky | 1 yr | June 8, '47 | New Orleans, La |
| 2 | Alexander, John B. | Private | May 19, 1846 | June 9, '46 | Louisville, Ky | 1 yr | June 8, '47 | New Orleans, La |
| 3 | Adkins, James | Private | May 19, 1846 | June 9, '46 | Louisville, Ky | 1 yr | June 8, '47 | New Orleans, La |
| 4 | Ashley, John R. | Private | May 19, 1846 | June 9, '46 | Louisville, Ky | 1 yr | June 8, '47 | New Orleans, La |
| 5 | Burns, Thomas | Private | May 19, 1846 | June 9, '46 | Louisville, Ky | 1 yr | June 8, '47 | New Orleans, La |
| 6 | Brown, William | Private | May 19, 1846 | June 9, '46 | Louisville, Ky | 1 yr | June 8, '47 | New Orleans, La |
| 7 | Bradshaw, Edward | Private | May 19, 1846 | June 9, '46 | Louisville, Ky | 1 yr | June 8, '47 | New Orleans, La |
| 8 | Bradshaw, John | Private | May 19, 1846 | June 9, '46 | Louisville, Ky | 1 yr | June 8, '47 | New Orleans, La |
| 9 | Bennett, William | Private | May 19, 1846 | June 9, '46 | Louisville, Ky | 1 yr | June 8, '47 | New Orleans, La |
| 10 | Creagh, Richard | Private | May 19, 1846 | June 9, '46 | Louisville, Ky | 1 yr | June 8, '47 | New Orleans, La |
| 11 | Cloyd, William | Private | May 19, 1846 | June 9, '46 | Louisville, Ky | 1 yr | June 8, '47 | New Orleans, La |
| 12 | Cloyd, John | Private | May 19, 1846 | June 9, '46 | Louisville, Ky | 1 yr | June 8, '47 | New Orleans, La |
| 13 | Crawford, John | Private | May 19, 1846 | June 9, '46 | Louisville, Ky | 1 yr | June 8, '47 | New Orleans, La |
| 14 | Curry, Mathew | Private | May 19, 1846 | June 9, '46 | Louisville, Ky | 1 yr | June 8, '47 | New Orleans, La |
| 15 | Chapman, Daniel | Private | May 19, 1846 | June 9, '46 | Louisville, Ky | 1 yr | June 8, '47 | New Orleans, La |
| 16 | Downey, William C. | Private | May 19, 1846 | June 9, '46 | Louisville, Ky | 1 yr | June 8, '47 | New Orleans, La |
| 17 | Downey, Hannibal | Private | May 19, 1846 | June 9, '46 | Louisville, Ky | 1 yr | June 8, '47 | New Orleans, La |
| 18 | Derlin, John | Private | May 19, 1846 | June 9, '46 | Louisville, Ky | 1 yr | June 8, '47 | New Orleans, La |
| 19 | Divine, Andrew | Private | May 19, 1846 | June 9, '46 | Louisville, Ky | 1 yr | June 8, '47 | New Orleans, La |
| 20 | Davis, Samuel | Private | May 19, 1846 | June 9, '46 | Louisville, Ky | 1 yr | June 8, '47 | New Orleans, La |
| 21 | Davison, Marion F. | Private | May 19, 1846 | June 9, '46 | Louisville, Ky | 1 yr | June 8, '47 | New Orleans, La |
| 22 | Edward, Archibald | Private | May 19, 1846 | June 9, '46 | Louisville, Ky | 1 yr | June 8, '47 | New Orleans, La |
| 23 | Fairman, John H. | Private | May 19, 1846 | June 9, '46 | Louisville, Ky | 1 yr | June 8, '47 | New Orleans, La |
| 24 | Gore, William | Private | May 19, 1846 | June 9, '46 | Louisville, Ky | 1 yr | June 8, '47 | New Orleans, La |
| 25 | Galligher, William | Private | May 19, 1846 | June 9, '46 | Louisville, Ky | 1 yr | June 8, '47 | New Orleans, La |
| 26 | Gray, Henry | Private | May 19, 1846 | June 9, '46 | Louisville, Ky | 1 yr | June 8, '47 | New Orleans, La |
| 27 | Howland, James T. | Private | May 19, 1846 | June 9, '46 | Louisville, Ky | 1 yr | June 8, '47 | New Orleans, La |
| 28 | Hungate, Davis | Private | May 19, 1846 | June 9, '46 | Louisville, Ky | 1 yr | June 8, '47 | New Orleans, La |
| 29 | Huff, William P. | Private | May 19, 1846 | June 9, '46 | Louisville, Ky | 1 yr | June 8, '47 | New Orleans, La |
| 30 | Johnson, Clarke | Private | May 19, 1846 | June 9, '46 | Louisville, Ky | 1 yr | June 8, '47 | New Orleans, La |
| 31 | Mays, Samuel J. | Private | May 19, 1846 | June 9, '46 | Louisville, Ky | 1 yr | June 8, '47 | New Orleans, La |
| 32 | Mann, James B. | Private | May 19, 1846 | June 9, '46 | Louisville, Ky | 1 yr | June 8, '47 | New Orleans, La |
| 33 | Neal, William H. | Private | May 19, 1846 | June 9, '46 | Louisville, Ky | 1 yr | June 8, '47 | New Orleans, La |
| 34 | Parr, William H. | Private | May 19, 1846 | June 9, '46 | Louisville, Ky | 1 yr | June 8, '47 | New Orleans, La |
| 35 | Ross, Reubin | Private | May 19, 1846 | June 9, '46 | Louisville, Ky | 1 yr | June 8, '47 | New Orleans, La |
| 36 | Rice, John | Private | May 19, 1846 | June 9, '46 | Louisville, Ky | 1 yr | June 8, '47 | New Orleans, La |
| 37 | Rice, George W. | Private | May 19, 1846 | June 9, '46 | Louisville, Ky | 1 yr | June 8, '47 | New Orleans, La |
| 38 | Satterwhite, Charles | Private | May 19, 1846 | June 9, '46 | Louisville, Ky | 1 yr | June 8, '47 | New Orleans, La |
| 39 | Springer, Charles P. | Private | May 19, 1846 | June 9, '46 | Louisville, Ky | 1 yr | June 8, '47 | New Orleans, La |

## MEXICAN WAR VETERANS.

## FOOT VOLUNTEERS—MEXICAN WAR—Continued.

| No. of each grade. | REMARKS. |
|---|---|
| 19 | Discharged at camp near Camargo, September 24th. Surgeon's certificate of disability. Order of Gen. Marshall. |
| 1 | Drowned in the Rio Grande above Burieta, Mexico, August 23d. |
| 2 | Died at camp near Camargo, October 22d. |
| 3 | Died at Matamoras, August 25th. |
| 4 | Died at Camp Rio Grande, August 13th. |
| 5 | Died at Matamoras, August 26th. |
| 1 | Appointed from private January 21st; killed in battle of Buena Vista, February 23d. |
| 1 | Killed in battle of Buena Vista, February 23d. |
| 2 | Killed in battle of Buena Vista, February 23d. |
| 1 | Deserted at Louisville, June 28th. |

## REGIMENT KENTUCKY FOOT VOLUNTEERS—MEXICAN WAR.

| | |
|---|---|
| 1 | |
| 1 | On detached service; Adjutant of Regiment from August 17th. Order of Col. McKee. |
| 1 | |
| 2 | Absent with leave from Gen. Taylor. Appointed from 1st Sergeant June 27th. |
| 1 | |
| 3 | |
| 4 | Appointed from Corporal March 12th. |
| 1 | |
| 2 | |
| 3 | |
| 4 | Appointed from private March 2d. |
| 1 | |
| 2 | |
| 3 | Absent sick at New Orleans since July 8th; has never rejoined company. |
| 4 | |
| 5 | |
| 6 | |
| 7 | |
| 8 | |
| 9 | |
| 10 | |
| 11 | Absent sick at New Orleans since July 8th; has never rejoined company. |
| 12 | |
| 13 | Absent on furlough; employed in Quartermaster Department in Mexico since May 8th. Order of Major Fry. |
| 14 | |
| 15 | Present; sick in New Orleans since June 7th. |
| 16 | Present; sick in New Orleans since June 7th. |
| 17 | |
| 18 | |
| 19 | |
| 20 | |
| 21 | |
| 22 | Absent on furlough; employed in Quartermaster Department in Mexico since May 8th. Order of Major Fry. |
| 23 | |
| 24 | |
| 25 | |
| 26 | |
| 27 | |
| 28 | |
| 29 | |
| 30 | |
| 31 | On detached service; Hospital Steward in Regiment from November 28th. Order of Col. McKee. |
| 32 | |
| 33 | |
| 34 | |
| 35 | |
| 36 | |
| 37 | |
| 38 | Absent on furlough since May 14th. Order of Major Fry. |
| 39 | |

## ROLL OF CAPTAIN PHILIP B. THOMPSON'S COMPANY [NO LETTER], SECOND

| No. of each grade. | Name. | Rank. | Enrolled. | Mustered In. When. | Mustered In. Where. | Period. | Mustered Out. When. | Mustered Out. Where. |
|---|---|---|---|---|---|---|---|---|
| 40 | Sharp, William | Private | May 19, 1846 | June 9, '46 | Louisville, Ky. | 1 yr. | June 8, '47 | New Orleans, La. |
| 41 | Settles, John | Private | May 19, 1846 | June 9, '46 | Louisville, Ky. | 1 yr. | June 8, '47 | New Orleans, La. |
| 42 | Tuggles, William | Private | May 19, 1846 | June 9, '46 | Louisville, Ky. | 1 yr. | June 8, '47 | New Orleans, La. |
| 43 | Turney, William | Private | May 19, 1846 | June 9, '46 | Louisville, Ky. | 1 yr. | June 8, '47 | New Orleans, La. |
| 44 | Tally, Reubin | Private | May 19, 1846 | June 9, '46 | Louisville, Ky. | 1 yr. | June 8, '47 | New Orleans, La. |
| 45 | Woods, Thomas C. | Private | May 19, 1846 | June 9, '46 | Louisville, Ky. | 1 yr. | June 8, '47 | New Orleans, La. |
| 46 | Walker, John | Private | May 19, 1846 | June 9, '46 | Louisville, Ky. | 1 yr. | June 8, '47 | New Orleans, La. |
| 47 | Walton, Caleb | Private | May 19, 1846 | June 9, '46 | Louisville, Ky. | 1 yr. | June 8, '47 | New Orleans, La. |
| 48 | Vaughn, Andrew J. | Private | May 19, 1846 | June 9, '46 | Louisville, Ky. | 1 yr. | June 8, '47 | New Orleans, La. |
|  | **Transferred.** |  |  |  |  |  |  |  |
| 1 | Barlow, Samuel | Private | May 19, 1846 | June 9, '46 | Louisville, Ky. | 1 yr. |  |  |
| 2 | Wheatly, John | Sergeant | May 19, 1846 | June 9, '46 | Louisville, Ky. | 1 yr. |  |  |
|  | **Discharged.** |  |  |  |  |  |  |  |
| 1 | Brenan, Francis M. | Sergeant | May 19, 1846 | June 9, '46 | Louisville, Ky. | 1 yr. |  |  |
| 2 | Bishop, Jacob K. | Private | May 19, 1846 | June 9, '46 | Louisville, Ky. | 1 yr. |  |  |
| 3 | Baldwin, William | Private | May 19, 1846 | June 9, '46 | Louisville, Ky. | 1 yr. |  |  |
| 4 | Graham, Archibald | Private | May 19, 1846 | June 9, '46 | Louisville, Ky. | 1 yr. |  |  |
| 5 | Hale, Samuel D. | Private | May 19, 1846 | June 9, '46 | Louisville, Ky. | 1 yr. |  |  |
| 6 | Mallay, James I. | Corporal | May 19, 1846 | June 9, '46 | Louisville, Ky. | 1 yr. |  |  |
| 7 | Duncan, Asa | Corporal | May 19, 1846 | June 9, '46 | Louisville, Ky. | 1 yr. |  |  |
| 8 | Bonta, Harry | Private | May 19, 1846 | June 9, '46 | Louisville, Ky. | 1 yr. |  |  |
| 9 | Coleman, John | Private | May 19, 1846 | June 9, '46 | Louisville, Ky. | 1 yr. |  |  |
| 10 | Garnett, Marco T. | Private | May 19, 1846 | June 9, '46 | Louisville, Ky. | 1 yr. |  |  |
| 11 | Halbert, George T. | Private | May 19, 1846 | June 9, '46 | Louisville, Ky. | 1 yr. |  |  |
| 12 | Lair, James | Private | May 19, 1846 | June 9, '46 | Louisville, Ky. | 1 yr. |  |  |
| 13 | Twyman, William | Private | May 19, 1846 | June 9, '46 | Louisville, Ky. | 1 yr. |  |  |
| 14 | Watts, William H. | Private | May 19, 1846 | June 9, '46 | Louisville, Ky. | 1 yr. |  |  |
| 15 | Withers, Joseph H. | Private | May 19, 1846 | June 9, '46 | Louisville, Ky. | 1 yr. |  |  |
| 16 | Posey, John | Private | May 19, 1846 | June 9, '46 | Louisville, Ky. | 1 yr. |  |  |
|  | **Deaths.** |  |  |  |  |  |  |  |
| 1 | Guthrie, Richard W. | Private | May 19, 1846 | June 9, '46 | Louisville, Ky. | 1 yr. |  |  |
| 2 | Wright, John G. | Private | May 19, 1846 | June 9, '46 | Louisville, Ky. | 1 yr. |  |  |
| 3 | Spriker, Joseph | Private | May 19, 1846 | June 9, '46 | Louisville, Ky. | 1 yr. |  |  |
| 4 | Hendron, Woodson | Private | May 19, 1846 | June 9, '46 | Louisville, Ky. | 1 yr. |  |  |
|  | **Killed in Battle.** |  |  |  |  |  |  |  |
| 1 | Williams, Sydney M. | Corporal | May 19, 1846 | June 9, '46 | Louisville, Ky. | 1 yr. |  |  |
| 1 | Booth, Micajah H. | Private | May 19, 1846 | June 9, '46 | Louisville, Ky. | 1 yr. |  |  |
| 2 | Burks, William | Private | May 19, 1846 | June 9, '46 | Louisville, Ky. | 1 yr. |  |  |
| 3 | Baker, Robert M. | Private | May 19, 1846 | June 9, '46 | Louisville, Ky. | 1 yr. |  |  |
| 4 | Moffat, John | Private | May 19, 1846 | June 9, '46 | Louisville, Ky. | 1 yr. |  |  |
|  | **Deserted.** |  |  |  |  |  |  |  |
| 1 | Burns, Harry J. | Private | May 19, 1846 | June 9, '46 | Louisville, Ky. | 1 yr. |  |  |
| 2 | Gore, Charles | Private | May 19, 1846 | June 9, '46 | Louisville, Ky. | 1 yr. |  |  |
| 3 | Merryman, William | Private | May 19, 1846 | June 9, '46 | Louisville, Ky. | 1 yr. |  |  |
| 4 | Peouler, Leonard | Private | May 19, 1846 | June 9, '46 | Louisville, Ky. | 1 yr. |  |  |
| 5 | Quinn, Robert | Private | May 19, 1846 | June 9, '46 | Louisville, Ky. | 1 yr. |  |  |

This Company was recruited at Harrodsburg, Ky.

# REGIMENT KENTUCKY FOOT VOLUNTEERS—MEXICAN WAR—Continued.

| No of each grade | REMARKS |
|---|---|
| 40 | Absent sick at New Orleans since July 8th; has never rejoined company. |
| 41 | |
| 42 | |
| 43 | |
| 44 | |
| 45 | |
| 46 | |
| 47 | |
| 48 | |
| 1 | Transferred to Col. H. Marshall's Regiment of Cavalry, date unknown. Whose order unknown. |
| 2 | Appointed on Regimental Staff, March 11th, from Sergeant, by order of Major Fry. |
| 1 | Reduced to Private from Sergeant, June 27th; dishonorably discharged at Louisville, Ky., June 28th. Order of Col. McKee. |
| 2 | Discharged at Camp Belknap, August 15th; Surgeon's certificate of disability. Order of Col. McKee. |
| 3 | Discharged at Camp Belknap, August 9th; Surgeon's certificate of disability. Order of Col. McKee. |
| 4 | Discharged at Camp Belknap, August 14th; Surgeon's certificate of disability. Order of Col. McKee. |
| 5 | Discharged at Camargo, September 8th; Surgeon's certificate of disability. Order of Col. McKee. |
| 6 | Discharged at Matamoras, February 1st; Surgeon's certificate of disability. Not known. |
| 7 | Discharged at Matamoras, September 24th; Surgeon's certificate of disability. Not known. |
| 8 | Discharged at Camargo, September 5th; Surgeon's certificate of disability. Order of Col. McKee. |
| 9 | Discharged at Matamoras, September 24th; Surgeon's certificate of disability. Whose order not known. |
| 10 | Discharged at Camargo, September 5th; Surgeon's certificate of disability. Order of Col. McKee. |
| 11 | Discharged at Camargo, September 23d; Surgeon's certificate of disability. Order of Col. McKee. |
| 12 | Discharged at Camargo, September 23d; Surgeon's certificate of disability. Order of Col. McKee. |
| 13 | Discharged at Monterey. Date not known. By whose order not known. |
| 14 | Discharged at Camargo, September 17th; Surgeon's certificate of disability. Order of Col. McKee. |
| 15 | Discharged at Camargo, October 23d; Surgeon's certificate of disability. Order of Col. McKee. |
| 16 | Discharged at Monterey on Surgeon's certificate of disability. Date, and by whose order, not known. |
| 1 | Died at New Orleans, July 9th. |
| 2 | Died on board ship "Sea Lion," July 17th. |
| 3 | Died at Matamoras, September 4th. |
| 4 | Died at Saltillo of wounds received in battle of February 23d. |
| 1 | Killed in battle of Buena Vista, February 23d. |
| 1 | Killed in battle of Buena Vista, February 23d. |
| 2 | Killed in battle of Buena Vista, February 23d. |
| 3 | Killed in battle of Buena Vista, February 23d. |
| 4 | Killed in battle of Buena Vista, February 23d. |
| 1 | Deserted at Louisville, Ky., June 26th. |
| 2 | Deserted at Louisville, Ky., June 28th. |
| 3 | Deserted at Louisville, Ky., June 12th. |
| 4 | Deserted at Louisville, Ky., June 20th. |
| 5 | Deserted at Louisville, Ky., June 13th. |

## ROLL OF THE FIELD AND STAFF FIRST REGIMENT

| No. of each grade | Name | Rank | Joined for Service | Mustered In. When | Mustered In. Where | Period | Mustered Out. When | Mustered Out. Where |
|---|---|---|---|---|---|---|---|---|
| 1 | Stephen Ormsby | Colonel | May 17, 1846 | May 17, '46 | Louisville, Ky. | 1 yr. | May 17, '47 | New Orleans Bks. |
| 2 | Jason Rogers | Lieut. Colonel | May 17, 1846 | May 17, '46 | Louisville, Ky. | 1 yr. | May 17, '47 | New Orleans Bks. |
| 3 | John B. Shepherd | Major | May 17, 1846 | May 17, '46 | Louisville, Ky. | 1 yr. | May 17, '47 | New Orleans Bks. |
| 4 | William Riddle | Adjutant | May 17, 1846 | May 17, '46 | Louisville, Ky. | 1 yr. | May 17, '47 | New Orleans Bks. |
| 5 | Henry C. Long | Quartermaster | May 17, 1846 | May 17, '46 | Louisville, Ky. | 1 yr. | May 17, '47 | New Orleans Bks. |
| 6 | Thomas L. Caldwell | Surgeon | May 17, 1846 | May 17, '46 | Louisville, Ky. | 1 yr. | May 17, '47 | New Orleans Bks. |
| 7 | John S. Matthews | Ass't Surgeon | May 17, 1846 | May 17, '46 | Louisville, Ky. | 1 yr. | May 17, '47 | New Orleans Bks. |
| 8 | William Duerson, Jr. | Ass't. Com'y | May 17, 1846 | May 17, '46 | Louisville, Ky. | 1 yr. | May 17, '47 | New Orleans Bks. |
|   | **Non-Com. Staff.** | | | | | | | |
| 1 | Thomas B. Ferguson | Sergeant Major | May 17, 1846 | May 17, '46 | Louisville, Ky. | 1 yr. | May 17, '47 | New Orleans Bks. |
| 2 | Henry C. Spurrier | Qr. M. Serg't | May 17, 1846 | May 17, '46 | Louisville, Ky. | 1 yr. | May 17, '47 | New Orleans Bks. |
|   | **Discharged.** | | | | | | | |
| 1 | Thomas W. Scott | Sergeant Major | May 17, 1846 | May 17, '46 | Louisville, Ky. | 1 yr. | May 17, '47 | New Orleans Bks. |

## ROLL OF COMPANY "A," FIRST REGIMENT KENTUCKY

| No. | Name | Rank | Joined for Service | Mustered In. When | Mustered In. Where | Period | Mustered Out. When | Mustered Out. Where |
|---|---|---|---|---|---|---|---|---|
| 1 | O. H. Harper | Captain | May 17, 1846 | May 17, '46 | Louisville, Ky. | 1 yr | May 17, '47 | New Orleans Bks. |
| 1 | W. A. Fisher | 1st Lieutenant | May 17, 1846 | May 17, '46 | Louisville, Ky. | 1 yr | May 17, '47 | New Orleans Bks. |
| 2 | L. B. White | 2d Lieutenant | May 17, 1846 | May 17, '46 | Louisville, Ky. | 1 yr | May 17, '47 | New Orleans Bks. |
| 3 | R. F. Maury | 2d Lieutenant | May 17, 1846 | May 17, '46 | Louisville, Ky. | 1 yr | May 17, '47 | New Orleans Bks. |
| 1 | James Hazlit | 1st Sergeant | May 17, 1846 | May 17, '46 | Louisville, Ky. | 1 yr | May 17, '47 | New Orleans Bks. |
| 2 | L. S. Mosby | 2d Sergeant | May 17, 1846 | May 17, '46 | Louisville, Ky. | 1 yr | May 17, '47 | New Orleans Bks. |
| 3 | Noah Grant | 3d Sergeant | May 17, 1846 | May 17, '46 | Louisville, Ky. | 1 yr | May 17, '47 | New Orleans Bks. |
| 4 | William Williams | 4th Sergeant | May 17, 1846 | May 17, '46 | Louisville, Ky. | 1 yr | May 17, '47 | New Orleans Bks. |
| 1 | Robt. W. Tompkins | 1st Corporal | May 17, 1846 | May 17, '46 | Louisville, Ky. | 1 yr | May 17, '47 | New Orleans Bks. |
| 2 | Theodore Bland | 2d Corporal | May 17, 1846 | May 17, '46 | Louisville, Ky. | 1 yr | May 17, '47 | New Orleans Bks. |
| 3 | James Simon | 3d Corporal | May 17, 1846 | May 17, '46 | Louisville, Ky. | 1 yr | May 17, '47 | New Orleans Bks. |
| 4 | Jeremiah Huber | 4th Corporal | May 17, 1846 | May 17, '46 | Louisville, Ky. | 1 yr | May 17, '47 | New Orleans Bks. |
| 1 | Austin, Felix | Private | May 17, 1846 | May 17, '46 | Louisville, Ky. | 1 yr | May 17, '47 | New Orleans Bks. |
| 2 | Allen, Charles | Private | May 17, 1846 | May 17, '46 | Louisville, Ky. | 1 yr | May 17, '47 | New Orleans Bks. |
| 3 | Armstrong, Geo. | Private | May 17, 1846 | May 17, '46 | Louisville, Ky. | 1 yr | May 17, '47 | New Orleans Bks. |
| 4 | Anderson, John | Private | May 17, 1846 | May 17, '46 | Louisville, Ky. | 1 yr | May 17, '47 | New Orleans Bks. |
| 5 | Broadwell, Silas | Private | May 17, 1846 | May 17, '46 | Louisville, Ky. | 1 yr | May 17, '47 | New Orleans Bks. |
| 6 | Bull, Jno. Randolph | Private | May 17, 1846 | May 17, '46 | Louisville, Ky. | 1 yr | May 17, '47 | New Orleans Bks. |
| 7 | Bell, Simeon P. | Private | May 17, 1846 | May 17, '46 | Louisville, Ky. | 1 yr | May 17, '47 | New Orleans Bks. |
| 8 | Barker, Sam'l W. | Private | May 17, 1846 | May 17, '46 | Louisville, Ky. | 1 yr | May 17, '47 | New Orleans Bks. |
| 9 | Bache, Franklin | Private | May 17, 1846 | May 17, '46 | Louisville, Ky. | 1 yr | May 17, '47 | New Orleans Bks. |
| 10 | Buck, Thomas H. | Private | May 17, 1846 | May 17, '46 | Louisville, Ky. | 1 yr | May 17, '47 | New Orleans Bks. |
| 11 | Birkhead, Nelson B. | Private | May 17, 1846 | May 17, '46 | Louisville, Ky. | 1 yr | May 17, '47 | New Orleans Bks. |
| 12 | Curry, Robert | Private | May 17, 1846 | May 17, '46 | Louisville, Ky. | 1 yr | May 17, '47 | New Orleans Bks. |
| 13 | Cox, Thomas | Private | May 17, 1846 | May 17, '46 | Louisville, Ky. | 1 yr | May 17, '47 | New Orleans Bks. |
| 14 | Clagett, Hezekiah | Private | May 17, 1846 | May 17, '46 | Louisville, Ky. | 1 yr | May 17, '47 | New Orleans Bks. |
| 15 | Clarke, Lafayette W. | Private | May 17, 1846 | May 17, '46 | Louisville, Ky. | 1 yr | May 17, '47 | New Orleans Bks. |
| 16 | Crawford, George W. | Private | May 17, 1846 | May 17, '46 | Louisville, Ky. | 1 yr | May 17, '47 | New Orleans Bks. |
| 17 | Cannon, Edward G. | Private | May 17, 1846 | May 17, '46 | Louisville, Ky. | 1 yr | May 17, '47 | New Orleans Bks. |
| 18 | Cooper, Archibald | Private | May 17, 1846 | May 17, '46 | Louisville, Ky. | 1 yr | May 17, '47 | New Orleana Bks. |
| 19 | Dashiell, Geo. W. | Private | May 17, 1846 | May 17, '46 | Louisville, Ky. | 1 yr | May 17, '47 | New Orleans Bks. |
| 20 | Fisher, Victor F. | Private | May 17, 1846 | May 17, '46 | Louisville, Ky. | 1 yr | May 17, '47 | New Orleans Bks. |
| 21 | Fuller, Benj. P. | Private | May 17, 1846 | May 17, '46 | Louisville, Ky. | 1 yr | May 17, '47 | New Orleans Bks. |
| 22 | Fox, Hugh | Private | May 17, 1846 | May 17, '46 | Louisville, Ky. | 1 yr | May 17, '47 | New Orleans Bks. |
| 23 | Grosh, Jacob | Private | May 17, 1846 | May 17, '46 | Louisville, Ky. | 1 yr | May 17, '47 | New Orleans Bks. |
| 24 | George, Theophelius | Private | May 17, 1846 | May 17, '46 | Louisville, Ky. | 1 yr | May 17, '47 | New Orleans Bks. |
| 25 | Gilliss, George | Private | May 17, 1846 | May 17, '46 | Louisville, Ky. | 1 yr | May 17, '47 | New Orleans Bks. |
| 26 | Graff, Felix | Private | May 17, 1846 | May 17, '46 | Louisville, Ky. | 1 yr | May 17, '47 | New Orleans Bks. |
| 27 | Green, James | Private | May 17, 1846 | May 17, '46 | Louisville, Ky. | 1 yr | May 17, '47 | New Orleans Bks. |
| 28 | Guinan, John | Private | May 17, 1846 | May 17, '46 | Louisville, Ky. | 1 yr | May 17, '47 | New Orleans Bks. |
| 29 | Huber, James H. | Private | May 17, 1846 | May 17, '46 | Louisville, Ky. | 1 yr | May 17, '47 | New Orleans Bks. |
| 30 | Hockersmith, Dan. J. | Private | May 17, 1846 | May 17, '46 | Louisville, Ky. | 1 yr | May 17, '47 | New Orleans Bks. |
| 31 | Herr, John F. | Private | May 17, 1846 | May 17, '46 | Louisville, Ky. | 1 yr | May 17, '47 | New Orleans Bks. |
| 32 | Kaye, Wm., Jr. | Private | May 17, 1846 | May 17, '46 | Louisville, Ky. | 1 yr | May 17, '47 | New Orleans Bks. |
| 33 | Kelly, James O. | Private | May 17, 1846 | May 17, '46 | Louisville, Ky. | 1 yr | May 17, '47 | New Orleans Bks. |
| 34 | Lighton, Andrew D. | Private | May 17, 1846 | May 17, '46 | Louisville, Ky. | 1 yr | May 17, '47 | New Orleans Bks. |
| 35 | Lacey, Wm. H. | Private | May 17, 1846 | May 17, '46 | Louisville, Ky. | 1 yr | May 17, '47 | New Orleans Bks. |
| 36 | Levering, Charles W. | Private | May 17, 1846 | May 17, '46 | Louisville, Ky. | 1 yr | May 17, '47 | New Orleans Bks. |
| 37 | Luke, Henry | Private | May 17, 1846 | May 17, '46 | Louisville, Ky. | 1 yr | May 17, '47 | New Orleans Bks. |
| 38 | McGarrity, James | Private | May 17, 1846 | May 17, '46 | Louisville, Ky. | 1 yr | May 17, '47 | New Orleans Bks. |
| 39 | McMichael, Andrew M. | Private | May 17, 1846 | May 17, '46 | Louisville, Ky. | 1 yr | May 17, '47 | New Orleans Bks. |
| 40 | Mercer, Henry O. | Private | May 17, 1846 | May 17, '46 | Louisville, Ky. | 1 yr | May 17, '47 | New Orleans Bks. |
| 41 | Mercer, James T. | Private | May 17, 1846 | May 17, '46 | Louisville, Ky. | 1 yr | May 17, '47 | New Orleans Bks. |

# KENTUCKY FOOT VOLUNTEERS—MEXICAN WAR.

| No. of each grade | REMARKS. |
|---|---|
| 1 | |
| 2 | |
| 3 | |
| 4 | |
| 5 | Absent on furlough for 60 days, from 14th December, 1846, and has not since joined the regiment. |
| 6 | Commissioned as Surgeon by the President of the United States. Not mustered out. |
| 7 | Commissioned as Assistant Surgeon by the President of the United States. Not mustered out. |
| 8 | Appointed by the President Commissary, with the rank of Captain, 9th March, 1847; promoted from 2d Lieutenant, "H" Company. Not [mustered out. |
| 1 | Appointed 1st September, 1846, from private, in Captain Harper's "A" Company. [has not yet been paid. |
| 2 | Acted as Commissary Sergeant in addition to his duty as Quartermaster Sergeant from 17th May, 1846, and 23d August, 1846, for which he |
| 1 | Discharged at Camargo, 26th August, 1847, on account of disability arising from disease in service. |

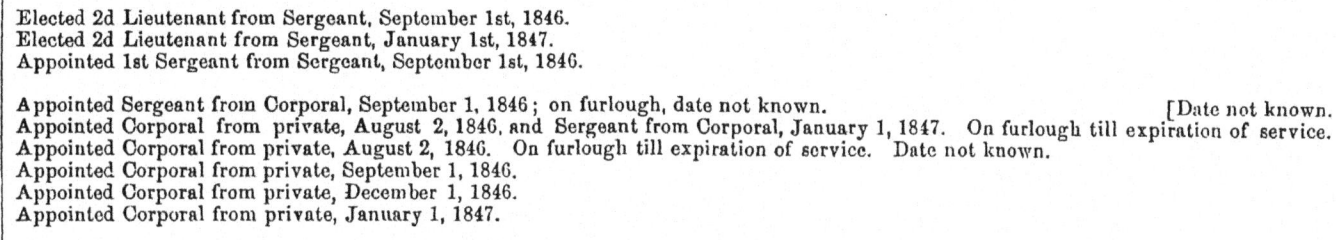

# FOOT VOLUNTEERS—MEXICAN WAR.

| | |
|---|---|
| 1 | |
| 1 | |
| 2 | Elected 2d Lieutenant from Sergeant, September 1st, 1846. |
| 3 | Elected 2d Lieutenant from Sergeant, January 1st, 1847. |
| 1 | Appointed 1st Sergeant from Sergeant, September 1st, 1846. |
| 2 | |
| 3 | Appointed Sergeant from Corporal, September 1, 1846; on furlough, date not known. [Date not known. |
| 4 | Appointed Corporal from private, August 2, 1846, and Sergeant from Corporal, January 1, 1847. On furlough till expiration of service. |
| 1 | Appointed Corporal from private, August 2, 1846. On furlough till expiration of service. Date not known. |
| 2 | Appointed Corporal from private, September 1, 1846. |
| 3 | Appointed Corporal from private, December 1, 1846. |
| 4 | Appointed Corporal from private, January 1, 1847. |
| 1 | |
| 2 | |
| 3 | |
| 4 | |
| 5 | |
| 6 | |
| 7 | |
| 8 | Furloughed to 17th May, 1847, since 28th April, 1847. Descriptive roll furnished him. |
| 9 | |
| 10 | |
| 11 | |
| 12 | |
| 13 | |
| 14 | |
| 15 | |
| 16 | In the hands of the enemy; captured near Marin, Mexico, February 24, 1847, whilst escorting wagon train. |
| 17 | |
| 18 | |
| 19 | |
| 20 | |
| 21 | |
| 22 | |
| 23 | |
| 24 | |
| 25 | |
| 26 | |
| 27 | |
| 28 | Furloughed to 17th May, 1847, since 28th April, 1847, and furnished with descriptive roll. |
| 29 | |
| 30 | |
| 31 | |
| 32 | |
| 33 | |
| 34 | |
| 35 | |
| 36 | |
| 37 | |
| 38 | Furloughed to 17th May, 1847, since 28th April, 1847, and furnished with descriptive roll. |
| 39 | |
| 40 | |
| 41 | |

## ROLL OF COMPANY "A," FIRST REGIMENT KENTUCKY

| No. of each grade. | Name. | Rank. | Joined for Service. | Mustered In. When. | Mustered In. Where. | Period | Mustered Out. When. | Mustered Out. Where. |
|---|---|---|---|---|---|---|---|---|
| 42 | Mackison, Richard | Private | May 17, 1846 | May 17, '46 | Louisville, Ky. | 1 yr. | May 17, '47 | New Orleans Bks. |
| 43 | Mills, Robert | Private | May 17, 1846 | May 17, '46 | Louisville, Ky. | 1 yr. | May 17, '47 | New Orleans Bks. |
| 44 | McClure, Solomon | Private | May 17, 1846 | May 17, '46 | Louisville, Ky. | 1 yr. | May 17, '47 | New Orleans Bks. |
| 45 | McCormeck, James T. | Private | May 17, 1846 | May 17, '46 | Louisville, Ky. | 1 yr. | May 17, '47 | New Orleans Bks. |
| 46 | Massie, James | Private | May 17, 1846 | May 17, '46 | Louisville, Ky. | 1 yr. | May 17, '47 | New Orleans Bks. |
| 47 | McMurtry, Geo. W. | Private | May 17, 1846 | May 17, '46 | Louisville, Ky. | 1 yr. | May 17, '47 | New Orleans Bks. |
| 48 | Owen, John L. | Private | May 17, 1846 | May 17, '46 | Louisville, Ky. | 1 yr. | May 17, '47 | New Orleans Bks. |
| 49 | Owen, L. D. | Private | May 17, 1846 | May 17, '46 | Louisville, Ky. | 1 yr. | May 17, '47 | New Orleans Bks. |
| 50 | Osborne, Charles | Private | May 17, 1846 | May 17, '46 | Louisville, Ky. | 1 yr. | May 17, '47 | New Orleans Bks. |
| 51 | Proctor, Wm. G. | Private | May 17, 1846 | May 17, '46 | Louisville, Ky. | 1 yr. | May 17, '47 | New Orleans Bks. |
| 52 | Poor, Standish F. | Private | May 17, 1846 | May 17, '46 | Louisville, Ky. | 1 yr. | May 17, '47 | New Orleans Bks. |
| 53 | Prather, James S. | Private | May 17, 1846 | May 17, '46 | Louisville, Ky. | 1 yr. | May 17, '47 | New Orleans Bks. |
| 54 | Henry, R. | Private | May 17, 1846 | May 17, '46 | Louisville, Ky. | 1 yr. | May 17, '47 | New Orleans Bks. |
| 55 | Phillips, John R. | Private | May 17, 1846 | May 17, '46 | Louisville, Ky. | 1 yr. | May 17, '47 | New Orleans Bks. |
| 56 | Parrent, John | Private | May 17, 1846 | May 17, '46 | Louisville, Ky. | 1 yr. | May 17, '47 | New Orleans Bks. |
| 57 | Phillips, Gilbert A. | Private | May 17, 1846 | May 17, '46 | Louisville, Ky. | 1 yr. | May 17, '47 | New Orleans Bks. |
| 58 | Pinkston, Thomas | Private | May 17, 1846 | May 17, '46 | Louisville, Ky. | 1 yr. | May 17, '47 | New Orleans Bks. |
| 59 | Seabough, John | Private | May 17, 1846 | May 17, '46 | Louisville, Ky. | 1 yr. | May 17, '47 | New Orleans Bks. |
| 60 | Stoy, David C. | Private | May 17, 1846 | May 17, '46 | Louisville, Ky. | 1 yr. | May 17, '47 | New Orleans Bks. |
| 61 | Stevenson, Sam'l G. | Private | May 17, 1846 | May 17, '46 | Louisville, Ky. | 1 yr. | May 17, '47 | New Orleans Bks. |
| 62 | Thompson, James A. | Private | May 17, 1846 | May 17, '46 | Louisville, Ky. | 1 yr. | May 17, '47 | New Orleans Bks. |
| 63 | Todd, John | Private | May 17, 1846 | May 17, '46 | Louisville, Ky. | 1 yr. | May 17, '47 | New Orleans Bks. |
| 64 | Williams, Alonzo | Private | May 17, 1846 | May 17, '46 | Louisville, Ky. | 1 yr. | May 17, '47 | New Orleans Bks. |
| 65 | Wigginton, E. G. | Private | May 17, 1846 | May 17, '46 | Louisville, Ky. | 1 yr. | May 17, '47 | New Orleans Bks. |
| 66 | Watson, John | Private | May 17, 1846 | May 17, '46 | Louisville, Ky. | 1 yr. | May 17, '47 | New Orleans Bks. |
| 67 | Woolfalk, E. H. T. | Private | May 17, 1846 | May 17, '46 | Louisville, Ky. | 1 yr. | May 17, '47 | New Orleans Bks. |
| 68 | Willard, George W. | Private | May 17, 1846 | May 17, '46 | Louisville, Ky. | 1 yr. | May 17, '47 | New Orleans Bks. |
| | **TRANSFERRED.** | | | | | | | |
| 1 | Butler, J. Russell | 2d Corporal | May 17, 1846 | May 17, '46 | Louisville, Ky. | 1 yr. | | |
| 2 | Ferguson, Thomas B. | Private | May 17, 1846 | May 17, '46 | Louisville, Ky. | 1 yr. | | |
| | **DISCHARGED.** | | | | | | | |
| 1 | Bower, R. F. | Private | May 17, 1846 | May 17, '46 | Louisville, Ky. | 1 yr. | | |
| 2 | Carey, Thomas | 1st Sergeant | May 17, 1846 | May 17, '46 | Louisville, Ky. | 1 yr. | | |
| 3 | Cress, Sam'l F. | Private | May 17, 1846 | May 17, '46 | Louisville, Ky. | 1 yr. | | |
| 4 | Dean, Austin E. | Private | May 17, 1846 | May 17, '46 | Louisville, Ky. | 1 yr. | | |
| 5 | Bibb, Loyd | Private | May 17, 1846 | May 17, '46 | Louisville, Ky. | 1 yr. | | |
| 6 | Taylor, James W. | Private | May 17, 1846 | May 17, '46 | Louisville, Ky. | 1 yr. | | |
| 7 | Gobin, Harrison A. | Private | May 17, 1846 | May 17, '46 | Louisville, Ky. | 1 yr. | | |
| 8 | Olivers, Thomas L. | Private | May 17, 1846 | May 17, '46 | Louisville, Ky. | 1 yr. | | |
| 9 | Fletcher, John | Private | May 17, 1846 | May 17, '46 | Louisville, Ky. | 1 yr. | | |
| 10 | Bligh, Delos F. | Private | May 17, 1846 | May 17, '46 | Louisville, Ky. | 1 yr. | | |
| 11 | Owings, Luther C. | Private | May 17, 1846 | May 17, '46 | Louisville, Ky. | 1 yr. | | |
| 12 | Schell, Francis M. | Private | May 17, 1846 | May 17, '46 | Louisville, Ky. | 1 yr. | | |
| 13 | Taylor, Lewis | Private | May 17, 1846 | May 17, '46 | Louisville, Ky. | 1 yr. | | |
| 14 | Cacke, Thomas | Private | May 17, 1846 | May 17, '46 | Louisville, Ky. | 1 yr. | | |
| 15 | Kaye, George | Private | May 17, 1846 | May 17, '46 | Louisville, Ky. | 1 yr. | | |
| 16 | Simmons, Harrison G. | Private | May 17, 1846 | May 17, '46 | Louisville, Ky. | 1 yr. | | |
| | **RESIGNED.** | | | | | | | |
| 1 | Joseph Peterson | 1st Lieutenant | May 17, 1846 | May 17, '46 | Louisville, Ky. | 1 yr. | | |
| | **DESERTED.** | | | | | | | |
| 1 | Longe, Anthony | Private | May 17, 1846 | May 17, '46 | Louisville, Ky. | 1 yr. | | |

## ROLL OF COMPANY "B," FIRST REGIMENT KENTUCKY

| | | | | | | | | |
|---|---|---|---|---|---|---|---|---|
| 1 | Frank Saunders | Captain | May 17, 1846 | May 17, '46 | Louisville, Ky. | 1 yr. | May 17, '47 | New Orleans Bks. |
| 1 | John J. Huff | 1st Lieutenant | May 17, 1846 | May 17, '46 | Louisville, Ky. | 1 yr. | May 17, '47 | New Orleans Bks. |
| 1 | W. E. Jones | 2d Lieutenant | May 17, 1846 | May 17, '46 | Louisville, Ky. | 1 yr. | May 17, '47 | New Orleans Bks. |
| 2 | C. W. Hilton | 2d Lieutenant | May 17, 1846 | May 17, '46 | Louisville, Ky. | 1 yr. | May 17, '47 | New Orleans Bks. |
| 1 | Robards, Squires S. | 1st Sergeant | May 17, 1846 | May 17, '46 | Louisville, Ky. | 1 yr. | May 17, '47 | New Orleans Bks. |
| 2 | Reid, Tilly W. | 2d Sergeant | May 17, 1846 | May 17, '46 | Louisville, Ky. | 1 yr. | May 17, '47 | New Orleans Bks. |
| 3 | Jones, Benjamin | 3d Sergeant | May 17, 1846 | May 17, '46 | Louisville, Ky. | 1 yr. | May 17, '47 | New Orleans Bks. |
| 4 | Aylward, John | 4th Sergeant | May 17, 1846 | May 17, '46 | Louisville, Ky. | 1 yr. | May 17, '47 | New Orleans Bks. |
| 1 | Britten, William | Corporal | May 17, 1846 | May 17, '46 | Louisville, Ky. | 1 yr. | May 17, '47 | New Orleans Bks. |
| 2 | Robison, William | Corporal | May 17, 1846 | May 17, '46 | Louisville, Ky. | 1 yr. | May 17, '47 | New Orleans Bks. |
| 3 | Pearson, Alonzo | Corporal | May 17, 1846 | May 17, '46 | Louisville, Ky. | 1 yr. | May 17, '47 | New Orleans Bks. |
| 4 | Moore, Peter | Corporal | May 17, 1846 | May 17, '46 | Louisville, Ky. | 1 yr. | May 17, '47 | New Orleans Bks. |

MEXICAN WAR VETERANS. 61

## FOOT VOLUNTEERS—MEXICAN WAR—Continued.

| No. of each grade | REMARKS. |
|---|---|
| 42 | |
| 43 | |
| 44 | |
| 45 | |
| 46 | |
| 47 | |
| 48 | |
| 49 | |
| 50 | |
| 51 | Hospital Steward to Regiment (10 Companies) since August 1, 1846. |
| 52 | |
| 53 | |
| 54 | |
| 55 | Furloughed from 28th April, 1847, to 17th May, 1847. Descriptive roll furnished him. |
| 56 | Left sick at Camargo, Mexico, September 6, 1846. |
| 57 | In the hands of the enemy; captured near Marin, Mexico, February 24, 1847, whilst escorting wagon train. |
| 58 | In the hands of the enemy; captured near Marin, Mexico, February 24, 1847, whilst escorting wagon train. |
| 59 | In the hands of the enemy; captured near Marin, Mexico, February 24, 1847, whilst escorting wagon train. |
| 60 | |
| 61 | Furloughed to 17th May, 1847, since 28th April, 1847, furnished with descriptive roll. |
| 62 | |
| 63 | |
| 64 | |
| 65 | |
| 66 | Sick at barracks hospital. |
| 67 | |
| 68 | |
| 1 | Appointed 2d Lieutenant in Captain Butler's (K) Company, 1st Regiment Kentucky Volunteers, July 8, 1846. |
| 2 | Appointed Sergeant Major September 1, 1846. |
| 1 | Discharged on Surgeon's certificate, July 31st, 1846, at Burieta, Mexico. |
| 2 | Discharged on Surgeon's certificate, August 2d, 1846, at Burieta, Mexico. |
| 3 | Discharged on Surgeon's certificate, August 2d, 1846, at Burieta, Mexico. |
| 4 | Discharged on Surgeon's certificate, August 2d, 1846, at Burieta, Mexico. |
| 5 | Discharged on Surgeon's certificate, August 2d, 1846, at Burieta, Mexico. |
| 6 | Discharged by order of Maj. Gen. Z. Taylor, August 2d, 1846, at Burieta, Mexico. |
| 7 | Discharged on Surgeon's certificate, August 2d, 1846 at Burieta, Mexico. |
| 8 | Discharged on Surgeon's certificate, August 29th, 1846, at Camargo, Mexico. |
| 9 | Discharged on Surgeon's certificate, August 29th, 1846, at Camargo, Mexico. |
| 10 | Discharged for disability at Monterey, Mexico, October 15th, 1846. |
| 11 | Discharged for disability at Camargo, Mexico, September 19th, 1846. |
| 12 | Discharged for disability at Camargo, Mexico, August 27th, 1846. |
| 13 | Had consent of proper officers for discharge, approved by Maj. Gen. Z. Taylor, August 27th, 1846. Left without certificate of discharge. |
| 14 | Discharged for disability at camp near Monterey, Mexico, November 30th, 1846. |
| 15 | Discharged by order of Major Gen. Thomas L. Hamer, camp near Monterey, Mexico, November 13th, 1846. |
| 16 | Discharged by order of Col. Ormsby, at Monterey, Mexico, April 5th, 1847. Descriptive roll furnished. |
| 1 | Resigned November 30th, 1846. |
| 1 | Furloughed for thirty days from September 6, 1846, by special requisition of G. H. Crossman, Assistant Quartermaster. Appointed by Col. Wm. R. McKee, 2d Regiment. Left without leave. |

## FOOT VOLUNTEERS—MEXICAN WAR.

| | |
|---|---|
| 1 | Absent since May 16, 1847, without leave. |
| 1 | Absent on leave at Camargo, since 10th April 1847. |
| 1 | Resigned 30th March, 1847, at Monterey, Mexico. |
| 2 | Promoted from 4th Sergeant from August 30, 1846. |
| 1 | First Sergeant from 17th May, 1846, to August 17, 1846. [master Department. |
| 2 | First Sergeant from 17th August to September 22, 1846; also First Sergeant December 5, 1846, to March 26, 1847; on furlough in Quarter- |
| 3 | First Sergeant 26th March, 1847, to this time. |
| 4 | Promoted from Corporal to Sergeant January 23, 1847; also from private to Corporal, 13th September, 1846. |
| 1 | Promoted from private to Corporal August —, 1846; on furlough at New Orleans till May 17, 1847. |
| 2 | |
| 3 | |
| 4 | Appointed Corporal from private 23d January, 1847; on furlough at Camargo till 17th May, 1847, as steamboat engineer. |

16

## MEXICAN WAR VETERANS.

### ROLL OF COMPANY "B," FIRST REGIMENT KENTUCKY

| No. of each grade | Name | Rank | Joined for Service | Mustered In. When | Mustered In. Where | Period | Mustered Out. When | Mustered Out. Where |
|---|---|---|---|---|---|---|---|---|
| 1 | Applegate, Elijah | Private | May 17, 1846 | May 17, '46 | Louisville, Ky. | 1 yr. | May 17, '47 | New Orleans Bks. |
| 2 | Arnold, Joshua | Private | May 17, 1846 | May 17, '46 | Louisville, Ky. | 1 yr. | May 17, '47 | New Orleans Bks. |
| 3 | Barth, Andrew | Private | May 17, 1846 | May 17, '46 | Louisville, Ky. | 1 yr. | May 17, '47 | New Orleans Bks. |
| 4 | Blevins, James | Private | May 17, 1846 | May 17, '46 | Louisville, Ky. | 1 yr. | May 17, '47 | New Orleans Bks. |
| 5 | Brown, William | Private | May 17, 1846 | May 17, '46 | Louisville, Ky. | 1 yr. | May 17, '47 | New Orleans Bks. |
| 6 | Berry, James M. | Private | May 17, 1846 | May 17, '46 | Louisville, Ky. | 1 yr. | May 17, '47 | New Orleans Bks. |
| 7 | Dolan, James | Private | May 17, 1846 | May 17, '46 | Louisville, Ky. | 1 yr. | May 17, '47 | New Orleans Bks. |
| 8 | Darkins, George | Private | May 17, 1846 | May 17, '46 | Louisville, Ky. | 1 yr. | May 17, '47 | New Orleans Bks. |
| 9 | Frederick, Charles | Private | May 17, 1846 | May 17, '46 | Louisville, Ky. | 1 yr. | May 17, '47 | New Orleans Bks. |
| 10 | Fox, Jacob | Private | May 17, 1846 | May 17, '46 | Louisville, Ky. | 1 yr. | May 17, '47 | New Orleans Bks. |
| 11 | Glass, William | Private | May 17, 1846 | May 17, '46 | Louisville, Ky. | 1 yr. | May 17, '47 | New Orleans Bks. |
| 12 | Graham, B. B. | Private | May 17, 1846 | May 17, '46 | Louisville, Ky. | 1 yr. | May 17, '47 | New Orleans Bks. |
| 13 | Howard, William | Private | May 17, 1846 | May 17, '46 | Louisville, Ky. | 1 yr. | May 17, '47 | New Orleans Bks. |
| 14 | Hughes, John | Private | May 17, 1846 | May 17, '46 | Louisville, Ky. | 1 yr. | May 17, '47 | New Orleans Bks. |
| 15 | Lyons, Leander | Private | May 17, 1846 | May 17, '46 | Louisville, Ky. | 1 yr. | May 17, '47 | New Orleans Bks. |
| 16 | Layton, John G. | Private | May 17, 1846 | May 17, '46 | Louisville, Ky. | 1 yr. | May 17, '47 | New Orleans Bks. |
| 17 | Mathorn, George | Private | May 17, 1846 | May 17, '46 | Louisville, Ky. | 1 yr. | May 17, '47 | New Orleans Bks. |
| 18 | Reynolds, George | Private | May 17, 1846 | May 17, '46 | Louisville, Ky. | 1 yr. | May 17, '47 | New Orleans Bks. |
| 19 | Richardson, John | Private | May 17, 1846 | May 17, '46 | Louisville, Ky. | 1 yr. | May 17, '47 | New Orleans Bks. |
| 20 | Richardson, Richard | Private | May 17, 1846 | May 17, '46 | Louisville, Ky. | 1 yr. | May 17, '47 | New Orleans Bks. |
| 21 | Shafar, Hugh S. | Private | May 17, 1846 | May 17, '46 | Louisville, Ky. | 1 yr. | May 17, '47 | New Orleans Bks. |
| 22 | Terrill, Uriah | Private | May 17, 1846 | May 17, '46 | Louisville, Ky. | 1 yr. | May 17, '47 | New Orleans Bks. |
| 23 | Wilcox, John | Private | May 17, 1846 | May 17, '46 | Louisville, Ky. | 1 yr. | May 17, '47 | New Orleans Bks. |
| 24 | Warren, Jael | Private | May 17, 1846 | May 17, '46 | Louisville, Ky. | 1 yr. | May 17, '47 | New Orleans Bks. |
| 25 | Columbus, T. | Private | May 17, 1846 | May 17, '46 | Louisville, Ky. | 1 yr. | May 17, '47 | New Orleans Bks. |
| 26 | Tilhart, Philip | Private | May 17, 1846 | May 17, '46 | Louisville, Ky. | 1 yr. | May 17, '47 | New Orleans Bks. |
| 27 | Swinney, Edmund | Private | June 4, 1846 | June 4, '46 | New Orleans, La. | 1 yr. | May 17, '47 | New Orleans Bks. |
| | **DISCHARGED.** | | | | | | | |
| 1 | Spurrier, Tevis | Private | May 17, 1846 | May 17, '46 | Louisville, Ky. | 1 yr. | | |
| 2 | Morrow, Alexander | Private | May 17, 1846 | May 17, '46 | Louisville, Ky. | 1 yr. | | |
| 3 | Ray, James | Private | May 17, 1846 | May 17, '46 | Louisville, Ky. | 1 yr. | | |
| 4 | Citizen, George | Private | May 17, 1846 | May 17, '46 | Louisville, Ky. | 1 yr. | | |
| 5 | Tuells, Charles | Private | May 17, 1846 | May 17, '46 | Louisville, Ky. | 1 yr. | | |
| 6 | Stafford, John | Private | May 17, 1846 | May 17, '46 | Louisville, Ky. | 1 yr. | | |
| 7 | Wisely, Robert | Private | May 17, 1846 | May 17, '46 | Louisville, Ky. | 1 yr. | | |
| 8 | Wells, William | Private | May 17, 1846 | May 17, '46 | Louisville, Ky. | 1 yr. | | |
| 9 | Bennett, John | Private | May 17, 1846 | May 17, '46 | Louisville, Ky. | 1 yr. | | |
| 10 | Stanfield, Joseph | Private | May 17, 1846 | May 17, '46 | Louisville, Ky. | 1 yr. | | |
| 11 | Tucker, George B. | Private | May 17, 1846 | May 17, '46 | Louisville, Ky. | 1 yr. | | |
| 12 | Triplett, Leroy | Private | May 17, 1846 | May 17, '46 | Louisville, Ky. | 1 yr. | | |
| 13 | Bailley, J. Q. A. | Private | May 17, 1846 | May 17, '46 | Louisville, Ky. | 1 yr. | | |
| 14 | Bird, Henry | Private | May 17, 1846 | May 17, '46 | Louisville, Ky. | 1 yr. | | |
| 15 | Delano, John | Private | May 17, 1846 | May 17, '46 | Louisville, Ky. | 1 yr. | | |
| 16 | Rutherford, Austin | Private | May 17, 1846 | May 17, '46 | Louisville, Ky. | 1 yr. | | |
| | **DIED.** | | | | | | | |
| 1 | Bookhart, John | Private | May 17, 1846 | May 17, '46 | Louisville, Ky. | 1 yr. | | |
| 2 | Brant, Jeremiah | Private | May 17, 1846 | May 17, '46 | Louisville, Ky. | 1 yr. | | |
| 3 | Brightbill, Thomas | Private | May 17, 1846 | May 17, '46 | Louisville, Ky. | 1 yr. | | |
| 4 | Minter, Joshua | Private | May 17, 1846 | May 17, '46 | Louisville, Ky. | 1 yr. | | |
| 5 | Wilkers, Parks | Private | May 17, 1846 | May 17, '46 | Louisville, Ky. | 1 yr. | | |
| 6 | Wiggins, James | Private | Aug. 17, 1846 | Aug. 17, '46 | Camargo, Mexico | 1 yr. | | |
| | **DESERTED.** | | | | | | | |
| 1 | Burrell, Walter | Private | May 17, 1846 | May 16, '46 | Louisville, Ky. | 1 yr. | | |
| 2 | Freeman, Finess | Private | May 17, 1846 | May 16, '46 | Louisville, Ky. | 1 yr. | | |
| 3 | McAllister, William | Private | May 17, 1846 | May 16, '46 | Louisville, Ky. | 1 yr. | | |
| 4 | Ross, John W. | Private | May 17, 1846 | May 16, '46 | Louisville, Ky. | 1 yr. | | |
| 5 | Morris, Daniel B. | Private | May 17, 1846 | May 16, '46 | Louisville, Ky. | 1 yr. | | |
| | **TRANSFERRED.** | | | | | | | |
| 1 | Dozier, Charles | Private | May 17, 1846 | May 17, '46 | Louisville, Ky. | 1 yr. | | |
| | **TAKEN PRISONER.** | | | | | | | |
| 1 | Cockrill, Robert | Private | May 17, 1846 | May 17, '46 | Louisville, Ky. | 1 yr. | | |

### ROLL OF COMPANY "C," FIRST REGIMENT KENTUCKY

| | | | | | | | | |
|---|---|---|---|---|---|---|---|---|
| 1 | Ebenezer B. Howe | Captain | May 17, 1846 | May 17, '46 | Louisville, Ky. | 1 yr. | May 17, '47 | New Orleans Bks. |
| 1 | George H. Sigler | 1st Lieutenant | May 17, 1846 | May 17, '46 | Louisville, Ky. | 1 yr. | May 17, '47 | New Orleans Bks. |

# MEXICAN WAR VETERANS. 63

## FOOT VOLUNTEERS—MEXICAN WAR—Continued.

| No. of each grade | REMARKS. |
|---|---|
| 1 | |
| 2 | |
| 3 | |
| 4 | |
| 5 | |
| 6 | |
| 7 | |
| 8 | |
| 9 | |
| 10 | |
| 11 | Sentenced by a general court-martial November 28, 1846, to forfeit all pay to that date, and to receive half pay during the remainder of his term of service; in arrest. |
| 12 | On furlough in Quartermaster Department at Monterey, till 17th May, 1847. |
| 13 | On furlough in Quartermaster Department at Camargo, till 17th May, 1847. |
| 14 | |
| 15 | On furlough in Quartermaster Department at Monterey, till 17th May, 1847. |
| 16 | |
| 17 | |
| 18 | |
| 19 | |
| 20 | |
| 21 | |
| 22 | |
| 23 | |
| 24 | |
| 25 | |
| 26 | |
| 27 | |
| | |
| 1 | Discharged August 2d, 1846, at Burieta, Mexico, on Surgeon's certificate. |
| 2 | Discharged August 2d, 1846, at Burieta, Mexico, on Surgeon's certificate. |
| 3 | Discharged August 2d, 1846, at Burieta, Mexico, on Surgeon's certificate. |
| 4 | Discharged August 17th, 1846, at Camargo, on Surgeon's certificate. |
| 5 | Discharged August 17th, 1846, at Camargo, on Surgeon's certificate. |
| 6 | Discharged August 17th, 1846, at Camargo, on Surgeon's certificate. |
| 7 | Discharged August 17th, 1846, at Camargo, on Surgeon's certificate. |
| 8 | Discharged August 17th, 1846, at Camargo, on Surgeon's certificate. |
| 9 | Discharged August 17th, 1846, at Camargo, on Surgeon's certificate. |
| 10 | Discharged August 17th, 1846, at Camargo, on Surgeon's certificate. |
| 11 | Discharged January 31st, 1847, at Monterey, Mexico, on Surgeon's certificate. |
| 12 | Discharged March 13th, 1847, at Monterey, Mexico, on Surgeon's certificate. |
| 13 | Discharged August 17, 1846, at Camargo, Mexico, on Surgeon's certificate. |
| 14 | Discharged August 17, 1846, at Camargo, Mexico, on Surgeon's certificate. |
| 15 | Discharged August 17, 1846, at Camargo, Mexico, on Surgeon's certificate. |
| 16 | Discharged November 11, 1846, at Monterey, Mexico, on Surgeon's certificate. |
| | |
| 1 | Died November 1, 1846, at Monterey, Mexico. |
| 2 | Died June 25, 1846, at hospital, Matamoras. |
| 3 | Died August 25, 1846, at Burieta, Mexico. |
| 4 | Died August 30, 1846, at Camargo. |
| 5 | Died August 1, 1846, at Burieta, Mexico. |
| 6 | Killed accidentally by officer of the day, March 20, 1847, at Monterey, Mexico. |
| | |
| 1 | Deserted June 4, 1846, at New Orleans, La. |
| 2 | Deserted June 4, 1846, at New Orleans, La. |
| 3 | Deserted June 4, 1846, at New Orleans, La. |
| 4 | Deserted June 4, 1846, at New Orleans, La. |
| 5 | Deserted at Monterey, Mexico, April 18, 1847. |
| | |
| 1 | Transferred to Company "E," 1st Regiment Kentucky Volunteers, at Brazos Santiago, 19th June, 1846, by order. |
| | |
| 1 | Taken prisoner by the Mexicans, near Marin, Mexico, February 24, 1847. Supposed to be in the city of Mexico. |

## FOOT VOLUNTEERS—MEXICAN WAR.

| | |
|---|---|
| 1 | |
| 1 | Promoted by election from Sergeant, March 2, 1847, vice Dearing, resigned. |

## MEXICAN WAR VETERANS.

### ROLL OF COMPANY "C," FIRST REGIMENT KENTUCKY

| No. of each grade. | Name. | Rank. | Joined for Service. | Mustered In. When. | Mustered In. Where. | Period. | Mustered Out. When. | Mustered Out. Where. |
|---|---|---|---|---|---|---|---|---|
| 1 | Samuel Withington | 2d Lieutenant | May 17, 1846. | May 17,'46. | Louisville, Ky. | 1 yr. | May 17,'47. | New Orleans Bks. |
| 1 | Marshall Brashear | 1st Sergeant | May 17, 1846. | May 17,'46. | Louisville, Ky. | 1 yr. | May 17,'47. | New Orleans Bks. |
| 2 | John Rhea | 2d Sergeant | May 17, 1846. | May 17,'46. | Louisville, Ky. | 1 yr. | May 17,'47. | New Orleans Bks. |
| 3 | William Miller | 3d Sergeant | May 17, 1846. | May 17,'46. | Louisville, Ky. | 1 yr. | May 17,'47. | New Orleans Bks. |
| 4 | John C. Harris | 4th Sergeant | June 19, 1846. | June 19,'46. | Louisville, Ky. | 1 yr. | May 17,'47. | New Orleans Bks. |
| 1 | Nooman L. Dixon | 1st Corporal | May 17, 1846. | May 17,'46. | Louisville, Ky. | 1 yr. | May 17,'47. | New Orleans Bks. |
| 2 | William S. Mathews | Corporal | May 17, 1846. | May 17,'46. | Louisville, Ky. | 1 yr. | May 17,'47. | New Orleans Bks. |
| 3 | John D. Jenkins | Corporal | May 17, 1846. | May 17,'46. | Louisville, Ky. | 1 yr. | May 17,'47. | New Orleans Bks. |
| 4 | William Parsons | Corporal | May 17, 1846. | May 17,'46. | Louisville, Ky. | 1 yr. | May 17,'47. | New Orleans Bks. |
| 1 | Armstrong, Robert | Private | May 17, 1846. | May 17,'46. | Louisville, Ky. | 1 yr. | May 17,'47. | New Orleans Bks. |
| 2 | Batman, William | Private | May 17, 1846. | May 17,'46. | Louisville, Ky. | 1 yr. | May 17,'47. | New Orleans Bks. |
| 3 | Beckwith, Elisha | Private | May 17, 1846. | May 17,'46. | Louisville, Ky. | 1 yr. | May 17,'47. | New Orleans Bks. |
| 4 | Brown, John A. | Private | May 17, 1846. | May 17,'46. | Louisville, Ky. | 1 yr | May 17,'47. | New Orleans Bks. |
| 5 | Burrett, George | Private | May 17, 1846. | May 17,'46. | Louisville, Ky. | 1 yr. | May 17,'47. | New Orleans Bks. |
| 6 | Buchholtz, Archibald | Private | May 17, 1846. | May 17,'46. | Louisville, Ky. | 1 yr. | May 17 '47. | New Orleans Bks. |
| 7 | Cox, Samuel | Private | May 17, 1846. | May 17,'46. | Louisville, Ky. | 1 yr. | May 17,'47. | New Orleans Bks. |
| 8 | Cabel, Jerry | Private | May 17, 1846. | May 17,'46. | Louisville, Ky. | 1 yr. | May 17,'47. | New Orleans Bks. |
| 9 | Croxton, William H. | Private | May 17, 1846. | May 17,'46. | Louisville, Ky. | 1 yr. | May 17,'47. | New Orleans Bks. |
| 10 | Davis, Cristopher C. | Private | May 17, 1846. | May 17,'46. | Louisville, Ky. | 1 yr. | May 17,'47. | New Orleans Bks. |
| 11 | Davis, John | Private | May 17, 1846. | May 17,'46. | Louisville, Ky. | 1 yr. | May 17,'47. | New Orleans Bks. |
| 12 | Double, Isaac | Private | May 17, 1846. | May 17,'46. | Louisville, Ky. | 1 yr. | May 17,'47. | New Orleans Bks. |
| 13 | Dougherty, John | Private | May 17, 1846. | May 17,'46. | Louisville, Ky. | 1 yr. | May 17,'47. | New Orleans Bks. |
| 14 | Exner, Casper | Private | May 17, 1846. | May 17,'46. | Louisville, Ky. | 1 yr. | May 17,'47. | New Orleans Bks. |
| 15 | Grey, Griffith | Private | May 17, 1846. | May 17,'46. | Louisville, Ky. | 1 yr. | May 17 '47 | New Orleans Bks. |
| 16 | Hann, Ferdinand | Private | May 17, 1846. | May 17,'46. | Louisville, Ky. | 1 yr. | May 17,'47 | New Orleans Bks. |
| 17 | Hale, James B. | Private | May 17, 1846. | May 17,'46. | Louisville, Ky. | 1 yr. | May 17,'47. | New Orleans Bks. |
| 18 | Harrison, Henry | Private | May 17, 1846. | May 17,'46. | Louisville, Ky. | 1 yr. | May 17,'47. | New Orleans Bks. |
| 19 | Jenkins, Horace | Private | May 17, 1846. | May 17,'46. | Louisville, Ky. | 1 yr. | May 17,'47. | New Orleans Bks. |
| 20 | Lyons, Fletcher | Private | May 17, 1846. | May 17,'46. | Louisville, Ky. | 1 yr. | May 17,'47. | New Orleans Bks. |
| 21 | Lybarger, Daniel | Private | May 17, 1846. | May 17,'46. | Louisville, Ky. | 1 yr. | May 17,'47. | New Orleans Bks. |
| 22 | Livers, Henry P. | Private | May 17, 1846. | May 17,'46. | Louisville, Ky. | 1 yr. | May 17,'47. | New Orleans Bks. |
| 23 | Lewis, Charles | Private | May 17, 1846 | May 17,'46. | Louisville, Ky. | 1 yr. | May 17,'47 | New Orleans Bks. |
| 24 | Mailey, Joseph | Private | May 17, 1846. | May 17,'46. | Louisville, Ky. | 1 yr. | May 17,'47 | New Orleans Bks. |
| 25 | Pangburn, John | Private | May 17, 1846. | May 17,'46. | Louisville, Ky. | 1 yr. | May 17,'47. | New Orleans Bks. |
| 26 | Pearman, Granville L. | Private | May 17, 1846. | May 17,'46. | Louisville, Ky. | 1 yr. | May 17,'47. | New Orleans Bks. |
| 27 | Quertermons, David B. | Private | May 17, 1846. | May 17,'46. | Louisville, Ky. | 1 yr. | May 17,'47. | New Orleans Bks. |
| 28 | Robinette, Moses | Private | May 17, 1846. | May 17,'46. | Louisville, Ky. | 1 yr. | May 17,'47. | New Orleans Bks. |
| 29 | Richard, John | Private | May 17, 1846. | May 17,'46 | Louisville, Ky. | 1 yr. | May 17,'47. | New Orleans Bks. |
| 30 | Smith, Madison M. | Private | May 17, 1846. | May 17,'46. | Louisville, Ky. | 1 yr. | May 17,'47. | New Orleans Bks. |
| 31 | Somers, Andrew | Private | May 17, 1846. | May 17,'46. | Louisville, Ky. | 1 yr. | May 17,'47. | New Orleans Bks. |
| 32 | Sweeny, Joseph J. | Private | May 17, 1846. | May 17,'46. | Louisville, Ky. | 1 yr. | May 17,'47. | New Orleans Bks. |
| 33 | Stephens, Thomas | Private | May 17, 1846. | May 17,'46. | Louisville, Ky. | 1 yr. | May 17,'47. | New Orleans Bks. |
| 34 | Shade, John | Private | May 17, 1846. | May 17,'46. | Louisville, Ky. | 1 yr. | May 17,'47. | New Orleans Bks. |
| 35 | Vetter, John | Private | May 17, 1846. | May 17,'46. | Louisville, Ky. | 1 yr. | May 17,'47. | New Orleans Bks. |
| 36 | Vittitoe, Samuel | Private | May 17, 1846. | May 17,'46. | Louisville, Ky. | 1 yr. | May 17,'47. | New Orleans Bks. |
| 37 | Waterfield, Tholbert | Private | May 17, 1846. | May 17,'46. | Louisville, Ky. | 1 yr. | May 17,'47. | New Orleans Bks. |
| 38 | Waterbery, Abitha | Private | May 17, 1846. | May 17,'46. | Louisville, Ky. | 1 yr. | May 17,'47. | New Orleans Bks. |
| 39 | Warmeck, James A. | Private | May 17, 1846. | May 17,'46. | Louisville, Ky. | 1 yr. | May 17,'47. | New Orleans Bks. |
| 40 | Welsh, John | Private | May 17, 1846. | May 17,'46. | Louisville, Ky. | 1 yr. | May 17,'47. | New Orleans Bks. |
| 41 | Wells, Richard | Private | May 17, 1846. | May 17,'46. | Louisville, Ky. | 1 yr. | May 17,'47. | New Orleans Bks. |
|  | DISCHARGED. |  |  |  |  |  |  |  |
| 1 | Boggess, William K. | Private | May 17, 1846. | May 17,'46. | Louisville, Ky. | 1 yr. |  |  |
| 2 | Brown, John H. | Private | May 17, 1846. | May 17,'46. | Louisville, Ky. | 1 yr. |  |  |
| 3 | Barhyat, Garrett | Private | May 17, 1846. | May 17,'46. | Louisville, Ky. | 1 yr. |  |  |
| 4 | Creason, Edward | Private | May 17, 1846. | May 17,'46. | Louisville, Ky. | 1 yr. |  |  |
| 5 | McCormack, Daniel | Private | May 17, 1846. | May 17,'46. | Louisville, Ky. | 1 yr. |  |  |
| 6 | Ditsler, John F. | Private | May 17, 1846. | May 17,'46. | Louisville, Ky. | 1 yr. |  |  |
| 7 | Fig, James | Private | May 17, 1846. | May 17,'46. | Louisville, Ky. | 1 yr. |  |  |
| 8 | Gettleman, George | Private | May 17, 1846. | May 17,'46. | Louisville, Ky. | 1 yr. |  |  |
| 9 | Gettis, James | Private | May 17, 1846. | May 17,'46. | Louisville, Ky. | 1 yr. |  |  |
| 10 | Heritage, Thomas R. | Private | May 17, 1846. | May 17,'46. | Louisville, Ky. | 1 yr. |  |  |
| 11 | Morry, John | Private | May 17, 1846. | May 17,'46. | Louisville, Ky. | 1 yr. |  |  |
| 12 | Merritt, James | Private | May 17, 1846. | May 17,'46. | Louisville, Ky. | 1 yr. |  |  |
| 13 | Nangle, Benjamin F. | Private | May 17, 1846. | May 17,'46. | Louisville, Ky. | 1 yr. |  |  |
| 14 | Sheriden, James | Private | May 17, 1846. | May 17,'46. | Louisville, Ky. | 1 yr. |  |  |
| 15 | Tolbert, Presly | Private | May 17, 1846. | May 17,'46. | Louisville, Ky. | 1 yr. |  |  |
| 16 | Williams, Edward | Sergeant | May 17, 1846. | May 17,'46. | Louisville, Ky. | 1 yr. |  |  |
| 17 | Kauffman, Richard | Private | May 17, 1846. | May 17,'46. | Louisville, Ky. | 1 yr. |  |  |
| 18 | Porter, Samuel W. | Corporal | May 17, 1846. | May 17,'46. | Louisville, Ky. | 1 yr. |  |  |
|  | DIED. |  |  |  |  |  |  |  |
| 1 | Clark, Dennis | Private | May 17, 1846. | May 17,'46. | Louisville, Ky. | 1 yr. |  |  |
| 2 | Herman, John | Private | May 17, 1846. | May 17,'46. | Louisville, Ky. | 1 yr. |  |  |

MEXICAN WAR VETERANS. 65

# FOOT VOLUNTEERS—MEXICAN WAR—Continued.

| No. of each grade | REMARKS. |
|---|---|
| 1 | Promoted by election from private, March 2, 1847. |
| 1 | Promoted March 1, 1847, by appointment to 1st Sergeant from Sergeant. |
| 2 | Promoted March 1, 1847, by appointment to 2d Sergeant. |
| 3 | Promoted March 1, 1847, by appointment to 3d Sergeant. [Order Gen. Taylor. |
| 4 | Promoted March 1, 1847, by appointment to 4th Sergeant from Corporal; joined by transfer from 2d Regiment, Kentucky Volunteers. |
| 1 | |
| 2 | Promoted Corporal from private, March 1, 1847, by appointment. |
| 3 | Appointed Corporal from private, March 1, 1847. |
| 4 | Appointed Corporal from private, April 7, 1847. |
| 1 | |
| 2 | |
| 3 | |
| 4 | |
| 5 | |
| 6 | |
| 7 | |
| 8 | |
| 9 | Joined the Regiment April 21, 1847, from detached service. |
| 10 | Left with train for Camargo from Monterey, Mexico, February 23, 1847, under command of Lieut. Barber, and since been made prisoner. |
| 11 | |
| 12 | |
| 13 | |
| 14 | |
| 15 | |
| 16 | |
| 17 | |
| 18 | |
| 19 | |
| 20 | |
| 21 | |
| 22 | |
| 23 | |
| 24 | |
| 25 | |
| 26 | |
| 27 | |
| 28 | |
| 29 | |
| 30 | |
| 31 | |
| 32 | |
| 33 | |
| 34 | |
| 35 | |
| 36 | |
| 37 | |
| 38 | Left with train for Camargo from Monterey, Mex., February 18, 1847, under command of Lieut. Barber, and since taken prisoner. |
| 39 | Left with train for Camargo from Monterey, Mex., February 18, 1847, under command of Lieut. Barber, and since taken prisoner. |
| 40 | Left with train for Camargo from Monterey, Mex., February 18, 1847, under command of Lieut. Barber, and since taken prisoner. |
| 41 | |
| 1 | Discharged by reason of Surgeon's certificate, at Monterey, Mex., January 28, 1847. |
| 2 | Discharged by reason of Surgeon's certificate, at Camargo, Mex., August 30, 1846. |
| 3 | Discharged by reason of Surgeon's certificate, at Camargo, Mex., August 30, 1846. |
| 4 | Discharged by reason of Surgeon's certificate, at Monterey, Mex., November 28, 1846. |
| 5 | Discharged by reason of Surgeon's certificate, at Algiers, La., May 30, 1846. |
| 6 | Discharged by reason of Surgeon's certificate, at Camargo, Mex., November 24, 1846. |
| 7 | Discharged by reason of Surgeon's certificate, at Monterey, Mex., January 28, 1846. |
| 8 | Discharged by reason of Surgeon's certificate, at Camargo, Mex., August 30, 1846. |
| 9 | Discharged by order of Col. Ormsby, at Matamoras, Mex., August 10, 1846. |
| 10 | Discharged by reason of Surgeon's certificate, at Monterey, Mex., October 7, 1846. |
| 11 | Discharged by special order Major-General Z. Taylor, December 15, 1846, at Monterey, Mex. |
| 12 | Discharged by reason of Surgeon's certificate, at Monterey, Mex., November 28, 1846. |
| 13 | Discharged by order of L. Thomas, Adjutant-General, Inspector, at Camargo, Mex., October 20, 1846. |
| 14 | Discharged by reason of Surgeon's certificate, at Camargo, Mex., November 24, 1846. |
| 15 | Discharged by reason of Surgeon's certificate, at Camargo, Mex., October 30, 1846. |
| 16 | Discharged by reason of Surgeon's certificate, at Camargo, Mex., October 30, 1846. |
| 17 | Discharged by order of Col. Ormsby, at Camargo, Mex., September —, 1846. |
| 18 | Discharged by order of Col. Ormsby, at Monterey, Mex., April 7, 1846. |
| 1 | Supposed to have been killed by the Mexicans, November 22, 1846, near Monterey, Mex. |
| 2 | Died in hospital at Monterey, Mex., January 3, 1847. |

## ROLL OF COMPANY "C," FIRST REGIMENT KENTUCKY

| No. of each grade | Name | Rank | Joined for Service | Mustered in When | Mustered in Where | Period | Mustered Out When | Mustered Out Where |
|---|---|---|---|---|---|---|---|---|
| | RESIGNED. | | | | | | | |
| 1 | Elias R. Dearing | 1st Lieutenant | May 17, 1846 | May 17,'46 | Louisville, Ky. | 1 yr. | | |
| 2 | John Johnson | 2d Lieutenant | May 17, 1846 | May 17,'46 | Louisville, Ky. | 1 yr. | | |
| 3 | William Littrell | 1st Lieutenant | May 17, 1846 | May 17,'46 | Louisville, Ky. | 1 yr. | | |
| | DESERTED. | | | | | | | |
| 1 | Dodson, Joseph | Private | May 17, 1846 | May 17,'46 | Louisville, Ky. | 1 yr. | | |
| 2 | Dillingham, John T. | Corporal | May 17, 1846 | May 17,'46 | Louisville, Ky. | 1 yr. | | |
| 3 | Fox, Austin T. | Private | May 17, 1846 | May 17,'46 | Louisville, Ky. | 1 yr. | | |
| 4 | Percy, Charles D. | Private | May 17, 1846 | May 17,'46 | Louisville, Ky. | 1 yr. | | |
| 5 | Remme, John H. | Private | May 17, 1846 | May 17,'46 | Louisville, Ky. | 1 yr. | | |

## ROLL OF COMPANY "D," FIRST REGIMENT KENTUCKY

| No. | Name | Rank | Joined for Service | Mustered in When | Mustered in Where | Period | Mustered Out When | Mustered Out Where |
|---|---|---|---|---|---|---|---|---|
| 1 | Kern, Florian | Captain | May 17, 1846 | May 17,'46 | Louisville, Ky. | 1 yr. | May 16,'47 | New Orleans Bks. |
| 1 | Albrecht, John | 1st Lieutenant | May 17, 1846 | May 17,'46 | Louisville, Ky. | 1 yr. | May 16,'47 | New Orleans Bks. |
| 1 | Becker, Louis | 2d Lieutenant | May 17, 1846 | May 17,'46 | Louisville, Ky. | 1 yr. | May 16,'47 | New Orleans Bks. |
| 2 | Pfalger, Jacob | 2d Lieutenant | May 17, 1846 | May 17,'46 | Louisville, Ky. | 1 yr. | May 16,'47 | New Orleans Bks. |
| 1 | Abers, William | 1st Sergeant | May 17, 1846 | May 17,'46 | Louisville, Ky. | 1 yr. | May 16,'47 | New Orleans Bks. |
| 2 | Seeman, Cornelius | Sergeant | May 17, 1846 | May 17,'46 | Louisville, Ky. | 1 yr. | May 16,'47 | New Orleans Bks. |
| 3 | Weber, Peter | Sergeant | May 17, 1846 | May 17,'46 | Louisville, Ky. | 1 yr. | May 16,'47 | New Orleans Bks. |
| 4 | Kub, William | Sergeant | May 17, 1846 | May 17,'46 | Louisville, Ky. | 1 yr. | May 16,'47 | New Orleans Bks. |
| 1 | Hilger, Andreas | Corporal | May 17, 1846 | May 17,'46 | Louisville, Ky. | 1 yr. | May 16,'47 | New Orleans Bks. |
| 2 | Fanning, Ed. Barnes | Corporal | May 17, 1846 | May 17,'46 | Louisville, Ky. | 1 yr. | May 16,'47 | New Orleans Bks. |
| 3 | Egbert, Joseph | Corporal | May 17, 1846 | May 17,'46 | Louisville, Ky. | 1 yr. | May 16,'47 | New Orleans Bks. |
| 4 | Fischer, Joseph | Corporal | May 17, 1846 | May 17,'46 | Louisville, Ky. | 1 yr. | May 16,'47 | New Orleans Bks. |
| 1 | Arweiler, Jacob | Private | May 17, 1846 | May 17,'46 | Louisville, Ky. | 1 yr. | May 16,'47 | New Orleans Bks. |
| 2 | Baumgaertner, Joseph | Private | May 17, 1846 | May 17,'46 | Louisville, Ky. | 1 yr. | May 16,'47 | New Orleans Bks. |
| 3 | Baumeister, George | Private | May 17, 1846 | May 17,'46 | Louisville, Ky. | 1 yr. | May 16,'47 | New Orleans Bks. |
| 4 | Deck, Michael | Private | May 17, 1846 | May 17,'46 | Louisville, Ky. | 1 yr. | May 16,'47 | New Orleans Bks. |
| 5 | Englemeier, Joseph | Private | May 17, 1846 | May 17,'46 | Louisville, Ky. | 1 yr. | May 16,'47 | New Orleans Bks. |
| 6 | Fleihofer, Frederick | Private | May 17, 1846 | May 17,'46 | Louisville, Ky. | 1 yr. | May 16,'47 | New Orleans Bks. |
| 7 | Gotti, Jacob | Private | May 17, 1846 | May 17,'46 | Louisville, Ky. | 1 yr. | May 16,'47 | New Orleans Bks. |
| 8 | Gehringer, Frederick | Private | May 17, 1846 | May 17,'46 | Louisville, Ky. | 1 yr. | May 16,'47 | New Orleans Bks. |
| 9 | Harter, Franz | Private | May 17, 1846 | May 17,'46 | Louisville, Ky. | 1 yr. | May 16,'47 | New Orleans Bks. |
| 10 | Herman, Jacob | Private | May 17, 1846 | May 17,'46 | Louisville, Ky. | 1 yr. | May 16,'47 | New Orleans Bks. |
| 11 | Kleinheintz, Michael | Private | May 17, 1846 | May 17,'46 | Louisville, Ky. | 1 yr. | May 16,'47 | New Orleans Bks. |
| 12 | Lambert, Joseph | Private | May 17, 1846 | May 17,'46 | Louisville, Ky. | 1 yr. | May 16,'47 | New Orleans Bks. |
| 13 | Naihart, Valentin | Private | May 17, 1846 | May 17,'46 | Louisville, Ky. | 1 yr. | May 16,'47 | New Orleans Bks. |
| 14 | Pfister, Heinrich | Private | May 17, 1846 | May 17,'46 | Louisville, Ky. | 1 yr. | May 16,'47 | New Orleans Bks. |
| 15 | Reichert, Franz | Private | May 17, 1846 | May 17,'46 | Louisville, Ky. | 1 yr. | May 16,'47 | New Orleans Bks. |
| 16 | Renz, Peter | Private | May 17, 1846 | May 17,'46 | Louisville, Ky. | 1 yr. | May 16,'47 | New Orleans Bks. |
| 17 | Ress, Conrad | Private | May 17, 1846 | May 17,'46 | Louisville, Ky. | 1 yr. | May 16,'47 | New Orleans Bks. |
| 18 | Semonis, John | Private | May 17, 1846 | May 17,'46 | Louisville, Ky. | 1 yr. | May 16,'47 | New Orleans Bks. |
| 19 | Schaefer, Christian | Private | May 17, 1846 | May 17,'46 | Louisville, Ky. | 1 yr. | May 16,'47 | New Orleans Bks. |
| 20 | Schwenk, Charles | Private | May 17, 1846 | May 17,'46 | Louisville, Ky. | 1 yr. | May 16,'47 | New Orleans Bks. |
| 21 | Siegel, Carl | Private | May 17, 1846 | May 17,'46 | Louisville, Ky. | 1 yr. | May 16,'47 | New Orleans Bks. |
| 22 | Ulrich, John | Private | May 17, 1846 | May 17,'46 | Louisville, Ky. | 1 yr. | May 16,'47 | New Orleans Bks. |
| 23 | Wild, John | Private | May 17, 1846 | May 17,'46 | Louisville, Ky. | 1 yr. | May 16,'47 | New Orleans Bks. |
| 24 | Werner, Anton | Private | May 17, 1846 | May 17,'46 | Louisville, Ky. | 1 yr. | May 16,'47 | New Orleans Bks. |
| 25 | Zeller, John | Private | May 17, 1846 | May 17,'46 | Louisville, Ky. | 1 yr. | May 16,'47 | New Orleans Bks. |
| | DESERTED. | | | | | | | |
| 1 | Duerr, Andreas | Private | May 17, 1846 | May 17,'46 | Louisville, Ky. | 1 yr. | | |
| 2 | Dorsch, Joseph | Private | May 17, 1846 | May 17,'46 | Louisville, Ky. | 1 yr. | | |
| 3 | Hoffman, John | Private | May 17, 1846 | May 17,'46 | Louisville, Ky. | 1 yr. | | |
| 4 | Jenger, Joseph | Private | May 17, 1846 | May 17,'46 | Louisville, Ky. | 1 yr. | | |
| 5 | Johartgen, Mathias | Private | May 17, 1846 | May 17,'46 | Louisville, Ky. | 1 yr. | | |
| 6 | Kraft, Christian | Private | May 17, 1846 | May 17,'46 | Louisville, Ky. | 1 yr. | | |
| 7 | Leohlifer, Georg | Private | May 17, 1846 | May 17,'46 | Louisville, Ky. | 1 yr. | | |
| 8 | Rickert, Andreas | Private | May 17, 1846 | May 17,'46 | Louisville, Ky. | 1 yr. | | |
| 9 | Rinkeler, Franz | Private | May 17, 1846 | May 17,'46 | Louisville, Ky. | 1 yr. | | |
| 10 | Stolger, Marx | Private | May 17, 1846 | May 17,'46 | Louisville, Ky. | 1 yr. | | |
| 11 | Schenke, William | Private | May 17, 1846 | May 17,'46 | Louisville, Ky. | 1 yr. | | |
| 12 | Storg, George J. | Private | May 17, 1846 | May 17,'46 | Louisville, Ky. | 1 yr. | | |
| 13 | Schweitzer, Joseph | Private | May 17, 1846 | May 17,'46 | Louisville, Ky. | 1 yr. | | |
| 14 | Sass, Conrad | Private | May 17, 1846 | May 17,'46 | Louisville, Ky. | 1 yr. | | |
| 15 | Volz, Joseph | Private | May 17, 1846 | May 17,'46 | Louisville, Ky. | 1 yr. | | |
| | DIED. | | | | | | | |
| 1 | Chalis, Andrew | Corporal | May 17, 1846 | May 17,'46 | Louisville, Ky. | 1 yr. | | |

# MEXICAN WAR VETERANS.

## FOOT VOLUNTEERS—MEXICAN WAR—Continued.

| No. of each grade. | REMARKS. |
|---|---|
| 1 | Resignation to take effect February 28, 1847. |
| 2 | Resignation to take effect February 28, 1847. |
| 3 | Resignation to take effect December 31, 1846. |
| | |
| 1 | Deserted at Algiers, La., June 5, 1846. |
| 2 | Deserted at Camargo. Mexico, September —, 1846. |
| 3 | Deserted at Algiers, La., June 5, 1846. |
| 4 | Deserted at Matamoras, Mexico, August 15, 1846. |
| 5 | Deserted at Algiers, La., June 5, 1846. |

## FOOT VOLUNTEERS—MEXICAN WAR.

| | |
|---|---|
| 1 | |
| 1 | Sick in New Orleans. |
| 1 | |
| 2 | |
| 1 | |
| 2 | On furlough at Camargo, Mex., from April 11th, to May 17, 1847, the date of the expiration of term of service; entitled to an honorable [discharge. |
| 3 | |
| 4 | On furlough from April 11th to May 17, 1847, the date of expiration of term of service; entitled to an honorable discharge. |
| 1 | |
| 2 | |
| 3 | |
| 4 | |
| 1 | |
| 2 | |
| 3 | |
| 4 | |
| 5 | Supposed to be taken prisoner by Mexican Lancers, February 24, 1847, near Marin, Mexico. |
| 6 | |
| 7 | |
| 8 | |
| 9 | |
| 10 | |
| 11 | |
| 12 | |
| 13 | Supposed to be taken prisoner by Mexican Lancers, February 24, 1847, near Marin, Mexico. |
| 14 | |
| 15 | |
| 16 | |
| 17 | |
| 18 | |
| 19 | On furlough from April 11th to May 17, 1847, the date of expiration of term of service; entitled to an honorable discharge. |
| 20 | |
| 21 | |
| 22 | On furlough from April 11th to May 17, 1847, the date of expiration of term of service; entitled to an honorable discharge. |
| 23 | |
| 24 | |
| 25 | |
| | |
| 1 | Deserted at New Orleans, La., June 3, 1846. |
| 2 | Deserted at New Orleans, La., June 3, 1846. |
| 3 | Deserted at New Orleans, La., June 3, 1846. |
| 4 | Deserted at New Orleans, La., June 3, 1846. |
| 5 | Deserted at New Orleans, La., June 3, 1846. |
| 6 | Deserted at New Orleans, La., June 3, 1846. |
| 7 | Deserted at New Orleans, La., June 3, 1846. |
| 8 | Deserted at New Orleans, La., June 3, 1846. |
| 9 | Deserted at New Orleans, La., June 3, 1846. |
| 10 | Deserted at New Orleans, La., June 3, 1846. |
| 11 | Deserted at New Orleans, La., June 3, 1846. |
| 12 | Deserted at New Orleans, La., June 3, 1846. |
| 13 | Deserted at New Orleans, La., June 3, 1846. |
| 14 | Deserted at New Orleans, La., June 3, 1846. |
| 15 | Deserted at New Orleans, La., June 3, 1846. |
| | |
| 1 | Died at Camargo, Mexico, September 18, 1846. |

## ROLL OF COMPANY "D," FIRST REGIMENT KENTUCKY

| No. of each grade. | Name. | Rank. | Joined for Service. | Mustered In. When. | Mustered In. Where. | Period. | Mustered Out. When. | Mustered Out. Where. |
|---|---|---|---|---|---|---|---|---|
| 2 | Fell, Treidrich | Private | May 17, 1846 | May 17, '46 | Louisville, Ky. | 1 yr. | | |
| 3 | Gebhard, John | Private | May 17, 1846 | May 17, '46 | Louisville, Ky. | 1 yr. | | |
| 4 | Grutsch, Henry | Private | May 17, 1846 | May 17, '46 | Louisville, Ky. | 1 yr. | | |
| 5 | Craft, Henry | Private | May 17, 1846 | May 17, '46 | Louisville, Ky. | 1 yr. | | |
| 6 | Spitznagel, Jacob | Private | May 17, 1846 | May 17, '46 | Louisville, Ky. | 1 yr. | | |
| 7 | Struthmann, Henry | Private | May 17, 1846 | May 17, '46 | Louisville, Ky. | 1 yr. | | |
| 8 | Kaegin, Ulrich | Private | May 17, 1846 | May 17, '46 | Louisville, Ky. | 1 yr. | | |
| | DISCHARGED. | | | | | | | |
| 1 | Brauer, John | Private | May 17, 1846 | May 17, '46 | Louisville, Ky. | 1 yr. | | |
| 2 | Eller, Michael | Private | May 17, 1846 | May 17, '46 | Louisville, Ky. | 1 yr. | | |
| 3 | Deckhard, Conrad | Private | May 17, 1846 | May 17, '46 | Louisville, Ky. | 1 yr. | | |
| 4 | Happ, Heinrich | Private | May 17, 1846 | May 17, '46 | Louisville, Ky. | 1 yr. | | |
| 5 | Haas, Michael | Private | May 17, 1846 | May 17, '46 | Louisville, Ky. | 1 yr. | | |
| 6 | Nieland, Herman | Private | May 17, 1846 | May 17, '46 | Louisville, Ky. | 1 yr. | | |
| 7 | Keller, John | Private | May 17, 1846 | May 17, '46 | Louisville, Ky. | 1 yr. | | |
| 8 | Piper, Ignatz | Private | May 17, 1846 | May 17, '46 | Louisville, Ky. | 1 yr. | | |
| 9 | Stumpf, John | Private | May 17, 1846 | May 17, '46 | Louisville, Ky. | 1 yr. | | |
| 10 | Vogel, Georg | Private | May 17, 1846 | May 17, '46 | Louisville, Ky. | 1 yr. | | |

## ROLL OF COMPANY "E," FIRST REGIMENT KENTUCKY

| No. | Name. | Rank. | Joined for Service. | Mustered In. When. | Mustered In. Where. | Period. | Mustered Out. When. | Mustered Out. Where. |
|---|---|---|---|---|---|---|---|---|
| 1 | Joseph C. Baird | 1st Lieutenant | May 17, 1846 | May 17, '46 | Louisville, Ky. | 1 yr. | May 17, '47 | New Orleans Bks. |
| 1 | David Black | 2d Lieutenant | May 17, 1846 | May 17, '46 | Louisville, Ky. | 1 yr. | May 17, '47 | New Orleans Bks. |
| 1 | John D. Pope | 1st Sergeant | May 17, 1846 | May 17, '46 | Louisville, Ky. | 1 yr. | May 17, '47 | New Orleans Bks. |
| 2 | George McKeag | Sergeant | May 17, 1846 | May 17, '46 | Louisville, Ky. | 1 yr. | May 17, '47 | New Orleans Bks. |
| 3 | James Gatton | Sergeant | May 17, 1846 | May 17, '46 | Louisville, Ky. | 1 yr. | May 17, '47 | New Orleans Bks. |
| 4 | David Q. Rasseau | Sergeant | May 17, 1846 | May 17, '46 | Louisville, Ky. | 1 yr. | May 17, '47 | New Orleans Bks. |
| 1 | James M. Clarke | Corporal | May 17, 1846 | May 17, '46 | Louisville, Ky. | 1 yr. | May 17, '47 | New Orleans Bks. |
| 2 | John B. Guthrie | Corporal | May 17, 1846 | May 17, '46 | Louisville, Ky. | 1 yr. | May 17, '47 | New Orleans Bks. |
| 3 | Joseph H. Hughs | Corporal | May 17, 1846 | May 17, '46 | Louisville, Ky. | 1 yr. | May 17, '47 | New Orleans Bks. |
| 1 | Anderson, Lafayette L. | Private | May 17, 1846 | May 17, '46 | Louisville, Ky. | 1 yr. | May 17, '47 | New Orleans Bks. |
| 2 | Boyd, Alfred | Private | May 17, 1846 | May 17, '46 | Louisville, Ky. | 1 yr. | May 17, '47 | New Orleans Bks. |
| 3 | Clark, Samuel F. | Private | May 17, 1846 | May 17, '46 | Louisville, Ky. | 1 yr. | May 17, '47 | New Orleans Bks. |
| 4 | Crump, Jesse W. | Private | May 17, 1846 | May 17, '46 | Louisville, Ky. | 1 yr. | May 17, '47 | New Orleans Bks. |
| 5 | Carmicial, David | Private | May 17, 1846 | May 17, '46 | Louisville, Ky. | 1 yr. | May 17, '47 | New Orleans Bks. |
| 6 | Devitt, James W. | Private | May 17, 1846 | May 17, '46 | Louisville, Ky. | 1 yr. | May 17, '47 | New Orleans Bks. |
| 7 | Gilbert, Benjamin | Private | May 17, 1846 | May 17, '46 | Louisville, Ky. | 1 yr. | May 17, '47 | New Orleans Bks. |
| 8 | Gossman, John | Private | May 17, 1846 | May 17, '46 | Louisville, Ky. | 1 yr. | May 17, '47 | New Orleans Bks. |
| 9 | Gilbert, Nathan | Private | May 17, 1846 | May 17, '46 | Louisville, Ky. | 1 yr. | May 17, '47 | New Orleans Bks. |
| 10 | Hicks, Thomas | Private | May 17, 1846 | May 17, '46 | Louisville, Ky. | 1 yr. | May 17, '47 | New Orleans Bks. |
| 11 | Humble, L. B. | Private | May 17, 1846 | May 17, '46 | Louisville, Ky. | 1 yr. | May 17, '47 | New Orleans Bks. |
| 12 | Henry, James | Private | May 17, 1846 | May 17, '46 | Louisville, Ky. | 1 yr. | May 17, '47 | New Orleans Bks. |
| 13 | Jewet, Josiah S. | Private | May 17, 1846 | May 17, '46 | Louisville, Ky. | 1 yr. | May 17, '47 | New Orleans Bks. |
| 14 | Lampton, William | Private | May 17, 1846 | May 17, '46 | Louisville, Ky. | 1 yr. | May 17, '47 | New Orleans Bks. |
| 15 | Lucas, Benjamin | Private | May 17, 1846 | May 17, '46 | Louisville, Ky. | 1 yr. | May 17, '47 | New Orleans Bks. |
| 16 | McAbee, John W. | Private | May 17, 1846 | May 17, '46 | Louisville, Ky. | 1 yr. | May 17, '47 | New Orleans Bks. |
| 17 | Marshall, William | Private | May 17, 1846 | May 17, '46 | Louisville, Ky. | 1 yr. | May 17, '47 | New Orleans Bks. |
| 18 | Marvin, William F. | Private | May 17, 1846 | May 17, '46 | Louisville, Ky. | 1 yr. | May 17, '47 | New Orleans Bks. |
| 19 | Marts, John L. | Private | May 17, 1846 | May 17, '46 | Louisville, Ky. | 1 yr. | May 17, '47 | New Orleans Bks. |
| 20 | O'Donald, Michael | Private | May 17, 1846 | May 17, '46 | Louisville, Ky. | 1 yr. | May 17, '47 | New Orleans Bks. |
| 21 | Phillips, Hiram | Private | May 17, 1846 | May 17, '46 | Louisville, Ky. | 1 yr. | May 17, '47 | New Orleans Bks. |
| 22 | Proudfit, James | Private | May 17, 1846 | May 17, '46 | Louisville, Ky. | 1 yr. | May 17, '47 | New Orleans Bks. |
| 23 | Patterson, Immanuel | Private | May 17, 1846 | May 17, '46 | Louisville, Ky. | 1 yr. | May 17, '47 | New Orleans Bks. |
| 24 | Reames, Obediah | Private | May 17, 1846 | May 17, '46 | Louisville, Ky. | 1 yr. | May 17, '47 | New Orleans Bks. |
| 25 | Rogerson, John | Private | May 17, 1846 | May 17, '46 | Louisville, Ky. | 1 yr. | May 17, '47 | New Orleans Bks. |
| 26 | Skidmore, John | Private | May 17, 1846 | May 17, '46 | Louisville, Ky. | 1 yr. | May 17, '47 | New Orleans Bks. |
| 27 | Smith, Augustus | Private | May 17, 1846 | May 17, '46 | Louisville, Ky. | 1 yr. | May 17, '47 | New Orleans Bks. |
| 28 | Thompson, Thomas | Private | May 17, 1846 | May 17, '46 | Louisville, Ky. | 1 yr. | May 17, '47 | New Orleans Bks. |
| 29 | Tibon, Theodore | Private | May 17, 1846 | May 17, '46 | Louisville, Ky. | 1 yr. | May 17, '47 | New Orleans Bks. |
| 30 | Twyman, Geo. R. | Private | May 17, 1846 | May 17, '46 | Louisville, Ky. | 1 yr. | May 17, '47 | New Orleans Bks. |
| 31 | Watsnider, Ellison | Private | May 17, 1846 | May 17, '46 | Louisville, Ky. | 1 yr. | May 17, '47 | New Orleans Bks. |
| 32 | Wells, Milton H. | Private | May 17, 1846 | May 17, '46 | Louisville, Ky. | 1 yr. | May 17, '47 | New Orleans Bks. |
| | DISCHARGED. | | | | | | | |
| 1 | John B. Onslow | Sergeant | May 17, 1846 | May 17, '46 | Louisville, Ky. | 1 yr. | | |
| 2 | Henry Bacon | Corporal | May 17, 1846 | May 17, '46 | Louisville, Ky. | 1 yr. | | |
| 3 | Jas. C. Benson | Corporal | May 17, 1846 | May 17, '46 | Louisville, Ky. | 1 yr. | | |
| 4 | Samuel Arnold | Private | May 17, 1846 | May 17, '46 | Louisville, Ky. | 1 yr. | | |
| 5 | David Barry | Private | May 17, 1846 | May 17, '46 | Louisville, Ky. | 1 yr. | | |
| 6 | Adam Clarke | Private | May 17, 1846 | May 17, '46 | Louisville, Ky. | 1 yr. | | |

## FOOT VOLUNTEERS—MEXICAN WAR—Continued.

| No. of each grade | REMARKS. |
|---|---|
| 2 | Killed by Mexican Lancers, February 26, 1847, near Aquafrio, Mexico. |
| 3 | Died at Camp Taylor, near Burieta, Mexico, July 28, 1846. |
| 4 | Killed by Mexican Lancers, February 24, 1847, near Marin, Mexico. |
| 5 | Died at Camargo, Mexico, August 27, 1846. |
| 6 | Died on board of steamboat on the Rio Grande, between Matamoras and Camargo, Mexico, August 23, 1846. |
| 7 | Killed by Mexican Lancers, February 26, 1847, near Aquafrio, Mexico. |
| 8 | Killed by Mexicans, near Monterey, Mexico, November 23, 1846. |
| | |
| 1 | Discharged at Camargo, Mexico, September 13, 1846, by reason of Surgeon's certificate. |
| 2 | Discharged at Camargo, Mexico, August 26, 1846, by reason of Surgeon's certificate. |
| 3 | Discharged at Monterey, Mexico, October 15, 1846, by reason of Surgeon's certificate. |
| 4 | Discharged at Camargo, Mexico, August 26, 1846, by reason of Surgeon's certificate. |
| 5 | Discharged at Camargo, Mexico, September 13, 1846, by reason of Surgeon's certificate. |
| 6 | Discharged at Camargo, Mexico, September 13, 1846, by reason of Surgeon's certificate. |
| 7 | Discharged at Camargo, Mexico, August 26, 1846, by reason of Surgeon's certificate. |
| 8 | Discharged at Camargo, Mexico, August 26, 1846, by reason of Surgeon's certificate. |
| 9 | Discharged at Camargo, Mexico, September 13, 1846, by reason of Surgeon's certificate. |
| 10 | Discharged at Camargo, Mexico, August 26, 1846, by reason of Surgeon's certificate. |

## FOOT VOLUNTEERS—MEXICAN WAR.

| No. of each grade | REMARKS. |
|---|---|
| 1 | Commanding company since April 1, 1847. Promoted 1st Lieutenant from 2d Lieutenant January 1, 1847. |
| 1 | Elected 2d Lieutenant from Corporal, September 1, 1846. |
| 1 | On furlough at Camargo, Mexico, from 17th April to expiration of service. |
| 2 | |
| 3 | On furlough at Camargo, Mexico, from 17th April to expiration of service. |
| 4 | Appointed Sergeant from Corporal April 4, 1847. |
| 1 | |
| 2 | |
| 3 | Appointed Corporal from private April 4, 1847. |
| 1 | On furlough at Camargo, Mexico, from 17th April to expiration of service. |
| 2 | |
| 3 | |
| 4 | On furlough at Camargo, Mexico, from 17th April to expiration of service. |
| 5 | On furlough at the mouth of the Rio Grande, Texas, from 17th April to expiration of service. |
| 6 | On furlough at the mouth of the Rio Grande, since 17th April, 1847. |
| 7 | |
| 8 | |
| 9 | Taken prisoner near Marin, Mexico, while on duty under Lieut. Barber. |
| 10 | |
| 11 | |
| 12 | |
| 13 | Taken prisoner near Marin, Mexico, while on duty under Lieut. Barber. |
| 14 | |
| 15 | |
| 16 | |
| 17 | |
| 18 | |
| 19 | |
| 20 | |
| 21 | |
| 22 | |
| 23 | |
| 24 | |
| 25 | |
| 26 | |
| 27 | |
| 28 | |
| 29 | |
| 30 | |
| 31 | |
| 32 | |
| | |
| 1 | Discharged at Monterey, Mexico, by order of Major-General Taylor, April 4, 1847. |
| 2 | Discharged at Burieta, Mexico, for disability, August 8, 1846. |
| 3 | Discharged at Camargo, Mexico, for disability, August 27, 1846. |
| 4 | Discharged at camp near Monterey, Mexico, for disability, October 15, 1846. |
| 5 | Discharged at Camargo, Mexico, for disability, August 8, 1846. |
| 6 | Discharged at Camargo, Mexico, for disability, August 25, 1846. |

## ROLL OF COMPANY "E," FIRST REGIMENT KENTUCKY

| No. of each grade | Name | Rank | Joined for Service | Mustered In When | Mustered In Where | Period | Mustered Out When | Mustered Out Where |
|---|---|---|---|---|---|---|---|---|
| 7 | Albert S. Calmes | Private | May 17, 1846 | May 17,'46 | Louisville, Ky. | 1 yr. | | |
| 8 | Elijah W. Gilbert | Private | May 17, 1846 | May 17,'46 | Louisville, Ky. | 1 yr. | | |
| 9 | Harrison Petit | Private | May 17, 1846 | May 17,'46 | Louisville, Ky. | 1 yr. | | |
| 10 | Geo. Siteason | Private | May 17, 1846 | May 17,'46 | Louisville, Ky. | 1 yr. | | |
| 11 | Daniel E. Litason | Private | May 17, 1846 | May 17,'46 | Louisville, Ky. | 1 yr. | | |
| 12 | Joseph Jeans | Private | May 17, 1846 | May 17,'46 | Louisville, Ky. | 1 yr. | | |
| 13 | Wilson Coke | Private | May 17, 1846 | May 17,'46 | Louisville, Ky. | 1 yr. | | |
| 14 | John B. Coke | Private | May 17, 1846 | May 17,'46 | Louisville, Ky. | 1 yr. | | |
| 15 | Wm. Douglass | Private | May 17, 1846 | May 17,'46 | Louisville, Ky. | 1 yr. | | |
| | **DIED.** | | | | | | | |
| 1 | A. J. Alexander | Private | May 17, 1846 | May 17,'46 | Louisville, Ky. | 1 yr. | | |
| 2 | John L. Henderson | Private | May 17, 1846 | May 17,'46 | Louisville, Ky. | 1 yr. | | |
| 3 | Silas E. Craig | Private | May 17, 1846 | May 17,'46 | Louisville, Ky. | 1 yr. | | |
| 4 | John Hargrave | Private | May 17, 1846 | May 17,'46 | Louisville, Ky. | 1 yr. | | |
| 5 | Richard E. Mattingly | Corporal | May 17, 1846 | May 17,'46 | Louisville, Ky. | 1 yr. | | |
| | **DESERTED.** | | | | | | | |
| 1 | G. W. Bloar | Private | May 17, 1846 | May 17,'46 | Louisville, Ky. | 1 yr. | | |
| 2 | James Hamilton | Private | May 17, 1846 | May 17,'46 | Louisville, Ky. | 1 yr. | | |
| 3 | W. L. Washington | Private | May 17, 1846 | May 17,'46 | Louisville, Ky. | 1 yr. | | |
| 4 | Malcolm Wright | Private | May 17, 1846 | May 17,'46 | Louisville, Ky. | 1 yr. | | |
| 5 | Robert Hicks | Private | May 17, 1846 | May 17,'46 | Louisville, Ky. | 1 yr. | | |
| 6 | Benjamin Smith | Private | May 17, 1846 | May 17,'46 | Louisville, Ky. | 1 yr. | | |

NOTE.—Captain Godfrey Pope received leave of absence for sixty days, from 29th July, 1846, when his resignation was to take effect. Lost at sea between Brazos Santiago and New Orleans, date not known.

Captain Wm. Minor promoted Captain from 1st Lieutenant, 1st of January, 1847, by General Marshall, and commissioned by the Governor of Kentucky. Resigned 1st April, 1847.

## ROLL OF COMPANY "F," FIRST REGIMENT KENTUCKY

| No. | Name | Rank | Joined for Service | Mustered In When | Mustered In Where | Period | Mustered Out When | Mustered Out Where |
|---|---|---|---|---|---|---|---|---|
| 1 | John Fuller | Captain | May 17, 1846 | May 17,'46 | Louisville, Ky. | 1 yr. | May 17,'47 | New Orleans Bks. |
| 1 | Patrick McPike | 1st Lieutenant | May 17, 1846 | May 17,'46 | Louisville, Ky. | 1 yr. | May 17,'47 | New Orleans Bks. |
| 1 | John Harrigan | 2d Lieutenant | May 17, 1846 | May 17,'46 | Louisville, Ky. | 1 yr. | May 17,'47 | New Orleans Bks. |
| 1 | Francis Nevin | 1st Sergeant | May 17, 1846 | May 17,'46 | Louisville, Ky. | 1 yr. | May 17,'47 | New Orleans Bks. |
| 2 | Daniel Mulholland | 2d Sergeant | May 17, 1846 | May 17,'46 | Louisville, Ky. | 1 yr. | May 17,'47 | New Orleans Bks. |
| 3 | Timothy Finn | 3d Sergeant | May 17, 1846 | May 17,'46 | Louisville, Ky. | 1 yr. | May 17,'47 | New Orleans Bks. |
| 4 | William Thompson | 4th Sergeant | May 17, 1846 | May 17,'46 | Louisville, Ky. | 1 yr. | May 17,'47 | New Orleans Bks. |
| 1 | Alexander Prouhet | Corporal | May 17, 1846 | May 17,'46 | Louisville, Ky. | 1 yr. | May 17,'47 | New Orleans Bks. |
| 2 | James Sullivan | Corporal | May 17, 1846 | May 17,'46 | Louisville, Ky. | 1 yr. | May 17,'47 | New Orleans Bks. |
| 3 | Nicholas Foley | Corporal | May 17, 1846 | May 17,'46 | Louisville, Ky. | 1 yr. | May 17,'47 | New Orleans Bks. |
| 4 | Cornelius Lyons | Corporal | May 17, 1846 | May 17,'46 | Louisville, Ky. | 1 yr. | May 17,'47 | New Orleans Bks. |
| 1 | Amslie, Hugh | Private | May 17, 1846 | May 17,'46 | Louisville, Ky. | 1 yr. | May 17,'47 | New Orleans Bks. |
| 2 | Brotherlin, Charles | Private | May 17, 1846 | May 17,'46 | Louisville, Ky. | 1 yr. | May 17,'47 | New Orleans Bks. |
| 3 | Brown, Alexander D. | Private | May 17, 1846 | May 17,'46 | Louisville, Ky. | 1 yr. | May 17,'47 | New Orleans Bks. |
| 4 | Callan, James | Private | May 17, 1846 | May 17,'46 | Louisville, Ky. | 1 yr. | May 17,'47 | New Orleans Bks. |
| 5 | Campbell, John | Private | May 17, 1846 | May 17,'46 | Louisville, Ky. | 1 yr. | May 17,'47 | New Orleans Bks. |
| 6 | Castellar, James | Private | May 17, 1846 | May 17,'46 | Louisville, Ky. | 1 yr. | May 17,'47 | New Orleans Bks. |
| 7 | Childs, James P. | Private | May 17, 1846 | May 17,'46 | Louisville, Ky. | 1 yr. | May 17,'47 | New Orleans Bks. |
| 8 | Davis, James | Private | May 17, 1846 | May 17,'46 | Louisville, Ky. | 1 yr. | May 17,'47 | New Orleans Bks. |
| 9 | Freeney, Patrick | Private | May 17, 1846 | May 17,'46 | Louisville, Ky. | 1 yr. | May 17,'47 | New Orleans Bks. |
| 10 | Hamilton, Ferdinand F. | Private | May 17, 1846 | May 17,'46 | Louisville, Ky. | 1 yr. | May 17,'47 | New Orleans Bks. |
| 11 | Hickey, Thomas | Private | May 17, 1846 | May 17,'46 | Louisville, Ky. | 1 yr. | May 17,'47 | New Orleans Bks. |
| 12 | Leahy, Dennis | Private | May 17, 1846 | May 17,'46 | Louisville, Ky. | 1 yr. | May 17,'47 | New Orleans Bks. |
| 13 | Laprin, Mitchell | Private | May 17, 1846 | May 17,'46 | Louisville, Ky. | 1 yr. | May 17,'47 | New Orleans Bks. |
| 14 | Laughlin, Alexander | Private | May 17, 1846 | May 17,'46 | Louisville, Ky. | 1 yr. | May 17,'47 | New Orleans Bks. |
| 15 | Medlicot, Joseph | Private | May 17, 1846 | May 17,'46 | Louisville, Ky. | 1 yr. | May 17,'47 | New Orleans Bks. |
| 16 | McGowan, Henry | Private | May 17, 1846 | May 17,'46 | Louisville, Ky. | 1 yr. | May 17,'47 | New Orleans Bks. |
| 17 | McGinnis, Patrick | Private | May 17, 1846 | May 17,'46 | Louisville, Ky. | 1 yr. | May 17,'47 | New Orleans Bks. |
| 18 | Murphy, William | Private | May 17, 1846 | May 17,'46 | Louisville, Ky. | 1 yr. | May 17,'47 | New Orleans Bks. |
| 19 | McCann, John | Private | May 17, 1846 | May 17,'46 | Louisville, Ky. | 1 yr. | May 17,'47 | New Orleans Bks. |
| 20 | McGeavery, John | Private | May 17, 1846 | May 17,'46 | Louisville, Ky. | 1 yr. | May 17,'47 | New Orleans Bks. |
| 21 | McLaughlin, Thomas | Private | May 17, 1846 | May 17,'46 | Louisville, Ky. | 1 yr. | May 17,'47 | New Orleans Bks. |
| 22 | McQuillan, Andrew | Private | May 17, 1846 | May 17,'46 | Louisville, Ky. | 1 yr. | May 17,'47 | New Orleans Bks. |
| 23 | Stone, Erastus | Private | May 17, 1846 | May 17,'46 | Louisville, Ky. | 1 yr. | May 17,'47 | New Orleans Bks. |
| 24 | Sharp, Josiah | Private | May 17, 1846 | May 17,'46 | Louisville, Ky. | 1 yr. | May 17,'47 | New Orleans Bks. |
| | **DISCHARGED.** | | | | | | | |
| 1 | Kelly, Michael | Private | May 17, 1846 | May 17,'46 | Louisville, Ky. | 1 yr. | | |
| 2 | Roach, Philip | Private | May 17, 1846 | May 17,'46 | Louisville, Ky. | 1 yr. | | |
| 3 | Russell, William | Private | May 17, 1846 | May 17,'46 | Louisville, Ky. | 1 yr. | | |

MEXICAN WAR VETERANS. 71

## FOOT VOLUNTEERS—MEXICAN WAR—Continued.

| No. of each grade. | REMARKS. |
|---|---|
| 7 | Discharged at Camargo, Mexico, for disability, August 27, 1846. |
| 8 | Discharged at Camargo, Mexico, for disability, August 27, 1846. |
| 9 | Discharged at Camargo, Mexico, for disability, August 8, 1846. |
| 10 | Discharged at Camargo, Mexico, for disability, August 8, 1846. |
| 11 | Discharged at Camargo, Mexico, for disability, August 27, 1846. |
| 12 | Discharged at camp near Monterey, Mexico. Order of Brigadier-General Hamer, October 9, 1846. |
| 13 | Discharged at Camargo, Mexico, for disability, December 17, 1846. |
| 14 | Discharged at Camargo, Mexico, for disability, August 8, 1846. |
| 15 | Discharged at Monterey, Mexico, by Surgeon's certificate. |
| 1 | Reported to have died in the hospital in Matamoras, Mexico, 1846. |
| 2 | Died in the hospital at Monterey, Mexico, January 18, 1847. |
| 3 | Reported to have died in the hospital at Matamoras, Mexico, 1847. |
| 4 | Drowned between the mouth of the Ohio and New Orleans, 27th May, 1846. |
| 5 | Died at New Orleans on the 12th of May, 1847. |
| 1 | Deserted at Algiers, La., June 3, 1846. |
| 2 | Deserted at Algiers, La., June 3, 1846. |
| 3 | Deserted between Matamoras and Camargo, August 18, 1846. |
| 4 | Deserted at Algiers, La., June 3, 1846. |
| 5 | Deserted at Algiers, La., June 3, 1846. |
| 6 | Deserted at Algiers, La., June 3, 1846. |

## FOOT VOLUNTEERS—MEXICAN WAR.

| No. of each grade. | REMARKS. |
|---|---|
| 1 | |
| 1 | |
| 1 | |
| 2 | Promoted from private to Sergeant, June, 1846. |
| 3 | Promoted from private to Sergeant, June 5, 1846. |
| 4 | Promoted from private to Sergeant, June 5, 1846. |
| 1 | |
| 2 | |
| 3 | |
| 4 | |
| 1 | |
| 2 | |
| 3 | |
| 4 | Left in confinement at Matamoras, Mexico. |
| 5 | |
| 6 | |
| 7 | |
| 8 | |
| 9 | |
| 10 | |
| 11 | |
| 12 | |
| 13 | |
| 14 | |
| 15 | |
| 16 | |
| 17 | |
| 18 | |
| 19 | |
| 20 | |
| 21 | |
| 22 | |
| 23 | |
| 24 | |
| 1 | Discharged at Camargo, Mexico, by Surgeon's certificate, August 30, 1846. |
| 2 | Discharged at Camargo, Mexico, by Surgeon's certificate, August 30, 1846. |
| 3 | Discharged at Camargo, Mexico, by Surgeon's certificate, August 30, 1846. |

MEXICAN WAR VETERANS.

## ROLL OF COMPANY "F," FIRST REGIMENT KENTUCKY

| No. of each grade. | Name. | Rank. | Joined for Service. | Mustered In. When. | Mustered In. Where. | Period. | Mustered Out. When. | Mustered Out. Where. |
|---|---|---|---|---|---|---|---|---|
| 4 | Roshier, George A. | Private | May 17, 1846 | May 17,'46. | Louisville, Ky. | 1 yr. | | |
| 5 | Roark, Elzy | Private | May 17, 1846. | May 17,'46. | Louisville, Ky. | 1 yr. | | |
| 6 | Armstrong, Thomas | Private | May 17, 1846. | May 17,'46. | Louisville, Ky. | 1 yr. | | |
| 7 | Smith, John | Private | May 17, 1846. | May 17,'46. | Louisville, Ky. | 1 yr. | | |
| 8 | McEvoy, Thomas | Private | May 17, 1846. | May 17,'46 | Louisville, Ky. | 1 yr. | | |
| 9 | Conner, James | Private | May 17, 1846. | May 17,'46. | Louisville, Ky. | 1 yr. | | |
| 10 | McDonald, George | Private | May 17, 1846. | May 17,'46. | Louisville, Ky. | 1 yr. | | |
| 11 | Ray, Patrick | Private | May 17, 1846. | May 17,'46. | Louisville, Ky. | 1 yr. | | |
| | DESERTED. | | | | | | | |
| 1 | McCleary, Thomas | Sergeant | May 17, 1846. | May 17,'46. | Louisville, Ky. | 1 yr. | | |
| 2 | Raveity, James | Sergeant | May 17, 1846. | May 17,'46. | Louisville, Ky. | 1 yr. | | |
| 1 | Butler, Peter | Private | May 17, 1846. | May 17,'46. | Louisville, Ky. | 1 yr. | | |
| 2 | Craumin, John | Private | May 17, 1846. | May 17,'46. | Louisville, Ky. | 1 yr. | | |
| 3 | Kennedy, Thomas | Private | May 17, 1846. | May 17,'46. | Louisville, Ky. | 1 yr. | | |
| 4 | Moore, John | Private | May 17, 1846. | May 17,'46. | Louisville, Ky. | 1 yr. | | |
| 5 | Munsriur, Jas. | Private | May 17, 1846. | May 17,'46. | Louisville, Ky. | 1 yr. | | |
| 6 | McEwin, Robert | Private | May 17, 1846. | May 17,'46. | Louisville, Ky. | 1 yr. | | |
| 7 | Hawley, John | Private | May 17, 1846 | May 17,'46. | Louisville, Ky. | 1 yr. | | |
| | TRANSFERRED. | | | | | | | |
| 1 | Russell, James | Private | May 17, 1846. | May 17,'46. | Louisville, Ky. | 1 yr. | | |
| | MISSING. | | | | | | | |
| 1 | McMahon, James | Private | May 17, 1846. | May 17,'46. | Louisville, Ky. | 1 yr. | | |
| | DIED. | | | | | | | |
| 1 | Dunn, Matthew | Private | May 17, 1846. | May 17,'46. | Louisville, Ky. | 1 yr. | | |
| | RESIGNED. | | | | | | | |
| 1 | Smith, James | 2d Lieutenant | May 17, 1846. | May 17,'46. | Louisville, Ky. | 1 yr. | | |
| | CAPTURED. | | | | | | | |
| 1 | Fogarty, John | Private | May 17, 1846. | May 17,'46. | Louisville, Ky. | 1 yr. | | |
| 2 | Newman, Darby | Private | May 17, 1846. | May 17,'46. | Louisville, Ky. | 1 yr. | | |

## ROLL OF COMPANY "G," FIRST REGIMENT KENTUCKY

| | Name | Rank | Joined for Service | Mustered In When | Mustered In Where | Period | Mustered Out When | Mustered Out Where |
|---|---|---|---|---|---|---|---|---|
| 1 | Conrad Shroeder | Captain | May 17, 1846. | May 17,'46. | Louisville, Ky. | 1 yr. | May 17,'47. | New Orleans Bks. |
| 1 | Wm. Riddle | 1st Lieutenant | May 17, 1846. | May 17,'46. | Louisville, Ky. | 1 yr. | May 17,'47. | New Orleans Bks. |
| 1 | C. Hadermann | 2d Lieutenant | May 17, 1846. | May 17,'46. | Louisville, Ky. | 1 yr. | May 17,'47. | New Orleans Bks. |
| 2 | Benedick Hubel | 2d Lieutenant | May 17, 1846. | May 17,'46. | Louisville, Ky. | 1 yr. | May 17,'47. | New Orleans Bks. |
| 1 | Richard Reubrecht | 1st Sergeant | May 17, 1846. | May 17,'46. | Louisville, Ky. | 1 yr. | May 17,'47. | New Orleans Bks. |
| 2 | Frederick Shroeder | Sergeant | May 17, 1846. | May 17,'46. | Louisville, Ky. | 1 yr. | May 17,'47. | New Orleans Bks. |
| 3 | Adam Knapp | Sergeant | May 17, 1846. | May 17,'46. | Louisville, Ky. | 1 yr. | May 17,'47. | New Orleans Bks. |
| 4 | Grieshaber Engelbert | Sergeant | May 17, 1846. | May 17,'46. | Louisville, Ky. | 1 yr. | May 17,'47. | New Orleans Bks. |
| 1 | Kaltenback Georg | Corporal | May 17, 1846. | May 17,'46. | Louisville, Ky. | 1 yr. | May 17,'47. | New Orleans Bks. |
| 2 | Sebastian Adams | Corporal | May 17, 1846. | May 17,'46. | Louisville, Ky. | 1 yr. | May 17,'47. | New Orleans Bks. |
| 3 | Anthony Martin | Corporal | May 17, 1846. | May 17,'46. | Louisville, Ky. | 1 yr. | May 17,'47. | New Orleans Bks. |
| 1 | Alheim, Lewis | Private | May 17, 1846. | May 17,'46. | Louisville, Ky. | 1 yr. | May 17,'47. | New Orleans Bks. |
| 2 | Ahrens, Frederick | Private | May 17, 1846. | May 17,'46. | Louisville, Ky. | 1 yr. | May 17,'47. | New Orleans Bks. |
| 3 | Algeier, Joseph | Private | May 17, 1846. | May 17,'46. | Louisville, Ky. | 1 yr. | May 17,'47. | New Orleans Bks. |
| 4 | Baumann, Frederick | Private | May 17, 1846 | May 17,'46 | Louisville, Ky. | 1 yr. | May 17,'47. | New Orleans Bks. |
| 5 | Buechle, Peter | Private | May 17, 1846. | May 17,'46. | Louisville, Ky. | 1 yr. | May 17,'47. | New Orleans Bks. |
| 6 | Dishler, Anton | Private | May 17, 1846. | May 17,'46. | Louisville, Ky. | 1 yr. | May 17,'47. | New Orleans Bks. |
| 7 | Deutsh, Georg | Private | May 17, 1846. | May 17,'46. | Louisville, Ky. | 1 yr. | May 17,'47. | New Orleans Bks. |
| 8 | Eisen, John | Private | May 17, 1846. | May 17,'46. | Louisville, Ky. | 1 yr. | May 17,'47. | New Orleans Bks. |
| 9 | Feldhaus, Frederick | Private | May 17, 1846. | May 17,'46. | Louisville, Ky. | 1 yr. | May 17,'47. | New Orleans Bks. |
| 10 | Frederick, Gossman | Private | May 17, 1846. | May 17,'46. | Louisville, Ky. | 1 yr. | May 17,'47. | New Orleans Bks. |
| 11 | Glotsbach, Sebastian | Private | May 17, 1846. | May 17,'46. | Louisville, Ky. | 1 yr. | May 17,'47. | New Orleans Bks. |
| 12 | Hoffmann, Thomas | Private | May 17, 1846. | May 17,'46. | Louisville, Ky. | 1 yr. | May 17,'47. | New Orleans Bks. |
| 13 | Heissmann, Henry | Private | May 17, 1846. | May 17,'46. | Louisville, Ky. | 1 yr. | May 17,'47. | New Orleans Bks. |
| 14 | Henry, Michael | Private | May 17, 1846. | May 17,'46. | Louisville, Ky. | 1 yr. | May 17,'47. | New Orleans Bks. |
| 15 | Hess, Georg | Private | May 17, 1846. | May 17,'46. | Louisville, Ky. | 1 yr. | May 17,'47. | New Orleans Bks. |
| 16 | Jurgens, Frank | Private | May 17, 1846. | May 17,'46. | Louisville, Ky. | 1 yr. | May 17,'47. | New Orleans Bks. |
| 17 | Ketterer, Friedrich | Private | May 17, 1846. | May 17,'46. | Louisville, Ky. | 1 yr. | May 17,'47 | New Orleans Bks. |
| 18 | Kuhn, Georg W. | Private | May 17, 1846. | May 17,'46. | Louisville, Ky. | 1 yr. | May 17,'47. | New Orleans Bks. |
| 19 | Leonhardt, John | Private | May 17, 1846. | May 17,'46. | Louisville, Ky. | 1 yr. | May 17,'47. | New Orleans Bks. |
| 20 | Lacker, Freidrich | Private | May 17, 1846. | May 17,'46. | Louisville, Ky. | 1 yr. | May 17,'47. | New Orleans Bks. |
| 21 | Miller, Henry | Private | May 17, 1846. | May 17,'46. | Louisville, Ky. | 1 yr. | May 17,'47. | New Orleans Bks. |
| 22 | Miller, Christofer | Private | May 17, 1846. | May 17,'46. | Louisville, Ky. | 1 yr. | May 17,'47. | New Orleans Bks. |

MEXICAN WAR VETERANS. 73

## FOOT VOLUNTEERS—MEXICAN WAR—Continued.

| No. of each grade | REMARKS. |
|---|---|
| 4 | Discharged at Camargo, Mexico, by Surgeon's certificate, August 30, 1846. |
| 5 | Discharged at Camargo, Mexico, by Surgeon's certificate, August 30, 1846. |
| 6 | Discharged at Monterey, Mexico, by Surgeon's certificate and certificate of pension, October 21, 1846. |
| 7 | Dishonorably discharged, sentence general court-martial; all pay forfeited to U. S., on 16th December, 1846, at camp near Monterey, Mex. |
| 8 | Discharged at Monterey, Mex., by Surgeon's certificate, January 30, 1847. |
| 9 | Discharged at Monterey, by request of Capt. Frazie-, to work in government employ, April 3, 1847. |
| 10 | Discharged at Monterey, by request of Capt. Montgomery, to work in government employ, April 4, 1847. |
| 11 | Discharged at Monterey, Mexico, by order, March 1, 1847. |
| 1 | Deserted at Algiers, La., June 4, 1846. |
| 2 | Deserted at Algiers, La., June 4, 1846. |
| 1 | Deserted at Algiers, La., June 4, 1846. |
| 2 | Deserted at Algiers, La., June 4, 1846. |
| 3 | Deserted at Algiers, La., June 4, 1846. |
| 4 | Deserted at Algiers, La., June 4, 1846. |
| 5 | Deserted at Algiers, La., June 4, 1846. |
| 6 | Deserted at Algiers, La., June 4, 1846. |
| 7 | Deserted from camp near Monterey, Mex., on the 15th day of November, 1846. |
| 1 | Recognized as a deserter from 1st Dragoons, August 14, 1846, by the name of James Welch, at Camargo. |
| 1 | Supposed to have been killed on the route from Camargo to Monterey, Mex., about the 7th or 8th of September, 1846. |
| 1 | Died at Camargo, Mex., on the 28th of April, 1847. |
| 1 | Elected from private to 2d additional Lieutenant, September 1, 1846; resigned his commission at Monterey, Mex., April 2, 1847. |
| 1 | Taken prisoner when on detached service under command of Lieut. Barber, as train guard, near Marin, Mex., February 24, 1847. |
| 2 | Taken prisoner when on detached service under command of Lieut. Barber, as train guard, near Marin, Mex., February 24, 1847. |

## FOOT VOLUNTEERS—MEXICAN WAR.

| No. of each grade | REMARKS. |
|---|---|
| 1 | |
| 1 | Regimental Adjutant. |
| 1 | On leave of absence since the 30th of August, 1846, for two months, by special order; leave of absence expires October 30, 1846. |
| 2 | Promoted from Sergeant the 1st of September, 1846. |
| 1 | Promoted from Sergeant the 1st of November, 1846. |
| 2 | |
| 3 | Promoted from Corporal 1st September, 1846. |
| 4 | Promoted from Corporal 1st September, 1846. |
| 1 | |
| 2 | Promoted from private 1st September, 1846. |
| 3 | Promoted from private 1st September, 1846. |
| 1 | |
| 2 | |
| 3 | |
| 4 | |
| 5 | |
| 6 | |
| 7 | |
| 8 | |
| 9 | |
| 10 | |
| 11 | Furloughed at Camargo, Mexico, till 17th day of May, on the 10th of April. |
| 12 | |
| 13 | Captured by the enemy February 24, 1847, near Marin, Mexico, with Lieutenant Barber, escorting train. |
| 14 | Sick in hospital. |
| 15 | |
| 16 | |
| 17 | |
| 18 | |
| 19 | |
| 20 | |
| 21 | |
| 22 | |
| 19 | |

## ROLL OF COMPANY "G," FIRST REGIMENT KENTUCKY

| No. of each grade | Name | Rank | Joined for Service | Mustered In When | Mustered In Where | Period | Mustered Out When | Mustered Out Where |
|---|---|---|---|---|---|---|---|---|
| 23 | Meissner, John | Private | May 17, 1846 | May 17,'46 | Louisville, Ky. | 1 yr. | May 17,'47 | New Orleans Bks. |
| 24 | Hinrich, Otto | Private | May 17, 1846 | May 17,'46 | Louisville, Ky. | 1 yr. | May 17,'47 | New Orleans Bks. |
| 25 | Riesenberger, Nicolaus | Private | May 17, 1846 | May 17,'46 | Louisville, Ky. | 1 yr. | May 17,'47 | New Orleans Bks. |
| 26 | Rush, David | Private | May 17, 1846 | May 17,'46 | Louisville, Ky. | 1 yr. | May 17,'47 | New Orleans Bks. |
| 27 | Reubeling, Henry | Private | May 17, 1846 | May 17,'46 | Louisville, Ky. | 1 yr. | May 17,'47 | New Orleans Bks. |
| 28 | Rudert, Frederick | Private | May 17, 1846 | May 17,'46 | Louisville, Ky. | 1 yr. | May 17,'47 | New Orleans Bks. |
| 29 | Rosing, Anthony W. | Private | May 17, 1846 | May 17,'46 | Louisville, Ky. | 1 yr. | May 17,'47 | New Orleans Bks. |
| 30 | Spirs, Leopold | Private | May 17, 1846 | May 17,'46 | Louisville, Ky. | 1 yr. | May 17,'47 | New Orleans Bks. |
| 31 | Schmidt, Nicolaus | Private | May 17, 1846 | May 17,'46 | Louisville, Ky. | 1 yr. | May 17,'47 | New Orleans Bks. |
| 32 | Schmidt, Michael | Private | May 17, 1846 | May 17,'46 | Louisville, Ky. | 1 yr. | May 17,'47 | New Orleans Bks. |
| 33 | Troxler, Wm. | Private | May 17, 1846 | May 17,'46 | Louisville, Ky. | 1 yr. | May 17,'47 | New Orleans Bks. |
| 34 | Weibel, Peter | Private | May 17, 1846 | May 17,'46 | Louisville, Ky. | 1 yr. | May 17,'47 | New Orleans Bks. |
| 35 | Wilker, Daniel | Private | May 17, 1846 | May 17,'46 | Louisville, Ky. | 1 yr. | May 17,'47 | New Orleans Bks. |
| 36 | Wrotmann, Wm. | Private | May 17, 1846 | May 17,'46 | Louisville, Ky. | 1 yr. | May 17,'47 | New Orleans Bks. |
| | **DISCHARGED.** | | | | | | | |
| 1 | Wiest, Friedrich | Private | May 17, 1846 | May 17,'46 | Louisville, Ky. | 1 yr. | | |
| 2 | Rehbein, Nicolaus | Private | May 17, 1846 | May 17,'46 | Louisville, Ky. | 1 yr. | | |
| 3 | Gramp, Charles | Sergeant | May 17, 1846 | May 17,'46 | Louisville, Ky. | 1 yr. | | |
| 4 | Marbaum, Heinrich | Corporal | May 17, 1846 | May 17,'46 | Louisville, Ky. | 1 yr. | | |
| 5 | Sauer, Henry | Private | May 17, 1846 | May 17,'46 | Louisville, Ky. | 1 yr. | | |
| 6 | Frank, John | Private | May 17, 1846 | May 17,'46 | Louisville, Ky. | 1 yr. | | |
| 7 | Krauss, Christopher | Private | May 17, 1846 | May 17,'46 | Louisville, Ky. | 1 yr. | | |
| 8 | Munpel, Jacob | Private | May 17, 1846 | May 17,'46 | Louisville, Ky. | 1 yr. | | |
| 9 | Hen, Phillipp | Private | May 17, 1846 | May 17,'46 | Louisville, Ky. | 1 yr. | | |
| 10 | Shlensky, Henry | Private | May 17, 1846 | May 17,'46 | Louisville, Ky. | 1 yr. | | |
| 11 | Burmann, Charles | Private | May 17, 1846 | May 17,'46 | Louisville, Ky. | 1 yr. | | |
| | **DIED.** | | | | | | | |
| 1 | Loeffler, John | Private | May 17, 1846 | May 17,'46 | Louisville, Ky. | 1 yr. | | |
| 2 | Nuber, John | Private | May 17, 1846 | May 17,'46 | Louisville, Ky. | 1 yr. | | |
| 3 | Miller, Jacob | Private | May 17, 1846 | May 17,'46 | Louisville, Ky. | 1 yr. | | |
| 4 | Hense, Charles | Private | May 17, 1846 | May 17,'46 | Louisville, Ky. | 1 yr. | | |
| 5 | Peter Anton | Private | May 17, 1846 | May 17,'46 | Louisville, Ky. | 1 yr. | | |
| 6 | Shuckardt, Francis | Private | May 17, 1846 | May 17,'46 | Louisville, Ky. | 1 yr. | | |
| 7 | Grief, William H. | Private | May 17, 1846 | May 17,'46 | Louisville, Ky. | 1 yr. | | |
| 8 | Shultz, Henry | Private | May 17, 1846 | May 17,'46 | Louisville, Ky. | 1 yr. | | |
| 9 | Hohmann, Andreas | Private | May 17, 1846 | May 17,'46 | Louisville, Ky. | 1 yr. | | |
| | **DESERTED.** | | | | | | | |
| 1 | Baumann, John | Private | May 17, 1846 | May 17,'46 | Louisville, Ky. | 1 yr. | | |
| 2 | Renboldt, Henry | Private | May 17, 1846 | May 17,'46 | Louisville, Ky. | 1 yr. | | |
| 3 | Fuchs, Jacob | Private | May 17, 1846 | May 17,'46 | Louisville, Ky. | 1 yr. | | |

## ROLL OF COMPANY "H," FIRST REGIMENT KENTUCKY

| No. | Name | Rank | Joined for Service | Mustered In When | Mustered In Where | Period | Mustered Out When | Mustered Out Where |
|---|---|---|---|---|---|---|---|---|
| 1 | F. F. C. Triplett | Captain | May 19, 1846 | June 9, '46 | Louisville, Ky. | 1 yr. | June 9, '47 | New Orleans Bks. |
| 1 | W. T. Barbour | 1st Lieutenant | May 19, 1846 | June 9, '46 | Louisville, Ky. | 1 yr. | June 9, '47 | New Orleans Bks. |
| 1 | William Duerson | 2d Lieutenant | May 19, 1846 | June 9, '46 | Louisville, Ky. | 1 yr. | June 9, '47 | New Orleans Bks. |
| 2 | R. Wolfe Taylor | 2d Lieutenant | May 19, 1846 | June 9, '46 | Louisville, Ky. | 1 yr. | June 9, '47 | New Orleans Bks. |
| 1 | John F. Johnson | 1st Sergeant | May 19, 1846 | June 9, '46 | Louisville, Ky. | 1 yr. | June 9, '47 | New Orleans Bks. |
| 2 | M. W. Oglesby | 2d Sergeant | May 19, 1846 | June 9, '46 | Louisville, Ky. | 1 yr. | June 9, '47 | New Orleans Bks. |
| 3 | W. T. Oglesby | 3d Sergeant | May 19, 1846 | June 9, '46 | Louisville, Ky. | 1 yr. | June 9, '47 | New Orleans Bks. |
| 1 | H. Guyan | Corporal | May 19, 1846 | June 9, '46 | Louisville, Ky. | 1 yr. | June 9, '47 | New Orleans Bks. |
| 2 | David Meade | Corporal | May 19, 1846 | June 9, '46 | Louisville, Ky. | 1 yr. | June 9, '47 | New Orleans Bks. |
| 3 | Thomas James | Corporal | May 19, 1846 | June 9, '46 | Louisville, Ky. | 1 yr. | June 9, '47 | New Orleans Bks. |
| 4 | H. M. Gazlay | Corporal | May 19, 1846 | June 9, '46 | Louisville, Ky. | 1 yr. | June 9, '47 | New Orleans Bks. |
| 1 | David Knowland | Drummer | May 19, 1846 | June 9, '46 | Louisville, Ky. | 1 yr. | June 9, '47 | New Orleans Bks. |
| 1 | Arnold, E. T. | Private | May 19, 1846 | June 9, '46 | Louisville, Ky. | 1 yr. | June 9, '47 | New Orleans Bks. |
| 2 | Bowman, J. G. | Private | May 19, 1846 | June 9, '46 | Louisville, Ky. | 1 yr. | June 9, '47 | New Orleans Bks. |
| 3 | Bibb, C. A. | Private | May 19, 1846 | June 9, '46 | Louisville, Ky. | 1 yr. | June 9, '47 | New Orleans Bks. |
| 4 | Brown, Thomas | Private | May 19, 1846 | June 9, '46 | Louisville, Ky. | 1 yr. | June 9, '47 | New Orleans Bks. |
| 5 | Boggs, John | Private | May 19, 1846 | June 9, '46 | Louisville, Ky. | 1 yr. | June 9, '47 | New Orleans Bks. |
| 6 | Coontz, J. G. W. | Private | May 19, 1846 | June 9, '46 | Louisville, Ky. | 1 yr. | June 9, '47 | New Orleans Bks. |
| 7 | Creem, W. L. | Private | May 19, 1846 | June 9, '46 | Louisville, Ky. | 1 yr. | June 9, '47 | New Orleans Bks. |
| 8 | Clore, R. B. | Private | May 19, 1846 | June 9, '46 | Louisville, Ky. | 1 yr. | June 9, '47 | New Orleans Bks. |
| 9 | Collins, John | Private | May 19, 1846 | June 9, '46 | Louisville, Ky. | 1 yr. | June 9, '47 | New Orleans Bks. |
| 10 | Callis, O. B. | Private | May 19, 1846 | June 9, '46 | Louisville, Ky. | 1 yr. | June 9, '47 | New Orleans Bks. |
| 11 | Callis, A. C. | Private | May 19, 1846 | June 9, '46 | Louisville, Ky. | 1 yr. | June 9, '47 | New Orleans Bks. |
| 12 | Calander, Abram | Private | May 19, 1846 | June 9, '46 | Louisville, Ky. | 1 yr. | June 9, '47 | New Orleans Bks. |
| 13 | Dawkins, J. G. | Private | May 19, 1846 | June 9, '46 | Louisville, Ky. | 1 yr. | June 9, '47 | New Orleans Bks. |

# FOOT VOLUNTEERS—MEXICAN WAR—Continued.

| No. of each grade | REMARKS. |
|---|---|
| 23 | |
| 24 | |
| 25 | |
| 26 | |
| 27 | |
| 28 | |
| 29 | |
| 30 | |
| 31 | |
| 32 | |
| 33 | |
| 34 | |
| 35 | |
| 36 | |
| 1 | Discharged 29th of May, 1846, at Algiers, La., on Surgeon's certificate. |
| 2 | Discharged at Brazos Santiago, Texas, June 21, 1846, on Surgeon's certificate. |
| 3 | Discharged at Camargo, Mexico, August 30, 1846, on Surgeon's certificate. |
| 4 | Discharged at Camargo, Mexico, August 30, 1846, on Surgeon's certificate. |
| 5 | Discharged at Camargo, Mexico, August 30, 1846, on Surgeon's certificate. |
| 6 | Discharged at Camargo, Mexico, September 13, 1846, on Surgeon's certificate. |
| 7 | Discharged at Camargo, Mexico, September 13, 1846, on Surgeon's certificate. |
| 8 | Discharged at camp near Monterey, Mexico, September 15, 1846, on Surgeon's certificate. |
| 9 | Discharged at Camargo, Mexico, November 2, 1846, on Surgeon's certificate. |
| 10 | Discharged at camp near Monterey, Mexico, November 17, 1846, on Surgeon's certificate. |
| 11 | Discharged at Camargo, Mexico, January 24, 1847, on Surgeon's certificate. |
| 1 | Died July 4, 1846, at Camp Taylor, near Burieta, Mex. |
| 2 | Died August 28, 1846, near Camargo, Mex. |
| 3 | Fell overboard on the night between the 27th and 28th of May, 1846, between Louisville, Ky., and New Orleans. |
| 4 | Died 30th August, 1846, near Camargo, Mex. |
| 5 | Died September 14, 1846, in hospital, Camargo, Mex. |
| 6 | Died September 17, 1846, in hospital, Matamoras, Mex. |
| 7 | Died November 23, 1846, in camp near Monterey. |
| 8 | Killed on February 23, 1847, at Saltillo, Mex., while on detached service with Lieut. Beard. |
| 9 | Died in hospital May 7, 1846, at New Orleans. |
| 1 | Deserted 3d of June, 1846, at Algiers, La. |
| 2 | Deserted 3d of June, 1846, at Algiers, La. |
| 3 | Deserted 4th of June, 1846, at Algiers, La. |

# FOOT VOLUNTEERS—MEXICAN WAR.

| No. of each grade | REMARKS. |
|---|---|
| 1 | |
| 1 | Taken prisoner by the Mexicans, February 24, 1847. Not heard from since. |
| 1 | Appointed Assistant Commissary with rank of Captain by the President—date not known. |
| 2 | |
| 1 | |
| 2 | |
| 3 | |
| 1 | Taken prisoner by the Mexicans, February 24, 1847. Not since heard from. |
| 2 | |
| 3 | Left sick in Monterey, Mexico; on furlough till June 9, 1847, when his term of service expires. |
| 4 | |
| 1 | |
| 1 | |
| 2 | Taken prisoner by the Mexicans February 24, 1847. Not since heard of. |
| 3 | |
| 4 | |
| 5 | |
| 6 | |
| 7 | Taken prisoner by the Mexicans February 24, 1847. Not heard from since. |
| 8 | |
| 9 | |
| 10 | |
| 11 | |
| 12 | |
| 13 | |

## MEXICAN WAR VETERANS.

### ROLL OF COMPANY "H," FIRST REGIMENT KENTUCKY

| No. of each grade | Name | Rank | Joined for Service | Mustered In When | Mustered In Where | Period | Mustered Out When | Mustered Out Where |
|---|---|---|---|---|---|---|---|---|
| 14 | Dick, David | Private | May 19, 1846 | June 9, '46 | Louisville, Ky. | 1 yr. | June 9, '47 | New Orleans Bks. |
| 15 | Densford, John | Private | May 19, 1846 | June 9, '46 | Louisville, Ky. | 1 yr. | June 9, '47 | New Orleans Bks. |
| 16 | Diefanbaugh, Henry | Private | May 19, 1846 | June 9, '46 | Louisville, Ky. | 1 yr. | June 9, '47 | New Orleans Bks. |
| 17 | Featheringale, J. T. | Private | May 19, 1846 | June 9, '46 | Louisville, Ky. | 1 yr. | June 9, '47 | New Orleans Bks. |
| 18 | Gwynn, J. T. | Private | May 19, 1846 | June 9, '46 | Louisville, Ky. | 1 yr. | June 9, '47 | New Orleans Bks. |
| 19 | Glass, John | Private | May 19, 1846 | June 9, '46 | Louisville, Ky. | 1 yr. | June 9, '47 | New Orleans Bks. |
| 20 | Glass, James | Private | May 19, 1846 | June 9, '46 | Louisville, Ky. | 1 yr. | June 9, '47 | New Orleans Bke. |
| 21 | Guillion, W. O. | Private | May 19, 1846 | June 9, '46 | Louisville, Ky. | 1 yr. | June 9, '47 | New Orleans Bks. |
| 22 | Hamilton, H. P. | Private | May 19, 1846 | June 9, '46 | Louisville, Ky. | 1 yr. | June 9, '47 | New Orleans Bks. |
| 23 | Hughes, John W. | Private | May 19, 1846 | June 9, '46 | Louisville, Ky. | 1 yr. | June 9, '47 | New Orleans Bks. |
| 24 | Harden, Owen | Private | May 19, 1846 | June 9, '46 | Louisville, Ky. | 1 yr. | June 9, '47 | New Orleans Bks. |
| 25 | Head, William | Private | May 19, 1846 | June 9, '46 | Louisville, Ky. | 1 yr. | June 9, '47 | New Orleans Bks. |
| 26 | Hanttzbaugh, Beverly | Private | May 19, 1846 | June 9, '46 | Louisville, Ky. | 1 yr. | June 9, '47 | New Orleans Bks. |
| 27 | James, D. W. | Private | May 19, 1846 | June 9, '46 | Louisville, Ky. | 1 yr | June 9, '47 | New Orleans Bks. |
| 28 | Kalfus, J. W. | Private | May 19, 1846 | June 9, '46 | Louisville, Ky. | 1 yr. | June 9, '47 | New Orleans Bks. |
| 29 | Lane, R. N. | Private | May 19, 1846 | June 9, '46 | Louisville, Ky. | 1 yr. | June 9, '47 | New Orleans Bks. |
| 30 | McDonald, W. P. | Private | May 19, 1846 | June 9, '46 | Louisville, Ky. | 1 yr. | June 9, '47 | New Orleans Bke. |
| 31 | Mercer, Levi | Private | May 19, 1846 | June 9, '46 | Louisville, Ky. | 1 yr. | June 9, '47 | New Orleans Bks |
| 32 | Moore, Robert | Private | May 19, 1846 | June 9, '46 | Louisville, Ky. | 1 yr. | June 9, '47 | New Orleans Bks. |
| 33 | Oglesby, R. M. | Private | May 19, 1846 | June 9, '46 | Louisville, Ky. | 1 yr. | June 9, '47 | New Orleans Bks. |
| 34 | Overstreet, J. M. | Private | May 19, 1846 | June 9, '46 | Louisville, Ky. | 1 yr. | June 9, '47 | New Orleans Bks. |
| 35 | Overstreet, S. W. | Private | May 19, 1846 | June 9, '46 | Louisville, Ky. | 1 yr. | June 9, '47 | New Orleans Bks. |
| 36 | Pemberton, R. H. | Private | May 19, 1846 | June 9, '46 | Louisville, Ky. | 1 yr. | June 9, '47 | New Orleans Bks. |
| 37 | Patterson, John | Private | May 19, 1846 | June 9, '46 | Louisville, Ky. | 1 yr. | June 9, '47 | New Orleans Bks. |
| 38 | Poixnett, John S. | Private | May 19, 1846 | June 9, '46 | Louisville, Ky. | 1 yr. | June 9, '47 | New Orleans Bks. |
| 39 | Roney, Hercules | Private | May 19, 1846 | June 9, '46 | Louisville, Ky. | 1 yr. | June 9, '47 | New Orleans Bks. |
| 40 | Roberts, Francis | Private | May 19, 1846 | June 9, '46 | Louisville, Ky. | 1 yr. | June 9, '47 | New Orleans Bks. |
| 41 | Raymond, J. B. | Private | May 19, 1846 | June 9, '46 | Louisville, Ky. | 1 yr. | June 9, '47 | New Orleans Bks. |
| 42 | Rice, W. M. | Private | May 19, 1846 | June 9, '46 | Louisville, Ky. | 1 yr. | June 9, '47 | New Orleans Bks. |
| 43 | Sage, Jesse | Private | May 19, 1846 | June 9, '46 | Louisville, Ky. | 1 yr. | June 9, '47 | New Orleans Bks. |
| 44 | Sneed, P. D. | Private | May 19, 1846 | June 9, '46 | Louisville, Ky. | 1 yr. | June 9, '47 | New Orleans Bks. |
| 45 | Smith, J. R. | Private | May 19, 1846 | June 9, '46 | Louisville, Ky. | 1 yr. | June 9, '47 | New Orleans Bks. |
| 46 | Sage, Jeremiah | Private | May 19, 1846 | June 9, '46 | Louisville Ky. | 1 yr. | June 9, '47 | New Orleans Bks. |
| 47 | Sibley, T. S. | Private | May 19, 1846 | June 9, '46 | Louisville, Ky. | 1 yr. | June 9, '47 | New Orleans Bks. |
| 48 | Snyder, Thomas | Private | May 19, 1846 | June 9, '46 | Louisville, Ky. | 1 yr. | June 9, '47 | New Orleans Bks. |
| 49 | Sudlow, William | Private | May 19, 1846 | June 9, '46 | Louisville, Ky. | 1 yr. | June 9, '47 | New Orleans Bks. |
| 50 | Stratton, D. P. H. | Private | May 19, 1846 | June 9, '46 | Louisville, Ky. | 1 yr. | June 9, '47 | New Orleans Bks. |
| 51 | Taylor, George A | Private | May 19, 1846 | June 9, '46 | Louisville, Ky. | 1 yr. | June 9, '47 | New Orleans Bks. |
| 52 | Taylor, W. J. | Private | May 19, 1846 | June 9, '46 | Louisville, Ky. | 1 yr. | June 9, '47 | New Orleans Bks. |
| 53 | Taylor, J. W. | Private | May 19, 1846 | June 9, '46 | Louisville, Ky. | 1 yr. | June 9, '47 | New Orleans Bks. |
| 54 | Tucker, Weston | Private | May 19, 1846 | June 9, '46 | Louisville, Ky. | 1 yr. | June 9, '47 | New Orleans Bks. |
| 55 | Vanse, Peter | Private | May 19, 1846 | June 9, '46 | Louisville, Ky. | 1 yr. | June 9, '47 | New Orleans Bks. |
| 56 | Wheeler, John H. | Private | May 19, 1846 | June 9, '46 | Louisville, Ky. | 1 yr. | June 9, '47 | New Orleans Bks. |
| 57 | Watson, John W. | Private | May 19, 1846 | June 9, '46 | Louisville, Ky. | 1 yr. | June 9, '47 | New Orleans Bks. |
| 58 | Watson, H. | Private | May 19, 1846 | June 9, '46 | Louisville, Ky. | 1 yr. | June 9, '47 | New Orleans Bks. |
| 59 | Williams, L. C. | Private | May 19, 1846 | June 9, '46 | Louisville, Ky. | 1 yr. | June 9, '47 | New Orleans Bks. |
| 60 | Williams, O. G. | Private | May 19, 1846 | June 9, '46 | Louisville, Ky. | 1 yr. | June 9, '47 | New Orleans Bks. |
| 61 | Wilhoite, A. N., 2d | Private | May 19, 1846 | June 9, '46 | Louisville, Ky. | 1 yr. | June 9, '47 | New Orleans Bks. |
| 62 | Howard, W. W. | Private | May 19, 1846 | June 9, '46 | Louisville, Ky. | 1 yr. | June 9, '47 | New Orleans Bks. |

**DISCHARGED.**

| | | | | | | | | |
|---|---|---|---|---|---|---|---|---|
| 1 | Armstrong, G. T. | Sergeant | May 19, 1846 | June 9, '46 | Louisville, Ky. | 1 yr. | | |
| 1 | Allen, J. B. | Corporal | May 19, 1846 | June 9, '46 | Louisville, Ky. | 1 yr. | | |
| 1 | Ashley, B. T. | Private | May 19, 1846 | June 9, '46 | Louisville, Ky. | 1 yr. | | |
| 2 | Berry, F. T. | Private | May 19, 1846 | June 9, '46 | Louisville, Ky. | 1 yr. | | |
| 3 | Cranch, B. T. | Private | May 19, 1846 | June 9, '46 | Louisville, Ky. | 1 yr. | | |
| 4 | Gibson, J. C. | Private | May 19, 1846 | June 9, '46 | Louisville, Ky. | 1 yr. | | |
| 5 | Griffith, J. W. D. | Private | May 19, 1846 | June 9, '46 | Louisville, Ky. | 1 yr. | | |
| 6 | Knowland, W. | Private | May 19, 1846 | June 9, '46 | Louisville, Ky. | 1 yr. | | |
| 7 | Parks, B. F. | Private | May 19, 1846 | June 9, '46 | Louisville, Ky. | 1 yr. | | |
| 8 | Gilpin, A. M. | Private | May 19, 1846 | June 9, '46 | Louisville, Ky. | 1 yr. | | |

**DIED.**

| | | | | | | | | |
|---|---|---|---|---|---|---|---|---|
| 1 | Austin, J. D. | Private | May 19, 1846 | June 9, '46 | Louisville, Ky. | 1 yr. | | |
| 2 | Button, R. Y. | Private | May 19, 1846 | June 9, '46 | Louisville, Ky. | 1 yr. | | |
| 3 | Glass, Thomas | Private | May 19, 1846 | June 9, '46 | Louisville, Ky. | 1 yr. | | |
| 4 | Harden, P. | Private | May 19, 1846 | June 9, '46 | Louisville, Ky. | 1 yr. | | |
| 5 | Jett, Henderson | Private | May 19, 1846 | June 9, '46 | Louisville, Ky. | 1 yr. | | |
| 6 | Overstreet, W. T. | Private | May 19, 1846 | June 9, '46 | Louisville, Ky. | 1 yr. | | |
| 7 | Pollard, J. C. | Private | May 19, 1846 | June 9, '46 | Louisville, Ky. | 1 yr. | | |
| 8 | Starks, A. | Private | May 19, 1846 | June 9, '46 | Louisville, Ky. | 1 yr. | | |
| 9 | Webber, Simpson | Private | May 19, 1846 | June 9, '46 | Louisville, Ky. | 1 yr. | | |
| 10 | Williams, A. | Private | May 19, 1846 | June 9, '46 | Louisville, Ky. | 1 yr. | | |

## FOOT VOLUNTEERS—MEXICAN WAR—Continued.

| No. of each grade | REMARKS. |
|---|---|
| 14 | |
| 15 | |
| 16 | |
| 17 | |
| 18 | |
| 19 | |
| 20 | On furlough in Monterey, Mexico, until 9th June, 1847. |
| 21 | Taken prisoner by Mexicans, February 24, 1847. Not since heard from. |
| 22 | |
| 23 | |
| 24 | |
| 25 | |
| 26 | |
| 27 | |
| 28 | |
| 29 | |
| 30 | |
| 31 | |
| 32 | |
| 33 | |
| 34 | |
| 35 | |
| 36 | |
| 37 | |
| 38 | |
| 39 | |
| 40 | |
| 41 | |
| 42 | |
| 43 | |
| 44 | |
| 45 | |
| 46 | |
| 47 | |
| 48 | |
| 49 | |
| 50 | |
| 51 | |
| 52 | Taken prisoner by Mexicans, February 24, 1847. Not heard from since. |
| 53 | On furlough until 9th June, 1847, when his term expires. |
| 54 | |
| 55 | |
| 56 | |
| 57 | |
| 58 | Left in Monterey, Mex., on furlough, until June 9, 1847, expiration term of service. |
| 59 | |
| 60 | |
| 61 | |
| 62 | |
| 1 | Discharged June, 1847, without the Captain's knowledge. |
| 1 | Discharged at Camargo, Mexico, September 14, 1846, on Surgeon's certificate. |
| 1 | Discharged at Monterey, Mexico, March 21, 1847, on Surgeon's certificate. |
| 2 | Discharged at Monterey, Mexico, December 13, 1846, order of Major-Gen. Taylor, for disability. |
| 3 | Discharged at Camargo, Mexico, September 14, 1846, on Surgeon's certificate. |
| 4 | Discharged at New Orleans, La., May 14, 1847, on Surgeon's certificate. |
| 5 | Discharged at Monterey, Mexico, October 23, 1846, on Surgeon's certificate. |
| 6 | Discharged at Camargo, Mexico, September 14, 1846, on Surgeon's certificate. |
| 7 | Discharged at Camargo, Mexico, September 14, 1846, on Surgeon's certificate. |
| 8 | Discharged at Camargo, Mexico, September 14, 1846, on Surgeon's certificate. |
| 1 | Died at Camargo, Mexico, 26th September, 1846. Sergeant from 1st to 8th September, 1846. |
| 2 | Died at Camargo, Mexico, 25th October, 1846. |
| 3 | Died at Camargo, Mexico, 6th September, 1846. |
| 4 | Killed by Mexicans, December 17, 1846. |
| 5 | Died at Monterey, Mexico, November 25, 1846. |
| 6 | Died at Monterey, Mexico, November 3, 1846. |
| 7 | Died at Burieta, Mexico, July 28, 1846. |
| 8 | Died at Matamoras, Mexico, in the month of September, 1846. Date not furnished. |
| 9 | Died at Monterey, Mexico, October 7, 1846. |
| 10 | Died at Paint Island, Texas, July 7, 1846. |

## MEXICAN WAR VETERANS.

### ROLL OF COMPANY "I," FIRST REGIMENT KENTUCKY

| No. of each grade | Name. | Rank. | Joined for Service. | Mustered In. When. | Mustered In. Where. | Period | Mustered Out. When. | Mustered Out. Where. |
|---|---|---|---|---|---|---|---|---|
| 1 | B. F. Stewart | Captain | May 17, 1846 | May 17,'46 | Louisville, Ky. | 1 yr. | May 17,'47 | New Orleans Bks. |
| 1 | William White | 1st Lieutenant | May 17, 1846 | May 17,'46 | Louisville, Ky. | 1 yr. | May 17,'47 | New Orleans Bks. |
| 1 | Levi White | 2d Lieutenant | May 17, 1846 | May 17,'46 | Louisville, Ky. | 1 yr. | May 17,'47 | New Orleans Bks. |
| 2 | G. D. Hooper | Adj't & 2d Lieut. | May 17, 1846 | May 17,'46 | Louisville, Ky. | 1 yr. | May 17,'47 | New Orleans Bks. |
| 1 | J. M. Fitzhenry | Sergeant | May 17, 1846 | May 17,'46 | Louisville, Ky. | 1 yr. | May 17,'47 | New Orleans Bks. |
| 1 | Sanford Welch | Corporal | May 17, 1846 | May 17,'46 | Louisville, Ky. | 1 yr. | May 17,'47 | New Orleans Bks. |
| 2 | William C. Williams | Corporal | May 17, 1846 | May 17,'46 | Louisville, Ky. | 1 yr. | May 17,'47 | New Orleans Bks. |
| 3 | Henry Stancer | Corporal | May 17, 1846 | May 17,'46 | Louisville, Ky. | 1 yr. | May 17,'47 | New Orleans Bks. |
| 1 | Aulger, Riley B. | Private | May 17, 1846 | May 17,'46 | Louisville, Ky. | 1 yr. | May 17,'47 | New Orleans Bks. |
| 2 | Bell, Jesse | Private | May 17, 1846 | May 17,'46 | Louisville, Ky. | 1 yr. | May 17,'47 | New Orleans Bks. |
| 3 | Camden, John | Private | May 17, 1846 | May 17,'46 | Louisville, Ky. | 1 yr. | May 17,'47 | New Orleans Bks. |
| 4 | Crandell, Joseph | Private | May 17, 1846 | May 17,'46 | Louisville, Ky. | 1 yr. | May 17,'47 | New Orleans Bks. |
| 5 | Cassiday, John I. | Private | May 17, 1846 | May 17,'46 | Louisville, Ky. | 1 yr. | May 17,'47 | New Orleans Bks. |
| 6 | Carpenter, William | Private | May 17, 1846 | May 17,'46 | Louisville, Ky. | 1 yr. | May 17,'47 | New Orleans Bks. |
| 7 | Duckworth, James F. | Private | May 17, 1846 | May 17,'46 | Louisville, Ky. | 1 yr. | May 17,'47 | New Orleans Bks. |
| 8 | Davis, Franklin | Private | May 17, 1846 | May 17,'46 | Louisville, Ky. | 1 yr. | May 17,'47 | New Orleans Bks. |
| 9 | Early, Napoleon B. | Private | May 17, 1846 | May 17,'46 | Louisville, Ky. | 1 yr. | May 17,'47 | New Orleans Bks. |
| 10 | Feuley, William H. | Private | May 17, 1846 | May 17,'46 | Louisville, Ky. | 1 yr. | May 17,'47 | New Orleans Bks. |
| 11 | Fanlac, Frederick A. | Private | May 17, 1846 | May 17,'46 | Louisville, Ky. | 1 yr. | May 17,'47 | New Orleans Bks. |
| 12 | Gwathmey, George | Private | May 17, 1846 | May 17,'46 | Louisville, Ky. | 1 yr. | May 17,'47 | New Orleans Bks. |
| 13 | Gafhart, Allen R. | Private | May 17, 1846 | May 17,'46 | Louisville, Ky. | 1 yr. | May 17,'47 | New Orleans Bks. |
| 14 | Hutchins, Milton | Private | May 17, 1846 | May 17,'46 | Louisville, Ky. | 1 yr. | May 17,'47 | New Orleans Bks. |
| 15 | Hand, James A. | Private | May 30, 1846 | May 30,'46 | New Orleans, La. | 1 yr. | May 17,'47 | New Orleans Bks. |
| 16 | Kimbree, Elijah R. | Private | May 17, 1846 | May 17,'46 | Louisville, Ky. | 1 yr. | May 17,'47 | New Orleans Bks. |
| 17 | Lhorton, Lewis | Private | May 17, 1846 | May 17,'46 | Louisville, Ky. | 1 yr. | May 17,'47 | New Orleans Bks. |
| 18 | Lewis, William | Private | May 17, 1846 | May 17,'46 | Louisville, Ky. | 1 yr. | May 17,'47 | New Orleans Bks. |
| 19 | McPherson, William L. | Private | May 17, 1846 | May 17,'46 | Louisville, Ky. | 1 yr. | May 17,'47 | New Orleans Bks |
| 20 | Myers, Jefferson W. H. | Private | May 17, 1846 | May 17,'46 | Louisville, Ky. | 1 yr. | May 17,'47 | New Orleans Bks. |
| 21 | Muller, Henry | Private | May 17, 1846 | May 17,'46 | Louisville, Ky. | 1 yr. | May 17,'47 | New Orleans Bks. |
| 22 | Powers, Jacob H. | Private | May 17, 1846 | May 17,'46 | Louisville, Ky. | 1 yr. | May 17,'47 | New Orleans Bks. |
| 23 | Piercy, Henry | Private | May 17, 1846 | May 17,'46 | Louisville, Ky. | 1 yr. | May 17,'47 | New Orleans Bks. |
| 24 | Polly, Thomas J. | Private | May 17, 1846 | May 17,'46 | Louisville, Ky. | 1 yr. | May 17,'47 | New Orleans Bks. |
| 25 | Ross, Joseph | Private | May 17, 1846 | May 17,'46 | Louisville, Ky. | 1 yr. | May 17,'47 | New Orleans Bks. |
| 26 | Redman, S. G. P. | Private | May 17, 1846 | May 17,'46 | Louisville, Ky. | 1 yr. | May 17,'47 | New Orleans Bks. |
| 27 | Rogers, George | Private | May 17, 1846 | May 17,'46 | Louisville, Ky. | 1 yr. | May 17,'47 | New Orleans Bks. |
| 28 | Robinson, Gabriel | Private | May 17, 1846 | May 17,'46 | Louisville, Ky. | 1 yr. | May 17,'47 | New Orleans Bks. |
| 29 | Smith, Sir Sidney | Private | May 17, 1846 | May 17,'46 | Louisville, Ky. | 1 yr. | May 17,'47 | New Orleans Bks. |
| 30 | Shoemate, Wm. H. | Private | May 17, 1846 | May 17,'46 | Louisville, Ky. | 1 yr. | May 17,'47 | New Orleans Bks. |
| 31 | Varble, Wm. | Private | May 17, 1846 | May 17,'46 | Louisville, Ky. | 1 yr. | May 17,'47 | New Orleans Bks. |
| 32 | Walt, Rufus | Private | May 17, 1846 | May 17,'46 | Louisville, Ky. | 1 yr. | May 17,'47 | New Orleans Bks. |
| 33 | Wood, Allen | Private | May 17, 1846 | May 17,'46 | Louisville, Ky. | 1 yr. | May 17,'47 | New Orleans Bks. |
|  | **Discharged.** | | | | | | | |
| 1 | Burnett, Robert | Private | May 17, 1846 | May 17,'46 | Louisville, Ky. | 1 yr | | |
| 2 | Boyden, Stephen | Private | May 17, 1846 | May 17,'46 | Louisville, Ky. | 1 yr | | |
| 3 | Elliott, Charles | Private | May 17, 1846 | May 17,'46 | Louisville, Ky. | 1 yr. | | |
| 4 | Gwartney, Micajah C. | Private | May 17, 1846 | May 17,'46 | Louisville, Ky. | 1 yr. | | |
| 5 | Kriel, Andrew | Private | May 17, 1846 | May 17,'46 | Louisville, Ky. | 1 yr. | | |
| 6 | Lucas, John | Private | May 17, 1846 | May 17,'46 | Louisville, Ky. | 1 yr. | | |
| 7 | McClenden, Milton R. | Private | May 17, 1846 | May 17,'46 | Louisville, Ky. | 1 yr. | | |
| 8 | Mosby, Thos. J. | Private | May 17, 1846 | May 17,'46 | Louisville, Ky. | 1 yr | | |
| 9 | Merrill, Micajah | Private | May 17, 1846 | May 17,'46 | Louisville, Ky. | 1 yr. | | |
| 10 | Smith, Philip | Private | May 17, 1846 | May 17,'46 | Louisville, Ky. | 1 yr. | | |
| 11 | Weller, W. L. | Private | May 17, 1846 | May 17,'46 | Louisville, Ky. | 1 yr. | | |
| 12 | Cloud, John A. W. | Private | May 17, 1846 | May 17,'46 | Louisville, Ky. | 1 yr. | | |
| 13 | Dougherty, Nathan | Private | May 17, 1846 | May 17,'46 | Louisville, Ky. | 1 yr. | | |
| 14 | Hair, Nathan G. | Private | May 17, 1846 | May 17,'46 | Louisville, Ky. | 1 yr | | |
| 15 | Morrison, James W. | Private | May 17, 1846 | May 17,'46 | Louisville, Ky. | 1 yr | | |
| 16 | Phillips, Jerome | Private | May 17, 1846 | May 17,'46 | Louisville, Ky. | 1 yr. | | |
| 17 | Carner, Pleasant | Private | May 17, 1846 | May 17,'46 | Louisville, Ky. | 1 yr. | | |
| 18 | Smyth, W. H. | Private | May 17, 1846 | May 17,'46 | Louisville, Ky. | 1 yr. | | |
|  | **On Furlough.** | | | | | | | |
| 1 | Elder, John C. | 1st Sergeant | May 17, 1846 | May 17,'46 | Louisville, Ky. | 1 yr. | | |
| 2 | Ashby, H. L. | Sergeant | May 17, 1846 | May 17,'46 | Louisville, Ky. | 1 yr. | | |
| 3 | Swan, Commodore | Private | May 17, 1846 | May 17,'46 | Louisville, Ky. | 1 yr. | | |
| 4 | Ward, Hugh | Private | May 17, 1846 | May 17,'46 | Louisville, Ky. | 1 yr. | | |
|  | **Captured.** | | | | | | | |
| 1 | Marsh, Jos. S. | Sergeant | May 17, 1846 | May 17,'46 | Louisville, Ky. | 1 yr. | | |
| 2 | Stewart, James | Corporal | May 17, 1846 | May 17,'46 | Louisville, Ky. | 1 yr. | | |
| 3 | Downing, Edward | Private | May 17, 1846 | May 17,'46 | Louisville, Ky. | 1 yr. | | |
|  | **Transferred.** | | | | | | | |
| 1 | Tucker, Isacher | Private | May 17, 1846 | May 17,'46 | Louisville, Ky. | 1 yr. | | |

## FOOT VOLUNTEERS MEXICAN WAR.

| No. of each grade | REMARKS. |
|---|---|
| 1 | Promoted Captain from 1st Lieutenant, September 1, 1846, vice W. L. Ball, deceased. |
| 1 | Promoted 1st Lieutenant from 2d Lieutenant, September 1, 1846, vice B. F. Stewart, promoted. |
| 1 | Promoted to 2d Lieutenant from 1st Sergeant, September 1, 1846, vice Wm. White, promoted. |
| 2 | Appointed additional 2d Lieutenant, September 1, 1846, from Sergeant. |
| 1 | |
| 1 | Promoted to Corporal from private, September 1, 1846. |
| 2 | |
| 3 | Promoted from private, February 1, 1847. |
| 1 | |
| 2 | On furlough since April 21, 1847. |
| 3 | |
| 4 | |
| 5 | |
| 6 | |
| 7 | |
| 8 | |
| 9 | |
| 10 | |
| 11 | |
| 12 | |
| 13 | |
| 14 | |
| 15 | |
| 16 | |
| 17 | |
| 18 | |
| 19 | |
| 20 | |
| 21 | |
| 22 | |
| 23 | |
| 24 | |
| 25 | On furlough since April 21, 1847. |
| 26 | |
| 27 | |
| 28 | |
| 29 | |
| 30 | |
| 31 | |
| 32 | |
| 33 | |
| 1 | By order of Gen. Taylor, April 4, 1847, at Monterey, Mexico. |
| 2 | For disability, at Saltillo, December 26, 1846. |
| 3 | By order of Gen. Taylor, April 4, 1847, at Monterey, Mexico. |
| 4 | For disability, at Monterey, April 10, 1847. |
| 5 | By order of Gen. Taylor, April 4, 1847, at Monterey, Mexico. |
| 6 | For disability, October 16, 1846, at Monterey, Mexico. |
| 7 | By order of Gen. Hamer, November 23, 1846, at Monterey, Mexico. |
| 8 | By order of Gen. Taylor, April 4, 1847, at Monterey, Mexico. |
| 9 | By order of Gen. Taylor, April 4, 1847, at Monterey, Mexico. |
| 10 | For disability, October 16, 1846, at Monterey, Mexico. |
| 11 | For disability, January 30 1847, at Monterey, Mexico. |
| 12 | For disability, August 30, 1846, at Camargo, Mexico. |
| 13 | For disability, August 30, 1846, at Camargo, Mexico. |
| 14 | For disability, August 30, 1846, at Camargo, Mexico. |
| 15 | For disability, August 30, 1846, at Camargo, Mexico. |
| 16 | For disability, August 30, 1846, at Camargo, Mexico. |
| 17 | For disability, May 30, 1846, at New Orleans, La. |
| 18 | For disability, May 30, 1846, at New Orleans, La. |
| 1 | On furlough at the mouth of the Rio Grande, in the employ of the Quartermaster since April 21, 1847. |
| 2 | On furlough at the mouth of the Rio Grande, in the employ of the Quartermaster since April 21, 1847. |
| 3 | On furlough at the mouth of the Rio Grande, in the employ of the Quartermaster since April 21, 1847. |
| 4 | On furlough at the mouth of the Rio Grande, in the employ of the Quartermaster since April 21, 1847. |
| 1 | By Mexicans, near Marin, Mexico, February 24, 1847, and now prisoner. |
| 2 | By Mexicans, near Marin, Mexico, February 24, 1847, and now prisoner. |
| 3 | By Mexicans, near Marin, Mexico, February 24, 1847, and now prisoner. |
| 1 | Transferred to 3d Regiment, U. S. A., August 7, 1846. |

MEXICAN WAR VETERANS.

## ROLL OF COMPANY "I," FIRST REGIMENT KENTUCKY

| No. of each grade | Name. | Rank. | Joined for Service. | Mustered In. When. | Mustered In. Where. | Period | Mustered Out. When. | Mustered Out. Where. |
|---|---|---|---|---|---|---|---|---|
| | DIED. | | | | | | | |
| 1 | Alexander, Benjamin | Private | May 17, 1846. | May 17, '46. | Louisville, Ky. | 1 yr. | | |
| 2 | Bartlett, Joseph | Private | May 17, 1846. | May 17, '46. | Louisville, Ky. | 1 yr. | | |
| 3 | Devley, Nicholas | Private | May 17, 1846. | May 17, '46. | Louisville, Ky. | 1 yr. | | |
| 4 | Bauchamp, Newell | Private | May 17, 1846. | May 17, '46. | Louisville, Ky. | 1 yr. | | |
| 5 | Simmers, Wm. P. | Private | May 17, 1846 | May 17, '46. | Louisville, Ky. | 1 yr. | | |
| 6 | Simms, Wm. | Private | May 17, 1846. | May 17, '46. | Louisville, Ky. | 1 yr. | | |
| 7 | Sharpe, German B. | Private | May 17, 1846. | May 17, '46. | Louisville, Ky. | 1 yr. | | |
| 8 | Herrick, David | Private | May 17, 1846. | May 17, '46. | Louisville, Ky. | 1 yr. | | |
| 9 | Ball, Wm. L. | Private | May 17, 1846. | May 17, '46. | Louisville, Ky. | 1 yr. | | |
| | DESERTED. | | | | | | | |
| 1 | Swinney, Jos. | Corporal | May 17, 1846. | May 17, '46. | Louisville, Ky. | 1 yr. | | |
| 2 | Sullivan, Wm. | Private | May 17, 1846. | May 17, '46. | Louisville, Ky. | 1 yr. | | |

## ROLL OF COMPANY "K," FIRST REGIMENT KENTUCKY

| No. | Name. | Rank. | Joined for Service. | Mustered In When. | Mustered In Where. | Period | Mustered Out When. | Mustered Out Where. |
|---|---|---|---|---|---|---|---|---|
| 1 | Charles W. Bullen | Captain | May 17, 1846. | May 17, '46. | Louisville, Ky. | 1 yr. | May 17, '47. | New Orleans Bks. |
| 1 | E. M. Stone | 1st Lieutenant | May 17, 1846. | May 17, '46. | Louisville, Ky. | 1 yr. | May 17, '47. | New Orleans Bks. |
| 1 | J. R. Butler | 2d Lieutenant | May 17, 1846. | May 17, '46. | Louisville, Ky. | 1 yr. | May 17, '47. | New Orleans Bks. |
| 2 | D. G. Swinney | 2d Lieutenant | May 17, 1846. | May 17, '46. | Louisville, Ky. | 1 yr. | May 17, '47. | New Orleans Bks. |
| 1 | Madison Powell | 1st Sergeant | May 17, 1846. | May 17, '46. | Louisville, Ky. | 1 yr. | May 17, '47. | New Orleans Bks. |
| 2 | Robert M. Buckner | 2d Sergeant | May 17, 1846. | May 17, '46. | Louisville, Ky. | 1 yr. | May 17, '47. | New Orleans Bks. |
| 3 | Wilson J. Green | 3d Sergeant | May 17, 1846. | May 17, '46. | Louisville, Ky. | 1 yr. | May 17, '47. | New Orleans Bks. |
| 4 | Lewis Roberts | 4th Sergeant | May 17, 1846. | May 17, '46. | Louisville, Ky. | 1 yr. | May 17, '47. | New Orleans Bks. |
| 1 | William M. Tilden | 1st Corporal | May 17, 1846. | May 17, '46. | Louisville, Ky. | 1 yr. | May 17, '47. | New Orleans Bks. |
| 2 | George Wright | 2d Corporal | May 17, 1846. | May 17, '46. | Louisville, Ky. | 1 yr. | May 17, '47. | New Orleans Bks. |
| 3 | Robert S. White | 3d Corporal | May 17, 1846. | May 17, '46. | Louisville, Ky. | 1 yr. | May 17, '47. | New Orleans Bks. |
| 4 | Richard D. Road | 4th Corporal | May 17, 1846. | May 17, '46. | Louisville, Ky. | 1 yr. | May 17, '47. | New Orleans Bks. |
| 1 | Abbott, Nelson | Private | May 17, 1846. | May 17, '46. | Louisville, Ky. | 1 yr | May 17, '47. | New Orleans Bks. |
| 2 | Anderson, George W. | Private | May 17, 1846. | May 17, '46. | Louisville, Ky. | 1 yr. | May 17, '47. | New Orleans Bks. |
| 3 | Brown, Peter S. | Private | May 17, 1846. | May 17, '46. | Louisville, Ky. | 1 yr. | May 17, '47. | New Orleans Bks. |
| 4 | Bradshaw, George W. | Private | May 17, 1846. | May 17, '46. | Louisville, Ky. | 1 yr. | May 17, '47. | New Orleans Bks. |
| 5 | Bayless, George W. | Private | May 17, 1846. | May 17, '46. | Louisville, Ky. | 1 yr. | May 17, '47. | New Orleans Bks. |
| 6 | Chambers, Alexander | Private | May 17, 1846. | May 17, '46 | Louisville, Ky. | 1 yr. | May 17, '47. | New Orleans Bks. |
| 7 | Densford, William | Private | May 17, 1846. | May 17, '46. | Louisville, Ky. | 1 yr. | May 17, '47. | New Orleans Bks. |
| 8 | Deutsch, Valentine | Private | May 17, 1846. | May 17, '46. | Louisville, Ky. | 1 yr. | May 17, '47. | New Orleans Bks. |
| 9 | Detch, Francis | Private | May 17, 1846. | May 17, '46. | Louisville, Ky. | 1 yr. | May 17, '47. | New Orleans Bks. |
| 10 | Davis, John T. | Private | June 6, 1846. | June 6, '46. | Algiers, La. | 1 yr. | May 17, '47. | New Orleans Bks. |
| 11 | Goff, W. S. | Private | May 17, 1846. | May 17, '46. | Louisville, Ky. | 1 yr. | May 17, '47. | New Orleans Bks. |
| 12 | Grable, Alfred | Private | May 17, 1846. | May 17, '46. | Louisville, Ky. | 1 yr. | May 17, '47. | New Orleans Bks. |
| 13 | Hatsell, David | Private | May 17, 1846. | May 17, '46. | Louisville, Ky. | 1 yr. | May 17, '47. | New Orleans Bks. |
| 14 | Hardin, Thomas P. | Private | May 17, 1846. | May 17, '46. | Louisville, Ky. | 1 yr. | May 17, '47. | New Orleans Bks. |
| 15 | Innis, Isaac | Private | May 17, 1846. | May 17, '46. | Louisville, Ky. | 1 yr. | May 17, '47. | New Orleans Bks. |
| 16 | Johnson, James | Private | May 17, 1846. | May 17, '46. | Louisville, Ky. | 1 yr. | May 17, '47. | New Orleans Bks. |
| 17 | Lampton, Joshua L. | Private | May 17, 1846. | May 17, '46. | Louisville, Ky. | 1 yr. | May 17, '47. | New Orleans Bks. |
| 18 | Lewis, John | Private | May 17, 1846. | May 17, '46. | Louisville, Ky. | 1 yr. | May 17, '47. | New Orleans Bks. |
| 19 | McCoy, George | Private | May 17, 1846. | May 17, '46. | Louisville, Ky. | 1 yr. | May 17, '47. | New Orleans Bks. |
| 20 | McCoy, Claiborne | Private | May 17, 1846. | May 17, '46. | Louisville, Ky. | 1 yr. | May 17, '47. | New Orleans Bks. |
| 21 | Mullen, John | Private | May 17, 1846. | May 17, '46. | Louisville, Ky. | 1 yr. | May 17, '47. | New Orleans Bks. |
| 22 | McDonald, William | Private | May 17, 1846. | May 17, '46. | Louisville, Ky. | 1 yr. | May 17, '47. | New Orleans Bks. |
| 23 | Moore, John A. | Private | May 17, 1846. | May 17, '46. | Louisville, Ky. | 1 yr. | May 17, '47. | New Orleans Bks. |
| 24 | Means, John H. | Private | May 17, 1846. | May 17, '46. | Louisville, Ky. | 1 yr. | May 17, '47. | New Orleans Bks. |
| 25 | McMillen, Hugh | Private | May 17, 1846. | May 17, '46 | Louisville, Ky. | 1 yr. | May 17, '47. | New Orleans Bks. |
| 26 | McHugh, Samuel | Private | May 17, 1846. | May 17, '46. | Louisville, Ky. | 1 yr. | May 17, '47. | New Orleans Bks. |
| 27 | Millarey, Daniel | Private | May 17, 1846. | May 17, '46. | Louisville, Ky. | 1 yr. | May 17, '47. | New Orleans Bks. |
| 28 | O'Niel, John P. | Private | May 17, 1846. | May 17, '46. | Louisville, Ky. | 1 yr. | May 17, '47. | New Orleans Bks. |
| 29 | Robards, Joseph | Private | May 17, 1846. | May 17, '46. | Louisville, Ky. | 1 yr. | May 17, '47. | New Orleans Bks. |
| 30 | Ritten, James | Private | May 17, 1846. | May 17, '46. | Louisville, Ky. | 1 yr. | May 17, '47. | New Orleans Bks. |
| 31 | Robertson, Arch | Private | May 17, 1846. | May 17, '46. | Louisville, Ky. | 1 yr. | May 17, '47. | New Orleans Bks. |
| 32 | Rhodes, John P. | Private | May 17, 1846. | May 17, '46 | Louisville, Ky. | 1 yr. | May 17, '47. | New Orleans Bks. |
| 33 | Spindler, Andy | Private | May 17, 1846. | May 17, '46. | Louisville, Ky. | 1 yr. | May 17, '47. | New Orleans Bks. |
| 34 | Stitt, John W. | Private | May 17, 1846. | May 17, '46. | Louisville, Ky. | 1 yr. | May 17, '47. | New Orleans Bks. |
| 35 | Scott, John | Private | May 17, 1846. | May 17, '46. | Louisville, Ky. | 1 yr. | May 17, '47. | New Orleans Bks. |
| 36 | Summers, T. T. | Private | May 17, 1846. | May 17, '46. | Louisville, Ky. | 1 yr. | May 17, '47. | New Orleans Bks. |
| 37 | Simpson, John F. | Private | May 17, 1846. | May 17, '46. | Louisville, Ky. | 1 yr. | May 17, '47. | New Orleans Bks. |
| 38 | Treloar, John | Private | May 17, 1846. | May 17, '46. | Louisville, Ky. | 1 yr. | May 17, '47. | New Orleans Bks. |
| 39 | Vail, Jacob G. | Private | May 17, 1846. | May 17, '46. | Louisville, Ky. | 1 yr. | May 17, '47. | New Orleans Bks. |
| 40 | Walton, John W. | Private | May 17, 1846. | May 17, '46. | Louisville, Ky. | 1 yr. | May 17, '47. | New Orleans Bks. |
| 41 | Wilcox, Stephen T. | Private | May 17, 1846. | May 17, '46. | Louisville, Ky. | 1 yr. | May 17, '47. | New Orleans Bks. |
| 42 | Wilkey, James | Private | May 17, 1846. | May 17, '46. | Louisville, Ky. | 1 yr. | May 17, '47. | New Orleans Bks. |

## FOOT VOLUNTEERS—MEXICAN WAR—Continued.

| No. of each grade | REMARKS. |
|---|---|
| 1 | Killed near Monterey, Mexico, November 25, 1846. |
| 2 | Died at Monterey, Mexico, October 2, 1846, from the effects of wounds received at the battle of Monterey. |
| 3 | Missing; supposed to have been murdered by Mexicans, near Monterey, Mexico, October 28, 1846. |
| 4 | Died at Matamoras, Mexico, September 1, 1846. |
| 5 | Died at Matamoras, Mexico, September 5, 1846. |
| 6 | Accidently drowned in the Rio Grande, near Burieta, Mexico, July 18, 1846. |
| 7 | Drowned in the Rio Grande near Burieta, Mexico, August 2, 1846. |
| 8 | Died at Camargo, Mexico, August 25, 1846. |
| 9 | Missing; supposed to have been murdered at or near Matamoras, Mexico, August 1, 1846. |
| 1 | Deserted at New Orleans, La., June 5, 1846. |
| 2 | Deserted at New Orleans, La., June 5, 1846. |

## FOOT VOLUNTEERS—MEXICAN WAR.

| No. of each grade | REMARKS. |
|---|---|
| 1 | |
| 1 | |
| 1 | Was appointed 2d Lieutenant July 7, 1846; now on furlough and aid to Gen. Butler. |
| 2 | Was promoted from a private September 1, 1846, to 2d Lieutenant. |
| 1 | Was promoted from private to Corporal September 1, 1846, and to 1st Sergeant January 6, 1847. |
| 2 | Was promoted from Corporal to Sergeant September 1, 1846. |
| 3 | Was promoted from Corporal to Sergeant September, 1, 1846. |
| 4 | Was promoted from private October 1, 1846. |
| 1 | Promoted from private January 7, 1847. |
| 2 | Promoted from private January 7, 1847. |
| 3 | Promoted from private September 1, 1847. |
| 4 | Promoted from private September 1, 1847. |
| 1 | |
| 2 | |
| 3 | |
| 4 | |
| 5 | |
| 6 | |
| 7 | |
| 8 | |
| 9 | |
| 10 | |
| 11 | |
| 12 | |
| 13 | |
| 14 | |
| 15 | |
| 16 | |
| 17 | |
| 18 | |
| 19 | |
| 20 | |
| 21 | |
| 22 | |
| 23 | |
| 24 | |
| 25 | |
| 26 | |
| 27 | |
| 28 | |
| 29 | |
| 30 | |
| 31 | |
| 32 | |
| 33 | |
| 34 | |
| 35 | |
| 36 | |
| 37 | |
| 38 | |
| 39 | |
| 40 | |
| 41 | |
| 42 | |

## ROLL OF COMPANY "K," FIRST REGIMENT KENTUCKY

| No. of each grade | Name | Rank | Joined for Service | Mustered In When | Mustered In Where | Period | Mustered Out When | Mustered Out Where |
|---|---|---|---|---|---|---|---|---|
| 43 | Wynne, Thomas | Private | May 17, 1846 | May 17, '46 | Louisville, Ky. | 1 yr. | May 17, '47 | New Orleans Bks. |
| 44 | Whetmeyer, Jacob | Private | May 17, 1846 | May 17, '46 | Louisville, Ky. | 1 yr. | May 17, '47 | New Orleans Bks. |
| | **On Furlough.** | | | | | | | |
| 1 | Branch, H. B. | Private | May 17, 1846 | May 17, '46 | Louisville, Ky. | 1 yr. | | |
| 2 | Lupton, Cy. C. | Private | May 17, 1846 | May 17, '46 | Louisville, Ky. | 1 yr. | | |
| 3 | Stephens, John | Private | May 17, 1846 | May 17, '46 | Louisville, Ky. | 1 yr. | | |
| 4 | Craig, Geo. W. | Private | Aug. 1, 1846 | Aug. 1, '46 | Camargo, Mexico | 1 yr. | | |
| | **Sick.** | | | | | | | |
| 1 | Benner, D. B. T. | Private | May 17, 1846 | May 17, '46 | Louisville, Ky. | 1 yr. | | |
| 2 | Grant, Jacob | Private | May 17, 1846 | May 17, '46 | Louisville, Ky. | 1 yr. | | |
| | **Captured.** | | | | | | | |
| 1 | Barry, Thomas I. | Private | May 17, 1846 | May 17, '46 | Louisville, Ky. | 1 yr. | | |
| 2 | Carpenter, W. W. | Private | May 17, 1846 | May 17, '46 | Louisville, Ky. | 1 yr. | | |
| 3 | Fairbanks, Flavius G. | Private | May 17, 1846 | May 17, '46 | Louisville, Ky. | 1 yr. | | |
| 4 | Miller, F. A. | Private | May 17, 1846 | May 17, '46 | Louisville, Ky. | 1 yr. | | |
| | **Discharged.** | | | | | | | |
| 1 | Atkinson, F. M. | Private | May 17, 1846 | May 17, '46 | Louisville, Ky. | 1 yr. | | |
| 2 | Allender, Thomas | Private | May 17, 1846 | May 17, '46 | Louisville, Ky. | 1 yr. | | |
| 3 | Ackley, W. M. | Private | May 17, 1846 | May 17, '46 | Louisville, Ky. | 1 yr. | | |
| 4 | Barnum, John W. | Private | May 17, 1846 | May 17, '46 | Louisville, Ky. | 1 yr. | | |
| 5 | Brown, Lindsey B. | Private | May 17, 1846 | May 17, '46 | Louisville, Ky. | 1 yr. | | |
| 6 | Deaver, Henry W. | Private | May 17, 1846 | May 17, '46 | Louisville, Ky. | 1 yr. | | |
| 7 | Davidson, William F. | Private | May 17, 1846 | May 17, '46 | Louisville, Ky. | 1 yr. | | |
| 8 | Dickson, Robert | Private | May 17, 1846 | May 17, '46 | Louisville, Ky. | 1 yr. | | |
| 9 | Dade, John | Private | May 17, 1846 | May 17, '46 | Louisville, Ky. | 1 yr. | | |
| 10 | Elder, William F. | Private | May 17, 1846 | May 17, '46 | Louisville, Ky. | 1 yr. | | |
| 11 | Flannery, George | Private | May 17, 1846 | May 17, '46 | Louisville, Ky. | 1 yr. | | |
| 12 | Johnson, Joseph C. | Private | May 17, 1846 | May 17, '46 | Louisville, Ky. | 1 yr. | | |
| 13 | Kilgour, John | Private | May 17, 1846 | May 17, '46 | Louisville, Ky. | 1 yr. | | |
| 14 | Moffitt, Eri | Private | June 6, 1846 | Sept. 1, '46 | Camargo, Mexico | 1 yr. | | |
| 15 | Melton, George W. | Private | May 17, 1846 | May 17, '46 | Louisville, Ky. | 1 yr. | | |
| 16 | Williams, W. W. | Private | May 17, 1846 | May 17, '46 | Louisville, Ky. | 1 yr. | | |
| 17 | Young, Lewis | Private | May 17, 1846 | May 17, '46 | Louisville, Ky. | 1 yr. | | |
| 18 | Jones, Harrison | 1st Sergeant | May 17, 1846 | May 17, '46 | Louisville, Ky. | 1 yr. | | |
| 19 | Baker, James H. | Sergeant | May 17, 1846 | May 17, '46 | Louisville, Ky. | 1 yr. | | |
| 20 | Hurst, Bolivar | Sergeant | May 17, 1846 | May 17, '46 | Louisville, Ky. | 1 yr. | | |
| 21 | Pittman, George W. | Corporal | May 17, 1846 | | | | | |
| | **Died.** | | | | | | | |
| 1 | Hoover, George D. | Private | May 17, 1846 | May 17, '46 | Louisville, Ky. | 1 yr. | | |
| 2 | Mackay, John | Private | May 17, 1846 | May 17, '46 | Louisville, Ky. | 1 yr. | | |
| 3 | Edwards, William H. | Private | May 17, 1846 | May 17, '46 | Louisville, Ky. | 1 yr. | | |
| | **Deserted.** | | | | | | | |
| 1 | Jeffries, James | Private | May 17, 1846 | May 17, '46 | Louisville, Ky. | 1 yr. | | |
| 2 | Lewis, William H. | Private | May 17, 1846 | May 17, '46 | Louisville, Ky. | 1 yr. | | |
| 3 | Shelton, Wiley A. | Private | May 17, 1846 | May 17, '46 | Louisville, Ky. | 1 yr. | | |
| 4 | Bemer, Benjamin H. | Private | May 17, 1846 | May 17, '46 | Louisville, Ky. | 1 yr. | | |

## ROLL OF THE FIELD AND STAFF THIRD REGIMENT

| | Name | Rank | Joined for Service | Mustered In When | Mustered In Where | Period | Mustered Out When | Mustered Out Where |
|---|---|---|---|---|---|---|---|---|
| 1 | Manlius V. Thompson | Colonel | Oct. 3, 1847 | Oct. 3, '47 | Louisville, Ky. | To serve during the war. | July 21, '48 | Louisville, Ky. |
| 1 | Thos. L. Crittenden | Lieut. Colonel | Oct. 4, 1847 | Oct. 4, '47 | Louisville, Ky. | | July 21, '48 | Louisville, Ky. |
| 1 | John C. Breckinridge | Major | Oct. 4, 1847 | Oct. 4, '47 | Louisville, Ky. | | July 21, '48 | Louisville, Ky. |
| 1 | Ben. F. Bradley | Adjutant | Oct. 3, 1847 | Oct. 4, '47 | Louisville, Ky. | | July 21, '48 | Louisville, Ky. |
| 1 | Enos H. Berry | 1st Lt. R. Q. M. | Nov. 27, 1847 | Oct. 4, '47 | Louisville, Ky. | | July 21, '48 | Louisville, Ky. |
| 1 | John A. Logan | 1st Lt. R. Com. | Oct. 20, 1847 | Oct. 5, '47 | Louisville, Ky. | | July 21, '48 | Louisville, Ky. |
| 1 | Wm. Cromwell | Ass't Surgeon | Oct. 14, 1847 | Oct. 16, '47 | Louisville, Ky. | | July 21, '48 | Louisville, Ky. |
| 1 | John T. Simerall | Sergeant Major | Mar. 21, 1848 | Oct. 5, '47 | Louisville, Ky. | | July 21, '48 | Louisville, Ky. |
| 1 | James Neal | Qr. M. Serg't | Apr. 30, 1848 | Oct. 4, '47 | Louisville, Ky. | | July 21, '48 | Louisville, Ky. |
| 1 | Thos. B. Martin | Prin'l Musician | Oct. 4, 1847 | Sept. 28, '47 | Louisville, Ky. | | July 21, '48 | Louisville, Ky. |
| 2 | Otho P. Simms | Prin'l Musician | Apr. 10, 1848 | Sept. 28, '47 | Louisville, Ky. | | July 21, '48 | Louisville, Ky. |
| | **Transferred.** | | | | | | | |
| 1 | Thomas H. Taylor | Ser. Major | Oct. 3, 1847 | Oct. 3, '47 | Louisville, Ky. | | July 21, '48 | Louisville, Ky. |

# FOOT VOLUNTEERS—MEXICAN WAR—Continued.

| No. of each grade | REMARKS. |
|---|---|
| 43 | |
| 44 | |
| | |
| 1 | On furlough at Monterey, Mex., in the employ of the Quartermaster, April 5, 1847. |
| 2 | On furlough at Monterey, Mex., in the employ of the Quartermaster, April 5, 1847. |
| 3 | On furlough at Monterey, Mex., in the employ of the Quartermaster, April 5, 1847. |
| 4 | On furlough at Monterey, Mex., as Hospital Steward. |
| | |
| 1 | Left sick at Monterey, April 12, 1847, in the hospital. |
| 2 | Left sick at Monterey, April 12, 1847, in the hospital. |
| | |
| 1 | Was captured at Marin, Mexico, February 24, 1847, with the train from Camargo. |
| 2 | Was captured at Marin, Mexico, February 24, 1847, with the train from Camargo. |
| 3 | Was captured at Marin, Mexico, February 24, 1847, with the train from Camargo. |
| 4 | Was captured at Marin, Mexico, February 24, 1847, with the train from Camargo. |
| | |
| 1 | Discharged at Camargo, Mexico, August 29, 1846, on Surgeon's certificate. |
| 2 | Discharged at Monterey, Mexico, December 18, 1846, on account of wounds received at the battle of Monterey, September 22, 1846. |
| 3 | Discharged at Camargo, Mexico, August 29, 1846, on Surgeon's certificate. |
| 4 | Discharged at Matamoras, Mexico, August 29, 1846, on Surgeon's certificate. |
| 5 | Discharged at Monterey, Mexico, December 5, 1846, on Surgeon's certificate. |
| 6 | Discharged at Camargo, Mexico, September 13, 1846, on Surgeon's certificate. |
| 7 | Discharged at Monterey, Mexico, January 16, on Surgeon's certificate. |
| 8 | Discharged at Monterey, Mexico, September 28, on Surgeon's certificate. |
| 9 | Discharged at Camargo, Mexico, August 29, on Surgeon's certificate. |
| 10 | Discharged at Camargo, Mexico, August 29, on Surgeon's certificate. |
| 11 | Discharged at Algiers, La., June 17, 1846, on Surgeon's certificate. |
| 12 | Discharged at Camargo, Mexico, August 29, 1846, on Surgeon's certificate. |
| 13 | Discharged at Camargo, Mexico, August 29, 1846, on Surgeon's certificate. |
| 14 | Discharged at Camargo, Mexico, September 10, 1846, on Surgeon's certificate. |
| 15 | Discharged at Camargo, Mexico, August 29, 1846, on Surgeon's certificate. |
| 16 | Discharged at Monterey, Mexico, November 6, 1846, on Surgeon's certificate. |
| 17 | Discharged at Monterey, Mexico, March 8, 1847, on Surgeon's certificate. |
| 18 | Discharged at Monterey, Mexico, September 28, 1846, on Surgeon's certificate. |
| 19 | Discharged at Camargo, Mexico, September 5, 1846, on Surgeon's certificate. |
| 20 | Discharged at Camargo, Mexico, August 29, 1846, on Surgeon's certificate. |
| 21 | Discharged at Camargo, Mexico, August 24, 1846, on Surgeon's certificate. |
| | |
| 1 | Died at Burieta, Mex., August 3, 1846. |
| 2 | Died of wounds received on the march from Monterey to Camargo, while in the line. |
| 3 | Killed at Saltillo, February 27, 1847, while on detached service. |
| | |
| 1 | Deserted at Algiers, La., June 7, 1846. |
| 2 | Deserted at Algiers, La., June 7, 1846. |
| 3 | Deserted at Louisville, Ky., May 25, 1846. |
| 4 | Deserted at Algiers, La., June 5, 1846. |

# KENTUCKY FOOT VOLUNTEERS—MEXICAN WAR.

| | |
|---|---|
| 1 | |
| 1 | |
| 1 | |
| 1 | Appointed by Col. Thompson, from Captain Smith's Company "A," in which he was enrolled 1st Lieutenant. |
| 1 | Appointed by Col. Thompson, from Captain Metcalf's Company "E," in which he was enrolled 1st Lieutenant. |
| 1 | Appointed by Col. Thompson, from Captain Todd's Company "I," in which he was enrolled 2d Lieutenant, promoted to 1st Lieutenant, February 27, 1848. |
| 1 | Accepted appointment October 14, 1847. |
| 1 | Appointed by Col. Thompson, March 21, 1848, from Company "B," in which he was enrolled and served a private to the date of appointment. |
| 1 | Appointed by Col. Thompson, April 30, 1848, from Company "E" (Captain Metcalf), in which he was enrolled and a private to date of appointment. |
| 1 | Appointed by Col. Thompson, October, 1848, from Captain Robinson's Company "C," in which he was enrolled and served as musician to date of appointment. |
| 2 | Appointed by Col. Thompson, April 10, 1848, from Captain Caldwell's Company "K." |
| | |
| 1 | Transferred by promotion, March 21, 1848, to 1st Lieutenant of Captain Caldwell's Company "K." |

## ROLL OF FIELD AND STAFF THIRD REGIMENT KENTUCKY

| No. of each grade | Name | Rank | Joined for Service | Mustered In When | Mustered In Where | Period | Mustered Out When | Mustered Out Where |
|---|---|---|---|---|---|---|---|---|
|   | DISCHARGED. |   |   |   |   |   |   |   |
| 1 | James O'Bannon | Q. M. Sergt. | Oct. 1, 1847 | Oct. 5, '47 | Louisville, Ky. | During war. | July 21, '48 | Louisville, Ky. |
| 2 | Thomas Holliday | Q. M. Sergt. | Nov. 26, 1847 | Oct. 4, '47 | Louisville, Ky. |   | July 21, '48 | Louisville, Ky. |
| 1 | John M. Stiners | Prin'l Musician | Oct. 4, 1847 | Sept. 28, '47 | Louisville, Ky. |   | July 21, '48 | Louisville, Ky. |

## ROLL OF COMPANY "A," THIRD REGIMENT KENTUCKY

| No. | Name | Rank | Joined for Service | Mustered In When | Mustered In Where | Period | Mustered Out When | Mustered Out Where |
|---|---|---|---|---|---|---|---|---|
| 1 | John R. Smith | Captain | Oct. 3, 1847 | Oct. 5, '47 | Louisville, Ky. | To serve during war. | July 21, '48 | Louisville, Ky. |
| 1 | Benjamin F. Bradley | 1st Lieutenant | Oct. 3, 1847 | Oct. 5, '47 | Louisville, Ky. |   | July 21, '48 | Louisville, Ky. |
| 1 | Eli Holtzclaw | 2d Lieutenant | Oct. 3, 1847 | Oct. 5, '47 | Louisville, Ky. |   | July 21, '48 | Louisville, Ky. |
| 2 | Will Edmonson | 2d Lieutenant | Oct. 3, 1847 | Oct. 5, '47 | Louisville, Ky. |   | July 21, '48 | Louisville, Ky. |
| 1 | Bela O. Bradford | 1st Sergeant | Oct. 3, 1847 | Oct. 5, '47 | Louisville, Ky. |   | July 21, '48 | Louisville, Ky. |
| 2 | Geo. W. Carter | Sergeant | Oct. 3, 1847 | Oct. 5, '47 | Louisville, Ky. |   | July 21, '48 | Louisville, Ky. |
| 3 | Cyrus M. Payne | Sergeant | Oct. 3, 1847 | Oct. 5, '47 | Louisville, Ky. |   | July 21, '48 | Louisville, Ky. |
| 4 | Lewis P. Thomson | Sergeant | Oct. 3, 1847 | Oct. 5, '47 | Louisville, Ky. |   | July 21, '48 | Louisville, Ky. |
| 1 | Thomas Holtzclaw | 1st Corporal | Oct. 3, 1847 | Oct. 5, '47 | Louisville, Ky. |   | July 21, '48 | Louisville, Ky. |
| 2 | Harrison Stanley | Corporal | Oct. 3, 1847 | Oct. 5, '47 | Louisville, Ky. |   | July 21, '48 | Louisville, Ky. |
| 3 | Samuel L. Glass | Corporal | Oct. 3, 1847 | Oct. 5, '47 | Louisville, Ky. |   | July 21, '48 | Louisville, Ky. |
| 4 | John H. Grigg | Corporal | Oct. 3, 1847 | Oct. 5, '47 | Louisville, Ky. |   | July 21, '48 | Louisville, Ky. |
| 1 | Daniel Neale | Musician | Oct. 3, 1847 | Oct. 5, '47 | Louisville, Ky. |   | July 21, '48 | Louisville, Ky. |
| 2 | John Hughes | Musician | Oct. 3, 1847 | Oct. 5, '47 | Louisville, Ky. |   | July 21, '48 | Louisville, Ky. |
| 1 | Awbery, Will | Private | Oct. 3, 1847 | Oct. 5, '47 | Louisville, Ky. |   | July 21, '48 | Louisville, Ky. |
| 2 | Awbery, French | Private | Oct. 3, 1847 | Oct. 5, '47 | Louisville, Ky. |   | July 21, '48 | Louisville, Ky. |
| 3 | Alsop, Leighton | Private | Oct. 3, 1847 | Oct. 5, '47 | Louisville, Ky. |   | July 21, '48 | Louisville, Ky. |
| 4 | Alsop, George | Private | Oct. 3, 1847 | Oct. 5, '47 | Louisville, Ky. |   | July 21, '48 | Louisville, Ky. |
| 5 | Anderson, Jas. W. | Private | Oct. 3, 1847 | Oct. 5, '47 | Louisville, Ky. |   | July 21, '48 | Louisville, Ky. |
| 6 | Bagby, John W. | Private | Oct. 3, 1847 | Oct. 5, '47 | Louisville, Ky. |   | July 21, '48 | Louisville, Ky. |
| 7 | Bennett, Jas. | Private | Oct. 3, 1847 | Oct. 5, '47 | Louisville, Ky. |   | July 21, '48 | Louisville, Ky. |
| 8 | Baldwin, Wm. H. | Private | Oct. 3, 1847 | Oct. 5, '47 | Louisville, Ky. |   | July 21, '48 | Louisville, Ky. |
| 9 | Beatey, Jas. | Private | Oct. 3, 1847 | Oct. 5, '47 | Louisville, Ky. |   | July 21, '48 | Louisville, Ky. |
| 10 | Bond, Waller G. | Private | Oct. 3, 1847 | Oct. 5, '47 | Louisville, Ky. |   | July 21, '48 | Louisville, Ky. |
| 11 | Bruner, John R. | Private | Oct. 3, 1847 | Oct. 5, '47 | Louisville, Ky. |   | July 21, '48 | Louisville, Ky. |
| 12 | Bennett, Richard | Private | Oct. 3, 1847 | Oct. 5, '47 | Louisville, Ky. |   | July 21, '48 | Louisville, Ky. |
| 13 | Crumbaugh, Henry | Private | Oct. 3, 1847 | Oct. 5, '47 | Louisville, Ky. |   | July 21, '48 | Louisville, Ky. |
| 14 | Covington, Zackariah | Private | Oct. 3, 1847 | Oct. 5, '47 | Louisville, Ky. |   | July 21, '48 | Louisville, Ky. |
| 15 | Crawford, Asa H. | Private | Oct. 3, 1847 | Oct. 5, '47 | Louisville, Ky. |   | July 21, '48 | Louisville, Ky. |
| 16 | Duvall, Theodore C. | Private | Oct. 3, 1847 | Oct. 5, '47 | Louisville, Ky. |   | July 21, '48 | Louisville, Ky. |
| 17 | Emmison, Joseph | Private | Oct. 3, 1847 | Oct. 5, '47 | Louisville, Ky. |   | July 21, '48 | Louisville, Ky. |
| 18 | Emison, John | Private | Oct. 3, 1847 | Oct. 5, '47 | Louisville, Ky. |   | July 21, '48 | Louisville, Ky. |
| 19 | Froste, Will P. | Private | Oct. 3, 1847 | Oct. 5, '47 | Louisville, Ky. |   | July 21, '48 | Louisville, Ky. |
| 20 | Foster, John W. | Private | Oct. 3, 1847 | Oct. 5, '47 | Louisville, Ky. |   | July 21, '48 | Louisville, Ky. |
| 21 | Green, Thomas | Private | Oct. 3, 1847 | Oct. 5, '47 | Louisville, Ky. |   | July 21, '48 | Louisville, Ky. |
| 22 | Guill, John M. | Private | Oct. 3, 1847 | Oct. 5, '47 | Louisville, Ky. |   | July 21, '48 | Louisville, Ky. |
| 23 | Hill, Henry | Private | Oct. 3, 1847 | Oct. 5, '47 | Louisville, Ky. |   | July 21, '48 | Louisville, Ky. |
| 24 | Herseng, Ben'j F. | Private | Oct. 3, 1847 | Oct. 5, '47 | Louisville, Ky. |   | July 21, '48 | Louisville, Ky. |
| 25 | Herndon, Thomas P. | Private | Oct. 3, 1847 | Oct. 5, '47 | Louisville, Ky. |   | July 21, '48 | Louisville, Ky. |
| 26 | Holtzclaw, Christopher | Private | Oct. 3, 1847 | Oct. 5, '47 | Louisville, Ky. |   | July 21, '48 | Louisville, Ky. |
| 27 | Ireland, Thomas | Private | Oct. 3, 1847 | Oct. 5, '47 | Louisville, Ky. |   | July 21, '48 | Louisville, Ky. |
| 28 | Jones, Stafford | Private | Oct. 3, 1847 | Oct. 5, '47 | Louisville, Ky. |   | July 21, '48 | Louisville, Ky. |
| 29 | Jarvis, Thompson | Private | Oct. 3, 1847 | Oct. 5, '47 | Louisville, Ky. |   | July 21, '48 | Louisville, Ky. |
| 30 | Jones, Robert B. | Private | Oct. 3, 1847 | Oct. 5, '47 | Louisville, Ky. |   | July 21, '48 | Louisville, Ky. |
| 31 | Jackson, Edward | Private | Oct. 3, 1847 | Oct. 5, '47 | Louisville, Ky. |   | July 21, '48 | Louisville, Ky. |
| 32 | Kemper, Samuel | Private | Oct. 3, 1847 | Oct. 5, '47 | Louisville, Ky. |   | July 21, '48 | Louisville, Ky. |
| 33 | Lindsay, Richard S. | Private | Oct. 3, 1847 | Oct. 5, '47 | Louisville, Ky. |   | July 21, '48 | Louisville, Ky. |
| 34 | Martin, Will. E. | Private | Oct. 3, 1847 | Oct. 5, '47 | Louisville, Ky. |   | July 21, '48 | Louisville, Ky. |
| 35 | Markham, Will. | Private | Oct. 3, 1847 | Oct. 5, '47 | Louisville, Ky. |   | July 21, '48 | Louisville, Ky. |
| 36 | Moody, Lewis | Private | Oct. 3, 1847 | Oct. 5, '47 | Louisville, Ky. |   | July 21, '48 | Louisville, Ky. |
| 37 | McFarland, Barthold | Private | Oct. 3, 1847 | Oct. 5, '47 | Louisville, Ky. |   | July 21, '48 | Louisville, Ky. |
| 38 | Morris, William O. | Private | Oct. 3, 1847 | Oct. 5, '47 | Louisville, Ky. |   | July 21, '48 | Louisville, Ky. |
| 39 | Nicholson, Henry | Private | Oct. 3, 1847 | Oct. 5, '47 | Louisville, Ky. |   | July 21, '48 | Louisville, Ky. |
| 40 | Offutt, Hezekiah | Private | Oct. 3, 1847 | Oct. 5, '47 | Louisville, Ky. |   | July 21, '48 | Louisville, Ky. |
| 41 | Price, Jackson | Private | Oct. 3, 1847 | Oct. 5, '47 | Louisville, Ky. |   | July 21, '48 | Louisville, Ky. |
| 42 | Peak, Jackson | Private | Oct. 3, 1847 | Oct. 5, '47 | Louisville, Ky. |   | July 21, '48 | Louisville, Ky. |
| 43 | Pettit, Charles B. | Private | Oct. 3, 1847 | Oct. 5, '47 | Louisville, Ky. |   | July 21, '48 | Louisville, Ky. |
| 44 | Stith, Thomas | Private | Oct. 3, 1847 | Oct. 5, '47 | Louisville, Ky. |   | July 21, '48 | Louisville, Ky. |
| 45 | Spiggle, Will. | Private | Oct. 3, 1847 | Oct. 5, '47 | Louisville, Ky. |   | July 21, '48 | Louisville, Ky. |
| 46 | Shipp, David R. | Private | Oct. 3, 1847 | Oct. 5, '47 | Louisville, Ky. |   | July 21, '48 | Louisville, Ky. |
| 47 | Srivers, John P. | Private | Oct. 3, 1847 | Oct. 5, '47 | Louisville, Ky. |   | July 21, '48 | Louisville, Ky. |
| 48 | Stubbs, Robert J. | Private | Oct. 3, 1847 | Oct. 5, '47 | Louisville, Ky. |   | July 21, '48 | Louisville, Ky. |
| 49 | Sullavan, John R. | Private | Oct. 3, 1847 | Oct. 5, '47 | Louisville, Ky. |   | July 21, '48 | Louisville, Ky. |
| 50 | Samuel, Arthur R. | Private | Oct. 3, 1847 | Oct. 5, '47 | Louisville, Ky. |   | July 21, '48 | Louisville, Ky. |

## FOOT VOLUNTEERS—MEXICAN WAR—Continued.

| No. of each grade. | REMARKS. |
|---|---|
| 1 | Discharged November 23, 1847, at Vera Cruz, on Surgeon's certificate of disability. |
| 2 | Discharged April 28, 1848, at the City of Mexico, on Surgeon's certificate of disability. |
| 1 | Discharged April 10, 1848, at the City of Mexico, on Surgeon's certificate of disability. |

## FOOT VOLUNTEERS—MEXICAN WAR.

| No. of each grade. | REMARKS. |
|---|---|
| 1 | |
| 1 | Regimental Adjutant. |
| 1 | |
| 2 | |
| 1 | |
| 2 | Appointed March 4, 1848, from private. |
| 3 | Reduced March 4, 1848; reinstated May 1, 1848. Missing; supposed to be killed by Mexicans June 2, 1848. |
| 4 | |
| 1 | |
| 2 | |
| 3 | |
| 4 | |
| 1 | |
| 2 | |
| 1 | |
| 2 | |
| 3 | |
| 4 | |
| 5 | |
| 6 | |
| 7 | |
| 8 | |
| 9 | |
| 10 | |
| 11 | |
| 12 | |
| 13 | |
| 14 | |
| 15 | |
| 16 | |
| 17 | Left in New Orleans as hospital attendant, July 8, 1848. |
| 18 | |
| 19 | |
| 20 | |
| 21 | |
| 22 | |
| 23 | |
| 24 | |
| 25 | |
| 26 | Left in confinement Vera Cruz, November 26, 1847. |
| 27 | |
| 28 | |
| 29 | |
| 30 | |
| 31 | |
| 32 | |
| 33 | |
| 34 | |
| 35 | |
| 36 | |
| 37 | |
| 38 | |
| 39 | |
| 40 | |
| 41 | |
| 42 | |
| 43 | |
| 44 | |
| 45 | |
| 46 | |
| 47 | |
| 48 | Left in confinement Vera Cruz, November 26, 1847. |
| 49 | |
| 50 | |

# MEXICAN WAR VETERANS.

## ROLL OF COMPANY "A," THIRD REGIMENT KENTUCKY

| No. of each grade. | Name. | Rank. | Joined for Service. | Mustered In. When. | Mustered In. Where. | Period | Mustered Out. When. | Mustered Out. Where. |
|---|---|---|---|---|---|---|---|---|
| 51 | Smith, John W. | Private | Oct. 3, 1847 | Oct. 5, '47 | Louisville, Ky. | | July 21, '48 | Louisville, Ky. |
| 52 | Suggeth, Samuel | Private | Oct. 3, 1847 | Oct. 5, '47 | Louisville, Ky. | | July 21, '48 | Louisville, Ky. |
| 53 | Smith, Hugh | Private | Oct. 3, 1847 | Oct. 5, '47 | Louisville, Ky. | | July 21, '48 | Louisville, Ky. |
| 54 | Theobold, Griffin | Private | Oct. 3, 1847 | Oct. 5, '47 | Louisville, Ky. | | July 21, '48 | Louisville, Ky. |
| 55 | Tormy, Thomas | Private | Oct. 3, 1847 | Oct. 5, '47 | Louisville, Ky. | | July 21, '48 | Louisville, Ky. |
| 56 | Vallandingham, Geo. | Private | Oct. 3, 1847 | Oct. 5, '47 | Louisville, Ky. | | July 21, '48 | Louisville, Ky. |
| 57 | Wells, Baswell | Private | Oct. 3, 1847 | Oct. 5, '47 | Louisville, Ky. | | July 21, '48 | Louisville, Ky. |
| 58 | Wolfe, Hervey | Private | Oct. 3, 1847 | Oct. 5, '47 | Louisville, Ky. | | July 21, '48 | Louisville, Ky. |
| 59 | Williams, Milton | Private | Oct. 3, 1847 | Oct. 5, '47 | Louisville, Ky. | | July 21, '48 | Louisville, Ky. |
| 60 | Wigginton, Elijah | Private | Oct. 3, 1847 | Oct. 5, '47 | Louisville, Ky. | | July 21, '48 | Louisville, Ky. |
| | **DIED.** | | | | | | | |
| 1 | Joseph Branham | Sergeant | Oct. 3, 1847 | Oct. 5, '47 | Louisville, Ky. | | | |
| 2 | Bradford Smith | Private | Oct. 3, 1847 | Oct. 5, '47 | Louisville, Ky. | | | |
| 3 | Jackson McMillen | Private | Oct. 3, 1847 | Oct. 5, '47 | Louisville, Ky. | | | |
| 4 | Minor P. Maitganery | Sergeant | Oct. 3, 1847 | Oct. 5, '47 | Louisville, Ky. | | | |
| 5 | William Finnie | Private | Oct. 3, 1847 | Oct. 5, '47 | Louisville, Ky. | To serve during the war. | | |
| 6 | Greenberry Bramlett | Private | Oct. 3, 1847 | Oct. 5, '47 | Louisville, Ky. | | | |
| 7 | William Young | Private | Oct. 3, 1847 | Oct. 5, '47 | Louisville, Ky. | | | |
| 8 | Will R. Glass | Private | Oct. 17, 1847 | Oct. 5, '47 | Louisville, Ky. | | | |
| 9 | Richard W. Park | Private | Oct. 3, 1847 | Oct. 5, '47 | Louisville, Ky. | | | |
| 10 | John Thawsen | Private | Oct. 3, 1847 | Oct. 5, '47 | Louisville, Ky. | | | |
| 11 | Robert M. Wiley | Private | Oct. 3, 1847 | Oct. 5, '47 | Louisville, Ky. | | | |
| | **DISCHARGED.** | | | | | | | |
| 1 | Samuel E. Glass | Private | Oct. 3, 1847 | Oct. 5, '47 | Louisville, Ky. | | | |
| 2 | Edward Long | Private | Oct. 3, 1847 | Oct. 5, '47 | Louisville, Ky. | | | |
| 3 | Gisham Morgan | Private | Oct. 3, 1847 | Oct. 5, '47 | Louisville, Ky. | | | |
| 4 | J. T. Megowan | Private | Oct. 3, 1847 | Oct. 5, '47 | Louisville, Ky. | | | |
| 5 | James McMannis | Private | Oct. 3, 1847 | Oct. 5, '47 | Louisville, Ky. | | | |
| 6 | Michael Grigg | Private | Oct. 3, 1847 | Oct. 5, '47 | Louisville, Ky. | | | |
| 7 | Ambrose Eaves | Private | Oct. 3, 1847 | Oct. 5, '47 | Louisville, Ky. | | | |
| 8 | Gabriel Stanton | Private | Oct. 3, 1847 | Oct. 5, '47 | Louisville, Ky. | | | |
| | **DESERTED.** | | | | | | | |
| 1 | George Jones | Private | Oct. 3, 1847 | Oct. 5, '47 | Louisville, Ky. | | | |
| 2 | Albert Munson | Private | Oct. 3, 1847 | Oct. 5, '47 | Louisville, Ky. | | | |
| 3 | James H. Sharron | Private | Oct. 3, 1847 | Oct. 5, '47 | Louisville, Ky. | | | |
| 4 | Johnson M. Suiter | Private | Oct. 3, 1847 | Oct. 5, '47 | Louisville, Ky. | | | |
| 5 | James Powell | Private | Oct. 3, 1847 | Oct. 5, '47 | Louisville, Ky. | | | |
| 6 | John Smith | Private | Oct. 3, 1847 | Oct. 5, '47 | Louisville, Ky. | | | |
| 7 | John E. Wade | Private | Oct. 3, 1847 | Oct. 5, '47 | Louisville, Ky. | | | |

This Company was organized by Capt. John R. Smith, at Georgetown, Ky., in the month of September, 1847, and marched thence to Louisville, where it arrived the 3d day of October, 1847, a distance of seventy miles.

## ROLL OF COMPANY "B," THIRD REGIMENT KENTUCKY

| | Name | Rank | Joined | Mustered In When | Mustered In Where | Period | Mustered Out When | Mustered Out Where |
|---|---|---|---|---|---|---|---|---|
| 1 | Leander M. Cox | Captain | Oct. 3, 1847 | Oct. 4, '47 | Louisville, Ky. | | July 21, '48 | Louisville, Ky. |
| 1 | William T. Walker | 1st Lieutenant | Oct. 3, 1847 | Oct. 4, '47 | Louisville, Ky. | | July 21, '48 | Louisville, Ky. |
| 2 | Walter J. Lacy | 1st Lieutenant | Oct. 3, 1847 | Oct. 4, '47 | Louisville, Ky. | | July 21, '48 | Louisville, Ky. |
| 1 | John M. Heddleson | 2d Lieutenant | Oct. 3, 1847 | Oct. 4, '47 | Louisville, Ky. | | July 21, '48 | Louisville, Ky. |
| 2 | Marshall L. Hone | 2d Lieutenant | Oct. 3, 1847 | Oct. 4, '47 | Louisville, Ky. | | July 21, '48 | Louisville, Ky. |
| 3 | Walter J. Lacy | 2d Lieutenant | Oct. 3, 1847 | Oct. 4, '47 | Louisville, Ky. | | July 21, '48 | Louisville, Ky. |
| 4 | Daniel Runyon | 2d Lieutenant | Oct. 3, 1847 | Oct. 4, '47 | Louisville, Ky. | | July 21, '48 | Louisville, Ky. |
| 1 | Crain, James L. | 1st Sergeant | Oct. 3, 1847 | Oct. 4, '47 | Louisville, Ky. | To serve during the war. | July 21, '48 | Louisville, Ky. |
| 2 | Markswell, Elias | Sergeant | Oct. 3, 1847 | Oct. 4, '47 | Louisville, Ky. | | July 21, '48 | Louisville, Ky. |
| 3 | Sweet, Samuel | Sergeant | Oct. 3, 1847 | Oct. 4, '47 | Louisville, Ky. | | July 21, '48 | Louisville, Ky. |
| 4 | Andrews, Alexander R. | Sergeant | Oct. 3, 1847 | Oct. 4, '47 | Louisville, Ky. | | July 21, '48 | Louisville, Ky. |
| 1 | Jones, John F. | Corporal | Oct. 3, 1847 | Oct. 4, '47 | Louisville, Ky. | | July 21, '48 | Louisville, Ky. |
| 2 | Wood, John | Corporal | Oct. 3, 1847 | Oct. 4, '47 | Louisville, Ky. | | July 21, '48 | Louisville, Ky. |
| 3 | Carpenter, Simon P. | Corporal | Oct. 3, 1847 | Oct. 4, '47 | Louisville, Ky. | | July 21, '48 | Louisville, Ky. |
| 4 | Evans, John M. | Corporal | Oct 3, 1847 | Oct. 4, '47 | Louisville, Ky. | | July 21, '48 | Louisville, Ky. |
| 1 | Morh, Frank C. | Musician | Oct. 3, 1847 | Oct. 4, '47 | Louisville, Ky. | | July 21, '48 | Louisville, Ky. |
| 2 | Goodwin, Milton | Musician | Oct. 3, 1847 | Oct. 4, '47 | Louisville, Ky. | | July 21, '48 | Louisville, Ky. |
| 1 | Asbury, Henry B. | Private | Oct. 3, 1847 | Oct. 4, '47 | Louisville, Ky. | | July 21, '48 | Louisville, Ky. |
| 2 | Alexander, Ambrose P. | Private | Oct. 3, 1847 | Oct. 4, '47 | Louisville, Ky. | | July 21, '48 | Louisville, Ky. |
| 3 | Atchison, James W. | Private | Oct. 3, 1847 | Oct. 4, '47 | Louisville, Ky. | | July 21, '48 | Louisville, Ky. |
| 4 | Beckner, William | Private | Oct. 3, 1847 | Oct. 4, '47 | Louisville, Ky. | | July 21, '48 | Louisville, Ky. |
| 5 | Bridges, William | Private | Oct. 3, 1847 | Oct. 4, '47 | Louisville, Ky. | | July 21, '48 | Louisville, Ky. |
| 6 | Bradley, Robert W. | Private | Oct. 3, 1847 | Oct. 4, '47 | Louisville, Ky. | | July 21, '48 | Louisville, Ky. |
| 7 | Barnaby, Edward | Private | Oct. 3, 1847 | Oct. 4, '47 | Louisville, Ky. | | July 21, '48 | Louisville, Ky. |

# FOOT VOLUNTEERS—MEXICAN WAR—Continued.

| No of each grade | REMARKS |
|---|---|
| 51 | |
| 52 | |
| 53 | |
| 54 | |
| 55 | |
| 56 | |
| 57 | |
| 58 | |
| 59 | |
| 60 | |
| 1 | Died in Puebla, Mexico, December 12, 1847. |
| 2 | Died in camp 18 miles west of Perote, Mexico, December 8, 1847. |
| 3 | Died at City of Mexico, February 11, 1848. |
| 4 | Died in hospital Mexico, March 22d, 1848. |
| 5 | Died in hospital Puebla, Mexico, February 24, 1848. |
| 6 | Died in hospital Puebla, Mexico, February 25, 1848. |
| 7 | Died in hospital Puebla, Mexico, February 21, 1848. |
| 8 | Died in hospital City of Mexico, March 24, 1848. |
| 9 | Died in hospital City of Mexico, May 24, 1848. |
| 10 | Died in New Orleans, June 24, 1848. |
| 11 | Died in hospital Jalapa. |
| 1 | Discharged October 6, 1847, for disability, Louisville, Ky. |
| 2 | Discharged by civil authority as a minor, Louisville, Ky., Oct. 25, 1847. |
| 3 | Discharged for disability, Louisville, Ky., November 1, 1847. |
| 4 | Discharged for disability, New Orleans, November 8, 1847. |
| 5 | Discharged for disability, Louisville, Ky., October 6, 1847. |
| 6 | Discharged on Surgeon's certificate of disability, Vera Cruz, January 18, 1848. |
| 7 | Discharged on Surgeon's certificate of disability, New Orleans, June 17, 1848. |
| 8 | Discharged on Surgeon's certificate of disability, New Orleans, June 17, 1848. |
| 1 | Deserted camp near Louisville, Ky., October 6, 1847. |
| 2 | Deserted camp near Louisville, Ky., October 17, 1847. |
| 3 | Deserted camp near Louisville, Ky., October 17, 1847. |
| 4 | Deserted camp near Louisville, Ky., October 24, 1847. |
| 5 | Deserted camp near Louisville, Ky., October 17, 1847. |
| 6 | Deserted camp near Louisville, Ky., October 6, 1847. |
| 7 | Deserted camp near Louisville, Ky., October 6, 1847. |

# FOOT VOLUNTEERS—MEXICAN WAR.

| | |
|---|---|
| 1 | |
| 1 | Resigned June 3, 1848, and was first Lieutenant from enrollment. |
| 2 | Promoted from 2d Lieutenant June 26, 1848, vice Walker, resigned. |
| 1 | Resigned January 12, 1848; was 2d Lieutenant from enrollment. |
| 2 | |
| 3 | Appointed from private January 12, 1848; promoted 1st Lieutenant as above. (No. 2.) |
| 4 | Appointed from private June 26, 1848; private from enrollment. |
| 1 | |
| 2 | |
| 3 | |
| 4 | Appointed from private January 10, 1848; was private from enrollment. |
| 1 | |
| 2 | |
| 3 | |
| 4 | |
| 1 | |
| 2 | Appointed Musician from private May 1, 1848; private from enrollment. |
| 1 | |
| 2 | |
| 3 | |
| 4 | |
| 5 | |
| 6 | |
| 7 | |

## ROLL OF COMPANY "B," THIRD REGIMENT KENTUCKY

| No. of each grade | Name | Rank | Joined for Service | Mustered In When | Mustered In Where | Period | Mustered Out When | Mustered Out Where |
|---|---|---|---|---|---|---|---|---|
| 8 | Bullion, John B. | Private | Oct. 3, 1847 | Oct. 4, '47 | Louisville, Ky. | | July 21, '48 | Louisville, Ky. |
| 9 | Byers, Alexander | Private | Oct. 3, 1847 | Oct. 4, '47 | Louisville, Ky. | | July 21, '48 | Louisville, Ky. |
| 10 | Clary, William P. | Private | Oct. 3, 1847 | Oct. 4, '47 | Louisville, Ky. | | July 21, '48 | Louisville, Ky. |
| 11 | Clary, Alfred | Private | Oct. 3, 1847 | Oct. 4, '47 | Louisville, Ky. | | July 21, '48 | Louisville, Ky. |
| 12 | Cary, Edmond | Private | Oct. 3, 1847 | Oct. 4, '47 | Louisville, Ky. | | July 21, '48 | Louisville, Ky. |
| 13 | Cole, Thomas | Private | Oct. 3, 1847 | Oct. 4, '47 | Louisville, Ky. | | July 21, '48 | Louisville, Ky. |
| 14 | Coleman, Moses | Private | Oct. 3, 1847 | Oct. 4, '47 | Louisville, Ky. | | July 21, '48 | Louisville, Ky. |
| 15 | Clark, Joseph S. | Private | Oct. 3, 1847 | Oct. 4, '47 | Louisville, Ky. | | July 21, '48 | Louisville, Ky. |
| 16 | Cary, James | Private | Oct. 3, 1847 | Oct. 4, '47 | Louisville, Ky. | | July 21, '48 | Louisville, Ky. |
| 17 | Craine, William A. | Private | Oct. 3, 1847 | Oct. 4, '47 | Louisville, Ky. | | July 21, '48 | Louisville, Ky. |
| 18 | Cox, William P. | Private | Oct. 3, 1847 | Oct. 4, '47 | Louisville, Ky. | | July 21, '48 | Louisville, Ky. |
| 19 | Crinzer, John | Private | Oct. 3, 1847 | Oct. 4, '47 | Louisville, Ky. | | July 21, '48 | Louisville, Ky. |
| 20 | Crair, Hiram P. | Private | Oct. 3, 1847 | Oct. 4, '47 | Louisville, Ky. | | July 21, '48 | Louisville, Ky. |
| 21 | Davis, Samuel | Private | Oct. 3, 1847 | Oct. 4, '47 | Louisville, Ky. | | July 21, '48 | Louisville, Ky. |
| 22 | Dixon, Darius | Private | Oct. 3, 1847 | Oct. 4, '47 | Louisville, Ky. | | July 21, '48 | Louisville, Ky. |
| 23 | Donaldson, John | Private | Oct. 3, 1847 | Oct. 4, '47 | Louisville, Ky. | | July 21, '48 | Louisville, Ky. |
| 24 | Donalson, William | Private | Oct. 3, 1847 | Oct. 4, '47 | Louisville, Ky. | | July 21, '48 | Louisville, Ky. |
| 25 | Fowler, William | Private | Oct. 3, 1847 | Oct. 4, '47 | Louisville, Ky. | | July 21, '48 | Louisville, Ky. |
| 26 | Fondry, Jefferson | Private | Oct. 3, 1847 | Oct. 4, '47 | Louisville, Ky. | | July 21, '48 | Louisville, Ky. |
| 27 | Foster, Joshua | Private | Oct. 3, 1847 | Oct. 4, '47 | Louisville, Ky. | To serve during war. | July 21, '48 | Louisville, Ky. |
| 28 | Gorman, Samuel | Private | Oct. 3, 1847 | Oct. 4, '47 | Louisville, Ky. | | July 21, '48 | Louisville, Ky. |
| 29 | Glass, Andrew | Private | Oct. 3, 1847 | Oct. 4, '47 | Louisville, Ky. | | July 21, '48 | Louisville, Ky. |
| 30 | Gale, Wallace | Private | Oct. 3, 1847 | Oct. 4, '47 | Louisville, Ky. | | July 21, '48 | Louisville, Ky. |
| 31 | Graham, Alfred | Private | Oct. 3, 1847 | Oct. 4, '47 | Louisville, Ky. | | July 21, '48 | Louisville, Ky. |
| 32 | Helvertine, Henry | Private | Oct. 3, 1847 | Oct. 4, '47 | Louisville, Ky. | | July 21, '48 | Louisville, Ky. |
| 33 | Henderson, Joseph W. | Private | Oct. 3, 1847 | Oct. 4, '47 | Louisville, Ky. | | July 21, '48 | Louisville, Ky. |
| 34 | Hedrick, Rolan T. | Private | Oct. 3, 1847 | Oct. 4, '47 | Louisville, Ky. | | July 21, '48 | Louisville, Ky. |
| 35 | Hedrick, James | Private | Oct. 3, 1847 | Oct. 4, '47 | Louisville, Ky. | | July 21, '48 | Louisville, Ky. |
| 36 | Hayden, Barnabas | Private | Oct. 3, 1847 | Oct. 4, '47 | Louisville, Ky. | | July 21, '48 | Louisville, Ky. |
| 37 | Hawes, Samuel | Private | Oct. 3, 1847 | Oct. 4, '47 | Louisville, Ky. | | July 21, '48 | Louisville, Ky. |
| 38 | Harper, Thomas | Private | Oct. 3, 1847 | Oct. 4, '47 | Louisville, Ky. | | July 21, '48 | Louisville, Ky. |
| 39 | Jones, William | Private | Oct. 3, 1847 | Oct. 4, '47 | Louisville, Ky. | | July 21, '48 | Louisville, Ky. |
| 40 | Kirkham, Ferdinand | Private | Oct. 3, 1847 | Oct. 4, '47 | Louisville, Ky. | | July 21, '48 | Louisville, Ky. |
| 41 | Kelly, William | Private | Oct. 3, 1847 | Oct. 4, '47 | Louisville, Ky. | | July 21, '48 | Louisville, Ky. |
| 42 | Linthicum, Hezekiah | Private | Oct. 3, 1847 | Oct. 4, '47 | Louisville, Ky. | | July 21, '48 | Louisville, Ky. |
| 43 | Lewis, Robert G. | Private | Oct. 3, 1847 | Oct. 4, '47 | Louisville, Ky. | | July 21, '48 | Louisville, Ky. |
| 44 | Mahan, Elijah | Private | Oct. 3, 1847 | Oct. 4, '47 | Louisville, Ky. | | July 21, '48 | Louisville, Ky. |
| 45 | Morrison, Robert W. | Private | Oct. 3, 1847 | Oct. 4, '47 | Louisville, Ky. | | July 21, '48 | Louisville, Ky. |
| 46 | McCracken, James | Private | Oct. 3, 1847 | Oct. 4, '47 | Louisville, Ky. | | July 21, '48 | Louisville, Ky. |
| 47 | McIntyre, George W. | Private | Oct. 3, 1847 | Oct. 4, '47 | Louisville, Ky. | | July 21, '48 | Louisville, Ky. |
| 48 | Nealis, James | Private | Oct. 3, 1847 | Oct. 4, '47 | Louisville, Ky. | | July 21, '48 | Louisville, Ky. |
| 49 | Nealis, James L. | Private | Oct. 3, 1847 | Oct. 4, '47 | Louisville, Ky. | | July 21, '48 | Louisville, Ky. |
| 50 | Obannon, William | Private | Oct. 3, 1847 | Oct. 4, '47 | Louisville, Ky. | | July 21, '48 | Louisville, Ky. |
| 51 | Prater, Parker V. | Private | Oct. 3, 1847 | Oct. 4, '47 | Louisville, Ky. | | July 21, '48 | Louisville, Ky. |
| 52 | Ringo, Robert | Private | Oct. 3, 1847 | Oct. 4, '47 | Louisville, Ky. | | July 21, '48 | Louisville, Ky. |
| 53 | Ringo, William M. | Private | Oct. 3, 1847 | Oct. 4, '47 | Louisville, Ky. | | July 21, '48 | Louisville, Ky. |
| 54 | Ringo, Thomas L. | Private | Oct. 3, 1847 | Oct. 4, '47 | Louisville, Ky. | | July 21, '48 | Louisville, Ky. |
| 55 | Ringo, James D. | Private | Oct. 3, 1847 | Oct. 4, '47 | Louisville, Ky. | | July 21, '48 | Louisville, Ky. |
| 56 | Roe, Jackson | Private | Oct. 3, 1847 | Oct. 4, '47 | Louisville, Ky. | | July 21, '48 | Louisville, Ky. |
| 57 | Ricketts, John | Private | Oct. 3, 1847 | Oct. 4, '47 | Louisville, Ky. | | July 21, '48 | Louisville, Ky. |
| 58 | Sutton, Nicholas | Private | Oct. 3, 1847 | Oct. 4, '47 | Louisville, Ky. | | July 21, '48 | Louisville, Ky. |
| 59 | Stockton, Hoblay | Private | Oct. 3, 1847 | Oct. 4, '47 | Louisville, Ky. | | July 21, '48 | Louisville, Ky. |
| 60 | Sullivan, William | Private | Oct. 3, 1847 | Oct. 4, '47 | Louisville, Ky. | | July 21, '48 | Louisville, Ky. |
| 61 | Schenck, Richard | Private | Oct. 3, 1847 | Oct. 4, '47 | Louisville, Ky. | | July 21, '48 | Louisville, Ky. |
| 62 | Schenck, John W. | Private | Oct. 6, 1847 | Oct. 6, '47 | Louisville, Ky. | | July 21, '48 | Louisville, Ky. |
| 63 | Taylor, James D. | Private | Oct. 3, 1847 | Oct. 4, '47 | Louisville, Ky. | | July 21, '48 | Louisville, Ky. |
| 64 | Traylor, Greenbury | Private | Oct. 3, 1847 | Oct. 4, '47 | Louisville, Ky. | | July 21, '48 | Louisville, Ky. |
| 65 | Umstedholt, John P. | Private | Oct. 3, 1847 | Oct. 4, '47 | Louisville, Ky. | | July 21, '48 | Louisville, Ky. |
| 66 | Wells, Mordecai | Private | Oct. 3, 1847 | Oct. 4, '47 | Louisville, Ky. | | July 21, '48 | Louisville, Ky. |
| 67 | Williams, Joseph M. | Private | Oct. 3, 1847 | Oct. 4, '47 | Louisville, Ky. | | July 21, '48 | Louisville, Ky. |
| 68 | Welch, William E. | Private | Oct. 3, 1847 | Oct. 4, '47 | Louisville, Ky. | | July 21, '48 | Louisville, Ky. |
| 69 | Wilson, Eli C. | Private | Oct. 3, 1847 | Oct. 4, '47 | Louisville, Ky. | | July 21, '48 | Louisville, Ky. |
| 70 | Zimmerman, Dillard | Private | Oct. 3, 1847 | Oct. 4, '47 | Louisville, Ky. | | July 21, '48 | Louisville, Ky. |
| | DISCHARGED. | | | | | | | |
| 1 | Balbs, John | Private | Oct. 3, 1847 | Oct. 4, '47 | Louisville, Ky. | | | |
| 2 | Pipper, William O. | Private | Oct. 3, 1847 | Oct. 4, '47 | Louisville, Ky. | | | |
| 3 | Markewell, George W. | Private | Oct. 3, 1847 | Oct. 4, '47 | Louisville, Ky. | | | |
| 4 | Kirk, Wilson T. | Private | Oct. 3, 1847 | Oct. 4, '47 | Louisville, Ky. | | | |
| 5 | Farris, John T. | Private | Oct. 3, 1847 | Oct. 4, '47 | Louisville, Ky. | | | |
| 6 | Rock, John B. | Sergeant | Oct. 3, 1847 | Oct. 4, '47 | Louisville, Ky. | | | |
| 7 | Combs, John D. | Private | Oct. 3, 1847 | Oct. 4, '47 | Louisville, Ky. | | | |
| | TRANSFERRED. | | | | | | | |
| 1 | Sumrall, John T. | Private | Oct. 3, 1847 | Oct. 4, '47 | Louisville, Ky. | | | |

# FOOT VOLUNTEERS—MEXICAN WAR—Continued.

| No. of each grade | REMARKS. |
|---|---|
| 8 | |
| 9 | |
| 10 | |
| 11 | |
| 12 | |
| 13 | |
| 14 | |
| 15 | |
| 16 | |
| 17 | |
| 18 | |
| 19 | |
| 20 | |
| 21 | |
| 22 | |
| 23 | |
| 24 | |
| 25 | |
| 26 | |
| 27 | |
| 28 | |
| 29 | |
| 30 | |
| 31 | |
| 32 | |
| 33 | |
| 34 | |
| 35 | |
| 36 | |
| 37 | |
| 38 | |
| 39 | |
| 40 | Detached on recruiting service. |
| 41 | |
| 42 | |
| 43 | |
| 44 | |
| 45 | |
| 46 | |
| 47 | |
| 48 | |
| 49 | |
| 50 | |
| 51 | |
| 52 | |
| 53 | |
| 54 | |
| 55 | |
| 56 | |
| 57 | |
| 58 | |
| 59 | |
| 60 | |
| 61 | |
| 62 | |
| 63 | |
| 64 | |
| 65 | |
| 66 | |
| 67 | |
| 68 | |
| 69 | |
| 70 | |
| 1 | Discharged at Vera Cruz, November 25, 1847; Surgeon's certificate of disability. |
| 2 | Discharged at Pueblo, December 12, 1847; Surgeon's certificate of disability. |
| 3 | Discharged at City of Mexico, January 15, 1847; Surgeon's certificate of disability. |
| 4 | Discharged at Vera Cruz, January 3, 1848; Surgeon's certificate of disability. |
| 5 | Discharged at Vera Cruz, January 10, 1848; Surgeon's certificate of disability. |
| 6 | Discharged at Vera Cruz, January 10, 1848; Surgeon's certificate of disability. |
| 7 | Discharged at New Orleans, June 17, 1848; Surgeon's certificate of disability. |
| 1 | Transferred to non-commissioned staff as Sergeant-Major, regimental orders No. 11, 1848. |

## ROLL OF COMPANY "B," THIRD REGIMENT KENTUCKY

| No. of each grade | Name | Rank | Joined for Service | Mustered in When | Mustered in Where | Period | Mustered Out When | Mustered Out Where |
|---|---|---|---|---|---|---|---|---|
| | DEATHS. | | | | | | | |
| 1 | Emmons, St. Clair | Private | Oct. 3, 1847 | Oct. 4, '47 | Louisville, Ky. | To serve during the war. | | |
| 2 | Dudley, Henry B. | Musician | Oct. 3, 1847 | Oct. 4, '47 | Louisville, Ky. | | | |
| 3 | Beatman, Thomas | Private | Oct. 3, 1847 | Oct. 4, '47 | Louisville, Ky. | | | |
| 4 | Markewell, Alvin | Private | Oct. 3, 1847 | Oct. 4, '47 | Louisville, Ky. | | | |
| 5 | Goodard, John | Private | Oct. 3, 1847 | Oct. 4, '47 | Louisville, Ky. | | | |
| 6 | Fondray, Washington | Private | Oct. 3, 1847 | Oct. 4, '47 | Louisville, Ky. | | | |
| 7 | Bradley, John | Private | Oct. 3, 1847 | Oct. 4, '47 | Louisville, Ky. | | | |
| 8 | Main, George | Private | Oct. 3, 1847 | Oct. 4, '47 | Louisville, Ky. | | | |
| 9 | Cline, Alfred | Private | Oct. 3, 1847 | Oct. 4, '47 | Louisville, Ky. | | | |
| 10 | Morgan, Silas | Private | Oct. 3, 1847 | Oct. 4, '47 | Louisville, Ky. | | | |
| 11 | Lawson, John | Private | Oct. 3, 1847 | Oct. 4, '47 | Louisville, Ky. | | | |
| 12 | Gross, John T. | Private | Oct. 3, 1847 | Oct. 4, '47 | Louisville, Ky. | | | |
| 13 | Allonder, James D. | Private | Oct. 3, 1847 | Oct. 4, '47 | Louisville, Ky. | | | |
| 14 | Reed, Elijah | Private | Oct. 3, 1847 | Oct. 4, '47 | Louisville, Ky. | | | |
| 15 | Helvestine, John P. J. | Private | Oct. 3, 1847 | Oct. 4, '47 | Louisville, Ky. | | | |
| 16 | Hughes, William | Private | Oct. 28, 1847 | Dec. 31, '47 | Mills Point | | | |
| 17 | Preston, Mordecai | Private | Oct. 3, 1847 | Oct. 4, '47 | Louisville, Ky. | | | |
| 18 | Cassidy, James | Private | Oct. 3, 1847 | Oct. 4, '47 | Louisville, Ky. | | | |
| 19 | Collins, William | Private | Oct. 3, 1847 | Oct. 4, '47 | Louisville, Ky. | | | |
| 20 | Snim, Thomas | Private | Oct. 3, 1847 | Oct. 4, '47 | Louisville, Ky. | | | |

This Company was organized by Captain L. M. Cox, at Flemingsburg, Ky., in September, 1847, and marched thence to Louisville, Ky., where it arrived on the 3d of October, a distance of one hundred and thirty-five miles.

## ROLL OF COMPANY "C," THIRD REGIMENT KENTUCKY

| No. | Name | Rank | Joined for Service | Mustered in When | Mustered in Where | Period | Mustered Out When | Mustered Out Where |
|---|---|---|---|---|---|---|---|---|
| 1 | Lawrence B. Robinson | Captain | Sept. 28, 1847 | Oct. 5, '47 | Louisville, Ky. | To serve during the war. | July 21, '48 | Louisville, Ky. |
| 2 | George S. Dodge | Captain | Sept. 28, 1847 | Oct. 5, '47 | Louisville, Ky. | | July 21, '48 | Louisville, Ky. |
| 1 | George S. Dodge | 1st Lieutenant | Sept. 28, 1847 | Oct. 5, '47 | Louisville, Ky. | | July 21, '48 | Louisville, Ky. |
| 2 | Wm. P. Morris | 1st Lieutenant | Sept. 28, 1847 | Oct. 5, '47 | Louisville, Ky. | | July 21, '48 | Louisville, Ky. |
| 1 | Wm. P. Morris | 2d Lieutenant | Sept. 28, 1847 | Oct. 5, '47 | Louisville, Ky. | | July 21, '48 | Louisville, Ky. |
| 2 | John B. Lee | 2d Lieutenant | Sept. 28, 1847 | Oct. 5, '47 | Louisville, Ky. | | July 21, '48 | Louisville, Ky. |
| 3 | Rigdon T. Barnhill | 2d Lieutenant | Sept. 28, 1847 | Oct. 5, '47 | Louisville, Ky. | | July 21, '48 | Louisville, Ky. |
| 4 | James H. Miller | 2d Lieutenant | Sept. 28, 1847 | Oct. 5, '47 | Louisville, Ky. | | July 21, '48 | Louisville, Ky. |
| 1 | Thos. Wilson | 1st Sergeant | Sept. 28, 1847 | Oct. 5, '47 | Louisville, Ky. | | July 21, '48 | Louisville, Ky. |
| 2 | Zackariah Shackleford | 2d Sergeant | Sept. 28, 1847 | Oct. 5, '47 | Louisville, Ky. | | July 21, '48 | Louisville, Ky. |
| 3 | Coleman Dixon | 3d Sergeant | Sept. 28, 1847 | Oct. 5, '47 | Louisville, Ky. | | July 21, '48 | Louisville, Ky. |
| 4 | Jeremiah Brown | 4th Sergeant | Sept. 28, 1847 | Oct. 5, '47 | Louisville, Ky. | | July 21, '48 | Louisville, Ky. |
| 1 | James Keiger | 1st Corporal | Sept. 28, 1847 | Oct. 5, '47 | Louisville, Ky. | | July 21, '48 | Louisville, Ky. |
| 2 | Johnson White | 2d Corporal | Sept. 28, 1847 | Oct. 5, '47 | Louisville, Ky. | | July 21, '48 | Louisville, Ky. |
| 3 | Wm. H. Taulbee | 3d Corporal | Sept. 28, 1847 | Oct. 5, '47 | Louisville, Ky. | | July 21, '48 | Louisville, Ky. |
| 4 | Benjamin Rossen | 4th Corporal | Sept. 28, 1847 | Oct. 5, '47 | Louisville, Ky. | | July 21, '48 | Louisville, Ky. |
| 1 | Clark M. Johnson | Drummer | Sept. 28, 1847 | Oct. 5, '47 | Louisville, Ky. | | July 21, '48 | Louisville, Ky. |
| 1 | Akhart, Alexander | Private | Sept. 28, 1847 | Oct. 5, '47 | Louisville, Ky. | | July 21, '48 | Louisville, Ky. |
| 2 | Brown, Samuel M. | Private | Sept. 28, 1847 | Oct. 5, '47 | Louisville, Ky. | | July 21, '48 | Louisville, Ky. |
| 3 | Blaize, William | Private | Sept. 28, 1847 | Oct. 5, '47 | Louisvil'e, Ky. | | July 21, '48 | Louisville, Ky. |
| 4 | Busick, Enok S. | Private | Sept. 28, 1847 | Oct. 5, '47 | Louisville, Ky. | | July 21, '48 | Louisville, Ky. |
| 5 | Ballance, James | Private | Sept. 28, 1847 | Oct. 5, '47 | Louisville, Ky. | | July 21, '48 | Louisville, Ky. |
| 6 | Bloodgood, Samuel | Private | Sept. 28, 1847 | Oct. 5, '47 | Louisville, Ky. | | Jul. 21, '48 | Louisville, Ky. |
| 7 | Compton, Levi F. | Private | Sept. 28, 1847 | Oct. 5, '47 | Louisville, Ky. | | July 21, '48 | Louisville, Ky. |
| 8 | Ceurson, Steward | Private | Sept. 28, 1847 | Oct. 5, '47 | Louisville, Ky. | | July 21, '48 | Louisville, Ky. |
| 9 | Coleman, Signat J. | Private | Sept. 28, 1847 | Oct. 5, '47 | Louisville, Ky. | | July 21, '48 | Louisville, Ky. |
| 10 | Church, Andrew J. | Private | Sept. 28, 1847 | Oct. 5, '47 | Louisville, Ky. | | July 21, '48 | Louisville, Ky. |
| 11 | Clark, Thomas | Private | Sept. 28, 1847 | Oct. 5, '47 | Louisville, Ky. | | July 21, '48 | Louisville, Ky. |
| 12 | Christopher, Thos. S. | Private | Sept. 28, 1847 | Oct. 5, '47 | Louisville, Ky. | | July 21, '48 | Louisville, Ky. |
| 13 | Columbus, Andrew J. | Private | Sept. 28, 1847 | Oct. 5, '47 | Louisville, Ky. | | July 21, '48 | Louisville, Ky. |
| 14 | Christopher, Wesley P. | Private | Sept. 28, 1847 | Oct. 5, '47 | Louisville, Ky. | | July 21, '48 | Louisville, Ky |
| 15 | Christopher, John W. | Private | Sept. 28, 1847 | Oct. 5, '47 | Louisville, Ky. | | July 21, '48 | Louisville, Ky. |
| 16 | Davis, Calvin | Private | Sept. 28, 1847 | Oct. 5, '47 | Louisville, Ky. | | July 21, '48 | Louisville, Ky. |
| 17 | Douglass Wm. | Private | Sept. 28, 1847 | Oct. 5, '47 | Louisville, Ky. | | July 21, '48 | Louisville, Ky. |
| 18 | Fulchur, Robert | Private | Sept. 28, 1847 | Oct. 5, '47 | Louisville, Ky. | | July 21, '48 | Louisville, Ky. |
| 19 | Forson, John | Private | Sept. 28, 1847 | Oct. 5, '47 | Louisville, Ky. | | July 21, '48 | Louisville, Ky. |
| 20 | Forster, David | Private | Sept. 28, 1847 | Oct. 5, '47 | Louisville, Ky. | | July 21, '48 | Louisville, Ky. |
| 21 | Finn, Henry | Private | Sept. 28, 1847 | Oct. 5, '47 | Louisville, Ky. | | July 21, '48 | Louisville, Ky. |
| 22 | Gordon, Charles | Private | Sept. 28, 1847 | Oct. 5, '47 | Louisville, Ky. | | July 21, '48 | Louisville, Ky. |
| 23 | Hasher, William A. | Private | Sept. 28, 1847 | Oct. 5, '47 | Louisville, Ky. | | July 21, '48 | Louisville, Ky. |
| 24 | Jones, David E. | Private | Sept. 28, 1847 | Oct. 5, '47 | Louisville, Ky. | | July 21, '48 | Louisville, Ky. |
| 25 | Johnson, Benjamin W. | Private | Sept. 28, 1847 | Oct 5, '47 | Louisville, Ky. | | July 21, '48 | Louisville, Ky. |
| 26 | Killinger, William H. | Private | Sept. 28, 1847 | Oct. 5, '47 | Louisville, Ky. | | July 21, '48 | Louisville, Ky. |
| 27 | Lilly, William B. | Private | Sept. 28, 1847 | Oct. 5, '47 | Louisville, Ky. | | July 21, '48 | Louisville, Ky. |
| 28 | Long, William | Private | Sept. 28, 1847 | Oct. 5, '47 | Louisville, Ky. | | July 21, '48 | Louisville, Ky. |

# FOOT VOLUNTEERS—MEXICAN WAR—Continued.

| No. of each grade | REMARKS. |
|---|---|
| 1 | Died December 10, 1847, at Jalapa. |
| 2 | Died December 12, 1847, at Jalapa. |
| 3 | Died December 12, 1847, at Jalapa. |
| 4 | Died December 12, 1847, at Pueblo. |
| 5 | Died December 13, 1847, at Pueblo. |
| 6 | Died December 13, 1847, at Pueblo. |
| 7 | Died December 14, 1847, at Pueblo. |
| 8 | Died December 25, 1847, at Pueblo. |
| 9 | Died December 28, 1847, at Pueblo. |
| 10 | Died December 24, 1847, at City of Mexico. |
| 11 | Died January 27, 1848, at City of Mexico. |
| 12 | Died January 26, 1848, at Pueblo. |
| 13 | Died January 29, 1848, at Pueblo. |
| 14 | Died February 3, 1848, at Pueblo. |
| 15 | Died March 4, 1848, at City of Mexico. |
| 16 | Died April 7, 1848, at City of Mexico. |
| 17 | Died April 25, 1848, at City of Mexico. |
| 18 | Died May 24, 1848, at City of Mexico. |
| 19 | Died June 9, 1848, at City of Perote. |
| 20 | Died July 2, 1848, on Gulf of Mexico. |

# FOOT VOLUNTEERS—MEXICAN WAR.

| No. of each grade | REMARKS. |
|---|---|
| 1 | Resignation accepted February 29, 1848. |
| 2 | Promoted from 1st Lieutenant, March 31, 1848, vice Robinson, resigned. |
| 1 | 1st Lieutenant from enrollment to March 31, 1848, when promoted. |
| 2 | Promoted from 2d Lieutenant, March 31, 1848, vice Dodge, promoted. |
| 1 | 2d Lieutenant from enrollment to March 31, 1848, when promoted. |
| 2 | Resignation accepted 6th May, 1848. |
| 3 | Promoted from private vice Morris, promoted March 31, 1848; private from enrollment to March 31, 1848. |
| 4 | Promoted from 1st Sergeant vice Lee, resigned, 6th May, 1848; 1st Sergeant from enrollment to May 6, 1848. |
| 1 | Promoted from private May 6, 1848; was private from enrollment. |
| 2 | |
| 3 | |
| 4 | |
| 1 | |
| 2 | |
| 3 | |
| 4 | |
| 1 | |
| 1 | |
| 2 | |
| 3 | |
| 4 | |
| 5 | |
| 6 | |
| 7 | |
| 8 | |
| 9 | |
| 10 | |
| 11 | |
| 12 | |
| 13 | |
| 14 | |
| 15 | |
| 16 | |
| 17 | |
| 18 | |
| 19 | |
| 20 | |
| 21 | Sick in hospital. |
| 22 | |
| 23 | |
| 24 | |
| 25 | |
| 26 | |
| 27 | |
| 28 | |

## MEXICAN WAR VETERANS.

### ROLL OF COMPANY "C," THIRD REGIMENT KENTUCKY

| No. of each grade | Name. | Rank. | Joined for Service. | Mustered In. When. | Mustered In. Where. | Period. | Mustered Out. When. | Mustered Out. Where. |
|---|---|---|---|---|---|---|---|---|
| 29 | Lamb, Reuben | Private | Sept. 28, 1847 | Oct. 5, '47 | Louisville, Ky. | | July 21, '48 | Louisville, Ky. |
| 30 | Lawson, Samuel | Private | Sept. 28, 1847 | Oct. 5, '47 | Louisville, Ky. | | July 21, '48 | Louisville, Ky. |
| 31 | Lenox, Moses | Private | Sept. 28, 1847 | Oct. 5, '47 | Louisville, Ky. | | July 21, '48 | Louisville, Ky. |
| 32 | Lane, Lucien B. | Private | Sept. 28, 1847 | Oct. 5, '47 | Louisville, Ky. | | July 21, '48 | Louisville, Ky. |
| 33 | Lawson, Andrew | Private | Sept. 28, 1847 | Oct. 5, '47 | Louisville | | July 21, '48 | Louisville, Ky. |
| 34 | McQuillin, Francis | Private | Sept. 28, 1847 | Oct. 5, '47 | Louisville, Ky. | | July 21, '48 | Louisville, Ky. |
| 35 | McDonald, William | Private | Sept. 28, 1847 | Oct. 5, '47 | Louisville, Ky | | July 21, '48 | Louisville, Ky. |
| 36 | McIntosh, William E. | Private | Sept. 28, 1847 | Oct. 5, '47 | Louisville, Ky. | | July 21, '48 | Louisville, Ky. |
| 37 | Maloney, James | Private | Sept. 28, 1847 | Oct. 5, '47 | Louisville, Ky. | | July 21, '48 | Louisville, Ky. |
| 38 | Mitchell, Thomas E. | Private | Sept. 28, 1847 | Oct. 5, '47 | Louisville, Ky. | | July 21, '48 | Louisville, Ky. |
| 39 | Moore, Harrison | Private | Sept. 28, 1847 | Oct. 5, '47 | Louisville, Ky. | | July 21, '48 | Louisville, Ky. |
| 40 | Metcalf, William | Private | Sept. 28, 1847 | Oct. 5, '47 | Louisville, Ky. | | July 21, '48 | Louisville, Ky. |
| 41 | McGran, Thomas L. | Private | Sept. 28, 1847 | Oct. 5, '47 | Louisville, Ky. | | July 21, '48 | Louisville, Ky. |
| 42 | McElwain, Alexander | Private | Sept. 28, 1847 | Oct. 5, '47 | Louisville, Ky. | | July 21, '48 | Louisville, Ky. |
| 43 | McQuoin, Zachariah | Private | Sept. 28, 1847 | Oct. 5, '47 | Louisville, Ky. | | July 21, '48 | Louisville, Ky. |
| 44 | Nethuby, John | Private | Sept. 28, 1847 | Oct. 5, '47 | Louisville, Ky. | | July 21, '48 | Louisville, Ky. |
| 45 | Oliver, Charles W. | Private | Sept. 28, 1847 | Oct. 5, '47 | Louisville, Ky. | | July 21, '48 | Louisville, Ky. |
| 46 | Patterson, Isaac | Private | Sept. 28, 1847 | Oct. 5, '47 | Louisville, Ky. | | July 21, '48 | Louisville, Ky. |
| 47 | Pankey, James S. | Private | Sept. 28, 1847 | Oct. 5, '47 | Louisville, Ky. | | July 21, '48 | Louisville, Ky. |
| 48 | Queen, Matthew | Private | Sept. 28, 1847 | Oct. 5, '47 | Louisville, Ky. | | July 21, '48 | Louisville, Ky. |
| 49 | Rogers, Cyrenius | Private | Sept. 28, 1847 | Oct. 5, '47 | Louisville, Ky. | | July 21, '48 | Louisville, Ky. |
| 50 | Sheridan, Alexander | Private | Sept. 28, 1847 | Oct. 5, '47 | Louisville, Ky. | | July 21, '48 | Louisville, Ky. |
| 51 | Sacre, Edmund | Private | Sept. 28, 1847 | Oct. 5, '47 | Louisville, Ky. | | July 21, '48 | Louisville, Ky. |
| 52 | Scott, Joab W. | Private | Sept. 28 1847 | Oct. 5, '47 | Louisville, Ky. | | July 21, '48 | Louisville, Ky. |
| 53 | Shaefer, Harrison L. | Private | Sept. 28, 1847 | Oct. 5, '47 | Louisville, Ky. | | July 21, '48 | Louisville, Ky. |
| 54 | Sohan, John | Private | Sept. 28, 1847 | Oct. 5, '47 | Louisville, Ky. | | July 21, '48 | Louisville, Ky. |
| 55 | Sebastian, Samuel | Private | Sept. 28, 1847 | Oct. 5, '47 | Louisville, Ky. | | July 21, '48 | Louisville, Ky. |
| 56 | Strawn, Edward J. | Private | Sept. 28, 1847 | Oct. 5, '47 | Louisville, Ky. | | July 21, '48 | Louisville, Ky. |
| 57 | Shields, John | Private | Sept. 28, 1847 | Oct. 5, '47 | Louisville, Ky. | | July 21, '48 | Louisville, Ky. |
| 58 | Tomlin, William N. | Private | Sept. 28, 1847 | Oct. 5, '47 | Louisville, Ky. | | July 21, '48 | Louisville, Ky. |
| 59 | Todd, David H. | Private | Sept. 28, 1847 | Oct. 5, '47 | Louisville, Ky. | | July 21, '48 | Louisville, Ky. |
| 60 | Udell, Henry E. | Private | Sept. 28, 1847 | Oct. 5, '47 | Louisville, Ky. | | July 21, '48 | Louisville, Ky. |
| 61 | White, Matthew C. | Private | Sept. 28, 1847 | Oct. 5, '47 | Louisville, Ky. | To serve during war. | July 21, '48 | Louisville, Ky. |
| 62 | Woldridge, Greenberry | Private | Sept. 28, 1847 | Oct. 5, '47 | Louisville, Ky. | | July 21, '48 | Louisville, Ky. |
| 63 | Williams, William J. | Private | Sept. 28, 1847 | Oct. 5, '47 | Louisville, Ky. | | July 21, '48 | Louisville, Ky. |
| | **DIED.** | | | | | | | |
| 1 | Balthis, Isaac | Private | Sept. 28, 1847 | Oct. 5, '47 | Louisville, Ky. | | | |
| 2 | Condit, Stephen R. | Private | Sept. 28, 1847 | Oct. 5, '47 | Louisville, Ky. | | | |
| 3 | Carlton, Andrew H. | Private | Sept. 28, 1847 | Oct. 5, '47 | Louisville, Ky. | | | |
| 4 | Copperass, John | Private | Sept. 28, 1847 | Oct. 5, '47 | Louisville, Ky. | | | |
| 5 | Defrance, Louis | Private | Sept. 28, 1847 | Oct. 5, '47 | Louisville, Ky. | | | |
| 6 | Higgins, James F. | Private | Sept. 28, 1847 | Oct. 5, '47 | Louisville, Ky. | | | |
| 7 | Jouett, Michael | Private | Sept. 28, 1847 | Oct. 5, '47 | Louisville, Ky. | | | |
| 8 | Michael, Thomas | Private | Sept. 28, 1847 | Oct. 5, '47 | Louisville, Ky. | | | |
| 9 | Meek, Lee | Private | Sept. 28, 1847 | Oct. 5, '47 | Louisville, Ky. | | | |
| 10 | Robinson, William | Private | Sept. 28, 1847 | Oct. 5, '47 | Louisville, Ky. | | | |
| 11 | McLin, David O. | Private | Sept. 28, 1847 | Oct. 5, '47 | Louisville, Ky. | | | |
| 12 | Rucker, Ezekiel | Private | Sept. 28, 1847 | Oct. 5, '47 | Louisville, Ky. | | | |
| | **DESERTED.** | | | | | | | |
| 1 | Moon, Robert | Private | Sept. 28, 1847 | Oct. 5, '47 | Louisville, Ky. | | | |
| 2 | Smith, William | Private | Sept. 28, 1847 | Oct. 5, '47 | Louisville, Ky. | | | |
| | **DISCHARGED.** | | | | | | | |
| 1 | Jos. J. Thornton | Sergeant | Sept. 28, 1847 | Oct. 5, '47 | Louisville, Ky. | | | |
| 1 | Dennis Fitzpatrick | Corporal | Sept. 28, 1847 | Oct. 5, '47 | Louisville, Ky. | | | |
| 1 | Brady, Philip | Private | Sept. 28, 1847 | Oct. 5, '47 | Louisville, Ky. | | | |
| 2 | Carl, Isahil T. | Private | Sept. 28, 1847 | Oct. 5, '47 | Louisville, Ky. | | | |
| 3 | Hutchinson, Richard | Private | Sept. 28, 1847 | Oct. 5, '47 | Louisville, Ky. | | | |
| 4 | Richardson, James | Private | Sept. 28, 1847 | Oct. 5, '47 | Louisville, Ky. | | | |
| 5 | Sebree, Muskin | Private | Sept. 28, 1847 | Oct. 5, '47 | Louisville, Ky. | | | |
| 6 | Winningham, Duffin | Private | Sept. 28, 1847 | Oct. 5, '47 | Louisville, Ky. | | | |
| 7 | Wicks, Nathaniel | Private | Sept. 28, 1847 | Oct. 5, '47 | Louisville, Ky. | | | |
| | **TRANSFERRED.** | | | | | | | |
| 1 | *John W. Stevens | Drummer | Sept. 28, 1847 | Oct. 5, '47 | Louisville, Ky. | | | |
| 2 | Thomas B. Martin | Fifer | Sept. 28, 1847 | Oct. 5, '47 | Louisville, Ky. | | | |

This Company was organized by Captain Lawrence B. Robinson, at Lexington, Kentucky, in the month of September, 1847, and marched thence to Louisville, Kentucky, where it arrived the 28th day of September, 1847, a distance of *seventy-five miles*.

## FOOT VOLUNTEERS—MEXICAN WAR—Continued.

| No. of each grade. | REMARKS. |
|---|---|
| 29 | |
| 30 | |
| 31 | |
| 32 | |
| 33 | |
| 34 | |
| 35 | |
| 36 | |
| 37 | |
| 38 | |
| 39 | |
| 40 | |
| 41 | |
| 42 | |
| 43 | |
| 44 | |
| 45 | |
| 46 | |
| 47 | |
| 48 | |
| 49 | |
| 50 | |
| 51 | |
| 52 | |
| 53 | |
| 54 | |
| 55 | |
| 56 | |
| 57 | |
| 58 | |
| 59 | |
| 60 | |
| 61 | |
| 62 | |
| 63 | |
| 1 | Assassinated by a Mexican, City of Mexico, March 12, 1848. |
| 2 | Died February 1, 1848, City of Mexico. |
| 3 | Died February 3, 1848, City of Mexico. |
| 4 | Jalapa hospital, March 20, 1848. Charged on descriptive roll. |
| 5 | Died in City of Mexico, January 26, 1848; assassinated by a Mexican. |
| 6 | Died in the City of Mexico, February 10, 1848. |
| 7 | Died in the City of Mexico, March 10, 1848. |
| 8 | Died in the city of Mexico, March 24, 1848. |
| 9 | Vera Cruz hospital; date unknown. Charged on descriptive roll. |
| 10 | Jalapa hospital, March 28, 1848. Charged on descriptive roll. |
| 11 | Perote hospital January 20, 1848. Charged on descriptive roll. |
| 12 | Died in the City of Mexico, February 7, 1848. |
| 1 | Louisville, Ky., October 7, 1847. |
| 2 | Louisville, Ky., October 6, 1847. |
| 1 | Mexico, April 11, 1848, Surgeon's certificate of disability. |
| 1 | Mexico, April 11, 1848, Surgeon's certificate of disability. |
| 1 | Louisville, October 20, 1847, Surgeon's certificate of disability. |
| 2 | New Orleans, November 6, 1847, Surgeon's certificate of disability. |
| 3 | Louisville, October, 1847, civil authority, being a minor. |
| 4 | New Orleans, November 7, 1847 Surgeon's certificate of disability. |
| 5 | Louisville, October 18, 1847, by civil authority, being a minor. |
| 6 | Vera Cruz, February 24, 1848, Surgeon's certificate of disability. |
| 7 | Louisville, October 10, 1847, by civil authority, being a minor. |
| 1 | Transferred to Regimental Staff, September 28, 1847. |
| 2 | Transferred to Regimental Staff, September 28, 1847. |

# MEXICAN WAR VETERANS.

## ROLL OF COMPANY "D," THIRD REGIMENT KENTUCKY

| No. of each grade | Name | Rank | Joined for Service | Mustered In. When | Mustered In. Where | Period | Mustered Out. When | Mustered Out. Where |
|---|---|---|---|---|---|---|---|---|
| 1 | James A. Pritchard | Captain | Oct. 4, 1847 | Oct. 5, '47 | Louisville, Ky. | | July 21, '48 | Louisville, Ky. |
| 1 | Hubart T. Buckner | 1st Lieutenant | Oct. 4, 1847 | Oct. 5, '47 | Louisville, Ky. | | July 21, '48 | Louisville, Ky. |
| 2 | Thomas C. Flournoy | 1st Lieutenant | Oct. 4, 1847 | Oct. 5, '47 | Louisville, Ky. | | July 21, '48 | Louisville, Ky. |
| 1 | James B. Casey | 2d Lieutenant | Oct. 4, 1847 | Oct. 5, '47 | Louisville, Ky. | | July 21, '48 | Louisville, Ky. |
| 2 | William G. Merrick | 2d 2d Lieutenant | Oct. 4, 1847 | Oct. 5, '47 | Louisville, Ky. | | July 21, '48 | Louisville, Ky. |
| 1 | Randolph B. Corbin | 1st Sergeant | Oct. 4, 1847 | Oct. 5, '47 | Louisville, Ky. | | July 21, '48 | Louisville, Ky. |
| 2 | Mason Cornelius | Sergeant | Oct. 4, 1847 | Oct. 5, '47 | Louisville, Ky. | | July 21, '48 | Louisville, Ky. |
| 3 | Joseph F. Martin | Sergeant | Oct. 4, 1847 | Oct. 5, '47 | Louisville, Ky. | | July 21, '48 | Louisville, Ky. |
| 4 | John N. Witt | Sergeant | Oct. 4, 1847 | Oct. 5, '47 | Louisville, Ky. | | July 21, '48 | Louisville, Ky. |
| 1 | Benjamin F. Triplett | Corporal | Oct. 4, 1847 | Oct. 5, '47 | Louisville, Ky. | | July 21, '48 | Louisville, Ky. |
| 2 | Pinckney P. Youell | Corporal | Oct. 4, 1847 | Oct. 5, '47 | Louisville, Ky. | | July 21, '48 | Louisville, Ky. |
| 3 | John C. Richards | Corporal | Oct. 4, 1847 | Oct. 5, '47 | Louisville, Ky. | | July 21, '48 | Louisville, Ky. |
| 4 | William H. Ruddle | Corporal | Oct. 4, 1847 | Oct. 5, '47 | Louisville, Ky. | | July 21, '48 | Louisville, Ky. |
| 1 | Jesse Coffer | Drummer | Oct. 4, 1847 | Oct. 5, '47 | Louisville, Ky. | | July 21, '48 | Louisville, Ky. |
| 2 | Albert Corbin | Fifer | Oct. 4, 1847 | Oct. 5, '47 | Louisville, Ky. | | July 21, '48 | Louisville, Ky. |
| 1 | Aydelott, Benjamin | Private | Oct. 4, 1847 | Oct. 5, '47 | Louisville, Ky. | | July 21, '48 | Louisville, Ky. |
| 2 | Baker, Adam | Private | Oct. 4, 1847 | Oct. 5, '47 | Louisville, Ky. | | July 21, '48 | Louisville, Ky. |
| 3 | Baldwin, David | Private | Oct. 4, 1847 | Oct. 5, '47 | Louisville, Ky. | | July 21, '48 | Louisville, Ky. |
| 4 | Bean, John | Private | Oct. 4, 1847 | Oct. 5, '47 | Louisville, Ky. | | July 21, '48 | Louisville, Ky. |
| 5 | Blackburn, James | Private | Oct. 4, 1847 | Oct. 5, '47 | Louisville, Ky. | | July 21, '48 | Louisville, Ky. |
| 6 | Bristow, James S. | Private | Oct. 4, 1847 | Oct. 5, '47 | Louisville, Ky. | | July 21, '48 | Louisville, Ky. |
| 7 | Britenham, Stephen | Private | Oct. 4, 1847 | Oct. 5, '47 | Louisville, Ky. | | July 21, '48 | Louisville, Ky. |
| 8 | Catterson, Robert W. | Private | Oct. 4, 1847 | Oct. 5, '47 | Louisville, Ky. | | July 21, '48 | Louisville, Ky. |
| 9 | Catterson, Thomas D. | Private | Oct. 4, 1847 | Oct. 5, '47 | Louisville, Ky. | | July 21, '48 | Louisville, Ky. |
| 10 | Childers, Elijah | Private | Oct. 4, 1847 | Oct. 5, '47 | Louisville, Ky. | | July 21, '48 | Louisville, Ky. |
| 11 | Corbin, Marion | Private | Oct. 4, 1847 | Oct. 5, '47 | Louisville, Ky. | | July 21, '48 | Louisville, Ky. |
| 12 | Crisler, Leonard | Private | Oct. 4, 1847 | Oct. 5, '47 | Louisville, Ky. | | July 21, '48 | Louisville, Ky. |
| 13 | Dean, Abial | Private | Oct. 4, 1847 | Oct. 5, '47 | Louisville, Ky. | | July 21, '48 | Louisville, Ky. |
| 14 | Ellis, James F. | Private | Oct. 4, 1847 | Oct. 5, '47 | Louisville, Ky. | | July 21, '48 | Louisville, Ky. |
| 15 | Ebbs, John W. | Private | Oct. 11, 1847 | Oct. 11, '47 | Louisville, Ky. | | July 21, '48 | Louisville, Ky. |
| 16 | Foley, Patrick | Private | Oct. 4, 1847 | Oct. 5, '47 | Louisville, Ky. | | July 21, '48 | Louisville, Ky. |
| 17 | Green, William V. | Private | Oct. 4, 1847 | Oct. 5, '47 | Louisville, Ky. | | July 21, '48 | Louisville, Ky. |
| 18 | Hardesty, John F. | Private | Oct. 4, 1847 | Oct. 5, '47 | Louisville, Ky. | To serve during the war. | July 21, '48 | Louisville, Ky. |
| 19 | Hardesty, Edward P. | Private | Oct. 4, 1847 | Oct. 5, '47 | Louisville, Ky. | | July 21, '48 | Louisville, Ky. |
| 20 | Hackney, John | Private | Oct. 4, 1847 | Oct. 5, '47 | Louisville, Ky. | | July 21, '48 | Louisville, Ky. |
| 21 | Hooker, John | Private | Oct. 4, 1847 | Oct. 5, '47 | Louisville, Ky. | | July 21, '48 | Louisville, Ky. |
| 22 | Huston, Thomas | Private | Oct. 4, 1847 | Oct. 5, '47 | Louisville, Ky. | | July 21, '48 | Louisville, Ky. |
| 23 | Huston, James | Private | Oct. 4, 1847 | Oct. 5, '47 | Louisville, Ky. | | July 21, '48 | Louisville, Ky. |
| 24 | Jackson, William | Private | Oct. 4, 1847 | Oct. 5, '47 | Louisville, Ky. | | July 21, '48 | Louisville, Ky. |
| 25 | Kendrick, Joseph L. | Private | Oct. 4, 1847 | Oct. 5, '47 | Louisville, Ky. | | July 21, '48 | Louisville, Ky. |
| 26 | Knotts, James B. | Private | Oct. 4, 1847 | Oct. 5, '47 | Louisville, Ky. | | July 21, '48 | Louisville, Ky. |
| 27 | Lancaster, James M. | Private | Oct. 4, 1847 | Oct. 5, '47 | Louisville, Ky. | | July 21, '48 | Louisville, Ky. |
| 28 | Lee, Henry | Private | Oct. 4, 1847 | Oct. 5, '47 | Louisville, Ky. | | July 21, '48 | Louisville, Ky. |
| 29 | Lee, Mathew | Private | Oct. 4, 1847 | Oct. 5, '47 | Louisville, Ky. | | July 21, '48 | Louisville, Ky. |
| 30 | Lore, Nathan | Private | Oct. 4, 1847 | Oct. 5, '47 | Louisville, Ky. | | July 21, '48 | Louisville, Ky. |
| 31 | Lore, Christopher C. | Private | Oct. 4, 1847 | Oct. 5, '47 | Louisville, Ky. | | July 21, '48 | Louisville, Ky. |
| 32 | Lynch, Joshua | Private | Oct. 4, 1847 | Oct. 5, '47 | Louisville, Ky. | | July 21, '48 | Louisville, Ky. |
| 33 | Mason, James T. | Private | Oct. 4, 1847 | Oct. 5, '47 | Louisville, Ky. | | July 21, '48 | Louisville, Ky. |
| 34 | Mason, John F. | Private | Oct. 4, 1847 | Oct. 5, '47 | Louisville, Ky. | | July 21, '48 | Louisville, Ky. |
| 35 | Marshall, William | Private | Oct. 4, 1847 | Oct. 5, '47 | Louisville, Ky. | | July 21, '48 | Louisville, Ky. |
| 36 | McNeill, John F. | Private | Oct. 4, 1847 | Oct. 5, '47 | Louisville, Ky. | | July 21, '48 | Louisville, Ky. |
| 37 | McAtee, John | Private | Oct. 4, 1847 | Oct. 5, '47 | Louisville, Ky. | | July 21, '48 | Louisville, Ky. |
| 38 | Moore, James L | Private | Oct. 4, 1847 | Oct. 5, '47 | Louisville, Ky. | | July 21, '48 | Louisville, Ky. |
| 39 | Myers, Michael | Private | Oct. 4, 1847 | Oct. 5, '47 | Louisville, Ky. | | July 21, '48 | Louisville, Ky. |
| 40 | Norton, William J. | Private | Oct. 4, 1847 | Oct. 5, '47 | Louisville, Ky. | | July 21, '48 | Louisville, Ky. |
| 41 | Percival, William E. | Private | Oct. 4, 1847 | Oct. 5, '47 | Louisville, Ky. | | July 21, '48 | Louisville, Ky. |
| 42 | Parnell, John | Private | Oct. 4, 1847 | Oct. 5, '47 | Louisville, Ky. | | July 21, '48 | Louisville, Ky. |
| 43 | Ramer, Lewis | Private | Oct. 4, 1847 | Oct. 5, '47 | Louisville, Ky. | | July 21, '48 | Louisville, Ky. |
| 44 | Richards, James D. | Private | Oct. 4, 1847 | Oct. 5, '47 | Louisville, Ky. | | July 21, '48 | Louisville, Ky. |
| 45 | Richardson, John V. | Private | Oct. 4, 1847 | Oct. 5, '47 | Louisville, Ky. | | July 21, '48 | Louisville, Ky. |
| 46 | Robinson, Marcellus M. | Private | Oct. 4, 1847 | Oct. 5, '47 | Louisville, Ky. | | July 21, '48 | Louisville, Ky. |
| 47 | Shultz, John H. | Private | Oct. 4, 1847 | Oct. 5, '47 | Louisville, Ky. | | July 21, '48 | Louisville, Ky. |
| 48 | Snyder, James | Private | Oct. 4, 1847 | Oct. 5, '47 | Louisville, Ky. | | July 21, '48 | Louisville, Ky. |
| 49 | Snyder, James S. | Private | Oct. 4, 1847 | Oct. 5, '47 | Louisville, Ky. | | July 21, '48 | Louisville, Ky. |
| 50 | Summers, Milton | Private | Oct. 4, 1847 | Oct. 5, '47 | Louisville, Ky. | | July 21, '48 | Louisville, Ky. |
| 51 | Thompson, George R. | Private | Oct. 4, 1847 | Oct. 5, '47 | Louisville, Ky. | | July 21, '48 | Louisville, Ky. |
| 52 | Utz, George M. | Private | Oct. 4, 1847 | Oct. 5, '47 | Louisville, Ky. | | July 21, '48 | Louisville, Ky. |
| 53 | Waters, Garland | Private | Oct. 4, 1847 | Oct. 5, '47 | Louisville, Ky. | | July 21, '48 | Louisville, Ky. |
| 54 | Whitaker, Julius | Private | Oct. 4, 1847 | Oct. 5, '47 | Louisville, Ky. | | July 21, '48 | Louisville, Ky. |
| 55 | Williams, Bennet | Private | Oct. 4, 1847 | Oct. 5, '47 | Louisville, Ky. | | July 21, '48 | Louisville, Ky. |
| 56 | Willson, Samuel | Private | Oct. 4, 1847 | Oct. 5, '47 | Louisville, Ky. | | July 21, '48 | Louisville, Ky. |
| 57 | Watts, John | Private | Oct. 4, 1847 | Oct. 5, '47 | Louisville, Ky. | | July 21, '48 | Louisville, Ky. |
| | DEATHS. | | | | | | | |
| 1 | McCracken, Stephen | Private | Oct. 4, 1847 | Oct. 5, '47 | Louisville, Ky. | | | |

## FOOT VOLUNTEERS—MEXICAN WAR.

| No. of each grade | REMARKS. |
|---|---|
| 1 | |
| 1 | Resigned May 6, 1848. |
| 2 | Promoted from 2d 2d Lieutenant to 1st Lieutenant, May 6, 1848, (vice Buckner, resigned.) He was 2d 2d Lieutenant from enrollment. |
| 1 | [Lieutenant May 6, 1848, (vice Flournoy, promoted.) |
| 2 | Was private from enrollment to 22d January, 1848, then Corporal to March 1, 1848, then Sergeant to May 6, 1848, then promoted to 2d 2d |
| 1 | |
| 2 | |
| 3 | |
| 4 | Was private from enrollment to January 22, 1848, then Corporal to May 6, 1848, then promoted to Sergeant M. |
| 1 | |
| 2 | |
| 3 | |
| 4 | Was private from enrollment to May 6, 1848, when appointed Corporal. |
| 1 | Was private from enrollment to May 1, 1848, when appointed Drummer. |
| 2 | |
| 1 | |
| 2 | |
| 3 | |
| 4 | |
| 5 | |
| 6 | |
| 7 | |
| 8 | |
| 9 | |
| 10 | |
| 11 | |
| 12 | |
| 13 | |
| 14 | |
| 15 | |
| 16 | |
| 17 | |
| 18 | |
| 19 | |
| 20 | |
| 21 | |
| 22 | |
| 23 | |
| 24 | |
| 25 | |
| 26 | |
| 27 | |
| 28 | |
| 29 | |
| 30 | |
| 31 | |
| 32 | |
| 33 | |
| 34 | |
| 35 | |
| 36 | |
| 37 | |
| 38 | |
| 39 | |
| 40 | |
| 41 | |
| 42 | |
| 43 | |
| 44 | |
| 45 | |
| 46 | Sick in hospital. |
| 47 | |
| 48 | |
| 49 | |
| 50 | |
| 51 | |
| 52 | |
| 53 | |
| 54 | |
| 55 | |
| 56 | |
| 57 | |
| 1 | Died at New Orleans, November 27, 1847. |

## ROLL OF COMPANY "D," THIRD REGIMENT KENTUCKY

| No. of each grade | Name. | Rank. | Joined for Service. | Mustered In. When. | Mustered In. Where. | Period | Mustered Out. When. | Mustered Out. Where. |
|---|---|---|---|---|---|---|---|---|
| 2 | Davis, Jesse | Private | Oct. 4, 1847 | Oct. 5, '47 | Louisville, Ky. | To serve during the war. | | |
| 3 | Powers, Samuel L. | Corporal | Oct. 4, 1847 | Oct. 5, '47 | Louisville, Ky. | | | |
| 4 | Beck, Samuel T. | Private | Oct. 4, 1847 | Oct. 5, '47 | Louisville, Ky. | | | |
| 5 | Adams, Benjamin | Private | Oct. 4, 1847 | Oct. 5, '47 | Louisville, Ky. | | | |
| 6 | Walker, John | Private | Oct. 4, 1847 | Oct. 5, '47 | Louisville, Ky. | | | |
| 7 | Waters, Thomas | Private | Oct. 4, 1847 | Oct. 5, '47 | Louisville, Ky. | | | |
| 8 | Wayman, Noble R. | Private | Oct. 4, 1847 | Oct. 5, '47 | Louisville, Ky. | | | |
| 9 | Nester, James | Private | Oct. 4, 1847 | Oct. 5, '47 | Louisville, Ky. | | | |
| 10 | Quinn, John | Private | Oct. 4, 1847 | Oct. 5, '47 | Louisville, Ky. | | | |
| 11 | Catterson, Wm. | Private | Oct. 4, 1847 | Oct. 5, '47 | Louisville, Ky. | | | |
| 12 | Elleston, Thomas | Private | Oct. 4, 1847 | Oct. 5, '47 | Louisville, Ky. | | | |
| 13 | Porter, John | Private | Oct. 4, 1847 | Oct. 5, '47 | Louisville, Ky. | | | |
| 14 | Williams, George W. | Private | Oct. 4, 1847 | Oct. 5, '47 | Louisville, Ky. | | | |
| 15 | Perry, Elijah | Private | Oct. 4, 1847 | Oct. 5, '47 | Louisville, Ky. | | | |
| 16 | Waugh, Thomas | Private | Oct. 4, 1847 | Oct. 5, '47 | Louisville, Ky. | | | |
| 17 | Garrison, Hiram | Private | Oct. 4, 1847 | Oct. 5, '47 | Louisville, Ky. | | | |
| 18 | Williams, John | Drummer | Oct. 4, 1847 | Oct. 5, '47 | Louisville, Ky. | | | |
| | **Deserted.** | | | | | | | |
| 1 | Willson, Edward | Private | Oct. 4, 1847 | Oct. 5, '47 | Louisville, Ky. | | | |
| 2 | Cunningham, Edward | Private | Oct. 4, 1847 | Oct. 5, '47 | Louisville, Ky. | | | |
| | **Discharged.** | | | | | | | |
| 1 | Jackson, Mathew E. | Private | Oct. 4, 1847 | Oct. 5, '47 | Louisville, Ky. | | | |
| 2 | Lebree, James | Private | Oct. 4, 1847 | Oct. 5, '47 | Louisville, Ky. | | | |
| 3 | Bills, John | Private | Oct. 4, 1847 | Oct. 5, '47 | Louisville, Ky. | | | |
| 4 | Bush, Joshua B. | Corporal | Oct. 4, 1847 | Oct. 5, '47 | Louisville, Ky. | | | |
| 5 | Phelphs, Edward H. | Corporal | Oct. 4, 1847 | Oct. 5, '47 | Louisville, Ky. | | | |
| 6 | Bills, Abram | Private | Oct. 4, 1847 | Oct. 5, '47 | Louisville, Ky. | | | |
| 7 | Ransom, William S. | Private | Oct. 4, 1847 | Oct. 5, '47 | Louisville, Ky. | | | |
| 8 | Burke, Patrick | Private | Oct. 4, 1847 | Oct. 5, '47 | Louisville, Ky. | | | |
| 9 | Connor, John T. | Private | Oct. 4, 1847 | Oct. 5, '47 | Louisville, Ky. | | | |
| 10 | Green, Joseph | Private | Oct. 4, 1847 | Oct. 5, '47 | Louisville, Ky. | | | |
| 11 | Jenkens, Joseph W. | Private | Oct. 4, 1847 | Oct. 5, '47 | Louisville, Ky. | | | |
| 12 | Franklin, James | Private | Oct. 4, 1847 | Oct. 5, '47 | Louisville, Ky. | | | |
| 13 | Gregory, Curtis | Private | Oct. 4, 1847 | Oct. 5, '47 | Louisville, Ky. | | | |
| 14 | Willson, Stephen | Private | Oct. 4, 1847 | Oct. 5, '47 | Louisville, Ky. | | | |
| 15 | Glacken, James W. | Private | Oct. 25, 1847 | Oct. 5, '47 | Louisville, Ky. | | | |

This Company was organized by Captain James A. Pritchard, at Burlington, Ky., in the month of September, 1847, and marched thence to Louisville, Ky., where it arrived the 4th day of October, a distance of one hundred and fifty miles.

## ROLL OF COMPANY "E," THIRD REGIMENT KENTUCKY

| No. | Name. | Rank. | Joined for Service. | Mustered In. When. | Mustered In. Where. | Period | Mustered Out. When. | Mustered Out. Where. |
|---|---|---|---|---|---|---|---|---|
| 1 | Leonidas Metcalf | Captain | Oct. 3, 1847 | Oct. 4, '47 | Louisville, Ky. | To serve during the war. | July 21, '48 | Louisville, Ky. |
| 1 | Enos H. Berry | 1st Lieutenant | Oct. 3, 1847 | Oct. 4, '47 | Louisville, Ky. | | July 21, '48 | Louisville, Ky. |
| 1 | James H. Halliday | 2d Lieutenant | Oct. 3, 1847 | Oct. 4, '47 | Louisville, Ky. | | July 21, '48 | Louisville, Ky. |
| 2 | John B. Halliday | 2d Lieutenant | Oct. 3, 1847 | Oct. 4, '47 | Louisville, Ky. | | July 21, '48 | Louisville, Ky. |
| 1 | William P. Robinson | 1st Sergeant | Oct. 3, 1847 | Oct. 4, '47 | Louisville, Ky. | | July 21, '48 | Louisville, Ky. |
| 2 | George W. Smart | Sergeant | Oct. 3, 1847 | Oct. 4, '47 | Louisville, Ky. | | July 21, '48 | Louisville, Ky. |
| 3 | William J. Stitt | Sergeant | Oct. 3, 1847 | Oct. 4, '47 | Louisville, Ky. | | July 21, '48 | Louisville, Ky. |
| 4 | William O. Chappel | Sergeant | Oct. 3, 1847 | Oct. 4, '47 | Louisville, Ky. | | July 21, '48 | Louisville, Ky. |
| 1 | William George | Corporal | Oct. 3, 1847 | Oct. 4, '47 | Louisville, Ky. | | July 21, '48 | Louisville, Ky. |
| 2 | Samuel Munson | Corporal | Oct. 3, 1847 | Oct. 4, '47 | Louisville, Ky. | | July 21, '48 | Louisville, Ky. |
| 3 | Preston M. C. Tuttle | Corporal | Oct. 3, 1847 | Oct. 4, '47 | Louisville, Ky. | | July 21, '48 | Louisville, Ky. |
| 4 | Napoleon B. Barrow | Corporal | Oct. 3, 1847 | Oct. 4, '47 | Louisville, Ky. | | July 21, '48 | Louisville, Ky. |
| 1 | James R. McCormick | Musician | Oct. 3, 1847 | Oct. 4, '47 | Louisville, Ky. | | July 21, '48 | Louisville, Ky. |
| 1 | Allen, George W. | Private | Oct. 3, 1847 | Oct. 4, '47 | Louisville, Ky. | | July 21, '48 | Louisville, Ky. |
| 2 | Allen, William | Private | Oct. 3, 1847 | Oct. 4, '47 | Louisville, Ky. | | July 21, '48 | Louisville, Ky. |
| 3 | Brown, Green B. | Private | Oct. 3, 1847 | Oct. 4, '47 | Louisville, Ky. | | July 21, '48 | Louisville, Ky. |
| 4 | Burgess, Henry | Private | Oct. 3, 1847 | Oct. 4, '47 | Louisville, Ky. | | July 21, '48 | Louisville, Ky. |
| 5 | Burns, John B. | Private | Oct. 3, 1847 | Oct. 4, '47 | Louisville, Ky. | | July 21, '48 | Louisville, Ky. |
| 6 | Burns, Samuel | Private | Oct. 3, 1847 | Oct. 4, '47 | Louisville, Ky. | | July 21, '48 | Louisville, Ky. |
| 7 | Blount, William H. | Private | Oct. 3, 1847 | Oct. 4, '47 | Louisville, Ky. | | July 21, '48 | Louisville, Ky. |
| 8 | Bland, James | Private | Oct. 3, 1847 | Oct. 4, '47 | Louisville, Ky. | | July 21, '48 | Louisville, Ky. |
| 9 | Bedford, Henry P. | Private | Oct. 3, 1847 | Oct. 4, '47 | Louisville, Ky. | | July 21, '48 | Louisville, Ky. |
| 10 | Campbell, James H. | Private | Oct. 3, 1847 | Oct. 4, '47 | Louisville, Ky. | | July 21, '48 | Louisville, Ky. |
| 11 | Campbell, James B. | Private | Oct. 3, 1847 | Oct. 4, '47 | Louisville, Ky. | | July 21, '48 | Louisville, Ky. |
| 12 | Conway, Henry W. | Private | Oct. 3, 1847 | Oct. 4, '47 | Louisville, Ky. | | July 21, '48 | Louisville, Ky. |
| 13 | Craddock, William W. | Private | Oct. 23, 1847 | Dec. 31, '47 | Louisville, Ky. | | July 21, '48 | Louisville, Ky. |
| 14 | Foster, Jackson | Private | Oct. 3, 1847 | Oct. 4, '47 | Louisville, Ky. | | July 21, '48 | Louisville, Ky. |
| 15 | Griffith, James H. | Private | Oct. 3, 1847 | Oct. 4, '47 | Louisville, Ky. | | July 21, '48 | Louisville, Ky. |
| 16 | Githens, James | Private | Oct. 3, 1847 | Oct. 4, '47 | Louisville, Ky. | | July 21, '48 | Louisville, Ky. |

## FOOT VOLUNTEERS—MEXICAN WAR—Continued.

| No. of each | REMARKS. |
|---|---|
| 2 | Died at Vera Cruz, November 25, 1847. |
| 3 | Died at Vera Cruz, November 28, 1847. |
| 4 | Died at Pueblo, Mexico, January 2, 1848. |
| 5 | Died at Pueblo, Mexico, January 23, 1848. |
| 6 | Died at Pueblo, Mexico, January 28, 1848. |
| 7 | Died at the City of Mexico, February 12, 1848. |
| 8 | Died at the City of Mexico, February 17, 1848. |
| 9 | Died at the City of Mexico, February 17, 1848. |
| 10 | Died at the City of Mexico, February 24, 1848. |
| 11 | Died at the City of Mexico, February 23, 1848. |
| 12 | Died at the City of Mexico, February 27, 1848. |
| 13 | Died at the City of Mexico, March 4, 1848. |
| 14 | Died at the City of Mexico, March 26, 1848. |
| 15 | Died at the City of Mexico, May 26, 1848. |
| 16 | Died at the City of Mexico, May 27, 1848. |
| 17 | Died at the City of Mexico, May 29, 1848. |
| 18 | Died at Pueblo, Mexico, the time not known. |
| 1 | Deserted at Louisville, Ky., October 28, 1847. |
| 2 | Deserted at New Orleans, La., November 9, 1847. |
| 1 | Discharged by civil authority as a minor at Louisville, Ky., October 28, 1847. |
| 2 | Discharged on Surgeon's certificate of disability, at Louisville, Ky., November 1, 1847. |
| 3 | Discharged on Surgeon's certificate of disability at Louisville, Ky., November 1, 1847. |
| 4 | Discharged on Surgeon's certificate of disability at the City of Mexico, January 12, 1848. |
| 5 | Discharged on Surgeon's certificate of disability, at the City of Mexico, January 12, 1848. |
| 6 | Discharged on Surgeon's certificate of disability, at the City of Mexico, February 17, 1848. |
| 7 | Discharged on Surgeon's certificate of disability, at Vera Cruz, January 2, 1848. |
| 8 | Discharged on Surgeon's certificate of disability, at Vera Cruz, January 25, 1848. |
| 9 | Discharged on Surgeon's certificate of disability, at New Orleans, April 3, 1848. |
| 10 | Discharged on Surgeon's certificate of disability, at New Orleans, April 3, 1848. |
| 11 | Discharged on Surgeon's certificate of disability, at New Orleans, April 3, 1848. |
| 12 | Discharged on Surgeon's certificate of disability, at Jalapa. Date unknown. |
| 13 | Discharged on Surgeon's certificate of disability, at New Orleans, January 17, 1848. |
| 14 | Discharged on Surgeon's certificate of disability, at New Orleans, June 29, 1848. |
| 15 | Discharged on Surgeon's certificate of disability, at Baton Rouge, May 2, 1848. |

## FOOT VOLUNTEERS—MEXICAN WAR.

| | |
|---|---|
| 1 | On the recruiting service from the 22d of January, 1848. |
| 1 | Regimental Quartermaster November 17, 1847. |
| 1 | |
| 2 | |
| 1 | |
| 2 | |
| 3 | |
| 4 | Appointed Sergeant from Corporal June 14, 1848; was Corporal from enrollment. |
| 1 | |
| 2 | |
| 3 | |
| 4 | Appointed Corporal from private June 14, 1848. |
| 1 | |
| 2 | |
| 3 | |
| 4 | |
| 5 | |
| 6 | |
| 7 | |
| 8 | |
| 9 | |
| 10 | |
| 11 | |
| 12 | |
| 13 | |
| 14 | |
| 15 | |
| 16 | |

## MEXICAN WAR VETERANS.

### ROLL OF COMPANY "E," THIRD REGIMENT KENTUCKY

| No. of each grade. | Name. | Rank. | Joined for Service. | Mustered In. When. | Mustered In. Where. | Period. | Mustered Out. When. | Mustered Out. Where. |
|---|---|---|---|---|---|---|---|---|
| 17 | Halladay, Joseph S. | Private | Oct. 3, 1847 | Oct. 4, '47 | Louisville, Ky. | | July 21, '48 | Louisville, Ky. |
| 18 | Hedrick, William | Private | Oct. 3, 1847 | Oct. 4, '47 | Louisville, Ky. | | July 21, '48 | Louisville, Ky. |
| 19 | Hackley, James A. | Private | Oct. 3, 1847 | Oct. 4, '47 | Louisville, Ky. | | July 21, '48 | Louisville, Ky. |
| 20 | Hughes, James M. | Private | Oct. 3, 1847 | Oct. 4, '47 | Louisville, Ky. | | July 21, '48 | Louisville, Ky. |
| 21 | Hornback, William H. | Private | Oct. 3, 1847 | Oct. 4, '47 | Louisville, Ky. | | July 21, '48 | Louisville, Ky. |
| 22 | Kimes, John | Private | Oct. 3, 1847 | Oct. 4, '47 | Louisville, Ky. | | July 21, '48 | Louisville, Ky. |
| 23 | Keen, James W. | Private | Oct. 3, 1847 | Oct. 4, '47 | Louisville, Ky. | | July 21, '48 | Louisville, Ky. |
| 24 | Kenton, Eldridge | Private | Oct. 3, 1847 | Oct. 4, '47 | Louisville, Ky. | | July 21, '48 | Louisville, Ky. |
| 25 | Lawrence, William | Private | Oct. 3, 1847 | Oct. 4, '47 | Louisville, Ky. | | July 21, '48 | Louisville, Ky. |
| 26 | Lawrence, Gibson | Private | Oct. 3, 1847 | Oct. 4, '47 | Louisville, Ky. | | July 21, '48 | Louisville, Ky. |
| 27 | Lewis, Orin M. | Private | Oct. 3, 1847 | Oct. 4, '47 | Louisville, Ky. | | July 21, '48 | Louisville, Ky. |
| 28 | Littlejohn, James W. | Private | Oct. 3, 1847 | Oct. 4, '47 | Louisville, Ky. | | July 21, '48 | Louisville, Ky. |
| 29 | Myers, David | Private | Oct. 3, 1847 | Oct. 4, '47 | Louisville, Ky. | | July 21, '48 | Louisville, Ky. |
| 30 | Myers, George, Jr. | Private | Oct. 3, 1847 | Oct. 4, '47 | Louisville, Ky. | | July 21, '48 | Louisville, Ky. |
| 31 | McFarland, Felix | Private | Oct. 3, 1847 | Oct. 4, '47 | Louisville, Ky. | | July 21, '48 | Louisville, Ky. |
| 32 | McCormack, John H. | Private | Oct. 3, 1847 | Oct. 4, '47 | Louisville, Ky. | | July 21, '48 | Louisville, Ky. |
| 33 | Miller, Washington | Private | Oct. 3, 1847 | Oct. 4, '47 | Louisville, Ky. | | July 21, '48 | Louisville, Ky. |
| 34 | Marshall, Silas | Private | Oct. 3, 1847 | Oct. 4, '47 | Louisville, Ky. | | July 21, '48 | Louisville, Ky |
| 35 | Murs, William L. | Private | Oct. 3, 1847 | Oct. 4, '47 | Louisville, Ky. | | July 21, '48 | Louisville, Ky. |
| 36 | Martin, John | Private | Oct. 3, 1847 | Oct. 4, '47 | Louisville, Ky. | | July 21, '48 | Louisville, Ky. |
| 37 | Morris, Lewis | Private | Oct. 3, 1847 | Oct. 4, '47 | Louisville, Ky. | | July 21, '48 | Louisville, Ky. |
| 38 | Moore, Calvin B. | Private | Oct. 3, 1847 | Oct. 4, '47 | Louisville, Ky. | | July 21, '48 | Louisville, Ky. |
| 39 | Moore, John | Private | Oct. 3, 1847 | Oct. 4, '47 | Louisville, Ky. | | July 21, '48 | Louisville, Ky |
| 40 | Miller, Joseph | Private | Oct. 3, 1847 | Oct. 4, '47 | Louisville, Ky. | | July 21, '48 | Louisville, Ky. |
| 41 | Miller, Isaiah | Private | Oct. 3, 1847 | Oct. 4, '47 | Louisville, Ky. | | July 21, '48 | Louisville, Ky. |
| 42 | Miller, John | Private | Oct. 3, 1847 | Oct. 4, '47 | Louisville, Ky. | | July 21, '48 | Louisville, Ky. |
| 43 | Morgan, Robert F. | Private | Oct. 3, 1847 | Oct. 4, '47 | Louisville, Ky. | | July 21, '48 | Louisville, Ky. |
| 44 | Neal, John | Private | Oct. 3, 1847 | Oct. 4, '47 | Louisville, Ky. | | July 21, '48 | Louisville, Ky. |
| 45 | Pope, William A. | Private | Oct. 3, 1847 | Oct. 4, '47 | Louisville, Ky. | | July 21, '48 | Louisville, Ky. |
| 46 | Ritchey, John W. | Private | Oct. 3, 1847 | Oct. 4, '47 | Louisville, Ky. | | July 21, '48 | Louisville, Ky. |
| 47 | Rankins, Edmond M. | Private | Oct. 3, 1847 | Oct. 4, '47 | Louisville, Ky. | | July 21, '48 | Louisville, Ky. |
| 48 | Roundtree, William | Private | Oct. 3, 1847 | Oct. 4, '47 | Louisville, Ky. | | July 21, '48 | Louisville, Ky. |
| 49 | Royse, John W. | Private | Oct. 3, 1847 | Oct. 4, '47 | Louisville, Ky. | | July 21, '48 | Louisville, Ky. |
| 50 | Ricketts, Benjamin | Private | Oct. 3, 1847 | Oct. 4, '47 | Louisville, Ky. | To serve during the war. | July 21, '48 | Louisville, Ky. |
| 51 | Reid, Samuel P. | Private | Oct. 3, 1847 | Oct. 4, '47 | Louisville, Ky. | | July 21, '48 | Louisville, Ky. |
| 52 | Simms, William | Private | Oct. 3, 1847 | Oct. 4, '47 | Louisville, Ky. | | July 21, '48 | Louisville, Ky. |
| 53 | Sandford, Granville | Private | Oct. 3, 1847 | Oct. 4, '47 | Louisville, Ky. | | July 21, '48 | Louisville, Ky. |
| 54 | Sonsby, Archibald | Private | Oct. 3, 1847 | Oct. 4, '47 | Louisville, Ky. | | July 21, '48 | Louisville, Ky. |
| 55 | Smart, Joseph | Private | Oct. 3, 1847 | Oct. 4, '47 | Louisville, Ky. | | July 21, '48 | Louisville, Ky. |
| 56 | Summers, James G. | Private | Oct. 31, 1847 | Dec. 31, '47 | Louisville, Ky. | | July 21, '48 | Louisville, Ky. |
| 57 | Tully, Joshua C. | Private | Oct. 3, 1847 | Oct. 4, '47 | Louisville, Ky. | | July 21, '48 | Louisville, Ky. |
| 58 | Watkins, Wm. | Private | Oct. 3, 1847 | Oct. 4, '47 | Louisville, Ky. | | July 21, '48 | Louisville, Ky. |
| 59 | Watkins, Burrell | Private | Oct. 3, 1847 | Oct. 4, '47 | Louisville, Ky. | | July 21, '48 | Louisville, Ky. |
| 60 | Watkins, Samuel | Private | Oct. 3, 1847 | Oct. 4, '47 | Louisville, Ky. | | July 21, '48 | Louisville, Ky. |
| 61 | Whitecraft, John E. | Private | Oct. 3, 1847 | Oct. 4, '47 | Louisville, Ky. | | July 21, '48 | Louisville, Ky. |
| 62 | Wheeler, Henry D. | Private | Oct. 3, 1847 | Oct. 4, '47 | Louisville, Ky. | | July 21, '48 | Louisville, Ky. |
| | DISCHARGED. | | | | | | | |
| 1 | Clay, Lewis A. | Private | Oct. 3, 1847 | Oct. 4, '47 | Louisville, Ky. | | | |
| 2 | Campbell, Wm. R. | Musician | Oct. 3, 1847 | Oct. 4, '47 | Louisville, Ky. | | | |
| 3 | Campbell, Thomas M. | Sergeant | Oct. 3, 1847 | Oct. 4, '47 | Louisville, Ky. | | | |
| 4 | Henry, John | Private | Oct. 3, 1847 | Oct. 4, '47 | Louisville, Ky. | | | |
| 5 | Kingcart, John | Private | Oct. 3, 1847 | Oct. 4, '47 | Louisville, Ky. | | | |
| 6 | Myers, Geo. (Sen.) | Private | Oct. 3, 1847 | Oct. 4, '47 | Louisville, Ky. | | | |
| 7 | Stewart, Henry | Private | Oct. 3, 1847 | Oct. 4, '47 | Louisville, Ky. | | | |
| 8 | Stephens, Alfred P. | Private | Oct. 3, 1847 | Oct. 4, '47 | Louisville, Ky. | | | |
| 9 | Scott, James M. | Private | Oct. 3, 1847 | Oct. 4, '47 | Louisville, Ky. | | | |
| | DEATHS. | | | | | | | |
| 1 | Alexander, Jesse F. | Private | Oct. 3, 1847 | Oct. 4, '47 | Louisville, Ky. | | | |
| 2 | Bishop, James H. | Private | Oct. 3, 1847 | Oct. 4, '47 | Louisville, Ky. | | | |
| 3 | Campbell, Daniel P. B. | Private | Oct. 3, 1847 | Oct. 4, '47 | Louisville, Ky. | | | |
| 4 | Coffman, Henry | Private | Oct. 3, 1847 | Oct. 4, '47 | Louisville, Ky. | | | |
| 5 | Eaton, Chas. | Private | Oct. 3, 1847 | Oct. 4, '47 | Louisville, Ky. | | | |
| 6 | Feeback, Mathew | Private | Oct. 3, 1847 | Oct. 4, '47 | Louisville, Ky. | | | |
| 7 | Hopkins, Eldridge | Private | Oct. 3, 1847 | Oct. 4, '47 | Louisville, Ky. | | | |
| 8 | Hoover, Chas. | Private | Oct. 3, 1847 | Oct. 4, '47 | Louisville, Ky. | | | |
| 9 | Hanlin, Thomas | Private | Oct. 3, 1847 | Oct. 4, '47 | Louisville, Ky. | | | |
| 10 | Jordan, Arthur B. | Private | Oct. 3, 1847 | Oct. 4, '47 | Louisville, Ky. | | | |
| 11 | Lindsay, Robert | Private | Oct. 3, 1847 | Oct. 4, '47 | Louisville, Ky. | | | |
| 12 | Lyons, Wm. | Private | Oct. 3, 1847 | Oct. 4, '47 | Louisville, Ky. | | | |
| 13 | McFarlan, Wm. | Private | Oct. 3, 1847 | Oct. 4, '47 | Louisville, Ky. | | | |
| 14 | Myers, Benjamin | Private | Oct. 3, 1847 | Oct. 4, '47 | Louisville, Ky. | | | |
| 15 | McCoun, Peter | Private | Oct. 3, 1847 | Oct. 4, '47 | Louisville, Ky. | | | |
| 16 | Ogden, Thomas | Private | Oct. 3, 1847 | Oct. 4, '47 | Louisville, Ky. | | | |

# FOOT VOLUNTEERS—MEXICAN WAR—Continued.

| No. of each grade | REMARKS. |
|---|---|
| 17 | |
| 18 | |
| 19 | |
| 20 | |
| 21 | |
| 22 | |
| 23 | |
| 24 | |
| 25 | Left sick at New Orleans, July 6, 1848, in hospital. |
| 26 | |
| 27 | |
| 28 | |
| 29 | |
| 30 | |
| 31 | |
| 32 | |
| 33 | |
| 34 | |
| 35 | |
| 36 | |
| 37 | |
| 38 | |
| 39 | |
| 40 | Left sick at Jalapa, December 6, 1847, in hospital. |
| 41 | |
| 42 | |
| 43 | |
| 44 | |
| 45 | |
| 46 | |
| 47 | |
| 48 | |
| 49 | |
| 50 | |
| 51 | |
| 52 | |
| 53 | |
| 54 | |
| 55 | |
| 56 | |
| 57 | |
| 58 | |
| 59 | |
| 60 | |
| 61 | |
| 62 | |
| 1 | At City of Mexico, January 12, 1848; Surgeon's certificate of disability. |
| 2 | At city of Mexico, March 4, 1848. Order of Major-General Butler. |
| 3 | By expiration of service at Newport, Ky., July 2, 1848. |
| 4 | At Pueblo, Mex., March 13, 1848; Surgeon's certificate of disability. |
| 5 | At City of Mexico, March 4, 1848. Order of Major-General Butler. |
| 6 | At City of Mexico, March 4, 1848. Order of Major-General Butler. |
| 7 | At Louisville, Ky., October 20, 1847, by civil authority, as a minor. |
| 8 | At City of Mexico, January 12, 1848; Surgeon's certificate of disability. |
| 9 | At New Orleans, March 15, 1848; Surgeon's certificate of disability. |
| 1 | At Vera Cruz, Mexico. November 26, 1847. |
| 2 | At City of Mexico, December 30, 1847. |
| 3 | At City of Vera Cruz, November 20, 1847. |
| 4 | At Pueblo, Mexico, February 2, 1848. |
| 5 | At Pueblo, Mexico. Not known. (Date.) |
| 6 | At Vera Cruz Mexico. Date unknown. |
| 7 | At City of Mexico, February 8, 1848. |
| 8 | At Jalapa, Mexico, April 15, 1848. |
| 9 | Joined Company February 28, 1848, from supposed desertion; died at the City of Mexico, April 1, 1848. |
| 10 | At Pueblo, March 11, 1848. |
| 11 | At City of Mexico, February 5, 1848. |
| 12 | At City of Mexico, February 10, 1848. |
| 13 | At Pueblo, Mexico. Date not known. |
| 14 | At City of Mexico, March 28, 1848. |
| 15 | At City of Mexico, April 10, 1848. |
| 16 | At camp ———, Mexico, June 26, 1848. |

## MEXICAN WAR VETERANS.

### ROLL OF COMPANY "E," THIRD REGIMENT KENTUCKY

| No. of each grade. | Name. | Rank. | Joined for Service. | Mustered In. When. | Mustered In. Where. | Period. | Mustered Out. When. | Mustered Out. Where. |
|---|---|---|---|---|---|---|---|---|
| 17 | Reid, Joseph | Private | Oct. 3, 1847 | Oct. 4, '47 | Louisville, Ky. | | | |
| 18 | Williams, Wm. | Private | Oct. 3, 1847 | Oct. 4, '47 | Louisville, Ky. | | | |
| 19 | Willoughby, Lewis | Private | Oct. 3, 1847 | Oct. 4, '47 | Louisville, Ky. | | | |
| 20 | Watson, Wm. | Private | Oct. 3, 1847 | Oct. 4, '47 | Louisville, Ky. | To serve during the war. | | |
| 21 | Walls, Armistead | Private | Oct. 3, 1847 | Oct. 4, '47 | Louisville Ky. | | | |
| 22 | Burden, Wm. | Private | Oct. 3, 1847 | Oct. 4, '47 | Louisville, Ky. | | | |
| 23 | Cassidy, Moses J. | Private | Oct. 3, 1847 | Oct. 4, '47 | Louisville, Ky | | | |
| 24 | Ritchey, Jos. M. | Private | Oct. 3, 1847 | Oct. 4, '47 | Louisville, Ky. | | | |
| 25 | Kimbrough, John | Sergeant | Oct. 3, 1847 | Oct. 4, '47 | Louisville, Ky. | | | |
| | **DESERTED.** | | | | | | | |
| 1 | Barker, Geo. | Private | Oct. 3, 1847 | Oct. 4, '47 | Louisville, Ky. | | | |
| 2 | Hanlin, Thos. | Private | Oct. 3, 1847 | Oct. 4, '47 | Louisville, Ky. | | | |
| | **TRANSFERRED.** | | | | | | | |
| 1 | Halladay, Thos. | Private | Oct. 3, 1847 | Oct. 4, '47 | Louisville, Ky. | | | |
| 2 | Neal, James | Private | Oct. 3, 1847 | Oct. 4, '47 | Louisville, Ky. | | | |

This Company was organized by Capt. Leonidas Metcalf, at Carlisle, Ky., in the month of September, 1847, and marched thence to Louisville, Ky., where it arrived on the 3d day of October, 1847, a distance of one hundred and ten miles.

### ROLL OF COMPANY "F," THIRD REGIMENT KENTUCKY

| No. | Name. | Rank. | Joined for Service. | Mustered In. When. | Mustered In. Where. | Period. | Mustered Out. When. | Mustered Out. Where. |
|---|---|---|---|---|---|---|---|---|
| 1 | Wm. P. Chiles | Captain | Oct. 3, 1847 | Oct. 6, '47 | Louisville, Ky. | | July 21, '48 | Louisville, Ky. |
| 1 | Henry H. Mize | 1st Lieutenant | Oct. 3, 1847 | Oct. 6, '47 | Louisville, Ky. | | July 21, '48 | Louisville, Ky. |
| 1 | Ansel D. Powell | 2d Lieutenant | Oct. 3, 1847 | Oct. 6, '47 | Louisville, Ky. | | July 21, '48 | Louisville, Ky. |
| 2 | Elisha B. Treadway | 2d Lieutenant | Oct. 3, 1847 | Oct. 6, '47 | Louisville, Ky. | | July 21, '48 | Louisville, Ky. |
| 1 | Berry B. Stone | 1st Sergeant | Oct. 3, 1847 | Oct. 6, '47 | Louisville, Ky. | | July 21, '48 | Louisville, Ky. |
| 2 | David McEver | Sergeant | Oct. 19, 1847 | Oct. 19, '47 | Louisville, Ky. | | July 21, '48 | Louisville, Ky. |
| 3 | Wm. Smallwood | Sergeant | Oct. 3, 1847 | Oct. 6, '47 | Louisville, Ky. | | July 21, '48 | Louisville, Ky. |
| 4 | Wm. E. Witt | Sergeant | Oct. 3, 1847 | Oct. 6, '47 | Louisville, Ky. | | July 21, '48 | Louisville, Ky. |
| 1 | Henry C. Thomas | 1st Corporal | Oct. 3, 1847 | Oct. 6, '47 | Louisville, Ky. | | July 21, '48 | Louisville, Ky. |
| 2 | James Hammons | Corporal | Oct. 3, 1847 | Oct. 6, '47 | Louisville, Ky. | | July 21, '48 | Louisville, Ky. |
| 3 | George W. Daniel | Corporal | Oct. 3, 1847 | Oct. 6, '47 | Louisville, Ky. | | July 21, '48 | Louisville, Ky. |
| 4 | John Brooks | Corporal | Oct. 3, 1847 | Oct. 6, '47 | Louisville, Ky. | | July 21, '48 | Louisville, Ky. |
| 1 | Napoleon B. Busby | Musician | Oct. 3, 1847 | Oct. 6, '47 | Louisville, Ky. | | July 21, '48 | Louisville, Ky. |
| 2 | Jacob W. Vanderpool | Musician | Oct. 3, 1847 | Oct. 6, '47 | Louisville, Ky. | | July 21, '48 | Louisville, Ky. |
| 1 | Anderson, James | Private | Oct. 3, 1847 | Oct. 6, '47 | Louisville, Ky. | | July 21, '48 | Louisville, Ky. |
| 2 | Ambrose, William | Private | Oct. 3, 1847 | Oct. 6, '47 | Louisville, Ky. | | July 21, '48 | Louisville, Ky. |
| 3 | Alverson, Mathew M. | Private | Oct. 3, 1847 | Oct. 6, '47 | Louisville, Ky. | | July 21, '48 | Louisville, Ky. |
| 4 | Benningfield, John | Private | Oct. 3, 1847 | Oct. 6, '47 | Louisville, Ky. | | July 21, '48 | Louisville, Ky. |
| 5 | Brandenburg, James | Private | Oct. 3, 1847 | Oct. 6, '47 | Louisville, Ky. | | July 21, '48 | Louisville Ky. |
| 6 | Bennett, Thomas H. | Private | Oct. 3, 1847 | Oct. 6, '47 | Louisville, Ky. | To serve during the war. | July 21, '48 | Louisville, Ky. |
| 7 | Brown, Caswell | Private | Oct. 3, 1847 | Oct. 6, '47 | Louisville, Ky. | | July 21, '48 | Louisville, Ky. |
| 8 | Bellis, William | Private | Oct. 3, 1847 | Oct. 6, '47 | Louisville, Ky. | | July 21, '48 | Louisville, Ky. |
| 9 | Bellis, Hiram | Private | Oct. 3, 1847 | Oct. 6, '47 | Louisville, Ky. | | July 21, '48 | Louisville, Ky. |
| 10 | Canter, William C. | Private | Oct. 3, 1847 | Oct. 6, '47 | Louisville, Ky. | | July 21, '48 | Louisville, Ky. |
| 11 | Campbell, William M. | Private | Oct. 3, 1847 | Oct. 6, '47 | Louisville, Ky. | | July 21, '48 | Louisville, Ky. |
| 12 | Clark, Christopher F. | Private | Oct. 3, 1847 | Oct. 6, '47 | Louisville, Ky. | | July 21, '48 | Louisville, Ky. |
| 13 | Crawford, Simpson | Private | Oct. 3, 1847 | Oct. 6, '47 | Louisville, Ky. | | July 21, '48 | Louisville, Ky. |
| 14 | Cole, William S. | Private | Oct. 3, 1847 | Oct. 6, '47 | Louisville, Ky. | | July 21, '48 | Louisville, Ky. |
| 15 | Cundiff, Stephen | Private | Oct. 3, 1847 | Oct. 6, '47 | Louisville, Ky. | | July 21, '48 | Louisville, Ky. |
| 16 | Drake, Francis S. | Private | Oct. 3, 1847 | Oct. 6, '47 | Louisville, Ky. | | July 21, '48 | Louisville, Ky. |
| 17 | Eads, Joel | Private | Oct. 3, 1847 | Oct. 6, '47 | Louisville, Ky. | | July 21, '48 | Louisville, Ky. |
| 18 | Eadens, Westley | Private | Oct. 3, 1847 | Oct. 6, '47 | Louisville, Ky. | | July 21, '48 | Louisville, Ky. |
| 19 | Evans, John | Private | Oct. 3, 1847 | Oct. 6, '47 | Louisville, Ky. | | July 21, '48 | Louisville, Ky. |
| 20 | Fraley, Henry | Private | Oct. 3, 1847 | Oct. 6, '47 | Louisville, Ky. | | July 21, '48 | Louisville, Ky. |
| 21 | Foreman, Richard S. | Private | Oct. 3, 1847 | Oct. 6, '47 | Louisville, Ky. | | July 21, '48 | Louisville, Ky. |
| 22 | Fraley, Greenbery | Private | Oct. 3, 1847 | Oct. 6, '47 | Louisville, Ky. | | July 21, '48 | Louisville, Ky. |
| 23 | Friar, Wm. | Private | Oct. 3, 1847 | Oct. 6, '47 | Louisville, Ky. | | July 21, '48 | Louisville, Ky. |
| 24 | Garner, John G. | Private | Oct. 3, 1847 | Oct. 6, '47 | Louisville, Ky. | | July 21, '48 | Louisville, Ky. |
| 25 | Gunn, John P. | Private | Oct. 3, 1847 | Oct. 6, '47 | Louisville, Ky. | | July 21, '48 | Louisville, Ky. |
| 26 | Goe, William | Private | Oct. 3, 1847 | Oct. 6, '47 | Louisville, Ky. | | July 21, '48 | Louisville, Ky. |
| 27 | Hubbard, Peter | Private | Oct. 3, 1847 | Oct. 6, '47 | Louisville, Ky. | | July 21, '48 | Louisville, Ky. |
| 28 | Hughs, Madison M. | Private | Oct. 3, 1847 | Oct. 6, '47 | Louisville, Ky. | | July 21, '48 | Louisville, Ky. |
| 29 | Hill, Moses | Private | Oct. 3, 1847 | Oct. 6, '47 | Louisville, Ky. | | July 21, '48 | Louisville, Ky. |
| 30 | Hill, Grandison | Private | Oct. 3, 1847 | Oct. 6, '47 | Louisville, Ky. | | July 21, '48 | Louisville, Ky. |
| 31 | Hammons, John | Private | Oct. 3, 1847 | Oct. 6, '47 | Louisville, Ky. | | July 21, '48 | Louisville, Ky. |
| 32 | Howard, Clement | Private | Oct. 3, 1847 | Oct. 6, '47 | Louisville, Ky. | | July 21, '48 | Louisville, Ky. |
| 33 | Horn, Wiley | Private | Oct. 3, 1847 | Oct. 6, '47 | Louisville, Ky. | | July 21, '48 | Louisville, Ky. |
| 34 | Hamilton, Jabez L. | Private | Oct. 3, 1847 | Oct. 6, '47 | Louisville, Ky. | | July 21, '48 | Louisville, Ky. |
| 35 | Han, James | Private | Oct. 3, 1847 | Oct. 6, '47 | Louisville, Ky. | | July 21, '48 | Louisville, Ky. |

## FOOT VOLUNTEERS—MEXICAN WAR—Continued.

| No. of each grade. | REMARKS. |
|---|---|
| 17 | At City of Mexico, March 14, 1848. |
| 18 | At Pueblo, Mexico, December 12, 1847. |
| 19 | At City of Mexico, February 7, 1848. |
| 20 | At City of Mexico, April 1, 1848. |
| 21 | At City of Mexico, May 13, 1848. |
| 22 | In camp near Pueblo, Mexico, June 4, 1848. |
| 23 | At New Orleans, on ship Palestine, July 5, 1848. |
| 24 | In camp near Jalapa, Mexico, June 10, 1848. |
| 25 | In camp at Enero, Mexico, June 13, 1848. |
| 1 | At Louisville, Ky., October 23, 1847. |
| 2 | At New Orleans, November 8, 1847. |
| 1 | To Regimental Staff as Quartermaster Sergeant, November 26, 1847. |
| 2 | To Regimental Staff as Quartermaster Sergeant, May 1, 1848. |

## FOOT VOLUNTEERS—MEXICAN WAR.

| No. | REMARKS. |
|---|---|
| 1 | |
| 1 | |
| 1 | |
| 2 | |
| 1 | Appointed 14th December, 1847; was private from enlistment. |
| 2 | Appointed 1st February, 1848; was private from enlistment. |
| 3 | |
| 4 | Appointed 1st March, 1848, from Corporal; was Corporal from January 1, 1848; was private from enlistment. |
| 1 | Appointed 1st February, 1848, from private. |
| 2 | Appointed 1st March, 1848, from private. |
| 3 | |
| 4 | |
| 1 | |
| 2 | |
| 1 | |
| 2 | Sick in hospital. |
| 3 | |
| 4 | |
| 5 | |
| 6 | |
| 7 | |
| 8 | Reduced from Sergeant 1st February, 1848, by Col. T.; absent on furlough from May 9th to June 28th. Order of Col. Thompson. |
| 9 | Reduced from Corporal 1st February, 1848, by Col. T.; absent on furlough from 28th May till 28th June, 1848. Order of Col. Thompson. |
| 10 | |
| 11 | |
| 12 | |
| 13 | |
| 14 | |
| 15 | |
| 16 | |
| 17 | |
| 18 | |
| 19 | |
| 20 | |
| 21 | Absent on furlough from 27th May till 28th June, by order of Col. Thompson. |
| 22 | Sick in hospital. |
| 23 | |
| 24 | |
| 25 | Absent on furlough from 27th May till 28th June, 1848. Order of Col. Thompson. |
| 26 | |
| 27 | |
| 28 | |
| 29 | |
| 30 | |
| 31 | Absent on furlough from 27th May till 28th June, 1848. Order of Col. Thompson. |
| 32 | |
| 33 | |
| 34 | |
| 35 | Absent on furlough from 8th May till 28th June, 1848. Order of Col. Thompson. |

## MEXICAN WAR VETERANS.

### ROLL OF COMPANY "F," THIRD REGIMENT KENTUCKY

| No. of each grade | Name | Rank | Joined for Service | Mustered In When | Mustered In Where | Period | Mustered Out When | Mustered Out Where |
|---|---|---|---|---|---|---|---|---|
| 36 | Hall, Green | Private | Oct. 3, 1847 | Oct. 6, '47 | Louisville, Ky. | | July 21, '48 | Louisville, Ky. |
| 37 | Hamilton, Wm. | Private | Oct. 3, 1847 | Oct. 6, '47 | Louisville, Ky. | | July 21, '48 | Louisville, Ky. |
| 38 | Howard, Montgomery | Private | Oct. 3, 1847 | Oct. 6, '47 | Louisville, Ky. | | July 21, '48 | Louisville, Ky. |
| 39 | James, Charles | Private | Oct. 3, 1847 | Oct. 6, '47 | Louisville, Ky. | | July 21, '48 | Louisville, Ky. |
| 40 | Kincaid, Socrates | Private | Oct. 3, 1847 | Oct. 6, '47 | Louisville, Ky. | | July 21, '48 | Louisville, Ky. |
| 41 | Keley, Wm. S. | Private | Oct. 3, 1847 | Oct. 6, '47 | Louisville, Ky. | | July 21, '48 | Louisville, Ky. |
| 42 | Lamberson, Joshua | Private | Oct. 3, 1847 | Oct. 6, '47 | Louisville, Ky. | | July 21, '48 | Louisville, Ky. |
| 43 | Lowry, Weedon S. | Private | Oct. 3, 1847 | Oct. 6, '47 | Louisville, Ky. | | July 21, '48 | Louisville, Ky. |
| 44 | McKinney, John | Private | Oct. 3, 1847 | Oct. 6, '47 | Louisville, Ky. | | July 21, '48 | Louisville, Ky. |
| 45 | Moore, Starling | Private | Oct. 3, 1847 | Oct. 6, '47 | Louisville, Ky. | | July 21, '48 | Louisville, Ky. |
| 46 | Muck, Humphrey | Private | Oct. 3, 1847 | Oct. 6, '47 | Louisville, Ky. | | July 21, '48 | Louisville, Ky. |
| 47 | Moore, John | Private | Oct. 3, 1847 | Oct. 6, '47 | Louisville, Ky. | | July 21, '48 | Louisville, Ky. |
| 48 | Muncy, James F. | Private | Oct. 3, 1847 | Oct. 6, '47 | Louisville, Ky. | | July 21, '48 | Louisville, Ky. |
| 49 | McKinney, Levi C. | Private | Oct. 3, 1847 | Oct. 6, '47 | Louisville, Ky. | | July 21, '48 | Louisville, Ky. |
| 50 | McKuney, James | Private | Oct. 3, 1847 | Oct. 6, '47 | Louisville, Ky. | | July 21, '48 | Louisville, Ky. |
| 51 | Noland, Obid | Private | Oct. 3, 1847 | Oct. 6, '47 | Louisville, Ky. | | July 21, '48 | Louisville, Ky. |
| 52 | Powell, Benjamin | Private | Oct. 3, 1847 | Oct. 6, '47 | Louisville, Ky. | | July 21, '48 | Louisville, Ky. |
| 53 | Parsons, Thomas W. | Private | Oct. 3, 1847 | Oct. 6, '47 | Louisville, Ky. | | July 21, '48 | Louisville, Ky. |
| 54 | Parsons, John W. | Private | Oct. 3, 1847 | Oct. 6, '47 | Louisville, Ky. | | July 21, '48 | Louisville, Ky. |
| 55 | Rogers, Isaac H. | Private | Oct. 3, 1847 | Oct. 6, '47 | Louisville, Ky. | | July 21, '48 | Louisville, Ky. |
| 56 | Rainey, Elihu L. | Private | Oct. 3, 1847 | Oct. 6, '47 | Louisville, Ky. | | July 21, '48 | Louisville, Ky. |
| 57 | Rowland, Robert | Private | Oct. 3, 1847 | Oct. 6, '47 | Louisville, Ky. | | July 21, '48 | Louisville, Ky. |
| 58 | Riddle, Adam | Private | Oct. 3, 1847 | Oct. 6, '47 | Louisville, Ky. | | July 21, '48 | Louisville, Ky. |
| 59 | Short, Pelly | Private | Oct. 3, 1847 | Oct. 6, '47 | Louisville, Ky. | To serve during the war. | July 21, '48 | Louisville, Ky. |
| 60 | Smith, William | Private | Oct. 3, 1847 | Oct. 6, '47 | Louisville, Ky. | | July 21, '48 | Louisville, Ky. |
| 61 | Shepherd, Ansel P. | Private | Oct. 3, 1847 | Oct. 6, '47 | Louisville, Ky. | | July 21, '48 | Louisville, Ky. |
| 62 | Shepherd, John B. | Private | Oct. 3, 1847 | Oct. 6, '47 | Louisville, Ky. | | July 21, '48 | Louisville, Ky. |
| 63 | Stackpole, Edward | Private | Oct. 3, 1847 | Oct. 6, '47 | Louisville, Ky. | | July 21, '48 | Louisville, Ky. |
| 64 | Smith, Henry | Private | Oct. 3, 1847 | Oct. 6, '47 | Louisville, Ky. | | July 21, '48 | Louisville, Ky. |
| 65 | Turpin, Smith | Private | Oct. 3, 1847 | Oct. 6, '47 | Louisville, Ky. | | July 21, '48 | Louisville, Ky. |
| 66 | Tillett, William | Private | Oct. 3, 1847 | Oct. 6, '47 | Louisville, Ky. | | July 21, '48 | Louisville, Ky. |
| 67 | White, Aquilla | Private | Oct. 3, 1847 | Oct. 6, '47 | Louisville, Ky. | | July 21, '48 | Louisville, Ky. |
| 68 | Watts, Jordan | Private | Oct. 3, 1847 | Oct. 6, '47 | Louisville, Ky. | | July 21, '48 | Louisville, Ky. |
| 69 | Woods, John B. | Private | Oct. 3, 1847 | Oct. 6, '47 | Louisville, Ky. | | July 21, '48 | Louisville, Ky. |
| | **DIED.** | | | | | | | |
| 1 | Watson, Riley W. | Private | Oct. 3, 1847 | Oct. 6, '47 | Louisville, Ky. | | | |
| 2 | Townsend, Westley | Private | Oct. 3, 1847 | Oct. 6, '47 | Louisville, Ky. | | | |
| 3 | Derickson, George M. | 4th Sergeant | Oct. 3, 1847 | Oct. 6, '47 | Louisville, Ky. | | | |
| 4 | Fullerlove, Clifton | Private | Oct. 3, 1847 | Oct. 6, '47 | Louisville, Ky. | | | |
| 5 | Crouch, Robert | Private | Oct. 3, 1847 | Oct. 6, '47 | Louisville, Ky. | | | |
| 6 | Munday, John | Private | Oct. 3, 1847 | Oct. 6, '47 | Louisville, Ky. | | | |
| 7 | Kincaid, Curtis | Private | Oct. 3, 1847 | Oct. 6, '47 | Louisville, Ky. | | | |
| 8 | Martin, George W. | Private | Oct. 3, 1847 | Oct. 6, '47 | Louisville, Ky. | | | |
| 9 | Ambrose, Thomas W. | Private | Oct. 3, 1847 | Oct. 6, '47 | Louisville, Ky. | | | |
| 10 | Cole, Aaron | Private | Oct. 3, 1847 | Oct. 6, '47 | Louisville, Ky. | | | |
| 11 | Richardson, Daniel | Private | Oct. 3, 1847 | Oct. 6, '47 | Louisville, Ky. | | | |
| 12 | Strong, John | Private | Oct. 3, 1847 | Oct. 6, '47 | Louisville, Ky. | | | |
| | **DISCHARGED.** | | | | | | | |
| 1 | Brenhager, Ansel | Private | Oct. 3, 1847 | Oct. 6, '47 | Louisville, Ky. | | | |
| 2 | Daniel, John M. | Private | Oct. 3, 1847 | Oct. 6, '47 | Louisville, Ky. | | | |
| 3 | Muck, Joseph | Private | Oct. 3, 1847 | Oct. 6, '47 | Louisville, Ky. | | | |
| 4 | McKinney, Pleasant B. | Private | Oct. 3, 1847 | Oct. 6, '47 | Louisville, Ky. | | | |
| 5 | Vanderpool, Isaac W. | Private | Oct. 3, 1847 | Oct. 6, '47 | Louisville, Ky. | | | |
| 6 | Campbell, Ebenezer | Private | Oct. 3, 1847 | Oct 6, '47 | Louisville, Ky. | | | |
| 7 | Mahaff, William C. | Private | Oct. 3, 1847 | Oct. 6, '47 | Louisville, Ky. | | | |
| 8 | Hamilton, Owen | Private | Oct. 3, 1847 | Oct. 6, '47 | Louisville, Ky. | | | |

This Company was organized by Captain William P. Chiles, in Estill county, Ky., September, 1847, and marched thence to Louisville, Ky., where it arrived on the 3d day of October, 1847, a distance of *one hundred and forty-four miles.*

### ROLL OF COMPANY "G," THIRD REGIMENT KENTUCKY

| | Name | Rank | Joined for Service | Mustered In When | Mustered In Where | Period | Mustered Out When | Mustered Out Where |
|---|---|---|---|---|---|---|---|---|
| 1 | James Ewing | Captain | Sept. 29, 1847 | Oct. 1, '47 | Louisville, Ky. | During war. | July 21, '48 | Louisville, Ky. |
| 1 | William C. Allen | 1st Lieutenant | Sept. 29, 1847 | Oct. 1, '47 | Louisville, Ky. | | July 21, '48 | Louisville, Ky. |
| 1 | Henry Herndon | 2d Lieutenant | Sept. 29, 1847 | Oct. 1, '47 | Louisville, Ky. | | July 21, '48 | Louisville, Ky. |
| 2 | B. D. Lacy | 2d Lieutenant | Sept. 29, 1847 | Oct. 1, '47 | Louisville, Ky. | | July 21, '48 | Louisville, Ky. |
| 3 | James T. Young | 2d Lieutenant | Sept. 29, 1847 | Oct. 1, '47 | Louisville, Ky. | | July 21, '48 | Louisville, Ky. |
| 1 | Hugh A. Young | 1st Sergeant | Sept. 29, 1847 | Oct. 1, '47 | Louisville, Ky. | | July 21, '48 | Louisville, Ky. |
| 2 | Jacob F. Trumbo | Sergeant | Sept. 29, 1847 | Oct. 1, '47 | Louisville, Ky. | | July 21, '48 | Louisville, Ky. |
| 3 | William H. Alexander | Sergeant | Sept. 29, 1847 | Oct. 1, '47 | Louisville, Ky. | | July 21, '48 | Louisville, Ky. |

# MEXICAN WAR VETERANS.

## FOOT VOLUNTEERS—MEXICAN WAR—Continued.

| No. of each grade | REMARKS. |
|---|---|
| 36 | |
| 37 | |
| 38 | Absent on furlough from 27th May till 28th June, 1848. Order of Col. Thompson. |
| 39 | |
| 40 | |
| 41 | |
| 42 | |
| 43 | Absent on furlough from 9th May till June 28, 1848. Order of Col. Thompson. |
| 44 | |
| 45 | |
| 46 | |
| 47 | |
| 48 | |
| 49 | |
| 50 | |
| 51 | |
| 52 | |
| 53 | |
| 54 | |
| 55 | |
| 56 | |
| 57 | |
| 58 | |
| 59 | |
| 60 | |
| 61 | Left sick at Vera Cruz, November 25, 1847; said to be discharged. |
| 62 | |
| 63 | |
| 64 | |
| 65 | |
| 66 | |
| 67 | |
| 68 | |
| 69 | Absent on furlough from 9th May till 28th June. Order of Col. Thompson.; was Corporal from enrollment till 1st February, 1848. |
| 1 | In General Hospital, Vera Cruz, December 31, 1847. |
| 2 | In Regimental Hospital, City of Mexico, 2d February, 1848. |
| 3 | In General Hospital, Pueblo, 30th January, 1848. |
| 4 | In General Hospital, Pueblo, 22d December, 1848. |
| 5 | In General Hospital, Pueblo, 21st December, 1848. |
| 6 | In General Hospital, Pueblo, 6th January, 1848. |
| 7 | In General Hospital, Pueblo, 7th February, 1848. |
| 8 | In General Hospital, Pueblo, 30th January, 1848. |
| 9 | In Regimental Hospital, City of Mexico, 23d March, 1848. |
| 10 | In Ayotla, Mexico, 1st June, 1848. |
| 11 | In Nopalucan, Mexico, 6th June, 1848. |
| 12 | On board steamer Missouri on her passage up Mississippi, 12th July, 1848. |
| 1 | At Louisville, 23d October, 1847; Surgeon's certificate of disability. |
| 2 | At City of Mexico, 12th January, 1848; Surgeon's certificate of disability. |
| 3 | At City of Mexico, 11th April, 1848; Surgeon's certificate of disability. |
| 4 | At City of Mexico, 11th April, 1848; Surgeon's certificate of disability. |
| 5 | At New Orleans, 9th March, 1848; Surgeon's certificate of disability. |
| 6 | At Vera Cruz, 15th February, 1848; Surgeon's certificate of disability. |
| 7 | At Vera Cruz, 15th February, 1848; Surgeon's certificate of disability. |
| 8 | At New Orleans, 17th June, 1848; Surgeon's certificate of disability. |

## FOOT VOLUNTEERS—MEXICAN WAR.

| | |
|---|---|
| 1 | |
| 1 | |
| 1 | Resigned per special No. 6; dated Headquarters Army of Mexico, January 11, 1848. |
| 2 | |
| 3 | Joined by promotion from Sergeant, February 13, 1848; was Sergeant from enrollment. |
| 1 | |
| 2 | |
| 3 | Appointed from private, April 8, 1848. |

## MEXICAN WAR VETERANS.

### ROLL OF COMPANY "G," THIRD REGIMENT KENTUCKY

| No. of each grade | Name. | Rank. | Joined for Service. | Mustered In. When. | Mustered In. Where. | Period. | Mustered Out. When. | Mustered Out. Where. |
|---|---|---|---|---|---|---|---|---|
| 4 | William P. Conner | Sergeant | Sept. 29, 1847 | Oct. 1, '47 | Louisville, Ky. | | July 21, '48 | Louisville, Ky. |
| 1 | William Bradshaw | Corporal | Sept. 29, 1847 | Oct. 1, '47 | Louisville, Ky. | | July 21, '48 | Louisville, Ky. |
| 2 | William Morgan | Corporal | Sept. 29, 1847 | Oct. 1, '47 | Louisville, Ky. | | July 21, '48 | Louisville, Ky. |
| 3 | Harrison K. Robinson | Corporal | Sept. 29, 1847 | Oct. 1, '47 | Louisville, Ky. | | July 21, '48 | Louisville, Ky. |
| 4 | Benjamin F. Burbridge | Corporal | Sept. 29, 1847 | Oct. 1, '47 | Louisville, Ky. | | July 21, '48 | Louisville, Ky. |
| 1 | William Horgis | Musician | Sept. 29, 1847 | Oct. 1, '47 | Louisville, Ky. | | July 21, '48 | Louisville, Ky. |
| 2 | Ambrose B. Cox | Musician | Sept. 29, 1847 | Oct. 1, '47 | Louisville, Ky. | | July 21, '48 | Louisville, Ky. |
| 1 | Bailey, John H. | Private | Sept. 29, 1847 | Oct. 1, '47 | Louisville, Ky. | | July 21, '48 | Louisville, Ky. |
| 2 | Barker, William | Private | Sept. 29, 1847 | Oct. 1, '47 | Louisville, Ky. | | July 21, '48 | Louisville, Ky. |
| 3 | Boon, John | Private | Sept. 29, 1847 | Oct. 1, '47 | Louisville, Ky. | | July 21, '48 | Louisville, Ky. |
| 4 | Boyd, John | Private | Sept. 29, 1847 | Oct. 1, '47 | Louisville, Ky. | | July 21, '48 | Louisville, Ky. |
| 5 | Bradshaw, David | Private | Sept. 29, 1847 | Oct. 1, '47 | Louisville, Ky. | | July 21, '48 | Louisville, Ky. |
| 6 | Bramlett, Marcus | Private | Sept. 29, 1847 | Oct. 1, '47 | Louisville, Ky. | | July 21, '48 | Louisville, Ky. |
| 7 | Brown, Eli | Private | Sept. 29, 1847 | Oct. 1, '47 | Louisville, Ky. | | July 21, '48 | Louisville, Ky. |
| 8 | Carson, John W. | Private | Sept. 29, 1847 | Oct. 1, '47 | Louisville, Ky. | | July 21, '48 | Louisville, Ky. |
| 9 | Chandler, Anderson | Private | Sept. 29, 1847 | Oct. 1, '47 | Louisville, Ky. | | July 21, '48 | Louisville, Ky. |
| 10 | Chrisman, Charles F. | Private | Sept. 29, 1847 | Oct. 1, '47 | Louisville, Ky. | | July 21, '48 | Louisville, Ky. |
| 11 | Cline, Levi W. | Private | Sept. 29, 1847 | Oct. 1, '47 | Louisville, Ky. | | July 21, '48 | Louisville, Ky. |
| 12 | Cook, Joseph | Private | Sept. 29, 1847 | Oct. 1, '47 | Louisville, Ky. | | July 21, '48 | Louisville, Ky. |
| 13 | Cope, William D. | Private | Sept. 29, 1847 | Oct. 1, '47 | Louisville, Ky. | | July 21, '48 | Louisville, Ky. |
| 14 | Copher, Jacob | Private | Sept. 29, 1847 | Oct. 1, '47 | Louisville, Ky. | | July 21, '48 | Louisville, Ky. |
| 15 | Copper, Rheuben | Private | Sept. 29, 1847 | Oct. 1, '47 | Louisville, Ky. | | July 21, '48 | Louisville, Ky. |
| 16 | Craig, John | Private | Sept. 29, 1847 | Oct. 1, '47 | Louisville, Ky. | | July 21, '48 | Louisville, Ky. |
| 17 | Castigan, Albert | Private | Sept. 29, 1847 | Oct. 1, '47 | Louisville, Ky. | | July 21, '48 | Louisville, Ky. |
| 18 | Cups, Jacob | Private | Sept. 29, 1847 | Oct. 1, '47 | Louisville, Ky. | | July 21, '48 | Louisville, Ky. |
| 19 | Crouch, Jonathan | Private | Sept. 29, 1847 | Oct. 1, '47 | Louisville, Ky. | | July 21, '48 | Louisville, Ky. |
| 20 | Davis, Silas | Private | Sept. 29, 1847 | Oct. 1, '47 | Louisville, Ky. | | July 21, '48 | Louisville, Ky. |
| 21 | Day, Joel A. | Private | Sept. 29, 1847 | Oct. 1, '47 | Louisville, Ky. | | July 21, '48 | Louisville, Ky. |
| 22 | Donalson, Walker R. | Private | Sept. 29, 1847 | Oct. 1, '47 | Louisville, Ky. | | July 21, '48 | Louisville, Ky. |
| 23 | Gill, Chiloah | Private | Sept. 29, 1847 | Oct. 1, '47 | Louisville, Ky. | | July 21, '48 | Louisville, Ky. |
| 24 | Ginter, Jacob | Private | Sept. 29, 1847 | Oct. 1, '47 | Louisville, Ky. | | July 21, '48 | Louisville, Ky. |
| 25 | Hopkins, William | Private | Sept. 29, 1847 | Oct. 1, '47 | Louisville, Ky. | | July 21, '48 | Louisville, Ky. |
| 26 | Hargis, Samuel | Private | Sept. 29, 1847 | Oct. 1, '47 | Louisville, Ky. | To serve during war. | July 21, '48 | Louisville, Ky. |
| 27 | Howard, Benjamin | Private | Sept. 29, 1847 | Oct. 1, '47 | Louisville, Ky. | | July 21, '48 | Louisville, Ky. |
| 28 | Howard, Joseph | Private | Sept. 29, 1847 | Oct. 1, '47 | Louisville, Ky. | | July 21, '48 | Louisville, Ky. |
| 29 | Ingram, John | Private | Sept. 29, 1847 | Oct. 1, '47 | Louisville, Ky. | | July 21, '48 | Louisville, Ky. |
| 30 | Ingram, William | Private | Sept. 29, 1847 | Oct. 1, '47 | Louisville, Ky. | | July 21, '48 | Louisville, Ky. |
| 31 | Jeaannery, John | Private | Sept. 29, 1847 | Oct. 1, '47 | Louisville, Ky. | | July 21, '48 | Louisville, Ky. |
| 32 | Jones, George W. | Private | Sept. 29, 1847 | Oct. 1, '47 | Louisville, Ky. | | July 21, '48 | Louisville, Ky. |
| 33 | Johnson, David | Private | Sept. 29, 1847 | Oct. 1, '47 | Louisville, Ky. | | July 21, '48 | Louisville, Ky. |
| 34 | Kyle, James | Private | Sept. 29, 1847 | Oct. 1, '47 | Louisville, Ky. | | July 21, '48 | Louisville, Ky. |
| 35 | Manley, Isaac | Private | Sept. 29, 1847 | Oct. 1, '47 | Louisville, Ky. | | July 21, '48 | Louisville, Ky. |
| 36 | Manley, William | Private | Sept. 29, 1847 | Oct. 1, '47 | Louisville, Ky. | | July 21, '48 | Louisville, Ky. |
| 37 | McIhenney, Beverly H. | Private | Sept. 29, 1847 | Oct. 1, '47 | Louisville, Ky. | | July 21, '48 | Louisville, Ky. |
| 38 | McGuire, Samuel W. | Private | Sept. 29, 1847 | Oct. 1, '47 | Louisville, Ky. | | July 21, '48 | Louisville, Ky. |
| 39 | McCure, David | Private | Sept. 29, 1847 | Oct. 1, '47 | Louisville, Ky. | | July 21, '48 | Louisville, Ky. |
| 40 | Norris, William | Private | Sept. 29, 1847 | Oct. 1, '47 | Louisville, Ky. | | July 21, '48 | Louisville, Ky. |
| 41 | North, Lafayette | Private | Sept. 29, 1847 | Oct. 1, '47 | Louisville, Ky. | | July 21, '48 | Louisville, Ky. |
| 42 | Oliver, Amos | Private | Sept. 29, 1847 | Oct. 1, '47 | Louisville, Ky. | | July 21, '48 | Louisville, Ky. |
| 43 | Oakley, James B. | Private | Sept. 29, 1847 | Oct. 1, '47 | Louisville, Ky. | | July 21, '48 | Louisville, Ky. |
| 44 | Oakly, Pleasant E. | Private | Sept. 29, 1847 | Oct. 1, '47 | Louisville, Ky. | | July 21, '48 | Louisville, Ky. |
| 45 | Pierce, William | Private | Sept. 29, 1847 | Oct. 1, '47 | Louisville, Ky. | | July 21, '48 | Louisville, Ky. |
| 46 | Pierce, George | Private | Sept. 29, 1847 | Oct. 1, '47 | Louisville, Ky. | | July 21, '48 | Louisville, Ky. |
| 47 | Power, John T. | Private | Sept. 29, 1847 | Oct. 1, '47 | Louisville, Ky. | | July 21, '48 | Louisville, Ky. |
| 48 | Power, Jackson | Private | Sept. 29, 1847 | Oct. 1, '47 | Louisville, Ky. | | July 21, '48 | Louisville, Ky. |
| 49 | Pergram, Robert C. | Private | Sept. 29, 1847 | Oct. 1, '47 | Louisville, Ky. | | July 21, '48 | Louisville, Ky. |
| 50 | Ralls, Daniel | Private | Sept. 29, 1847 | Oct. 1, '47 | Louisville, Ky. | | July 21, '48 | Louisville, Ky. |
| 51 | Snediger, James | Private | Sept. 29, 1847 | Oct. 1, '47 | Louisville, Ky. | | July 21, '48 | Louisville, Ky. |
| 52 | Sorrell, Augustus | Private | Sept. 29, 1847 | Oct. 1, '47 | Louisville, Ky. | | July 21, '48 | Louisville, Ky. |
| 53 | Stinsar, James | Private | Sept. 29, 1847 | Oct. 1, '47 | Louisville, Ky. | | July 21, '48 | Louisville, Ky. |
| 54 | Spence, William | Private | Sept. 29, 1847 | Oct. 1, '47 | Louisville, Ky. | | July 21, '48 | Louisville, Ky. |
| 55 | Fincher, Franklin | Private | Sept. 29, 1847 | Oct. 1, '47 | Louisville, Ky. | | July 21, '48 | Louisville, Ky. |
| 56 | Thompson, Thomas A. | Private | Sept. 29, 1847 | Oct. 1, '47 | Louisville, Ky. | | July 21, '48 | Louisville, Ky. |
| 57 | Wells, Alfred | Private | Sept. 29, 1847 | Oct. 1, '47 | Louisville, Ky. | | July 21, '48 | Louisville, Ky. |
| 58 | Wells, Oliver P. | Private | Sept. 29, 1847 | Oct. 1, '47 | Louisville, Ky. | | July 21, '48 | Louisville, Ky. |
| 59 | Wells, Richard | Private | Sept. 29, 1847 | Oct. 1, '47 | Louisville, Ky. | | July 21, '48 | Louisville, Ky. |
| 60 | Williams, Drury B. | Private | Sept. 29, 1847 | Oct. 1, '47 | Louisville, Ky. | | July 21, '48 | Louisville, Ky. |
| 61 | Wright, Calvin A. | Private | Sept. 29, 1847 | Oct. 1, '47 | Louisville, Ky. | | July 21, '48 | Louisville, Ky. |
| 62 | Wright, Thomas | Private | Sept. 29, 1847 | Oct. 1, '47 | Louisville, Ky. | | July 21, '48 | Louisville, Ky. |
| 63 | Yarbrough, Harrison | Private | Sept. 29, 1847 | Oct. 1, '47 | Louisville, Ky. | | July 21, '48 | Louisville, Ky. |
| 64 | Yarbrough, Jackson | Private | Sept. 29, 1847 | Oct. 1, '47 | Louisville, Ky. | | July 21, '48 | Louisville, Ky. |
| 65 | Yarbough, Alfred | Private | Sept. 29, 1847 | Oct. 1, '47 | Louisville, Ky. | | July 21, '48 | Louisville, Ky. |
| | DIED. | | | | | | | |
| 1 | James Moran | Private | Sept. 29, 1847 | Oct. 1, '47 | Louisville, Ky. | | | |

## FOOT VOLUNTEERS—MEXICAN WAR—Continued.

| No. of each grade. | REMARKS. |
|---|---|
| 4 | Appointed from private, February 14, 1848. |
| 1 | |
| 2 | Appointed from private, April 1, 1848. |
| 3 | Sick in hospital. |
| 4 | |
| 1 | Left sick at Jalapa, December 6, 1847. |
| 2 | |
| 1 | |
| 2 | |
| 3 | |
| 4 | |
| 5 | |
| 6 | |
| 7 | |
| 8 | Left sick at Vera Cruz, November 26, 1847. |
| 9 | |
| 10 | |
| 11 | Sick in hospital. |
| 12 | |
| 13 | |
| 14 | |
| 15 | |
| 16 | |
| 17 | |
| 18 | Left sick at Vera Cruz, November 26, 1847. |
| 19 | |
| 20 | |
| 21 | |
| 22 | |
| 23 | |
| 24 | |
| 25 | |
| 26 | |
| 27 | |
| 28 | |
| 29 | |
| 30 | |
| 31 | |
| 32 | |
| 33 | |
| 34 | |
| 35 | |
| 36 | Sick in hospital. |
| 37 | |
| 38 | |
| 39 | |
| 40 | |
| 41 | |
| 42 | |
| 43 | |
| 44 | |
| 45 | |
| 46 | |
| 47 | |
| 48 | |
| 49 | |
| 50 | |
| 51 | |
| 52 | |
| 53 | |
| 54 | |
| 55 | |
| 56 | |
| 57 | |
| 58 | |
| 59 | |
| 60 | |
| 61 | |
| 62 | |
| 63 | |
| 64 | |
| 65 | |
| 1 | Killed by a Mexican in the City of Mexico, December 21, 1847. |

## ROLL OF COMPANY "G," THIRD REGIMENT KENTUCKY

| No. of each grade. | Name. | Rank. | Joined for Service. | Mustered In. When. | Mustered In. Where. | Period. | Mustered Out. When. | Mustered Out. Where. |
|---|---|---|---|---|---|---|---|---|
| 2 | Anderson Powell | Private | Sept. 29, 1847 | Oct. 1, '47 | Louisville, Ky. | To serve during the war. | | |
| 3 | Wm. Reynolds | Private | Sept. 29, 1847 | Oct. 1, '47 | Louisville, Ky. | | | |
| 4 | John R. Bedell | Private | Sept. 29, 1847 | Oct. 1, '47 | Louisville, Ky. | | | |
| 5 | Franklin Bedell | Private | Sept. 29, 1847 | Oct. 1, '47 | Louisville, Ky. | | | |
| 6 | James B. Daniel | Private | Sept. 29, 1847 | Oct. 1, '47 | Louisville, Ky. | | | |
| 7 | Allen Garner | Private | Sept. 29, 1847 | Oct. 1, '47 | Louisville, Ky. | | | |
| 8 | Jackson Staten | Private | Sept. 29, 1847 | Oct. 1, '47 | Louisville, Ky. | | | |
| 9 | Geo. Foy | Private | Sept. 29, 1847 | Oct. 1, '47 | Louisville, Ky. | | | |
| 10 | John P. Graubb | Private | Sept. 29, 1847 | Oct. 1, '47 | Louisville, Ky. | | | |
| 11 | Robert Gregory | Private | Sept. 29, 1847 | Oct. 1, '47 | Louisville, Ky. | | | |
| 12 | Francis M. Hopkins | Private | Sept. 29, 1847 | Oct. 1, '47 | Louisville, Ky. | | | |
| 13 | Henry Perkins | Private | Sept. 29, 1847 | Oct. 1, '47 | Louisville, Ky. | | | |
| 14 | Geo. Raidon | Private | Sept. 29, 1847 | Oct. 1, '47 | Louisville, Ky. | | | |
| 15 | Wm. Templeman | Private | Sept. 29, 1847 | Oct. 1, '47 | Louisville, Ky. | | | |
| 16 | Isaac Vice | Private | Sept. 29, 1847 | Oct. 1, '47 | Louisville, Ky. | | | |
| 17 | Wm. P. Bedell | Private | Sept. 29, 1847 | Oct. 1, '47 | Louisville, Ky. | | | |
| 18 | Felix McIlhenney | Private | Sept. 29, 1847 | Oct. 1, '47 | Louisville, Ky. | | | |
| 19 | Daniel Cupps | Private | Sept. 29, 1847 | Oct. 1, '47 | Louisville, Ky. | | | |
|  | **DISCHARGED.** | | | | | | | |
| 1 | James Bohannan | Private | Sept. 29, 1847 | Oct. 1, '47 | Louisville, Ky. | | | |
| 2 | George Oakley | Private | Sept. 29, 1847 | Oct. 1, '47 | Louisville, Ky. | | | |
| 3 | Peter Crouch | Corporal | Sept. 29, 1847 | Oct. 1, '47 | Louisville, Ky. | | | |
| 4 | Wm. Barnett | Private | Sept. 29, 1847 | Oct. 1, '47 | Louisville, Ky. | | | |
| 5 | Robert Glover | Private | Sept. 29, 1847 | Oct. 1, '47 | Louisville, Ky. | | | |
|  | **TRANSFERRED.** | | | | | | | |
| 1 | James T. Young | Sergeant | Sept. 29, 1847 | Oct. 1, '47 | Louisville, Ky. | | | |

This Company was organized by Capt. James Ewing, at Owingsville, Ky., in the month of September, 1847, and marched thence to Louisville, Ky., where it arrived on the 29th day of September, 1847, a distance of one hundred and fifty miles.

## ROLL OF COMPANY "H," THIRD REGIMENT KENTUCKY

| No. | Name. | Rank. | Joined for Service. | Mustered In. When. | Mustered In. Where. | Period. | Mustered Out. When. | Mustered Out. Where. |
|---|---|---|---|---|---|---|---|---|
| 1 | W. E. Simms | Captain | Oct. 3, '47 | Oct. 3, '47 | Louisville, Ky. | To serve during the war. | July 21, '48 | Louisville, Ky. |
| 1 | Wm. P. Bramlett | 1st Lieutenant | Oct. 3, '47 | Oct. 3, '47 | Louisville, Ky. | | July 21, '48 | Louisville, Ky. |
| 1 | Churchill G. Campbell | 2d Lieutenant | Oct. 3, '47 | Oct. 3, '47 | Louisville, Ky. | | July 21, '48 | Louisville, Ky. |
| 2 | James H. Waller | 2d Lieutenant | Oct. 3, '47 | Oct. 3, '47 | Louisville, Ky. | | July 21, '48 | Louisville, Ky. |
| 2 | Wm. E. Fish | 2d Lieutenant | Oct. 3, '47 | Oct. 3, '47 | Louisville, Ky. | | July 21, '48 | Louisville, Ky. |
| 1 | Isaac H. Skillman | 1st Sergeant | Oct. 3, '47 | Oct. 3, '47 | Louisville, Ky. | | July 21, '48 | Louisville, Ky. |
| 2 | Leroy C. Hughes | Sergeant | Oct. 3, '47 | Oct. 3, '47 | Louisville, Ky. | | July 21, '48 | Louisville, Ky. |
| 3 | Reuben Sanford | Sergeant | Oct. 3, 1847 | Oct. 3, '47 | Louisville, Ky. | | July 21, '48 | Louisville, Ky. |
| 4 | Wm. L. Samuel | Sergeant | Oct. 3, 1847 | Oct. 3, '47 | Louisville, Ky. | | July 21, '47 | Louisville, Ky. |
| 1 | James T. Taylor | Corporal | Oct. 3, 1847 | Oct. 3, '47 | Louisville, Ky. | | July 21, '48 | Louisville, Ky. |
| 2 | Berry Kennedey | Corporal | Oct. 3, 1847 | Oct. 3, '47 | Louisville, Ky. | | July 21, '48 | Louisville, Ky. |
| 3 | Henry Turnbull | Corporal | Oct. 3, 1847 | Oct. 3, '47 | Louisville, Ky. | | July 21, '48 | Louisville, Ky. |
| 4 | Wm. T. Murphy | Corporal | Oct. 3, 1847 | Oct. 3, '47 | Louisville, Ky. | | July 21, '48 | Louisville, Ky. |
| 1 | Geo. W. Lemon | Musician | Oct. 3, 1847 | Oct. 3, '47 | Louisville, Ky. | | July 21, '48 | Louisville, Ky. |
| 2 | Benjamin Ford | Musician | Oct. 3, 1847 | Oct. 3, '47 | Louisville, Ky. | | July 21, '48 | Louisville, Ky. |
| 1 | Adair, Wm. | Private | Oct. 3, 1847 | Oct. 3, '47 | Louisville, Ky. | | July 21, '48 | Louisville, Ky. |
| 2 | Aubry, Jackson | Private | Oct. 3, 1847 | Oct. 3, '47 | Louisville, Ky. | | July 21, '48 | Louisville, Ky. |
| 3 | Anderson, John | Private | Oct. 3, 1847 | Oct. 3, '47 | Louisville, Ky. | | July 21, '48 | Louisville, Ky. |
| 4 | Bethars, Pascal M. C. | Private | Oct. 3, 1847 | Oct. 3, '47 | Louisville, Ky. | | July 21, '48 | Louisville, Ky. |
| 5 | Bivens, Valney H. | Private | Oct. 3, 1847 | Oct. 3, '47 | Louisville, Ky. | | July 21, '48 | Louisville, Ky. |
| 6 | Banta, DeWitt C. | Private | Oct. 3, 1847 | Oct. 3, '47 | Louisville, Ky. | | July 21, '48 | Louisville, Ky. |
| 7 | Burdin, Benjamin F. | Private | Oct. 3, 1847 | Oct. 3, '47 | Louisville, Ky. | | July 21, '48 | Louisville, Ky. |
| 8 | Barnett, Charles | Private | Oct. 3, 1847 | Oct. 3, '47 | Louisville, Ky. | | July 21, '48 | Louisville, Ky. |
| 9 | Briscoe, Wm. | Private | Oct. 3, 1847 | Oct. 3, '47 | Louisville, Ky. | | July 21, '48 | Louisville, Ky. |
| 10 | Boswell, James | Private | Oct. 3, 1847 | Oct. 3, '47 | Louisville, Ky. | | July 21, '48 | Louisville, Ky. |
| 11 | Collins, Foster | Private | Oct. 3, 1847 | Oct. 3, '47 | Louisville, Ky. | | July 21, '48 | Louisville, Ky. |
| 12 | Cole, Andrew | Private | Oct. 3, 1847 | Oct. 3, '47 | Louisville, Ky. | | July 21, '48 | Louisville, Ky. |
| 13 | Craddock, John | Private | Oct. 3, 1847 | Oct. 3, '47 | Louisville, Ky. | | July 21, '48 | Louisville, Ky. |
| 14 | Cravins, James | Private | Oct. 3, 1847 | Oct. 3, '47 | Louisville, Ky. | | July 21, '48 | Louisville, Ky. |
| 15 | Coons, Peter E. | Private | Oct. 3, 1847 | Oct. 3, '47 | Louisville, Ky. | | July 21, '48 | Louisville, Ky. |
| 16 | Durgeon, Andrew | Private | Oct. 15, 1847 | Dec. 31, '47 | City of Mexico | | July 21, '48 | Louisville, Ky. |
| 17 | Delance, Joseph | Private | Oct. 3, 1847 | Oct. 3, '47 | Louisville, Ky. | | July 21, '48 | Louisville, Ky. |
| 18 | Ennis, James | Private | Oct. 3, 1847 | Oct. 3, '47 | Louisville, Ky. | | July 21, '48 | Louisville, Ky. |
| 19 | Fowl, N. W. | Private | Oct. 3, 1847 | Oct. 3, '47 | Louisville, Ky. | | July 21, '48 | Louisville, Ky. |
| 20 | Gibson, Joseph | Private | Oct. 3, 1847 | Oct. 3, '47 | Louisville, Ky. | | July 21, '48 | Louisville, Ky. |
| 21 | Gallaspie, Isaac | Private | Oct. 3, 1847 | Oct. 3, '47 | Louisville, Ky. | | July 21, '48 | Louisville, Ky. |
| 22 | Howell, Lewis M. | Private | Oct. 3, 1847 | Oct. 3, '47 | Louisville, Ky. | | July 21, '48 | Louisville, Ky. |

# FOOT VOLUNTEERS—MEXICAN WAR—Continued.

| No. of each grade | REMARKS. |
|---|---|
| 2 | Died at Vera Cruz, November 9, 1847. |
| 3 | Died at Camp Butler, near Louisville, Ky., October 24, 1847. |
| 4 | Died at City of Mexico, February 21, 1848. |
| 5 | Died at City of Mexico, January 7, 1848. |
| 6 | Died at City of Mexico, February 9, 1848. |
| 7 | Died at City of Mexico, January 15, 1848. |
| 8 | Died at City of Mexico, January 15, 1848. |
| 9 | Died at City of Mexico, January 22, 1848. |
| 10 | Died at Pueblo, Mexico, February 14, 1848. |
| 11 | Died at City of Mexico, March 13, 1848. |
| 12 | Died at Pueblo, January 14, 1848. |
| 13 | Died at Pueblo, January 25, 1848. |
| 14 | Died at City of Mexico, March 25, 1848. |
| 15 | Died at Vera Cruz, December—, 1847. Date unknown. |
| 16 | Died at City of Mexico, May 20, 1848. |
| 17 | Died at City of Mexico, May 1, 1848. |
| 18 | Died at City of Mexico, May 3, 1848. |
| 19 | Died on Transport Merchant, off Vera Cruz, June 28, 1848. |
| 1 | Discharged at Louisville, Ky., October 25, 1847, for disability. |
| 2 | Discharged at City of Mexico, 12th January, 1848, Surgeon's certificate of disability. |
| 3 | Discharged at Vera Cruz, February 8, 1848, Surgeon's certificate of disability. |
| 4 | Discharged at Vera Cruz, February 8, 1848, Surgeon's certificate of disability. |
| 5 | Discharged at Vera Cruz, March 28, 1848, Surgeon's certificate of disability. |
| 1 | Transferred by promotion to 2d Lieutenant of the Company, February 13, 1848. |

# FOOT VOLUNTEERS—MEXICAN WAR.

| | |
|---|---|
| 1 | |
| 1 | |
| 1 | |
| 2 | Resigned November 26, 1847. |
| 2 | Sergeant from enrollment. Promoted 2d Lieutenant, November 26, 1847, vice Waller, resigned. |
| 1 | Appointed 1st Sergeant January 1st, order of Col. Thompson, from Corporal, vice J. R. Foreman, reduced; was Corporal from enrollment. |
| 2 | |
| 3 | Corporal from enrollment, appointed Sergeant, July 1, 1848. Order of Col. Thompson, vice John H. Thompson, died. |
| 4 | Appointed Corporal from private, January 1st 1848, vice Isaac H. Skillman, promoted; appointed Sergeant from vice Ewalt, deceased. Order of Col. Thompson. |
| 1 | |
| 2 | Appointed Corporal from private, January 1, 1848 Order of Col. Thompson, vice John H. Thompson, promoted. |
| 3 | Appointed Corporal from private, July 1, 1848. Order of Col. Thompson, vice Reuben Sanford, promoted. |
| 4 | Appointed Corporal from private, July 9, 1848. Order of Col. Thompson, vice Wm. S. Samuel, promoted. |
| 1 | |
| 2 | Appointed Musician, May 1, 1848, from private, vice Wilson Lewis, discharged. Order of Col. Thompson. |
| 1 | |
| 2 | |
| 3 | |
| 4 | |
| 5 | |
| 6 | |
| 7 | |
| 8 | |
| 9 | |
| 10 | |
| 11 | |
| 12 | |
| 13 | |
| 14 | |
| 15 | |
| 16 | |
| 17 | |
| 18 | |
| 19 | |
| 20 | |
| 21 | |
| 22 | |

# MEXICAN WAR VETERANS.

## ROLL OF COMPANY "H," THIRD REGIMENT KENTUCKY

| No. of each grade | Name. | Rank. | Joined for Service. | Mustered In. When. | Mustered In. Where. | Period. | Mustered Out. When. | Mustered Out. Where. |
|---|---|---|---|---|---|---|---|---|
| 23 | Hitchins, Caleb A. | Private | Oct. 3, 1847 | Oct. 3, '47 | Louisville, Ky. | | July 21, '48 | Louisville, Ky. |
| 24 | Hutcherson, James | Private | Oct. 3, 1847 | Oct. 3, '47 | Louisville, Ky. | | July 21, '48 | Louisville, Ky. |
| 25 | Henry, James R. | Private | Oct. 3, 1847 | Oct. 3, '47 | Louisville, Ky. | | July 21, '48 | Louisville, Ky. |
| 26 | Hall, Francis | Private | Oct. 3, 1847 | Oct. 3, '47 | Louisville, Ky. | | July 21, '48 | Louisville, Ky. |
| 27 | Hughes, Perry A. | Private | Oct. 3, 1847 | Oct. 3, '47 | Louisville, Ky. | | July 21, '48 | Louisville, Ky. |
| 28 | Hulett, Alfred | Private | Oct. 3, 1847 | Oct. 3, '47 | Louisville, Ky. | | July 21, '48 | Louisville, Ky. |
| 29 | Hampton, Perry | Private | Oct. 3, 1847 | Oct. 3, '47 | Louisville, Ky. | | July 21, '48 | Louisville, Ky. |
| 30 | Henry, James W. | Private | Oct. 3, 1847 | Oct. 3, '47 | Louisville, Ky. | | July 21, '48 | Louisville, Ky. |
| 31 | Hogg, Joseph | Private | Oct. 3, 1847 | Oct. 3, '47 | Louisville, Ky. | | July 21, '48 | Louisville, Ky. |
| 32 | Kenney, George M. | Private | Oct. 3, 1847 | Oct. 3, '47 | Louisville, Ky. | | July 21, '48 | Louisville, Ky. |
| 33 | Kenney, Jeff. | Private | Oct. 15, 1847 | Dec. 31, '47 | City of Mexico | | July 21, '48 | Louisville, Ky. |
| 34 | Long, David | Private | Oct. 3, 1847 | Oct. 3, '47 | Louisville, Ky. | | July 21, '48 | Louisville, Ky. |
| 35 | McDonald, Robert G. | Private | Oct. 3, 1847 | Oct. 3, '47 | Louisville, Ky. | | July 21, '48 | Louisville, Ky. |
| 36 | Morton, John | Private | Oct. 3, 1847 | Oct. 3, '47 | Louisville, Ky. | | July 21, '48 | Louisville, Ky. |
| 37 | McCracken, —— | Private | Oct. 15, 1847 | Dec. 31, '47 | City of Mexico | | July 21, '48 | Louisville, Ky. |
| 38 | Mullins, Samuel | Private | Oct. 3, 1847 | Oct. 3, '47 | Louisville, Ky. | | July 21, '48 | Louisville, Ky. |
| 39 | Numan, James | Private | Oct. 3, 1847 | Oct. 3, '47 | Louisville, Ky. | | July 21, '48 | Louisville, Ky. |
| 40 | Norton, Wm. H. | Private | Oct. 3, 1847 | Oct. 3, '47 | Louisville, Ky. | | July 21, '48 | Louisville, Ky. |
| 41 | Ryan, Thomas | Private | Oct. 3, 1847 | Oct. 3, '47 | Louisville, Ky. | | July 21, '48 | Louisville, Ky. |
| 42 | Ross, Ludwell | Private | Oct. 3, 1847 | Oct. 3, '47 | Louisville, Ky. | | July 21, '48 | Louisville, Ky. |
| 43 | Stokely, Jacob | Private | Oct. 3, 1847 | Oct. 3, '47 | Louisville, Ky. | | July 21, '48 | Louisville, Ky. |
| 44 | See, John H. | Private | Oct. 3, 1847 | Oct. 3, '47 | Louisville, Ky. | | July 21, '48 | Louisville, Ky. |
| 45 | Shields, Robert | Private | Oct. 3, 1847 | Oct. 3, '47 | Louisville, Ky. | | July 21, '48 | Louisville, Ky. |
| 46 | Scott, Samuel | Private | Oct. 3, 1847 | Oct. 3, '47 | Louisville, Ky. | | July 21, '48 | Louisville, Ky. |
| 47 | Sharp, William | Private | Oct. 3, 1847 | Oct. 3, '47 | Louisville, Ky. | | July 21, '48 | Louisville, Ky. |
| 48 | Swartz, Philip | Private | Oct. 3, 1847 | Oct. 3, '47 | Louisville, Ky. | | July 21, '48 | Louisville, Ky. |
| 49 | Sample, Thomas H. | Private | Oct. 15, 1847 | Dec. 31, '47 | City of Mexico | | July 21, '48 | Louisville, Ky. |
| 50 | Sharp, Henry | Private | Oct. 3, 1847 | Oct. 3, '47 | Louisville, Ky. | | July 21, '48 | Louisville, Ky. |
| 51 | Terry, John T. | Private | Oct. 3, 1847 | Oct. 3, '47 | Louisville, Ky. | | July 21, '48 | Louisville, Ky. |
| 52 | Talbot, Horatio | Private | Oct. 3, 1847 | Oct. 3, '47 | Louisville, Ky. | | July 21, '48 | Louisville, Ky. |
| 53 | Thompson, Joseph | Private | Oct. 3, 1847 | Oct. 3, '47 | Louisville, Ky. | To serve during the war. | July 21, '48 | Louisville, Ky. |
| 54 | True, Claban H. | Private | Oct. 3, 1847 | Oct. 3, '47 | Louisville, Ky. | | July 21, '48 | Louisville, Ky. |
| 55 | Thomas, Jourdan | Private | Oct. 3, 1847 | Oct. 3, '47 | Louisville, Ky. | | July 21, '48 | Louisville, Ky. |
| 56 | Utterback, Ben'j. | Private | Oct. 3, 1847 | Oct. 3, '47 | Louisville, Ky. | | July 21, '48 | Louisville, Ky. |
| 57 | Way, Elias | Private | Oct. 3, 1847 | Oct. 3, '47 | Louisville, Ky. | | July 21, '48 | Louisville, Ky. |
| 58 | Watkins, John | Private | Oct. 3, 1847 | Oct. 3, '47 | Louisville, Ky. | | July 21, '48 | Louisville, Ky. |
| 59 | Wells, Wm. T. | Private | Oct. 3, 1847 | Oct. 3, '47 | Louisville, Ky. | | July 21, '48 | Louisville, Ky. |
| 60 | Wyman, Lewis | Private | Oct. 3, 1847 | Oct. 3, '47 | Louisville, Ky. | | July 21, '48 | Louisville, Ky. |
| 61 | Welkins, Henry | Private | Oct. 3, 1847 | Oct. 3, '47 | Louisville, Ky. | | July 21, '48 | Louisville, Ky. |
| 62 | Wood, Burril | Private | Oct. 3, 1847 | Oct. 3, '47 | Louisville, Ky. | | July 21, '48 | Louisville, Ky. |
| 63 | Weighart, Andrew | Private | Oct. 3, 1847 | Oct. 3, '47 | Louisville, Ky. | | July 21, '48 | Louisville, Ky. |
| 64 | Weighart, Lorran | Private | Oct. 3, 1847 | Oct. 3, '47 | Louisville, Ky. | | July 21, '48 | Louisville, Ky. |
| 65 | Young, James | Private | Oct. 3, 1847 | Oct. 3, '47 | Louisville, Ky. | | July 21, '48 | Louisville, Ky. |
| | **Died.** | | | | | | | |
| 1 | Thompson, John H. | Sergeant | Oct. 3, 1847 | Oct. 3, '47 | Louisville, Ky. | | | |
| 2 | Ewalt, Wm. | Sergeant | Oct. 3, 1847 | Oct. 3, '47 | Louisville, Ky. | | | |
| 3 | Loyd, John T. | Private | Oct. 3, 1847 | Oct. 3, '47 | Louisville, Ky. | | | |
| 4 | Laughlin, Mark W. | Private | Oct. 3, 1847 | Oct. 3, '47 | Louisville, Ky. | | | |
| 5 | Hall, Jesse T. | Private | Oct. 3, 1847 | Oct. 3, '47 | Louisville, Ky. | | | |
| 6 | Higgins, James M. B | Private | Oct. 3, 1847 | Oct. 3, '47 | Louisville, Ky. | | | |
| 7 | Martin, John | Private | Oct. 3, 1847 | Oct. 3, '47 | Louisville, Ky. | | | |
| 8 | Humble, Harvey | Private | Oct. 3, 1847 | Oct. 3, '47 | Louisville, Ky. | | | |
| 9 | Hedges, John W. | Private | Oct. 3, 1847 | Oct. 3, '47 | Louisville, Ky. | | | |
| | **Deserted.** | | | | | | | |
| 1 | Lowry, Hugh | Private | Oct. 15, 1847 | Dec. 31, '47 | City of Mexico | | | |
| | **Discharged** | | | | | | | |
| 1 | Fowle, Isaac | Private | Oct. 3, 1847 | Oct. 3, '47 | Louisville, Ky. | | | |
| 2 | Fisher, Ambrose R. | Private | Oct. 3, 1847 | Oct. 3, '47 | Louisville, Ky. | | | |
| 3 | Bush, Ambrose E. | Private | Oct. 3, 1847 | Oct. 3, '47 | Louisville, Ky. | | | |
| 4 | Spires, Andrew | Private | Oct. 3, 1847 | Oct. 3, '47 | Louisville, Ky. | | | |
| 5 | True, Elijah | Private | Oct. 3, 1847 | Oct. 3, '47 | Louisville, Ky. | | | |
| 6 | Williams, Joseph | Private | Oct. 3, 1847 | Oct. 3, '47 | Louisville, Ky. | | | |
| 7 | Browning, Wm. T. | Private | Oct. 3, 1847 | Oct. 3, '47 | Louisville, Ky. | | | |
| 8 | Wilson, Lewis M. | Musician | Oct. 3, 1847 | Oct. 3, '47 | Louisville, Ky. | | | |
| 9 | Ball, Thomas P. | Private | Oct. 3, 1847 | Oct. 3, '47 | Louisville, Ky. | | | |
| 10 | Forman, Joseph R. | Private | Oct. 3, 1847 | Oct. 3, '47 | Louisville, Ky. | | | |
| 11 | Stivers, John B. | Private | Oct. 3, 1847 | Oct. 3, '47 | Louisville, Ky. | | | |
| 12 | Stivers, Joseph W. | Private | Oct. 3, 1847 | Oct. 3, '47 | Louisville, Ky. | | | |

This Company was organized by Captain W. E. Simms, at Paris, Ky., in the month of September, 1847, and marched thence to Louisville, Ky., where it arrived the 3d day of October, 1847, a distance of one hundred miles.

## FOOT VOLUNTEERS—MEXICAN WAR—Continued.

| No. of each grade | REMARKS. |
|---|---|
| 23 | |
| 24 | |
| 25 | |
| 26 | |
| 27 | |
| 28 | |
| 29 | |
| 30 | |
| 31 | |
| 32 | |
| 33 | |
| 34 | |
| 35 | |
| 36 | |
| 37 | |
| 38 | |
| 39 | |
| 40 | |
| 41 | |
| 42 | |
| 43 | |
| 44 | |
| 45 | |
| 46 | |
| 47 | |
| 48 | |
| 49 | |
| 50 | |
| 51 | |
| 52 | |
| 53 | |
| 54 | |
| 55 | |
| 56 | |
| 57 | |
| 58 | |
| 59 | |
| 60 | |
| 61 | |
| 62 | |
| 63 | |
| 64 | |
| 65 | |
| 1 | Died June 24, 1848, at Encerro, Mexico; appointed Sergeant January 1, 1848, vice Corporal W. E. Fisher, promoted. |
| 2 | Died at New Orleans, July 8, 1848; Sergeant from enrollment. |
| 3 | Died at the City of Mexico, December 19, 1847. |
| 4 | Died in hospital, Louisville, Ky., December, 1847. |
| 5 | Died at City of Mexico, February 10, 1848. |
| 6 | Died at City of Mexico, February 11, 1848. |
| 7 | Died in City of Mexico, April 19, 1848. |
| 8 | Died in General Hospital, Jalapa, June 5, 1848. |
| 9 | Died at Encerro, Mexico, May 25, 1848. |
| 1 | Deserted at the City of Mexico, May 25, 1848. |
| 1 | November 8, 1847, at Louisville, Ky.; Surgeon's certificate of disability. |
| 2 | November 26, 1847, at Vera Cruz; Surgeon's certificate of disability. |
| 3 | November 26, 1847, at Vera Cruz; Surgeon's certificate of disability. |
| 4 | November 26, 1847, at Vera Cruz; Surgeon's certificate of disability. |
| 5 | February 1, 1848, at Vera Cruz; Surgeon's certificate of disability. |
| 6 | February 15, 1848, at Vera Cruz; Surgeon's certificate of disability. |
| 7 | Date not known. At Vera Cruz; Surgeon's certificate of disability. |
| 8 | At Jalapa. Date not known; Surgeon's certificate of disability. |
| 9 | June 21, 1848, at New Orleans; Surgeon's certificate of disability. |
| 10 | June 21, 1848, at New Orleans; Surgeon's certificate of disability. Reduced to private January 1, 1848. |
| 11 | June 29, 1848, at New Orleans; Surgeon's certificate of disability. |
| 12 | June 29, 1848, at New Orleans; Surgeon's certificate of disability. |

## MEXICAN WAR VETERANS.

### ROLL OF COMPANY "I," THIRD REGIMENT KENTUCKY

| No. of each grade | Name. | Rank. | Joined for Service. | Mustered In. When. | Mustered In. Where. | Period | Mustered Out. When. | Mustered Out. Where. |
|---|---|---|---|---|---|---|---|---|
| 1 | Thomas Todd | Captain | Oct. 1, 1847 | Oct. 1, '47 | Louisville, Ky. | | July 21, '48 | Louisville, Ky. |
| 1 | H. P. Johnson | 1st Lieutenant | Oct. 1, 1847 | Oct. 1, '47 | Louisville, Ky. | | July 21, '48 | Louisville, Ky. |
| 2 | John A. Logan | 1st Lieutenant | Oct. 1, 1847 | Oct. 1, '47 | Louisville, Ky. | | July 21, '48 | Louisville, Ky. |
| 1 | Walter C. Whitaker | 2d Lieutenant | Oct. 1, 1847 | Oct. 1, '47 | Louisville, Ky. | | July 21, '48 | Louisville, Ky |
| 2 | Jos. C. Dear | 2d Lieutenant | Oct. 1, 1847 | Oct. 1, '47 | Louisville, Ky. | | July 21, '48 | Louisville, Ky. |
| 1 | David R. Stockton | 1st Sergeant | Oct. 1, 1847 | Oct. 1, '47 | Louisville, Ky. | | July 21, '48 | Louisville, Ky. |
| 2 | Joseph Lake | Sergeant | Oct. 1, 1847 | Oct. 1, '47 | Louisville, Ky. | | July 21, '48 | Louisville, Ky. |
| 3 | Silas McClung | Sergeant | Oct. 1, 1847 | Oct. 1, '47 | Louisville, Ky. | | July 21, '48 | Louisville, Ky. |
| 4 | Jonathan R. Gore | Sergeant | Oct. 1, 1847 | Oct. 1, '47 | Louisville, Ky. | | July 21, '48 | Louisville, Ky. |
| 1 | James M. Thompson | Corporal | Oct. 1, 1847 | Oct. 1, '47 | Louisville, Ky. | | July 21, '48 | Louisville, Ky. |
| 2 | Thomas A. Tyler | Corporal | Oct. 1, 1847 | Oct. 1, '47 | Louisville, Ky. | | July 21, '48 | Louisville, Ky. |
| 3 | Benjamin. Robinson | Corporal | Oct. 1, 1847 | Oct. 1, '47 | Louisville, Ky. | | July 21, '48 | Louisville, Ky. |
| 4 | John Banfield | Corporal | Oct. 1, 1847 | Oct. 1, '47 | Louisville, Ky. | | July 21, '48 | Louisville, Ky. |
| 1 | Maddox, George C. | Musician | Oct. 1, 1847 | Oct. 1, '47 | Louisville, Ky. | | July 21, '48 | Louisville, Ky. |
| 1 | Ashby, William | Private | Oct. 1, 1847 | Oct. 1, '47 | Louisville, Ky. | | July 21, '48 | Louisville, Ky. |
| 2 | Ashmore, David | Private | Oct. 1, 1847 | Oct. 1, '47 | Louisville, Ky. | | July 21, '48 | Louisville, Ky. |
| 3 | Baker, Benjamin | Private | Oct. 1, 1847 | Oct. 1, '47 | Louisville, Ky. | | July 21, '48 | Louisville, Ky. |
| 4 | Branham, Bradford | Private | Oct. 1, 1847 | Oct. 1, '47 | Louisville, Ky. | | July 21, '48 | Louisville, Ky. |
| 5 | Corley, James | Private | Oct. 1, 1847 | Oct. 1, '47 | Louisville, Ky. | | July 21, '48 | Louisville, Ky. |
| 6 | Cosby, William | Private | Oct. 1, 1847 | Oct. 1, '47 | Louisville, Ky. | | July 21, '48 | Louisville, Ky. |
| 7 | Dear, Ephraim G. | Private | Oct. 1, 1847 | Oct. 1, '47 | Louisville, Ky. | | July 21, '48 | Louisville, Ky. |
| 8 | Davis, John C. | Private | Oct. 1, 1847 | Oct. 1, '47 | Louisville, Ky. | | July 21, '48 | Louisville, Ky. |
| 9 | Eakin, William | Private | Oct. 1, 1847 | Oct. 1, '47 | Louisville, Ky. | | July 21, '48 | Louisville, Ky. |
| 10 | Gregory, George W. | Private | Oct. 1, 1847 | Oct. 1, '47 | Louisville, Ky. | | July 21, '48 | Louisville, Ky. |
| 11 | Gibbs, Joshua | Private | Oct. 1, 1847 | Oct. 1, '47 | Louisville, Ky. | | July 21, '48 | Louisville, Ky. |
| 12 | Hilbert, Michael | Private | Oct. 1, 1847 | Oct. 1, '47 | Louisville, Ky. | | July 21, '48 | Louisville, Ky. |
| 13 | Jone, Frederick | Private | Oct. 1, 1847 | Oct. 1, '47 | Louisville, Ky. | | July 21, '48 | Louisville, Ky. |
| 14 | Jones, Charles | Private | Oct. 18, 1847 | Oct. 18, '47 | Louisville, Ky. | | July 21, '48 | Louisville, Ky. |
| 15 | James, Richard | Private | Oct. 1, 1847 | Oct. 1, '47 | Louisville, Ky. | | July 21, '48 | Louisville, Ky. |
| 16 | Kelly, James | Private | Oct. 1, 1847 | Oct. 1, '47 | Louisville, Ky. | | July 21, '48 | Louisville, Ky. |
| 17 | Lowell, William | Private | Oct. 1, 1847 | Oct. 1, '47 | Louisville, Ky. | | July 21, '48 | Louisville, Ky. |
| 18 | Livingston, Wm. J. | Private | Oct. 1, 1847 | Oct. 1, '47 | Louisville, Ky. | To serve during war. | July 21, '48 | Louisville, Ky. |
| 19 | Long, James M. | Private | Oct. 1, 1847 | Oct. 1, '47 | Louisville, Ky. | | July 21, '48 | Louisville, Ky. |
| 20 | Morris, William | Private | Oct. 1, 1847 | Oct. 1, '47 | Louisville, Ky. | | July 21, '48 | Louisville, Ky. |
| 21 | McDonald, Hiram | Private | Oct. 1, 1847 | Oct. 1, '47 | Louisville, Ky. | | July 21, '48 | Louisville, Ky. |
| 22 | Miller, Wm. | Private | Oct. 1, 1847 | Oct. 1, '47 | Louisville, Ky. | | July 21, '48 | Louisville, Ky. |
| 23 | Moore, Jas. | Private | Oct. 1, 1847 | Oct. 1, '47 | Louisville, Ky. | | July 21, '48 | Louisville, Ky. |
| 24 | McCarty, Blair | Private | Oct. 1, 1847 | Oct. 1, '47 | Louisville, Ky. | | July 21, '48 | Louisville, Ky. |
| 25 | Magruder, Cornelius C. | Private | Oct. 1, 1847 | Oct. 1, '47 | Louisville, Ky. | | July 21, '48 | Louisville, Ky. |
| 26 | McBath, John | Private | Oct. 1, 1847 | Oct. 1, '47 | Louisville, Ky. | | July 21, '48 | Louisville, Ky. |
| 27 | McLemore, Hiram G. | Private | Oct. 1, 1847 | Oct. 1, '47 | Louisville, Ky. | | July 21, '48 | Louisville, Ky. |
| 28 | Niel, Wm. G. | Private | Oct. 1, 1847 | Oct. 1, '47 | Louisville, Ky. | | July 21, '48 | Louisville, Ky. |
| 29 | Roswell, John C. | Private | Oct. 1, 1847 | Oct. 1, '47 | Louisville, Ky. | | July 21, '48 | Louisville, Ky. |
| 30 | Smith, Jackson J. | Private | Oct. 1, 1847 | Oct. 1, '47 | Louisville, Ky. | | July 21, '48 | Louisville, Ky. |
| 31 | Schweitser, Benjamin | Private | Oct. 1, 1847 | Oct. 1, '47 | Louisville, Ky. | | July 21, '48 | Louisville, Ky. |
| 32 | Thompson, Wm. F. | Private | Oct. 1, 1847 | Oct. 1, '47 | Louisville, Ky. | | July 21, '48 | Louisville, Ky. |
| 33 | Thompson, James | Private | Oct. 1, 1847 | Oct. 1, '47 | Louisville, Ky. | | July 21, '48 | Louisville, Ky. |
| 34 | Teasley, Wm. | Private | Oct. 1, 1847 | Oct. 1, '47 | Louisville, Ky. | | July 21, '48 | Louisville, Ky. |
| 35 | Taylor, John W. | Private | Oct. 1, 1847 | Oct. 1, '47 | Louisville, Ky. | | July 21, '48 | Louisville, Ky. |
| 36 | Thompson, Wm. H. | Private | Oct. 1, 1847 | Oct. 1, '47 | Louisville, Ky. | | July 21, '48 | Louisville, Ky. |
| 37 | Thompson, Wm. A. | Private | Oct. 1, 1847 | Oct. 1, '47 | Louisville, Ky. | | July 21, '48 | Louisville, Ky. |
| 38 | Teasley, Presley D. | Private | Oct. 1, 1847 | Oct. 1, '47 | Louisville, Ky. | | July 21, '48 | Louisville, Ky. |
| 39 | Thomasson, Allen | Private | Oct. 18, 1847 | Oct. 18, '47 | Louisville, Ky. | | July 21, '48 | Louisville, Ky. |
| 40 | Vaughn, James R. | Private | Oct. 1, 1847 | Oct. 1, '47 | Louisville, Ky. | | July 21, '48 | Louisville, Ky. |
| 41 | Webb, James | Private | Oct. 1, 1847 | Oct. 1, '47 | Louisville, Ky. | | July 21, '48 | Louisville, Ky. |
| 42 | Wise, George | Private | Oct. 1, 1847 | Oct. 1, '47 | Louisville, Ky. | | July 21, '48 | Louisville, Ky. |
| 43 | Wayne, David | Private | Oct. 1, 1847 | Oct. 1, '47 | Louisville, Ky. | | July 21, '48 | Louisville, Ky. |
| 44 | Storts, Chas. H. | Private | Oct. 1, 1847 | Oct. 1, '47 | Louisville, Ky. | | July 21, '48 | Louisville, Ky. |
| | **TRANSFERRED.** | | | | | | | |
| 1 | Armistead, John P. | Private | Oct. 1, 1847 | Oct. 1, '47 | Louisville, Ky. | | | |
| 2 | Allender, James C. | Private | Oct. 1, 1847 | Oct. 1, '47 | Louisville, Ky. | | | |
| 3 | Atchison, James W. | Private | Oct. 1, 1847 | Oct. 1, '47 | Louisville, Ky | | | |
| 4 | Crane, Hiram P. | Private | Oct. 1, 1847 | Oct. 1, '47 | Louisville, Ky. | | | |
| 5 | Cassidy, James B. | Private | Oct. 1, 1847 | Oct. 1, '47 | Louisville, Ky. | | | |
| 6 | Gales, Wallace | Private | Oct. 1, 1847 | Oct. 1, '47 | Louisville, Ky. | | | |
| 7 | Lawson, John | Private | Oct. 1, 1847 | Oct. 1, '47 | Louisville, Ky. | | | |
| 8 | McKracken, James | Private | Oct. 1, 1847 | Oct. 1, '47 | Louisville, Ky. | | | |
| 9 | Markwell, Alvin | Private | Oct. 1, 1847 | Oct. 1, '47 | Louisville, Ky. | | | |
| 10 | Prater, Parker B. | Private | Oct. 1, 1847 | Oct. 1, '47 | Louisville, Ky. | | | |
| 11 | Wilson, Eli C. | Private | Oct. 1, 1847 | Oct. 1, '47 | Louisville, Ky. | | | |
| 12 | William, John | Private | Oct. 1, 1847 | Oct. 1, '47 | Louisville, Ky. | | | |
| | **DISCHARGED.** | | | | | | | |
| 1 | Demaree, Allen | Private | Oct. 1, 1847 | Oct. 1, '47 | Louisville, Ky. | | | |

## FOOT VOLUNTEERS—MEXICAN WAR.

| No. of each grade | REMARKS. |
|---|---|
| 1 | |
| 1 | Resigned February 29, 1848, per special No. 6; dated Headquarters Army of Mexico. |
| 2 | Promoted from 2d Lieutenant, February 29, 1848, vice Johnson, resigned. 2d Lieutenant from enrollment. |
| 1 | Promoted from 2d Lieutenant, February 29, 1848. vice Logan, promoted. 2d 2d Lieutenant from enrollment. |
| 2 | Promoted from Sergeant, February 29, 1848. Sergeant from enrollment. |
| 1 | Appointed 1st Sergeant, May 1, 1848. Sergeant from enrollment. |
| 2 | Appointed from private, March 1, 1848. Private from enrollment. |
| 3 | Appointed from private, February 4, 1848. Private from enrollment. |
| 4 | Appointed from Corporal, May 1, 1848. Corporal from enrollment. |
| 1 | |
| 2 | Appointed from private, January 1, 1848. Private from enrollment. |
| 3 | |
| 4 | Appointed from private May 1, 1848. Private from enrollment. |
| 1 | |
| 1 | |
| 2 | |
| 3 | Reported sick by Surgeon in hospital in New Orleans. |
| 4 | |
| 5 | |
| 6 | |
| 7 | |
| 8 | |
| 9 | |
| 10 | |
| 11 | |
| 12 | |
| 13 | |
| 14 | |
| 15 | |
| 16 | |
| 17 | |
| 18 | |
| 19 | |
| 20 | |
| 21 | |
| 22 | |
| 23 | |
| 24 | |
| 25 | |
| 26 | |
| 27 | |
| 28 | |
| 29 | |
| 30 | |
| 31 | |
| 32 | |
| 33 | |
| 34 | |
| 35 | |
| 36 | |
| 37 | |
| 38 | |
| 39 | |
| 40 | Appointed 1st Sergeant, November 19, 1847; was private from enrollment; resigned as 1st Sergeant May 1, 1848. |
| 41 | |
| 42 | |
| 43 | |
| 44 | Hospital Steward. |
| 1 | Transferred to Company B, 3d Ky. Volunteer Infantry, November 1, 1847. |
| 2 | Transferred to Company B, 3d Ky. Volunteer Infantry, November 1, 1847. |
| 3 | Transferred to Company B, 3d Ky. Volunteer Infantry, November 1, 1847. |
| 4 | Transferred to Company B, 3d Ky. Volunteer Infantry, November 1, 1847. |
| 5 | Transferred to Company B, 3d Ky. Volunteer Infantry, November 1, 1847. |
| 6 | Transferred to Company B, 3d Ky. Volunteer Infantry, November 1, 1847. |
| 7 | Transferred to Company B, 3d Ky. Volunteer Infantry, November 1, 1847. |
| 8 | Transferred to Company B, 3d Ky. Volunteer Infantry, November 1, 1847. |
| 9 | Transferred to Company B, 3d Ky. Volunteer Infantry, November 1, 1847. |
| 10 | Transferred to Company B, 3d Ky. Volunteer Infantry, November 1, 1847. |
| 11 | Transferred to Company B, 3d Ky. Volunteer Infantry, November 1, 1847. |
| 12 | Transferred to Company D, 4th Ky. Infantry, 15th October, 1847. |
| 1 | Discharged on Surgeon's certificate of disability, at Vera Cruz, November 23, 1847. |

## MEXICAN WAR VETERANS.

### ROLL OF COMPANY "I," THIRD REGIMENT KENTUCKY

| No. of each grade. | Name. | Rank. | Joined for Service. | Mustered In. When. | Mustered In. Where. | Period. | Mustered Out. When. | Mustered Out. Where. |
|---|---|---|---|---|---|---|---|---|
| 2 | O'Bannon, James | Private | Oct. 1, 1847 | Oct. 1, '47 | Louisville, Ky. | | | |
| 3 | Venable, Joseph W. | Private | Oct. 1, 1847 | Oct. 1, '47 | Louisville, Ky. | | | |
| 4 | Eubank, Harrison | Corporal | Oct. 1, 1847 | Oct. 1, '47 | Louisville, Ky. | | | |
| 5 | Myles, Stephen G. | Private | Oct. 1, 1847 | Oct. 1, '47 | Louisville, Ky. | | | |
| 6 | Ragland, Nathaniel J. T. | Private | Oct. 1, 1847 | Oct. 1, '47 | Louisville, Ky. | | | |
| 7 | Easton, John | Private | Oct. 1, 1847 | Oct. 1, '47 | Louisville, Ky. | | | |
| 8 | Dougherly, James W. | Private | Oct. 1, 1847 | Oct. 1, '47 | Louisville, Ky. | | | |
| 9 | Davis, Joseph D. | Private | Oct. 1, 1847 | Oct. 1, '47 | Louisville, Ky. | | | |
| | **Died.** | | | | | | | |
| 1 | Booth, William E. | 1st Sergeant | Oct. 1, 1847 | Oct. 1, '47 | Louisville, Ky. | | | |
| 2 | Bright, Warfield | Sergeant | Oct. 1, 1847 | Oct. 1, '47 | Louisville, Ky. | | | |
| 3 | Ashley, James B. | Corporal | Oct. 1, 1847 | Oct. 1, '47 | Louisville, Ky. | | | |
| 4 | Drake, John C. | Private | Oct. 1, 1847 | Oct. 1, '47 | Louisville, Ky. | | | |
| 5 | Pifer, Nathan M. | Private | Oct. 1, 1847 | Oct. 1, '47 | Louisville, Ky. | To serve during the war. | | |
| 6 | Tilley, James B. | Private | Oct. 1, 1847 | Oct. 1, '47 | Louisvil'e, Ky. | | | |
| 7 | Still, Adam C. | Private | Oct. 1, 1847 | Oct. 1, '47 | Louisville, Ky. | | | |
| 8 | Garnett, Moses R. | Private | Oct. 1, 1847 | Oct. 1, '47 | Louisville, Ky. | | | |
| 9 | Doss, Cyranus W. | Private | Oct. 1, 1847 | Oct. 1, '47 | Louisville, Ky. | | | |
| 10 | Williamson, John J. | Private | Oct. 1, 1847 | Oct. 1, '47 | Louisville, Ky. | | | |
| 11 | Berry, John W. | Private | Oct. 1, 1847 | Oct. 1, '47 | Louisville, Ky. | | | |
| 12 | Brown, Ezekiel | Private | Oct. 1, 1847 | Oct. 1, '47 | Louisville, Ky. | | | |
| 13 | Truill, John L. | Private | Oct. 1, 1847 | Oct. 1, '47 | Louisville, Ky. | | | |
| 14 | Thurman, John J. | Private | Oct. 1, 1847 | Oct. 1, '47 | Louisville, Ky. | | | |
| 15 | Steele, George | Private | Oct. 1, 1847 | Oct. 1, '47 | Louisville, Ky. | | | |
| 16 | Sullivan, James | Musician | Oct. 1, 1847 | Oct. 1, '47 | Louisville, Ky. | | | |
| 17 | Harris, Sanford | Private | Oct. 1, 1847 | Oct. 1, '47 | Louisville, Ky. | | | |
| 18 | Jaquitt, Isaac | Private | Oct. 1, 1847 | Oct. 1, '47 | Louisville, Ky. | | | |
| 19 | Levi, David A. | Private | Oct. 1, 1847 | Oct. 1, '47 | Louisville, Ky. | | | |
| 20 | Mitchell, John | Private | Oct. 1, 1847 | Oct. 1, '47 | Louisville, Ky. | | | |
| 21 | Smith, Isham O. | Private | Oct. 1, 1847 | Oct. 1, '47 | Louisville, Ky. | | | |
| 22 | Wise, Charley | Private | Oct. 1, 1847 | Oct. 1, '47 | Louisville, Ky. | | | |
| | **Deserted.** | | | | | | | |
| 1 | Clemmons, John | Private | Oct. 1, 1847 | Oct. 1, '47 | Louisville, Ky. | | | |
| 2 | Driskin, Charles | Private | Oct. 1, 1847 | Oct. 1, '47 | Louisville, Ky. | | | |
| 3 | Stumpfs, John | Private | Oct. 1, 1847 | Oct. 1, '47 | Louisville, Ky. | | | |
| 4 | Sly, Zebedee | Private | Oct. 1, 1847 | Oct. 1, '47 | Louisville, Ky. | | | |
| 5 | Warren, Charles | Private | Oct. 1, 1847 | Oct. 1, '47 | Louisville, Ky. | | | |

This Company was organized by Captain T. Todd at Shelbyville, Ky., in the month of September, 1847.

### ROLL OF COMPANY "K," THIRD REGIMENT KENTUCKY

| | Name | Rank | Joined for Service | Mustered In When | Mustered In Where | Period | Mustered Out When | Mustered Out Where |
|---|---|---|---|---|---|---|---|---|
| 1 | A. F. Coldwell | Captain | Oct. 5, 1847 | Oct. 5, '47 | Louisville, Ky. | | July 21, '48 | Louisville, Ky. |
| 1 | Jesse B. Davis | 1st Lieutenant | Oct. 5, 1847 | Oct. 5, '47 | Louisville, Ky. | | July 21, '48 | Louisville, Ky. |
| 1 | Thomas H. Taylor | 1st Lieutenant | Oct. 5, 1847 | Oct. 5, '47 | Louisville, Ky. | | July 21, '48 | Louisville, Ky. |
| 1 | John Brock | 2d Lieutenant | Oct. 5, 1847 | Oct 5, '47 | Louisville, Ky. | | July 21, '48 | Louisville, Ky. |
| 1 | James Kendall | 2d Lieutenant | Oct. 5, 1847 | Oct. 5, '47 | Louisville, Ky. | | July 21, '48 | Louisville, Ky. |
| 2 | Wm. M. Faris | 2d Lieutenant | Oct. 5, 1847 | Oct. 5, '47 | Louisville, Ky. | | July 21, '48 | Louisville, Ky. |
| 2 | John P. Thatcher | 2d Lieutenant | Oct. 5, 1847 | Oct. 5, '47 | Louisville, Ky. | | July 21, '48 | Louisville, Ky. |
| 1 | John A. Westerfield | 1st Sergeant | Oct. 5, 1847 | Oct. 5, '47 | Louisville, Ky. | | July 21, '48 | Louisville, Ky. |
| 2 | Josiah Davis | Sergeant | Oct. 5, 1847 | Oct. 5, '47 | Louisville, Ky. | To serve during the war. | July 21, '48 | Louisville, Ky. |
| 3 | Wesley Acton | Sergeant | Oct. 5, 1847 | Oct. 5, '47 | Louisville, Ky. | | July 21, '48 | Louisville, Ky. |
| 4 | James L. Mitchell | Sergeant | Oct. 5, 1847 | Oct. 5, '47 | Louisville, Ky. | | July 21, '48 | Louisville, Ky. |
| 1 | Zimri Box | Corporal | Oct. 5, 1847 | Oct. 5, '47 | Louisville, Ky. | | July 21, '48 | Louisville, Ky. |
| 2 | Joseph G. Faris | Corporal | Oct. 5, 1847 | Oct. 5, '47 | Louisville, Ky. | | July 21, '48 | Louisville, Ky. |
| 3 | James R. Cox | Corporal | Oct. 5, 1847 | Oct. 5, '47 | Louisville, Ky. | | July 21, '48 | Louisville, Ky. |
| 4 | Andrew J. Veach | Corporal | Oct. 5, 1847 | Oct. 5, '47 | Louisville, Ky. | | July 21, '48 | Louisville, Ky. |
| 1 | Arthur, Edward | Private | Oct. 5, 1847 | Oct. 5, '47 | Louisville, Ky. | | July 21, '48 | Louisville, Ky. |
| 2 | Adkins, Christopher B. | Private | Oct. 5, 1847 | Oct. 5, '47 | Louisville, Ky. | | July 21, '48 | Louisville, Ky. |
| 3 | Astley, John W. | Private | Oct. 8, 1847 | Oct. 8, '47 | Louisville, Ky. | | July 21, '48 | Louisville, Ky. |
| 4 | Browner, William C. | Private | Oct. 5, 1847 | Oct. 5, '47 | Louisville, Ky. | | July 21, '48 | Louisville, Ky. |
| 5 | Brotherlin, Charles | Private | Oct. 8, 1847 | Oct. 8, '47 | Louisville, Ky. | | July 21, '48 | Louisville, Ky. |
| 6 | Brown, William | Private | Oct. 5, 1847 | Oct. 5, '47 | Louisville, Ky. | | July 21, '48 | Louisville, Ky. |
| 7 | Ballinger, Joseph | Private | Oct. 5, 1847 | Oct. 5, '47 | Louisville, Ky. | | July 21, '48 | Louisville, Ky. |
| 8 | Bearnes, William | Private | Oct. 5, 1847 | Oct. 5, '47 | Louisville, Ky. | | July 21, '48 | Louisville, Ky. |
| 9 | Burkhard, John | Private | Oct. 5, 1847 | Oct. 5, '47 | Louisville, Ky. | | July 21, '48 | Louisville, Ky. |
| 10 | Coleman, Skelton | Private | Oct. 5, 1847 | Oct. 5, '47 | Louisville, Ky. | | July 21, '48 | Louisville, Ky. |
| 11 | Craven, Hiram F. | Private | Oct. 5, 1847 | Oct. 5, '47 | Louisville, Ky. | | July 21, '48 | Louisville, Ky. |
| 12 | Comstock, Alexander | Private | Oct. 5, 1847 | Oct. 5, '47 | Louisville, Ky. | | July 21, '48 | Louisville, Ky. |

## MEXICAN WAR VETERANS.

## FOOT VOLUNTEERS—MEXICAN WAR—Continued.

| No. of each grade | REMARKS. |
|---|---|
| 2 | Discharged on Surgeon's certificate of disability, at Vera Cruz, November 23, 1847. |
| 3 | Discharged by civil authority as a minor at Louisville, October 1, 1847. |
| 4 | Discharged on Surgeon's certificate of disability, at Vera Cruz, 6th January, 1848. |
| 5 | Discharged on Surgeon's certificate of disability, at Vera Cruz, 6th January, 1848. |
| 6 | Discharged on Surgeon's certificate of disability, at City of Mexico, January 12, 1848. |
| 7 | Discharged on Surgeon's certificate of disability, at Vera Cruz, March 3, 1848. |
| 8 | Discharged on Surgeon's certificate of disability, at New Orleans, January 17, 1848. |
| 9 | Discharged May 6, 1848, having been appointed a Lieutenant 11th Infantry, U. S. A. (Transferred.) |
| 1 | Died 18th November, 1847, at Vera Cruz. |
| 2 | Died 4th February, 1848, at City of Mexico. |
| 3 | Died 16th November, 1847, at Vera Cruz. |
| 4 | Died 16th November, 1847, at Vera Cruz. |
| 5 | Died 20th November, 1847, at Vera Cruz. |
| 6 | Died 16th November, 1847, at Vera Cruz. |
| 7 | Died 20th November, 1847, at Vera Cruz. |
| 8 | Died 9th January, 1848, at Vera Cruz |
| 9 | Died 18th February, 1848, at City of Mexico. |
| 10 | Died 25th February, 1848, at City of Mexico. |
| 11 | Died 25th January, 1848, at Pueblo, Mexico. |
| 12 | Died 25th January, 1848, at Pueblo, Mexico. |
| 13 | Died 20th March, 1848, at City of Mexico. |
| 14 | Died 8th April, 1848, at City of Mexico. |
| 15 | Died 11th April, 1848, at City of Mexico. |
| 16 | Died 8th July, 1848, at New Orleans. |
| 17 | Died 12th June, 1848, at Jalapa. |
| 18 | Died 25th May, 1848, at City of Mexico. |
| 19 | Died 25th May, 1848, at City of Mexico. |
| 20 | Died 13th June 1848, at Encero, Mexico. |
| 21 | Died June 6th, 1848, at Amasoque, Mexico. |
| 22 | Died 20th March, 1848, at Pueblo. Transferred from Capt. Bartlett's Company " D," 4th Regiment Ky. Infantry, 15th October, 1847. |
| 1 | Deserted at Louisville, Ky., October 8, 1847. |
| 2 | Deserted at Louisville, Ky., October 30, 1847. |
| 3 | Deserted at Louisville, Ky., October 9, 1847. |
| 4 | Deserted at Louisville, Ky., October 6, 1847. |
| 5 | Deserted at Louisville, Ky., October 9, 1847. |

## FOOT VOLUNTEERS—MEXICAN WAR.

| No. of each grade | REMARKS. |
|---|---|
| 1 | |
| 1 | Died in City of Mexico, March 9, 1848. |
| 1 | Appointed from Sergeant-Major, March 21, 1848, vice Jesse B. Davis, deceased; Sergeant-Major from enrollment. |
| 1 | Died 19th March, 1848. |
| 1 | Appointed from private, April 5, 1848, vice Wm. M. Faris, resigned; private from enrollment. |
| 2 | Resigned April 5, 1848. |
| 2 | Appointed from Sergeant, June 1, 1848; Sergeant from enrollment. |
| 1 | |
| 2 | |
| 3 | Promoted from private to Sergeant, June 1, 1848, vice Thacker, promoted; private from enrollment. |
| 4 | Promoted from private to Sergeant, June 22, 1848, vice Westerfield, promoted; private from enrollment. |
| 1 | |
| 2 | |
| 3 | |
| 4 | |
| 1 | |
| 2 | |
| 3 | Absent, sick in New Orleans since November 7, 1847. |
| 4 | |
| 5 | |
| 6 | |
| 7 | |
| 8 | |
| 9 | |
| 10 | |
| 11 | |
| 12 | |

# MEXICAN WAR VETERANS.

## ROLL OF COMPANY "K," THIRD REGIMENT KENTUCKY

| No. of each grade | Name. | Rank. | Joined for Service. | Mustered In. When. | Mustered In. Where. | Period | Mustered Out. When. | Mustered Out. Where. |
|---|---|---|---|---|---|---|---|---|
| 13 | Dunsil, Thomas | Private | Oct. 5, 1847 | Oct. 5, '47 | Louisville, Ky. | | July 21, '48 | Louisville, Ky. |
| 14 | Flinn, William | Private | Oct. 5, 1847 | Oct. 5, '47 | Louisville, Ky. | | July 21, '48 | Louisville, Ky. |
| 15 | Fugate, William | Private | Oct. 5, 1847 | Oct. 5, '47 | Louisville, Ky. | | July 21, '48 | Louisville, Ky. |
| 16 | Goens, Kenneday | Private | Oct. 5, 1847 | Oct. 5, '47 | Louisville, Ky. | | July 21, '48 | Louisville, Ky. |
| 17 | Hick, Edwin | Private | Oct. 5, 1847 | Oct. 5, '47 | Louisville, Ky. | | July 21, '48 | Louisville, Ky. |
| 18 | Hennersy, Patrick | Private | Oct. 24, 1847 | Dec. 31, '47 | City of Mexico | | July 21, '48 | Louisville, Ky. |
| 19 | Jackson, Isaac D. | Private | Oct. 5, 1847 | Oct. 5, '47 | Louisville, Ky. | | July 21, '48 | Louisville, Ky. |
| 20 | Jones, Wiley | Private | Oct. 5, 1847 | Oct. 5, '47 | Louisville, Ky. | | July 21, '48 | Louisville, Ky. |
| 21 | Jones, George | Private | Oct. 5, 1847 | Oct. 5, '47 | Louisville, Ky. | | July 21, '48 | Louisville, Ky. |
| 22 | Knight, Granville P. | Private | Oct. 5, 1847 | Oct. 5, '47 | Louisville, Ky | | July 21, '48 | Louisville, Ky. |
| 23 | Lunsford, Tarlton | Private | Oct. 5, 1847 | Oct. 5, '47 | Louisville, Ky. | | July 21, '48 | Louisville, Ky. |
| 24 | Leftridge, Harvey | Private | Oct. 5, 1847 | Oct. 5, '47 | Louisville, Ky. | | July 21, '48 | Louisville, Ky. |
| 25 | Lime, James | Private | Oct. 22, 1847 | Dec. 31, '47 | City of Mexico | | July 21, '48 | Louisville, Ky. |
| 26 | Lime, William | Private | Oct. 22, 1847 | Dec. 31, '47 | City of Mexico | | July 21, '48 | Louisville, Ky. |
| 27 | Marcum, Joseph | Private | Oct. 5, 1847 | Oct. 5, '47 | Louisville, Ky. | | July 21, '48 | Louisville, Ky. |
| 28 | McCarty, Charles | Private | Oct. 5, 1847 | Oct. 5, '47 | Louisville, Ky. | | July 21, '48 | Louisville, Ky. |
| 29 | Maloney, Edward | Private | Oct. 5, 1847 | Oct. 5, '47 | Louisville, Ky. | | July 21, '48 | Louisville, Ky. |
| 30 | Morgan, Robert | Private | Oct. 5, 1847 | Oct. 5, '47 | Louisville, Ky. | | July 21, '48 | Louisville, Ky. |
| 31 | Meadows, George W. B. | Private | Oct. 5, 1847 | Oct. 5, '47 | Louisville, Ky. | | July 21, '48 | Louisville, Ky. |
| 32 | Martin, Joel | Private | Oct. 5, 1847 | Oct. 5, '47 | Louisville, Ky. | | July 21, '48 | Louisville, Ky. |
| 33 | Martin, Henry | Private | Oct. 8, 1847 | Oct. 8, '47 | Louisville, Ky. | | July 21, '48 | Louisville, Ky. |
| 34 | Nix, John | Private | Oct. 5, 1847 | Oct. 5, '47 | Louisville, Ky. | | July 21, '48 | Louisville, Ky. |
| 35 | Nix, Joseph D. | Private | Oct. 5, 1847 | Oct. 5, '47 | Louisville, Ky. | | July 21, '48 | Louisville, Ky. |
| 36 | Randall, James S. | Private | Oct. 5, 1847 | Oct. 5, '47 | Louisville, Ky. | | July 21, '48 | Louisville, Ky. |
| 37 | Sullivan, Lasser | Private | Oct. 5, 1847 | Oct. 5, '47 | Louisville, Ky. | | July 21, '48 | Louisville, Ky. |
| 38 | Sexton, Preston | Private | Oct. 5, 1847 | Oct. 5, '47 | Louisville, Ky. | | July 21, '48 | Louisville, Ky. |
| 39 | Shryock, Andrew J. | Private | Oct. 5, 1847 | Oct. 5, '47 | Louisville, Ky. | | July 21, '48 | Louisville, Ky. |
| 40 | Sears, Peter | Private | Oct. 5, 1847 | Oct. 5, '47 | Louisville, Ky. | | July 21, '48 | Louisville, Ky. |
| 41 | Wood, Allison M. | Private | Oct. 5, 1847 | Oct. 5, '47 | Louisville, Ky. | | July 21, '48 | Louisville, Ky. |
| 42 | Wood, William L. | Private | Oct. 5, 1847 | Oct. 5, '47 | Louisville, Ky. | | July 21, '48 | Louisville, Ky. |
| 43 | Young, Richard | Private | Oct. 5, 1847 | Oct. 5, '47 | Louisville, Ky. | | July 21, '48 | Louisville, Ky. |
| 44 | Richardson, James | Private | Oct. 5, 1847 | Oct. 5, '47 | Louisville, Ky. | | July 21, '48 | Louisville, Ky. |
| | **Discharged.** | | | | | To serve during the war. | | |
| 1 | Thomas Milican | Private | Oct. 5, 1847 | Oct. 5, '47 | Louisville, Ky. | | | |
| 2 | Jarvis J. Carnifax | Private | Oct. 5, 1847 | Oct. 5, '47 | Louisville, Ky. | | | |
| 3 | John Canada | Private | Oct. 5, 1847 | Oct. 5, '47 | Louisville, Ky. | | | |
| 4 | Josiah Sullivan | Private | Oct. 5, 1847 | Oct. 5, '47 | Louisville, Ky. | | | |
| 5 | Austin Pickett | Private | Oct. 5, 1847 | Oct. 5, '47 | Louisville, Ky. | | | |
| 6 | Charles Poteete | Private | Oct. 5, 1847 | Oct. 5, '47 | Louisville, Ky. | | | |
| 7 | Henry Myers | Private | Oct. 5, 1847 | Oct. 5, '47 | Louisville, Ky. | | | |
| 8 | Calvin Wells | Private | Oct. 5, 1847 | Oct. 5, '47 | Louisville, Ky. | | | |
| 9 | John M. Englin | Private | Oct. 5, 1847 | Oct. 5, '47 | Louisville, Ky. | | | |
| 10 | Thomas R. Harmon | 1st Sergeant | Oct. 5, 1847 | Oct. 5, '47 | Louisville, Ky. | | | |
| 11 | Alexander Frazier | Private | Oct. 5, 1847 | Oct. 5, '47 | Louisville, Ky. | | | |
| 12 | Robert Morgan | Private | Oct. 5, 1847 | Oct. 5, '47 | Louisville, Ky. | | | |
| 13 | Alonzo L. Byron | Private | Oct. 5, 1847 | Oct. 5, '47 | Louisville, Ky. | | | |
| | **Deserted.** | | | | | | | |
| 1 | Solomon Edwards | Private | Oct. 11, 1847 | Oct. 11, '47 | Louisville, Ky. | | | |
| | **Died.** | | | | | | | |
| 1 | James Barr | Private | Oct. 12, 1847 | Oct. 12, '47 | Louisville, Ky. | | | |
| 2 | John R. Boling | Private | Oct. 8, 1847 | Oct. 8, '47 | Louisville, Ky. | | | |
| 3 | Andrew C. Burke | Private | Oct. 5, 1847 | Oct. 5, '47 | Louisville, Ky. | | | |
| 4 | James Wells | Sergeant | Oct. 5, 1847 | Oct. 5, '47 | Louisville, Ky. | | | |
| 5 | John Tuttle | Fifer | Oct. 5, 1847 | Oct. 5, '47 | Louisville, Ky. | | | |
| 6 | Henry N. Canlin | Private | Oct. 5, 1847 | Oct. 5, '47 | Louisville, Ky. | | | |
| 7 | Bazil Brawner | Private | Oct. 5, 1847 | Oct. 5, '47 | Louisville, Ky. | | | |
| 8 | Granville P. Murry | Private | Oct. 5, 1847 | Oct. 5, '47 | Louisville, Ky. | | | |
| 9 | William R. Ellison | Private | Oct. 5, 1847 | Oct. 5, '47 | Louisville, Ky. | | | |
| 10 | Pinckney A. Hall | Private | Oct. 5, 1847 | Oct. 5, '47 | Louisville, Ky. | | | |
| 11 | John Kerr | Private | Oct. 5, 1847 | Oct. 5, '47 | Louisville, Ky. | | | |
| 12 | Wymer Still | Private | Oct. 5, 1847 | Oct. 5, '47 | Louisville, Ky. | | | |
| 13 | Harris Boyd | Private | Oct. 24, 1847 | Dec. 31, '47 | City of Mexico | | | |
| 14 | Luther McCarty | Private | Oct. 5, 1847 | Oct. 5, '47 | Louisville, Ky. | | | |
| 15 | Beverly Matthews | Private | Oct. 5, 1847 | Oct. 5, '47 | Louisville, Ky. | | | |
| 16 | Francis Sears | Private | Oct. 5, 1847 | Oct. 5, '47 | Louisville, Ky. | | | |
| 17 | Levi Napier | Private | Oct. 5, 1847 | Oct. 5, '47 | Louisville, Ky. | | | |
| 18 | Alfred Young | Private | Oct. 5, 1847 | Oct. 5, '47 | Louisville, Ky. | | | |
| 19 | Reuben Meadows | Private | Oct. 5, 1847 | Oct. 5, '47 | Louisville, Ky. | | | |
| 20 | Zackariah Smith | Private | Oct. 5, 1847 | Oct. 5, '47 | Louisville, Ky. | | | |
| 21 | John H. Grebe | Private | Oct. 11, 1847 | Oct. 11, '47 | Louisville, Ky. | | | |
| 22 | Samuel Young | Private | Oct. 5, 1847 | Oct. 5, '47 | Louisville, Ky. | | | |
| 23 | William Rogers | Private | Oct. 5, 1847 | Oct. 5, '47 | Louisville, Ky. | | | |

## FOOT VOLUNTEERS—MEXICAN WAR—Continued.

| No. of each grade | REMARKS. |
|---|---|
| 13 | |
| 14 | |
| 15 | |
| 16 | |
| 17 | |
| 18 | |
| 19 | |
| 20 | |
| 21 | |
| 22 | |
| 23 | |
| 24 | |
| 25 | |
| 26 | |
| 27 | |
| 28 | |
| 29 | |
| 30 | Absent sick; sent from City of Mexico. |
| 31 | |
| 32 | |
| 33 | |
| 34 | |
| 35 | |
| 36 | |
| 37 | |
| 38 | |
| 39 | |
| 40 | |
| 41 | |
| 42 | |
| 43 | |
| 44 | |
| 1 | Discharged October 18, 1847; Surgeon's certificate of disability, at Louisville, Ky. |
| 2 | Discharged October 22, 1847, by civil authority, at Louisville, Ky. |
| 3 | Discharged January 12, 1848; Surgeon's certificate of disability, in City of Mexico. |
| 4 | Discharged January 12, 1848; Surgeon's certificate of disability, in City of Mexico. |
| 5 | Discharged January 15, 1848; Surgeon's certificate of disability, in Vera Cruz. |
| 6 | Discharged February 17, 1848; Surgeon's certificate of disability, in City of Mexico. |
| 7 | In Pueblo, March 18, 1848; Surgeon's certificate of disability. |
| 8 | In Pueblo, February, 1848; Surgeon's certificate of disability. |
| 9 | In New Orleans, on Surgeon's certificate of disability, March 15, 1848. |
| 10 | In New Orleans, on Surgeon's certificate of disability. Date unknown. |
| 11 | In New Orleans, on Surgeon's certificate of disability. Date unknown. |
| 12 | In New Orleans, on Surgeon's certificate of disability. Date unknown. |
| 13 | In New Orleans, on Surgeon's certificate of disability. Date unknown. |
| 1 | At Louisville; not heard of since. |
| 1 | At Vera Cruz, December 12, 1847. |
| 2 | In Pueblo, December 17, 1847. |
| 3 | In Pueblo, December 20, 1847. |
| 4 | In Pueblo, December 24, 1847. |
| 5 | In Jalapa, December 25, 1847. |
| 6 | No official report. |
| 7 | In Pueblo, January 16, 1848. |
| 8 | In City of Mexico, January 16, 1848. |
| 9 | In City of Mexico, January 29, 1848. |
| 10 | In City of Mexico, January 29, 1848. |
| 11 | In City of Mexico, January 30, 1848. |
| 12 | In City of Mexico, February 5, 1848. |
| 13 | In City of Mexico, February 6, 1848. |
| 14 | In City of Mexico, February 9, 1848. |
| 15 | In City of Mexico, February 16, 1848. |
| 16 | In City of Mexico, February 25, 1848. |
| 17 | In Vera Cruz. Date unknown. No official report. |
| 18 | In City of Mexico, March 2, 1848. |
| 19 | City of Mexico, March 2, 1848. |
| 20 | City of Mexico, March 31, 1848. |
| 21 | City of Mexico, May 25, 1848. |
| 22 | City of Mexico, April 22, 1848. |
| 23 | City of Mexico, May 20, 1848. |

## ROLL OF COMPANY "K," THIRD REGIMENT KENTUCKY

| No. of each grade | Name | Rank | Joined for Service | Mustered In When | Mustered In Where | Period | Mustered Out When | Mustered Out Where |
|---|---|---|---|---|---|---|---|---|
| 24 | John W. Rickerson | Private | Oct. 11, 1847 | Oct. 11, '47 | Louisville, Ky. | During the war. | | |
| 25 | Joshua Hendrickson | Private | Oct. 5, 1847 | Oct. 5, '47 | Louisville, Ky. | | | |
| 26 | William Bryant | Private | Oct. 5, 1847 | Oct. 5, '47 | Louisville, Ky. | | | |
| 27 | Willis Suttles | Private | Oct. 5, 1847 | Oct. 5, '47 | Louisville, Ky. | | | |
| 28 | William Sullivan | Private | Oct. 5, 1847 | Oct. 5, '47 | Louisville, Ky. | | | |
| | TRANSFERRED. | | | | | | | |
| 1 | Otho P. Simms | Drummer | Oct. 5, 1847 | Oct. 5, '47 | Louisville, Ky. | | | |
| 2 | James Cameron | Private | Oct. 5, 1847 | Oct. 5, '47 | Louisville, Ky. | | | |
| 3 | Jacob Lehman | Private | Oct. 8, 1847 | Oct. 8, '47 | Louisville, Ky. | | | |

This Company was organized by Captain A. F. Coldwell at London, Ky., in the month of September, 1847, and marched thence to Louisville, Ky., where it arrived on the 5th day of October, 1847, a distance of *one hundred and forty-three miles.*

## ROLL OF THE FIELD AND STAFF FOURTH REGIMENT

| | Name | Rank | Joined for Service | Mustered In When | Mustered In Where | Period | Mustered Out When | Mustered Out Where |
|---|---|---|---|---|---|---|---|---|
| 1 | John S. Williams | Colonel | Sept. 20, 1847 | Oct. 4, '47 | Louisville, Ky. | To serve during the war. | July 25, '48 | Louisville, Ky. |
| 1 | Wm. Preston | Lieut. Colonel | Sept. 20, 1847 | Oct. 4, '47 | Louisville, Ky. | | July 25, '48 | Louisville, Ky. |
| 1 | Wm. F. Ward | Major | Sept. 20, 1847 | Oct. 4, '47 | Louisville, Ky. | | July 25, '48 | Louisville, Ky. |
| 1 | Chas. H. Creel | Adjutant | Apr. 26, 1848 | Oct. 4, '47 | Louisville, Ky. | | July 25, '48 | Louisville, Ky. |
| 1 | Joseph G. Roberts | Surgeon | Sept. 8, 1847 | Oct. 4, '47 | Louisville, Ky. | | July 25, '48 | Louisville, Ky. |
| 1 | Zebalon C. Bishop | Capt. & A. Q. M. | Sept. 9, 1847 | Oct. 4, '47 | Louisville, Ky. | | July 25, '48 | Louisville, Ky. |
| 1 | Reuben L. Nance | Capt. A. C. S. | Sept. 8, 1847 | Oct. 4, '47 | Louisville, Ky. | | July 25, '48 | Louisville, Ky. |
| 1 | John R. Steele | Ass't Surgeon | Sept. 8, 1847 | Oct. 4, '47 | Louisville, Ky. | | July 25, '48 | Louisville, Ky. |
| 1 | Harry A. Kane | Ser. Major | Oct. 4, 1847 | Oct. 4, '47 | Smithland, Ky. | | July 25, '48 | Louisville, Ky. |
| 1 | Chas. W. Ball | Qr. M. Serg't | Oct. 1, 1847 | Oct. 4, '47 | Louisville, Ky. | | July 25, '48 | Louisville, Ky. |
| 1 | Chas. H. Fieldbush | Prin'l Musician | | | Louisville, Ky. | | July 25, '48 | Louisville, Ky. |
| 2 | James Beaty | Prin'l Musician | | | Louisville, Ky. | | July 25, '48 | Louisville, Ky. |
| | DEATHS. | | | | | | | |
| 1 | Shelby A. Ray | Sergeant Major | Oct. 4, 1847 | Oct 4, '47 | Louisville, Ky. | | | |
| | DISCHARGED. | | | | | | | |
| 1 | Davis L. Adair | Qr. M. Serg't | Oct. 4, 1847 | Oct. 4, '47 | Louisville, Ky. | | | |
| | TRANSFERRED. | | | | | | | |
| | Robert P. Trabue | Adjutant | Oct. 4, 1847 | Oct. 4, '47 | Louisville, Ky. | | | |

## ROLL OF COMPANY "A," FOURTH REGIMENT KENTUCKY

| | Name | Rank | Joined for Service | Mustered In When | Mustered In Where | Period | Mustered Out When | Mustered Out Where |
|---|---|---|---|---|---|---|---|---|
| 1 | Timothy Keating | Captain | Oct. 4, 1847 | Oct. 4, '47 | Louisville, Ky. | To serve during the war. | July 25, '48 | Louisville, Ky. |
| 1 | Wm. E. Woodruff | 1st Lieutenant | Oct. 4, 1847 | Oct. 4, '47 | Louisville, Ky. | | July 25, '48 | Louisville, Ky. |
| 1 | Presley Talbott | 2d Lieutenant | Oct. 4, 1847 | Oct. 4, '47 | Louisville, Ky. | | July 25, '48 | Louisville, Ky. |
| 2 | Levi White | 2d Lieutenant | Oct. 4, 1847 | Oct. 4, '47 | Louisville, Ky. | | July 25, '48 | Louisville, Ky. |
| 1 | John H. Johnson | 1st Sergeant | Oct. 4, 1847 | Oct. 4, '47 | Louisville, Ky. | | July 25, '48 | Louisville, Ky. |
| 2 | Edward S. Mopps | Sergeant | Oct. 4, 1847 | Oct. 4, '47 | Louisville, Ky. | | July 25, '48 | Louisville, Ky. |
| 3 | Wm. D. Labbree | Sergeant | Oct. 4, 1847 | Oct. 4, '47 | Louisville, Ky. | | July 25, '48 | Louisville, Ky. |
| 4 | Edmund H. McDonald | Sergeant | Oct. 4, 1847 | Oct. 4, '47 | Louisville, Ky. | | July 25, '48 | Louisville, Ky. |
| 1 | Franklin M. Hughes | Corporal | Oct. 4, 1847 | Oct. 4, '47 | Louisville, Ky. | | July 25, '48 | Louisville, Ky. |
| 2 | Thomas J. Smith | Corporal | Oct. 4, 1847 | Oct. 4, '47 | Louisville, Ky. | | July 25, '48 | Louisville, Ky. |
| 3 | Geo. P. Albert | Corporal | Oct. 4, 1847 | Oct. 4, '47 | Louisville, Ky. | | July 25, '48 | Louisville, Ky. |
| 4 | Geo. T. Hubbard | Corporal | Oct. 4, 1847 | Oct. 4, '47 | Louisville, Ky. | | July 25, '48 | Louisville, Ky. |
| 1 | Franz Kirkhai | Musician | Oct. 4, 1847 | Oct. 4, '47 | Louisville, Ky. | | July 25, '48 | Louisville, Ky. |
| 2 | Robert R. Kirkpatrick | Musician | Oct. 4, 1847 | Oct. 4, '47 | Louisville, Ky. | | July 25, '48 | Louisville, Ky. |
| 1 | Arthur, Thomas | Private | Oct. 4, 1847 | Oct. 4, '47 | Louisville, Ky. | | July 25, '48 | Louisville, Ky. |
| 2 | Atwell, John | Private | Oct. 11, 1847 | Oct. 4, '47 | Louisville, Ky. | | July 25, '48 | Louisville, Ky. |
| 3 | Abbott, Wm. H. | Private | Oct. 4, 1847 | Oct. 4, '47 | Louisville, Ky. | | July 25, '48 | Louisville, Ky. |
| 4 | Brown, Daniel | Private | Oct. 4, 1847 | Oct. 4, '47 | Louisville, Ky. | | July 25, '48 | Louisville, Ky. |
| 5 | Batman, Wm. | Private | Oct. 4, 1847 | Oct. 4, '47 | Louisville, Ky. | | July 25, '48 | Louisville, Ky. |
| 6 | Brown, James T. | Private | Oct. 4, 1847 | Oct. 4, '47 | Louisville, Ky. | | July 25, '48 | Louisville, Ky. |
| 7 | Basham, Daniel | Private | Oct. 4, 1847 | Oct. 4, '47 | Louisville, Ky. | | July 25, '48 | Louisville, Ky. |
| 8 | Batsom, Wesley | Private | Oct. 30, 1847 | Dec. 31, '47 | City of Mexico | | July 25, '48 | Louisville, Ky. |
| 9 | Cox, Lorenzo D. | Private | Oct. 4, 1847 | Oct. 4, '47 | Louisville, Ky. | | July 25, '48 | Louisville, Ky. |
| 10 | Child, Conrad | Private | Oct. 4, 1847 | Oct. 4, '47 | Louisville, Ky. | | July 25, '48 | Louisville, Ky. |
| 11 | Creighton, John | Private | Oct. 4, 1847 | Oct. 4, '47 | Louisville, Ky. | | July 25, '48 | Louisville, Ky. |
| 12 | Caswell, Herter A. | Private | Oct. 7, 1847 | Oct. 4, '47 | Louisville, Ky. | | July 25, '48 | Louisville, Ky. |
| 13 | Carmichael, David | Private | Oct. 4, 1847 | Oct. 4, '47 | Louisville, Ky. | | July 25, '48 | Louisville, Ky. |
| 14 | Davis, Wm. | Private | Oct. 4, 1847 | Oct. 4, '47 | Louisville, Ky. | | July 25, '48 | Louisville, Ky. |

# FOOT VOLUNTEERS—MEXICAN WAR—Continued.

| No. of each grade | REMARKS. |
|---|---|
| 24 | City of Mexico, May 31, 1848. |
| 25 | City of Mexico, April 8, 1848. |
| 26 | City of Jalapa, May 29, 1848. |
| 27 | At San Antonio, June 8, 1848. |
| 28 | On the steamer Missouri, Mississippi river, July 11, 1848. |
| 1 | Transferred to non-commissioned staff, April 2, 1848, as principal Musician. |
| 2 | Transferred to 12th Infantry, as a deserter, April 4, 1848. |
| 3 | Transferred to 4th Infantry, as a deserter, April 25, 1848. |

# KENTUCKY FOOT VOLUNTEERS—MEXICAN WAR.

| | |
|---|---|
| 1 | |
| 1 | |
| 1 | |
| 1 | Appointed from 2d Lieutenant, Company "B," vice R. P. Trabue, resigned and transferred; was 2d Lieutenant from enrollment. |
| 1 | Joined for duty at Louisville, Ky., 4th October, 1847. |
| 1 | Transferred from Regiment, January 14, 1848. General orders No. 20. |
| 1 | On furlough since April 7, 1848. General orders No. 33. |
| 1 | Joined for duty at Louisville, Ky., October 4, 1847. |
| 1 | Appointed from Sergeant, Company "E," March 20, 1848, vice Shelby A. Ray, deceased; was Sergeant from enrollment. |
| 1 | Appointed from private, Company "D," January 1, 1848, vice D. L. Adair, discharged. |
| 1 | |
| 2 | |
| 1 | Died in the City of Mexico, March 20, 1848. |
| 1 | Discharged from the service at City of Mexico, January 8, 1848; Surgeon's certificate of disability. |
| | Resigned from Regimental Staff and transferred to Company "B," 4th Regiment, Ky. Volunteers, April 26, 1848. |

# FOOT VOLUNTEERS—MEXICAN WAR.

| | |
|---|---|
| 1 | |
| 1 | |
| 1 | |
| 2 | |
| 1 | Appointed 1st Sergeant, October 9, 1847, vice Shelby A. Ray, transferred to N. C. Staff; Sergeant from enrollment. |
| 2 | |
| 3 | Appointed Sergeant from Corporal, March 1, 1848, vice W. H. Abbott, reduced; Corporal from enrollment. |
| 4 | |
| 1 | |
| 2 | |
| 3 | |
| 4 | Appointed Corporal from private, March 1, 1848, vice Wm. B. Labbree, appointed Sergeant. |
| 1 | |
| 2 | Appointed Musician from private, vice James Beatty, transferred to N. C. Staff, October 4, 1847. |
| 1 | |
| 2 | |
| 3 | Reduced to ranks from Sergeant, March 1, 1848. |
| 4 | |
| 5 | |
| 6 | |
| 7 | |
| 8 | Joined Company at City of Mexico. |
| 9 | |
| 10 | |
| 11 | |
| 12 | |
| 13 | |
| 14 | |

# MEXICAN WAR VETERANS.

## ROLL OF COMPANY "A," FOURTH REGIMENT KENTUCKY

| No. of each grade. | Name. | Rank. | Joined for Service. | Mustered In. When. | Mustered In. Where. | Period. | Mustered Out. When. | Mustered Out. Where. |
|---|---|---|---|---|---|---|---|---|
| 15 | Delisle, John | Private | Oct. 4, 1847 | Oct. 4, '47 | Louisville, Ky. | | July 25, '48 | Louisville, Ky. |
| 16 | Devine, James | Private | Oct. 4, 1847 | Oct. 4, '47 | Louisville, Ky. | | July 25, '48 | Louisville, Ky. |
| 17 | Dunlap, John | Private | Oct. 4, 1847 | Oct. 4, '47 | Louisville, Ky. | | July 25, '48 | Louisville, Ky. |
| 18 | Debonish, Mathew | Private | Oct. 4, 1847 | Oct. 4, '47 | Louisville, Ky. | | July 25, '48 | Louisville, Ky. |
| 19 | Dunn, Edward | Private | Oct. 4, 1847 | Oct. 4, '47 | Louisville, Ky. | | July 25, '48 | Louisville, Ky. |
| 20 | Degarris, Wm. | Private | Oct. 11, 1847 | Oct. 11, '47 | Louisville, Ky. | | July 25, '48 | Louisville, Ky. |
| 21 | Eames, George W. | Private | Oct. 4, 1847 | Oct. 4, '47 | Louisville, Ky. | | July 25, '48 | Louisville, Ky. |
| 22 | Frederick, Richard | Private | Oct. 4, 1847 | Oct. 4, '47 | Louisville, Ky. | | July 25, '48 | Louisville, Ky. |
| 23 | Foster, Alonzo | Private | Oct. 4, 1847 | Oct. 4, '47 | Louisville, Ky. | | July 25, '48 | Louisville, Ky. |
| 24 | Fanllin, Thomas P. | Private | Oct. 4, 1847 | Oct. 4, '47 | Louisville, Ky. | | July 25, '48 | Louisville, Ky. |
| 25 | Flowers, George W. | Private | Oct. 4, 1847 | Oct. 4, '47 | Louisville, Ky. | | July 25, '48 | Louisville, Ky. |
| 26 | Gilbraith, Edward | Private | Oct. 4, 1847 | Oct. 4, '47 | Louisville, Ky. | | July 25, '48 | Louisville, Ky. |
| 27 | Gamble, Jeremiah | Private | Oct. 4, 1847 | Oct. 4, '47 | Louisville, Ky. | | July 25, '48 | Louisville, Ky. |
| 28 | Garrett, Benjamin | Private | Oct. 4, 1847 | Oct. 4, '47 | Louisville, Ky. | | July 25, '48 | Louisville, Ky. |
| 29 | Garnett, Alexander | Private | Oct. 4, 1847 | Oct. 4, '47 | Louisville, Ky. | | July 25, '48 | Louisville, Ky. |
| 30 | Gray, Robert | Private | Oct. 4, 1847 | Oct. 4, '47 | Louisville, Ky. | | July 25, '48 | Louisville, Ky. |
| 31 | Hickey, Thomas | Private | Oct. 4, 1847 | Oct. 4, '47 | Louisville, Ky. | | July 25, '48 | Louisville, Ky. |
| 32 | Hausenburg, Frederk | Private | Oct. 4, 1847 | Oct. 4, '47 | Louisville, Ky. | | July 25, '48 | Louisville, Ky. |
| 33 | Hogan, John A. | Private | Oct. 4, 1847 | Oct. 4, '47 | Louisville, Ky. | | July 25, '48 | Louisville, Ky. |
| 34 | Hahn, Samuel | Private | Oct. 4, 1847 | Oct. 4, '47 | Louisville, Ky. | | July 25, '48 | Louisville, Ky. |
| 35 | Hogan, Green | Private | Oct. 4, 1847 | Oct. 4, '47 | Louisville, Ky. | | July 25, '48 | Louisville, Ky. |
| 36 | Hauck, Christian | Private | Oct. 4, 1847 | Oct. 4, '47 | Louisville, Ky. | | July 25, '48 | Louisville, Ky. |
| 37 | Hecock, Joel | Private | Oct. 4, 1847 | Oct. 4, '47 | Louisville, Ky. | | July 25, '48 | Louisville, Ky. |
| 38 | Harney, Benjamin | Private | Oct. 4, 1847 | Oct. 4, '47 | Louisville, Ky. | | July 25, '48 | Louisville, Ky. |
| 39 | Johnson, Sidney L. | Private | Oct. 4, 1847 | Oct. 4, '47 | Louisville, Ky. | | July 25, '48 | Louisville, Ky. |
| 40 | Jenkins, Horace | Private | Oct. 4, 1847 | Oct. 4, '47 | Louisville, Ky. | | July 25, '48 | Louisville, Ky. |
| 41 | Johnson, John W. | Private | Oct. 28, 1847 | Dec. 31, '47 | City of Mexico | | July 25, '48 | Louisville, Ky. |
| 42 | Jones, Edward | Private | Oct. 4, 1847 | Oct. 4, '47 | Louisville, Ky. | | July 25, '48 | Louisville, Ky. |
| 43 | Kracht, Samuel | Private | Oct. 4, 1847 | Oct. 4, '47 | Louisville, Ky. | | July 25, '48 | Louisville, Ky. |
| 44 | Lampton, James S. | Private | Oct. 4, 1847 | Oct. 4, '47 | Louisville, Ky. | | July 25, '48 | Louisville, Ky. |
| 45 | Lacomb, John | Private | Oct. 4, 1847 | Oct. 4, '47 | Louisville, Ky. | | July 25, '48 | Louisville, Ky. |
| 46 | Lane, William B. | Private | July 16, 1846 | July 16, '46 | Bedford, Ky. | | July 25, '48 | Louisville, Ky. |
| 47 | McMurry, William | Private | Oct. 4, 1847 | Oct. 4, '47 | Louisville, Ky. | To serve during war. | July 25, '48 | Louisville, Ky. |
| 48 | Mayer, William D. | Private | Oct. 4, 1847 | Oct. 4, '47 | Louisville, Ky. | | July 25, '48 | Louisville, Ky. |
| 49 | Miller, John A. | Private | Oct. 4, 1847 | Oct. 4, '47 | Louisville, Ky. | | July 25, '48 | Louisville, Ky. |
| 50 | Minor, George G. | Private | June 15, 1846 | June 15, '46 | Columbus, Ohio | | July 25, '48 | Louisville, Ky. |
| 51 | Mearing, Christopher | Private | Oct. 4, 1847 | Oct. 4, '47 | Louisville, Ky. | | July 25, '48 | Louisville, Ky. |
| 52 | McGaw, Hugh B. | Private | Oct. 4, 1847 | Oct. 4, '47 | Louisville, Ky. | | July 25, '48 | Louisville, Ky. |
| 53 | Mitchell, Charles | Private | Oct. 4, 1847 | Oct. 4, '47 | Louisville, Ky. | | July 25, '48 | Louisville, Ky. |
| 54 | Means, William C. | Private | Oct. 4, 1847 | Oct. 4, '47 | Louisville, Ky. | | July 25, '48 | Louisville, Ky. |
| 55 | Myers, Stephen | Private | Oct. 4, 1847 | Oct. 4, '47 | Louisville, Ky. | | July 25, '48 | Louisville, Ky. |
| 56 | Morrison, Joseph | Private | Oct. 4, 1847 | Oct. 4, '47 | Louisville, Ky. | | July 25, '48 | Louisville, Ky. |
| 57 | Merryman, Walton | Private | Oct. 4, 1847 | Oct. 4, '47 | Louisville, Ky. | | July 25, '48 | Louisville, Ky. |
| 58 | McCain, Wm. H. H. | Private | Oct. 16, 1847 | Oct. 16, '47 | Louisville, Ky. | | July 25, '48 | Louisville, Ky. |
| 59 | O'Sullivan, Eugene | Private | Oct. 4, 1847 | Oct. 4, '47 | Louisville, Ky. | | July 25, '48 | Louisville, Ky. |
| 60 | Peark, Joseph | Private | Oct. 4, 1847 | Oct. 4, '47 | Louisville, Ky. | | July 25, '48 | Louisville, Ky. |
| 61 | Passier, Wm. | Private | Jan. 1, 1848 | Jan. 1, '48 | City of Mexico | | July 25, '48 | Louisville, Ky. |
| 62 | Southern, Stephen | Private | Oct. 4, 1847 | Oct. 4, '47 | Louisville, Ky. | | July 25, '48 | Louisville, Ky. |
| 63 | Saunders, Benedict J. | Private | Oct. 4, 1847 | Oct. 4, '47 | Louisville, Ky. | | July 25, '48 | Louisville, Ky. |
| 64 | Seibman, John A. | Private | Oct. 4, 1847 | Oct. 4, '47 | Louisville, Ky. | | July 25, '48 | Louisville, Ky. |
| 65 | Simpson, Thomas A. | Private | Oct. 4, 1847 | Oct. 4, '47 | Louisville, Ky. | | July 25, '48 | Louisville, Ky. |
| 66 | Stewart, Benjamin | Private | Oct. 4, 1847 | Oct. 4, '47 | Louisville, Ky. | | July 25, '48 | Louisville, Ky. |
| 67 | St. Clair, Archibald | Private | Oct. 4, 1847 | Oct. 4, '47 | Louisville, Ky. | | July 25, '48 | Louisville, Ky. |
| 68 | Terry, Michael | Private | Oct. 4, 1847 | Oct. 4, '47 | Louisville, Ky. | | July 25, '48 | Louisville, Ky. |
| 69 | Turner, Milton | Private | Oct. 4, 1847 | Oct. 4, '47 | Louisville, Ky. | | July 25, '48 | Louisville, Ky. |
| 70 | Thompson, Alexander | Private | Oct. 4, 1847 | Oct. 4, '47 | Louisville, Ky. | | July 25, '48 | Louisville, Ky. |
| 71 | Thompson, Joseph | Private | Oct. 18, 1847 | Oct. 18, '47 | Louisville, Ky. | | July 25, '48 | Louisville, Ky. |
| 72 | Weaver, John | Private | Oct. 4, 1847 | Oct. 4, '47 | Louisville, Ky. | | July 25, '48 | Louisville, Ky. |
| 73 | Walker, Alexander | Private | Oct. 4, 1847 | Oct. 4, '47 | Louisville, Ky. | | July 25, '48 | Louisville, Ky. |
| 74 | Wells, Richard | Private | Oct. 4, 1847 | Oct. 4, '47 | Louisville, Ky. | | July 25, '48 | Louisville, Ky. |
| 75 | Yeck, Wm. | Private | Oct. 4, 1847 | Oct. 4, '47 | Louisville, Ky. | | July 25, '48 | Louisville, Ky. |
| | DISCHARGED. | | | | | | | |
| 1 | Limebaugh, Daniel | Private | Oct. 4, 1847 | Oct. 4, '47 | Louisville, Ky. | | | |
| 2 | Price, Jonathan | Private | Oct. 4, 1847 | Oct. 4, '47 | Louisville, Ky. | | | |
| 3 | Collins, John | Private | Oct. 4, 1847 | Oct. 4, '47 | Louisville, Ky. | | | |
| 4 | Wilson, James A. | Private | Oct. 4, 1847 | Oct. 4, '47 | Louisville, Ky. | | | |
| 5 | Davis, George | Private | Oct. 30, 1847 | Oct. 30, '47 | Louisville, Ky. | | | |
| 6 | Pangburn, John | Private | Oct. 4, 1847 | Oct. 4, '47 | Louisville, Ky. | | | |
| 7 | Hartmann, Peter | Private | Jan. 1, 1848 | Jan. 1, '48 | City of Mexico | | | |
| 8 | Kennedy, Thomas J. | Private | Oct. 4, 1847 | Oct. 4, '47 | Louisville, Ky. | | | |
| 9 | Durbins, George | Private | Oct. 4, 1847 | Oct. 4, '47 | Louisville, Ky. | | | |
| | TRANSFERRED. | | | | | | | |
| 1 | Rowham, Daniel C. | Private | Oct. 4, 1847 | Oct. 4, '47 | Louisville, Ky. | | | |
| 2 | Ray, Shelby A. | Sergeant | Oct. 4, 1847 | Oct. 4, '47 | Louisville, Ky. | | | |

## FOOT VOLUNTEERS—MEXICAN WAR—Continued.

| No. of each grade | REMARKS. |
|---|---|
| 15 | |
| 16 | |
| 17 | |
| 18 | |
| 19 | |
| 20 | |
| 21 | |
| 22 | |
| 23 | |
| 24 | Left sick at Vera Cruz, Mexico, November 26, 1847, and not heard of since. |
| 25 | |
| 26 | |
| 27 | |
| 28 | |
| 29 | |
| 30 | |
| 31 | |
| 32 | |
| 33 | |
| 34 | |
| 35 | |
| 36 | |
| 37 | |
| 38 | |
| 39 | |
| 40 | |
| 41 | Joined at City of Mexico. |
| 42 | |
| 43 | |
| 44 | |
| 45 | |
| 46 | Transferred from Regt. M. Rifles to Co. "A," 4th Ky. Vols., in place of Daniel C. Rowham, January 1, 1848. |
| 47 | |
| 48 | |
| 49 | |
| 50 | |
| 51 | |
| 52 | |
| 53 | |
| 54 | |
| 55 | |
| 56 | |
| 57 | |
| 58 | |
| 59 | |
| 60 | |
| 61 | |
| 62 | |
| 63 | |
| 64 | |
| 65 | |
| 66 | |
| 67 | On extra duty as Hospital Steward since December 5, 1847. |
| 68 | |
| 69 | |
| 70 | |
| 71 | |
| 72 | |
| 73 | |
| 74 | |
| 75 | |
| 1 | Discharged at Louisville, Ky., by civil authority, he being a minor. |
| 2 | Discharged at Louisville, Ky., on a writ of habeas corpus. |
| 3 | Discharged at City of Mexico, February 23, 1848, on Surgeon's certificate of disability. |
| 4 | Discharged at City of Mexico, February 23, 1848, on Surgeon's certificate of disability. |
| 5 | Discharged per special order No. 15, Headquarters U. S. Army, City of Mexico, April 22, 1848. |
| 6 | Discharged at hospital, New Orleans, March 13, 1848, Surgeon's certificate of disability. |
| 7 | Discharged at City of Mexico, March 1, 1848, Surgeon's certificate of disability. |
| 8 | Discharged at Jalapa, Mexico (not reported); Surgeon's certificate of disability. |
| 9 | Discharged at New Orleans, July 6, 1848, Surgeon's certificate of disability. |
| 1 | Transferred to Reg't M. Rifles January 1, 1848, in place of Wm. B. Lane. Special order Headquarters U. S. A. |
| 2 | Transferred to non-commissioned staff, 4th Kentucky Volunteers, October 9, 1847. |

120 MEXICAN WAR VETERANS.

## ROLL OF COMPANY "A," FOURTH REGIMENT KENTUCKY

| No. of each grade | Name | Rank | Joined for Service | Mustered In When | Mustered In Where | Period | Mustered Out When | Mustered Out Where |
|---|---|---|---|---|---|---|---|---|
| 3 | Beatty, James | Musician | Oct. 4, 1847 | Oct. 4, '47 | Louisville, Ky. | | | |
| | **Deserted.** | | | | | | | |
| 1 | McCarthy, Patrick | Private | Oct. 4, 1847 | Oct. 4, '47 | Louisville, Ky. | | | |
| 2 | Davis, John | Private | Oct. 4, 1847 | Oct. 4, '47 | Louisville, Ky. | | | |
| 3 | Fix, Frederick | Private | Oct. 4, 1847 | Oct. 4, '47 | Louisville, Ky. | | | |
| 4 | Grant, Washington | Private | Oct. 4, 1847 | Oct. 4, '47 | Louisville, Ky. | | | |
| 5 | Hunn, Dominick | Musician | Oct. 4, 1847 | Oct. 4, '47 | Louisville, Ky. | To serve during the war. | | |
| 6 | McGhee, Joseph | Private | Oct. 4, 1847 | Oct. 4, '47 | Louisville, Ky. | | | |
| 7 | Egan, Mathew | Private | Oct. 4, 1847 | Oct. 4, '47 | Louisville, Ky. | | | |
| | **Died.** | | | | | | | |
| 1 | Peterson, Charles | Private | Oct. 4, 1847 | Oct. 4, '47 | Louisville, Ky. | | | |
| 2 | Rogers, George | Private | Oct. 4, 1847 | Oct. 4, '47 | Louisville, Ky. | | | |
| 3 | Flannery, George F. | Private | Oct. 4, 1847 | Oct. 4, '47 | Louisville, Ky. | | | |
| 4 | Rogers, Joseph | Private | Oct. 4, 1847 | Oct. 4, '47 | Louisville, Ky. | | | |
| 5 | Morse, Benjamin | Private | Oct. 4, 1847 | Oct. 4, '47 | Louisville, Ky. | | | |
| 6 | Atwell, Samuel | Private | Oct. 4, 1847 | Oct. 4, '47 | Louisville, Ky. | | | |
| 7 | Ieder, Benjamin | Private | Oct. 4, 1847 | Oct. 4, '47 | Louisville, Ky. | | | |
| 8 | Sansberry, Giles | Private | Oct. 4, 1847 | Oct. 4, '47 | Louisville, Ky. | | | |
| 9 | Boyden, Stephen | Private | Oct. 4, 1847 | Oct. 4, '47 | Louisville, Ky. | | | |
| 10 | Bermer, Nicholas | Private | Oct. 26, 1847 | Oct. 26, '47 | Louisville, Ky. | | | |

This Company was organized by Capt. Timothy Keating, in the month of September, 1847, at Louisville, Ky.

## ROLL OF COMPANY "B," FOURTH REGIMENT KENTUCKY

| | Name | Rank | Joined for Service | Mustered In When | Mustered In Where | Period | Mustered Out When | Mustered Out Where |
|---|---|---|---|---|---|---|---|---|
| 1 | John S. Squires | Captain | Oct. 2, 1847 | Oct. 4, '47 | Louisville, Ky. | | | |
| 2 | Hamilton N. Owens | Captain | Oct. 2, 1847 | Oct. 4, '47 | Louisville, Ky. | | July 25, '48 | Louisville, Ky. |
| 1 | Robert P. Trabue | 1st Lieutenant | Oct. 2, 1847 | Oct. 4, '47 | Louisville, Ky. | | July 25, '48 | Louisville, Ky. |
| 1 | Charles H. Creel | 2d Lieutenant | Oct. 2, 1847 | Oct. 4, '47 | Louisville, Ky. | | July 25, '48 | Louisville, Ky. |
| 2 | William E. Russell | 2d 2d Lieut. | Oct. 2, 1847 | Oct. 4, '47 | Louisville, Ky. | | July 25, '48 | Louisville, Ky. |
| 1 | Allen G. Overton | 1st Sergeant | Oct. 2, 1847 | Oct. 4, '47 | Louisville, Ky. | | July 25, '48 | Louisville, Ky. |
| 2 | James O. Nelson | 2d Sergeant | Oct. 2, 1847 | Oct. 4, '47 | Louisville, Ky. | | July 25, '48 | Louisville, Ky. |
| 3 | George W. Deloney | 3d Sergeant | Oct. 2, 1847 | Oct. 4, '47 | Louisville, Ky. | | July 25, '48 | Louisville, Ky. |
| 4 | Francis Patrum | 4th Sergeant | Oct. 2, 1847 | Oct. 4, '47 | Louisville, Ky. | | July 25, '48 | Louisville, Ky. |
| 1 | William C. Turk | Corporal | Oct. 2, 1847 | Oct. 4, '47 | Louisville, Ky. | | July 25, '48 | Louisville, Ky. |
| 2 | Benj. M. Hutcherson | Corporal | Oct. 2, 1847 | Oct. 4, '47 | Louisville, Ky. | | July 25, '48 | Louisville, Ky. |
| 3 | Winslow C. Simpson | Corporal | Oct. 2, 1847 | Oct. 4, '47 | Louisville, Ky. | | July 25, '48 | Louisville, Ky. |
| 4 | William T. Epperson | Corporal | Oct. 2, 1847 | Oct. 4, '47 | Louisville, Ky. | | July 25, '48 | Louisville, Ky. |
| 1 | John Eubank | Musician | Oct. 2, 1847 | Oct. 4, '47 | Louisville, Ky. | | July 25, '48 | Louisville, Ky. |
| 2 | Richard Cundiff | Musician | Oct. 2, 1847 | Oct. 4, '47 | Louisville, Ky. | | July 25, '48 | Louisville, Ky. |
| 1 | Atkinson, Daniel S. | Private | Oct. 2, 1847 | Oct. 4, '47 | Louisville, Ky. | | July 25, '48 | Louisville, Ky. |
| 2 | Bennett, Robert | Private | Oct. 2, 1847 | Oct. 4, '47 | Louisville, Ky. | | July 25, '48 | Louisville, Ky. |
| 3 | Bennett, Oliver P. | Private | Oct. 2, 1847 | Oct. 4, '47 | Louisville, Ky. | | July 25, '48 | Louisville, Ky. |
| 4 | Bell, Thomas A. | Private | Oct. 2, 1847 | Oct. 4, '47 | Louisville, Ky. | | July 25, '48 | Louisville, Ky. |
| 5 | Clark, Leonard W. | Private | Oct. 2, 1847 | Oct. 4, '47 | Louisville, Ky. | | July 25, '48 | Louisville, Ky. |
| 6 | Craig, Joseph M. | Private | Oct. 2, 1847 | Oct. 4, '47 | Louisville, Ky. | | July 25, '48 | Louisville, Ky. |
| 7 | Cabbell, William | Private | Oct. 2, 1847 | Oct. 4, '47 | Louisville, Ky. | To serve during the war. | July 25, '48 | Louisville, Ky. |
| 8 | Campbell, James | Private | Oct. 2, 1847 | Oct. 4, '47 | Louisville, Ky. | | July 25, '48 | Louisville, Ky. |
| 9 | Carson, John | Private | Oct. 2, 1847 | Oct. 4, '47 | Louisville, Ky. | | July 25, '48 | Louisville, Ky. |
| 10 | Cain, Adam | Private | Oct. 2, 1847 | Oct. 4, '47 | Louisville, Ky. | | July 25, '48 | Louisville, Ky. |
| 11 | Craig, James | Private | Oct. 2, 1847 | Oct. 4, '47 | Louisville, Ky. | | July 25, '48 | Louisville, Ky. |
| 12 | Dearing, George H. | Private | Oct. 2, 1847 | Oct. 4, '47 | Louisville, Ky. | | July 25, '48 | Louisville, Ky. |
| 13 | Day, Elisha | Private | Oct. 2, 1847 | Oct. 4, '47 | Louisville, Ky. | | July 25, '48 | Louisville, Ky. |
| 14 | Escue, John | Private | Oct. 2, 1847 | Oct. 4, '47 | Louisville, Ky. | | July 25, '48 | Louisville, Ky. |
| 15 | Edington, William W. | Private | Oct. 2, 1847 | Oct. 4, '47 | Louisville, Ky. | | July 25, '48 | Louisville, Ky. |
| 16 | Earles, William | Private | Oct. 2, 1847 | Oct. 4, '47 | Louisville, Ky. | | July 25, '48 | Louisville, Ky. |
| 17 | East, John | Private | Oct. 2, 1847 | Oct. 4, '47 | Louisville, Ky. | | July 25, '48 | Louisville, Ky. |
| 18 | Fletcher, John C. | Private | Oct. 2, 1847 | Oct. 4, '47 | Louisville, Ky. | | July 25, '48 | Louisville, Ky. |
| 19 | Fletcher, Wm. T. | Private | Oct. 2, 1847 | Oct. 4, '47 | Louisville, Ky. | | July 25, '48 | Louisville, Ky. |
| 20 | Grady, Caleb | Private | Oct. 2, 1847 | Oct. 4, '47 | Louisville, Ky. | | July 25, '48 | Louisville, Ky. |
| 21 | Hardin, Jackson W. | Private | Oct. 2, 1847 | Oct. 4, '47 | Louisville, Ky. | | July 25, '48 | Louisville, Ky. |
| 22 | Hurt, Oliver M. | Private | Oct. 2, 1847 | Oct. 4, '47 | Louisville, Ky. | | July 25, '48 | Louisville, Ky. |
| 23 | Hood, Jesse | Private | Oct. 2, 1847 | Oct. 4, '47 | Louisville, Ky. | | July 25, '48 | Louisville, Ky. |
| 24 | Hedspeth, Wm. | Private | Oct. 2, 1847 | Oct. 4, '47 | Louisville, Ky. | | July 25, '48 | Louisville, Ky. |
| 25 | Harris, Joseph F. | Private | Oct. 2, 1847 | Oct. 4, '47 | Louisville, Ky. | | July 25, '48 | Louisville, Ky. |
| 26 | Heberson, John | Private | Nov. 2, 1847 | Dec. 31, '47 | City of Mexico | | July 25, '48 | Louisville, Ky. |
| 27 | Janes, Wm. D. | Private | Oct. 2, 1847 | Oct. 4, '47 | Louisville, Ky. | | July 25, '48 | Louisville, Ky. |
| 28 | Judd, Andrew J. | Private | Oct. 2, 1847 | Oct. 4, '47 | Louisville, Ky. | | July 25, '48 | Louisville, Ky. |
| 29 | Janes, Greenup | Private | Oct. 2, 1847 | Oct. 4, '47 | Louisville, Ky. | | July 25, '48 | Louisville, Ky. |
| 30 | Montgomery, Frank Z. | Private | Oct. 2, 1847 | Oct. 4, '47 | Louisville, Ky. | | July 25, '48 | Louisville, Ky. |

## FOOT VOLUNTEERS—MEXICAN WAR—Continued.

REMARKS.

| No. of each grade | |
|---|---|
| 3 | Transferred to non-commissioned staff, 4th Kentucky Volunteers, October 9, 1847. |
| 1 | Deserted at Louisville, Ky., October 11, 1847. |
| 2 | Deserted at Louisville, Ky., October 26, 1847. |
| 3 | Deserted at Louisville, Ky., October 26, 1847. |
| 4 | Deserted at Louisville, Ky., October 26, 1847. |
| 5 | Deserted at Louisville, Ky., November 1, 1847. |
| 6 | Deserted at mouth of Mississippi river, November 11, 1847. |
| 7 | Deserted at Louisville, Ky., November 1, 1847. |
| 1 | Accidentally shot at Oho de Auqua, Mexico, December 9, 1847. |
| 2 | Murdered in the city of Mexico by Mexicans, December 22, 1847. |
| 3 | Died at the City of Pueblo, in hospital, January 23, 1848. |
| 4 | Died at the City of Pueblo, in hospital, ———. |
| 5 | Died at the City of Mexico, in hospital, March 21, 1848. |
| 6 | Supposed to have been assassinated on the route from Pueblo to the City of Mexico. |
| 7 | Died in hospital, City of Mexico, April 18, 1848. |
| 8 | Died in hospital, New Orleans, May 10, 1848. |
| 9 | Died in hospital at Jalapa, ———. |
| 10 | Died in hospital at Jalapa, ———. |

## FOOT VOLUNTEERS—MEXICAN WAR.

| | |
|---|---|
| 1 | Died in the City of Mexico, 20th March, 1848.                    [Ky., July 19, 1848; was 1st Lieutenant from enrollment. |
| 2 | Promoted Captain from 1st Lieutenant 21st March, 1848, in place of Capt Squires, died, and from 1st Lieutenant for duty at Louisville, |
| 1 | Promoted 1st Lieutenant from 2d Lieutenant, vice 1st Lieutenant Owens, promoted, 21st March, 1848. |
| 1 | |
| 2 | Promoted from 1st Sergeant, vice second 2d Lieutenant Creel, promoted; was 1st Sergeant from enrollment. |
| 1 | Appointed 1st from 4th Sergeant in place of William E. Russell, promoted, 21st March, 1884. |
| 2 | |
| 3 | |
| 4 | Appointed from Corporal, March 21, 1848, and was Corporal from 15th February, 1848, and private from enrollment. |
| 1 | |
| 2 | Appointed from ranks, 21st March, 1848. |
| 3 | |
| 4 | Appointed from ranks 21st March, 1848. |
| 1 | |
| 2 | |
| 1 | |
| 2 | |
| 3 | |
| 4 | |
| 5 | |
| 6 | |
| 7 | |
| 8 | |
| 9 | |
| 10 | |
| 11 | |
| 12 | |
| 13 | |
| 14 | |
| 15 | |
| 16 | |
| 17 | |
| 18 | |
| 19 | |
| 20 | |
| 21 | |
| 22 | |
| 23 | |
| 24 | |
| 25 | |
| 26 | |
| 27 | |
| 28 | |
| 29 | |
| 30 | |
| 31 | |

## ROLL OF COMPANY "B," FOURTH REGIMENT KENTUCKY

| No. of each grade | Name | Rank | Joined for Service | Mustered in When | Mustered in Where | Period | Mustered Out When | Mustered Out Where |
|---|---|---|---|---|---|---|---|---|
| 31 | Matney, Thomas J. | Private | Oct. 2, 1847 | Oct. 4, '47 | Louisville, Ky. | | July 25, '48 | Louisville, Ky. |
| 32 | Nepp, Wm. | Private | Oct. 2, 1847 | Oct. 4, '47 | Louisville, Ky. | | July 25, '48 | Louisville, Ky. |
| 33 | Payne, Wm. P. | Private | Oct. 2, 1847 | Oct. 4, '47 | Louisville, Ky. | | July 25, '48 | Louisville, Ky. |
| 34 | Powell, Edley | Private | Oct. 2, 1847 | Oct. 4, '47 | Louisville, Ky. | | July 25, '48 | Louisville, Ky. |
| 35 | Powell, Benjamin | Private | Oct. 2, 1847 | Oct. 4, '47 | Louisville, Ky. | | July 25, '48 | Louisville, Ky. |
| 36 | Privett, John H. | Private | Oct. 2, 1847 | Oct. 4, '47 | Louisville, Ky. | | July 25, '48 | Louisville, Ky. |
| 37 | Perkins, Willis | Private | Oct. 2, 1847 | Dec. 31, '47 | City of Mexico | | July 25, '48 | Louisville, Ky. |
| 38 | Preston, Otho | Private | Oct. 2, 1847 | Oct. 4, '47 | Louisville, Ky. | | July 25, '48 | Louisville, Ky. |
| 39 | Rogers, Wm. | Private | Oct. 2, 1847 | Oct. 4, '47 | Louisville, Ky. | | July 25, '48 | Louisville, Ky. |
| 40 | Rucker, Wm. C. | Private | Oct. 2, 1847 | Oct. 4, '47 | Louisville, Ky. | | July 25, '48 | Louisville, Ky. |
| 41 | Ross, Henry | Private | Oct. 2, 1847 | Oct. 4, '47 | Louisville, Ky. | | July 25, '48 | Louisville, Ky. |
| 42 | Robertson, Joseph S. | Private | Oct. 2, 1847 | Oct. 4, '47 | Louisville, Ky. | | July 25, '48 | Louisville, Ky. |
| 43 | Russell, Joseph | Private | Oct. 2, 1847 | Oct. 4, '47 | Louisville, Ky. | | July 25, '48 | Louisville, Ky. |
| 44 | Richardson, Richard B. | Private | Oct. 2, 1847 | Oct. 4, '47 | Louisville, Ky. | | July 25, '48 | Louisville, Ky. |
| 45 | Ross, John | Private | Oct. 2, 1847 | Oct. 4, '47 | Louisville, Ky. | | July 25, '48 | Louisville, Ky. |
| 46 | Simms, Andrew J. | Private | Oct. 2, 1847 | Oct. 4, '47 | Louisville, Ky. | | July 25, '48 | Louisville, Ky. |
| 47 | Sexton, John N. | Private | Oct. 2, 1847 | Oct. 4, '47 | Louisville, Ky. | | July 25, '48 | Louisville, Ky. |
| 48 | Stotts, John | Private | Oct. 2, 1847 | Oct. 4, '47 | Louisville, Ky. | | July 25, '48 | Louisville, Ky. |
| 49 | Stotts, George W. | Private | Oct. 2, 1847 | Oct. 4, '47 | Louisville, Ky. | | July 25, '48 | Louisville, Ky. |
| 50 | Smith, Robert C. | Private | Oct. 2, 1847 | Oct. 4, '47 | Louisville, Ky. | | July 25, '48 | Louisville, Ky. |
| 51 | Stillwell, John | Private | Oct. 2, 1847 | Oct. 4, '47 | Louisville, Ky. | | July 25, '48 | Louisville, Ky. |
| 52 | Smith, John C. | Private | Oct. 2, 1847 | Oct. 4, '47 | Louisville, Ky. | | July 25, '48 | Louisville, Ky. |
| 53 | Smith, Wm. T. | Private | Oct. 2, 1847 | Oct. 4, '47 | Louisville, Ky. | | July 25, '48 | Louisville, Ky. |
| 54 | Sexton, James W. | Private | Oct. 2, 1847 | Oct. 4, '47 | Louisville, Ky. | | July 25, '48 | Louisville, Ky. |
| 55 | Smith, Cyrus | Private | Oct. 2, 1847 | Oct. 4, '47 | Louisville, Ky. | To serve during the war. | July 25, '48 | Louisville, Ky. |
| 56 | Todd, William | Private | Oct. 2, 1847 | Oct. 4, '47 | Louisville, Ky. | | July 25, '48 | Louisville, Ky. |
| 57 | Terrell, James W. | Private | Oct. 2, 1847 | Oct. 4, '47 | Louisville, Ky. | | July 25, '48 | Louisville, Ky. |
| 58 | Vanmetre, William P. | Private | Oct. 2, 1847 | Oct. 4, '47 | Louisville, Ky. | | July 25, '48 | Louisville, Ky. |
| 59 | Vigus, William T. | Private | Oct. 2, 1847 | Oct. 4, '47 | Louisville, Ky. | | July 25, '48 | Louisville, Ky. |
| 60 | Watson, Henry | Private | Oct. 2, 1847 | Oct. 4, '47 | Louisville, Ky. | | July 25, '48 | Louisville, Ky. |
| 61 | Wheat, William | Private | Oct. 2, 1847 | Oct. 4, '47 | Louisville, Ky. | | July 25, '48 | Louisville, Ky. |
| 62 | Ward, Campbell | Private | Oct. 2, 1847 | Oct. 4, '47 | Louisville, Ky. | | July 25, '48 | Louisville, Ky. |
| 63 | Watson, Warren | Private | Oct. 2, 1847 | Oct. 4, '47 | Louisville, Ky. | | July 25, '48 | Louisville, Ky. |
| 64 | Walker, Elzey C. | Private | Oct. 2, 1847 | Oct. 4, '47 | Louisville, Ky. | | July 25, '48 | Louisville, Ky. |
| | **DIED.** | | | | | | | |
| 1 | Absher, Granville A. | Sergeant | Oct. 2, 1847 | Oct. 4, '47 | Louisville, Ky. | | | |
| 2 | Buckner, Harry T. | Private | Oct. 2, 1847 | Oct. 4, '47 | Louisville, Ky. | | | |
| 3 | Barbee, Joseph W. | Private | Oct. 2, 1847 | Oct. 4, '47 | Louisville, Ky. | | | |
| 4 | Burnett, Charles T. | Private | Oct. 2, 1847 | Oct. 4, '47 | Louisville, Ky. | | | |
| 5 | Curry, Robert W. | Private | Oct. 2, 1847 | Oct. 4, '47 | Louisville, Ky. | | | |
| 6 | Judd, George W. | Private | Oct. 2, 1847 | Oct. 4, '47 | Louisville, Ky. | | | |
| 7 | McDonald, William H. | Private | Oct. 2, 1847 | Oct. 4, '47 | Louisville, Ky. | | | |
| 8 | McKamy, Alexander | Private | Oct. 2, 1847 | Oct. 4, '47 | Louisville, Ky. | | | |
| 9 | Montgomery, James B. | Private | Oct. 2, 1847 | Oct. 4, '47 | Louisville, Ky. | | | |
| 10 | Nelson, Joseph C. | Private | Oct. 2, 1847 | Oct. 4, '47 | Louisville, Ky. | | | |
| 11 | Rogers, John W. | Private | Oct. 2, 1847 | Oct. 4, '47 | Louisville, Ky. | | | |
| 12 | Todd, Samuel | Private | Oct. 2, 1847 | Oct. 4, '47 | Louisville, Ky. | | | |
| 13 | McDonald, John C. | Private | Oct. 2, 1847 | Oct. 4, '47 | Louisville, Ky. | | | |
| | **DISCHARGED.** | | | | | | | |
| 1 | Cave, William D. | Private | Oct. 2, 1847 | Oct. 4, '47 | Louisville, Ky. | | | |
| 2 | Childers, William H. | Private | Oct. 2, 1847 | Oct. 4, '47 | Louisville, Ky. | | | |
| 3 | Gilchrist, William | Private | Oct. 2, 1847 | Oct. 4, '47 | Louisville, Ky. | | | |
| 4 | McElroy, Malaki | Private | Oct. 2, 1847 | Oct. 4, '47 | Louisville, Ky. | | | |
| 5 | Janes, Preston B. | Private | Oct. 2, 1847 | Oct. 4, '47 | Louisville, Ky. | | | |
| 6 | Smith, George W. | Private | Oct. 2, 1847 | Oct. 4, '47 | Louisville, Ky. | | | |
| 7 | Skeen, John | Private | Oct. 2, 1847 | Oct. 4, '47 | Louisville, Ky. | | | |

This Company was organized by Capt. John C. Squires, at Columbia, Ky., in the month of September, 1847, and marched thence to Louisville, Ky., where it arrived the 2d day of October, 1847, a distance of one hundred miles.

## ROLL OF COMPANY "C," FOURTH REGIMENT KENTUCKY

| | Name | Rank | Joined for Service | Mustered in When | Mustered in Where | Period | Mustered Out When | Mustered Out Where |
|---|---|---|---|---|---|---|---|---|
| 1 | B. Rowan Hardin | Captain | Oct. 3, 1847 | Oct. 3, '47 | Louisville, Ky. | | July 25, '48 | Louisville, Ky. |
| 1 | Jesse Davis | 1st Lieutenant | Oct. 3, 1847 | Oct. 3, '47 | Louisville, Ky. | | July 25, '48 | Louisville, Ky. |
| 1 | Chas. D. Pennebaker | 2d Lieutenant | Oct. 3, 1847 | Oct. 3, '47 | Louisville, Ky. | During war. | July 25, '48 | Louisville, Ky. |
| 2 | Wm. G. Johnson | 2d Lieutenant | Oct. 3, 1847 | Oct. 3, '47 | Louisville, Ky. | | July 25, '48 | Louisville, Ky. |
| 1 | Preston F. Samuels | 1st Sergeant | Oct. 3, 1847 | Oct. 3, '47 | Louisville, Ky. | | July 25, '48 | Louisville, Ky. |
| 2 | Remus V. Long | 2d Sergeant | Oct. 3, 1847 | Oct. 3, '47 | Louisville, Ky. | | July 25, '48 | Louisville, Ky. |
| 3 | John T. Ballard | 3d Sergeant | Oct. 3, 1847 | Oct. 3, '47 | Louisville, Ky. | | July 25, '48 | Louisville, Ky. |

## FOOT VOLUNTEERS—MEXICAN WAR—Continued.

| No. of each grade | REMARKS |
|---|---|
| 31 | |
| 32 | |
| 33 | |
| 34 | |
| 35 | |
| 36 | |
| 37 | |
| 38 | |
| 39 | |
| 40 | |
| 41 | |
| 42 | |
| 43 | |
| 44 | |
| 45 | |
| 46 | |
| 47 | |
| 48 | |
| 49 | |
| 50 | |
| 51 | |
| 52 | |
| 53 | |
| 54 | |
| 55 | |
| 56 | |
| 57 | |
| 58 | |
| 59 | |
| 60 | |
| 61 | |
| 62 | |
| 63 | |
| 64 | |
| 1 | Died in the City of Mexico, 1st March, 1848. |
| 2 | Died in the City of Vera Cruz, 20th November, 1847. |
| 3 | Died in the City of Mexico, 11th January, 1848. |
| 4 | Died in the City of Vera Cruz, 4th December, 1847. |
| 5 | Died in the City of Vera Cruz, 9th January, 1848. |
| 6 | Died in New Orleans, 12th November, 1847. |
| 7 | Died in the City of Mexico, 20th January, 1848. |
| 8 | Died in the City of Mexico, 8th February, 1848. |
| 9 | Died in the City of Vera Cruz, 14th December, 1847. |
| 10 | Fell overboard from steamer Archer, on route to Louisville, 17th July, 1848. |
| 11 | Died in Jalapa, Mexico, May 22, 1848. |
| 12 | Died in the City of Mexico, 27th February, 1848. |
| 13 | Died at Louisville, Ky., 20th July, 1848. |
| 1 | Discharged from hospital at Louisville. Time unknown. Left in hospital 28th October, 1847. Not heard from since. |
| 2 | Discharged at Plaquemine, La., July, 1848, on passage up the Mississippi river, by expiration of term of service. |
| 3 | Discharged from hospital at Jalapa, Mexico. Time unknown. On Surgeon's certificate of disability. Left in hospital December 5, 1847. |
| 4 | Discharged from hospital at Jalapa, Mexico. Time unknown. On Surgeon's certificate of disability. Left in hospital December 5, 1847. |
| 5 | Discharged at City of Mexico, January 14, 1848; on Surgeon's certificate of disability. |
| 6 | Discharged at City of Mexico, January 28, 1848; on Surgeon's certificate of disability. |
| 7 | Discharged at Jalapa, Mexico. Time unknown. Left in hospital 5th December, 1847; on Surgeon's certificate of disability. |

## FOOT VOLUNTEERS—MEXICAN WAR.

| | |
|---|---|
| 1 | |
| 1 | Detailed on recruiting service. Order of Col. Williams; stationed Bardstown, Ky., since October 29, 1847, and rejoined company at Jalapa, Mexico, June 11, 1848. |
| 1 | Detailed as Regimental Quartermaster and Commissary since March 20, 1848. Order of Col. Williams. |
| 2 | |
| 1 | |
| 2 | |
| 3 | |

## MEXICAN WAR VETERANS.

### ROLL OF COMPANY "C," FOURTH REGIMENT KENTUCKY

| No. of each grade | Name | Rank | Joined for Service | Mustered In When | Mustered In Where | Period | Mustered Out When | Mustered Out Where |
|---|---|---|---|---|---|---|---|---|
| 4 | Hugh J. Dunavan | 4th Sergeant | Oct. 3, 1847 | Oct. 3, '47 | Louisville, Ky. | | July 25, '48 | Louisville, Ky. |
| 1 | William May | Corporal | Oct. 3, 1847 | Oct. 3, '47 | Louisville, Ky. | | July 25, '48 | Louisville, Ky. |
| 2 | Jas. W. Williams | Corporal | Oct. 3, 1847 | Oct. 3, '47 | Louisville, Ky. | | July 25, '48 | Louisville, Ky. |
| 3 | John P. Haynes | Corporal | Oct. 3, 1847 | Oct. 3, '47 | Louisville, Ky. | | July 25, '48 | Louisville, Ky. |
| 4 | Richard Constantine | Corporal | Oct. 3, 1847 | Oct. 3, '47 | Louisville, Ky. | | July 25, '48 | Louisville, Ky. |
| 1 | John Osborne | Musician | Oct. 3, 1847 | Oct. 3, '47 | Louisville, Ky. | | July 25, '48 | Louisville, Ky. |
| 2 | Calvin Winsett | Musician | Oct. 3, 1847 | Oct. 3, '47 | Louisville, Ky. | | July 25, '48 | Louisville, Ky. |
| 1 | Atwood, John V. | Private | Oct. 3, 1847 | Oct. 3, '47 | Louisville, Ky. | | July 25, '48 | Louisville, Ky. |
| 2 | Ash, Levi | Private | Oct. 3, 1847 | Oct. 3, '47 | Louisville, Ky. | | July 25, '48 | Louisville, Ky. |
| 3 | Bissett, Thomas F. | Private | Oct. 3, 1847 | Oct. 3, '47 | Louisville, Ky. | | July 25, '48 | Louisville, Ky. |
| 4 | Ballard, Thomas B. | Private | Oct. 3, 1847 | Oct. 3, '47 | Louisville, Ky. | | July 25, '48 | Louisville, Ky. |
| 5 | Baker, Jacob | Private | Oct. 3, 1847 | Oct. 3, '47 | Louisville, Ky. | | July 25, '48 | Louisville, Ky. |
| 6 | Bailey, Andrew J. | Private | Oct. 3, 1847 | Oct. 3, '47 | Louisville, Ky. | | July 25, '48 | Louisville, Ky. |
| 7 | Bailey, Wm. A. | Private | Oct. 3, 1847 | Oct. 3, '47 | Louisville, Ky. | | July 25, '48 | Louisville, Ky. |
| 8 | Bean, John | Private | Oct. 3, 1847 | Oct. 3, '47 | Louisville, Ky. | | July 25, '48 | Louisville, Ky. |
| 9 | Bethel, Christopher | Private | Oct. 3, 1847 | Oct. 3, '47 | Louisville, Ky. | | July 25, '48 | Louisville, Ky. |
| 10 | Bodine, Charles | Private | Oct. 3, 1847 | Oct. 3, '47 | Louisville, Ky. | | July 25, '48 | Louisville, Ky. |
| 11 | Bond, Marion | Private | Oct. 3, 1847 | Oct. 3, '47 | Louisville, Ky. | | July 25, '48 | Louisville, Ky. |
| 12 | Conner, James C. | Private | Oct. 3, 1847 | Oct. 3, '47 | Louisville, Ky. | | July 25, '48 | Louisville, Ky. |
| 13 | Conner, Franklin | Private | Oct. 3, 1847 | Oct. 3, '47 | Louisville, Ky. | | July 25, '48 | Louisville, Ky. |
| 14 | Cronin, Daniel | Private | Oct. 3, 1847 | Oct. 3, '47 | Louisville, Ky. | | July 25, '48 | Louisville, Ky. |
| 15 | Cravin, George W. | Private | Oct. 3, 1847 | Oct. 3, '47 | Louisville, Ky. | | July 25, '48 | Louisville, Ky. |
| 16 | Campbell, Joseph E. | Private | Oct. 3, 1847 | Oct. 3, '47 | Louisville, Ky. | | July 25, '48 | Louisville, Ky. |
| 17 | Calhoun, Richard | Private | Oct. 3, 1847 | Oct. 3, '47 | Louisville, Ky. | | July 25, '48 | Louisville, Ky. |
| 18 | Calvert, Harrison | Private | Oct. 3, 1847 | Oct. 3, '47 | Louisville, Ky. | | July 25, '48 | Louisville, Ky. |
| 19 | Dewell, George | Private | Oct. 3, 1847 | Oct. 3, '47 | Louisville, Ky. | | July 25, '48 | Louisville, Ky. |
| 20 | Dewell, John | Private | Oct. 3, 1847 | Oct. 3, '47 | Louisville, Ky. | | July 25, '48 | Louisville, Ky. |
| 21 | Duncan, Benjamin | Private | Oct. 3, 1847 | Oct. 3, '47 | Louisville, Ky. | | July 25, '48 | Louisville, Ky. |
| 22 | Duncan, Jepthah | Private | Oct. 3, 1847 | Oct. 3, '47 | Louisville, Ky. | | July 25, '48 | Louisville, Ky. |
| 23 | Davis, Thomas M. | Private | Oct. 3, 1847 | Oct. 3, '47 | Louisville, Ky. | | July 25, '48 | Louisville, Ky. |
| 24 | Duvall, Gabriel | Private | Oct. 3, 1847 | Oct. 3, '47 | Louisville, Ky. | | July 25, '48 | Louisville, Ky. |
| 25 | Dyer, James | Private | Oct. 3, 1847 | Oct. 3, '47 | Louisville, Ky. | To serve during the war. | July 25, '48 | Louisville, Ky. |
| 26 | Dews, Thomas J. | Private | Oct. 3, 1847 | Oct. 3, '47 | Louisville, Ky. | | July 25, '48 | Louisville, Ky. |
| 27 | Dean, Job A. | Private | Oct. 3, 1847 | Oct. 3, '47 | Louisville, Ky. | | July 25, '48 | Louisville, Ky. |
| 28 | Dever, Milton | Private | Oct. 3, 1847 | Oct. 3, '47 | Louisville, Ky. | | July 25, '48 | Louisville, Ky. |
| 29 | Evans, John L. | Private | Oct. 3, 1847 | Oct. 3, '47 | Louisville, Ky. | | July 25, '48 | Louisville, Ky. |
| 30 | Franklin, Benjamin B. | Private | Oct. 3, 1847 | Oct. 3, '47 | Louisville, Ky. | | July 25, '48 | Louisville, Ky. |
| 31 | Flanders, Oliver P. | Private | Oct. 3, 1847 | Oct. 3, '47 | Louisville, Ky. | | July 25, '48 | Louisville, Ky. |
| 32 | Guthrie, David B. | Private | Oct. 3, 1847 | Oct. 3, '47 | Louisville, Ky. | | July 25, '48 | Louisville, Ky. |
| 33 | Graham, Robert A. | Private | Oct. 3, 1847 | Oct. 3, '47 | Louisville, Ky. | | July 25, '48 | Louisville, Ky. |
| 34 | Graham, Joseph | Private | Oct. 3, 1847 | Oct. 3, '47 | Louisville, Ky. | | July 25, '48 | Louisville, Ky. |
| 35 | Haydon, Thomas E. | Private | Oct. 3, 1847 | Oct. 3, '47 | Louisville, Ky. | | July 25, '48 | Louisville, Ky. |
| 36 | Hagan, Charles L. | Private | Oct. 3, 1847 | Oct. 3, '47 | Louisville, Ky. | | July 25, '48 | Louisville, Ky. |
| 37 | Hardisty, David A. | Private | Oct. 3, 1847 | Oct. 3, '47 | Louisville, Ky. | | July 25, '48 | Louisville, Ky. |
| 38 | Hogan, William P. | Private | Oct. 3, 1847 | Oct. 3, '47 | Louisville, Ky. | | July 25, '48 | Louisville, Ky. |
| 39 | Holsclaw, William H. | Private | Oct. 3, 1847 | Oct. 3, '47 | Louisville, Ky. | | July 25, '48 | Louisville, Ky. |
| 40 | Hartley, Hamilton | Private | Oct. 3, 1847 | Oct. 3, '47 | Louisville, Ky. | | July 25, '48 | Louisville, Ky. |
| 41 | Jenkins, Ambrose Y. | Private | Oct. 3, 1847 | Oct. 3, '47 | Louisville, Ky. | | July 25, '48 | Louisville, Ky. |
| 42 | Kelly, William E. | Private | Oct. 3, 1847 | Oct. 3, '47 | Louisville, Ky. | | July 25, '48 | Louisville, Ky. |
| 43 | Lefler, William | Private | Oct. 3, 1847 | Oct. 3, '47 | Louisville, Ky. | | July 25, '48 | Louisville, Ky. |
| 44 | Leake, Gabriel | Private | Oct. 3, 1847 | Oct. 3, '47 | Louisville, Ky. | | July 25, '48 | Louisville, Ky. |
| 45 | Larue, Warren J. | Private | Oct. 3, 1847 | Oct. 3, '47 | Louisville, Ky. | | July 25, '48 | Louisville, Ky. |
| 46 | Love, James M. | Private | Oct. 3, 1847 | Oct. 3, '47 | Louisville, Ky. | | July 25, '48 | Louisville, Ky. |
| 47 | Lane, Monroe | Private | Oct. 3, 1847 | Oct. 3, '47 | Louisville, Ky. | | July 25, '48 | Louisville, Ky. |
| 48 | Murphy, John L. | Private | Oct. 3, 1847 | Oct. 3, '47 | Louisville, Ky. | | July 25, '48 | Louisville, Ky. |
| 49 | Murphy, Bryant Y. | Private | Oct. 3, 1847 | Oct. 3, '47 | Louisville, Ky. | | July 25, '48 | Louisville, Ky. |
| 50 | Marshall, George A. | Private | Oct. 3, 1847 | Oct. 3, '47 | Louisville, Ky. | | July 25, '48 | Louisville, Ky. |
| 51 | Marshall, Franklin | Private | Oct. 3, 1847 | Oct. 3, '47 | Louisville, Ky. | | July 25, '48 | Louisville, Ky. |
| 52 | Marshall, Madison | Private | Oct. 3, 1847 | Oct. 3, '47 | Louisville, Ky. | | July 25, '48 | Louisville, Ky. |
| 53 | Muir, Jasper W. | Private | Oct. 3, 1847 | Oct. 3, '47 | Louisville, Ky. | | July 25, '48 | Louisville, Ky. |
| 54 | Muir, John M. | Private | Oct. 3, 1847 | Oct. 3, '47 | Louisville, Ky. | | July 25, '48 | Louisville, Ky. |
| 55 | Moore, George W. | Private | Oct. 3, 1847 | Oct. 3, '47 | Louisville, Ky. | | July 25, '48 | Louisville, Ky. |
| 56 | Moore, John | Private | Oct. 3, 1847 | Oct. 3, '47 | Louisville, Ky. | | July 25, '48 | Louisville, Ky. |
| 57 | Millan, James | Private | Oct. 3, 1847 | Oct. 3, '47 | Louisville, Ky. | | July 25, '48 | Louisville, Ky. |
| 58 | Miller, John | Private | Oct. 3, 1847 | Oct. 3, '47 | Louisville, Ky. | | July 25, '48 | Louisville, Ky. |
| 59 | Mason, William L. | Private | Oct. 3, 1847 | Oct. 3, '47 | Louisville, Ky. | | July 25, '48 | Louisville, Ky. |
| 60 | Mason, Augustus E. | Private | Oct. 3, 1847 | Oct. 3, '47 | Louisville, Ky. | | July 25, '48 | Louisville, Ky. |
| 61 | McIntire, Benjamin | Private | Oct. 3, 1847 | Oct. 3, '47 | Louisville, Ky. | | July 25, '48 | Louisville, Ky. |
| 62 | Neil, George W. | Private | Oct. 3, 1847 | Oct. 3, '47 | Louisville, Ky. | | July 25, '48 | Louisville, Ky. |
| 63 | Nourse, Charles E. | Private | Oct. 3, 1847 | Oct. 3, '47 | Louisville, Ky. | | July 25, '48 | Louisville, Ky. |
| 64 | Parrott, Moses | Private | Oct. 3, 1847 | Oct. 3, '47 | Louisville, Ky. | | July 25, '48 | Louisville, Ky. |
| 65 | Pottinger, Samuel | Private | Oct. 3, 1847 | Oct. 3, '47 | Louisville, Ky. | | July 25, '48 | Louisville, Ky. |
| 66 | Price, John | Private | Oct. 3, 1847 | Oct. 3, '47 | Louisville, Ky. | | July 25, '48 | Louisville, Ky. |
| 67 | Presnall, Meshack | Private | Oct. 3, 1847 | Oct. 3, '47 | Louisville, Ky. | | July 25, '48 | Louisville, Ky. |
| 68 | Ricketts, Samuel A. | Private | Oct. 3, 1847 | Oct. 3, '47 | Louisville, Ky. | | July 25, '48 | Louisville, Ky. |

## FOOT VOLUNTEERS—MEXICAN WAR—Continued.

| No. of each grade | REMARKS. |
|---|---|
| 4 | Promoted from Corporal, March 20, 1848; was Corporal from enrollment. |
| 1 | |
| 2 | |
| 3 | Promoted from ranks, February 7, 1848. |
| 4 | Promoted from ranks, March 20, 1848. |
| 1 | Promoted from ranks, March 29, 1848. |
| 2 | |
| 1 | |
| 2 | |
| 3 | |
| 4 | |
| 5 | |
| 6 | |
| 7 | |
| 8 | |
| 9 | |
| 10 | |
| 11 | |
| 12 | |
| 13 | |
| 14 | |
| 15 | |
| 16 | |
| 17 | |
| 18 | |
| 19 | |
| 20 | |
| 21 | |
| 22 | Reduced from Musician, March 29, 1848; was Musician from enrollment. |
| 23 | |
| 24 | |
| 25 | |
| 26 | |
| 27 | |
| 28 | |
| 29 | |
| 30 | |
| 31 | |
| 32 | |
| 33 | |
| 34 | |
| 35 | |
| 36 | |
| 37 | |
| 38 | |
| 39 | |
| 40 | |
| 41 | |
| 42 | |
| 43 | |
| 44 | |
| 45 | |
| 46 | |
| 47 | |
| 48 | |
| 49 | |
| 50 | |
| 51 | |
| 52 | |
| 53 | |
| 54 | |
| 55 | |
| 56 | |
| 57 | |
| 58 | |
| 59 | |
| 60 | |
| 61 | |
| 62 | |
| 63 | Reduced from Sergeant 20th March, 1848, and furloughed from 20th March; rejoined Company 21st July, 1848. |
| 64 | |
| 65 | |
| 66 | |
| 67 | |
| 68 | |

126                  MEXICAN WAR VETERANS.

## ROLL OF COMPANY "C," FOURTH REGIMENT KENTUCKY

| No. of each grade | Name | Rank | Joined for Service | Mustered In When | Mustered In Where | Period | Mustered Out When | Mustered Out Where |
|---|---|---|---|---|---|---|---|---|
| 69 | Roby, William O. | Private | Oct. 3, 1847 | Oct. 3, '47 | Louisville, Ky. | | July 25, '48 | Louisville, Ky. |
| 70 | Runner, Samuel H. | Private | Oct. 3, 1847 | Oct. 3, '47 | Louisville, Ky. | | July 25, '48 | Louisville, Ky. |
| 71 | Rachford, Henry | Private | Oct. 3, 1847 | Oct. 3, '47 | Louisville, Ky. | | July 25, '48 | Louisville, Ky. |
| 72 | Roney, John M. | Private | Oct. 3, 1847 | Oct. 3, '47 | Louisville, Ky. | | July 25, '48 | Louisville, Ky. |
| 73 | Rooney, James B. | Private | Oct. 3, 1847 | Oct. 3, '47 | Louisville, Ky. | | July 25, '48 | Louisville, Ky. |
| 74 | Redman, Thomas | Private | Oct. 3, 1847 | Oct. 3, '47 | Louisville, Ky. | | July 25, '48 | Louisville, Ky. |
| 75 | Slaughter, Philip I. | Private | Oct. 3, 1847 | Oct. 3, '47 | Louisville, Ky. | | July 25, '48 | Louisville, Ky. |
| 76 | Soerell, John | Private | Oct. 3, 1847 | Oct. 3, '47 | Louisville, Ky. | | July 25, '48 | Louisville, Ky. |
| 77 | Smith, Stephen D. | Private | Oct. 3, 1847 | Oct. 3, '47 | Louisville, Ky. | | July 25, '48 | Louisville, Ky. |
| 78 | Steuart, Charles | Private | Oct. 3, 1847 | Oct. 3, '47 | Louisville, Ky. | | July 25, '48 | Louisville, Ky. |
| 79 | Stephens, William N. | Private | Oct. 3, 1847 | Oct. 3, '47 | Louisville, Ky. | | July 25, '48 | Louisville, Ky. |
| 80 | Talbott, Lyttleton | Private | Oct. 3, 1847 | Oct. 3, '47 | Louisville, Ky. | | July 25, '48 | Louisville, Ky. |
| 81 | Talbott, John | Private | Oct. 3, 1847 | Oct. 3, '47 | Louisville, Ky. | | July 25, '48 | Louisville, Ky. |
| 82 | Tilford, Robert B. | Private | Oct. 3, 1847 | Oct. 3, '47 | Louisville, Ky. | | July 25, '48 | Louisville, Ky. |
| 83 | Wright, William F. | Private | Oct. 3, 1847 | Oct. 3, '47 | Louisville, Ky. | | July 25, '48 | Louisville, Ky. |
| 84 | Wright, William | Private | Oct. 3, 1847 | Oct. 3, '47 | Louisville, Ky. | To serve during war | July 25, '48 | Louisville, Ky. |
| 85 | Willett, Robert A. | Private | Oct. 3, 1847 | Oct. 3, '47 | Louisville, Ky. | | July 25, '48 | Louisvil'e, Ky. |
| 86 | Weller, David R. | Private | Oct. 3, 1847 | Oct. 3, '47 | Louisville, Ky. | | July 25, '48 | Louisville, Ky. |
| 87 | Ward, Legran R. | Private | Oct. 3, 1847 | Oct. 3, '47 | Louisville, Ky. | | July 25, '48 | Louisville, Ky. |
| | **DISCHARGED.** | | | | | | | |
| 1 | Hagan, Joseph F. | Private | Oct. 3, 1847 | Oct. 3, '47 | Louisville, Ky. | | | |
| 2 | Marshal, George W. | Private | Oct. 3, 1847 | Oct. 3, '47 | Louisville, Ky. | | | |
| 3 | Millan, Alexander | Private | Oct. 3, 1847 | Oct. 3, '47 | Louisville, Ky. | | | |
| 4 | Hoffman, John | Private | Oct. 3, 1847 | Oct. 3, '47 | Louisville, Ky. | | | |
| 5 | Cooper, William H. | Private | Oct. 3, 1847 | Oct. 3, '47 | Louisville, Ky. | | | |
| | **DIED.** | | | | | | | |
| 1 | Davis, Newton | Corporal | Oct. 3, 1847 | Oct. 3, '47 | Louisville, Ky. | | | |
| 2 | Hardy, William D. | Private | Oct. 3, 1847 | Oct. 3, '47 | Louisville, Ky. | | | |
| 3 | Hopewell, Erasmus | Private | Oct. 3, 1847 | Oct. 3, '47 | Louisville, Ky. | | | |
| 4 | Shanklin, John B. | Private | Oct. 3, 1847 | Oct. 3, '47 | Louisville, Ky. | | | |
| 5 | Seifers, James | Private | Oct. 3, 1847 | Oct. 3, '47 | Louisville, Ky. | | | |
| 6 | Mason, Anderson G. | Private | Oct. 3, 1847 | Oct. 3, '47 | Louisville, Ky. | | | |
| 7 | Slaughter, Edwin R. | Private | Oct. 3, 1847 | Oct. 3, '47 | Louisville, Ky. | | | |
| 8 | Duncan, John B. | Private | Oct. 3, 1847 | Oct. 3, '47 | Louisville, Ky. | | | |
| 9 | Hogland, John | Private | Oct. 3, 1847 | Oct. 3, '47 | Louisville, Ky. | | | |
| 10 | Bond, William | Private | Oct. 3, 1847 | Oct. 3, '47 | Louisville, Ky. | | | |
| 11 | Davis, George W. | Private | Oct. 3, 1847 | Oct. 3, '47 | Louisville, Ky. | | | |
| 12 | Huffman, William | Private | Oct. 3, 1847 | Oct. 3, '47 | Louisville, Ky. | | | |
| 13 | Murray, Daniel | Private | Oct. 3, 1847 | Oct. 3, '47 | Louisville, Ky. | | | |

This Company was organized by Captain B. Rowan Hardin, at Bardstown, Ky., in the month of September, 1847, and marched thence to Louisville, Ky., where it arrived on the 3d of October, 1847, a distance of forty miles.

## ROLL OF COMPANY "D," FOURTH REGIMENT KENTUCKY

| | Name | Rank | Joined for Service | Mustered In When | Mustered In Where | Period | Mustered Out When | Mustered Out Where |
|---|---|---|---|---|---|---|---|---|
| 1 | Anthony W. Bartlett | Captain | Oct. 2, 1847 | Oct. 2, '47 | Louisville, Ky. | | July 25, '48 | Louisville, Ky. |
| 1 | John W. Hughes | 1st Lieutenant | Oct. 2, 1847 | Oct. 2, '47 | Louisville, Ky. | | July 25, '48 | Louisville, Ky. |
| 1 | Titus P. A. Bibb | 2d Lieutenant | Oct. 2, 1847 | Oct. 2, '47 | Louisville, Ky. | | July 25, '48 | Louisville, Ky. |
| 2 | Christopher C. Robbins | 2d 2d Lieut. | Oct. 2, 1847 | Oct. 2, '47 | Louisville, Ky. | | July 25, '48 | Louisville, Ky. |
| 3 | Noah Z. Chapline | 2d 2d Lieut. | Oct. 2, 1847 | Oct. 2, '47 | Louisville, Ky. | | July 25, '48 | Louisville, Ky. |
| 1 | William H. Kalfus | 1st Sergeant | Oct. 2, 1847 | Oct. 2, '47 | Louisville, Ky. | | July 25, '48 | Louisville, Ky. |
| 2 | John B. Ellis | 2d Sergeant | Oct. 2, 1847 | Oct. 2, '47 | Louisville, Ky. | To serve during the war | July 25, '48 | Louisville, Ky. |
| 3 | Joseph Whiteley | 3d Sergeant | Oct. 2, 1847 | Oct. 2, '47 | Louisville, Ky. | | July 25, '48 | Louisville, Ky. |
| 4 | Thomas C. Ireland | 4th Sergeant | Oct. 2, 1847 | Oct. 2, '47 | Louisville, Ky. | | July 25, '48 | Louisville, Ky. |
| 1 | Jefferson Toombs | 1st Corporal | Oct. 2, 1847 | Oct. 2, '47 | Louisville, Ky. | | July 25, '48 | Louisville, Ky. |
| 2 | Samuel P. Duncan | 2d Corporal | Oct. 2, 1847 | Oct. 2, '47 | Louisville, Ky. | | July 25, '48 | Louisville, Ky. |
| 3 | John M. Floyd | 3d Corporal | Oct. 2, 1847 | Oct. 2, '47 | Louisville, Ky. | | July 25, '48 | Louisville, Ky. |
| 4 | Milton Adams | 4th Corporal | Oct. 2, 1847 | Oct. 2, '47 | Louisville, Ky. | | July 25, '48 | Louisville, Ky. |
| 1 | Newton Foote | Musician | Oct. 2, 1847 | Oct. 2, '47 | Louisville, Ky. | | July 25, '48 | Louisville, Ky. |
| 2 | James E. Sudduth | Musician | Oct. 2, 1847 | Oct. 2, '47 | Louisville, Ky. | | July 25, '48 | Louisville, Ky. |
| 1 | Adams, Henry | Private | Oct. 2, 1847 | Oct. 2, '47 | Louisville, Ky. | | July 25, '48 | Louisville, Ky. |
| 2 | Adams, Preston | Private | Oct. 2, 1847 | Oct. 2, '47 | Louisville, Ky. | | July 25, '48 | Louisville, Ky. |
| 3 | Barnes, Nathan | Private | Oct. 2, 1847 | Oct. 2, '47 | Louisville, Ky. | | July 25, '48 | Louisville, Ky. |
| 4 | Bricknell, Chris. V. | Private | Oct. 2, 1847 | Oct. 2, '47 | Louisville, Ky. | | July 25, '48 | Louisville, Ky. |
| 5 | Bailey, Barnet E. | Private | Oct. 2, 1847 | Oct. 2, '47 | Louisville, Ky. | | July 25, '48 | Louisville, Ky. |
| 6 | Buchannan, Ferd'nd A. | Private | Oct. 2, 1847 | Oct. 2, '47 | Louisville, Ky. | | July 25, '48 | Louisville, Ky. |
| 7 | Bightol, Joshua | Private | Oct. 2, 1847 | Oct. 2, '47 | Louisville, Ky. | | July 25, '48 | Louisville, Ky. |
| 8 | Chowning, Thomas S. | Private | Oct. 2, 1847 | Oct. 2, '47 | Louisville, Ky. | | July 25, '48 | Louisville, Ky. |
| 9 | Conn, William | Private | Oct. 2, 1847 | Oct. 2, '47 | Louisville, Ky. | | July 25, '48 | Louisville, Ky. |

## FOOT VOLUNTEERS—MEXICAN WAR—Continued.

| No. of each grade | REMARKS |
|---|---|
| 69 | |
| 70 | |
| 71 | |
| 72 | |
| 73 | |
| 74 | |
| 75 | |
| 76 | |
| 77 | |
| 78 | |
| 79 | |
| 80 | |
| 81 | |
| 82 | |
| 83 | |
| 84 | |
| 85 | |
| 86 | |
| 87 | |
| 1 | Discharged on Surgeon's certificate of disability, at City of Mexico. Order of Major-General Butler, February 21, 1848. |
| 2 | Discharged on Surgeon's certificate of disability, at Vera Cruz, January 24, 1848. |
| 3 | Discharged on Surgeon's certificate of disability, at Vera Cruz, February 29, 1848. |
| 4 | Discharged on Surgeon's certificate of disability, February 24, 1848. |
| 5 | Discharged on Surgeon's certificate of disability, at New Orleans, 10th July, 1848. |
| 1 | Died in hospital, City of Mexico, February 7, 1848. |
| 2 | Died in hospital, City of Mexico, January 24, 1848. |
| 3 | Died in hospital, City of Mexico, February 11, 1848. |
| 4 | Died in hospital, Pueblo, 24th December, 1847. |
| 5 | Died in hospital, Pueblo, 25th January, 1848. |
| 6 | Died in hospital, New Orleans, November 25, 1847. |
| 7 | Died in hospital, New Orleans, December 2, 1847. |
| 8 | Died in hospital, Pueblo, date unknown; Surgeon failed to send certificate of death. |
| 9 | Died in hospital, Pueblo, February 1, 1848. |
| 10 | Died in hospital, City of Mexico, March 9, 1848. |
| 11 | Died in hospital, City of Mexico, April 8, 1848. |
| 12 | Died in hospital, City of Mexico, April 23, 1848. |
| 13 | Died in hospital, City of Mexico, May 28, 1848. |

## FOOT VOLUNTEERS—MEXICAN WAR.

| | |
|---|---|
| 1 | |
| 1 | |
| 1 | |
| 2 | Resigned May 1, 1848; was 2d Lieutenant from enrollment. |
| 3 | Promoted from 1st Sergeant, May 1, 1848; was 1st Sergeant from enrollment. |
| 1 | Promoted from May 1, 1848; was 2d Sergeant from enrollment. |
| 2 | Promoted from private to Sergeant, December 20, 1847. |
| 3 | Promoted from private to Sergeant, March 1, 1848. |
| 4 | Promoted from private to Sergeant, May 1, 1848. |
| 1 | |
| 2 | Promoted from private to Corporal, November 22, 1847. |
| 3 | |
| 4 | |
| 1 | Promoted from private, March 1, 1848. |
| 2 | |
| 1 | |
| 2 | |
| 3 | |
| 4 | |
| 5 | |
| 6 | |
| 7 | Killed or taken prisoner at Encerro, by Mexicans, with his gun and accoutrements. |
| 8 | |
| 9 | |

## MEXICAN WAR VETERANS.

### ROLL OF COMPANY "D," FOURTH REGIMENT KENTUCKY

| No. of each grade | Name. | Rank. | Joined for Service. | Mustered In. When. | Mustered In. Where. | Period | Mustered Out. When. | Mustered Out. Where. |
|---|---|---|---|---|---|---|---|---|
| 10 | Coleman, Jesse L. | Private | Oct. 2, 1847 | Oct. 2, '47 | Louisville, Ky. | | July 25, '48 | Louisville, Ky. |
| 11 | Caplinger, Paul | Private | Oct. 2, 1847 | Oct. 2, '47 | Louisville, Ky. | | July 25, '48 | Louisville, Ky. |
| 12 | Duggins, Daniel | Private | Oct. 2, 1847 | Oct. 2, '47 | Louisville, Ky. | | July 25, '48 | Louisville, Ky. |
| 13 | Ellis, Richard B. | Private | Oct. 2, 1847 | Oct. 2, '47 | Louisville, Ky. | | July 25, '48 | Louisville, Ky. |
| 14 | Fitzgerald, Smith | Private | Oct. 2, 1847 | Oct. 2, '47 | Louisville, Ky. | | July 25, '48 | Louisville, Ky. |
| 15 | Ford, James W. | Private | Oct. 2, 1847 | Oct. 2, '47 | Louisville, Ky. | | July 25, '48 | Louisville, Ky. |
| 16 | Ford, John P. | Private | Oct. 2, 1847 | Oct. 2, '47 | Louisville, Ky. | | July 25, '48 | Louisville, Ky. |
| 17 | Gibson, Achilles K. | Private | Oct. 2, 1847 | Oct. 2, '47 | Louisville, Ky. | | July 25, '48 | Louisville, Ky. |
| 18 | Grady, James M. | Private | Oct. 2, 1847 | Oct. 2, '47 | Louisville, Ky. | | July 25, '48 | Louisville, Ky. |
| 19 | Green, Hugh J. | Private | Oct. 2, 1847 | Oct. 2, '47 | Louisville, Ky. | | July 25, '48 | Louisville, Ky. |
| 20 | Harlow, Nathaniel | Private | Oct. 2, 1847 | Oct. 2, '47 | Louisville, Ky. | | July 25, '48 | Louisville, Ky. |
| 21 | Henderson, Andrew J. | Private | Oct. 2, 1847 | Oct. 2, '47 | Louisville, Ky. | | July 25, '48 | Louisville, Ky. |
| 22 | Ireland, Thomas S. | Private | Oct. 2, 1847 | Oct. 2, '47 | Louisville, Ky. | | July 25, '48 | Louisville, Ky. |
| 23 | Jones, Griffith | Private | Oct. 2, 1847 | Oct. 2, '47 | Louisville, Ky. | | July 25, '48 | Louisville, Ky. |
| 24 | King, William P. | Private | Oct. 2, 1847 | Oct. 2, '47 | Louisville, Ky. | | July 25, '48 | Louisville, Ky. |
| 25 | Keynon, William M. | Private | Oct. 2, 1847 | Oct. 2, '47 | Louisville, Ky. | | July 25, '48 | Louisville, Ky. |
| 26 | Kelley, George M. | Private | Oct. 25, 1847 | Dec. 31, '47 | City of Mexico | | July 25, '48 | Louisville, Ky. |
| 27 | Law, John | Private | Oct. 2, 1847 | Oct. 2, '47 | Louisville, Ky. | | July 25, '48 | Louisville, Ky. |
| 28 | Lamaster, Thomas | Private | Oct. 2, 1847 | Oct. 2, '47 | Louisville, Ky. | | July 25, '48 | Louisville, Ky. |
| 29 | Matlock, John | Private | Oct. 2, 1847 | Oct. 2, '47 | Louisville, Ky. | | July 25, '48 | Louisville, Ky. |
| 30 | Milner, Lafayette | Private | Oct. 2, 1847 | Oct. 2, '47 | Louisville, Ky. | | July 25, '48 | Louisville, Ky. |
| 31 | Mobley, Allen | Private | Oct. 2, 1847 | Oct. 2, '47 | Louisville, Ky. | | July 25, '48 | Louisville, Ky. |
| 32 | Mullen, Harry | Private | Oct. 2, 1847 | Oct. 2, '47 | Louisville, Ky. | | July 25, '48 | Louisville, Ky. |
| 33 | Marshall, William | Private | Oct. 2, 1847 | Oct. 2, '47 | Louisville, Ky. | | July 25, '48 | Louisville, Ky. |
| 34 | Norvell, Leonard S. | Private | Oct. 2, 1847 | Oct. 2, '47 | Louisville, Ky. | | July 25, '48 | Louisville, Ky. |
| 35 | Perkins, Pleasant | Private | Oct. 2, 1847 | Oct. 2, '47 | Louisville, Ky. | | July 25, '48 | Louisville, Ky. |
| 36 | Pierse, William W. | Private | Oct. 2, 1847 | Oct. 2, '47 | Louisville, Ky. | | July 25, '48 | Louisville, Ky. |
| 37 | Price, John C. | Private | Oct. 2 1847 | Oct. 2, '47 | Louisville, Ky. | | July 25, '48 | Louisville, Ky. |
| 38 | Rose, John W. | Private | Oct. 2, 1847 | Oct. 2, '47 | Louisville, Ky. | | July 25, '48 | Louisville, Ky. |
| 39 | Robertson, William | Private | Oct. 2, 1847 | Oct. 2, '47 | Louisville, Ky. | | July 25, '48 | Louisville, Ky. |
| 40 | Roberts, William G. | Private | Oct. 2, 1847 | Oct. 2, '47 | Louisville, Ky. | | July 25, '48 | Louisville, Ky. |
| 41 | Ronner, Greenbury | Private | Oct. 2, 1847 | Oct. 2, '47 | Louisville, Ky. | To serve during the war. | July 25, '48 | Louisville, Ky. |
| 42 | Smith, John L. | Private | Oct. 2, 1847 | Oct. 2, '47 | Louisville, Ky. | | July 25, '48 | Louisville, Ky. |
| 43 | Sale, Elijah D. | Private | Oct. 2, 1847 | Oct. 2, '47 | Louisville, Ky. | | July 25, '48 | Louisville, Ky. |
| 44 | Shuck, David | Private | Oct. 2, 1847 | Oct. 2, '47 | Louisville, Ky. | | July 25, '48 | Lou'sville, Ky. |
| 45 | Stewart, Enoch | Private | Oct. 2, 1847 | Oct. 2, '47 | Louisville, Ky. | | July 25, '48 | Louisville, Ky. |
| 46 | Stewart, John | Private | Oct. 2, 1847 | Oct. 2, '47 | Louisville, Ky. | | July 25, '48 | Louisville, Ky. |
| 47 | Sanders, James | Private | Oct. 2, 1847 | Oct. 2, '47 | Louisville, Ky. | | July 25, '48 | Louisville, Ky. |
| 48 | Satterwhite, William M. | Private | Oct. 2, 1847 | Oct. 2, '47 | Louisville, Ky. | | July 25, '48 | Louisville, Ky. |
| 49 | Tagan, Joseph | Private | Oct. 2, 1847 | Oct. 2, '47 | Louisville, Ky. | | July 25, '48 | Louisville, Ky. |
| 50 | Winbourne, Andrew J. | Private | Oct. 2, 1847 | Oct. 2, '47 | Louisville, Ky. | | July 25, '48 | Louisville, Ky. |
| 51 | Whiteley, Burr H. | Private | Oct. 2, 1847 | Oct. 2, '47 | Louisville, Ky. | | July 25, '48 | Louisville, Ky. |
| 52 | Wilson, Harrison | Private | Oct. 2, 1847 | Oct. 2, '47 | Louisville, Ky. | | July 25, '48 | Louisville, Ky. |
| 53 | Wright, Robert | Private | Oct. 2 1847 | Oct. 2, '47 | Louisville, Ky. | | July 25, '48 | Louisville, Ky. |
| 54 | Williams, John W. | Private | Oct. 2, 1847 | Oct. 2, '47 | Louisville, Ky. | | July 25, '48 | Louisville, Ky. |
| 55 | Shonty, Greenberry | Private | Oct. 2, 1847 | Oct. 2, '47 | Louisville, Ky. | | July 25, '48 | Louisville, Ky. |
| 56 | Charles M. Norris | Private | Oct. 2 1847 | Oct. 2, '47 | Louisville, Ky. | | July 25, '48 | Louisville, Ky. |
| 57 | Estice, William | Private | Oct. 2, 1847 | Oct 2, '47 | Louisville, Ky. | | July 25, '48 | Louisville, Ky. |
| | **Discharged** | | | | | | | |
| 1 | Lewis F. Montague | 4th Sergeant | Oct. 2, 1847 | Oct. 2, '47 | Louisville, Ky. | | | |
| 2 | Robert Caplinger | Private | Oct. 2, 1847 | Oct. 2, '47 | Louisville, Ky. | | | |
| 3 | Elijah Miller | Private | Oct. 2, 1847 | Oct. 2, '47 | Louisville, Ky. | | | |
| 4 | Falconer James | Private | Oct. 2, 1847 | Oct. 2, '47 | Louisville, Ky. | | | |
| 5 | James L. Ronner | Private | Oct. 2, 1847 | Oct. 2, '47 | Louisville, Ky. | | | |
| 6 | Freeborn Olmstead | Private | Oct. 2, 1847 | Oct. 2, '47 | Louisville, Ky. | | | |
| 7 | John Parks | Private | Oct. 2, 1847 | Oct. 2, '47 | Louisville, Ky. | | | |
| 8 | Granville Ward | Private | Oct. 2, 1847 | Oct. 2, '47 | Louisville, Ky. | | | |
| | **Died.** | | | | | | | |
| 1 | Arnold, Jackson | Private | Oct. 2, 1847 | Oct. 2, '47 | Louisville, Ky. | | | |
| 2 | Calbert, Logan | Private | Oct. 2, 1847 | Oct. 2, '47 | Louisville, Ky. | | | |
| 3 | Forquer, James | Private | Oct. 2, 1847 | Oct. 2, '47 | Louisville, Ky. | | | |
| 4 | Logan, Oscar D. | Private | Oct. 2, 1847 | Oct. 2, '47 | Louisville, Ky. | | | |
| 5 | Naylor, Simeon | Private | Oct. 2, 1847 | Oct. 2, '47 | Louisville, Ky. | | | |
| 6 | Stilwell, John | Private | Oct. 2, 1847 | Oct. 2, '47 | Louisville, Ky. | | | |
| 7 | Smith, Albert G. | Private | Oct. 2, 1847 | Oct. 2, '47 | Louisville, Ky. | | | |
| 8 | Sullinger, James | Private | Oct. 2, 1847 | Oct. 2, '47 | Louisville, Ky. | | | |
| 9 | Ashburn, William H. | Private | Oct. 2, 1847 | Oct. 2, '47 | Louisville, Ky. | | | |
| 10 | Bicknel, Bolin G. | Private | Oct. 2, 1847 | Oct. 2, '47 | Louisville, Ky. | | | |
| 11 | Hitt, James K. | Private | Oct. 2, 1847 | Oct. 2, '47 | Louisville, Ky. | | | |
| 12 | Green, Doctor F. | Private | Oct. 2, 1847 | Oct. 2, '47 | Louisville, Ky. | | | |
| 13 | Harlon, Giles | Private | Oct. 2, 1847 | Oct. 2, '47 | Louisville, Ky. | | | |
| 14 | Mitchell, Andrew J. | Private | Oct. 2 1847 | Oct. 2, '47 | Louisville, Ky. | | | |
| 15 | Penn, Nimrod | Private | Oct. 2, 1847 | Oct. 2, '47 | Louisville, Ky. | | | |

## FOOT VOLUNTEERS—MEXICAN WAR—Continued.

| No. of each grade | REMARKS. |
|---|---|
| 10 | |
| 11 | |
| 12 | |
| 13 | On extra daily duty as Commissary Sergeant, from October 21, 1847. |
| 14 | |
| 15 | |
| 16 | |
| 17 | |
| 18 | |
| 19 | |
| 20 | |
| 21 | |
| 22 | |
| 23 | |
| 24 | |
| 25 | |
| 26 | |
| 27 | |
| 28 | |
| 29 | |
| 30 | |
| 31 | |
| 32 | |
| 33 | |
| 34 | Was Sergeant to the 20th of December, 1847. |
| 35 | |
| 36 | |
| 37 | |
| 38 | |
| 39 | |
| 40 | |
| 41 | |
| 42 | |
| 43 | |
| 44 | |
| 45 | |
| 46 | |
| 47 | |
| 48 | |
| 49 | |
| 50 | |
| 51 | |
| 52 | |
| 53 | |
| 54 | |
| 55 | Left sick at Louisville, November 1, 1847; not heard from since. |
| 56 | Joined at Jalapa, from Recruiting Depot, January 15, 1848. |
| 57 | |
| | |
| 1 | Discharged from hospital, New Orleans, date unknown. |
| 2 | Discharged from hospital at Vera Cruz, date unknown. |
| 3 | Discharged at New Orleans, July 8, 1848. Order of Commanding-General Butler. |
| 4 | Discharged from hospital, City of Mexico, March 4, 1848; Surgeon's certificate of disability. |
| 5 | Discharged from hospital, City of Mexico, March 4, 1848; Surgeon's certificate of disability. |
| 6 | Discharged from hospital, Jalapa, date unknown; Surgeon's certificate of disability. |
| 7 | Discharged from hospital, Vera Cruz, March 28, 1848; Surgeon's certificate of disability. |
| 8 | Discharged from hospital, New Orleans, March 16, 1848; Surgeon's certificate of disability. |
| | |
| 1 | Died in hospital at Pueblo, date unknown. |
| 2 | Died in hospital, City of Mexico, May 3, 1848. |
| 3 | Died at Encerro, in camp, June 13, 1848. |
| 4 | Died at Jalapa, in hospital, date unknown. |
| 5 | Died in hospital, City of Mexico, of ordinary sickness. |
| 6 | Died in hospital, Pueblo, date unknown. |
| 7 | Drowned at New Orleans, July 5, 1848. |
| 8 | Died in hospital, Pueblo, date unknown. |
| 9 | Died in hospital, City of Mexico, March 24, 1848. |
| 10 | Died in quarters, City of Mexico, February 21, 1848. |
| 11 | Died at Vera Cruz, November 21, 1847; Corporal from enrollment to November 21, 1847. |
| 12 | Died at City of Mexico, in hospital, April 15, 1848. |
| 13 | Died at City of Mexico, January 3, 1848. |
| 14 | Died at City of Mexico, March 4, 1848. |
| 15 | Died at City of Mexico, March 13, 1848. |

## MEXICAN WAR VETERANS.

### ROLL OF COMPANY "D," FOURTH REGIMENT KENTUCKY

| No. of each grade | Name. | Rank. | Joined for Service. | Mustered In. When. | Mustered In. Where. | Period. | Mustered Out. When. | Mustered Out. Where. |
|---|---|---|---|---|---|---|---|---|
| 16 | Robbins, David D. | Private | Oct. 2, 1847 | Oct. 2, '47 | Louisville, Ky. | During the war. | | |
| 17 | Trout, Daniel B. | Private | Oct. 2, 1847 | Oct. 2, '47 | Louisville, Ky. | | | |
|  | TRANSFERRED. | | | | | | | |
| 1 | Charles Storts | Private | Oct. 2, 1847 | Oct. 2, '47 | Louisville, Ky. | | | |
| 2 | Charles W. Ball | Private | Oct. 2, 1847 | Oct. 2, '47 | Louisville, Ky. | | | |
| 3 | Charles Wise | Private | Oct. 2, 1847 | Oct. 2, '47 | Louisville, Ky. | | | |

This Company was organized by Captain Anthony W. Bartlett, at Bedford, Trimble county, Ky., in the month of September, 1847, and marched thence to Louisville, Ky., where it arrived on the 2d day of October, 1847, a distance of fifty miles.

### ROLL OF COMPANY "E," FOURTH REGIMENT KENTUCKY

| No. | Name. | Rank. | Joined for Service. | Mustered In When. | Mustered In Where. | Period | Mustered Out When. | Mustered Out Where. |
|---|---|---|---|---|---|---|---|---|
| 1 | George B. Cook | Captain | Oct. 4, 1847 | Oct. 4, '47 | Smithland, Ky. | To serve during the war. | July 25, '48 | Louisville, Ky. |
| 1 | Edgar D. Barbour | 1st Lieutenant | Oct. 4, 1847 | Oct. 4, '47 | Smithland, Ky. | | July 25, '48 | Louisville, Ky. |
| 1 | John W. Snyder | 2d Lieutenant | Oct. 4, 1847 | Oct. 4, '47 | Smithland, Ky. | | July 25, '48 | Louisville, Ky. |
| 2 | Benjamin F. Egan | 2d Lieutenant | Oct. 4, 1847 | Oct. 4, '47 | Smithland, Ky. | | July 25, '48 | Louisville, Ky. |
| 1 | Frederick C. Stump | 1st Sergeant | Oct. 4, 1847 | Oct. 4, '47 | Smithland, Ky. | | July 25, '48 | Louisville, Ky. |
| 2 | John W. Bowen | Sergeant | Oct. 4, 1847 | Oct. 4, '47 | Smithland, Ky. | | July 25, '48 | Louisville, Ky. |
| 3 | James Phelps | Sergeant | Oct. 4, 1847 | Oct. 4, '47 | Smithland, Ky. | | July 25, '48 | Louisville, Ky. |
| 4 | Francis M. Procter | Sergeant | Oct. 4, 1847 | Oct. 4, '47 | Smithland, Ky. | | July 25, '48 | Louisville, Ky. |
| 1 | John P. Roberts | Corporal | Oct. 4, 1847 | Oct. 4, '47 | Smithland, Ky. | | July 25, '48 | Louisville, Ky. |
| 2 | William A. Swails | Corporal | Oct. 4, 1847 | Oct. 4, '47 | Smithland, Ky. | | July 25, '48 | Louisville, Ky. |
| 3 | Henry E. Ford | Corporal | Oct. 4, 1847 | Oct. 4, '47 | Smithland, Ky. | | July 25, '48 | Louisville, Ky. |
| 4 | Owen McGinnis | Corporal | Oct. 4, 1847 | Oct. 4, '47 | Smithland, Ky. | | July 25, '48 | Louisville, Ky. |
| 1 | James Thomas | Musician | Oct. 4, 1847 | Oct. 4, '47 | Smithland, Ky. | | July 25, '48 | Louisville, Ky. |
| 2 | James P. Roach | Musician | Oct. 4, 1847 | Oct. 4, '47 | Smithland, Ky. | | July 25, '48 | Louisville, Ky. |
| 1 | Akinson, Appleton | Private | Oct. 4, 1847 | Oct. 4, '47 | Smithland, Ky. | | July 25, '48 | Louisville, Ky. |
| 2 | Bishop, Joseph | Private | Oct. 4, 1847 | Oct. 4, '47 | Smithland, Ky. | | July 25, '48 | Louisville, Ky. |
| 3 | Berry, Simon | Private | Oct. 4, 1847 | Oct. 4, '47 | Smithland, Ky. | | July 25, '48 | Louisville, Ky. |
| 4 | Brinsfield, Littleberry G. | Private | Oct. 4, 1847 | Oct. 4, '47 | Smithland, Ky. | | July 25, '48 | Louisville, Ky. |
| 5 | Bohanan, George | Private | Oct. 4, 1847 | Oct. 4, '47 | Smithland, Ky. | | July 25, '48 | Louisville, Ky. |
| 6 | Bohanan, James W. | Private | Oct. 4, 1847 | Oct. 4, '47 | Smithland, Ky. | | July 25, '48 | Louisville, Ky. |
| 7 | Bohanan, Jefferson | Private | Oct. 4, 1847 | Oct. 4, '47 | Smithland, Ky. | | July 25, '48 | Louisville, Ky. |
| 8 | Bohanan, Nathan | Private | Oct. 4, 1847 | Oct. 4, '47 | Smithland, Ky. | | July 25, '48 | Louisville, Ky. |
| 9 | Boyd, George G. | Private | Oct. 4, 1847 | Oct. 4, '47 | Smithland, Ky. | | July 25, '48 | Louisville, Ky. |
| 10 | Barnett, Lee | Private | Oct. 4, 1847 | Oct. 4, '47 | Smithland, Ky. | | July 25, '48 | Louisville, Ky. |
| 11 | Buil, Archibald | Private | Oct. 4, 1847 | Oct. 4, '47 | Smithland, Ky. | | July 25, '48 | Louisville, Ky. |
| 12 | Brown, William S. | Private | Oct. 4, 1847 | Oct. 4, '47 | Smithland, Ky. | | July 25, '48 | Louisville, Ky. |
| 13 | Baty, James | Private | Nov. 26, 1847 | Feb. 19, '48 | Newport Bks. | | July 25, '48 | Louisville, Ky. |
| 14 | Champion, Henry | Private | Oct. 4, 1847 | Oct. 4, '47 | Smithland, Ky. | | July 25, '48 | Louisville, Ky. |
| 15 | Carrack, Thomas | Private | Oct. 4, 1847 | Oct. 4, '47 | Smithland, Ky. | | July 25, '48 | Louisville, Ky. |
| 16 | Conley, Neil | Private | Oct. 4, 1847 | Oct. 4, '47 | Smithland, Ky. | | July 25, '48 | Louisville, Ky. |
| 17 | Curtis, Alexander | Private | Oct. 4, 1847 | Oct. 4, '47 | Smithland, Ky. | | July 25, '48 | Louisville, Ky. |
| 18 | Carter, George C. | Private | Oct. 4, 1847 | Oct. 4, '47 | Smithland, Ky. | | July 25, '48 | Louisville, Ky. |
| 19 | Ezell, William M. | Private | Oct. 4, 1847 | Oct. 4, '47 | Smithland, Ky. | | July 25, '48 | Louisville, Ky. |
| 20 | Fogg, James B. | Private | Oct. 4, 1847 | Oct. 4, '47 | Smithland, Ky. | | July 25, '48 | Louisville, Ky. |
| 21 | Fatrell, Wiley | Private | Oct. 4, 1847 | Oct. 4, '47 | Smithland, Ky. | | July 25, '48 | Louisville, Ky. |
| 22 | Gill, Richard | Private | Oct. 4, 1847 | Oct. 4, '47 | Smithland, Ky. | | July 25, '48 | Louisville, Ky. |
| 23 | Gibbs, William D. | Private | Dec. 3, 1847 | Feb. 19, '48 | Newport Bks., Ky. | | July 25, '48 | Louisville, Ky. |
| 24 | Heath, James H. | Private | Oct. 4, 1847 | Oct. 4, '47 | Smithland, Ky. | | July 25, '48 | Louisville, Ky. |
| 25 | Hamilton, John | Private | Oct. 4, 1847 | Oct. 4, '47 | Smithland, Ky. | | July 25, '48 | Louisville, Ky. |
| 26 | Hasty, John | Private | Oct. 4, 1847 | Oct. 4, '47 | Smithland, Ky. | | July 25, '48 | Louisville, Ky. |
| 27 | Hodge, Littleberry | Private | Oct. 4, 1847 | Oct. 4, '47 | Smithland, Ky. | | July 25, '48 | Louisville, Ky. |
| 28 | Hursk, George W. | Private | Oct. 4, 1847 | Oct. 4, '47 | Smithland, Ky. | | July 25, '48 | Louisville, Ky. |
| 29 | Hursk, Benjamin F. | Private | Oct. 4, 1847 | Oct. 4, '47 | Smithland, Ky. | | July 25, '48 | Louisville, Ky. |
| 30 | Harley, Moses | Private | Oct. 4, 1847 | Oct. 4, '47 | Smithland, Ky. | | July 25, '48 | Louisville, Ky. |
| 31 | Hiette, Wesley | Private | Oct. 4, 1847 | Oct. 4, '47 | Smithland, Ky. | | July 25, '48 | Louisville, Ky. |
| 32 | Hiette, George P. | Private | Oct. 4, 1847 | Oct. 4, '47 | Smithland, Ky. | | July 25, '48 | Louisville, Ky. |
| 33 | Johnson, William H. | Private | Oct. 4, 1847 | Oct. 4, '47 | Smithland, Ky. | | July 25, '48 | Louisville, Ky. |
| 34 | Jones, Newton | Private | Nov. 6, 1847 | Dec. 31, '47 | City of Mexico | | July 25, '48 | Louisville, Ky. |
| 35 | King, William C. | Private | Oct. 4, 1847 | Oct. 4, '47 | Smithland, Ky. | | July 25, '48 | Louisville, Ky. |
| 36 | Kelly, Robert C. | Private | Nov. 1, 1847 | Feb. 19, '48 | Newport Bks., Ky. | | July 25, '48 | Louisville, Ky. |
| 37 | Lucas, George W. | Private | Oct. 16, 1847 | Oct. 4, '47 | Smithland, Ky. | | July 25, '48 | Louisville, Ky. |
| 38 | Matthews, Caleb S. | Private | Oct. 4, 1847 | Oct. 4, '47 | Smithland, Ky. | | July 25, '48 | Louisville, Ky. |
| 39 | Montgomery, Robert | Private | Oct. 4, 1847 | Oct. 4, '47 | Smithland, Ky. | | July 25, '48 | Louisville, Ky. |
| 40 | Morant, Robert | Private | Oct. 4, 1847 | Oct. 4, '47 | Smithland, Ky. | | July 25, '48 | Louisville, Ky. |
| 41 | Molloy, Pinckney C. | Private | Oct. 4, 1847 | Oct. 4, '47 | Smithland, Ky. | | July 25, '48 | Louisville, Ky. |
| 42 | McCanna, James | Private | Oct. 4, 1847 | Oct. 4, '47 | Smithland, Ky. | | July 25, '48 | Louisville, Ky. |
| 43 | Mohundro, William O. | Private | Oct. 4, 1847 | Oct. 4, '47 | Smithland, Ky. | | July 25, '48 | Louisville, Ky. |
| 44 | Morse, Berry | Private | Oct. 16, 1847 | Oct. 4, '47 | Smithland, Ky. | | July 25, '48 | Louisville, Ky. |
| 45 | McMullins, Daniel | Private | Oct. 27, 1847 | Dec. 31, '47 | City of Mexico | | July 25, '48 | Louisville, Ky. |

## FOOT VOLUNTEERS—MEXICAN WAR—Continued.

| No. of each grade | REMARKS. |
|---|---|
| 16 | Died at New Orleans, December 10, 1847. |
| 17 | Died at City of Mexico, March 2, 1848. |
| 1 | Transferred to Company "I," Captain Todd's Company, 3d Regiment Ky. Volunteers. Date unknown. |
| 2 | Appointed Quartermaster Sergeant and transferred to non-commissioned staff, January 12, 1848. |
| 3 | Transferred to Captain Todd's Company, 3d Regiment Ky. Volunteers. Date unknown. |

## FOOT VOLUNTEERS—MEXICAN WAR.

| No. | REMARKS. |
|---|---|
| 1 | |
| 1 | |
| 1 | |
| 2 | |
| 1 | |
| 2 | Corporal from 1st muster; promoted from Corporal to Sergeant, 24th February, 1848. |
| 3 | Corporal from 1st muster; promoted from Corporal to Sergeant, 20th March 1848. |
| 4 | |
| 1 | |
| 2 | |
| 3 | Promoted from ranks to Corporal, 24th February, 1848. |
| 4 | Promoted from ranks to Corporal, 20th March, 1848. |
| 1 | |
| 2 | Appointed from ranks Musician, 1st March, 1848. |
| 1 | |
| 2 | |
| 3 | |
| 4 | |
| 5 | |
| 6 | |
| 7 | |
| 8 | |
| 9 | |
| 10 | |
| 11 | |
| 12 | |
| 13 | |
| 14 | |
| 15 | |
| 16 | |
| 17 | |
| 18 | |
| 19 | |
| 20 | |
| 21 | |
| 22 | |
| 23 | |
| 24 | |
| 25 | |
| 26 | |
| 27 | |
| 28 | |
| 29 | |
| 30 | |
| 31 | |
| 32 | Absent sick in hospital at Natchez, Miss., since November 4, 1847. No information concerning him received since. |
| 33 | Absent sick in General Hospital, New Orleans, since November 7, 1847. No information could be obtained concerning him. |
| 34 | |
| 35 | |
| 36 | |
| 37 | |
| 38 | |
| 39 | |
| 40 | |
| 41 | |
| 42 | |
| 43 | |
| 44 | |
| 45 | Joined by transfer 25th April, 1848, at City of Mexico, from Company "I," 4th Kentucky Regiment. |

## ROLL OF COMPANY "E," FOURTH REGIMENT KENTUCKY

| No. of each grade | Name | Rank | Joined for Service | Mustered In When | Mustered In Where | Period | Mustered Out When | Mustered Out Where |
|---|---|---|---|---|---|---|---|---|
| 46 | Newman, Nel D. | Private | Oct. 4, 1847 | Oct. 4, '47 | Smithland, Ky. | | July 25, '48 | Louisville, Ky. |
| 47 | Patterson, John S. | Private | Oct. 4, 1847 | Oct. 4, '47 | Smithland, Ky. | | July 25, '48 | Louisville, Ky. |
| 48 | Procter, Rowan P. | Private | Oct. 4, 1847 | Oct. 4, '47 | Smithland, Ky. | | July 25, '48 | Louisville, Ky. |
| 49 | Pertecte, Ezekiel | Private | Oct. 4, 1847 | Oct. 4, '47 | Smithland, Ky. | | July 25, '48 | Louisville, Ky. |
| 50 | Parke, William | Private | Oct. 4, 1847 | Oct. 4, '47 | Smithland, Ky. | | July 25, '48 | Louisville, Ky. |
| 51 | Scallen, Matthew R. | Private | Oct. 4, 1847 | Oct. 4, '47 | Smithland, Ky. | | July 25, '48 | Louisville, Ky. |
| 52 | Starnes, Robert | Private | Oct. 4, 1847 | Oct. 4, '47 | Smithland, Ky. | | July 25, '48 | Louisville, Ky. |
| 53 | Stevenson, Elias E. | Private | Oct. 4, 1847 | Oct. 4, '47 | Smithland, Ky. | | July 25, '48 | Louisville, Ky. |
| 54 | Surratt, William P. | Private | Oct. 4, 1847 | Oct. 4, '47 | Smithland, Ky. | | July 25, '48 | Louisville, Ky. |
| 55 | Scatten, William | Private | Oct. 16, 1847 | Oct. 16, '47 | Smithland, Ky. | | July 25, '48 | Louisville, Ky. |
| 56 | Tegner, John W. | Private | Oct. 4, 1847 | Oct. 4, '47 | Smithland, Ky. | | July 25, '48 | Louisville, Ky. |
| 57 | Tracey, James | Private | Oct. 4, 1847 | Oct. 4, '47 | Smithland, Ky. | | July 25, '48 | Louisville, Ky. |
| 58 | Verhines, James | Private | Oct. 4, 1847 | Oct. 4, '47 | Smithland, Ky. | | July 25, '48 | Louisville, Ky. |
| 59 | Wilson, Robert C. | Private | Oct. 4, 1847 | Oct. 4, '47 | Smithland, Ky. | | July 25, '48 | Louisville, Ky. |
| 60 | Warren, Henry C. | Private | Oct. 4, 1847 | Oct. 4, '47 | Smithland, Ky. | | July 25, '48 | Louisville, Ky. |
| 61 | White, James | Private | Feb. 19, 1848 | Feb. 19, '48 | Newport Bks., Ky. | | July 25, '48 | Louisville, Ky. |

**DISCHARGED.**

| | | | | | | | | |
|---|---|---|---|---|---|---|---|---|
| 1 | William H. Greenwood | Musician | Oct. 4, 1847 | Oct. 4, '47 | Smithland, Ky. | To serve during the war. | | |
| 2 | John J. Bennett | Private | Oct. 4, 1847 | Oct. 4, '47 | Smithland, Ky. | | | |
| 3 | Allen Holt | Private | Oct. 4, 1847 | Oct. 4, '47 | Smithland, Ky. | | | |
| 4 | James G. N. Moore | Private | Oct. 4, 1847 | Oct. 4, '47 | Smithland, Ky. | | | |
| 5 | George E. Riley | Private | Oct. 4, 1847 | Oct. 4, '47 | Smithland, Ky. | | | |
| 6 | John H. Hammonds | Private | Oct. 4, 1847 | Oct. 4, '47 | Smithland, Ky. | | | |
| 7 | Thomas Bryt | Private | Oct. 4, 1847 | Oct. 4, '47 | Smithland, Ky. | | | |
| 8 | Goodrich E. Lightfoot | Private | Oct. 4, 1847 | Oct. 4, '47 | Smithland, Ky. | | | |
| 9 | John T. Stone | Private | Oct. 4, 1847 | Oct. 4, '47 | Smithland, Ky. | | | |

**TRANSFERRED.**

| | | | | | | | | |
|---|---|---|---|---|---|---|---|---|
| 1 | Henry A. Kane | Sergeant | Oct. 4, 1847 | Oct. 4, '47 | Smithland, Ky. | | | |
| 2 | John C. Stevenson | Private | Dec. 3, 1847 | Feb. 19, '48 | Newport Bks., Ky. | | | |

**DIED.**

| | | | | | | | | |
|---|---|---|---|---|---|---|---|---|
| 1 | Francis Myrick | Private | Oct. 4, 1847 | Oct. 4, '47 | Smithland, Ky. | | | |
| 2 | John Adams | Private | Oct. 4, 1847 | Oct. 4, '47 | Smithland, Ky. | | | |
| 3 | Dempsey W. Goodrich | Private | Oct. 4, 1847 | Oct. 4, '47 | Smithland, Ky. | | | |
| 4 | Alfred Martin | Private | Oct. 4, 1847 | Oct. 4, '47 | Smithland, Ky. | | | |
| 5 | Littleberry B. Ford | Private | Oct. 4, 1847 | Oct. 4, '47 | Smithland, Ky. | | | |
| 6 | Jacob Chrismore | Private | Oct. 4, 1847 | Oct. 4, '47 | Smithland, Ky. | | | |
| 7 | Isaac McElroy | Private | Oct. 4, 1847 | Oct. 4, '47 | Smithland, Ky. | | | |
| 8 | William P. Hardin | Private | Oct. 4, 1847 | Oct. 4, '47 | Smithland, Ky. | | | |
| 9 | Griffin L. Lackman | Private | Oct. 4, 1847 | Oct. 4, '47 | Smithland, Ky. | | | |
| 10 | George W. L. Reeves | Private | Oct. 4, 1847 | Oct. 4, '47 | Smithland, Ky. | | | |
| 11 | Peter R. Hughes | Sergeant | Oct. 4, 1847 | Oct. 4, '47 | Smithland, Ky. | | | |
| 12 | George W. L. Pace | Private | Oct. 4, 1847 | Oct. 4, '47 | Smithland, Ky. | | | |
| 13 | William C. Cooksey | Private | Oct. 4, 1847 | Oct. 4, '47 | Smithland, Ky. | | | |
| 14 | John L. Bolton | Private | Oct. 4, 1847 | Oct. 4, '47 | Smithland, Ky. | | | |
| 15 | John W. O. Mohundro | Private | Oct. 4, 1847 | Oct. 4, '47 | Smithland, Ky. | | | |
| 16 | Twitty R. Pace | Private | Oct. 4, 1847 | Oct. 4, '47 | Smithland, Ky. | | | |
| 17 | George R. Orr | Private | Oct. 4, 1847 | Oct. 4, '47 | Smithland, Ky. | | | |
| 18 | Lewis V. Ralston | Private | Oct. 4, 1847 | Oct. 4, '47 | Smithland, Ky. | | | |

**DESERTED.**

| | | | | | | | | |
|---|---|---|---|---|---|---|---|---|
| 1 | Rufus L. Thompson | Private | Oct. 4, 1847 | Oct. 4, '47 | Smithland, Ky. | | | |

This Company was organized by Captain George B. Cook, at Smithland, Ky., in the month of September, 1847.

## ROLL OF COMPANY "F," FOURTH REGIMENT KENTUCKY

| | Name | Rank | Joined for Service | Mustered In When | Mustered In Where | Period | Mustered Out When | Mustered Out Where |
|---|---|---|---|---|---|---|---|---|
| 1 | Dennis McCreery | Captain | Oct. 4, 1847 | Oct. 6, '47 | Louisville, Ky. | During war. | July 25, '48 | Louisville, Ky. |
| 1 | William Bristow | 1st Lieutenant | Oct. 4, 1847 | Oct. 6, '47 | Louisville, Ky. | | July 25, '48 | Louisville, Ky. |
| 1 | William P. D. Bush | 2d Lieutenant | Oct. 4, 1847 | Oct. 6, '47 | Louisville, Ky. | | July 25, '48 | Louisville, Ky. |
| 2 | Isaac P. Washburn | 2d Lieutenant | Oct. 4, 1847 | Oct. 6, '47 | Louisville, Ky. | | July 25, '48 | Louisville, Ky. |
| 1 | Hiram Lenour | 1st Sergeant | Oct. 4, 1847 | Oct. 6, '47 | Louisville, Ky. | | July 25, '48 | Louisville, Ky. |
| 2 | George J. Markes | Sergeant | Oct. 4, 1847 | Oct. 6, '47 | Louisville, Ky. | | July 25, '48 | Louisville, Ky. |
| 3 | Benjamin Tanner | Sergeant | Oct. 4, 1847 | Oct. 6, '47 | Louisville, Ky. | | July 25, '48 | Louisville, Ky. |
| 4 | James A. Hunter | Sergeant | Oct. 4, 1847 | Oct. 6, '47 | Louisville, Ky. | | July 25, '48 | Louisville, Ky. |
| 1 | William D. Tanner | Corporal | Oct. 4, 1847 | Oct. 6, '47 | Louisville, Ky. | | July 25, '48 | Louisville, Ky. |
| 2 | Mortimer C. Crow | Corporal | Oct. 4, 1847 | Oct. 6, '47 | Louisville, Ky. | | July 25, '48 | Louisville, Ky. |
| 3 | Allen B. Burton | Corporal | Oct. 4, 1847 | Oct. 6, '47 | Louisville, Ky. | | July 25, '48 | Louisville, Ky. |
| 4 | John L. Chambers | Corporal | Oct. 4, 1847 | Oct. 6, '47 | Louisville, Ky. | | July 25, '48 | Louisville, Ky. |

## FOOT VOLUNTEERS—MEXICAN WAR—Continued.

| No. of each grade | REMARKS |
|---|---|
| 46 | |
| 47 | |
| 48 | |
| 49 | |
| 50 | |
| 51 | Left sick in hospital at New Orleans, 9th July, 1848. To be discharged there. |
| 52 | |
| 53 | |
| 54 | |
| 55 | Left as attendant in hospital at New Orleans, 9th July, 1848. To be discharged. |
| 56 | |
| 57 | |
| 58 | |
| 59 | |
| 60 | |
| 61 | Recruit from General Depot; assigned to Company. Joined 7th June, 1848. |
| | |
| 1 | Discharged at Vera Cruz, December 24, 1847; Surgeon's certificate of ordinary disability. |
| 2 | Discharged at City of Mexico, March 5, 1848; Surgeon's certificate of disability. |
| 3 | Discharged at City of Mexico, March 5, 1848; Surgeon's certificate of disability. |
| 4 | Discharged at City of Mexico, March 5, 1848; Surgeon's certificate of disability. |
| 5 | Discharged at Vera Cruz, 14th February, 1848; Surgeon's certificate of disability. |
| 6 | Discharged at Vera Cruz; Surgeon's certificate of disability. |
| 7 | Discharged at New Orleans, June, 1848; Surgeon's certificate of disability. |
| 8 | Discharged at New Orleans, 17th June, 1848; Surgeon's certificate of disability. |
| 9 | Discharged at New Orleans, 17th June, 1848; Surgeon's certificate of disability. |
| | |
| 1 | Sergeant from 1st muster. Transferred to Regimental Staff; appointed Sergeant-Major March 20, 1848. |
| 2 | Transferred to Company "I," 4th Regiment Kentucky Volunteers, at City of Mexico, April 25, 1848; recruit from General Depot; assigned to Company "E," April 24, 1848. |
| | |
| 1 | Died at City of Mexico, 25th December, 1847. |
| 2 | Died at City of Mexico, 27th December, 1847. |
| 3 | Died at City of Mexico, 27th January, 1848. |
| 4 | Died in General Hospital, in Vera Cruz, 1st January, 1848. |
| 5 | Died in City of Mexico, January 24, 1848. |
| 6 | Died in City of Mexico, February 20, 1848. |
| 7 | Died in General Hospital, Vera Cruz, January 28, 1848. |
| 8 | Died in General Hospital, Pueblo, January 26, 1848. |
| 9 | Died in General Hospital, Pueblo, December 20, 1847. |
| 10 | Died in General Hospital, Pueblo, December 18, 1847. |
| 11 | Died in General Hospital, Pueblo. February 11, 1848. |
| 12 | Died in General Hospital, at Pueblo, January 20, 1848. |
| 13 | Died in General Hospital, at Jalapa, Mexico, December 27, 1847. |
| 14 | Died in General Hospital, at Pueblo, January 3, 1848. |
| 15 | Died in City of Mexico, May 24 1848. |
| 16 | Died at Encerro, Mexico, June 18, 1848. |
| 17 | Died on board U. S. Transport, 15th July, 1848. |
| 18 | Died in General Hospital, at Jalapa, Mexico, April 20, 1848. |
| | |
| 1 | Deserted from hospital, at New Orleans, La., January, 22, 1848. |

## FOOT VOLUNTEERS—MEXICAN WAR.

| | |
|---|---|
| 1 | |
| 1 | |
| 1 | |
| 2 | |
| 1 | |
| 2 | |
| 3 | Private till 17th February, 1848, from enrollment, then promoted to Sergeant. |
| 4 | |
| 1 | |
| 2 | |
| 3 | |
| 4 | |

## MEXICAN WAR VETERANS.

### ROLL OF COMPANY "F," FOURTH REGIMENT KENTUCKY

| No. of each grade. | NAME. | RANK. | JOINED FOR SERVICE. | MUSTERED IN. When. | MUSTERED IN. Where. | Period. | MUSTERED OUT. When. | MUSTERED OUT. Where. |
|---|---|---|---|---|---|---|---|---|
| 1 | Dozier B. Lewis | Fifer | Oct. 4, 1847 | Oct. 6, '47 | Louisville, Ky. | | July 25, '48 | Louisville, Ky |
| 2 | Shipman Samuel | Drummer | Oct. 4, 1847 | Oct. 6, '47 | Louisville, Ky. | | July 25, '48 | Louisville, Ky. |
| 1 | Aldridge, John | Private | Oct. 4, 1847 | Oct. 6, '47 | Louisville, Ky. | | July 25, '48 | Louisville, Ky. |
| 2 | Adams, Lloyd C. | Private | Oct. 4, 1847 | Oct. 6, '47 | Louisville, Ky. | | July 25, '48 | Louisville, Ky. |
| 3 | Adams, Eli | Private | Oct. 4, 1847 | Oct. 6, '47 | Louisville, Ky. | | July 25, '48 | Louisville, Ky. |
| 4 | Baker, Frederick | Private | Oct. 4, 1847 | Oct. 6, '47 | Louisville, Ky. | | July 25, '48 | Louisville, Ky. |
| 5 | Bishop, William L. | Private | Oct. 4, 1847 | Oct. 6, '47 | Louisville, Ky. | | July 25, '48 | Louisville, Ky. |
| 6 | Bivins, John L. | Private | Oct. 4, 1847 | Oct. 6, '47 | Louisville, Ky. | | July 25, '48 | Louisville, Ky. |
| 7 | Cruse, James B. | Private | Oct. 4, 1847 | Oct. 6, '47 | Louisville, Ky. | | July 25, '48 | Louisville, Ky. |
| 8 | Cameron, George | Private | Oct. 4, 1847 | Oct. 6, '47 | Louisville, Ky. | | July 25, '48 | Louisville, Ky. |
| 9 | Collins, Bartlett | Private | Oct. 4, 1847 | Oct. 6, '47 | Louisville, Ky. | | July 25, '48 | Louisville, Ky. |
| 10 | Cameron, James A. | Private | Oct. 4, 1847 | Oct. 6, '47 | Louisville, Ky. | | July 25, '48 | Louisville, Ky. |
| 11 | Dean, Thomas | Private | Oct. 4, 1847 | Oct. 6, '47 | Louisville, Ky. | | July 25, '48 | Louisville, Ky. |
| 12 | Eggleston, Ferdinand | Private | Oct. 4, 1847 | Oct. 6, '47 | Louisville, Ky. | | July 25, '48 | Louisville, Ky. |
| 13 | Field, Logan | Private | Oct. 4, 1847 | Oct. 6, '47 | Louisville, Ky. | | July 25, '48 | Louisville, Ky. |
| 14 | Farmer, John | Private | Oct. 4, 1847 | Oct. 6, '47 | Louisville, Ky. | | July 25, '48 | Louisville, Ky. |
| 15 | Farmer, Harrison | Private | Oct. 4, 1847 | Oct. 6, '47 | Louisville, Ky. | | July 25, '48 | Louisville, Ky. |
| 16 | Freels, Isaac M. | Private | Oct. 4, 1847 | Oct. 6, '47 | Louisville, Ky. | | July 25, '48 | Louisville, Ky. |
| 17 | Griffin, John | Private | Oct. 4, 1847 | Oct. 6, '47 | Louisville, Ky. | | July 25, '48 | Louisville, Ky. |
| 18 | Gautier, Leonard | Private | Oct. 4, 1847 | Oct. 6, '47 | Louisville, Ky. | | July 25, '48 | Louisville, Ky. |
| 19 | Green, John W. | Private | Oct. 4, 1847 | Oct. 6, '47 | Louisville, Ky. | | July 25, '48 | Louisville, Ky. |
| 20 | Harbart, Obediah B. | Private | Oct. 4, 1847 | Oct. 6, '47 | Louisville, Ky. | | July 25, '48 | Louisville, Ky. |
| 21 | Hollingsworth, J. R. | Private | Oct. 4, 1847 | Oct. 6, '47 | Louisville, Ky. | | July 25, '48 | Louisville, Ky. |
| 22 | Harrison, William D. | Private | Oct. 4, 1847 | Oct. 6, '47 | Louisville, Ky. | | July 25, '48 | Louisville, Ky. |
| 23 | Hendricks, Thomas | Private | Oct. 4, 1847 | Oct. 6, '47 | Louisville, Ky. | | July 25, '48 | Louisville, Ky. |
| 24 | Hyatt, Conradus | Private | Oct. 4, 1847 | Oct. 6, '47 | Louisville, Ky. | | July 25, '48 | Louisville, Ky. |
| 25 | Hemmingway, Silas | Private | Oct. 4, 1847 | Oct. 6, '47 | Louisville, Ky. | To serve during the war. | July 25, '48 | Louisville, Ky. |
| 26 | Kimberlin, William | Private | Oct. 4, 1847 | Oct. 6, '47 | Louisville, Ky. | | July 25, '48 | Louisville, Ky. |
| 27 | Kenney, James H. | Private | Oct. 4, 1847 | Oct. 6, '47 | Louisville, Ky. | | July 25, '48 | Louisville, Ky. |
| 28 | Kimberlin, John | Private | Oct. 4, 1847 | Oct. 6, '47 | Louisville, Ky. | | July 25, '48 | Louisville, Ky. |
| 29 | Megowan, James F. | Private | Oct. 4, 1847 | Oct. 6, '47 | Louisville, Ky. | | July 25, '48 | Louisville, Ky. |
| 30 | May, Barney | Private | Oct. 4, 1847 | Oct. 6, '47 | Louisville, Ky. | | July 25, '48 | Louisville, Ky. |
| 31 | Miles, Albert | Private | Oct. 4, 1847 | Oct. 6, '47 | Louisville, Ky. | | July 25, '48 | Louisville, Ky. |
| 32 | Marshall, James M. | Private | Oct. 4, 1847 | Oct. 6, '47 | Louisville, Ky. | | July 25, '48 | Louisville, Ky. |
| 33 | Miller, James Q. | Private | Oct. 4, 1847 | Oct. 6, '47 | Louisville, Ky. | | July 25, '48 | Louisville, Ky. |
| 34 | McQuady, Edmund | Private | Oct. 4, 1847 | Oct. 6, '47 | Louisville, Ky. | | July 25, '48 | Louisville, Ky. |
| 35 | McGhee, Meredith | Private | Oct. 4, 1847 | Oct. 6, '47 | Louisville, Ky. | | July 25, '48 | Louisville, Ky. |
| 36 | McNamer, Philip | Private | Oct. 4, 1847 | Oct. 6, '47 | Louisville, Ky. | | July 25, '48 | Louisville, Ky. |
| 37 | Newman, William | Private | Oct. 4, 1847 | Oct. 6, '47 | Louisville, Ky. | | July 25, '48 | Louisville, Ky. |
| 38 | Nichols, John | Private | Oct. 4, 1847 | Oct. 6, '47 | Louisville, Ky. | | July 25, '48 | Louisville, Ky. |
| 39 | Newman, Richard | Private | Oct. 4, 1847 | Oct. 6, '47 | Louisville, Ky. | | July 25, '48 | Louisville, Ky. |
| 40 | Odom, John George W. | Private | Oct. 4, 1847 | Oct. 6, '47 | Louisville, Ky. | | July 25, '48 | Louisville, Ky. |
| 41 | Overstreet, Samuel W. | Private | Oct. 4, 1847 | Oct. 6, '47 | Louisville, Ky. | | July 25, '48 | Louisville, Ky. |
| 42 | Oldham, George M. | Private | Oct. 4, 1847 | Oct. 6, '47 | Louisville, Ky. | | July 25, '48 | Louisville, Ky. |
| 43 | Peak, Joseph H. | Private | Oct. 4, 1847 | Oct. 6, '47 | Louisville, Ky. | | July 25, '48 | Louisville, Ky. |
| 44 | Preast, James M. | Private | Oct. 4, 1847 | Oct. 6, '47 | Louisville, Ky. | | July 25, '48 | Louisville, Ky. |
| 45 | Pirtle, Samuel S. | Private | Oct. 4, 1847 | Oct. 6, '47 | Louisville, Ky. | | July 25, '48 | Louisville, Ky. |
| 46 | Peak, William L. | Private | Oct. 4, 1847 | Oct. 6, '47 | Louisville, Ky. | | July 25, '48 | Louisville, Ky. |
| 47 | Peak, Hezekiah | Private | Oct. 4, 1847 | Oct. 6, '47 | Louisville, Ky. | | July 25, '48 | Louisville, Ky. |
| 48 | Porter, William H. | Private | Oct. 4, 1847 | Oct. 6, '47 | Louisville, Ky. | | July 25, '48 | Louisville, Ky. |
| 49 | Richardson, Richard | Private | Oct. 4, 1847 | Oct. 6, '47 | Louisville, Ky. | | July 25, '48 | Louisville, Ky. |
| 50 | Richmond, James H. | Private | Oct. 4, 1847 | Oct. 6, '47 | Louisville, Ky. | | July 25, '48 | Louisville, Ky. |
| 51 | Rogers, William | Private | Oct. 4, 1847 | Oct. 6, '47 | Louisville, Ky. | | July 25, '48 | Louisville, Ky. |
| 52 | Sale, Josiah B. | Private | Oct. 4, 1847 | Oct. 6, '47 | Louisville, Ky. | | July 25, '48 | Louisville, Ky. |
| 53 | Scott, William J. | Private | Oct. 4, 1847 | Oct. 6, '47 | Louisville, Ky. | | July 25, '48 | Louisville, Ky. |
| 54 | Spray, Jefferson | Private | Oct. 16, 1847 | Oct. 16, '47 | Louisville, Ky. | | July 25, '48 | Louisville, Ky. |
| 55 | Thompson, John W. | Private | Oct. 4, 1847 | Oct. 6, '47 | Louisville, Ky. | | July 25, '48 | Louisville, Ky. |
| 56 | Tucker, Nelson B. | Private | Oct. 4, 1847 | Oct. 6, '47 | Louisville, Ky. | | July 25, '48 | Louisville, Ky. |
| 57 | Tanner, Benjamin F. | Private | Oct. 4, 1847 | Oct. 6, '47 | Louisville, Ky. | | July 25, '48 | Louisville, Ky. |
| 58 | Travis, Charles | Private | Oct. 16, 1847 | Oct. 16, '47 | Louisville, Ky. | | July 25, '48 | Louisville, Ky. |
| 59 | Ward, Joseph T. | Private | Oct. 4, 1847 | Oct. 6, '47 | Louisville, Ky. | | July 25, '48 | Louisville, Ky. |
| 60 | Wright, Washington | Private | Oct. 4, 1847 | Oct. 6, '47 | Louisville, Ky. | | July 25, '48 | Louisville, Ky. |
| 61 | Williams, John | Private | Oct. 4, 1847 | Oct. 6, '47 | Louisville, Ky. | | July 25, '48 | Louisville, Ky. |
| 62 | Watson, Thomas J. | Private | Oct. 4, 1847 | Oct. 6, '47 | Louisville, Ky. | | July 25, '48 | Louisville, Ky. |
| 63 | Waller, Amos J. | Private | Oct. 4, 1847 | Oct. 6, '47 | Louisville, Ky. | | July 25, '48 | Louisville, Ky. |
| 64 | Weedon, John | Private | Oct. 4, 1847 | Oct. 6, '47 | Louisville, Ky. | | July 25, '48 | Louisville, Ky. |
| 65 | Yewell, John | Private | Oct. 4, 1847 | Oct. 6, '47 | Louisville, Ky. | | July 25, '48 | Louisville, Ky. |
| | DIED. | | | | | | | |
| 1 | Joshua Murphy | Drummer | Oct. 4, 1847 | Oct. 6, '47 | Louisville, Ky. | | | |
| 2 | Davis, John M. | Private | Oct. 4, 1847 | Oct. 6, '47 | Louisville, Ky. | | | |
| 3 | Dennis, George W. | Private | Oct. 4, 1847 | Oct. 6, '47 | Louisville, Ky. | | | |
| 4 | Field, William | Private | Oct. 4, 1847 | Oct. 6, '47 | Louisville, Ky. | | | |
| 5 | Mempel, Adam | Private | Oct. 15, 1847 | Oct. 15, '47 | Louisville, Ky. | | | |
| 6 | Snyder, Edley B. | Private | Oct. 4, 1847 | Oct. 6, '47 | Louisville, Ky. | | | |

## FOOT VOLUNTEERS—MEXICAN WAR—Continued.

| No. of each grade. | REMARKS. |
|---|---|
| 1 | |
| 2 | |
| 1 | |
| 2 | |
| 3 | |
| 4 | |
| 5 | |
| 6 | |
| 7 | |
| 8 | |
| 9 | |
| 10 | |
| 11 | |
| 12 | |
| 13 | |
| 14 | |
| 15 | |
| 16 | |
| 17 | |
| 18 | |
| 19 | |
| 20 | |
| 21 | |
| 22 | |
| 23 | |
| 24 | |
| 25 | |
| 26 | |
| 27 | |
| 28 | |
| 29 | |
| 30 | |
| 31 | |
| 32 | |
| 33 | |
| 34 | |
| 35 | |
| 36 | |
| 37 | |
| 38 | |
| 39 | |
| 40 | |
| 41 | |
| 42 | |
| 43 | |
| 44 | |
| 45 | |
| 46 | |
| 47 | |
| 48 | |
| 49 | |
| 50 | |
| 51 | |
| 52 | |
| 53 | |
| 54 | |
| 55 | |
| 56 | |
| 57 | |
| 58 | |
| 59 | |
| 60 | |
| 61 | |
| 62 | |
| 63 | |
| 64 | |
| 65 | |
| 1 | Died at Pueblo, January 6, 1848. |
| 2 | Died at City of Mexico, 29th December, 1847. |
| 3 | Died at Vera Cruz, 14th December, 1847. |
| 4 | Died at New Orleans, 23d November, 1847. |
| 5 | Died at Pueblo, 7th January, 1848. |
| 6 | Died at City of Mexico, 30th May, 1848. |

## MEXICAN WAR VETERANS.

### ROLL OF COMPANY "F," FOURTH REGIMENT KENTUCKY

| No. of each grade | NAME. | RANK. | JOINED FOR SERVICE. | MUSTERED IN. When. | MUSTERED IN. Where. | Period | MUSTERED OUT. When. | MUSTERED OUT. Where. |
|---|---|---|---|---|---|---|---|---|
| 7 | Snyder, William D. | Private | Oct. 4, 1847 | Oct. 6, '47 | Louisville, Ky. | | | |
| 8 | Sublett, Jerred | Private | Oct. 4, 1847 | Oct. 6, '47 | Louisville, Ky. | | | |
| | DISCHARGED. | | | | | | | |
| 1 | Allen, James | Private | Oct. 4, 1847 | Oct. 6, '47 | Louisville, Ky. | | | |
| 2 | Bishop, John | Private | Oct. 4, 1847 | Oct. 6, '47 | Louisville, Ky. | | | |
| 3 | Cummings, William P. | Private | Oct. 4, 1847 | Oct. 6, '47 | Louisville, Ky. | To serve during the war. | | |
| 4 | Clements, Charles O. | Private | Oct. 4, 1847 | Oct. 6, '47 | Louisville, Ky. | | | |
| 5 | Hile, John | Private | Oct. 4, 1847 | Oct. 6, '47 | Louisville, Ky. | | | |
| 6 | McGhee, William J. | Private | Oct. 4, 1847 | Oct. 6, '47 | Louisville, Ky. | | | |
| 7 | Pool, Allen | Private | Oct. 4, 1847 | Oct. 6, '47 | Louisville, Ky. | | | |
| 8 | Richmond, Sylvester R. | Private | Oct. 4, 1847 | Oct. 6, '47 | Louisville, Ky. | | | |
| 9 | Thomas, John | Private | Oct. 4, 1847 | Oct. 6, '47 | Louisville, Ky. | | | |
| 10 | Westbrook, Thomas H. | Private | Oct. 20, 1847 | Oct. 20, '47 | Louisville, Ky. | | | |
| | TRANSFERRED. | | | | | | | |
| 1 | Davis L. Adair | Sergeant | Oct. 4, 1847 | Oct. 6, '47 | Louisville, Ky. | | | |
| | DESERTED. | | | | | | | |
| 1 | Sowerby, George | Private | Oct. 4, 1847 | Oct. 6, '47 | Louisville, Ky. | | | |

This Company was organized by Captain Dennis McCreery, at Owensboro, Daviess county, Ky., in the month of September, 1847, and marched thence to Louisville, Ky., where it arrived on the 4th day of October, 1847, a distance of one hundred and sixty miles.

### ROLL OF COMPANY "G," FOURTH REGIMENT KENTUCKY

| No. | NAME. | RANK. | JOINED FOR SERVICE. | MUSTERED IN. When. | MUSTERED IN. Where. | Period | MUSTERED OUT. When. | MUSTERED OUT. Where. |
|---|---|---|---|---|---|---|---|---|
| 1 | Joseph S. Conn | Captain | Oct. 3, 1847 | Oct. 4 '47 | Smithland, Ky. | | July 25, '48 | Louisville, Ky. |
| 1 | Jeremiah F. Dorries | 1st Lieutenant | Oct. 3, 1847 | Oct. 4, '47 | Smithland, Ky. | | July 25, '48 | Louisville, Ky. |
| 1 | John M. Massey | 2d Lieutenant | Oct. 3, 1847 | Oct. 4, '47 | Smithland, Ky. | | July 25, '48 | Louisville, Ky. |
| 2 | Noah M. Watkins | 2d Lieutenant | Oct. 3, 1847 | Oct. 4, '47 | Smithland, Ky. | | July 25, '48 | Louisville, Ky. |
| 3 | John B. Waddington | 2d Lieutenant | Oct. 3, 1847 | Oct. 4, '47 | Smithland, Ky. | | | |
| 4 | Cyrus A. Scott | 2d Lieutenant | Oct. 3, 1847 | Oct. 4, '47 | Smithland, Ky. | | | |
| 1 | Erastus R. Pickering | 1st Sergeant | Oct. 3, 1847 | Oct. 4, '47 | Smithland, Ky. | | July 25, '48 | Louisville, Ky. |
| 2 | Shelton Jones | 2d Sergeant | Oct. 3, 1847 | Oct. 4, '47 | Smithland, Ky. | | July 25, '48 | Louisville, Ky. |
| 3 | John P. Gulp | 3d Sergeant | Oct. 3, 1847 | Oct. 4, '47 | Smithland, Ky. | | July 25, '48 | Louisville, Ky. |
| 4 | William A. Prime | 4th Sergeant | Oct. 3, 1847 | Oct. 4, '47 | Smithland, Ky. | | July 25, '48 | Louisville, Ky. |
| 1 | Morrison D. Wilcox | Corporal | Oct. 3, 1847 | Oct. 4, '47 | Smithland, Ky. | | July 25, '48 | Louisville, Ky. |
| 2 | David R. Piden | Corporal | Oct. 3, 1847 | Oct. 4, '47 | Smithland, Ky. | | July 25, '48 | Louisville, Ky. |
| 3 | George W. Bond | Corporal | Oct. 3, 1847 | Oct. 4, '47 | Smithland, Ky. | | July 25, '48 | Louisville, Ky. |
| 4 | John W. Hanks | Corporal | Oct. 3, 1847 | Oct. 4, '47 | Smithland, Ky. | | July 25, '48 | Louisville, Ky. |
| 1 | Erastus Morrison | Drummer | Oct. 3, 1847 | Oct. 4, '47 | Smithland, Ky. | | July 25, '48 | Louisville, Ky. |
| 2 | West A Mettan | Fifer | Oct. 3, 1847 | Oct. 4, '47 | Smithland, Ky. | To serve during the war. | July 25, '48 | Louisville, Ky. |
| 1 | Armstrong, William A. | Private | Oct. 3, 1847 | Oct. 4, '47 | Smithland, Ky. | | July 25, '48 | Louisville, Ky. |
| 2 | Brewster, James P. | Private | Oct. 3, 1847 | Oct. 4, '47 | Smithland, Ky. | | July 25, '48 | Louisville, Ky. |
| 3 | Brewer, Etna M. | Private | Oct. 3, 1847 | Oct. 4, '47 | Smithland, Ky. | | July 25, '48 | Louisville, Ky. |
| 4 | Bruitin, Madison | Private | Oct. 3, 1847 | Oct. 4, '47 | Smithland, Ky. | | July 25, '48 | Louisville, Ky. |
| 5 | Bradley, Amos K. | Private | Oct. 3, 1847 | Oct. 4, '47 | Smithland, Ky. | | July 25, '48 | Louisville, Ky. |
| 6 | Bradley, Edward L. | Private | Oct. 3, 1847 | Oct. 4, '47 | Smithland, Ky. | | July 25, '48 | Louisville, Ky. |
| 7 | Cardwell, Thomas R. | Private | Oct. 3, 1847 | Oct. 4, '47 | Smithland, Ky. | | July 25, '48 | Louisville, Ky. |
| 8 | Chambers, James T. | Private | Oct. 3, 1847 | Oct. 4, '47 | Smithland, Ky. | | July 25, '48 | Louisville, Ky. |
| 9 | Cravens, James L. | Private | Oct. 3, 1847 | Oct. 4, '47 | Smithland, Ky. | | July 25, '48 | Louisville, Ky. |
| 10 | Cook, Joseph P. | Private | Oct. 3, 1847 | Oct. 4, '47 | Smithland, Ky. | | July 25, '48 | Louisville, Ky. |
| 11 | Cook, Robert | Private | Oct. 3, 1847 | Oct. 4, '47 | Smithland, Ky. | | July 25, '48 | Louisville, Ky. |
| 12 | Cook, Henry A. | Private | Oct. 3, 1847 | Oct. 4, '47 | Smithland, Ky. | | July 25, '48 | Louisville, Ky. |
| 13 | Catlett, James H. | Private | Oct. 3, 1847 | Oct. 4, '47 | Smithland, Ky. | | July 25, '48 | Louisville, Ky. |
| 14 | Campbell Thomas W. | Private | Oct. 3, 1847 | Oct. 4, '47 | Smithland, Ky. | | July 25, '48 | Louisville, Ky. |
| 15 | Davidge, Robert | Private | Oct. 3, 1847 | Oct. 4, '47 | Smithland, Ky. | | July 25, '48 | Louisville, Ky. |
| 16 | Dunn, Andrew F. | Private | Oct. 3, 1847 | Oct. 4, '47 | Smithland, Ky. | | July 25, '48 | Louisville, Ky. |
| 17 | Davis, Alfred P. | Private | Oct. 3, 1847 | Oct. 4, '47 | Smithland, Ky. | | July 25, '48 | Louisville, Ky. |
| 18 | Davis, Henry H. | Private | Oct. 3, 1847 | Oct. 4, '47 | Smithland, Ky. | | July 25, '48 | Louisville, Ky. |
| 19 | Eisen, James C. | Private | Oct. 3, 1847 | Oct. 4, '47 | Smithland, Ky. | | July 25, '48 | Louisville, Ky. |
| 20 | Freer, Charles W. | Private | Oct. 3, 1847 | Oct. 4, '47 | Smithland, Ky. | | July 25, '48 | Louisville, Ky. |
| 21 | Ferguson, Thomas | Private | Oct. 3, 1847 | Oct. 4, '47 | Smithland, Ky. | | July 25, '48 | Louisville, Ky. |
| 22 | Fawn, James R. | Private | Oct. 3, 1847 | Oct. 4, '47 | Smithland, Ky. | | July 25, '48 | Louisville, Ky. |
| 23 | Gore, Augustus A. | Private | Oct. 3, 1847 | Oct. 4, '47 | Smithland, Ky. | | July 25, '48 | Louisville, Ky. |
| 24 | Glass, James | Private | Oct. 3, 1847 | Oct. 4, '47 | Smithland, Ky. | | July 25, '48 | Louisville, Ky. |
| 25 | Goodler, Joseph A. | Private | Oct. 3, 1847 | Oct. 4, '47 | Smithland, Ky. | | July 25, '48 | Louisville, Ky. |
| 26 | Gregory, John W. | Private | Oct. 3, 1847 | Oct. 4, '47 | Smithland, Ky. | | July 25, '48 | Louisville, Ky. |
| 27 | Hanks, Samuel | Private | Oct. 3, 1847 | Oct. 4, '47 | Smithland, Ky. | | July 25, '48 | Louisville, Ky. |
| 28 | Hanks, Richard W. | Private | Oct. 3, 1847 | Oct. 4, '47 | Smithland, Ky. | | July 25, '48 | Louisville, Ky. |
| 29 | Head, William H. | Private | Oct. 3, 1847 | Oct. 4, '47 | Smithland, Ky. | | July 25, '48 | Louisville, Ky. |

# FOOT VOLUNTEERS—MEXICAN WAR—Continued.

| No. of each grade | REMARKS. |
|---|---|
| 7 | Died at Pueblo, but not officially reported. |
| 8 | Died at City of Mexico, 17th March, 1848. |
| 1 | Discharged at City of Mexico, March 4, 1848, for disability. |
| 2 | Discharged at New Orleans, March, 1848. Not officially reported. |
| 3 | Discharged at New Or'eans, March 17, 1848, for disability. |
| 4 | Discharged at New Orleans, March 17, 1848, but not reported. |
| 5 | Discharged at New Orleans, April 3, 1848, for disability. |
| 6 | Discharged at Vera Cruz, February 19, 1848, for disability. |
| 7 | Discharged at City of Mexico, March 4, 1848, for disability. |
| 8 | Discharged at New Orleans, March 17, 1848, for disability. |
| 9 | Discharged at Louisville, Ky., October 8, 1847, for disability. |
| 10 | Discharged at Louisville, October 8, 1847, but not reported. |
| 1 | Appointed Quartermaster Sergeant October 6, 1847, order Col. Williams. Discharged at City of Mexico, January 8, 1848, for disability. |
| 1 | Deserted at Camp Butler, near Louisville, October 28, 1847; apprehended City of Mexico, by Sergeant Lenour, 22d ———, 1848, and joined his Company May 8th; transferred to the 2d Ohio Volunteers, order of Brig. Gen. Marshall, June 13, 1848. Debtor to the U. S. $30 for apprehension. |

# FOOT VOLUNTEERS—MEXICAN WAR.

| | |
|---|---|
| 1 | |
| 1 | |
| 1 | Promoted from 1st Sergeant, 15th February, 1848; was Sergeant from enrollment. |
| 2 | Promoted from Sergeant 31st May; was private from enrollment to February 9, then 1st Sergeant. |
| 3 | Resigned at City of Mexico, 21st March, 1848. Ill health. |
| 4 | Died at City of Mexico, February 7, 1848. |
| 1 | |
| 2 | |
| 3 | |
| 4 | |
| 1 | |
| 2 | |
| 3 | |
| 4 | |
| 1 | |
| 2 | |
| 1 | |
| 2 | |
| 3 | |
| 4 | |
| 5 | |
| 6 | |
| 7 | |
| 8 | |
| 9 | |
| 10 | |
| 11 | |
| 12 | |
| 13 | |
| 14 | |
| 15 | |
| 16 | |
| 17 | |
| 18 | |
| 19 | |
| 20 | |
| 21 | |
| 22 | |
| 23 | |
| 24 | |
| 25 | |
| 26 | |
| 27 | |
| 28 | |
| 29 | |

## MEXICAN WAR VETERANS.

### ROLL OF COMPANY "G," FOURTH REGIMENT KENTUCKY

| No. of each grade. | Name. | Rank. | Joined for Service. | Mustered In. When. | Mustered In. Where. | Period | Mustered Out. When. | Mustered Out. Where. |
|---|---|---|---|---|---|---|---|---|
| 30 | Hayworth, John A. | Private | Oct. 3, 1847 | Oct. 4, '47 | Smithland, Ky. | | July 25, '48 | Louisville, Ky. |
| 31 | Jones, Joseph I. | Private | Oct. 3, 1847 | Oct. 4, '47 | Smithland, Ky. | | July 25, '48 | Louisville, Ky. |
| 32 | Johns, Thomas | Private | Oct. 3, 1847 | Oct. 4, '47 | Smithland, Ky. | | July 25, '48 | Louisville, Ky. |
| 33 | Johnson, Thomas F. | Private | Oct. 3, 1847 | Oct. 4, '47 | Smithland, Ky. | | July 25, '48 | Louisville, Ky. |
| 34 | Jordan, Benjamin | Private | Oct. 3, 1847 | Oct. 4, '47 | Smithland, Ky. | | July 25, '48 | Louisville, Ky. |
| 35 | Kendrick, James W. | Private | Oct. 3, 1847 | Oct. 4, '47 | Smithland, Ky. | | July 25, '48 | Louisville, Ky. |
| 36 | Kena, James | Private | Oct. 3, 1847 | Oct. 4, '47 | Smithland, Ky. | | July 25, '48 | Louisville, Ky. |
| 37 | Lambert, William H. | Private | Oct. 3, 1847 | Oct. 4, '47 | Smithland, Ky. | | July 25, '48 | Louisville, Ky. |
| 38 | Lewis, Henry | Private | Oct. 3, 1847 | Oct. 4, '47 | Smithland, Ky. | | July 25, '48 | Louisville, Ky. |
| 39 | Lewis, John H. | Private | Oct. 3, 1847 | Oct. 4, '47 | Smithland, Ky. | | July 25, '48 | Louisville, Ky. |
| 40 | Lamb, Archibald | Private | Oct. 3, 1847 | Oct. 4, '47 | Smithland, Ky. | | July 25, '48 | Louisville, Ky. |
| 41 | Ladyman, George W. | Private | Oct. 3, 1847 | Oct. 4, '47 | Smithland, Ky. | | July 25, '48 | Louisville, Ky. |
| 42 | Ladd, Henry | Private | Oct. 3, 1847 | Oct. 4, '47 | Smithland, Ky. | | July 25, '48 | Louisville, Ky. |
| 43 | Lang, Patrick A. | Private | Oct. 3, 1847 | Oct. 4, '47 | Smithland, Ky. | | July 25, '48 | Louisville, Ky. |
| 44 | Lynn, James | Private | Oct. 3, 1847 | Oct. 4, '47 | Smithland, Ky. | | July 25, '48 | Louisville, Ky. |
| 45 | Martin, Benjamin | Private | Oct. 3, 1847 | Oct. 4, '47 | Smithland, Ky. | | July 25, '48 | Louisville, Ky. |
| 46 | Martin, John | Private | Oct. 3, 1847 | Oct. 4, '47 | Smithland, Ky. | | July 25, '48 | Louisville, Ky. |
| 47 | Mercer, John E. | Private | Oct. 3, 1847 | Oct. 4, '47 | Smithland, Ky. | | July 25, '48 | Louisville, Ky. |
| 48 | May, Coleman C. | Private | Oct. 3, 1847 | Oct. 4, '47 | Smithland, Ky. | | July 25, '48 | Louisville, Ky. |
| 49 | Mitchell, James | Private | Oct. 3, 1847 | Oct. 4, '47 | Smithland, Ky. | | July 25, '48 | Louisville, Ky. |
| 50 | Moneymaker, Wilson | Private | Oct. 3, 1847 | Oct. 4, '47 | Smithland, Ky. | | July 25, '48 | Louisville, Ky. |
| 51 | McCaslin, William H. | Private | Oct. 3, 1847 | Oct. 4, '47 | Smithland, Ky. | | July 25, '48 | Louisville, Ky. |
| 52 | Owens, William | Private | Oct. 3, 1847 | Oct. 4, '47 | Smithland, Ky. | | July 25, '48 | Louisville, Ky. |
| 53 | Pierce, James M. | Private | Oct. 3, 1847 | Oct. 4, '47 | Smithland, Ky. | | July 25, '48 | Louisville, Ky. |
| 54 | Pruity, Joseph B. | Private | Oct. 3, 1847 | Oct. 4, '47 | Smithland, Ky. | | July 25, '48 | Louisville, Ky. |
| 55 | Robinson, Thornton | Private | Oct. 3, 1847 | Oct. 4, '47 | Smithland, Ky. | | July 25, '48 | Louisville, Ky. |
| 56 | Robertson, James | Private | Oct. 3, 1847 | Oct. 4, '47 | Smithland, Ky. | | July 25, '48 | Louisville, Ky. |
| 57 | Ray, Benjamin | Private | Oct. 3, 1847 | Oct. 4, '47 | Smithland, Ky. | | July 25, '48 | Louisville, Ky. |
| 58 | Salirro, Clement C. | Private | Oct. 3, 1847 | Oct. 4, '47 | Smithland, Ky. | | July 25, '48 | Louisville, Ky. |
| 59 | Scott, William | Private | Oct. 3, 1847 | Oct. 4, '47 | Smithland, Ky. | | July 25, '48 | Louisville, Ky. |
| 60 | Scott, Columbus M. | Private | Oct. 8, 1847 | Oct. 4, '47 | Smithland, Ky. | To serve during the war. | July 25, '48 | Louisville, Ky. |
| 61 | Stevens, William | Private | Oct. 3, 1847 | Oct. 4, '47 | Smithland, Ky. | | July 25, '48 | Louisville, Ky. |
| 62 | Smith, Josiah | Private | Oct. 3, 1847 | Oct. 4, '47 | Smithland, Ky. | | July 25, '48 | Louisville, Ky. |
| 63 | Trotter, Charles L. | Private | Oct. 3, 1847 | Oct. 4, '47 | Smithland, Ky. | | July 25, '48 | Louisville, Ky. |
| 64 | Walker, Silas G. | Private | Oct. 3, 1847 | Oct. 4, '47 | Smithland, Ky. | | July 25, '48 | Louisville, Ky. |
| 65 | Whittington, Richard | Private | Oct. 3, 1847 | Oct. 4, '47 | Smithland, Ky. | | July 25, '48 | Louisville, Ky. |
| 66 | Wiley, James | Private | Oct. 3, 1847 | Oct. 4, '47 | Smithland, Ky. | | July 25, '48 | Louisville, Ky. |
| 67 | Williams, William | Private | Oct. 3, 1847 | Oct. 4, '47 | Smithland, Ky. | | July 25, '48 | Louisville, Ky. |
| 68 | Williams, George | Private | Oct. 3, 1847 | Oct. 4, '47 | Smithland, Ky. | | July 25, '48 | Louisville, Ky. |
| 69 | Welker, Daniel | Private | Feb. 9, 1848 | Feb. 9, '48 | City of Mexico | | July 25, '48 | Louisville, Ky. |
| 70 | Young, Franklin | Private | Oct. 3, 1847 | Oct. 3, '47 | Smithland, Ky. | | July 25, '48 | Louisville, Ky. |
| | **Discharged.** | | | | | | | |
| 1 | McGuire, George | Private | Oct. 3, 1847 | Oct. 3, '47 | Smithland, Ky. | | | |
| 2 | Lyon, Matthew M. | Private | Oct. 3, 1847 | Oct. 3, '47 | Smithland, Ky. | | | |
| 3 | White, Benjamin | Private | Oct. 3, 1847 | Oct. 3, '47 | Smithland, Ky. | | | |
| 4 | Ward, Pleasant P. | Private | Oct. 3, 1847 | Oct. 3, '47 | Smithland, Ky. | | | |
| 5 | Chandler, King S. | Private | Oct. 8, 1847 | Oct. 3, '47 | Smithland, Ky. | | | |
| 6 | Spratt, Baylor I. | Private | Oct. 3, 1847 | Oct. 3, '47 | Smithland, Ky. | | | |
| 7 | Lambert, Robert B. | Private | Oct. 3, 1847 | Oct. 3, '47 | Smithland, Ky. | | | |
| 8 | Armstrong, Benj. F. | Private | Oct. 3, 1847 | Oct. 3, '47 | Smithland, Ky. | | | |
| 9 | Fox, Benjamin S. | Private | Oct. 3, 1847 | Oct. 3, '47 | Smithland, Ky. | | | |
| 10 | Krone, Benjamin | Private | Oct. 3, 1847 | Oct. 3, '47 | Smithland, Ky. | | | |
| 11 | Davis M. Waddington | Private | Oct. 3, 1847 | Oct. 3, '47 | Smithland, Ky. | | | |
| 12 | Bradford, Cantrell | Private | Oct. 3, 1847 | Oct. 3, '47 | Smithland, Ky. | | | |
| | **Deserted.** | | | | | | | |
| 1 | Ellenwood, William | Private | Feb. 15, 1848 | Feb. 29, '48 | City of Mexico | | | |
| 2 | Fisher, Joseph | Private | Feb. 9, 1848 | Feb. 29, '48 | City of Mexico | | | |
| 3 | Bailey, W. D. | Private | Oct. 3, 1847 | Oct. 4, '47 | Smithland, Ky. | | | |
| | **Died.** | | | | | | | |
| 1 | Blick, Willis N. | Private | Oct. 3, 1847 | Oct. 4, '47 | Smithland, Ky. | | | |
| 2 | Brooks, John H. | Private | Oct. 3, 1847 | Oct. 4, '47 | Smithland, Ky. | | | |
| 3 | Bridges, James | Private | Oct. 3, 1847 | Oct. 4, '47 | Smithland, Ky. | | | |
| 4 | Beard, Ezekiel | Private | Oct. 3, 1847 | Oct. 4, '47 | Smithland, Ky. | | | |
| 5 | Cannon, John | Private | Oct. 3, 1847 | Oct. 4, '47 | Smithland, Ky. | | | |
| 6 | Cookery, James W. | Private | Oct. 3, 1847 | Oct. 4, '47 | Smithland, Ky. | | | |
| 7 | Calvert, Spencer M. | Private | Oct. 3, 1847 | Oct. 4, '47 | Smithland, Ky. | | | |
| 8 | Hewlett, Martin | Private | Oct. 3, 1847 | Oct. 4, '47 | Smithland, Ky. | | | |
| 9 | Hunter, John M. | Private | Oct. 3, 1847 | Oct. 4, '47 | Smithland, Ky. | | | |
| 10 | Hunter, James | Private | Oct. 3, 1847 | Oct. 4, '47 | Smithland, Ky. | | | |
| 11 | Clinton, William | Private | Oct. 3, 1847 | Oct. 4, '47 | Smithland, Ky. | | | |
| 12 | Jones, Monroe | Private | Oct. 3, 1847 | Oct. 4, '47 | Smithland, Ky. | | | |
| 13 | Lamb, Wiley | Private | Oct. 3, 1847 | Oct. 4, '47 | Smithland, Ky. | | | |

## FOOT VOLUNTEERS—MEXICAN WAR—Continued.

| No. of each grade | REMARKS. |
|---|---|
| 30 | |
| 31 | |
| 32 | |
| 33 | |
| 34 | |
| 35 | |
| 36 | |
| 37 | |
| 38 | |
| 39 | |
| 40 | |
| 41 | |
| 42 | |
| 43 | |
| 44 | |
| 45 | Left sick in hospital, New Orleans, June 28, 1848; died 10th July, 1848. |
| 46 | Left as nurse in hospital, New Orleans, July 7, 1848. |
| 47 | |
| 48 | |
| 49 | |
| 50 | |
| 51 | |
| 52 | |
| 53 | |
| 54 | |
| 55 | |
| 56 | |
| 57 | |
| 58 | |
| 59 | |
| 60 | |
| 61 | |
| 62 | |
| 63 | |
| 64 | |
| 65 | |
| 66 | |
| 67 | |
| 68 | |
| 69 | Mustered as substitute for D. M. Waddington; order of Commander-in-Chief. |
| 70 | |
| 1 | Discharged at Smithland, Ky., November 1, 1847; Surgeon's certificate. |
| 2 | Discharged at New Orleans (not reported); Surgeon's certificate. |
| 3 | Discharged at Pueblo (not reported); Surgeon's certificate. |
| 4 | Discharged at City of Mexico, January 13, 1848; Surgeon's certificate. |
| 5 | Discharged at Vera Cruz (not reported); Surgeon's certificate. |
| 6 | Discharged at Vera Cruz, February 6, 1848; Surgeon's certificate. |
| 7 | Discharged at City of Mexico, March 31, 1848; Surgeon's certificate. |
| 8 | Discharged at New Orleans in June; time not reported. |
| 9 | Discharged at New Orleans, March 14, 1848; not fully reported. |
| 10 | Discharged at Jalapa, March 14, 1848; not fully reported. |
| 11 | Discharged, order of Commander-in-Chief, at City of Mexico, February 9, 1848, on furnishing substitute. |
| 12 | Discharged, order of Commander-in-Chief, at City of Mexico, February 9, 1848, on furnishing substitute. |
| 1 | Deserted at the City of Mexico, May 29, 1848. |
| 2 | Deserted (2d time) at the City of Mexico, in April, 1848. |
| 3 | Deserted from hospital in New Orleans, time unknown. |
| 1 | Died at Smithland, October 24, 1847. No pay. |
| 2 | Died at City of Mexico, December 28, 1847. No pay. |
| 3 | Died at City of Mexico, January 25, 1848, and pay to 21st December, 1847. |
| 4 | Died at Vera Cruz, March 11, 1848. Pay unknown. |
| 5 | Died at City of Mexico, January 11, 1848, and pay to December 31, 1847. |
| 6 | Died at City of Mexico, January 27, 1848, and pay to December 31, 1847. |
| 7 | Died at Pueblo, February 28, 1848. Pay unknown. |
| 8 | Died at City of Mexico, January 28, 1848. No pay. |
| 9 | Died at City of Mexico, January 21, 1848, and pay to December 31, 1847. |
| 10 | Died at City of Mexico, February 7, 1848, and pay to December 31, 1847. |
| 11 | Died on board ship in June. Unknown. |
| 12 | Died at City of Mexico, January 6, 1848. No pay. |
| 13 | Died at City of Mexico, January 3, 1848. No pay. |

## MEXICAN WAR VETERANS.

### ROLL OF COMPANY "G," FOURTH REGIMENT KENTUCKY

| No. of each grade | Name | Rank | Joined for Service | Mustered In When | Mustered In Where | Period | Mustered Out When | Mustered Out Where |
|---|---|---|---|---|---|---|---|---|
| 14 | Sells, Charles | Private | Oct. 3 1847 | Oct. 4, '47 | Smithland, Ky | During war | | |
| 15 | McFarland, James | Private | Oct. 3, 1847 | Oct. 4, '47 | Smithland, Ky | | | |
| 16 | Miller, William | Private | Oct. 3, 1847 | Oct. 4, '47 | Smithland, Ky | | | |
| 17 | Moore, Collin B. | Private | Oct. 3, 1847 | Oct. 4, '47 | Smithland, Ky | | | |
| 18 | Shepley, Joseph | Private | Oct. 3, 1847 | Oct. 4, '47 | Smithland, Ky | | | |
| 19 | Shaw, Washington | Private | Oct. 3, 1847 | Oct. 4, '47 | Smithland, Ky | | | |
| 20 | Stone, Henry F. | Private | Oct. 3, 1847 | Oct. 4, '47 | Smithland, Ky | | | |
| 21 | McCaslin, John G. | Private | Oct. 3, 1847 | Oct. 4, '47 | Smithland, Ky | | | |
| 22 | Wheatley, Mark | Private | Oct. 3 1847 | Oct. 4, '47 | Smithland, Ky | | | |
| 23 | White, Joshua | Private | Oct. 3, 1847 | Oct. 4, '47 | Smithland, Ky | | | |
| 24 | West, Balser B. | Private | Oct. 3, 1847 | Oct. 4, '47 | Smithland, Ky | | | |

This Company was organized by Captain James S. Conn, at Princeton, Kentucky, in the month of September, 1847, and marched thence to Smithland, where it arrived the 3d day of October, 1847, a distance of fifty-three miles.

### ROLL OF COMPANY "H," FOURTH REGIMENT KENTUCKY

| No. | Name | Rank | Joined for Service | Mustered In When | Mustered In Where | Period | Mustered Out When | Mustered Out Where |
|---|---|---|---|---|---|---|---|---|
| 1 | John G. Lair | Captain | Oct. 3 1847 | Oct. 4, '47 | Louisville, Ky. | To serve during the war | July 25, '48 | Somerset, Ky. |
| 1 | Milford Elliott | 1st Lieutenant | Oct. 3, 1847 | Oct. 4, '47 | Louisville, Ky. | | July 25, '48 | Somerset, Ky. |
| 1 | Cyrenius W. Gilmore | 2d Lieutenant | Oct. 3, 1847 | Oct. 4, '47 | Louisville, Ky. | | July 25, '48 | Somerset, Ky. |
| 2 | Samuel D. Cowan | 2d Lieutenant | Oct. 3, 1847 | Oct. 4, '47 | Louisville, Ky. | | July 25, '48 | Somerset, Ky. |
| 1 | James M. Cowan | 1st Sergeant | Oct. 3, 1847 | Oct. 4, '47 | Louisville, Ky. | | July 25, '48 | Somerset, Ky. |
| 2 | Isaac Smith | Sergeant | Oct. 3, 1847 | Oct. 4, '47 | Louisville, Ky. | | July 25, '48 | Somerset, Ky. |
| 3 | Charles P. Hays | Sergeant | Oct. 3 1847 | Oct. 4, '47 | Louisville, Ky. | | July 25, '48 | Somerset, Ky. |
| 4 | Andrew H. Campbell | Sergeant | Oct. 3 1847 | Oct. 4, '47 | Louisville, Ky. | | July 25, '48 | Somerset, Ky. |
| 1 | Addison Beatty | Corporal | Oct. 3, 1847 | Oct. 4, '47 | Louisville, Ky. | | July 25, '48 | Somerset, Ky. |
| 2 | Tunstall Q. Jasper | Corporal | Oct. 3, 1847 | Oct. 4, '47 | Louisville, Ky. | | July 25, '48 | Somerset, Ky. |
| 3 | William W. Arnett | Corporal | Oct. 3, 1847 | Oct. 4, '47 | Louisville, Ky. | | July 25, '48 | Somerset, Ky. |
| 4 | Lewis C. Grubb | Corporal | Oct. 3, 1847 | Oct. 4, '47 | Louisville, Ky. | | July 25, '48 | Somerset, Ky. |
| 1 | William S. Turpin | Musician | Oct. 3, 1847 | Oct. 4, '47 | Louisville, Ky. | | July 25, '48 | Somerset, Ky. |
| 2 | Robert Gunnell | Musician | Oct. 3, 1847 | Oct. 4, '47 | Louisville, Ky. | | July 25, '48 | Somerset, Ky. |
| 1 | Adkins, Benjamin | Private | Oct. 3, 1847 | Oct. 4, '47 | Louisville, Ky. | | July 25, '48 | Somerset, Ky. |
| 2 | Alexander, Thomas | Private | Oct. 3, 1847 | Oct. 4, '47 | Louisville Ky. | | July 25, '48 | Somerset, Ky. |
| 3 | Armstrong, William H. | Private | Oct. 13, 1847 | Oct. 13, '47 | Louisville, Ky. | | July 25, '48 | Somerset, Ky. |
| 4 | Burger, Jackson | Private | Oct. 3, 1847 | Oct. 4, '47 | Louisville, Ky. | | July 25, '48 | Somerset, Ky. |
| 5 | Blacklidge, Woodruff | Private | Oct. 3, 1847 | Oct. 4, '47 | Louisville, Ky. | | July 25, '48 | Somerset, Ky. |
| 6 | Brown, William | Private | Oct. 3, 1847 | Oct. 4, '47 | Louisville, Ky. | | July 25, '48 | Somerset, Ky. |
| 7 | Black, Calvan | Private | Oct. 3, 1847 | Oct. 4, '47 | Louisville, Ky. | | July 25, '48 | Somerset, Ky. |
| 8 | Barnett, James T. W. | Private | Oct. 3, 1847 | Oct. 4, '47 | Louisville, Ky. | | July 25, '48 | Somerset, Ky. |
| 9 | Baker, John A. | Private | Oct. 3, 1847 | Oct. 4, '47 | Louisville, Ky. | | July 25, '48 | Somerset, Ky. |
| 10 | Blankenship, Noah | Private | Oct. 3, 1847 | Oct. 4, '47 | Louisville, Ky. | | July 25, '48 | Somerset, Ky. |
| 11 | Carrigan, James M. | Private | Oct. 3, 1847 | Oct. 4, '47 | Louisville, Ky. | | July 25, '48 | Somerset, Ky. |
| 12 | Cundiff, Martin V. | Private | Oct. 3, 1847 | Oct. 4, '47 | Louisville, Ky. | | July 25, '48 | Somerset, Ky. |
| 13 | Crain, John L. | Private | Oct. 3, 1847 | Oct. 4, '47 | Louisville, Ky. | | July 25, '48 | Somerset, Ky. |
| 14 | Carrigan, John | Private | Oct. 3, 1847 | Oct. 4, '47 | Louisville, Ky. | | July 25, '48 | Somerset, Ky. |
| 15 | Christian, John C. | Private | Oct. 3, 1847 | Oct. 4, '47 | Louisville, Ky. | | July 25, '48 | Somerset, Ky. |
| 16 | Collyer, Cyrenius W. | Private | Oct. 3, 1847 | Oct. 4, '47 | Louisville, Ky. | | July 25, '48 | Somerset, Ky. |
| 17 | Denham, Samuel | Private | Oct. 3 1847 | Oct. 4, '47 | Louisville, Ky. | | July 25, '48 | Somerset, Ky. |
| 18 | Estis, Patrick H. | Private | Oct. 3, 1847 | Oct. 4, '47 | Louisville, Ky. | | July 25, '48 | Somerset, Ky. |
| 19 | Evans, James | Private | Oct. 3, 1847 | Oct. 4, '47 | Louisville, Ky. | | July 25, '48 | Somerset, Ky. |
| 20 | Elder, Jessee T. | Private | Oct. 3, 1847 | Oct. 4, '47 | Louisville, Ky. | | July 25, '48 | Somerset, Ky. |
| 21 | Fisher, Erasmus D. | Private | Oct. 3, 1847 | Oct. 4 '47 | Louisville, Ky. | | July 25, '48 | Somerset, Ky. |
| 22 | Faris, Tunstall Q. | Private | Oct. 3, 1847 | Oct. 4, '47 | Louisville, Ky. | | July 25, '48 | Somerset, Ky. |
| 23 | Freeman, Stephen L. | Private | Oct. 3, 1847 | Oct. 4, '47 | Louisville, Ky. | | July 25, '48 | Somerset, Ky. |
| 24 | Freeman, Green C. | Private | Oct. 3, 1847 | Oct. 4, '47 | Louisville, Ky. | | July 25, '48 | Somerset, Ky. |
| 25 | Faris, Thomas C. | Private | Oct. 3, 1847 | Oct. 4, '47 | Louisville, Ky. | | July 25, '48 | Somerset, Ky. |
| 26 | Goggin, David | Private | Oct. 3, 1847 | Oct. 4, '47 | Louisville, Ky. | | July 25, '48 | Somerset, Ky. |
| 27 | Gains, Thomas | Private | Oct. 3, 1847 | Oct. 4, '47 | Louisville, Ky. | | July 25, '48 | Somerset, Ky. |
| 28 | Gilmore, James | Private | Oct. 3, 1847 | Oct. 4, '47 | Louisville, Ky. | | July 25, '48 | Somerset, Ky. |
| 29 | Hendricks, James | Private | Oct. 3, 1847 | Oct. 4, '47 | Louisville Ky. | | July 25, '48 | Somerset, Ky. |
| 30 | Haman, William | Private | Oct. 3, 1847 | Oct. 4, '47 | Louisville, Ky. | | July 25, '48 | Somerset, Ky. |
| 31 | Hoskins, Gideon | Private | Oct. 3, 1847 | Oct. 4, '47 | Louisville, Ky. | | July 25, '48 | Somerset, Ky. |
| 32 | Hays, Isaac | Private | Oct. 3, 1847 | Oct. 4, '47 | Louisville, Ky. | | July 25, '48 | Somerset, Ky. |
| 33 | Hargiss, Thomas | Private | Oct. 3, 1847 | Oct. 4, '47 | Louisville, Ky. | | July 25, '48 | Somerset, Ky. |
| 34 | Hinds, Joel | Private | Oct. 3, 1847 | Oct. 4, '47 | Louisville, Ky. | | July 25, '48 | Somerset, Ky. |
| 35 | Higgins, Cornelius | Private | Oct. 3, 1847 | Oct. 4, '47 | Louisville, Ky. | | July 25, '48 | Somerset, Ky. |
| 36 | Harris, John L | Private | Oct. 3, 1847 | Oct. 4, '47 | Louisville, Ky. | | July 25, '48 | Somerset, Ky. |
| 37 | Lamb, James M. | Private | Oct. 3, 1847 | Oct. 4, '47 | Louisville, Ky. | | July 25, '48 | Somerset, Ky. |
| 38 | Morgan, William | Private | Oct. 3 1847 | Oct. 4, '47 | Louisville, Ky. | | July 25, '48 | Somerset, Ky. |
| 39 | McGinnis, James C. | Private | Oct. 3, 1847 | Oct. 4, '47 | Louisville, Ky. | | July 25, '48 | Somerset, Ky. |
| 40 | Mills, Samuel F. | Private | Oct. 3, 1847 | Oct. 4, '47 | Louisville, Ky. | | July 25, '48 | Somerset, Ky. |
| 41 | McKinney, William M. | Private | Oct. 3, 1847 | Oct. 4, '47 | Louisville, Ky. | | July 25, '48 | Somerset, Ky. |

## FOOT VOLUNTEERS—MEXICAN WAR—Continued.

| No. of each grade. | REMARKS. |
|---|---|
| 14 | Died at City of Mexico, January 5, 1848. No pay. |
| 15 | Died at Pueblo, January 6, 1848. Unknown. |
| 16 | Died at Pueblo, March 20, 1848. Unknown. |
| 17 | Died at Pueblo, January 21, 1848. Unknown. |
| 18 | Died at Acajeta, December 11, 1848. No pay. |
| 19 | Died at City of Mexico, January 9, 1848. |
| 20 | Died at City of Mexico, January 13, 1848, and pay to December 31, 1847. |
| 21 | Died at Pueblo, March 21, 1848. Pay unknown. |
| 22 | Died at City of Mexico, January 13, 1848, and pay to December 31, 1847. |
| 23 | Died at City of Mexico, January 26, 1848, and pay to December 31, 1847. |
| 24 | Died at City of Mexico, May 10, 1848; paid to 29th February, 1848. |

## FOOT VOLUNTEERS—MEXICAN WAR.

| | |
|---|---|
| 1 | |
| 1 | Absent on recruiting service since October 22, 1847. Order Col. Williams. Station, Somerset, Ky. |
| 1 | |
| 2 | |
| 1 | |
| 2 | |
| 3 | Appointed from private, 9th December, 1847. Order Col. Williams. |
| 4 | |
| 1 | Appointed from private, December 9, 1847. Order of Col. Williams. |
| 2 | |
| 3 | Appointed from private, 24th March, 1848. Order of Col. Williams. |
| 4 | |
| 1 | |
| 2 | Appointed from private March 1, 1848. |
| 1 | |
| 2 | |
| 3 | |
| 4 | |
| 5 | |
| 6 | Left sick in hospital at Jalapa, December 6, 1847. |
| 7 | |
| 8 | |
| 9 | Entitled to pay as hospital cook from 5th April, 1848, to June 1, 1848. Detailed by Dr. Roberts. |
| 10 | |
| 11 | |
| 12 | |
| 13 | |
| 14 | |
| 15 | |
| 16 | Reduced from Corporal March 24, 1848. Order of Col. Williams. Was Corporal from enrollment. |
| 17 | |
| 18 | |
| 19 | |
| 20 | |
| 21 | Reduced to ranks from Sergeant, December 9, 1847, order of Col. Williams. Was Sergeant from enrollment. |
| 22 | |
| 23 | |
| 24 | |
| 25 | |
| 26 | |
| 27 | |
| 28 | |
| 29 | |
| 30 | |
| 31 | |
| 32 | Sent sick to Jalapa, April 13, 1848. |
| 33 | |
| 34 | |
| 35 | |
| 36 | |
| 37 | |
| 38 | |
| 39 | |
| 40 | |
| 41 | |

## MEXICAN WAR VETERANS.

### ROLL OF COMPANY "H," FOURTH REGIMENT KENTUCKY

| No. of each grade | Name | Rank | Joined for Service | Mustered In When | Mustered In Where | Period | Mustered Out When | Mustered Out Where |
|---|---|---|---|---|---|---|---|---|
| 42 | Meed, Harvey J. | Private | Oct. 3, 1847 | Oct. 4, '47 | Louisville, Ky. | | July 25, '48 | Somerset, Ky. |
| 43 | Mounce, Greenup R. | Private | Oct. 3, 1847 | Oct. 4, '47 | Louisville, Ky. | | July 25, '48 | Somerset, Ky. |
| 44 | McClure, Hosea C. | Private | Oct. 3, 1847 | Oct. 4, '47 | Louisville, Ky. | | July 25, '48 | Somerset, Ky. |
| 45 | Nance, Jesse | Private | Oct. 3, 1847 | Oct. 4, '47 | Louisville, Ky. | | July 25, '48 | Somerset, Ky. |
| 46 | Nunnelly, William B. | Private | Oct. 3, 1847 | Oct. 4, '47 | Louisville, Ky. | | July 25, '48 | Somerset, Ky. |
| 47 | Owens, David D. | Private | Oct. 3, 1847 | Oct. 4, '47 | Louisville, Ky. | | July 25, '48 | Somerset, Ky. |
| 48 | Peters, Harrison | Private | Oct. 3, 1847 | Oct. 4, '47 | Louisville, Ky. | | July 25, '48 | Somerset, Ky. |
| 49 | Parker, Chrisman H. | Private | Oct. 3, 1847 | Oct. 4, '47 | Louisville, Ky. | | July 25, '48 | Somerset, Ky. |
| 50 | Porch, Henry S. | Private | Oct. 3, 1847 | Oct. 4, '47 | Louisville, Ky. | | July 25, '48 | Somerset, Ky. |
| 51 | Quinton, John | Private | Oct. 3, 1847 | Oct. 4, '47 | Louisville, Ky. | | July 25, '48 | Somerset, Ky. |
| 52 | Roberts, Montgomery | Private | Oct. 3, 1847 | Oct. 4, '47 | Louisville, Ky. | | July 25, '48 | Somerset, Ky. |
| 53 | Rosseau, James A. | Private | Oct. 3, 1847 | Oct. 4, '47 | Louisville, Ky. | | July 25, '48 | Somerset, Ky. |
| 54 | Rousseau, Lawrence H. | Private | Oct. 3, 1847 | Oct. 4, '47 | Louisville, Ky. | | July 25, '48 | Somerset, Ky. |
| 55 | Sadler, Edward | Private | Oct. 3, 1847 | Oct. 4, '47 | Louisville, Ky. | | July 25, '48 | Somerset, Ky. |
| 56 | Stogsdill, John | Private | Oct. 3, 1847 | Oct. 4, '47 | Louisville, Ky. | | July 25, '48 | Somerset, Ky. |
| 57 | Snodgrass, Seneca | Private | Oct. 3, 1847 | Oct. 4, '47 | Louisville, Ky. | | July 25, '48 | Somerset, Ky. |
| 58 | Stringer, Charles | Private | Oct. 3, 1847 | Oct. 4, '47 | Louisville, Ky. | | July 25, '48 | Somerset, Ky. |
| 59 | Stringer, Cyremus W. | Private | Oct. 3, 1847 | Oct. 4, '47 | Louisville, Ky. | | July 25, '48 | Somerset, Ky. |
| 60 | Stewart, George B. | Private | Oct. 3, 1847 | Oct 4, '47 | Louisville, Ky. | | July 25, '48 | Somerset, Ky. |
| 61 | Surber, Galen C. | Private | Oct. 3, 1847 | Oct. 4, '47 | Louisville, Ky. | | July 25, '48 | Somerset, Ky. |
| 62 | Tarter, Caleb | Private | Oct. 3, 1847 | Oct. 4, '47 | Louisville, Ky. | | July 25, '48 | Somerset, Ky. |
| 63 | Tarter, Alvadas | Private | Oct. 3, 1847 | Oct. 4, '47 | Louisville, Ky. | | July 25, '48 | Somerset, Ky. |
| 64 | Thacker, James | Private | Oct. 3, 1847 | Oct. 4, '47 | Louisville, Ky. | To serve during the war. | July 25, '48 | Somerset, Ky. |
| 65 | Taylor, Jarvis | Private | Oct. 3, 1847 | Oct. 4, '47 | Louisville, Ky. | | July 25, '48 | Somerset, Ky. |
| 66 | Vaught, Stephen | Private | Oct. 3, 1847 | Oct. 4, '47 | Louisville, Ky. | | July 25, '48 | Somerset, Ky. |
| 67 | Wells, John M. | Private | Oct. 3, 1847 | Oct. 4, '47 | Louisville, Ky. | | July 25, '48 | Somerset, Ky. |
| 68 | Williams, George B. | Private | Oct. 3, 1847 | Oct. 4, '47 | Louisville, Ky. | | July 25, '48 | Somerset, Ky. |
| 69 | Woodal, John | Private | Oct. 3, 1847 | Oct. 4, '47 | Louisville, Ky. | | July 25, '48 | Somerset, Ky. |
| 70 | Weddle, Daniel | Private | Oct. 3, 1847 | Oct. 4, '47 | Louisville, Ky. | | July 25, '48 | Somerset, Ky. |
| 71 | Wilson, Benjamin | Private | Oct. 3, 1847 | Oct. 4, '47 | Louisville, Ky. | | July 25, '48 | Somerset, Ky. |
| 72 | Warren, Alexander | Private | Oct. 3, 1847 | Oct. 4, '47 | Louisville, Ky. | | July 25, '48 | Somerset, Ky. |
| | **DISCHARGED.** | | | | | | | |
| 1 | Cox, Thomas | Private | Oct. 3, 1847 | Oct. 4, '47 | Louisville, Ky. | | | |
| 2 | Hamon, Daniel S. | Private | Oct. 3, 1847 | Oct. 4, '47 | Louisville, Ky. | | | |
| 3 | Merrick, James T. | Private | Oct. 3, 1847 | Oct. 4, '47 | Louisville, Ky. | | | |
| 4 | Turpin, William F. | Musician | Oct. 3, 1847 | Oct. 4, '47 | Louisville, Ky. | | | |
| | **DIED.** | | | | | | | |
| 1 | Bratton, Richard C. | Private | Oct. 3, 1847 | Oct. 4, '47 | Louisville, Ky. | | | |
| 2 | Bowyers, James | Private | Oct. 3, 1847 | Oct. 4, '47 | Louisville, Ky. | | | |
| 3 | Buckner, Bennet B. | Private | Oct. 3, 1847 | Oct. 4, '47 | Louisville, Ky. | | | |
| 4 | Durman, Green | Private | Oct. 3, 1847 | Oct. 4, '47 | Louisville, Ky. | | | |
| 5 | Durham, William | Private | Oct. 3, 1847 | Oct. 4, '47 | Louisville, Ky. | | | |
| 6 | Fugate, Martin H. | Private | Oct. 3, 1847 | Oct. 4, '47 | Louisville, Ky. | | | |
| 7 | Hunt, Silas | Private | Oct. 3, 1847 | Oct. 4, '47 | Louisville, Ky. | | | |
| 8 | Jasper, Merrill | Private | Oct. 3, 1847 | Oct. 4, '47 | Louisville, Ky. | | | |
| 9 | Jasper, John | Private | Oct. 3, 1847 | Oct. 4, '47 | Louisville, Ky. | | | |
| 10 | May, Jesse | Private | Oct. 3, 1847 | Oct. 4, '47 | Louisville, Ky. | | | |
| 11 | Pence, William | Private | Oct. 3, 1847 | Oct. 4, '47 | Louisville, Ky. | | | |
| 12 | Price, Noah | Private | Oct. 3, 1847 | Oct. 4, '47 | Louisville, Ky. | | | |
| 13 | Silvers, Westley | Private | Oct. 3, 1847 | Oct. 4, '47 | Louisville, Ky | | | |
| 14 | Tayman, Elisha G. | Private | Oct. 3, 1847 | Oct. 4, '47 | Louisville, Ky. | | | |
| | **DESERTED.** | | | | | | | |
| 1 | Pumphrey, Andrew | Private | Oct. 3, 1847 | Oct. 4, '47 | Louisville, Ky. | | | |
| 2 | Swinney, Daniel B. F. | Private | Oct. 3, 1847 | Oct. 4, '47 | Louisville, Ky. | | | |

This Company was organized by Captain John G. Lair, at Somerset, Ky., in the month of September, 1847, and marched thence to Louisville, Ky., where it arrived the 3d day of October, 1847, a distance of one hundred and thirty miles.

### ROLL OF COMPANY "I," FOURTH REGIMENT KENTUCKY

| | Name | Rank | Joined for Service | Mustered In When | Mustered In Where | Period | Mustered Out When | Mustered Out Where |
|---|---|---|---|---|---|---|---|---|
| 1 | Mark R. Hardin | Captain | Oct. 4, 1847 | Oct. 4, '47 | Louisville, Ky. | | July 25, '48 | Louisville, Ky. |
| 1 | Andrew D. Carey | 1st Lieutenant | Oct. 4, 1847 | Oct. 4, '47 | Louisville, Ky. | | July 25, '48 | Louisville, Ky. |
| 1 | James M. Shackleford | 2d Lieutenant | Oct. 4, 1847 | Oct. 4, '47 | Louisville, Ky. | During the war. | July 25, '48 | Louisville, Ky. |
| 2 | John D. Cosby | 2d Lieutenant | Oct. 4, 1847 | Oct. 4, '47 | Louisville, Ky. | | July 25, '48 | Louisville, Ky. |
| 1 | Michael Handley | 1st Sergeant | Oct. 4, 1847 | Oct. 4, '47 | Louisville, Ky. | | July 25, '48 | Louisville, Ky. |
| 2 | Henry Hix | Sergeant | Oct. 4, 1847 | Oct. 4, '47 | Louisville, Ky. | | July 25, '48 | Louisville, Ky. |
| 3 | Ezra W. Gray | Sergeant | Oct. 4, 1847 | Oct. 4, '47 | Louisville, Ky. | | July 25, '48 | Louisville, Ky. |
| 4 | Henry Moore | Sergeant | Oct. 4, 1847 | Oct. 4, '47 | Louisville, Ky. | | July 25, '48 | Louisville, Ky. |
| 1 | James H. Casey | Corporal | Oct. 4, 1847 | Oct. 4, '47 | Louisville, Ky. | | July 25, '48 | Louisville, Ky. |

## FOOT VOLUNTEERS—MEXICAN WAR—Continued.

| No. of each grade | REMARKS |
|---|---|
| 42 | |
| 43 | |
| 44 | |
| 45 | |
| 46 | |
| 47 | |
| 48 | |
| 49 | |
| 50 | Reduced from Corporal, December 9, 1847, order of Col. Williams; was Corporal from enrollment. |
| 51 | [dered on the march. |
| 52 | Left sick at Vera Cruz, November 22, 1847; returned for duty November 29, 1847, and left Vera Cruz, and is supposed to have been mur- |
| 53 | |
| 54 | |
| 55 | |
| 56 | |
| 57 | |
| 58 | |
| 59 | |
| 60 | |
| 61 | |
| 62 | |
| 63 | |
| 64 | Missing in the City of Mexico, May 31, 1848; supposed to have been murdered by the Mexicans. |
| 65 | |
| 66 | |
| 67 | |
| 68 | |
| 69 | |
| 70 | |
| 71 | |
| 72 | |
| 1 | Discharged on Surgeon's certificate of disability, January, 1848, at Pueblo, Mexico. |
| 2 | Discharged on Surgeon's certificate of disability, July 7, 1848, at New Orleans. |
| 3 | Discharged on Surgeon's certificate of disability, March 8, 1848, at New Orleans. |
| 4 | Discharged on Surgeon's certificate of disability, February 28, 1848, at City of Mexico. |
| 1 | Died in hospital, at Jalapa, January 6, 1848. |
| 2 | Died in hospital, at Pueblo, January 31, 1848. |
| 3 | Died in hospital, at City of Mexico, May 29, 1848. |
| 4 | Died in hospital, at City of Mexico, January 14, 1848 |
| 5 | Died in hospital, at City of Mexico, February 14, 1848. |
| 6 | Died in hospital, at Jalapa, June 6, 1848. |
| 7 | Died in hospital, at City of Mexico, February 2, 1848. |
| 8 | Died in hospital, at City of Mexico, February 13, 1848. |
| 9 | Died in hospital, at City of Mexico, March 30, 1848. |
| 10 | Died on march, near Vera Cruz, June 29, 1848. |
| 11 | Died in hospital, at New Orleans, November 22, 1847. |
| 12 | Died in hospital, at City of Mexico, March 30, 1848. |
| 13 | Died in barracks, City of Mexico, December 24, 1847. |
| 14 | Died in camp at Encerro, Mexico, June 22, 1848. |
| 1 | Deserted at Louisville, Ky., October 13, 1847. |
| 2 | Deserted at Louisville, Ky., October 13, 1847. |

## FOOT VOLUNTEERS—MEXICAN WAR.

| No. of each grade | REMARKS |
|---|---|
| 1 | |
| 1 | |
| 1 | |
| 2 | |
| 1 | |
| 2 | |
| 3 | Appointed Sergeant from ranks, May 10, 1848. |
| 4 | |
| 1 | |

## MEXICAN WAR VETERANS.

### ROLL OF COMPANY "I," FOURTH REGIMENT KENTUCKY

| No. of each grade | Name | Rank | Joined for Service | Mustered in When | Mustered in Where | Period | Mustered Out When | Mustered Out Where |
|---|---|---|---|---|---|---|---|---|
| 2 | Thomas Gaither | Corporal | Oct. 4, 1847 | Oct. 4, '47 | Louisville, Ky. | | July 25, '48 | Louisville, Ky. |
| 3 | Uriah Robeson | Corporal | Oct. 4, 1847 | Oct. 4, '47 | Louisville, Ky. | | July 25, '48 | Louisville, Ky. |
| 4 | Jesse Peters | Corporal | Oct. 4, 1847 | Oct. 4, '47 | Louisville, Ky. | | July 25, '48 | Louisville, Ky. |
| 1 | Armenius Peter | Musician | Oct. 4, 1847 | Oct. 4, '47 | Louisville, Ky. | | July 25, '48 | Louisville, Ky. |
| 2 | Thomas Britton | Musician | Oct. 26, 1847 | Dec. 3, '47 | City of Mexico | | July 25, '48 | Louisville, Ky. |
| 1 | Arvin, Thomas | Private | Oct. 4, 1847 | Oct. 4, '47 | Louisville, Ky. | | July 25, '48 | Louisville, Ky. |
| 2 | Aubery, Gabriel | Private | Oct. 4, 1847 | Oct 4, '47 | Louisville, Ky. | | July 25, '48 | Louisville, Ky. |
| 3 | Basham, Joel | Private | Oct. 4, 1847 | Oct. 4, '47 | Louisville, Ky. | | July 25, '48 | Louisville, Ky. |
| 4 | Basham, Solomell | Private | Oct. 4, 1847 | Oct. 4, '47 | Louisville, Ky. | | July 25, '48 | Louisville, Ky. |
| 5 | Blayez, John | Private | Oct. 4, 1847 | Oct. 4, '47 | Louisville, Ky. | | July 25, '48 | Louisville, Ky. |
| 6 | Berry, Philip G. | Private | Oct. 4, 1847 | Oct. 4, '47 | Louisville, Ky. | | July 25, '48 | Louisville, Ky. |
| 7 | Cooper, Thomas | Private | Oct. 4, 1847 | Oct. 4, '47 | Louisville, Ky. | | July 25, '48 | Louisville, Ky. |
| 8 | Crutcher, Cortes | Private | Oct. 4, 1847 | Oct. 4, '47 | Louisville, Ky. | | July 25, '48 | Louisville, Ky. |
| 9 | Campbell, Morten M. | Private | Oct. 4, 1847 | Oct. 4, '47 | Louisville, Ky. | | July 25, '48 | Louisville, Ky. |
| 10 | Cox, Nathaniel | Private | Oct. 4, 1847 | Oct. 4, '47 | Louisville, Ky. | | July 25, '48 | Louisville, Ky. |
| 11 | Corley, John | Private | Oct. 4, 1847 | Oct. 4, '47 | Louisville, Ky. | | July 25, '48 | Louisville, Ky. |
| 12 | Cheatham, John D. | Private | Oct. 4, 1847 | Oct. 4, '47 | Louisville, Ky. | | July 25, '48 | Louisville, Ky. |
| 13 | Cleveland Geo. W. | Private | Oct. 25, 1847 | Dec 31, '47 | City of Mexico | | July 25, '48 | Louisville, Ky. |
| 14 | Cotter, Wm. | Private | Oct. 4, 1847 | Oct. 4, '47 | Louisville, Ky. | | July 25, '48 | Louisville, Ky. |
| 15 | Cauman, Andrew | Private | Oct. 4, 1847 | Oct. 4, '47 | Louisville, Ky. | | July 25, '48 | Louisville, Ky. |
| 16 | Dugan, Henry | Private | Jan. 30, 1848 | Jan. 30, '48 | City of Mexico | | July 25, '48 | Louisville, Ky. |
| 17 | Graham, Matthew | Private | Oct. 4, 1847 | Oct. 4, '47 | Louisville, Ky. | | July 25, '48 | Louisville, Ky. |
| 18 | Green, Henry | Private | Oct. 4, 1847 | Oct. 4, '47 | Louisville, Ky. | | July 25, '48 | Louisville, Ky. |
| 19 | Green, Thomas | Private | Oct. 4, 1847 | Oct. 4, '47 | Louisville, Ky. | | July 25, '48 | Louisville, Ky. |
| 20 | Hardin, Thomas | Private | Oct. 4, 1847 | Oct. 4, '47 | Louisville, Ky. | | July 25, '48 | Louisville, Ky. |
| 21 | Hedges, Elias | Private | Oct. 4, 1847 | Oct. 4, '47 | Louisville, Ky. | | July 25, '48 | Louisville, Ky. |
| 22 | Hilburn, Edwin | Private | Oct. 4, 1847 | Oct. 4, '47 | Louisville, Ky. | | July 25, '48 | Louisville, Ky. |
| 23 | Hupp, Wm. I. | Private | Oct. 4, 1847 | Oct. 4, '47 | Louisville, Ky. | | July 25, '48 | Louisville, Ky. |
| 24 | Hendren, James M. | Private | Oct. 4, 1847 | Oct. 4, '47 | Louisville, Ky. | | July 25, '48 | Louisville, Ky. |
| 25 | Heather, James H. | Private | Oct. 4, 1847 | Oct. 4, '47 | Louisville, Ky. | | July 25, '48 | Louisville, Ky. |
| 26 | Higgs, James | Private | Oct. 4, 1847 | Oct. 4, '47 | Louisville, Ky. | | July 25, '48 | Louisville, Ky. |
| 27 | Hayes, James | Private | Oct. 4, 1847 | Oct. 4, '47 | Louisville, Ky. | To serve during the war | July 25, '48 | Louisville, Ky. |
| 28 | Hodges, Thomas D. | Private | Oct. 4, 1847 | Oct. 4, '47 | Louisville, Ky. | | July 25, '48 | Louisville, Ky. |
| 29 | Hatten, James | Private | Oct. 4, 1847 | Oct. 4, '47 | Louisville, Ky. | | July 25, '48 | Louisville, Ky. |
| 30 | Harisly, Wm. | Private | Oct. 4, 1847 | Oct. 4, '47 | Louisville, Ky. | | July 25, '48 | Louisville, Ky. |
| 31 | Jones, Jonathan | Private | Oct. 4, 1847 | Oct. 4, '47 | Louisville, Ky. | | July 25, '48 | Louisville, Ky. |
| 32 | Jarboe, Walter S. | Private | Oct. 4, 1847 | Oct. 4, '47 | Louisville, Ky. | | July 25, '48 | Louisville, Ky. |
| 33 | Johnston, Hamilton P. | Private | Mar. 11, 1848 | Apr. 30, '48 | City of Mexico | | July 25, '48 | Louisville, Ky. |
| 34 | Lamb, John | Private | Oct. 4, 1847 | Oct. 4, '47 | Louisville, Ky. | | July 25, '48 | Louisville, Ky. |
| 35 | Luke, Wm. | Private | Oct. 4, 1847 | Oct. 4, '47 | Louisville, Ky. | | July 25, '48 | Louisville, Ky. |
| 36 | Lambert, Geo. W. | Private | Oct. 4, 1847 | Oct. 4, '47 | Louisville, Ky. | | July 25, '48 | Louisville, Ky. |
| 37 | Meriman, John | Private | Oct. 4, 1847 | Oct. 4, '47 | Louisville, Ky. | | July 25, '48 | Louisville, Ky. |
| 38 | Morris, James | Private | Oct. 4, 1847 | Oct. 4, '47 | Louisville, Ky. | | July 25, '48 | Louisville, Ky. |
| 39 | Maddox, Andrew J. | Private | Oct. 4, 1847 | Oct. 4, '47 | Louisville, Ky. | | July 25, '48 | Louisville, Ky. |
| 40 | McKitrick, Joseph C. | Private | Oct. 4, 1847 | Oct. 4, '47 | Louisville, Ky. | | July 25, '48 | Louisville, Ky. |
| 41 | McKitrick, Felix | Private | Oct. 4, 1847 | Oct. 4, '47 | Louisville, Ky. | | July 25, '48 | Louisville, Ky. |
| 42 | McDonald, James | Private | Oct. 4, 1847 | Oct. 4, '47 | Louisville, Ky. | | July 25, '48 | Louisville, Ky. |
| 43 | Mudd, Paul | Private | Oct. 6, 1847 | Dec. 31, '47 | City of Mexico | | July 25, '48 | Louisville, Ky. |
| 44 | Montgomery, Paul | Private | Oct. 4, 1847 | Oct. 4, '47 | Louisville, Ky. | | July 25, '48 | Louisville, Ky. |
| 45 | Mayes, Allen H. | Private | Oct. 4, 1847 | Oct. 4, '47 | Louisville, Ky. | | July 25, '48 | Louisville, Ky. |
| 46 | Maddox, Edward C. | Private | Oct. 4, 1847 | Oct. 4, '47 | Louisville, Ky. | | July 25, '48 | Louisville, Ky. |
| 47 | McAlister, John | Private | Oct. 4, 1847 | Oct. 4, '47 | Louisville, Ky. | | July 25, '48 | Louisville, Ky. |
| 48 | Northern, Russel H. | Private | Oct. 4, 1847 | Oct. 4, '47 | Louisville, Ky. | | July 25, '48 | Louisville, Ky. |
| 49 | Orin, William H. | Private | Oct. 4, 1847 | Oct. 4, '47 | Louisville, Ky. | | July 25, '48 | Louisville, Ky. |
| 50 | Osburn, Francis | Private | Oct. 4, 1847 | Oct. 4, '47 | Louisville, Ky. | | July 25, '48 | Louisville, Ky. |
| 51 | Platt, Thomas W. | Private | Oct. 4, 1847 | Oct. 4, '47 | Louisville, Ky. | | July 25, '48 | Louisville, Ky. |
| 52 | Pope, William W. | Private | Oct. 4, 1847 | Oct. 4, '47 | Louisville, Ky. | | July 25, '48 | Louisville, Ky. |
| 53 | Ross, James | Private | Oct. 4, 1847 | Oct. 4, '47 | Louisville, Ky. | | July 25, '48 | Louisville, Ky. |
| 54 | Simpson, Elias W. | Private | Oct. 4, 1847 | Oct. 4, '47 | Louisville, Ky. | | July 25, '48 | Louisville, Ky. |
| 55 | Sinithart, John | Private | Oct. 4, 1847 | Oct. 4, '47 | Louisville, Ky. | | July 25, '48 | Louisville, Ky. |
| 56 | Seay, James L. | Private | Oct. 4, 1847 | Oct. 4, '47 | Louisville, Ky. | | July 25, '48 | Louisville, Ky. |
| 57 | Smith, James R. | Private | Oct. 4, 1847 | Oct. 4, '47 | Louisville, Ky. | | July 25, '48 | Louisville, Ky. |
| 58 | Smith, Edward K. | Private | Oct. 4, 1847 | Oct. 4, '47 | Louisville, Ky. | | July 25, '48 | Louisville, Ky. |
| 59 | Shackleford, George | Private | Oct. 4, 1847 | Oct. 4, '47 | Louisville, Ky. | | July 25, '48 | Louisville, Ky. |
| 60 | Stephenson, John | Private | Dec. 23, 1847 | Apr. 30, '48 | City of Mexico | | July 25, '48 | Louisville, Ky. |
| 61 | Thomas, Ruban | Private | Oct. 4, 1847 | Oct. 4, '47 | Louisville, Ky. | | July 25, '48 | Louisville, Ky. |
| 62 | Thompson, Jeroam A. | Private | Oct. 4, 1847 | Oct. 4, '47 | Louisville, Ky. | | July 25, '48 | Louisville, Ky. |
| 63 | Thompson, William | Private | Oct. 4, 1847 | Oct. 4, '47 | Louisville, Ky. | | July 25, '48 | Louisville, Ky. |
| 64 | Townsend, Eli | Private | Oct. 4, 1847 | Oct. 4, '47 | Louisville, Ky. | | July 25, '48 | Louisville, Ky. |
| 65 | Townson, William | Private | Oct. 4, 1847 | Oct. 4, '47 | Louisville, Ky. | | July 25, '48 | Louisville, Ky. |
| 66 | Thornhill, Henry | Private | May 10, 1848 | May 10, '48 | City of Mexico | | July 25, '48 | Louisville, Ky. |
| 67 | Wheatley, Richard | Private | Oct. 4, 1847 | Oct. 4, '47 | Louisville, Ky. | | July 25, '48 | Louisville, Ky. |
| 68 | Wright, Harrison | Private | Oct. 4, 1847 | Oct. 4, '47 | Louisville, Ky. | | July 25, '48 | Louisville, Ky. |
| 69 | White, Richard | Private | Oct. 4, 1847 | Oct. 4, '47 | Louisville, Ky. | | July 25, '48 | Louisville, Ky. |
| 70 | Young, James H. | Private | Oct. 4, 1847 | Oct. 4, '47 | Louisville, Ky. | | July 25, '48 | Louisville, Ky. |

## FOOT VOLUNTEERS—MEXICAN WAR—Continued.

| No. of each grade. | REMARKS. |
|---|---|
| 2 | Absent sick at New Orleans, since July 8, 1848. |
| 3 | |
| 4 | Appointed Corporal from ranks March 1, 1848. |
| 1 | Appointed Musician from ranks February 20, 1848. |
| 2 | Appointed Musician from ranks February 20, 1848. |
| 1 | |
| 2 | |
| 3 | |
| 4 | |
| 5 | |
| 6 | |
| 7 | |
| 8 | |
| 9 | |
| 10 | |
| 11 | |
| 12 | |
| 13 | |
| 14 | |
| 15 | |
| 16 | |
| 17 | |
| 18 | |
| 19 | |
| 20 | |
| 21 | |
| 22 | |
| 23 | |
| 24 | |
| 25 | |
| 26 | |
| 27 | |
| 28 | |
| 29 | |
| 30 | |
| 31 | |
| 32 | |
| 33 | |
| 34 | |
| 35 | |
| 36 | |
| 37 | |
| 38 | |
| 39 | Musician reduced to ranks, February 20, 1848, by order. |
| 40 | |
| 41 | |
| 42 | |
| 43 | |
| 44 | |
| 45 | |
| 46 | |
| 47 | |
| 48 | |
| 49 | |
| 50 | |
| 51 | Detached on recruiting service from enrollment until June 16, 1848, when joined his Company at Jalapa. |
| 52 | |
| 53 | |
| 54 | |
| 55 | |
| 56 | |
| 57 | |
| 58 | |
| 59 | |
| 60 | Transferred from Company " E," by regimental order No. 20, April, 1848. |
| 61 | |
| 62 | |
| 63 | |
| 64 | |
| 65 | |
| 66 | |
| 67 | |
| 68 | |
| 69 | |
| 70 | |

## ROLL OF COMPANY "I," FOURTH REGIMENT KENTUCKY

| No. of each grade. | Name. | Rank. | Joined for Service. | Mustered In. When. | Mustered In. Where. | Period | Mustered Out. When. | Mustered Out. Where. |
|---|---|---|---|---|---|---|---|---|
| | **DIED.** | | | | | | | |
| 1 | Fowler, William | Private | Oct. 3, 1847 | Oct. 4, '47 | Louisville, Ky. | | | |
| 2 | Robert Hardin | Private | Oct. 4, 1847 | Oct. 4, '47 | Louisville, Ky. | | | |
| 3 | William Shield | Private | Oct. 4, 1847 | Oct. 4, '47 | Louisville, Ky. | | | |
| 4 | Thomas Fulkinson | Private | Oct. 4, 1847 | Oct. 4, '47 | Louisville, Ky. | | | |
| 5 | Robert G. Pitts | Private | Oct. 4, 1847 | Oct. 4, '47 | Louisville, Ky. | | | |
| 6 | James W. Sappington | Private | Oct. 4, 1847 | Oct. 4, '47 | Louisville, Ky. | | | |
| 7 | James Burch | Private | Oct. 4, 1847 | Oct. 4, '47 | Louisville, Ky. | To serve during the war. | | |
| 8 | Robert Mullin | Private | Oct. 4, 1847 | Oct. 4, '47 | Louisville, Ky. | | | |
| 9 | Wm. P. Pullin | Private | Oct. 4, 1847 | Oct. 4, '47 | Louisville, Ky. | | | |
| 10 | Felix Doyle | Private | Oct. 4, 1847 | Oct. 4, '47 | Louisville, Ky. | | | |
| 11 | George Launaser | Private | Oct. 4, 1847 | Oct. 4, '47 | Louisville, Ky. | | | |
| 12 | Cox, William | Private | Oct. 4, 1847 | Oct. 4, '47 | Louisville, Ky. | | | |
| | **DISCHARGED.** | | | | | | | |
| 1 | Jackson Bird | Private | Oct. 4, 1847 | Oct. 4, '47 | Louisville, Ky. | | | |
| 2 | Edward T. Hughes | Private | Oct. 4, 1847 | Oct. 4, '47 | Louisville, Ky. | | | |
| 3 | Thomas Phelps | Private | Oct. 4, 1847 | Oct. 4, '47 | Louisville, Ky. | | | |
| 4 | John Schuling | Private | Oct. 4, 1847 | Oct. 4, '47 | Louisville, Ky. | | | |
| 5 | Squire Montgomery | Private | Oct. 4, 1847 | Oct. 4, '47 | Louisville, Ky. | | | |
| 6 | James Hillard | Private | Oct. 4, 1847 | Oct. 4, '47 | Louisville, Ky. | | | |
| 7 | Thomas Strang | Private | Oct. 4, 1847 | Oct. 4, '47 | Louisville, Ky. | | | |
| 8 | James Young | Private | Oct. 4, 1847 | Oct. 4, '47 | Louisville, Ky. | | | |
| 9 | Matthew Young | Private | Oct. 4, 1847 | Oct. 4, '47 | Louisville, Ky. | | | |
| | **DESERTED.** | | | | | | | |
| 1 | Richard Crutcher | Private | Oct. 4, 1847 | Oct. 4, '47 | Louisville, Ky. | | | |
| 2 | Buford McGowan | Private | Oct. 4, 1847 | Oct. 4, '47 | Louisville, Ky. | | | |
| 3 | John Williams | Private | Feb. 7, 1848 | Feb. 7, '48 | City of Mexico | | | |
| 4 | William White | Private | Jan. 30, 1848 | Jan. 30, '48 | City of Mexico | | | |
| | **TRANSFERRED.** | | | | | | | |
| 1 | Daniel McMullin | Private | Oct. 27, 1847 | Dec. 1, '47 | City of Mexico | | | |

This Company was organized by Captain Mark R. Hardin, at Springfield, Ky., in the month of September, 1847, and marched thence to Louisville, Ky., where it arrived on the 3d day of October, 1848, a distance of sixty miles.

## ROLL OF COMPANY "K," FOURTH REGIMENT KENTUCKY

| | Name | Rank | Joined for Service | Mustered In When | Mustered In Where | Period | Mustered Out When | Mustered Out Where |
|---|---|---|---|---|---|---|---|---|
| 1 | Patrick H. Gardner | Captain | Sept. 28, 1847 | Oct. 1, '47 | Louisville, Ky. | | | |
| 2 | Thomas Mayfield | Captain | Sept. 28, 1847 | Oct. 1, '47 | Louisville, Ky. | | July 25, '48 | Louisville, Ky. |
| 1 | Henry D. Nevill | 1st Lieutenant | Sept. 28, 1847 | Oct. 1, '47 | Louisville, Ky. | | July 25, '48 | Louisville, Ky. |
| 2 | John Donan | 1st Lieutenant | Sept. 28, 1847 | Oct. 1, '47 | Louisville, Ky. | | July 25, '48 | Louisville, Ky. |
| 1 | Harvey Woodward | 2d Lieutenant | Sept. 28, 1847 | Oct. 1, '47 | Louisville, Ky. | | July 25, '48 | Louisville, Ky. |
| 2 | Charles A. Wickliffe | 2d Lieutenant | Apr. 13, 1848 | Apr. 13, '48 | City of Mexico | | July 25, '48 | Louisville, Ky. |
| 1 | Jeptha G. Collins | 1st Sergeant | Sept. 28, 1847 | Oct. 1, '47 | Louisville, Ky. | | July 25, '48 | Louisville, Ky. |
| 2 | Orill Mayfield | Sergeant | Sept. 28, 1847 | Oct. 1, '47 | Louisville, Ky. | | July 25, '48 | Louisville, Ky. |
| 3 | Arthur Gardner | Sergeant | Oct. 30, 1847 | Dec. 31, '47 | City of Mexico | | July 25, '48 | Louisville, Ky. |
| 4 | Jesse J. Craddock | Sergeant | Sept. 28, 1847 | Oct. 1, '47 | Louisville, Ky. | | July 25, '48 | Louisville, Ky. |
| 1 | Samuel C. Handley | Corporal | Sept. 28, 1847 | Oct. 1, '47 | Louisville, Ky. | | July 25, '48 | Louisville, Ky. |
| 2 | Thomas D. Woodson | Corporal | Sept. 28, 1847 | Oct. 1, '47 | Louisville, Ky. | To serve during war. | July 25, '48 | Louisville, Ky. |
| 3 | James R. Neale | Corporal | Sept. 28, 1847 | Oct. 1, '47 | Louisville, Ky. | | July 25, '48 | Louisville, Ky. |
| 4 | William F. Rolston | Corporal | Sept. 28, 1847 | Oct. 1, '47 | Louisville, Ky. | | July 25, '48 | Louisville, Ky. |
| 1 | Allen, Arthur R. | Private | Sept. 28, 1847 | Oct. 1, '47 | Louisville, Ky. | | July 25, '48 | Louisville, Ky. |
| 2 | Anderson, Meredith | Private | Sept. 28, 1847 | Oct. 1, '47 | Louisville, Ky. | | July 25, '48 | Louisville, Ky. |
| 3 | Ashworth, Stephen G. | Private | Sept. 28, 1847 | Oct. 1, '47 | Louisville, Ky. | | July 25, '48 | Louisville, Ky. |
| 4 | Burris, John B. | Private | Sept. 28, 1847 | Oct. 1, '47 | Louisville, Ky. | | July 25, '48 | Louisville, Ky. |
| 5 | Butler, James | Private | Sept. 28, 1847 | Oct. 1, '47 | Louisville, Ky. | | July 25, '48 | Louisville, Ky. |
| 6 | Burris, Albert G. | Private | Sept. 28, 1847 | Oct. 1, '47 | Louisville, Ky. | | July 25, '48 | Louisville, Ky. |
| 7 | Craddock, Alexander G. | Private | Sept. 28, 1847 | Oct. 1, '47 | Louisville, Ky. | | July 25, '48 | Louisville, Ky. |
| 8 | Clevedence, Jonathan | Private | Sept. 28, 1847 | Oct. 1, '47 | Louisville, Ky. | | July 25, '48 | Louisville, Ky. |
| 9 | Critchlow, Grafton J. | Private | Sept. 28, 1847 | Oct. 1, '47 | Louisville, Ky. | | July 25, '48 | Louisville, Ky. |
| 10 | Crump, Joshua A. | Private | Sept. 28, 1847 | Oct. 1, '47 | Louisville, Ky. | | July 25, '48 | Louisville, Ky. |
| 11 | Corder, Reuben | Private | Sept. 28, 1847 | Oct. 1, '47 | Louisville, Ky. | | July 25, '48 | Louisville, Ky. |
| 12 | Dunagan, John D. | Private | Sept. 28, 1847 | Oct. 1, '47 | Louisville, Ky. | | July 25, '48 | Louisville, Ky. |
| 13 | Fletcher Elias | Private | Sept. 28, 1847 | Oct. 1, '47 | Louisville, Ky. | | July 25, '48 | Louisville, Ky. |
| 14 | Garvin, John L. | Private | Sept. 28, 1847 | Oct. 1, '47 | Louisville, Ky. | | July 25, '48 | Louisville, Ky. |
| 15 | Gunn, Abraham | Private | Sept. 28, 1847 | Oct. 1, '47 | Louisville, Ky. | | July 25, '48 | Louisville, Ky. |
| 16 | Gardner, Wm. E. | Private | Sept. 28, 1847 | Oct. 1, '47 | Louisville, Ky. | | July 25, '48 | Louisville, Ky. |
| 17 | Harper, Wm. B. | Private | Sept. 28, 1847 | Oct. 1, '47 | Louisville, Ky. | | July 25, '48 | Louisville, Ky. |
| 18 | Handley, David H. | Private | Sept. 28, 1847 | Oct. 1, '47 | Louisville, Ky. | | July 25, '48 | Louisville, Ky. |
| 19 | Hendrick, Edward H. | Private | Sept. 28, 1847 | Oct. 1, '47 | Louisville, Ky. | | July 25, '48 | Louisville, Ky. |

## FOOT VOLUNTEERS—MEXICAN WAR—Continued.

| No. of each grade | REMARKS. |
|---|---|
| 1 | Died at Jalapa, December 2, 1847. |
| 2 | Died City of Mexico, February 11, 1848. |
| 3 | Died City of Mexico, ordinary sickness, July 29, 1848. |
| 4 | Died City of Mexico, February 12, 1848. |
| 5 | Died in hospital at Pueblo, January 23, 1848. |
| 6 | Died in hospital at Pueblo, January 11, 1848. |
| 7 | Died in hospital at Jalapa, of ordinary sickness, December 29, 1847. |
| 8 | Died at the City of Mexico, April 17, 1848. |
| 9 | Died March 11, 1848, in hospital at Jalapa. |
| 10 | Died in hospital Jalapa, about June 17, 1848. |
| 11 | Died July 16, 1848, on board steamer St. Landry, Mississippi river. |
| 12 | Died July 17, 1848, on board steamer St. Landry, Mississippi river. |
| | |
| 1 | Discharged on writ of habeas corpus, October 15, 1847, at Louisville, Ky. Order of Judge Wm. Bullock. |
| 2 | Discharged on writ of habeas corpus, November 1, 1847, at Louisville, Ky. Order of Judge Wm. Bullock. |
| 3 | Discharged April 13, 1848, City of Mexico, special order, No. not known; Headquarters, City of Mexico. |
| 4 | Discharged April 13, 1848, City of Mexico, for disability; on Surgeon's certificate. |
| 5 | Discharged March 31. 1848, by special order, not known; Headquarters, City of Mexico. |
| 6 | Discharged at the hospital at Jalapa, June, 1848. |
| 7 | Discharged May, 1848, on Surgeon's certificate, at hospital, New Orleans. |
| 8 | Discharged at the City of New Orleans, on Surgeon's certificate. Time not known. |
| 9 | Discharged at the City of New Orleans, on Surgeon's certificate. Time not known. |
| | |
| 1 | Deserted at Louisville, October 10, 1847. |
| 2 | Deserted at Danville, Ky., October 15, 1847. |
| 3 | Deserted February 20, 1848, in City of Mexico. |
| 4 | Deserted February 20, 1848, in City of Mexico. |
| | |
| 1 | Transferred to Company "E," by Regimental order No. 20, April 21, 1848. |

## FOOT VOLUNTEERS—MEXICAN WAR.

| | |
|---|---|
| 1 | Resigned 13th April, 1848. |
| 2 | Promoted from 2d Lieutenant 13th April, 1848, vice Gardner, resigned; 2d Lieutenant from enrollment. |
| 1 | Dropped 13th April, 1848; never joined the Company. |
| 2 | Promoted from 2d Lieutenant April 13, 1848, vice Nevill, dropped; was 2d Lieutenant from enrollment. |
| 1 | Promoted from private April 13, 1848, vice Donan, promoted. Volunteer aid to Gen. Butler; pay due as from February 29th to promotion. |
| 2 | Appointed April 13, 1848, vice Mayfield, promoted, at City of Mexico. |
| 1 | |
| 2 | |
| 3 | |
| 4 | |
| 1 | |
| 2 | |
| 3 | |
| 4 | |
| 1 | |
| 2 | |
| 3 | |
| 4 | |
| 5 | |
| 6 | |
| 7 | |
| 8 | |
| 9 | |
| 10 | |
| 11 | |
| 12 | |
| 13 | |
| 14 | |
| 15 | |
| 16 | |
| 17 | |
| 18 | |
| 19 | |

## MEXICAN WAR VETERANS.

### ROLL OF COMPANY "K," FOURTH REGIMENT KENTUCKY

| No. of each grade | Name. | Rank. | Joined for Service. | Mustered In. When. | Mustered In. Where. | Period | Mustered Out. When. | Mustered Out. Where. |
|---|---|---|---|---|---|---|---|---|
| 20 | Hardin, William P... | Private... | Sept. 28, 1847. | Oct. 1, '47. | Louisville, Ky... | | July 25, '48 | Louisville, Ky... |
| 21 | Jolly, Charles... | Private... | Sept. 28, 1847. | Oct. 1, '47. | Louisville, Ky... | | July 25, '48 | Louisville, Ky... |
| 22 | Jones, Robert G... | Private... | Sept. 28, 1847. | Oct. 1, '47. | Louisville, Ky... | | July 25, '48. | Louisville, Ky... |
| 23 | Key, Albert M... | Private... | Sept. 28, 1847 | Oct. 1, '47. | Louisville, Ky... | | July 25, '48. | Louisville, Ky... |
| 24 | Kerr, James D... | Private... | Sept. 28 1847 | Oct. 1, '47. | Louisville, Ky... | | July 25, '48. | Louisville, Ky... |
| 25 | Kelly, David L... | Private... | Sept. 28, 1847. | Oct. 1, '47. | Louisville, Ky... | | July 25, '48. | Louisville, Ky... |
| 26 | Knight, Benjamin... | Private... | Sept. 28, 1847. | Oct. 1, '47. | Louisville, Ky... | | July 25, '48. | Louisville, Ky... |
| 27 | Lard, Thomas G... | Private... | Sept. 28, 1847. | Oct. 1, '47. | Louisville, Ky... | | July 25, '48. | Louisville, Ky... |
| 28 | Lard, Robert... | Private... | Sept. 28, 1847. | Oct. 1, '47. | Louisville, Ky... | | July 25, '48. | Louisville, Ky... |
| 29 | Meredith, William... | Private... | Sept. 28, 1847. | Oct. 1, '47. | Louisville, Ky... | | July 25, '48. | Louisville, Ky... |
| 30 | Mansfield, Washington | Private... | Sept. 28, 1847. | Oct. 1, '47. | Louisville, Ky... | | July 25, '48. | Louisville, Ky... |
| 31 | Murray, Samuel A... | Private... | Sept. 28, 1847. | Oct. 1, '47. | Louisville, Ky... | | July 25, '48. | Louisville, Ky... |
| 32 | Martin, James W... | Private... | Sept. 28, 1847. | Oct. 1, '47. | Louisville, Ky... | | July 25, '48. | Louisville, Ky... |
| 33 | Mayfield, Beverly C... | Private... | Sept. 28, 1847. | Oct. 1, '47. | Louisville, Ky... | | July 25, '48. | Louisville, Ky... |
| 34 | Monin, Rawleigh M... | Private... | Sept. 28, 1847. | Oct. 1, '47. | Louisville, Ky... | | July 25, '48. | Louisville, Ky... |
| 35 | Monin, Joseph N... | Private... | Sept. 28, 1847 | Oct. 1, '47. | Louisville, Ky... | | July 25, '48 | Louisville, Ky... |
| 36 | Maxey, Ephraim... | Private... | Oct. 30, 1847. | Dec. 31, 47. | City of Mexico... | | July 25, '48. | Louisville, Ky... |
| 37 | McKinney, Marion... | Private... | Dec. 3, 1847. | Not known. | Not known... | | | |
| 38 | Newton, Isaac... | Private... | Sept. 28, 1847. | Oct. 1, '47. | Louisville, Ky... | | July 25, '48. | Louisville, Ky... |
| 39 | Oldham, Caleb... | Private... | Sept. 28, 1847. | Oct. 1, '47. | Louisville, Ky... | | July 25, '48. | Louisville, Ky... |
| 40 | Price, John M... | Private... | Sept. 28, 1847. | Oct. 1, '47. | Louisville, Ky... | | July 25, '48. | Louisville, Ky... |
| 41 | Perry, Miles J... | Private... | Sept. 28, 1847. | Oct. 1, '47. | Louisville, Ky... | | July 25, '48. | Louisville, Ky... |
| 42 | Parker, William H... | Private... | Sept. 28, 1847 | Oct. 1, '47. | Louisville, Ky... | | July 25, '48. | Louisville, Ky... |
| 43 | Rainey, Robert... | Private... | Sept. 28, 1847. | Oct. 1, '47. | Louisville, Ky... | | July 25, '48. | Louisville, Ky... |
| 44 | Roundtree, James W... | Private... | Sept. 28, 1847. | Oct. 1, '47. | Louisville, Ky... | | July 25, '48. | Louisville, Ky... |
| 45 | Rolston, John... | Private... | Sept. 28, 1847. | Oct. 1, '47. | Louisville, Ky... | | July 25, '48. | Louisville, Ky... |
| 46 | Ragland, Hugh... | Private... | Sept. 28, 1847. | Oct. 1, '47. | Louisville, Ky... | | July 25, '48. | Louisville, Ky... |
| 47 | Robertson, Louis... | Private... | Sept. 28, 1847. | Oct. 1, '47. | Louisville, Ky... | | July 25, '48. | Louisville, Ky... |
| 48 | Robertson, Uriah... | Private... | Sept. 28, 1847. | Oct. 1, '47. | Louisville, Ky... | | July 25, '48. | Louisville, Ky... |
| 49 | Sturgeon, Willis... | Private... | Sept. 28, 1847 | Oct. 1, '47. | Louisville, Ky... | | July 25, '48. | Louisville, Ky... |
| 50 | Smith, Robert... | Private... | Sept. 28, 1847. | Oct. 1, '47. | Louisville, Ky... | | July 25, '48. | Louisville, Ky... |
| 51 | Smith, Peter... | Private... | Oct. 28, 1847. | Dec. 31, '47. | City of Mexico... | To serve during the war. | July 25, '48. | Louisville, Ky... |
| 52 | Smith, Nicholas... | Private... | Nov. 12, 1847. | Dec. 31, '47. | City of Mexico. | | July 25, '48. | Louisville, Ky... |
| 53 | Sims, Joseph C... | Private... | Sept. 28, 1847. | Oct. 1, '47. | Louisville, Ky... | | July 25, '48. | Louisville, Ky... |
| 54 | Welsh, Edgar... | Private... | Sept. 28, 1847. | Oct. 1, '47. | Louisville, Ky... | | July 25, '48. | Louisville, Ky... |
| 55 | Waddle, Jacob... | Private... | Sept. 28, 1847. | Oct. 1, '47. | Louisville, Ky... | | July 25, '48. | Louisville, Ky... |
| 56 | Wilson, Washington... | Private... | Sept. 28, 1847. | Oct. 1, '47. | Louisville, Ky... | | July 25, '48. | Louisville, Ky... |
| 57 | Wilson, John E... | Private... | Sept. 28, 1847. | Oct. 1, '47. | Louisville, Ky... | | July 25, '48 | Louisville, Ky... |
| 58 | Witherspoon, John L... | Private... | Sept. 28, 1847. | Oct. 1, '47. | Louisville, Ky... | | July 25, '48. | Louisville, Ky... |
| 59 | Webb, Benjamin F... | Private... | Sept. 28, 1847. | Oct. 1, '47. | Louisville, Ky... | | July 25, '48. | Louisville, Ky... |
| 60 | Wilhelm, Jacob... | Private... | Sept. 28, 1847. | Oct. 1, '47. | Louisville, Ky... | | July 25, '48. | Louisville, Ky... |
| 61 | Wooden, William... | Private... | Sept. 28, 1847. | Oct. 1, '47. | Louisville, Ky... | | July 25, '48. | Louisville, Ky... |
| 62 | Williams, Joseph P... | Private... | Sept. 28, 1847. | Oct. 1, '47. | Louisville, Ky... | | July 25, '48. | Louisville, Ky... |
| 63 | Wells, David... | Private... | Sept. 28, 1847. | Oct. 1, '47. | Louisville, Ky... | | July 25, '48. | Louisville, Ky... |
| 64 | Yates, James G... | Private... | Sept. 28, 1847. | Oct. 1, '47. | Louisville, Ky... | | July 25, '48. | Louisville, Ky... |
| | **DISCHARGED.** | | | | | | | |
| 1 | Craddock, Samuel A... | Private... | Sept. 28, 1847. | Oct. 1, '47. | Louisville, Ky... | | | |
| 2 | Mansfield, James L... | Private... | Sept. 28, 1847. | Oct. 1, '47. | Louisville, Ky... | | | |
| 3 | Murray, Jesse M... | Sergeant... | Sept. 28, 1847. | Oct. 1, '47. | Louisville, Ky... | | | |
| 4 | Carden, James... | Private... | Sept. 28, 1847. | Oct. 1, '47. | Louisville, Ky... | | | |
| 5 | Palmer, Manley F... | Private... | Sept. 28, 1847. | Oct. 1, '47. | Louisville, Ky... | | | |
| 6 | Rolston, George J... | Private... | Sept. 28, 1847. | | | | | |
| | **DIED.** | | | | | | | |
| 1 | Adcock, Joseph... | Private... | Sept. 28, 1847. | Oct. 1, '47. | Louisville, Ky... | | | |
| 2 | Mansfield, James L... | Private... | Sept. 28, 1847. | Oct. 1, '47. | Louisville, Ky... | | | |
| 3 | Murray, Jesse M... | Private... | Sept. 28, 1847. | Oct. 1, '47. | Louisville, Ky... | | | |
| 4 | Jones, James A... | Private... | Sept. 28, 1847. | Oct. 1, '47. | Louisville, Ky... | | | |
| 5 | Clever, Hiram... | Private... | Oct. 28, 1847. | Dec. 31, '47. | City of Mexico... | | | |
| 6 | Huston, Robert W... | Private... | Sept. 28, 1847. | Oct. 1, '47. | Louisville, Ky... | | | |
| 7 | Brashears, Greenberry. | Private... | Sept. 28, 1847. | Oct. 1, '47. | Louisville, Ky... | | | |
| 8 | Stewart, Milton... | Private... | Sept. 28, 1847. | Oct. 1, '47. | Louisville, Ky... | | | |
| 9 | Farris, Cyrus... | Private... | Sept. 28, 1847. | Oct. 1, '47. | Louisville, Ky... | | | |
| 10 | Reynolds, Rolly W... | Private... | Sept. 28, 1847. | Oct. 1, '47. | Louisville, Ky... | | | |
| 11 | Roundtree, Wm. H... | Private... | Sept. 28, 1847. | Oct. 1, '47. | Louisville, Ky... | | | |
| 12 | Oldham, Allen... | Private... | Sept. 28, 1847. | Oct. 1, '47. | Louisville, Ky... | | | |
| 13 | Jeffries, Thomas A... | Private... | Sept. 28, 1847. | Oct. 1, '47. | Louisville, Ky... | | | |
| 14 | Walters, Walter B... | Private... | Sept. 28, 1847. | Oct. 1, '47. | Louisville, Ky... | | | |
| 15 | Rainey, John W... | Private... | Sept. 28, 1847. | Oct. 1, '47. | Louisville, Ky... | | | |
| 16 | Crump, David... | Private... | Sept. 28, 1847. | Oct. 1, '47. | Louisville, Ky... | | | |
| 17 | Cully, John L... | Private... | Sept. 28, 1847. | Oct. 1, '47. | Louisville, Ky... | | | |
| 18 | Farlee, Ansolem... | Private... | Sept. 28, 1847. | Oct. 1, '47. | Louisville, Ky... | | | |

## FOOT VOLUNTEERS—MEXICAN WAR—Continued.

| No. of each grade. | REMARKS. |
|---|---|
| 20 | |
| 21 | |
| 22 | |
| 23 | |
| 24 | |
| 25 | |
| 26 | |
| 27 | |
| 28 | |
| 29 | |
| 30 | |
| 31 | |
| 32 | |
| 33 | |
| 34 | |
| 35 | |
| 36 | |
| 37 | |
| 38 | Joined; assigned to Company, Encerro, Mex., June 18, 1848. |
| 39 | |
| 40 | |
| 41 | |
| 42 | |
| 43 | |
| 44 | |
| 45 | |
| 46 | |
| 47 | |
| 48 | |
| 49 | |
| 50 | |
| 51 | |
| 52 | |
| 53 | |
| 54 | |
| 55 | |
| 56 | |
| 57 | |
| 58 | |
| 59 | |
| 60 | |
| 61 | |
| 62 | |
| 63 | |
| 64 | |
| 1 | Discharged at Louisville, Ky., October 30, 1847; Surgeon's certificate of physical disability. |
| 2 | Discharged at Louisville, Ky., October 4, 1847, by civil authority, as a minor. |
| 3 | Discharged at Jalapa, Mexico, January 9, 1848; Surgeon's certificate of physical disability. |
| 4 | Discharged at Jalapa, Mexico (date unknown), upon Surgeon's certificate of ordinary disability. |
| 5 | Discharged at Vera Cruz, Mexico; date not known. |
| 6 | Discharged at New Orleans, La., July 5, 1848; Surgeon's certificate of physical disability. |
| 1 | Died at Pueblo, December 13, 1847. |
| 2 | Died in City of Mexico, January 8, 1848. |
| 3 | Died in City of Mexico, January 18, 1848. |
| 4 | Died at Pueblo, January 19, 1848. |
| 5 | Died at City of Mexico, January 23, 1848. |
| 6 | Died at City of Mexico, January 26, 1848. |
| 7 | Died at City of Mexico, January 29, 1848. |
| 8 | Died at City of Mexico, February 2, 1848. |
| 9 | Died at City of Mexico, February 10, 1848. |
| 10 | Died at City of Mexico, February 15, 1848. |
| 11 | Died at City of Mexico, February 20, 1848. |
| 12 | Died at Pueblo, March 1, 1848. |
| 13 | Died at City of Mexico, March 4, 1848. |
| 14 | Died at City of Mexico, March 21, 1848. |
| 15 | Died at City of Mexico, April 9, 1848. |
| 16 | Died at City of Mexico, April 16, 1848. |
| 17 | Died at City of Mexico, April 25, 1848. |
| 18 | Died at City of Mexico, May 20, 1848. |

## MEXICAN WAR VETERANS.

### ROLL OF COMPANY "K," FOURTH REGIMENT KENTUCKY

| No. of each grade | Name. | Rank. | Joined for Service. | Mustered In. When. | Mustered In. Where. | Period. | Mustered Out. When. | Mustered Out. Where. |
|---|---|---|---|---|---|---|---|---|
| | DESERTED. | | | | | | | |
| 1 | West Gardner | Musician | Sept. 28, 1847. | Oct. 1, '47. | Louisville, Ky. | During war. | | |
| 2 | Nathan, Levi | Private | Dec. 12, 1847. | | | | | |

This Company was organized by Capt. P. H. Gardner, at Munfordsville, Ky., in the month of September, 1847, and marched thence to Louisville, Ky., where it arrived on the 28th day of September, 1847, a distance of seventy-five miles.

### ROLL OF A DETACHMENT OF RECRUITS OF FOURTH REGIMENT KENTUCKY

| | Name | Rank | Joined | Mustered In Where | | Mustered Out When | Mustered Out Where |
|---|---|---|---|---|---|---|---|
| 1 | Anderson, Thomas J. | Private | Nov. 30, 1847. | Monticello, Ky. | Never mustered into service. | June 20, '48. | Newport Bks., Ky. |
| 2 | Anderson, John W. | Private | Nov. 16, 1847. | Somerset, Ky. | | June 20, '48. | Newport Bks., Ky. |
| 3 | Blair, Madison | Private | Mar. 22, 1848. | Somerset, Ky. | | June 20, '48. | Newport Bks., Ky. |
| 4 | Davenport, Milford E. | Private | Jan. 21, 1848. | Somerset, Ky. | | June 20, '48. | Newport Bks., Ky. |
| 5 | Davis, David Allen | Private | Feb. 1, 1848. | Somerset, Ky. | | June 20, '48. | Newport Bks., Ky. |
| 6 | Estepp, James W. | Private | Apr. 12, 1848. | Somerset, Ky. | | June 20, '48. | Newport Bks., Ky. |
| 7 | Elder, William J. | Private | Feb. 1, 1848. | Somerset, Ky. | | June 20, '48. | Newport Bks., Ky. |
| 8 | Hall, William | Private | Jan. 1, 1848. | Somerset, Ky. | To serve during the war. | June 20, '48. | Newport Bks., Ky. |
| 9 | Jasper, Teral | Private | Jan. 21, 1848. | Somerset, Ky. | | June 20, '48. | Newport Bks., Ky. |
| 10 | Jasper, John | Private | Mar. 2, 1848. | Somerset, Ky. | | June 20, '48. | Newport Bks., Ky. |
| 11 | Maxey, Jeremiah | Private | Nov. 8, 1847. | Somerset, Ky. | | June 20, '48. | Newport Bks., Ky. |
| 12 | Maxey, Larkin | Private | Dec. 21, 1847. | Somerset, Ky. | | June 20, '48. | Newport Bks., Ky. |
| 13 | Meredith, Randol | Private | Nov. 30, 1847. | Monticello, Ky. | | June 20, '48. | Newport Bks., Ky. |
| 14 | Minton, James R. | Private | Jan. 1, 1848. | Casey county, Ky. | | June 20, '48. | Newport Bks., Ky. |
| 15 | Minton, Jonathan | Private | Mar. 22, 1848. | Casey county, Ky. | | June 20, '48. | Newport Bks., Ky. |
| 16 | Meeks, Robert | Private | Mar. 23, 1848. | Casey county, Ky. | | June 20, '48. | Newport Bks., Ky. |
| 17 | Meeks, John | Private | Mar. 22, 1848. | Casey county, Ky. | | June 20, '48. | Newport Bks., Ky. |
| 18 | Meeks, William | Private | Nov. 13, 1847. | Casey county, Ky. | | June 20, '48. | Newport Bks., Ky. |
| 19 | Night, Weston | Private | Mar. 23, 1848. | Somerset, Ky. | | June 20, '48. | Newport Bks., Ky. |
| 20 | Pumphrey, Andrew J. | Private | Nov. 8, 1847. | Somerset, Ky. | | June 20, '48. | Newport Bks., Ky. |
| 21 | Ross, Levi | Private | Mar. 11, 1848. | Casey county, Ky. | | June 20, '48. | Newport Bks, Ky. |
| 22 | Swinea, Stephen | Private | May 5, 1848. | Somerset, Ky. | | June 20, '48. | Newport Bks., Ky. |
| 23 | Tarter, James | Private | Mar. 23, 1848. | Casey county, Ky. | | June 20, '48. | Newport Bks., Ky. |
| 24 | Woolsey, Richard | Private | Apr. 12, 1848. | Somerset, Ky. | | June 20, '48. | Newport Bks., Ky. |

### ROLL OF CAPT. JOHN S. WILLIAMS' INDEPENDENT

| | Name | Rank | Joined for Service | Mustered In When | Mustered In Where | Period | Mustered Out When | Mustered Out Where |
|---|---|---|---|---|---|---|---|---|
| 1 | John S. Williams | Captain | June 13, 1846. | June 15, '46. | Louisville, Ky. | 1 yr. | May 27, '47. | New Orleans, La. |
| 1 | Roger W. Hanson | 1st Lieutenant | June 13, 1846. | June 15, '46. | Louisville, Ky. | 1 yr. | May 27, '47. | New Orleans, La. |
| 1 | Wm. A. McConnell | 2d Lieutenant | June 13, 1846. | June 15, '46. | Louisville, Ky. | 1 yr. | May 27, '47. | New Orleans, La. |
| 2 | Geo. S. Sutherland | 2d Lieutenant | June 13, 1846. | June 15, '46. | Louisville, Ky. | 1 yr. | May 27, '47. | New Orleans, La. |
| 1 | Allen T. Mocabee | 1st Sergeant | June 13, 1846. | June 15, '46. | Louisville, Ky. | 1 yr. | May 27, '47. | New Orleans, La. |
| 2 | Jesse H. Patton | Sergeant | June 13, 1846. | June 15, '46. | Louisville, Ky. | 1 yr. | May 27, '47. | New Orleans, La. |
| 3 | Roger T. Quissenbury | Sergeant | June 13, 1846. | June 15, '46. | Louisville, Ky. | 1 yr. | May 27, '47. | New Orleans, La. |
| 4 | William T. Rice | Sergeant | June 13, 1846. | June 15, '46. | Louisville, Ky. | 1 yr. | May 27, '47. | New Orleans, La. |
| 1 | William M. Bush | Corporal | June 13, 1846. | June 15, '46. | Louisville, Ky. | 1 yr. | May 27, '47. | New Orleans, La. |
| 2 | William R. Tutt | Corporal | June 13, 1846. | June 15, '46. | Louisville, Ky. | 1 yr. | May 27, '47. | New Orleans, La. |
| 3 | Leslie C. Webster | Corporal | June 13, 1846. | June 15, '46. | Louisville, Ky. | 1 yr. | May 27, '47. | New Orleans, La. |
| 4 | Willis F. Martin | Corporal | June 13, 1846. | June 15, '46. | Louisville, Ky. | 1 yr. | May 27, '47. | New Orleans, La. |
| 1 | Adams, Joshua | Private | June 13, 1846. | June 15, '46. | Louisville, Ky. | 1 yr. | May 27, '47. | New Orleans, La. |
| 2 | Baher, Stanley | Private | June 13, 1846. | June 15, '46. | Louisville, Ky. | 1 yr. | May 27, '47. | New Orleans, La. |
| 3 | Bruner, Henry | Private | June 13, 1846. | June 15, '46. | Louisville, Ky. | 1 yr. | May 27, '47. | New Orleans, La. |
| 4 | Bruce, Eli | Private | June 13, 1846. | June 15, '46. | Louisville, Ky. | 1 yr. | May 27, '47. | New Orleans, La. |
| 5 | Ballad, Wm. | Private | June 13, 1846. | June 15, '46. | Louisville, Ky. | 1 yr. | May 27, '47. | New Orleans, La. |
| 6 | Barly, Timothy | Private | June 13, 1846. | June 15, '46. | Louisville, Ky. | 1 yr. | May 27, '47. | New Orleans, La. |
| 7 | Battail, Bird W. | Private | June 13, 1846. | June 15, '46. | Louisville, Ky. | 1 yr. | May 27, '47. | New Orleans, La. |
| 8 | Bruce, William | Private | June 13, 1846. | June 15, '46. | Louisville, Ky. | 1 yr. | May 27, '47. | New Orleans, La. |
| 9 | Brewer, Francis M. | Private | June 13, 1846. | June 15, '46. | Louisville, Ky. | 1 yr. | May 27, '47. | New Orleans, La. |
| 10 | Curtis, James J. | Private | June 13, 1846. | June 15, '46. | Louisville, Ky. | 1 yr. | May 27, '47. | New Orleans, La. |
| 11 | Courtright, Wm. | Private | June 13, 1846. | June 15, '46. | Louisville, Ky. | 1 yr. | May 27, '47. | New Orleans, La. |
| 12 | Clark, John T. | Private | June 13, 1846. | June 15, '46. | Louisville, Ky. | 1 yr. | May 27, '47. | New Orleans, La. |
| 13 | Curtis, D. Dudley | Private | June 13, 1846. | June 15, '46. | Louisville, Ky. | 1 yr. | May 27, '47. | New Orleans, La. |
| 14 | Culbertson, David | Private | June 13, 1846. | June 15, '46. | Louisville, Ky. | 1 yr. | May 27, '47. | New Orleans, La. |
| 15 | Cruiz, Theodore | Private | June 13, 1846. | June 15, '46. | Louisville, Ky. | 1 yr. | May 27, '47. | New Orleans, La. |
| 16 | Chism, William | Private | June 13, 1846. | June 15, '46. | Louisville, Ky. | 1 yr. | May 27, '47. | New Orleans, La. |
| 17 | Crow, David S. | Private | June 13, 1846. | June 15, '46. | Louisville, Ky. | 1 yr. | May 27, '47. | New Orleans, La. |
| 18 | Curry, Joseph E. | Private | June 13, 1846. | June 15, '46. | Louisville, Ky. | 1 yr. | May 27, '47. | New Orleans, La. |
| 19 | Duncan, John | Private | June 13, 1846. | June 15, '46. | Louisville, Ky. | 1 yr. | May 27, '47. | New Orleans, La. |
| 20 | Emerson, Rufus S. | Private | June 13, 1846. | June 15, '46. | Louisville, Ky. | 1 yr. | May 27, '47. | New Orleans, La. |

## FOOT VOLUNTEERS—MEXICAN WAR—Continued.

| No. of each grade | REMARKS. |
|---|---|
| 1 | Deserted at the City of Mexico, December 22, 1847—supposed. |
| 2 | Deserted at the City of Mexico, December 27, 1847. |

## FOOT VOLUNTEERS, COLONEL JOHN S. WILLIAMS—MEXICAN WAR.

| | |
|---|---|
| 1 | Pay due from enrollment. |
| 2 | Pay due from enrollment. |
| 3 | Pay due from enrollment. |
| 4 | Pay due from enrollment. |
| 5 | Pay due from enrollment. |
| 6 | Pay due from enrollment. |
| 7 | Pay due from enrollment. |
| 8 | Pay due from enrollment. |
| 9 | Pay due from enrollment. |
| 10 | Pay due from enrollment. |
| 11 | Pay due from enrollment. |
| 12 | Pay due from enrollment. |
| 13 | Pay due from enrollment. |
| 14 | Pay due from enrollment. |
| 15 | Pay due from enrollment. |
| 16 | Pay due from enrollment. |
| 17 | Pay due from enrollment. |
| 18 | Pay due from enrollment. |
| 19 | Pay due from enrollment. |
| 20 | Pay due from enrollment. |
| 21 | Pay due from enrollment. |
| 22 | Pay due from enrollment. |
| 23 | Pay due from enrollment. |
| 24 | Pay due from enrollment. |

## COMPANY, KENTUCKY VOLUNTEERS—MEXICAN WAR.

| | |
|---|---|
| 1 | |
| 1 | |
| 1 | |
| 2 | Wounded severely in battle of Cerro Gordo, April 18, 1847. |
| 1 | Wounded severely in battle of Cerro Gordo, April 18, 1847. |
| 2 | Sick in hospital at Jalapa, May 6, 1847. |
| 3 | |
| 4 | |
| 1 | |
| 2 | |
| 3 | |
| 4 | Appointed Corporal April 18, 1847. |
| 1 | Absent; sick at San Antonio, Texas, September 26, 1846. Order of Gen. Wool. |
| 2 | |
| 3 | Wounded severely in battle of Cerro Gordo, April 18, 1847. |
| 4 | |
| 5 | |
| 6 | |
| 7 | |
| 8 | |
| 9 | |
| 10 | |
| 11 | |
| 12 | |
| 13 | |
| 14 | |
| 15 | Absent; sick in Louisville, Ky., from June 29, 1846. Order of Col. McKee. |
| 16 | |
| 17 | |
| 18 | |
| 19 | Absent; sick in Louisville, Ky., since June 29, 1846. Order of Col. McKee. |
| 20 | |

## MEXICAN WAR VETERANS.

### ROLL OF CAPT. JOHN S. WILLIAMS' INDEPENDENT COMPANY

| No. of each grade | Name. | Rank. | Joined for Service. | Mustered In. When. | Mustered In. Where. | Period | Mustered Out. When. | Mustered Out. Where. |
|---|---|---|---|---|---|---|---|---|
| 21 | Freeman, William F. | Private | June 13, 1846. | June 15, '46. | Louisville, Ky. | 1 yr. | May 27, '47. | New Orleans, La. |
| 22 | Hampton, James | Private | June 13, 1846. | June 15, '46. | Louisville, Ky. | 1 yr. | May 27, '47. | New Orleans, La. |
| 23 | Hon, Simpson | Private | June 13, 1846. | June 15, '46. | Louisville, Ky. | 1 yr. | May 27, '47. | New Orleans, La. |
| 24 | Haggard, Bartlett S. | Private | June 13, 1846. | June 15, '46. | Louisville, Ky. | 1 yr. | May 27, '47. | New Orleans, La. |
| 25 | Hogan, James | Private | June 13, 1846. | June 15, '46. | Louisville, Ky. | 1 yr. | May 27, '47. | New Orleans, La. |
| 26 | Harlow, George | Private | June 13, 1846. | June 15, '46. | Louisville, Ky. | 1 yr. | May 27, '47. | New Orleans, La. |
| 27 | Jones, Jesse W. | Private | June 13, 1846. | June 15, '46. | Louisville, Ky. | 1 yr. | May 27, '47. | New Orleans, La. |
| 28 | Keith, Nathaniel W. | Private | June 13, 1846. | June 15, '46. | Louisville, Ky. | 1 yr. | May 27, '47 | New Orleans, La. |
| 29 | Langston, Joseph G. | Private | June 13, 1846. | June 15, '46. | Louisville, Ky. | 1 yr. | May 27, '47. | New Orleans, La. |
| 30 | Lawrence, William S. | Private | June 13, 1846. | June 15, '46. | Louisville, Ky. | 1 yr. | May 27, '47. | New Orleans, La. |
| 31 | Lyle, Francis M. | Private | June 13, 1846. | June 15, '46. | Louisville, Ky. | 1 yr. | May 27, '47. | New Orleans, La. |
| 32 | Muir, James | Private | June 13, 1846. | June 15, '46. | Louisville, Ky. | 1 yr. | May 27, '47. | New Orleans, La. |
| 33 | March, Japtha R. | Private | June 13, 1846. | June 15, '46. | Louisville, Ky. | 1 yr. | May 27, '47. | New Orleans, La. |
| 34 | Mulhall, Robert | Private | June 13, 1846. | June 15, '46. | Louisville, Ky. | 1 yr. | May 27, '47. | New Orleans, La. |
| 35 | Nelson, Robert | Private | June 13, 1846. | June 15, '46. | Louisville, Ky. | 1 yr. | May 27, '47. | New Orleans, La. |
| 36 | Oden, Creason | Private | June 13, 1846. | June 15, '46. | Louisville, Ky. | 1 yr. | May 27, '47. | New Orleans, La. |
| 37 | Peddicord, James | Private | June 13, 1846. | June 15, '46. | Louisville, Ky. | 1 yr. | May 27, '47. | New Orleans, La. |
| 38 | Riggs, Caleb F. | Private | June 13, 1846 | June 15, '46. | Louisville, Ky. | 1 yr. | May 27, '47. | New Orleans, La. |
| 39 | Ralls, Eli | Private | June 13, 1846. | June 15, '46. | Louisville, Ky. | 1 yr. | May 27, '47. | New Orleans, La. |
| 40 | Risen, Josiah | Private | June 13, 1846. | June 15, '46. | Louisville, Ky. | 1 yr. | May 27, '47. | New Orleans, La. |
| 41 | Smith, Minor T. | Private | June 13, 1846. | June 15, '46. | Louisville, Ky. | 1 yr. | May 27, '47. | New Orleans, La. |
| 42 | Stuart, John W. | Private | June 13, 1846. | June 15, '46. | Louisville, Ky. | 1 yr. | May 27, '47. | New Orleans, La. |
| 43 | Snyder, Peter | Private | June 13, 1846. | June 15, '46. | Louisville, Ky. | 1 yr. | May 27, '47. | New Orleans, La. |
| 44 | Sutherland, James | Private | June 13, 1846. | June 15, '46. | Louisville, Ky. | 1 yr. | May 27, '47. | New Orleans, La. |
| 45 | Sutherland, Frederick | Private | June 13, 1846. | June 15, '46. | Louisville, Ky. | 1 yr. | May 27, '47. | New Orleans, La. |
| 46 | Snyder, John | Private | June 13, 1846. | June 15, '46. | Louisville, Ky. | 1 yr. | May 27, '47. | New Orleans, La. |
| 47 | Twyman, Allen H. | Private | June 13 1846. | June 15, '46. | Louisville, Ky. | 1 yr. | May 27, '47. | New Orleans, La. |
| 48 | Tate, George W. | Private | June 13, 1846. | June 15, '46. | Louisville, Ky. | 1 yr. | May 27, '47. | New Orleans, La. |
| 49 | Thompson, William | Private | June 13, 1846. | June 15, '46. | Louisville, Ky. | 1 yr. | May 27, '47. | New Orleans, La. |
| 50 | White, Fielding W. | Private | June 13, 1846. | June 15, '46. | Louisville, Ky. | 1 yr. | May 27, '47. | New Orleans, La. |
| 51 | Williams, William A. | Private | June 13, 1846. | June 15, '46. | Louisville, Ky. | 1 yr. | May 27, '47. | New Orleans, La. |
| 52 | Williams, Henry D. | Private | June 13, 1846. | June 15, '46. | Louisville, Ky. | 1 yr. | May 27, '47. | New Orleans, La. |
| 53 | Wright, William | Private | June 13, 1846. | June 15, '46. | Louisville, Ky. | 1 yr. | May 27, '47. | New Orleans, La. |
| 54 | Wright, James | Private | June 13, 1846. | June 15, '46. | Louisville, Ky. | 1 yr. | May 27, '47. | New Orleans, La. |
| | **Died.** | | | | | | | |
| 1 | William T. Bush | 1st Sergeant | June 13, 1846. | June 15, '46. | Louisville, Ky. | 1 yr. | | |
| 1 | Elkin, William P. | Corporal | June 13, 1846. | June 15, '46. | Louisville, Ky. | 1 yr. | | |
| 1 | Birch, Silas J. | Private | June 13, 1846. | June 15 '46. | Louisville, Ky. | 1 yr. | | |
| 2 | Berry, Landon T. | Private | June 13, 1846 | June 15, '46. | Louisville, Ky. | 1 yr. | | |
| 3 | Durham, William | Private | June 13, 1846 | June 15, '46 | Louisville, Ky. | 1 yr. | | |
| 4 | Devary, Benjamin F. | Private | June 13, 1846. | June 15, '46. | Louisville, Ky. | 1 yr. | | |
| 5 | Haggard, James | Private | June 13, 1846. | June 15, '46. | Louisville, Ky. | 1 yr. | | |
| 6 | Hatton, Alfred | Private | June 13, 1846. | June 15, '46. | Louisville, Ky. | 1 yr. | | |
| 7 | Storm, Ira | Private | June 13, 1846. | June 15, '46. | Louisville, Ky. | 1 yr. | | |
| 8 | Thomas, Samuel | Private | June 13, 1846. | June 15, '46. | Louisville, Ky. | 1 yr. | | |
| 9 | Tuttle, James A. | Private | June 13, 1846. | June 15, '46. | Louisville, Ky. | 1 yr. | | |
| 10 | Worrel, John | Private | June 13, 1846. | June 15, '46. | Louisville, Ky. | 1 yr. | | |
| | **Discharged.** | | | | | | | |
| 1 | Abbott, John B. | Private | June 13, 1846. | June 15, '46. | Louisville, Ky. | 1 yr. | | |
| 2 | Artis, Robert | Private | June 13, 1846. | June 15, '46. | Louisville, Ky. | 1 yr. | | |
| 3 | Burris, William T. | Private | June 13, 1846. | June 15, '46. | Louisville, Ky. | 1 yr. | | |
| 4 | Kirby, James | Private | June 13, 1846. | June 15, '46. | Louisville, Ky. | 1 yr. | | |
| 5 | Goodrich, William T. | Private | June 13, 1846. | June 15, '46. | Louisville, Ky. | 1 yr. | | |
| 6 | Lon, William | Private | June 13, 1846 | June 15, '46. | Louisville, Ky. | 1 yr. | | |
| 7 | Mitchell, Adison | Private | June 13, 1846. | June 15, '46. | Louisville, Ky. | 1 yr. | | |
| | **Deserted.** | | | | | | | |
| 1 | Clem, Albert G. | Private | June 13, 1846. | June 15, '46. | Louisville, Ky. | 1 yr. | | |
| 2 | Hampton, Ambrose W. | Private | June 13, 1846. | June 15, '46. | Louisville, Ky. | 1 yr. | | |

NOTE.—Clem Estis, as appears on original muster roll, was mustered into the service with the Company, which I am satisfied is a mistake, as he was examined by Surgeon Robert Hunt, and pronounced physically unable, and was rejected by the mustering officer.

JOHN S. WILLIAMS, *Captain.*

# KENTUCKY VOLUNTEERS—MEXICAN WAR—Continued.

| No. of each grade | REMARKS. |
|---|---|
| 21 | |
| 22 | |
| 23 | Absent; at sick Lavacca, Texas, since August 13, 1846. Order of Capt. Williams. |
| 24 | |
| 25 | |
| 26 | [self for sixty-two days. |
| 27 | Was sick at Lavacca, Texas, 13th August, 1846, and was unable to join the camp, which was in the interior of Mexico. Subsisted him- |
| 28 | Wounded severely in battle of Cerro Gordo, April 18, 1847; in hospital Jalapa, Mexico. |
| 29 | Wounded severely in battle of Cerro Gordo, April 18, 1847. |
| 30 | |
| 31 | Absent as hospital nurse, Jalapa, Mexico, May 6, 1847. Order of Col. Haskell. |
| 32 | Absent sick in hospital at Jalapa, from May 6, 1847. |
| 33 | |
| 34 | |
| 35 | |
| 36 | |
| 37 | |
| 38 | |
| 39 | |
| 40 | |
| 41 | Wounded severely in battle of Cerro Gordo, April 18, 1847; in hospital Jalapa, Mexico. |
| 42 | |
| 43 | |
| 44 | |
| 45 | |
| 46 | Joined by transfer from Capt. Turpin's Company, 2d Regt. Ky. Vols. Order of Col. McKee, July 7, 1846. |
| 47 | |
| 48 | |
| 49 | |
| 50 | |
| 51 | |
| 52 | Wounded severely in battle of Cerro Gordo, April 18, 1847. |
| 53 | |
| 54 | Absent; sick at San Antonio, Texas, September 26, 1846. |
| | |
| 1 | Died at Lavacca, Texas, July 25, 1846. |
| 1 | Killed in battle of Cerro Gordo, April 18, 1847. |
| 1 | Died at Monterey, February 11, 1847. |
| 2 | Died at Jalapa, May 6, 1847. |
| 3 | Killed in battle of Cerro Gordo, April 18, 1847. |
| 4 | Died at Lavacca, August 1, 1846. |
| 5 | Killed accidentally while on post as sentinel at Saltillo, January 3, 1847. |
| 6 | Killed in battle of Cerro Gordo, April 18, 1847. |
| 7 | Died at Jalapa, May 4, 1847, of wounds received in battle of Cerro Gordo, April 18, 1847. |
| 8 | Died at Vera Cruz, March 10, 1847. |
| 9 | Died at Vera Cruz, March 17, 1847. |
| 10 | Died at Palo Alto, February 15, 1847. |
| | |
| 1 | Discharged August 13, 1846, for physical disability, at Lavacca, Texas. Order Capt. Williams. |
| 2 | Discharged August 13, 1846, for physical disability, at Lavacca, Texas. Order Capt. Williams. |
| 3 | Discharged August 13, 1846, for physical disability, at Lavacca, Texas. Order Capt. Williams. |
| 4 | Discharged Louisville, Ky., for disobedience of orders, improper and immoral conduct. Order of Gen. Wool, June 29, 1846. |
| 5 | Discharged at San Antonio, Texas, for physical disability, September 10, 1846. Order of Gen. Wool. |
| 6 | Discharged at San Antonio, Texas, for physical disability, September 10, 1846. Order of Gen. Wool. |
| 7 | Discharged at San Antonio, Texas, for physical disability, September 16, 1846. Order of Gen. Wool. |
| | |
| 1 | Deserted at Louisville, June 29, 1846. |
| 2 | Deserted at New Orleans, July 9, 1846. |

## MEXICAN WAR VETERANS.

# ROLL OF COMPANY "B," SIXTEENTH REGIMENT U. S. INFANTRY, COL.
## UNDER ACT OF CONGRESS OF FEBRUARY

| No. of each grade | NAME. | RANK. | Date of commission | Enlisted When. | Enlisted Where. | Period | Mustered Out When. | Mustered Out Where. |
|---|---|---|---|---|---|---|---|---|
| 1 | John T. Hughes | Captain | Date of commission not stated. | | | To serve during the war. | | |
| 1 | Edward C. Berry | 1st Lieutenant | | | | | | |
| 1 | William Garrard | 2d Lieutenant | | | | | | |
| 1 | Charles Wickliffe | Captain | | | | | | |
| 1 | Edward Curd | 1st Lieutenant | | | | | | |
| 1 | Burwell B. Irvan | 2d Lieutenant | | | | | | |
| 2 | Thomas P. Hawkins | 2d Lieutenant | | | | | | |
| 1 | William C. Miller | 1st Sergeant | | April 5, '47 | Benton, Ky. | | Aug. 7, '48 | Newport, Ky. |
| 2 | Walter C. Austin | Sergeant | | April 5, '47 | Benton, Ky. | | Aug. 7, '48 | Newport, Ky. |
| 3 | John Curd | Sergeant | | April 3, '47 | Murray, Ky. | | Aug. 7, '48 | Newport, Ky. |
| 1 | Arthur H. W. Perry | Corporal | | April 5, '47 | Benton, Ky. | | Aug. 7, '48 | Newport, Ky. |
| 2 | John A. Poindexter | Corporal | | May 18, '47 | Newport, Ky. | | | |
| 3 | Littleton Helm | Corporal | | April 10, '47 | Benton, Ky | | Aug. 7, '47 | Newport, Ky. |
| 1 | George W. Barton | Drummer | | May 3, '47 | Murray, Ky. | | Aug. 7, '48 | Newport, Ky |
| 2 | Andrew T. Suter | Fifer | | May 25, '47 | Owenton, Ky. | | Aug. 7, '48 | Newport, Ky. |
| 1 | Adamson, Charles | Private | | April 24, '47 | Bardstown, Ky. | | Aug. 7, '48 | Newport. Ky. |
| 2 | Adams, Thomas | Private | | April 26, '47 | Murray, Ky. | | Aug. 7, '48 | Newport, Ky. |
| 3 | Beecher, George M. | Private | | Mar. 13, '47 | Chicago, Ill. | | Aug. 7, '48 | Newport, Ky. |
| 4 | Beck, Reddick D. | Private | | April 17, '47 | Murray, Ky. | | Aug. 7, '48 | Newport, Ky. |
| 5 | Bennett, Wesley | Private | | May 25, '47 | Owenton, Ky. | | Aug. 7, '48 | Newport, Ky. |
| 6 | Boulton, John W. | Private | | May 25, '47 | Owenton, Ky. | | Aug. 7, '48 | Newport, Ky. |
| 7 | Bogard, Benjamin F. | Private | | April 17, '47 | Murray, Ky. | | Aug. 7, '48 | Newport, Ky. |
| 8 | Bell, Mahlen | Private | | May 12, '47 | Fort Wayne, Ind. | | Aug. 7, '48 | Newport, Ky. |
| 9 | Blake, John | Private | | July 9, '47 | Louisville, Ky. | | Aug. 7, '48 | Newport, Ky. |
| 10 | Becket, Alexander | Private | | July 8, '47 | Louisville, Ky. | | Aug. 7, '48 | Newport, Ky. |
| 11 | Brown, Richard | Private | | July 11, '47 | Louisville, Ky. | | Aug. 7, '48 | Newport, Ky. |
| 12 | Crabtree, James H. | Private | | April 24, '47 | Murray, Ky. | | Aug. 7, '48 | Newport, Ky. |
| 13 | Castleman, Richard | Private | | May 13, '47 | Fort Wayne, Ind. | | Aug. 7, '48 | Newport. Ky. |
| 14 | Cunningham, Isaac L. | Private | | April 8, '47 | Madison, | | Aug. 7, '48 | Newport, Ky. |
| 15 | Dawson, John | Private | | May 25, '47 | Owenton, Ky. | | Aug. 7, '48 | Newport, Ky. |
| 16 | Dickson, John | Private | | April 10, '47 | Murray, Ky. | | Aug. 7, '48 | Newport, Ky. |
| 17 | Ellison, Paris M. | Private | | April 1, '47 | Murray, Ky. | | Aug. 7, '48 | Newport, Ky. |
| 18 | Gore, Notley D. | Private | | April 1, '47 | Murray, Ky. | | | |
| 19 | Guilliland, David | Private | | May 2, '47 | Blandville, Ky. | | Aug. 7, '48 | Newport. Ky. |
| 20 | Grey, Lafayette W. | Private | | May 2, '47 | Newport, Ky. | | Aug. 7, '48 | Newport, Ky. |
| 21 | Haumer, John E. | Private | | Apr. 9, '47 | Blandville, Ky. | | Aug. 7, '48 | Newport, Ky. |
| 22 | Hagan, John T. | Private | | Apr. 25, '47 | Bardstown, Ky. | | Aug. 7, '48 | Newport, Ky. |
| 23 | Hart, Samuel H. | Private | | Apr. 24, '47 | Murray, Ky. | | Aug. 7, '48 | Newport, Ky. |
| 24 | Hawkins, Benjamin H. | Private | | May 25, '47 | Owenton, Ky. | | Aug. 7, '48 | Newport, Ky. |
| 25 | Hutchins, Thomas W. | Private | | Apr. 24, '47 | Murray, Ky. | | Aug. 7, '48 | Newport, Ky. |
| 26 | Hunter, Angress | Private | | May 22, '47 | New Liberty, Ky. | | Aug. 7, '48 | Newport, Ky. |
| 27 | Harrington, A. M. | Private | | May 4, '47 | Cairo, Ill. | | Aug. 7, '48 | Newport, Ky. |
| 28 | Householder, Solomon | Private | | May 14, '47 | Fort Wayne, Ind. | | Aug. 7, '48 | Newport, Ky. |
| 29 | Jupin, James H. | Private | | May 2, '47 | Blandville, Ky. | | Aug. 7, '48 | Newport, Ky. |
| 30 | Jones, Jackson A. | Private | | May 21, '47 | Owenton, Ky. | | Aug. 7, '48 | Newport, Ky. |
| 31 | Kelly, Joseph | Private | | Apr. 20, '47 | Murray, Ky. | | | |
| 32 | Ligon, John B. | Private | | May 25, '47 | Carrollton, Ky. | | Aug. 7, '8 | Newport, Ky. |
| 33 | Littlejohn, Charles | Private | | Apr. 5, '47 | Benton, Ky. | | Aug. 7, '48 | Newport, Ky. |
| 34 | Lelland, John A. | Private | | Aug. 28, '47 | Louisville, Ky. | | Aug. 7, '48 | Newport, Ky. |
| 35 | Marberry, William W. | Private | | Apr. 22, '47 | Murray, Ky. | | Aug. 7, '48 | Newport, Ky. |
| 36 | McCarty, William H. | Private | | July 15, '47 | Louisville, Ky. | | Aug. 7, '48 | Newport, Ky. |
| 37 | McCarty, George W. | Private | | Apr. 3, '47 | Murray, Ky. | | Aug. 7, '48 | Newport, Ky. |
| 38 | McCarty, Benjamin | Private | | April 7, '47 | Murray, Ky. | | Aug. 7, '48 | Newport, Ky. |
| 39 | McCarty, James | Private | | Apr. 29, '47 | Blandville, Ky. | | Aug. 7, '48 | Newport, Ky. |
| 40 | McCormick, Joseph | Private | | May 11, '47 | Fort Wayne, Ind. | | Aug. 7, '48 | Newport, Ky. |
| 41 | McKnight, Samuel | Private | | Apr. 24, '47 | Murray, Ky. | | Aug. 7, '48 | Newport, Ky. |
| 42 | McNute, George W. | Private | | Apr. 2, '47 | Murray, Ky. | | Aug. 7, '48 | Newport, Ky. |
| 43 | Morgan, Daniel W. | Private | | July 15, '47 | Benton, Ky. | | Aug. 7, '48 | Newport, Ky. |
| 44 | Morgan, Daniel | Private | | July 15, '47 | Louisville, Ky. | | Aug. 7, '48 | Newport, Ky. |
| 45 | Melton, Seth P. | Private | | Apr. 1, '47 | Murray, Ky. | | Aug. 7, '48 | Newport, Ky. |
| 46 | Meyer, Jacob | Private | | Aug. 4, '47 | Louisville, Ky. | | Aug. 7, '48 | Newport, Ky. |
| 47 | Norman, William B. | Private | | Apr. 10, '47 | Benton, Ky. | | Aug. 7, '48 | Newport, Ky. |
| 48 | Ormes, Nelson | Private | | May 3, '47 | St. Marys | | Aug. 7, '48 | Newport, Ky. |
| 49 | Padgett, Durett | Private | | Apr. 17, '47 | Murray, Ky. | | Aug. 7, '48 | Newport, Ky. |
| 50 | Parrish, John N. | Private | | Sept. 15, '47 | Harrodsburg, Ky. | | Aug. 7, '48 | Newport, Ky. |
| 51 | Ratcliffe, Reason P. | Private | | Apr. 5, '47 | Benton, Ky. | | Aug. 7, '48 | Newport, Ky. |
| 52 | Reaves, William | Private | | Apr. 5, '47 | Benton, Ky. | | Aug. 7, '48 | Newport, Ky. |
| 53 | Rhey, John | Private | | May 21, '47 | Owenton, Ky. | | Aug. 7, '48 | Newport, Ky. |
| 54 | Rose, William S. | Private | | July 23, '47 | Louisville, Ky. | | Aug. 7, '48 | Newport, Ky. |
| 55 | Reigler, Leonard | Private | | Oct. 7, '47 | Louisville, Ky. | | Aug. 7, '48 | Newport, Ky. |
| 56 | Sample, John L. | Private | | Apr. 5, '47 | Benton, Ky. | | Aug. 7, '48 | Newport, Ky. |

# JOHN W. TIBBATTS, CALLED INTO SERVICE OF UNITED STATES 11, 1847, FOR WAR AGAINST MEXICO.

| No. of each grade | REMARKS. |
|---|---|
| 1 | Promoted Captain " B " Company, February 12, 1848. |
| 1 | Promoted 1st Lieutenant " B " Company, October 12, 1847. |
| 1 | Assigned to " B," Company, March, 1848. |
| 1 | Promoted Major 14th Infantry, February 12, 1848. |
| 1 | Promoted Captain of " G " Company, 16th Infantry, October 12, 1847. |
| 1 | Promoted 1st Lieutenant of Company " K," 16th Infantry, February 12, 1848. |
| 2 | Transferred to " K " Company, 16th Infantry, by order No. 2, Headquarters 16th Infantry, July 11, 1847. |
| 1 | Appointed Corporal, April 16, 1847; appointed Sergeant, November 21, 1847, and 1st Sergeant May 9, 1848. |
| 2 | Appointed Sergeant, March 1, 1848. |
| 3 | Appointed Corporal, April 16, 1847; appointed Sergeant, November 21, 1847. |
| 1 | Appointed Sergeant April 16, 1847; reduced and appointed Corporal, November 21, 1847. |
| 2 | Appointed Corporal, May 9, 1848; absent sick, in charge of Surgeon Berry, "en route" for Newport. |
| 3 | Appointed Corporal, May 9, 1848. |
| 1 | Appointed Drummer, July 1, 1847. |
| 2 | Appointed Fifer, January 1, 1848. |
| 1 | |
| 2 | |
| 3 | |
| 4 | |
| 5 | |
| 6 | |
| 7 | |
| 8 | |
| 9 | See manuscript Muster Roll. |
| 10 | |
| 11 | |
| 12 | |
| 13 | |
| 14 | |
| 15 | |
| 16 | |
| 17 | |
| 18 | |
| 19 | |
| 20 | |
| 21 | |
| 22 | |
| 23 | |
| 24 | |
| 25 | |
| 26 | |
| 27 | |
| 28 | |
| 29 | |
| 30 | |
| 31 | Absent sick, in charge of Surgeon Berry, "en route" for Newport. |
| 32 | |
| 33 | |
| 34 | |
| 35 | |
| 36 | |
| 37 | |
| 38 | |
| 39 | |
| 40 | |
| 41 | |
| 42 | |
| 43 | |
| 44 | |
| 45 | |
| 47 | |
| 46 | |
| 48 | |
| 49 | |
| 50 | |
| 51 | |
| 52 | |
| 53 | |
| 54 | |
| 55 | |
| 56 | |

## ROLL OF COMPANY "B," SIXTEENTH REGIMENT U. S. INFANTRY, COL. JOHN W.
## CONGRESS OF FEBRUARY 11, 1847, FOR

| No. of each grade. | Name. | Rank. | Enlisted. When. | Enlisted. Where. | Period. | Mustered Out. When. | Mustered Out. Where. |
|---|---|---|---|---|---|---|---|
| 57 | Schroader, Lafayette | Private | Apr. 17, '47 | Murray, Ky. | | Aug. 7, '48 | Newport, Ky. |
| 58 | Sheffield, Richard H. | Private | Apr. 5, '47 | Benton, Ky. | | Aug. 7, '48 | Newport, Ky. |
| 59 | Shelburn, Pascal R. | Private | Apr. 17, '47 | Blandville, Ky. | | Aug. 7, '48 | Newport, Ky. |
| 60 | Shirley, Ezekiel A. | Private | Apr. 24, '47 | Murray, Ky. | | Aug. 7, '48 | Newport, Ky. |
| 61 | Sherban, Enoch | Private | May 2, '47 | Owenton, Ky. | | Aug. 7, '48 | Newport, Ky. |
| 62 | Stamper, Geo. R. | Private | May 24, '47 | Owenton, Ky. | | Aug. 7, '48 | Newport, Ky. |
| 63 | Steele, Tillman H. | Private | Apr. 5, '47 | Benton, Ky. | | Aug. 7, '48 | Newport, Ky. |
| 64 | Smith, John | Private | July 9, '47 | Louisville, Ky. | | Aug. 7, '48 | Newport, Ky. |
| 65 | Staucer, Henry | Private | Aug. 7, '47 | Louisville, Ky. | | Aug. 7, '48 | Newport, Ky. |
| 66 | Steigler, Jacob | Private | Aug. 7, '47 | Louisville, Ky. | | Aug. 7, '48 | Newport, Ky. |
| 67 | Shaeffer, Christian | Private | Aug. 14, '47 | Louisville, Ky. | | Aug. 7, '48 | Newport, Ky. |
| 68 | Taylor, Geo. W. (No. 1) | Private | Apr. 24, '47 | Murray, Ky. | | Aug. 7, '48 | Newport, Ky. |
| 69 | Taylor, Geo. W. (No. 2) | Private | Apr. 2, '47 | Blandville, Ky. | | Aug. 7, '48 | Newport, Ky. |
| 70 | Taylor, Creed | Private | Apr. 24, '47 | Murray, Ky. | | Aug. 7, '48 | Newport, Ky. |
| 71 | Tome, Jacob | Private | July 8, '47 | Louisville, Ky. | | Aug. 7, '48 | Newport, Ky. |
| 72 | Watkins, Benjamin | Private | May 4, '47 | Murray, Ky. | | Aug. 7, '48 | Newport, Ky. |
| 73 | Wells, Julius C. | Private | Apr. 3, '47 | Murray, Ky. | | Aug. 7, '48 | Newport, Ky. |
| 74 | Wells, James | Private | June 23, '47 | Louisville, Ky. | | Aug. 7, '48 | Newport, Ky. |
| 75 | Wicker, David | Private | May 4, '47 | Murray, Ky. | | Aug. 7, '48 | Newport, Ky. |
| 76 | Williamson, E. G. | Private | Apr. 1, '47 | Murray, Ky. | | Aug. 7, '48 | Newport, Ky. |
| 77 | Wilburn, Miles W. | Private | Apr. 17, '47 | Murray, Ky. | | Aug. 7, '48 | Newport, Ky. |
| 78 | Wilburn, Francis G. | Private | Apr. 20, '47 | Murray, Ky. | | Aug. 7, '48 | Newport, Ky. |
| 79 | Woodruff, Hiram | Private | May 12, '47 | St. Marys, Ky. | | Aug. 7, '48 | Newport, Ky. |
| 80 | Wray, John G. | Private | Apr. 24, '47 | Murray, Ky. | | Aug. 7, '48 | Newport, Ky. |
| 81 | Williams, Geo. W. | Private | July 15, '47 | Louisville, Ky. | | Aug. 7, '48 | Newport, Ky. |
| 82 | Williams, Morrison | Private | July 17, '47 | Galena, Ill. | | Aug. 7, '48 | Newport, Ky. |
| 83 | Whitton, Robert | Private | July 3, '47 | Louisville, Ky. | | Aug. 7, '48 | Newport, Ky. |
| 84 | Wise, George | Private | Aug. 21, '47 | Louisville, Ky. | To serve during the war. | Aug. 7, '48 | Newport, Ky. |
| 85 | Thomas, George W. | Private | Apr. 3, '47 | Blandville, Ky. | | Aug. 7, '48 | Newport, Ky. |

### DISCHARGED.

| | | | | | | | |
|---|---|---|---|---|---|---|---|
| 1 | Abernethy, Moses F. | Private | | Aug. 24, '47 | Galena, Ill. | | | |
| 2 | Ezell, Herbert O. | Private | | Aug. 26, '47 | Murray, Ky. | | | |
| 3 | Fry, Robert | Private | | Aug. 20, '47 | Blandville, Ky. | | | |
| 4 | Hayes, Jesse H. | Sergeant | | Aug. 8, '47 | Blandville, Ky. | | | |
| 5 | Henry, Alexander H. | Private | | Aug. 1, '47 | Blandville, Ky. | | | |
| 6 | Herridge, Tillman T. | Private | | Aug 5, '47 | Benton, Ky. | | | |
| 7 | Joyner, William J. | Private | | May 4, '47 | Cairo, Ill. | | | |
| 8 | King, William | Private | | May 25, '47 | Carrollton, Ky. | | | |
| 9 | Lynch, James M. M. | Private | | Apr. 16, '47 | Murray, Ky. | | | |
| 10 | Myers, John | Private | | Apr. 15, '47 | Blandville, Ky. | | | |
| 11 | Moss, Joel | Private | | Apr. 1, '47 | Murray, Ky. | | | |
| 12 | Pennington, Marcus | Private | | May 2, '47 | Blandville, Ky. | | | |
| 13 | Powell, Hilrah | Private | | May 8, '47 | Fort Wayne, Ind. | | | |
| 14 | Phillips, William | Private | | Sept. 27, '47 | Harrodsburg, Ky. | | | |
| 15 | Ratcliffe, James | Private | | Apr. 5, '47 | Benton, Ky. | | | |
| 16 | Richardson, James E. | Private | | May 12, '47 | Carrollton, La. | | | |
| 17 | Stratton, Peter A. | Private | | Apr. 10, '47 | Blandville, Ky. | | | |
| 18 | Terrell, Paul W. | Private | | Apr 20, '47 | Blandville, Ky. | | | |
| 19 | Thompson, David | Private | | Apr. 20, '47 | Murray, Ky. | | | |
| 20 | Ward, Matthew | Private | | Apr. 24, '47 | Murray, Ky. | | | |
| 21 | Woodfin, John | Sergeant | | Apr. 2, '47 | Newport, Ky. | | | |

### TRANSFERRED.

| | | | | | | | |
|---|---|---|---|---|---|---|---|
| 1 | Luna, Anastasio | Private | | June 25, '48 | Monterey, Mexico | | | |
| 2 | Stringfellow, Chris. F. | Private | | Apr. 22, '47 | Bardstown, Ky. | | | |

### DIED.

| | | | | | | | |
|---|---|---|---|---|---|---|---|
| 1 | Cole, Peter R. | Private | | May 4, '47 | Murray, Ky. | | | |
| 2 | Flora, William | Private | | Apr. 3, '47 | Blandville, Ky. | | | |
| 3 | Humphries, George | Private | | Apr. 1, '47 | Murray, Ky. | | | |
| 4 | Hendley, Edmund J. C. | Private | | Apr. 24, '47 | Murray, Ky. | | | |
| 5 | Johnson, Henry M. | Sergeant | | Apr. 5, '47 | Benton, Ky. | | | |
| 6 | McCarty, John D. | Private | | Apr. 12, '47 | Murray, Ky. | | | |
| 7 | Scruggs, Chesley G. | Private | | Apr. 2, '47 | Murray, Ky. | | | |
| 8 | Schools, Joseph | Private | | Apr. 1, '47 | Blandville, Ky. | | | |
| 9 | Walker, Jesse | Private | | Apr. 5, '47 | Blandville, Ky. | | | |

### DESERTED.

| | | | | | | | |
|---|---|---|---|---|---|---|---|
| | Martin, Henry H. | Private | | Apr. 15, '47 | Blandville, Ky. | | | |

This Company formed a part of a battalion of four Companies of the 16th U. S. Infantry, organized in Kentucky for the Mexican War; the officers of said Regiment being appointed by the President of the United States. Act of Congress February 11, 1847.

# TIBBATTS, CALLED INTO SERVICE OF THE UNITED STATES UNDER ACT OF THE WAR AGAINST MEXICO—Continued.

| No. of each grade | REMARKS. |
|---|---|
| 57 | |
| 58 | |
| 59 | |
| 60 | |
| 61 | |
| 62 | |
| 63 | |
| 64 | |
| 65 | |
| 66 | |
| 67 | |
| 68 | |
| 69 | Corporal from April 16, 1847, to June 17, 1848. |
| 70 | |
| 71 | |
| 72 | |
| 73 | |
| 74 | |
| 75 | |
| 76 | |
| 77 | |
| 78 | |
| 79 | |
| 80 | |
| 81 | |
| 82 | |
| 83 | |
| 84 | |
| 85 | |
| 1 | Papers for discharge made out and sent to New Orleans, July, 1848. |
| 2 | Discharged at Monterey, December 5th, 1847. |
| 3 | Discharged at Monterey, January 3d, 1848. |
| 4 | Discharged at Monterey, December 5, 1847. Sergeant from April 16, 1847. |
| 5 | Discharged at Monterey, October 3, 1847. |
| 6 | Discharged at Monterey, December 5, 1847. |
| 7 | Discharged at Monterey, March 8, 1848. |
| 8 | Discharged at Ceralvo, November 16, 1847. |
| 9 | Discharged at Monterey, December 5, 1847. |
| 10 | Discharged at Monterey, December 5, 1847. |
| 11 | Discharged at Monterey, December 5, 1847. |
| 12 | Discharged at Monterey, December 5, 1847. |
| 13 | Discharged at Brazos Santiago, July 8, 1848. Order of Maj. Gen. Wool. |
| 14 | Papers made out and sent to New Orleans, July, 1848. |
| 15 | Discharged at Ceralvo, December 12, 1847. |
| 16 | Discharged at Brazos Santiago, July 8, 1848. Order of Maj. Gen. Wool. |
| 17 | Discharged at Monterey, February 8, 1848. |
| 18 | Discharged at ———, December 5, 1847. |
| 19 | Discharged at ———, December 5, 1847. |
| 20 | Discharged at ———, December 5, 1847. |
| 21 | Discharged at Brazos Santiago, July 8, 1847, by order of Major Gen Wool. In "C" Company from May 22 to Oct. 1, 1847; Sergeant in "B" Company from May 9, 1848. |
| 1 | Transferred to "I" Co., May 11, 1848, by order Col. Tibbatts. |
| 2 | Transferred to "C" Co., May 11, 1848, by order Col. Tibbatts. Corporal from November 21, 1847, to February —, 1848. |
| 1 | Died June 2, 1847, at San Franciso, Mex. |
| 2 | Died November 27, 1847, at Monterey, Mex. |
| 3 | Died August 14, 1847, at Mier, Mex. |
| 4 | Died November 20, 1847, at Monterey, Mex. |
| 5 | Died June 13, 1847, at Camargo, Mex. Sergeant from April 16, 1847. |
| 6 | Died October 28, 1847, at Monterey, Mex. |
| 7 | Died ——— —, at Point Isabel, Mex., date not known; supposed to have died in May or June, 1847. |
| 8 | Died May 8, 1847, Mississippi river—drowned. |
| 9 | Died May 29, 1847, at Point Isabel. |
| 1 | Deserted May 15, 1847, at Carrolton, La. |

## MEXICAN WAR VETERANS.

158

ROLL OF COMPANY "E," SIXTEENTH REGIMENT U. S. INFANTRY, COL. JOHN
WAR, BEING ONE OF THE BATTALION OF FOUR COMPANIES,
OF THE UNITED STATES. ACT

| No. of each grade | Name. | Rank. | Mustered In. When. | Mustered In. Where. | Period | Mustered Out. When. | Mustered Out. Where. |
|---|---|---|---|---|---|---|---|
| 1 | Theodore T. Garrard | Captain | | | | | |
| 1 | Charles J. Helm | 1st Lieutenant | | | | | |
| 1 | Bernard H. Garrett | 2d Lieutenant | | | | | |
| 2 | James M. Smith | 2d Lieutenant | | | | | |
| 1 | Hugh L. White | 1st Sergeant | Apr. 5, '47 | Manchester | | Aug. 5, '48 | Newport, Ky. |
| 2 | Samuel B. Tod | 2d Sergeant | Apr. 19, '47 | Newport | | Aug. 5, '48 | Newport, Ky. |
| 3 | John W. Keller | 3d Sergeant | Apr. 12, '47 | Prestonsburg | | Aug. 5, '48 | Newport, Ky. |
| 4 | James T. Price | 4th Sergeant | Apr. 24, '47 | Manchester | | Aug. 5, '48 | Newport, Ky. |
| 1 | Philip Singleton | 1st Corporal | Mar. 27, '47 | Mt. Vernon | | Aug. 5, '48 | Newport, Ky. |
| 2 | Jarvis C. Jackson | 2d Corporal | Apr. 5, '47 | Manchester | | Aug. 5, '48 | Newport, Ky. |
| 3 | Mathew Parker | 3d Corporal | Apr. 26, '47 | Newport | | Aug. 5, '48 | Newport, Ky. |
| 4 | James F. Amis | 4th Corporal | Apr. 5, '47 | Manchester | | Aug. 5, '48 | Newport, Ky. |
| 1 | John Tirk | Musician | Apr. 26, '47 | Newport | | Aug. 5, '48 | Newport, Ky. |
| 1 | Allison, William | Private | May 17, '47 | Newport | | Aug. 5, '48 | Newport, Ky. |
| 2 | Byerly, John | Private | Apr. 16, '47 | Manchester | | Aug. 5, '48 | Newport, Ky. |
| 3 | Baldwin, John R. | Private | Apr. 24, '47 | Manchester | | Aug. 5, '48 | Newport, Ky. |
| 4 | Bowlin, Graham | Private | Apr. 25, '47 | Manchester | | Aug. 5, '48 | Newport, Ky. |
| 5 | Bowlin, John | Private | Apr. 25, '47 | Manchester | | Aug. 5, '48 | Newport, Ky. |
| 6 | Baker, James A. | Private | Apr. 13, '47 | Booneville | | Aug. 5, '48 | Newport, Ky. |
| 7 | Beck, James S. | Private | May 9, '47 | Newport | | Aug. 5, '48 | Newport, Ky. |
| 8 | Brown, Robert | Private | Apr. 12, '47 | Prestonsburg | | Aug. 5, '48 | Newport, Ky. |
| 9 | Crutchfield, J. M. | Private | Apr. 12, '47 | London | | Aug. 5, '48 | Newport, Ky. |
| 10 | Carter, Tunstell D. | Private | Apr. 19, '47 | Somerset | | | |
| 11 | Cole, George | Private | Apr. 19, '47 | Manchester | | Aug. 5, '48 | Newport, Ky. |
| 12 | Crook, Wiley | Private | Apr. 5, '47 | Manchester | | Aug. 5, '48 | Newport, Ky. |
| 13 | Coleman, Joseph | Private | Apr. 24, '47 | Algers | | Aug. 5, '48 | Newport, Ky. |
| 14 | Cain, James | Private | May 3, '47 | Newport | | Aug. 5, '48 | Newport, Ky. |
| 15 | Duggar, William | Private | Apr 24, '47 | Mt. Vernon | | | |
| 16 | Devlin, Peter | Private | Apr. 15, '47 | Newport | | Aug. 5, '48 | Newport, Ky. |
| 17 | Delaney, Michael | Private | July 5, '47 | Louisville, Ky. | To serve during the war. | Aug. 5, '48 | Newport, Ky. |
| 18 | Dunegin, Joseph | Private | June 1, '47 | Louisville, Ky. | | Aug. 5, '48 | Newport, Ky. |
| 19 | Davenport, Charles | Private | Aug. 1, '47 | Louisville, Ky. | | Aug. 5, '48 | Newport, Ky. |
| 20 | Davis, Joseph | Private | July 29, '47 | Louisville, Ky. | | Aug. 5, '48 | Newport, Ky. |
| 21 | Eastland, William W. | Private | July 5, '47 | Louisville, Ky. | | Aug. 5, '48 | Newport, Ky. |
| 22 | Foster, Charles | Private | Apr. 28 '47 | Louisa | | Aug. 5, '48 | Newport, Ky. |
| 23 | Flowers, John W. | Private | May 5, '47 | Newport, Ky. | | Aug. 5, '48 | Newport, Ky. |
| 24 | Furgerson, James | Private | July 6, '47 | Louisville | | Aug. 5, '48 | Newport, Ky. |
| 25 | Gullett, Isaac | Private | Apr. 21, '47 | Manchester | | Aug. 5, '48 | Newport, Ky. |
| 26 | Grutz, Richard | Private | Apr. 5, '47 | Louisville | | Aug. 5, '48 | Newport, Ky. |
| 27 | Graham, John R. | Private | July 27, '47 | Louisville | | Aug. 5, '48 | Newport, Ky. |
| 28 | Herd, John W. | Private | Apr. 24, '47 | Manchester | | Aug. 5, '48 | Newport, Ky. |
| 29 | Hamptons, Livingston | Private | Apr. 20, '47 | Manchester | | Aug. 5, '48 | Newport, Ky. |
| 30 | Hibbard, Theophilus | Private | Apr. 20, '47 | Manchester | | Aug. 5, '48 | Newport, Ky. |
| 31 | Harris, James | Private | Apr. 24, '47 | Mt. Vernon | | Aug. 5, '48 | Newport, Ky. |
| 32 | Howard, Louis G. | Private | Apr. 19, '47 | Somerset | | Aug. 5, '48 | Newport, Ky. |
| 33 | Hill, Alexander | Private | Apr. 22, '47 | Newport | | | |
| 34 | Hawkins, Elihuo | Private | Apr. 15, '47 | Prestonsburg | | Aug. 5, '48 | Newport, Ky. |
| 35 | Hart, Thomas D. | Private | Apr. 19, '47 | Prestonsburg | | Aug. 5, '48 | Newport, Ky. |
| 36 | Hadley, William W. | Private | Oct. —, '47 | Jacksonville | | | |
| 37 | Hyde, John | Private | Sept. 23, '47 | Jacksonville | | Aug. 5, '48 | Newport, Ky. |
| 38 | Jones, Hartsville F. | Private | Apr. 21, '47 | Manchester | | | |
| 39 | Johnson, Charles | Private | Apr. 5, '47 | Manchester | | Aug. 5, '48 | Newport, Ky. |
| 40 | Jackson, Thomas | Private | May 4, '47 | Newport | | Aug. 5, '48 | Newport, Ky. |
| 41 | Lucas, John | Private | Apr. 24, '47 | Manchester | | Aug. 5, '48 | Newport, Ky. |
| 42 | Lunsford, Jesse | Private | Apr. 25, '47 | Manchester | | Aug. 5, '48 | Newport, Ky. |
| 43 | Lefferd, Samuel | Private | Apr. 27, '47 | Madison Co. | | Aug. 5, '48 | Newport, Ky. |
| 44 | Lendengen, Silas | Private | July 26, '47 | Galena | | Aug. 5, '48 | Newport, Ky. |
| 45 | Mershon, Andrew J. | Private | Apr. 27, '47 | Madison Co. | | Aug. 5, '48 | Newport, Ky. |
| 46 | McCoy, Sanders | Private | Apr. 8, '47 | Newport | | Aug. 5, '48 | Newport, Ky. |
| 47 | Madans, Sanders | Private | Apr. 30, '47 | Newport | | Aug. 5, '48 | Newport, Ky. |
| 48 | Noe, Felix G. | Private | Apr. 20, '47 | Manchester | | Aug. 5, '48 | Newport, Ky. |
| 49 | Neil, Daniel | Private | Apr. 20, '47 | Manchester | | Aug. 5, '48 | Newport, Ky. |
| 50 | Neely, William W. | Private | Apr. 24, '47 | Mt. Vernon | | Aug. 5, '48 | Newport, Ky. |
| 51 | Nickel, William | Private | May 3, '47 | Newport | | Aug. 5, '48 | Newport, Ky. |
| 52 | Osburn, Robert J. | Private | Apr. 6, '47 | Newport | | Aug. 5, '48 | Newport, Ky. |
| 53 | Price, Daniel G. | Private | Apr. 12, '47 | Boonville | | Aug. 5, '48 | Newport, Ky. |
| 54 | Powel, Stephen | Private | Apr. 24, '47 | Manchester | | Aug. 5, '48 | Newport, Ky. |
| 55 | Pruette, John | Private | Apr. 24, '47 | Mt. Vernon | | Aug. 5, '48 | Newport, Ky. |
| 56 | Reid, James | Private | Apr. 5, '47 | Manchester | | Aug. 5, '48 | Newport, Ky. |
| 57 | Roark, Saul | Private | Apr. 5, '47 | Manchester | | Aug. 5, '48 | Newport, Ky. |
| 58 | Roark, John | Private | Apr. 25, '47 | Manchester | | Aug. 5, '48 | Newport, Ky. |

## MEXICAN WAR VETERANS. 159

**W. TIBBATTS, CALLED INTO THE SERVICE OF THE U. S. FOR THE MEXICAN ORGANIZED IN KENTUCKY, AND OFFICERED BY THE PRESIDENT OF CONGRESS, FEBRUARY 11, 1847.**

| No. of each grade. | REMARKS. |
|---|---|
| 1 | |
| 1 | On duty at Washington, D. C. |
| 1 | |
| 2 | Dismissed, September 14, 1847, by General Court-martial. |
| 1 | |
| 2 | |
| 3 | Appointed Sergeant, January 1, 1848. |
| 4 | Appointed Sergeant, March 1, 1848. |
| 1 | |
| 2 | |
| 3 | Appointed Corporal, August 1, 1847. |
| 4 | Appointed Corporal, January 1, 1848. |
| 1 | |
| 1 | Joined Company from Regimental Depot, June 24, 1847. |
| 2 | |
| 3 | |
| 4 | |
| 5 | |
| 6 | |
| 7 | Joined Company from Regimental Depot, June 24, 1847. |
| 8 | |
| 9 | |
| 10 | Left with Surgeon Berry; arrived since muster. |
| 11 | |
| 12 | |
| 13 | Joined from Voltiguers, May 21, 1847. |
| 14 | Joined from Regimental Depot, June 24, 1847. |
| 15 | Sick; left with Surgeon Berry. |
| 16 | |
| 17 | Joined from Regimental Depot, January 30, 1848. |
| 18 | Joined from Regimental Depot, January 30, 1848. |
| 19 | Joined from Regimental Depot, January 30, 1848. |
| 20 | Joined from Regimental Depot, January 30, 1848. |
| 21 | Joined from Regimental Depot, January 30, 1848. |
| 22 | Joined from Regimental Depot. January 30, 1848. |
| 23 | Joined from Regimental Depot, June 24, 1847. |
| 24 | |
| 25 | |
| 26 | Transferred from Company "K," July 10, 1847. |
| 27 | Joined from Regimental Depot, January 30, 1848. |
| 28 | |
| 29 | |
| 30 | |
| 31 | |
| 32 | |
| 33 | Left with Surgeon Berry at New Orleans. |
| 34 | |
| 35 | |
| 36 | Joined from Regimental Depot, January 30, 1848. Sick with Surgeon Berry at N. O. |
| 37 | |
| 38 | Left with Surgeon Berry as attendant. Now at N. O. |
| 39 | |
| 40 | Joined from Regimental Depot, June 30, 1847. |
| 41 | |
| 42 | |
| 43 | |
| 44 | Joined from Regimental Depot, January 30, 1848. |
| 45 | |
| 46 | Reduced to ranks, August 1, 1847. |
| 47 | |
| 48 | |
| 49 | |
| 50 | |
| 51 | Joined from Regimental Depot, June 24, 1847. |
| 52 | See manuscript roll of this Company. |
| 53 | |
| 54 | |
| 55 | |
| 56 | |
| 57 | |
| 58 | |

## MEXICAN WAR VETERANS.

### ROLL OF COMPANY "E," SIXTEENTH REGIMENT U. S. INFANTRY, COL. JOHN WAR, BEING ONE OF THE BATTALION OF FOUR COMPANIES, OF THE UNITED STATES. ACT

| No. of each grade | Name. | Rank. | | Mustered In. When. | Mustered In. Where. | Period | Mustered Out. When. | Mustered Out. Where. |
|---|---|---|---|---|---|---|---|---|
| 59 | Ragle, John A. | Private | | May 24, '47. | Manchester | | Aug. 5, '48. | Newport, Ky. |
| 60 | Robinson, Stephen | Private | | May 25, '47. | Manchester | | Aug. 5, '48. | Newport, Ky. |
| 61 | Robinson, Hugh L. | Private | | May 12, '47. | Boonville | | Aug. 5, '48. | Newport, Ky. |
| 62 | Redmond, Washington | Private | | May 10, '47. | Manchester | | Aug. 5, '48. | Newport, Ky. |
| 63 | Reynolds, John | Private | | May 17, '47. | Mt. Vernon | | Aug. 5, '48. | Newport, Ky. |
| 64 | Stuard, Ranson | Private | | May 21, '47. | Manchester | | Aug. 5, '48. | Newport, Ky. |
| 65 | Suttles, Andrew J. | Private | | May 27, '47. | Madison county | | Aug. 5, '48. | Newport, Ky. |
| 66 | Stotsworth, John | Private | | May 17, '47. | Mt. Vernon | | Aug. 5, '48. | Newport, Ky. |
| 67 | Shanks, George T. | Private | | May 26, '47. | Newport | | Aug. 5, '48. | Newport, Ky. |
| 68 | Smith, Jabel | Private | | May 17, '47. | Manchester | | Aug. 5, '48. | Newport, Ky. |
| 69 | Sommer, Julius | Private | | May 10, '47. | Newport | | Aug. 5, '48. | Newport, Ky. |
| 70 | Shrader, Herman | Private | | May 17, '47. | Newport | | Aug. 5, '48. | Newport, Ky. |
| 71 | Snyder, Henry | Private | | May 8, '47. | Newport | | Aug. 5, '48. | Newport, Ky. |
| 72 | Taylor, Jesse | Private | | Apr. 11, '47. | London | | Aug. 5, '48. | Newport, Ky. |
| 73 | Thompson, John | Private | | Apr. 21, '47. | Louisville | | Aug. 5, '48. | Newport, Ky. |
| 74 | Turry, W. H. | Private | | May 8, '47. | Springfield | | Aug. 5, '48. | Newport, Ky. |
| 75 | Vandergrift, John | Private | | July 26, '47. | Galena | | Aug. 5, '48. | Newport, Ky. |
| 76 | Whitley, W. J. | Private | | Apr. 12, '47. | Prestonsburg | | Aug. 5, '48. | Newport, Ky. |
| 77 | White, William H. | Private | | Apr. 19, '47. | Newport | | Aug. 5, '48. | Newport, Ky. |
| 78 | Williams, James | Private | | May 17, '47. | Newport | | Aug. 5, '48. | Newport, Ky. |
| 79 | Wysner, Hiram | Private | | July 4, '47. | Galena | | Aug. 5, '48. | Newport, Ky. |
| 80 | Zink, John H. | Private | | Apr. 29, '47. | Newport | | Aug. 5, '48. | Newport, Ky. |
| | **Deaths.** | | | | | | | |
| 1 | Ballinger, John | Private | | Apr. 10, '47. | Manchester | To serve during the war. | | |
| 2 | Carver, Wickliff | Private | | Apr. 28, '47. | Richmond | | | |
| 3 | Bullock, Charles | Private | | Apr. 15, '47. | Newport | | | |
| 4 | Allison, James | Private | | Apr 22, '47. | Manchester | | | |
| 5 | Evans, Jerome | Private | | Apr. 24, '47. | Newport | | | |
| 6 | Allen, John | Private | | May 5, '47. | Newport | | | |
| 7 | Penell, William J. | Private | | Apr. 26, '47. | Newport | | | |
| 8 | Noe, Nixon | Private | | Apr. 20, '47. | Manchester | | | |
| 9 | Crawford, H. T. | Private | | May 2, '47. | Louisville | | | |
| 10 | Roark, Lewis A. | Private | | Apr. 5, '47. | Manchester | | | |
| 11 | Devall, Daniel | Private | | Apr 16, '47. | Newport | | | |
| 12 | Brown, John H. | Private | | Apr. 28, '47. | Louisa | | | |
| | **Transferred.** | | | | | | | |
| 1 | Hamblin, James | Private | | Apr. 24, '47. | Lawrenceburg | | | |
| 2 | Norris, George | Private | | Apr. 24, '47. | Lawrenceburg | | | |
| 3 | Perry, William | Private | | Apr. 22, '47. | Lawrenceburg | | | |
| 4 | Park, Samuel | Private | | Apr. 23, '47. | Lawrenceburg | | | |
| 5 | Reep, Pleasantfield | Private | | Apr. 17, '47. | Madison | | | |
| 6 | Reep, Farmerkey | Private | | Apr. 19, '47. | Madison | | | |
| 7 | Vinzant, Jacob | Private | | Apr. 20, '47. | Madison | | | |
| 8 | Young, Hezekiah | Private | | Apr. 22, '47. | Lawrenceburg | | | |
| 9 | Zimmerman, Jos. | Private | | Apr. 24, '47. | Lawrenceburg | | | |
| 10 | Kettle, Daniel A. | Private | | Apr. 20, '47. | Lawrenceburg | | | |
| 11 | Crouch, Levi | Private | | Apr. 26, '47. | Newport | | | |
| 12 | Brown, Ludwin | Private | | Apr. 12, '47. | Louisville | | | |
| 13 | Haynes, John | Private | | Apr. 20, '47. | Louisville | | | |
| 14 | Hill, David | Private | | Apr. 20, '47. | Louisville | | | |
| 15 | Holmes, James | Private | | Apr. 20, '47. | Louisville | | | |
| 16 | Lowman, Didrick | Private | | Apr. 20, '47. | Louisville | | | |
| 17 | Richardson, W. | Private | | Apr. 17, '47. | Louisville | | | |
| 18 | Riley, Owen | Private | | Apr. 21, '47. | Louisville | | | |
| 19 | Thompson, John | Private | | Apr. 21, '47. | Louisville | | | |
| 20 | O'Dorherty, P. | Private | | May 6, 47. | Newport | | | |
| 21 | Wilbank, Edwin | Private | | May 20, 47. | Newport | | | |
| 22 | Hadley, J. S. | Private | | Sept. 24, '47. | Jacksonville | | | |
| | **Discharged.** | | | | | | | |
| 1 | Reynolds, Joseph | Private | | May 6, 47. | Newport | | | |
| 2 | Smallwood, W. | Private | | Apr. 6, '47. | Mt. Vernon | | | |
| 3 | Bates, Thomas J. | Private | | Apr. 17, '47. | Mt. Vernon | | | |
| 4 | Crawford, A. | Private | | Aug. 7, '47. | Louisville | | | |
| 5 | Frollick, Frederick | Private | | Apr. 10, '47. | Newport | | | |
| 6 | Perry, Daniel | Private | | May 6, '47. | Newport | | | |
| 7 | Baldwin, R. N. | Private | | Apr. 12, '47. | Boonville | | | |
| 8 | Hening, Robert | Private | | May 4, '47. | Newport | | | |
| 9 | Garard, Wm. | Sergeant | | Apr. 24, '47. | Manchester | | | |

W. TIBBATTS, CALLED INTO THE SERVICE OF THE U. S. FOR THE MEXICAN ORGANIZED IN KENTUCKY, AND OFFICERED BY THE PRESIDENT OF CONGRESS, FEBRUARY 11, 1847.

| No. of each grade | REMARKS. |
|---|---|
| 59 | |
| 60 | |
| 61 | |
| 62 | |
| 63 | |
| 64 | |
| 65 | |
| 66 | |
| 67 | |
| 68 | |
| 69 | |
| 70 | Joined from Regimental Depot, June 24, 1847. |
| 71 | Joined from Regimental Depot, June 24, 1847. |
| 72 | |
| 73 | Joined by transfer, June 3, 1848. |
| 74 | |
| 75 | |
| 76 | |
| 77 | |
| 78 | Joined Company from Regimental Depot, June 24, 1848. |
| 79 | Joined Company from Regimental Depot, January 30, 1848. |
| 80 | |
| 1 | Died June 22, 1847, at camp opposite Camargo, Mexico. Ordinary. |
| 2 | Died July 11, 1847, at camp opposite Camargo, Mexico. Ordinary. |
| 3 | Died July 13, 1847, at camp opposite Camargo, Mexico. Ordinary. |
| 4 | Died July 25, 1847, at Mier, Mexico. Ordinary. |
| 5 | Died August 6, 1847, at Mier, Mexico. Ordinary. |
| 6 | Died August 7, 1847, at Mier, Mexico. Ordinary. |
| 7 | Died August 9, 1847, at Mier, Mexico. Ordinary. |
| 8 | Died August 18, 1847, at camp near Mier, Mexico. Ordinary. |
| 9 | Died August 26, 1847, en route from Mier to Ceralvo, Mexico. Ordinary. |
| 10 | Died August 28, 1847, Mier, Mexico. |
| 11 | Died July 31, 1847, at Mier, Mexico. Ordinary. |
| 12 | Died July 26, 1848, near mouth of Salt river, in Ohio river. |
| 1 | Transferred to "C" Company, May 19, 1847, at Palo Alto. |
| 2 | Transferred to "C" Company, May 19, 1847, at Palo Alto. |
| 3 | Transferred to "C" Company, May 19, 1847, at Palo Alto. |
| 4 | Transferred to "C" Company, May 19, 1847, at Palo Alto. |
| 5 | Transferred to "C" Company, May 19, 1847, at Palo Alto. |
| 6 | Transferred to "C" Company, May 19, 1847, at Palo Alto. |
| 7 | Transferred to "C" Company, May 19, 1847, at Palo Alto. |
| 8 | Transferred to "C" Company, May 19, 1847, at Palo Alto. |
| 9 | Transferred to "C" Company, May 19, 1847, at Palo Alto. |
| 10 | Transferred to "C" Company, May 19, 1847, at Palo Alto. |
| 11 | Transferred to "K" Company, May 19, 1847, at Palo Alto. |
| 12 | Transferred to "K" Company, May 19, 1847. |
| 13 | Transferred to "K" Company, May 19, 1847. |
| 14 | Transferred to "K" Company, May 19, 1847. |
| 15 | Transferred to "K" Company, May 19, 1847. |
| 16 | Transferred to "K" Company, May 19, 1847. |
| 17 | Transferred to "K" Company, May 19, 1847. |
| 18 | Transferred to "K" Company, May 19, 1847. |
| 19 | Transferred to "K" Company, May 19, 1847. |
| 20 | Transferred to "G" Company, May 10, 1848. |
| 21 | Transferred to "C" Company, May 18, 1848. |
| 22 | Transferred to "C" Company, June 3, 1848. |
| 1 | Discharged May 1, 1848; Surgeon's certificate of disability. |
| 2 | Discharged July 2, 1848, by order of Gen. Wool. |
| 3 | Discharged July 2, 1848, by order of Gen. Wool. |
| 4 | Discharged July 2, 1848. |
| 5 | Discharged February 5, 1848; Surgeon's certificate of disability. |
| 6 | Discharged September 17, 1848; Surgeon's certificate of disability. |
| 7 | Discharged February 8, 1848; Surgeon's certificate of disability. |
| 8 | Discharged February 29, 1848; Surgeon' certificate of disability. |
| 9 | Appointed Lieutenant in the 16th Regiment U. S. Infantry, 22d February, 1848. |

## MEXICAN WAR VETERANS.

ROLL OF COMPANY "E," SIXTEENTH REGIMENT U. S. INFANTRY, COL. JOHN WAR, BEING ONE OF THE BATTALION OF FOUR COMPANIES, OF THE UNITED STATES. ACT

| No. of each grade | Name. | Rank. | Mustered In. When. | Mustered In. Where. | Period | Mustered Out. When. | Mustered Out. Where. |
|---|---|---|---|---|---|---|---|
| | DESERTED. | | | | | | |
| 1 | Hocket, Elijah | Private | May 4, '47 | Newport | During war | | |
| 2 | Smith, John | | May 3, '47 | Newport | | | |
| 3 | Hath, Sanboun | | Apr. 19, '47 | Newport | | | |
| | TRANSFERRED. | | | | | | |
| 1 | DeWitt Collins | 2d Sergeant | Mar. 23, '47 | Newport | | | |

ROLL OF COMPANY "F," SIXTEENTH REGIMENT, U. S. INFANTRY, COL. JOHN WAR, BEING ONE OF THE BATTALION OF FOUR BY THE PRESIDENT OF THE U. S.

| | Name. | Rank. | When. | Where. | | When. | Where. |
|---|---|---|---|---|---|---|---|
| 1 | E. A. Granes | Captain | | | | | |
| 2 | H. K. Ramsey | 1st. Lieutenant | | | | | |
| 3 | Francis McMordie | 2d Lieutenant | | | | | |
| 1 | P. H. Harris | 1st Lieutenant | | | | | |
| 2 | E. C. Berry | 2d Lieutenant | | | | | |
| 1 | Hardy, Arnold S. | 1st Sergeant | Apr. 3, '47 | Lebanon, Ky. | | Aug. 5, '48 | Newport, Ky. |
| 2 | Chrisman, Abraham | 2d Sergeant | Apr. 6, '47 | Harrodsburg, Ky. | | Aug. 5, '48 | Newport, Ky. |
| 3 | Collins, James R. | 3d Sergeant | Mch. 27, '47 | Newport, Ky. | | Aug. 5, '48 | Newport, Ky. |
| 4 | Ellis, James L. W. | 4th Sergeant | April 1, '47 | Lebanon, Ky. | | Aug. 5, '48 | Newport, Ky. |
| 1 | Fletcher, Squire | 1st Corporal | Mch. 27, '47 | Harrodsburg, Ky. | | Aug. 5, '48 | Newport, Ky. |
| 2 | Spaulding, Joseph | 2d Corporal | Apr. 3, '47 | Lebanon, Ky. | | Aug. 5, '48 | Newport, Ky. |
| 3 | McElvoy, Benjamin H. | 3d Corporal | Apr. 17, '47 | Willisburg, Ky. | | Aug. 5, '48 | Newport, Ky. |
| 4 | Reed, James | 4th Corporal | April 8, '47 | Willisburg, Ky. | | Aug. 5, '48 | Newport, Ky. |
| 1 | Hill, Frederick M. | Musician | Apr. 30, '47 | Newport, Ky. | | Aug. 5, '48 | Newport, Ky. |
| 2 | Knott, Timothy C. | Musician | Apr. 15, '47 | Lebanon, Ky. | | Aug. 5, '48 | Newport, Ky. |
| 1 | Able, Joshua | Private | Apr. 5, '47 | Lebanon, Ky. | To serve during the war | Aug. 5, '48 | Newport, Ky. |
| 2 | Allen, Cyrus | Private | April 10, '47 | Raywick, Ky. | | Aug. 5, '48 | Newport, Ky. |
| 3 | Brock, Micajah | Private | April 15, '47 | Liberty, Ky. | | Aug. 5, '48 | Newport, Ky. |
| 4 | Beedles, Robert C. | Private | Apr. 10, '47 | Harrodsburg, Ky. | | Aug. 5, '48 | Newport, Ky. |
| 5 | Birch, William A. | Private | Apr. 5, '47 | Harrodsburg, Ky. | | Aug. 5, '48 | Newport, Ky. |
| 6 | Beard, Joseph | Private | April 10, '47 | Raywick, Ky. | | Aug. 5, '48 | Newport, Ky. |
| 7 | Brown, Andrew J. | Private | April 15, '47 | Lebanon, Ky. | | Aug. 5, '48 | Newport, Ky. |
| 8 | Burk, James | Private | Sept. 24, '47 | Harrodsburg, Ky | | Aug. 5, '48 | Newport, Ky. |
| 9 | Coffman, Eyres A. | Private | Apr. 12, '47 | Harrodsburg, Ky. | | Aug. 5, '48 | Newport, Ky. |
| 10 | Clark, William H. | Private | Apr. 6, '47 | Harrodsburg, Ky. | | Aug. 5, '48 | Newport, Ky. |
| 11 | Clark, Joseph | Private | Apr. 12, '47 | Lebanon, Ky. | | Aug. 5, '48 | Newport, Ky. |
| 12 | Cambron, John | Private | Apr. 13, '47 | Lebanon, Ky. | | Aug. 5, '48 | Newport, Ky. |
| 13 | Corper, James A. | Private | Apr. 19, '47 | Lebanon, Ky. | | Aug. 5, '48 | Newport, Ky. |
| 14 | Clark, John | Private | Mch. 31, '47 | Louisville, Ky. | | Aug. 5, '48 | Newport, Ky. |
| 15 | Clemmons, William | Private | May 11, '47 | Maryville, Ky. | | Aug. 5, '48 | Newport, Ky. |
| 16 | Dean, Newton | Private | Apr. 28, '47 | Harrodsburg, Ky. | | Aug. 5, '48 | Newport, Ky. |
| 17 | Eakin, Charles W. | Private | Aug. 9, '47 | Harrodsburg, Ky. | | Aug. 5, '48 | Newport, Ky. |
| 18 | Easey, Abraham | Private | Sept. 14, '47 | Harrodsburg, Ky. | | Aug. 5, '48 | Newport, Ky. |
| 19 | Fenwick, Cornelius M. | Private | Apr. 10, '47 | Raywick, Ky. | | Aug. 5, '48 | Newport, Ky. |
| 20 | Farris, Jeremiah V. | Private | Apr. 9, '47 | Willisburg, Ky. | | Aug. 5, '48 | Newport, Ky. |
| 21 | Fitzsimmons, James | Private | May 24, '47 | Harrodsburg, Ky. | | Aug. 5, '48 | Newport, Ky. |
| 22 | Flowers, Roling | Private | May 10, '47 | Willisburg, Ky. | | Aug. 5, '48 | Newport, Ky. |
| 23 | Giles, John P. | Private | Apr. 15, '47 | Liberty, Ky. | | Aug. 5, '48 | Newport, Ky. |
| 24 | Giles, James W. | Private | April 9, '47 | Harrodsburg, Ky. | | Aug. 5, '48 | Newport, Ky. |
| 25 | Glasscock, Hall | Private | Apr. 24, '47 | Harrodsburg, Ky. | | Aug. 5, '48 | Newport, Ky. |
| 26 | Gallaher, Charles | Private | Apr. 26, '47 | Frankfort, Ky. | | Aug. 5, '48 | Newport, Ky. |
| 27 | Hearring, John A. | Private | Apr. 3, '47 | Harrodsburg, Ky. | | Aug. 5, '48 | Newport, Ky. |
| 28 | Haggarty, John | Private | Apr. 24, '47 | Harrodsburg, Ky. | | Aug. 5, '48 | Newport, Ky. |
| 29 | Hankla, George C. | Private | Apr. 10, '47 | Harrodsburg, Ky. | | Aug. 5, '48 | Newport, Ky. |
| 30 | Hamilton, Edward B. | Private | Apr. 3, '47 | Lebanon, Ky. | | Aug. 5, '48 | Newport, Ky. |
| 31 | Hinton, Joseph | Private | Apr. 10, '47 | Lebanon, Ky. | | Aug. 5, '48 | Newport, Ky. |
| 32 | Hall, Stephen W. | Private | May 6, '47 | Lebanon, Ky. | | Aug. 5, '48 | Newport, Ky. |
| 33 | Haynes, Hardin P. | Private | Aug. 9, '47 | Harrodsburg, Ky. | | Aug. 5, '48 | Newport, Ky. |
| 34 | Jackson, William O. | Private | Apr. 10, '47 | Harrodsburg, Ky. | | Aug. 5, '48 | Newport, Ky. |
| 35 | Kinkton, Vinson F. | Private | Apr. 14, '47 | Lawrenceburg, Ky. | | Aug. 5, '48 | Newport, Ky. |
| 36 | Landrum, Joel | Private | April 7, '47 | Harrodsburg, Ky. | | Aug. 5, '48 | Newport, Ky. |
| 37 | Lucas, Henry | Private | Apr. 18, '47 | Liver Spring, Ky. | | Aug. 5, '48 | Newport, Ky. |
| 38 | Lanham, John | Private | Apr. 12, '47 | Harrodsburg, Ky. | | Aug. 5, '48 | Newport, Ky. |
| 39 | Lanham, Samuel | Private | April 8, '47 | Willisburg, Ky. | | Aug. 5, '48 | Newport, Ky. |

## MEXICAN WAR VETERANS.

W. TIBBATTS, CALLED INTO THE SERVICE OF THE U. S. FOR THE MEXICAN ORGANIZED IN KENTUCKY, AND OFFICERED BY THE PRESIDENT OF CONGRESS, FEBRUARY 11, 1847.

| No. of each grade | REMARKS. |
|---|---|
| 1 | July 2d, 1847, at Nine Mile Ranch, near Camargo. |
| 2 | August 23, 1847, Mier, Mexico. |
| 3 | January 6, 1848, Ceralvo, Mexico. |
| 1 | Appointed Quartermaster Sergeant, December 23, 1847. |

W. TIBBATTS, CALLED INTO THE SERVICE OF THE U. S. FOR THE MEXICAN COMPANIES ORGANIZED IN KENTUCKY, AND OFFICERED ACT OF CONGRESS, FEBRUARY 11, 1847.

| | |
|---|---|
| 1 | |
| 2 | Promoted to 1st Lieutenant June 14, 1847, and assigned to Company "F." |
| 3 | |
| 1 | Promoted to Captain June 14, 1847, and assigned to Company " B." |
| 2 | Promoted to 1st Lieutenant June 14, 1847. |
| 1 | Appointed 1st Sergeant April 3, 1847. |
| 2 | Appointed 2d Sergeant April 16, 1847. |
| 3 | Appointed 3d Sergeant April 15, 1847. |
| 4 | Appointed Corporal April 29, 1847, and promoted to Sergeant June 14, 1847. |
| 1 | Appointed Corporal March 27, 1847. |
| 2 | Appointed Corporal May 1, 1847. |
| 3 | Appointed Corporal November 7, 1847. |
| 4 | Appointed Corporal May 12, 1848. |
| 1 | Appointed Musician May 31, 1847. |
| 2 | Appointed Musician January 1, 1848; paid only as private. |
| 1 | |
| 2 | |
| 3 | Four months' pay to be stopped by sentence of general court-martial. |
| 4 | |
| 5 | |
| 6 | |
| 7 | |
| 8 | Joined from Regimental Depot, 21st December, 1847. |
| 9 | |
| 10 | |
| 11 | |
| 12 | |
| 13 | Appointed Corporal September 3, 1847, and reduced to the ranks May 11, 1848. Order of Col. Tibbatts. |
| 14 | Joined by transfer from Company " K," July 14, 1847. |
| 15 | |
| 16 | |
| 17 | Joined from Regimental Depot, December 21, 1847. |
| 18 | |
| 19 | |
| 20 | |
| 21 | Joined from Regimental Depot, July 11, 1847. |
| 22 | Joined from Regimental Depot, July 11, 1847. |
| 23 | |
| 24 | |
| 25 | |
| 26 | |
| 27 | |
| 28 | |
| 29 | |
| 30 | |
| 31 | |
| 32 | Joined from Regimental Depot, July 11, 1847. |
| 33 | Joined from Regimental Depot, July 21, 1847. |
| 34 | |
| 35 | |
| 36 | |
| 37 | |
| 38 | |
| 39 | |

## MEXICAN WAR VETERANS.

### ROLL OF COMPANY "F," SIXTEENTH REGIMENT U. S. INFANTRY, COL. JOHN WAR, BEING ONE OF THE BATTALION OF FOUR BY THE PRESIDENT OF THE U. S.

| No. of each grade | Name. | Rank. | | Mustered In. When. | Mustered In. Where. | Period. | Mustered Out. When. | Mustered Out. Where. |
|---|---|---|---|---|---|---|---|---|
| 40 | McWhorter, James B. | Private | | April 15, '47. | Liberty, Ky. | | Aug. 5, '48. | Newport, Ky. |
| 41 | McKitrick, Fielding | Private | | April 8, '47. | Maxville, Ky. | | Aug. 5, '48. | Newport, Ky. |
| 42 | Murphy, Joseph K. | Private | | Apr. 5, '47. | Lebanon, Ky. | | Aug. 5, '48. | Newport, Ky. |
| 43 | Murphy, Kenelian | Private | | Apr. 23, '47. | Lebanon, Ky. | | Aug. 5, '48. | Newport, Ky. |
| 44 | Mills, John | Private | | Apr. 22, '47. | Lebanon, Ky. | | Aug. 5, '48. | Newport, Ky. |
| 45 | May, Wm. R. | Private | | May 4, '47. | Lebanon, Ky. | | Aug. 5, '48. | Newport, Ky. |
| 46 | Napier, Clabourn | Private | | Apr. 13, '47. | Liberty, Ky. | | Aug. 5, '48. | Newport, Ky. |
| 47 | Peavler, Leonard | Private | | Apr. 20, '47. | Harrodsburg, Ky. | | Aug. 5, '48. | Newport, Ky. |
| 48 | Rhuark, Wm. | Private | | Apr. 6, '47. | Harrodsburg, Ky. | | Aug. 5, '48. | Newport, Ky. |
| 49 | Riney, Edward G. | Private | | Apr. 20, '47. | Lebanon, Ky. | | Aug. 5, '48. | Newport, Ky. |
| 50 | Raley, John J. | Private | | April 3, '47. | Lebanon, Ky. | | Aug. 5, '48. | Newport, Ky. |
| 51 | Ray, Absalom | Private | | Apr. 10, '47. | Raywick, Ky. | | Aug. 5, '48. | Newport, Ky. |
| 52 | Rogers, Ransom | Private | | April 8, '47. | Willisburg, Ky. | | Aug. 5, '48. | Newport, Ky. |
| 53 | Rogers, Henry | Private | | April 8, '47. | Willisburg, Ky. | | Aug. 5, '48. | Newport, Ky. |
| 54 | Rigney, Ferdinand | Private | | Apr. 20, '47. | Harrodsburg, Ky. | | Aug. 5, '48. | Newport, Ky. |
| 55 | Rose, George | Private | | April 25, '47. | Oregon, Ky. | | Aug. 5, '48. | Newport, Ky. |
| 56 | Rogers, Geo. A. | Private | | May 6, '47. | Lebanon, Ky. | | Aug 5, '48. | Newport, Ky. |
| 57 | Reed, Winkfield | Private | | May 10, '47. | Willisburg, Ky. | | Aug. 5, '48. | Newport, Ky. |
| 58 | Riley, James | Private | | May 19, '47. | Harrodsburg, Ky. | | Aug. 5, '48. | Newport, Ky. |
| 59 | Smith, Philip | Private | | Apr. 6, '47. | Harrodsburg, Ky. | | Aug. 5, '48. | Newport, Ky. |
| 60 | Smith, John | Private | | Apr. 16, '47. | Bradfordsville, Ky. | | Aug. 5, '48 | Newport, Ky. |
| 61 | Spalding, John A. | Private | | Apr. 12, '47. | Lebanon, Ky. | | Aug. 5, '48. | Newport, Ky. |
| 62 | Scott, John B. | Private | | Apr. 5, '47. | Lebanon. Ky. | | Aug. 5, '48. | Newport, Ky. |
| 63 | Sutton, Alexander | Private | | Apr. 25, '47. | Oregon, Ky. | | Aug. 5, '48. | Newport, Ky. |
| 64 | Sumpter, Andrew J. | Private | | Apr. 17, '47 | Willisburg, Ky. | | Aug. 5 '48. | Newport, Ky. |
| 65 | Sutton, Armsted | Private | | Apr. 16, '47. | Harrodsburg, Ky. | | Aug. 5, '48. | Newport, Ky. |
| 66 | Sanderfur, Andrew J. | Private | | Apr. 13, '47. | Harrodsburg, Ky. | | Aug. 5, '48. | Newport, Ky. |
| 67 | Taylor, Jas. | Private | | Apr. 23, '47. | Harrodsburg, Ky. | | Aug. 5, '48. | Newport, Ky. |
| 68 | Thomas, Benedict | Private | | Apr. 5, '47. | Lebanon, Ky. | | Aug. 5, '48. | Newport, Ky. |
| 69 | Thompson, Hilory M. | Private | | Apr. 10, '47. | Raywick, Ky. | | Aug. 5, '48 | Newport, Ky. |
| 70 | Thompson, Jas. H. | Private | | Apr. 15, '47. | Raywick, Ky. | | Aug. 5, '48. | Newport, Ky. |
| 71 | Thompson, Elijah | Private | | Apr. 17, '47. | Willisburg, Ky. | | Aug. 5, '48. | Newport, Ky. |
| 72 | Thompson, James | Private | | Apr. 8, '47. | Willisburg, Ky. | | Aug. 5, '48. | Newport, Ky. |
| 73 | Vanfleet, John | Private | | May 24, '47. | Harrodsburg, Ky. | | Aug. 5, '48 | Newport, Ky. |
| 74 | Whittle, John | Private | | Apr. 19, '47. | Harrodsburg, Ky. | | Aug. 5, '48. | Newport, Ky. |
| 75 | Whitesides, Wm. B. | Private | | Apr. 19, '47. | Harrodsburg, Ky. | | Aug. 5, '48. | Newport, Ky. |
| 76 | Wilkerson, Stith | Private | | Apr. 20, '47. | Harrodsburg, Ky. | | Aug. 5, '48 | Newport, Ky. |
| 77 | Whitfield, James W. | Private | | Apr. 13, '47. | Lebanon, Ky. | | Aug. 5, '48. | Newport, Ky. |
| 78 | Whitefield, Edward | Private | | Apr. 10, '47. | Lebanon, Ky. | | Aug. 5, '48. | Newport, Ky. |
| 79 | Wilson, John T. | Private | | Sept. 22, '47. | Harrodsburg, Ky. | | Aug. 5, '48. | Newport, Ky. |
| 80 | Yates, Elijah | Private | | Apr. 5, '47. | Harrodsburg, Ky. | | Aug 5, '48. | Newport, Ky. |
| 81 | Young, John | Private | | May 11, '47. | Maxville, Ky. | | Aug. 5 '48. | Newport, Ky. |
| 82 | Yates, William | Private | | Sept. 22, '47. | Harrodsburg, Ky. | | Aug. 5, '48. | Newport, Ky. |
| | **DISCHARGED.** | | | | | | | |
| 1 | Akin, John B. | Corporal | | Apr. 12, '47. | Lawrenceburg, Ky. | | | |
| 2 | Childers, Henry | Private | | Apr. 23, '47. | Lebanon, Ky. | | | |
| 3 | Hohimer, Benjamin | Private | | Apr. 24, '47. | Willisburg, Ky. | | | |
| 4 | Mason, James | Private | | Apr. 14, '47. | Liberty, Ky. | | | |
| 5 | Drain, John M. | Private | | Mar. 17, '47. | Louisville, Ky. | | | |
| 6 | Hightower, Joshua | Private | | May 18, '47. | Harrodsburg, Ky. | | Joined from | Regt. Dep. July 11, '47 |
| 7 | Monohon, Samuel | Private | | Aug. 18, '47. | Louisville, Ky. | | Joined from | Regt. Dep. Jan. 3, '47 |
| 8 | Oliver, Richard | Private | | Sept. 13, '47. | Harrodsburg, Ky. | | Joined from | Regt. Dep. Jan. 12, '47 |
| 9 | Phillips, Benjamin T. | Private | | Apr. 16, '47. | Newport, Ky. | | | |
| 10 | Roberts, James T. | Private | | Apr. 16, '47. | Harrodsburg, Ky. | | | |
| 11 | Rhuark, Elza | Private | | Apr. 6, '47. | Harrodsburg, Ky. | | | |
| 12 | Samples, Samuel | Private | | May 6, '47. | Lebanon, Ky. | | Joined from | Regt. Dep. July 11, '47 |
| 13 | Thompson, Geo. H. | Private | | May 6, '47. | Lebanon, Ky. | | Joined from | Regt. Dep. July 11, '47 |
| 14 | Thompson, Green B. | Private | | Aug. 17, '47. | Louisville, Ky. | | Joined from | Regt. Dep. Jan. 3, '47 |
| | **TRANSFERRED.** | | | | | | | |
| 1 | Davis, George C. | Private | | Mch. 26, '47. | Harrodsburg, Ky. | | | |
| 2 | Castillo, Pablo | Private | | Dec. 5, '47. | Monterey, Mex. | | Joined from | Regt. Dep. Jan. 16, '48 |
| 3 | Gonzales, Benancio | Private | | Jan. 16, '48. | Monterey, Mex. | | Joined from | Regt. Dep. Jan. 16, '48 |
| 4 | Moon, Jas. W. | Private | | Apr. 17, '47. | Harrodsburg, Ky. | | | |
| | **DIED.** | | | | | | | |
| 1 | Moon, Samuel | 4th Sergeant | | Apr. 5, '47. | Harrodsburg, Ky. | | | |
| 2 | Barton, Samuel | Private | | Apr. 18, '47. | Harrodsburg, Ky. | | | |
| 3 | Barton, Owen | Private | | Apr. 15, '47. | Liberty, Ky. | | | |
| 4 | Barton, Milton | Private | | Apr. 13, '47. | Liberty, Ky. | | | |

*To serve during the war.*

W. TIBBATTS, CALLED INTO THE SERVICE OF THE U. S. FOR THE MEXICAN
COMPANIES ORGANIZED IN KENTUCKY, AND OFFICERED
ACT OF CONGRESS, FEBRUARY 11, 1847.

| No. of each grade. | REMARKS. |
|---|---|
| 40 | |
| 41 | |
| 42 | |
| 43 | |
| 44 | |
| 45 | Joined from Regimental Depot, July 11, 1847. |
| 46 | |
| 47 | |
| 48 | |
| 49 | |
| 50 | |
| 51 | |
| 52 | |
| 53 | |
| 54 | |
| 55 | |
| 56 | Joined from Regimental Depot, July 11, 1847. |
| 57 | Joined from Regimental Depot, July 11, 1847. |
| 58 | Joined from Regimental Depot, July 11, 1847. |
| 59 | Appointed Corporal, May 1, 1847, and reduced to ranks September 3, 1847. Order of Col. Tibbatts. |
| 60 | Two weeks' pay to be stopped by sentence of General Court-martial. |
| 61 | |
| 62 | |
| 63 | |
| 64 | |
| 65 | |
| 66 | |
| 67 | |
| 68 | |
| 69 | |
| 70 | |
| 71 | Appointed Musician May 31, 1847, and reduced to the ranks December 1, 1847. Order of Col. Tibbatts. |
| 72 | |
| 73 | Joined from Regimental Depot, July 11, 1847. |
| 74 | |
| 75 | |
| 76 | |
| 77 | |
| 78 | |
| 79 | Joined from Regimental Depot, December 21, 1847. |
| 80 | |
| 81 | Joined from Regimental Depot, July 11, 1847. |
| 82 | Joined from Regimental Depot, December 21, 1847. |
| 1 | Appointed Corporal 12th April, 1847; discharged November 6, 1847; Surgeon's certificate of disability, at Monterey, Mexico. |
| 2 | Discharged July 2, 1848, expiration of service, to enlist in 2d Dragoons, at Camargo, Mexico. |
| 3 | Discharged November 5, 1847; Surgeon's certificate of disability, at Monterey, Mexico. |
| 4 | Discharged November 6, 1847; Surgeon's certificase of disability, at Monterey, Mexico. |
| 5 | Discharged October 1, 1847; Surgeon's certificate of disability, at Monterey, Mexico. |
| 6 | Discharged February 5, 1848; Surgeon's certificate of disability, at Monterey, Mexico. |
| 7 | Discharged July 2, 1848, expiration of service, and to re-enlist in the 2d Dragoons, at Monterey, Mexico. |
| 8 | Discharged July 5, 1848; Surgeon's certificate of disability, at New Orleans. |
| 9 | Discharged July 6, 1848; Surgeon's certificate of disability, at Newport, Ky. |
| 10 | Discharged July 2, 1848; to re-enlist in the 2d Dragoons, at Camargo. |
| 11 | Discharged July 5, 1848; Surgeon's certificate of disability, at New Orleans. |
| 12 | Discharged April 13, 1848; Surgeon's certificate of disability, at Monterey. |
| 13 | Discharged April 13, 1848; Surgeon's certificate of disability, at Monterey. |
| 14 | Discharged January, 1848; order of Gen. Wool, cause, insanity, at Monterey. |
| 1 | Transferred July 14, 1847; exchanged to Company "K," at Mier, Mexico. |
| 2 | Transferred May 10, 1848, to Company "H," at Monterey, Mexico. |
| 3 | Transferred March 11, 1848, to Regimental Band, at Monterey, Mexico. |
| 4 | Transferred July 14, 1847; exchanged to Company "K," at Mexico. |
| 1 | Appointed Sergeant 15th April, 1847 and died June 13, 1847, at Camargo, Mexico. Inflammatory rheumatism. |
| 2 | Died at hospital, Mier, Mexico, July 26, 1847. Measles. |
| 3 | Died at hospital, Mier, Mexico, July 24, 1847. Measles. |
| 4 | Died at hospital, Mier, Mexico, October 2, 1847. Continued fever. |

## MEXICAN WAR VETERANS.

ROLL OF COMPANY "F," SIXTEENTH REGIMENT U. S. INFANTRY, COL. JOHN WAR, BEING ONE OF THE BATTALION OF FOUR COMPANIES, OF THE UNITED STATES. ACT

| No. of each grade | Name. | Rank. | | Mustered In. When. | Mustered In. Where. | Period | Mustered Out. When. | Mustered Out. Where. |
|---|---|---|---|---|---|---|---|---|
| 5 | Brock, Leonard | Private | | Apr. 15, '47. | Liberty, Ky. | During the war. | | |
| 6 | Davis, Samuel | Private | | Apr. 10, '47. | Raywick, Ky. | | | |
| 7 | Griffin, Daniel | Private | | Apr. 5, '47 | Harrodsburg, Ky. | | | |
| 8 | Glascock, Wharton | Private | | Apr. 16, '47. | Harrodsburg, Ky. | | | |
| 9 | Gaitwood, Robert | Private | | Oct. 27, '47. | Harrodsburg, Ky. | | | |
| 10 | Moor, John | Private | | Apr. 2, '47. | Lebanon, Ky. | | | |
| 11 | Madden, Benedict J. | Private | | Apr. 13, '47. | Lebanon, Ky. | | | |
| 12 | Mullus, Richard | Private | | Apr. 12, '47. | Bardstown, Ky. | | | |
| 13 | Mattingly, Sabastian C. | Private | | Apr. 10, '47. | Raywick, Ky. | | | |
| 14 | Thomas, William A. | Private | | Apr. 21, '47. | Lebanon, Ky. | | | |

ROLL OF COMPANY "K," SIXTEENTH REGIMENT U. S. INFANTRY, COL. JOHN WAR, BEING ONE OF THE BATTALION OF FOUR COMPANIES, OF THE UNITED STATES. ACT

| | Name. | Rank. | | When. | Where. | | When. | Where. |
|---|---|---|---|---|---|---|---|---|
| 1 | James W. Brannon | Captain | | Mar. 10, '47. | Louisville | | | |
| 2 | B. B. Irvan | 1st Lieutenant | | | | | | |
| | Pyth. Holcomb | 2d Lieutenant | | | | | | |
| | Thomas T. Hawkins | 2d Lieutenant | | | | | | |
| | **Transferred.** | | | | | | | |
| | George W. Singleton | 1st Lieutenant | | Mar. 10, '47. | | | | |
| | John T. Hughes | 1st Lieutenant | | | | | | |
| | A. Evans | 2d Lieutenant | | | | | | |
| | Thos. M. Winston | 2d Lieutenant | | | | | | |
| 1 | Robert H. Barker | 1st Sergeant | | Mar. 12, '47. | Louisville | To serve during the war. | Aug. 2, '48. | Newport, Ky. |
| 2 | William H. Parker | 2d Sergeant | | Mar. 12, '47. | Louisville | | Aug. 2, '48 | Newport, Ky. |
| 3 | Henry G. Marshall | Sergeant | | Mar. 12, '47. | Louisville | | Aug. 2, '48 | Newport, Ky. |
| 4 | George Wilcox | Sergeant | | Apr. 7, '47. | Louisville | | Aug. 2, '48 | Newport, Ky. |
| 1 | Tarlton Caldwell | Corporal | | Apr. 7, '47. | Madison, Ind. | | Aug. 2, '48 | Newport, Ky. |
| 2 | Chasteen Donavan | Corporal | | Mar. 19, '47. | Louisville | | Aug. 2, '48 | Newport, Ky. |
| 3 | Thomas B. Mattingly | Corporal | | Mar. 12, '47. | Louisville | | Aug. 2, '48 | Newport, Ky. |
| 4 | Richard Conquest | Corporal | | May 22, '47. | Harrisonville | | Aug. 2, '48 | Newport, Ky. |
| 1 | James Figg | Drummer | | Apr. 28, '47. | Louisville | | Aug. 2, '48 | Newport, Ky. |
| 2 | Ira L. Derby | Fifer | | Sept. 13, '47. | Galena | | Aug. 2, '48 | Newport, Ky. |
| 1 | Adams, John | Private | | Apr. 28, '47. | Louisville | | Aug. 2, '48 | Newport, Ky. |
| 2 | Adams, James | Private | | Apr. 5, '47. | Columbus | | Aug. 2, '48 | Newport, Ky. |
| 3 | Anderson, Aaron | Private | | July 28, '47. | Galena | | Aug. 2, '48 | Newport, Ky. |
| 4 | Bowen, David T. | Private | | Mar. 17, '47. | Chicago | | Aug. 2, '48 | Newport, Ky. |
| 5 | Brown, Ludwing | Private | | Apr. 22, '47. | Louisville | | Aug. 2, '48 | Newport, Ky. |
| 6 | Boswell, Lewis | Private | | Aug. 20, '47. | Meredocio | | Aug. 2, '48 | Newport, Ky. |
| 7 | Bernard, Richard | Private | | July 8, '47. | Potosi | | Aug. 2, '48 | Newport, Ky. |
| 8 | Buck, Jerome B. | Private | | Sept. 28, '47. | Galena | | Aug. 2, '48 | Newport, Ky. |
| 9 | Bollen, Daniel | Private | | Sept. 25, '47. | Galena | | Aug. 2, '48 | Newport, Ky. |
| 10 | Burton, George W. | Private | | July 16, '47. | Bloomington, Ind. | | | |
| 11 | Crook, John W. | Private | | Mar. 29, '47 | Louisville | | | |
| 12 | Conner, Nathaniel H. | Private | | Mar. 31, '47. | Louisville | | Aug. 2, '48. | Newport, Ky. |
| 13 | Charles, Samuel | Private | | May 15, '47. | Natchez, Miss. | | Aug. 2, '48. | Newport, Ky. |
| 14 | Clark, Lewis P. | Private | | Apr. 12, '47. | Chicago | | Aug. 2, '48. | Newport, Ky. |
| 15 | Cox, Champlain | Private | | Sept. 28, '47. | Bloomington | | Aug. 2, '48. | Newport, Ky. |
| 16 | Calvert, William | Private | | Sept. 20, '47. | Galena | | Aug. 2, '48. | Newport, Ky. |
| 17 | Denslow, John W. | Private | | Mar. 20, '47 | Louisville | | Aug. 2, '48. | Newport, Ky. |
| 18 | Daily, John D. | Private | | May 13, '47. | Louisville | | Aug. 2, '48. | Newport, Ky. |
| 19 | Duckworth, William | Private | | Apr. 17, '47. | Mt. Vernon, Ind. | | Aug. 2, '48. | Newport, Ky. |
| 20 | Dovan, Andrew | Private | | Aug. 8, '47. | Louisville | | Aug. 2, '48. | Newport, Ky. |
| 21 | Doty, Samuel | Private | | Aug. 19, '47. | Bardstown, Ky. | | Aug. 2, '48. | Newport, Ky. |
| 22 | Driscall, William N. | Private | | July 14, '47. | Louisville | | Aug. 2, '48. | Newport, Ky. |
| 23 | Davidson, Marion T. | Private | | Sept. 15, '47. | Harrodsburg | | Aug. 2, '48. | Newport, Ky. |
| 24 | Edmundson, John W. | Private | | July 23, '47. | Galena | | Aug. 2, '48. | Newport, Ky. |
| 25 | Foster, Joseph | Private | | Mar. 17, '47 | Louisville | | Aug. 2, '48. | Newport, Ky. |
| 26 | Ficklin, Charles | Private | | Apr. 7, '47 | Louisville | | Aug. 2, '48. | Newport, Ky. |
| 27 | Ferry, Charles F. | Private | | Mar. 18, '47. | Madison | | Aug. 2, '48. | Newport, Ky. |
| 28 | Hepting, Paul | Private | | Mar. 17, '47 | Louisville | | Aug. 2, '48. | Newport, Ky. |
| 29 | Hardingbrook, Lewis | Private | | Apr. 2, '47. | Madison | | Aug. 2, '48. | Newport, Ky. |
| 30 | Hughes, Claburn | Private | | Apr. 5, '47 | Louisville | | Aug. 2, '48. | Newport, Ky. |
| 31 | Haynes, John | Private | | Apr 20, '47. | Louisville | | Aug. 2, '48. | Newport, Ky. |
| 32 | Henning, John S. | Private | | Mar. 22, '47. | Louisville | | Aug. 2, '48. | Newport, Ky. |

# MEXICAN WAR VETERANS.

## W. TIBBATTS, CALLED INTO THE SERVICE OF THE U. S. FOR THE MEXICAN ORGANIZED IN KENTUCKY, AND OFFICERED BY THE PRESIDENT OF CONGRESS, FEBRUARY 11, 1847—Continued.

| No. of each grade. | REMARKS. |
|---|---|
| 5 | Died at hospital, Mier, Mexico, August 12, 1847. Measles. |
| 6 | Died at hospital, Mier, Mexico, July 15, 1847. Measles. |
| 7 | Died at hospital, Mier, Mexico, July 11, 1847. Measles. |
| 8 | Died in camp near Camargo, Mexico, June 20, 1847. Measles. |
| 9 | Joined from Regimental Depot, December 21, 1847 and died at Monterey, Mexico, June 4, 1848. Typhoid fever. |
| 10 | Died in hospital, Mier, August 3, 1847. Diarrhœa. |
| 11 | Died in hospital, Mier, July 30, 1847. Diarrhœa. |
| 12 | Died at camp near Camargo, June 18, 1847. Inflammation of brain. |
| 13 | Died in hospital, Mier, Mexico, August 31, 1847. Fever. |
| 14 | Died in camp near Mier, Mexico, August 13, 1847. Fever. |

## W. TIBBATTS, CALLED INTO THE SERVICE OF THE U. S. FOR THE MEXICAN ORGANIZED IN KENTUCKY, AND OFFICERED BY THE PRESIDENT OF CONGRESS, FEBRUARY 11, 1847.

| | |
|---|---|
| 1 | |
| 2 | Joined by transfer from Company "B," at Monterey; order 26, dated 28th April, 1848. Col. Tibbatts. On duty as Adjutant of the Regiment since March 15, 1848; order No. 6. Mustered on Field and Staff. |
| | Transferred to Company "C," at Mier, July 8, 1847. Order No. 4. [at Monterey. |
| | Joined by transfer from Company "C," order No. 11, July 25, 1847, at Mier; transferred to Company "B," order 26, dated April, 1848, |
| | Transferred to Company "C," Mier, order No. 11, 25th July, 1847. |
| | Transferred to Company "I," Monterey, order No. 8, 16th March, 1848. |
| 1 | Appointed 2d Sergeant, 11th April, 1847; promoted to 1st Sergeant 11th July, at Mier, Mexico. Order of Col. Tibbatts. |
| 2 | Appointed 1st Sergeant, 11th April, 1847; reduced to 2d Sergeant, 11th July, 1847. Order of Col. Tibbatts. |
| 3 | Appointed Sergeant, 11th April, 1847, at Mier, Mexico. Order of Col. Tibbatts. |
| 4 | Appointed Sergeant, 11th April, 1847; reduced to Corporal, 11th July, 1847, from Sergeant; September 21, 1847. [Alto. |
| 1 | Joined by transfer from Company "C," 11th July, 1847, at Mier, Mexico; order of Col. Tibbatts; appointed Corporal May 2, 1847, Palo |
| 2 | Appointed Corporal, 21st September, 1847. |
| 3 | Appointed Corporal, 11th April, 1847; reduced to ranks 11th July; appointed Corporal 25th March, 1848. |
| 4 | Appointed Corporal, 30th March, 1848; joined from Regimental Depot, at Mier, July 11, 1847. [January 26, 1847. |
| 1 | Transferred to Regimental Band, 11th August, 1847; rejoined Company, 18th November, 1847, Monterey; joined from Regimental Depot, |
| 2 | Joined from Regimental Depot, 24th December, 1847, at Monterey. |
| 1 | Joined from Regimental Depot June 26, 1847, at Camargo Mexico. |
| 2 | Joined by transfer from Company "C," at Monterey. 24th December, 1847. |
| 3 | Joined from Regimental Depot, Newport, Ky., 24th December, 1847. |
| 4 | Joined by transfer from Company "G," at Mier, 11th July, 1847. |
| 5 | Joined by transfer from Company "E," at Palo Alto, 21st May, 1847. Order of Major Talbott. |
| 6 | Joined from Regimental Depot, Newport, Ky., at Monterey, Mexico, 24th December, 1847. Col. Tibbatts. |
| 7 | Joined from Regimental Depot, Newport, Ky., at Monterey, Mexico, 24th December, 1847. Col. Tibbatts. |
| 8 | Joined from Regimental Depot, Newport, Ky., at Monterey, Mexico, 24th December, 1847. Col. Tibbatts. |
| 9 | Joined from Regimental Depot, Newport, Ky., at Monterey, Mexico, 24th December, 1847. Col. Tibbatts. |
| 10 | Joined from Regimental Depot, Newport, Ky., at Monterey, Mexico, 24th December, 1847. Sick in New Orleans. |
| 11 | Joined from Regimental Depot, Newport, Ky., at Monterey, Mexico, 24th December, 1847. Sick in New Orleans. |
| 12 | Appointed Corporal, at Mier, Mexico, 21st September, 1847; resigned as Corporal, 25th March, 1848. |
| 13 | Joined from Regimental Depot, at Mier, July 11, 1847. |
| 14 | Joined by transfer from Company "G," at Mier, July 11, 1847. |
| 15 | Joined from Regimental Depot, at Monterey, 24th December, 1847. |
| 16 | Joined from Regimental Depot, at Monterey, 24th December, 1847; March, 1848. Col. Tibbatts. |
| 17 | Appointed Corporal, 11th July, 1847; reduced to ranks 21st September, 1847. Col. Tibbatts. |
| 18 | Joined from Regimental Depot, at Camargo, 26th June, 1847. Col. Tibbatts. |
| 19 | Joined by transfer from Company "D," at Mier, 11th July, 1847. Col. Tibbatts. |
| 20 | Joined from Regimental Depot, at Monterey, 21st December, 1847. |
| 21 | Joined from Regimental Depot, at Monterey, 21st December, 1847. |
| 22 | Joined from Regimental Depot, at Monterey, 21st December, 1847. |
| 23 | Joined from Regimental Depot, at Monterey, 21st December, 1847. |
| 24 | Joined from Regimental Depot, at Monterey, 21st December, 1847. |
| 25 | Joined from Regimental Depot, at Monterey, 21st December, 1847. |
| 26 | |
| 27 | Joined by transfer from Company "C," at Monterey, 2d June, 1848. Col. Tibbatts. |
| 28 | |
| 29 | Joined by transfer from Company "C," at Mier, July 11, 1847; appointed Corporal same day; reduced to ranks, 22d November, 1847. |
| 30 | |
| 31 | Joined by transfer from Company "E," at Palo Alto, 21st May, 1847. Order of Major Talbott. |
| 32 | |

## 168            MEXICAN WAR VETERANS.

ROLL OF COMPANY "K," SIXTEENTH REGIMENT U. S. INFANTRY, COL. JOHN WAR, BEING ONE OF THE BATTALION OF FOUR COMPANIES, OF THE UNITED STATES. ACT

| No. of each grade | Name. | Rank. | Mustered In. When. | Mustered In. Where. | Period | Mustered Out. When. | Mustered Out. Where. |
|---|---|---|---|---|---|---|---|
| 33 | Holmes, James | Private | Apr. 20, '47 | Louisville | | Aug. 2, '48 | Newport, Ky. |
| 34 | Holmes, Benjamin R. | Private | Mar. 16, '47 | Madison | | Aug. 2, '48 | Newport, Ky. |
| 35 | Harlan, James M. | Private | Apr. 26, '47 | Frankfort, Ind. | | Aug. 2, '48 | Newport, Ky. |
| 36 | Harper, George W. | Private | Apr. 1, '47 | Boonville | | Aug. 2, '48 | Newport, Ky. |
| 37 | Harris, Benjamin G. | Private | Apr. 19, '47 | Louisville | | Aug. 2, '48 | Newport, Ky. |
| 38 | Hearn, Franklin | Private | May 25, '47 | Owenton, Ky. | | Aug. 2, '48 | Newport, Ky. |
| 39 | Horr, John A. | Private | Apr. 20, '47 | Chicago, Ill. | | Aug. 2, '48 | Newport, Ky. |
| 40 | Ivey, Jesse | Private | May 25, '47 | Carrollton, Ky. | | Aug. 2, '48 | Newport, Ky. |
| 41 | Jett, Benjamin F. | Private | May 4, '47 | Mt. Vernon | | Aug. 2, '48 | Newport, Ky. |
| 42 | Joslin, James | Private | Aug. 19, '47 | Louisville | | Aug. 2, '48 | Newport, Ky. |
| 43 | Joslin, Almond | Private | Apr. 30, '47 | Cairo, Ill. | | Aug. 2, '48 | Newport, Ky. |
| 44 | Keeler, Joseph C. | Private | Mar. 12, '47 | Louisville | | Aug. 2, '48 | Newport, Ky. |
| 45 | Knip, Joel K. | Private | Sept. 1, '47 | Meredccio | | Aug. 2, '48 | Newport, Ky. |
| 46 | Knott, Samuel | Private | Oct. 6, '47 | Louisville | | Aug. 2, '48 | Newport, Ky. |
| 47 | Lemonds, Nelson | Private | May 27, '47 | Springfield | | Aug. 2, '48 | Newport, Ky. |
| 48 | Little, James | Private | June 23, '47 | Galena | | Aug. 2, '48 | Newport, Ky. |
| 49 | Logston, Dougherty | Private | July 15, '47 | Nashville | | Aug. 2, '48 | Newport, Ky. |
| 50 | Murray, Winfield S. | Private | Mar. 29, '47 | Louisville | | Aug. 2, '48 | Newport, Ky. |
| 51 | Mahon, George T. | Private | Apr. 10, '47 | Louisville | | Aug. 2, '48 | Newport, Ky. |
| 52 | Mercer, James T. | Private | Apr. 27, '47 | Louisville | | Aug. 2, '48 | Newport, Ky. |
| 53 | Middleton, John | Private | Apr. 7, '47 | Evansville | | Aug. 2, '48 | Newport, Ky. |
| 54 | Morgan, John | Private | May 21, '47 | Owenton | | Aug. 2, '48 | Newport, Ky. |
| 55 | Miles, James M. | Private | Oct. 1, '47 | Galena | | Aug. 2, '48 | Newport, Ky. |
| 56 | McDonald, John B. | Private | Mar. 15, '47 | Louisville | | Aug. 2, '48 | Newport, Ky. |
| 57 | McDonald, George | Private | June 30, '47 | Platteville | | Aug. 2, '48 | Newport, Ky. |
| 58 | McQuiddy, Alex. A. | Private | Aug. 2, '47 | Galena | | Aug. 2, '48 | Newport, Ky. |
| 59 | McAttee, Ferdinand | Private | Aug. 21, '47 | Galena | | Aug. 2, '48 | Newport, Ky. |
| 60 | McCombs, Anderson | Private | Aug. 9, '47 | Jacksonville | To serve during the war. | Aug. 2, '48 | Newport, Ky. |
| 61 | Parks, John C. | Private | Mar. 18, '47 | Chicago | | Aug. 2, '48 | Newport, Ky. |
| 62 | Parker, Cal. C. | Private | Oct. 4, '47 | Bloomington | | Aug. 2, '48 | Newport, Ky. |
| 63 | Power, John | Private | Sept. 22, '47 | Galena | | Aug. 2, '48 | Newport, Ky. |
| 64 | Power, William | Private | Sept. 24, '47 | Galena | | Aug. 2, '48 | Newport, Ky. |
| 65 | Poe, John F. | Private | Sept. 9, '47 | Louisville | | Aug. 2, '48 | Newport, Ky. |
| 66 | Quick, William | Private | Aug. 24, '47 | Bloomington | | Aug. 2, '48 | Newport, Ky. |
| 67 | Reagan, William H. | Private | Mar. 13, '47 | Louisville | | Aug. 2, '48 | Newport, Ky. |
| 68 | Rourge, John O. | Private | Apr. 6, '47 | Louisville | | Aug. 2, '48 | Newport, Ky. |
| 69 | Russell, Newell | Private | Apr. 7, '47 | Louisville | | Aug. 2, '48 | Newport, Ky. |
| 70 | Russell, Alexander | Private | May 5, '47 | Wilshire | | Aug. 2, '48 | Newport, Ky. |
| 71 | Reed, Phelps | Private | May 8, '47 | Springville | | Aug. 2, '48 | Newport, Ky. |
| 72 | Repp, Farmer K. | Private | Apr. 19, '47 | Madison | | Aug. 2, '48 | Newport, Ky. |
| 73 | Repp, Pleaston F. | Private | Apr. 17, '47 | Madison | | Aug. 2, '48 | Newport, Ky. |
| 74 | Rutherford, John | Private | July 28, '47 | Galena | | Aug. 2, '48 | Newport, Ky. |
| 75 | Shiplar, Stephenson | Private | Mar. 12, '47 | Louisville | | Aug. 2, '48 | Newport, Ky. |
| 76 | Shiplar, John W. | Private | Mar. 24, '47 | Louisville | | Aug. 2, '48 | Newport, Ky. |
| 77 | Scrugg, William R. | Private | Mar. 12, '47 | Louisville | | Aug. 2, '48 | Newport, Ky. |
| 78 | Shaver, Peter A. | Private | Apr. 7, '47 | Louisville | | Aug. 2, '48 | Newport, Ky. |
| 79 | Southworth, George T. | Private | Mar. 17, '47 | Louisville | | Aug. 2, '48 | Newport, Ky. |
| 80 | Slaughter, John | Private | May 12, '47 | Bloomington | | Aug. 2, '48 | Newport, Ky. |
| 81 | Sapers, John | Private | Sept. 23, '47 | Jacksonville | | Aug. 2, '48 | Newport, Ky. |
| 82 | Smith, Aaron | Private | Aug. 2, '47 | Mineral Point | | Aug. 2, '48 | Newport, Ky. |
| 83 | Simms, William | Private | June 23, '47 | Louisville | | Aug. 2, '48 | Newport, Ky. |
| 84 | Truman, James W. | Private | Apr. 7, '47 | Louisville | | Aug. 2, '48 | Newport, Ky. |
| 85 | Tullis, Thomas | Private | Apr. 27, '47 | Louisville | | Aug. 2, '48 | Newport, Ky. |
| 86 | Todlock, James B. | Private | Sept. 15, '47 | Harrodsburg | | Aug. 2, '48 | Newport, Ky. |
| 87 | Vickers, Jackson | Private | May 24, '47 | Natchez | | Aug. 2, '48 | Newport, Ky. |
| 88 | Veatch, Absalom | Private | Aug. 17, '47 | Bloomington | | Aug. 2, '48 | Newport, Ky. |
| 89 | Winright, John | Private | Apr. 3, '47 | Louisville | | Aug. 2, '48 | Newport, Ky. |
| 90 | Wallace, William | Private | Apr. 10, '47 | Louisville | | Aug. 2, '48 | Newport, Ky. |
| 91 | Wilson, William | Private | Apr. 5, '47 | N. Harmony | | Aug. 2, '48 | Newport, Ky. |
| 92 | Waters, Joseph | Private | May 3, '47 | St. Marys | | Aug. 2, '48 | Newport, Ky. |
| 93 | Wetherill, Richard | Private | May 13, '47 | Louisville | | Aug. 2, '48 | Newport, Ky. |
| 94 | Williams, John | Private | Mar. 22, '47 | Dupont | | Aug. 2, '48 | Newport, Ky. |
| 95 | Wheatley, Elam | Private | July 17, '47 | Louisville | | Aug. 2, '48 | Newport, Ky. |
| | DIED. | | | | | | |
| 1 | John C. Devore | Private | Mar. 19, '47 | Louisville, Ky. | | | |
| 2 | David F. Johnson | Private | Apr. 10, '47 | Louisville, Ky. | | | |
| 3 | William McKeag | Private | Mar. 18, '47 | Louisville, Ky. | | | |
| 4 | Ellison Williams | Private | Apr. 26, '47 | N. Harmony | | Joined from | Co. "D.," Aug. 1, '47. |
| 5 | James W. Moore | Private | Apr. 29, '47 | Harrodsburg | | Joined from | Co. "E, Aug. 1, '47. |

## MEXICAN WAR VETERANS.

**W. TIBBATTS, CALLED INTO THE SERVICE OF THE U. S. FOR THE MEXICAN ORGANIZED IN KENTUCKY, AND OFFICERED BY THE PRESIDENT OF CONGRESS, FEBRUARY 11, 1847—Continued.**

| No. of each grade | REMARKS. |
|---|---|
| 33 | |
| 34 | Joined by transfer from Company "C," at Monterey, 2d January, 1848. Order of Col. Tibbatts; due U. S. clothing $3.86. |
| 35 | Joined by transfer from Company "D," at Mier, 11th July, 1847. Order of Col. Tibbatts. |
| 36 | Joined by transfer from Company "I," at Mier, 11th July, 1847. Order of Col. Tibbatts. |
| 37 | Joined from Regimental Depot, at Camargo, 26th June, 1847. Order of Col. Tibbatts. |
| 38 | Joined from Regimental Depot, at Mier, 11th July, 1847. Order of Col. Tibbatts. |
| 39 | Joined by transfer from Company "G," 11th July, 1847. Order of Col. Tibbatts. |
| 40 | Joined from Regimental Depot, 11th July, 1847. Order of Col. Tibbatts. |
| 41 | Joined from Company "D," by transfer, 11th July, 1847. Order of Col. Tibbatts. |
| 42 | Joined from Regimental Depot, Monterey, 24th December, 1847. Order of Col. Tibbatts. |
| 43 | Joined from Company "G," by transfer, Monterey, 7th January, 1848. Order of Col. Tibbatts. |
| 44 | |
| 45 | Joined from Regimental Depot, Monterey, 24th December, 1847. Order of Col. Tibbatts. |
| 46 | Joined from Regimental Depot, Monterey, 24th December, 1847. Order of Col. Tibbatts. |
| 47 | Joined from Regimental Depot, Mier, 11th July, 1847. Order of Col. Tibbatts. |
| 48 | Joined from Regimental Depot, Monterey, 24th December, 1847. Order of Col. Tibbatts. |
| 49 | |
| 50 | |
| 51 | |
| 52 | Joined from Regimental Depot, Camargo, 26th June, 1847. Order of Col. Tibbatts. |
| 53 | Joined from Company "I," Mier, 11th July, 1847. Order of Col. Tibbatts. |
| 54 | Joined from Regimental Depot, Mier, 11th July, 1847. Order of Col. Tibbatts. |
| 55 | Joined from Regimental Depot, Monterey, 24th December, 1847. Order of Col. Tibbatts. |
| 56 | |
| 57 | Joined from Regimental Depot, Monterey, 24th December, 1847. Order of Col. Tibbatts. |
| 58 | Joined from Regimental Depot, Monterey, 24th December, 1847. Order of Col. Tibbatts. |
| 59 | Joined from Regimental Depot, Monterey, 24th December, 1847. Order of Col Tibbatts. |
| 60 | Joined from Regimental Depot, Monterey, 24th December, 1847. Order of Col. Tibbatts. |
| 61 | Joined by transfer from Company "G," as Sergeant, at Mier, 11th July, 1847; reduced to ranks 21st Sept., 1847. Order of Col. Tibbatts. |
| 62 | Joined from Regimental Depot, Monterey, 24th December, 1847. Order of Col. Tibbatts. |
| 63 | Joined from Regimental Depot, Monterey, 24th December, 1847. Order of Col. Tibbatts. |
| 64 | Joined from Regimental Depot, Monterey, 24th December, 1847. Order of Col. Tibbatts. |
| 65 | |
| 66 | Joined from Regimental Depot, Monterey, 24th December, 1847. Order of Col. Tibbatts. |
| 67 | |
| 68 | |
| 69 | |
| 70 | Joined from Regimental Depot, Mier, July 11, 1847. Order of Col. Tibbatts. |
| 71 | Joined from Regimental Depot, Mier, July 11, 1847. Order of Col. Tibbatts. |
| 72 | Joined from Company "C;" appointed Corporal 22d November, 1847; resigned Corporal 30th March, 1847. Order of Col. Tibbatts. |
| 73 | Joined from Company "C," July 11, 1847. Order of Col. Tibbatts. |
| 74 | Joined from Regimental Depot, December 24, 1847. Order of Col. Tibbatts. |
| 75 | |
| 76 | |
| 77 | |
| 78 | |
| 79 | |
| 80 | Joined from Regimental Depot, at Mier, 11th July, 1847. Order of Col. Tibbatts. |
| 81 | Joined from Regimental Depot, at Monterey, 24th December, 1847. Order of Col. Tibbatts. |
| 82 | Joined from Regimental Depot, at Monterey, 24th December, 1847. Order of Col. Tibbatts. |
| 83 | Joined from Regimental Depot, at Monterey, 24th December, 1847. Order of Col. Tibbatts. |
| 84 | |
| 85 | Joined from Regimental Depot, at Camargo, 26th June, 1847. Order of Col. Tibbatts. |
| 86 | Joined from Regimental Depot at Monterey, 24th December, 1847. Order of Col. Tibbatts. |
| 87 | Joined from Regimental Depot at Mier, 11th July, 1847. Order of Col. Tibbatts. |
| 88 | Joined from Regimental Depot at Monterey, 24th December, 1847. Order of Col. Tibbatts. |
| 89 | |
| 90 | |
| 91 | Joined from Company "D" at Mier, 11th July, 1847. Order of Col. Tibbatts. |
| 92 | Joined from Regimental Depot at Mier, 11th July, 1847. Order of Col. Tibbatts. |
| 93 | Joined from Regimental Depot at Camargo, June 26, 1847. Order of Col. Tibbatts. |
| 94 | Joined from Company "C" at Mier, 11th July, 1847. Order of Col. Tibbatts. |
| 95 | Joined from Regimental Depot at Monterey, 24th December, 1847. Order of Col. Tibbatts. |
| 1 | At Matamoras, Mex., May 27, 1847. Typhoid fever. |
| 2 | At Matamoras, Mex., June 3, 1847. Dysentery. |
| 3 | At Camargo, Mex., June 8, 1847. Dysentery. |
| 4 | At Mier, Mex., September 11, 1847. Left in hospital at Mier, 22d August, 1847. |
| 5 | At Mier, Mex., September 18, 1847. Dysentery. |

170                  MEXICAN WAR VETERANS.

ROLL OF COMPANY "K," SIXTEENTH REGIMENT U. S. INFANTRY, COL. JOHN WAR, BEING ONE OF THE BATTALION OF FOUR BY THE PRESIDENT OF THE U. S.

| No. of each grade | Name. | Rank. | | Mustered In. When. | Mustered In. Where. | Period. | Mustered Out. When. | Mustered Out. Where. |
|---|---|---|---|---|---|---|---|---|
| | **DESERTED.** | | | | | | | |
| 1 | Thomas Hambleton | Private | | Apr. 3 '47 | Louisville | | | |
| 2 | John Tyson | Private | | Mar. 26, '47 | Louisville | | | |
| 3 | Richard H. Padder | Private | | Apr. 8, '47 | Louisville | | | |
| 4 | George C. Davis | Private | | Mar. 26, '47 | Harrodsburg | | Joined by | transfer Co. "F," 11th July, 1847. |
| | **DISCHARGED.** | | | | | | | |
| 1 | Silas Evans | Private | | Mar. 12, '47 | Louisville | | | |
| 2 | James T. Hamlin | Private | | Apr. 24, '47 | Lawrenceburg | | Joined from | Co. "C" 11th July, '47. |
| 3 | Robert R. Hirons | Private | | Apr. 10, '47 | Louisville, Ky. | | | |
| 4 | Jacobs Cryster | Private | | Mar. 23, '47 | Dupont | | Joined from | Co. "C," 11th July, '47 |
| 5 | John Blain | Private | | Mar. 25, '47 | Bloomington | | Joined from | Co. "I," 11th July, '47 |
| 6 | Jacob Tague | Private | | Mar. 30, '47 | Madison | | Joined from | Co. "C," 11th July, '47 |
| 7 | William Hearn | Private | | May 25, '47 | Owenton | | Joined from | Regt. Dep. July 11,'47 |
| 8 | Francis Metcalf | Private | | Sept. 14, '47 | Louisville | | Joined from | Regt. Dep. July 24,'47 |
| 9 | Veatchele Parish | Private | | Sept. 15, '47 | Harrodsburg | | Joined from | Regt. Dep. July 24,'47 |
| 10 | John Tyson | Private | | Mar. 24, '47 | Louisville | | | |
| | **TRANSFERRED.** | | | | | | | |
| 1 | John N. Tranchl | Private | | Mch. 31, '47 | Louisville | | | |
| 2 | Tom Hall | Private | | Apr. 5, '47 | Louisville | | | |
| 3 | John W. Wright | Private | | Mar. 24, '47 | Louisville | | | |
| 4 | James H. Thorpe | Private | | Apr. 5, '47 | Louisville | | | |
| 5 | Alexander Belmont | Private | | Mch. 12, '47 | Louisville | | | |
| 6 | James M. Baughn | Private | | Apr. 9, '47 | Louisville | | | |
| 7 | Sam'l M. Benson | Private | | Mch 12. '47 | Louisville | To serve during the war. | | |
| 8 | John Beakman | Private | | April 27,'47 | Louisville | | Joined from | Regt. Dep. June 26,'47 |
| 9 | James T. Charlton | Private | | Mch. 15, '47 | Louisville | | | |
| 10 | Levi Crouch | Private | | Apr. 26, '47 | Newport, Ky. | | Joined Co. | "E," May 21, '47 |
| 11 | John Clark | Private | | Mar. 31, '47 | Louisville | | | |
| 12 | George Digier | Private | | Mar. 19, '47 | Louisville | | | |
| 13 | William Doll | Private | | Mar. 28, '47 | Louisville | | | |
| 14 | John M. Drain | Private | | Mar. 17, '47 | Louisville | | | |
| 15 | Thomas Edrington | Private | | Mar. 12 '47 | Louisville | | | |
| 16 | Thomas Evans | Private | | Mar. 12, '47 | Louisville | | | |
| 17 | John Fetcher | Private | | Mar. 12, '47 | Louisville | | | |
| 18 | John Fogler | Private | | May 11, '47 | Louisville | | Joined from | Regt. Dep. June 26,'47 |
| 19 | Allen Fox | Private | | Apr. 28, '47 | Louisville | | Joined from | Regt. Dep. June 26,'47 |
| 20 | Henry T. Glass | Private | | Mar. 12, '47 | Louisville | | | |
| 21 | Charles Genet | Private | | Apr. 5, '47 | Louisville | | | |
| 22 | Alfred Genverely | Private | | Apr. 10, '47 | Louisville | | | |
| 23 | Richard Grutz | Private | | Apr. 5, '47 | Louisville | | | |
| 24 | Carl Goldsmith | Private | | Mar. 12, '47 | Louisville | | | |
| 25 | Benjamin T. Hoadley | Private | | Mar. 29, '47 | Louisville | | | |
| 26 | James M. Howe | Private | | Mar. 20, '47 | Louisville | | | |
| 27 | DeWitt C. Hewitt | Private | | Mar. 23, '47 | Louisville | | | |
| 28 | David Hill | Private | | Apr. 20, '47 | Louisville | | Joined by | Transfer Co."E," May 21, '47] |
| 29 | John Hamilton | Private | | Mar. 19, '47 | Louisville | | | |
| 30 | John T. Hall | Private | | Apr. 6 '47 | Louisville | | | |
| 31 | Alexander Kent | Private | | Mar. 12, '47 | Louisville | | | |
| 32 | James Kelley | Private | | Mar. 12, '47 | Louisville | | | |
| 33 | George W. Lawson | Private | | Mar. 27, '47 | Louisville | | | |
| 34 | Diedrick Lomon | Private | | Apr. 20, '47 | Louisville | | Joined by | Transfer Co."E," May 21, '47] |
| 35 | Moses L. McClure | Private | | Mar. 16, '47 | Louisville | | | |
| 36 | William Morris | Private | | Mar. 29, '47 | Louisville | | | |
| 37 | Thomas Murrey | Private | | May 12, '47 | Louisville | | Joined from | Regt. Dep. 26 June,'47 |
| 38 | Columb C. Ott | Private | | Mar. 12, '47 | Louisville | | | |
| 39 | Bryant C. O'Neil | Private | | May 24, '47 | Louisville | | | |

MEXICAN WAR VETERANS. 171

W. TIBBATTS, CALLED INTO THE SERVICE OF THE U. S. FOR THE MEXICAN COMPANIES ORGANIZED IN KENTUCKY, AND OFFICERED ACT OF CONGRESS, FEBRUARY 11, 1847—Continued.

| No. of each grade | REMARKS. |
|---|---|
| 1 | At Louisville, Ky., March 31, 1847. Joined Company at Mier, Mex., August 1, 1847. |
| 2 | At Louisville, Ky., March 31, 1847. |
| 3 | At Camargo, Mex., July 1, 1847. |
| 4 | At Mier, Mex., December 24, 1847. Had been left sick at general hospital. |
|  |  |
| 1 | At New Orleans, April 18, 1847; Surgeon's certificate of disability. |
| 2 | At Mier, Mex., September 17, 1847; Surgeon's certificate of disability. |
| 3 | At Monterey, Mex., September 25, 1847; Surgeon's certificate of disability. |
| 4 | At Monterey, Mex., November 24, 1847; Surgeon's certificate of disability. |
| 5 | At Monterey, Mex., December 7, 1847; Surgeon's certificate of disability. |
| 6 | At Monterey, Mex., April 11, 1848; Surgeon's certificate of disability. |
| 7 | At Monterey, Mex., April 11, 1848; Surgeon's certificate of disability. |
| 8 | At Monterey, Mex., April 11, 1848; Surgeon's certificate of disability. |
| 9 | At Monterey, Mex., April 11, 1848; Surgeon's certificate of disability. [Wood. |
| 10 | Desertion; drummed out of service by sentence of a General Court-martial, dated 6th March, 1848, at Monterey, Mex. Order of Gen. |
|  |  |
| 1 | Transferred to Company "C," 16th Infantry, 12th April, 1847, at Louisville. Order Col. Tibbatts, 16th Infantry. |
| 2 | Transferred to Company "C," 16th Infantry, 12th April, 1847, at Louisville. Order of Col. Tibbatts, 16th Infantry. |
| 3 | Transferred to Company "C," 16th Infantry, 12th April, 1847, at Louisville. Order of Col. Tibbatts, 16th Infantry. |
| 4 | Transferred to Crutchell's Company, Voltigeurs, May 22, 1847, at Palo Alto, Mexico. |
| 5 | Transferred to Company "C," 16th Infantry, July 11, 1847, at Mier, Mexico. Order Col. Tibbatts. |
| 6 | Transferred to Company "C," 16th Infantry, July 11, 1847, at Mier, Mexico. Order Col. Tibbatts. |
| 7 | Transferred to Company "C," 16th Infantry, July 11, 1847, at Mier, Mexico. Order Col. Tibbatts. |
| 8 | Transferred to Company "C," 16th Infantry, July 11, 1847, at Mier, Mexico. Order Col. Tibbatts. |
| 9 | Transferred to Company "C," 16th Infantry, July 11, 1847, at Mier, Mexico. Order Col. Tibbatts. |
| 10 | Transferred to Company "C," 16th Infantry, July 11, 1847, at Mier, Mexico. Order Col. Tibbatts. |
| 11 | Transferred to Company "F," 16th Infantry, July 11, 1847, at Mier, Mexico. Order Col. Tibbatts. |
| 12 | Transferred to Company "C," 16th Infantry, July 11, 1847, at Mier, Mexico. Order Col. Tibbatts. |
| 13 | Transferred to Company "C," 16th Infantry, July 11, 1847, at Mier, Mexico. Order Col. Tibbatts. |
| 14 | Transferred to Company "F," 16th Infantry, July 11, 1847, at Mier, Mexico. Order Col. Tibbatts. |
| 15 | Transferred to Company "C," 16th Infantry, July 11, 1847, at Mier, Mexico. Order Col. Tibbatts. |
| 16 | Transferred to Company "C," 16th Infantry, July 11, 1847, at Mier, Mexico. Order Col. Tibbatts. |
| 17 | Transferred to Company "C," 16th Infantry, July 11, 1847, at Mier, Mexico. Order Col. Tibbatts. |
| 18 | Transferred to Company "C," 16th Infantry, July 11, 1847, at Mier, Mexico. Order Col. Tibbatts. |
| 19 | Transferred to Company "C," 16th Infantry, July 11, 1847, at Mier, Mexico. Order Col. Tibbatts. |
| 20 | Transferred to Company "C," 16th Infantry, July 11, 1847, at Mier, Mexico. Order Col. Tibbatts. |
| 21 | Transferred to Company "C," 16th Infantry, July 11, 1847, at Mier, Mexico. Order Col. Tibbatts. |
| 22 | Transferred to Company "C," 16th Infantry, July 11, 1847, at Mier, Mexico. Order Col. Tibbatts. |
| 23 | Transferred to Company "E," 16th Infantry, July 11, 1847, at Mier, Mexico. Order Col. Tibbatts. |
| 24 | Transferred to Company "D," 16th Infantry, July 11, 1847, at Mier, Mexico. Order Col. Tibbatts. |
| 25 | Transferred to Company "C," 16th Infantry, July 11, 1847, at Mier, Mexico. Order Col. Tibbatts. |
| 26 | Transferred to Company "C," 16th Infantry, July 11, 1847, at Mier, Mexico. Order Col. Tibbatts. |
| 27 | Transferred to Company "C," 16th Infantry, July 11, 1847, at Mier, Mexico. Order Col. Tibbatts. |
| 28 | Transferred to Company "C," 16th Infantry, July 11, 1847, at Mier, Mexico. Order Col. Tibbatts. |
| 29 | Transferred to Company "C," 16th Infantry, July 11, 1847, at Mier, Mexico. Order Col. Tibbatts |
| 30 | Transferred to Company "C," 16th Infantry, July 11, 1847, at Mier, Mexico. Order Col. Tibbatts. |
| 31 | Transferred to Company "C," 16th Infantry, July 11, 1847, at Mier, Mexico. Order Col. Tibbatts. |
| 32 | Transferred to Company "C," 16th Infantry, July 11, 1847, at Mier, Mexico. Order Col. Tibbatts. |
| 33 | Transferred to Company "C," 16th Infantry, July 11, 1847, at Mier, Mexico. Order Col. Tibbatts. |
| 34 | Transferred to Company "C," 16th Infantry, July 11, 1847, at Mier, Mexico. Order Col. Tibbatts. |
| 35 | Transferred to Company "C," 16th Infantry, July 11, 1847, at Mier, Mex. Order Col. Tibbatts. |
| 36 | Transferred to Company "C," 16th Infantry, July 11, 1847, at Mier, Mex. Order Col. Tibbatts. |
| 37 | Transferred to Company "C," 16th Infantry, July 11, 1847, at Mier, Mex. Order Col. Tibbatts. |
| 38 | Transferred to Company "C," 16th Infantry, July 11, 1847, at Mier, Mex. Order Col. Tibbatts. |
| 39 | Transferred to Company "C," 16th Infantry, July 11, 1847, at Mier, Mex. Order Col. Tibbatts. |

# APPENDIX.

# MEXICAN WAR VETERANS.

## ROLL OF A DETACHMEMT OF RECRUITS OF

| No. of each grade | Name. | Rank. | Joined for Service. | Mustered In. When. | Mustered In. Where. | Period. | Mustered Out. When. | Mustered Out. Where. |
|---|---|---|---|---|---|---|---|---|
| 1 | Cornelius, Lorenz D. | Private | Apr. 4, 1848 | Not stated. | Not stated. | To serve during the war. | June 20,'48 | Newport Bks. |
| 2 | Cornelius, William | Private | Apr. 4, 1848 | | | | June 20,'48 | Newport Bks. |
| 3 | Cornelius, John | Private | Apr. 4, 1848 | | | | June 20,'48 | Newport Bks. |
| 4 | Davidson, James H. | Private | Apr. 13, 1848 | | | | June 20,'48 | Newport Bks. |
| 5 | Flanary, Wm. H. | Private | May 24, 1848 | | | | June 20,'48 | Newport Bks. |
| 6 | Hutchman, Gillaspie | Private | May 3, 1848 | | | | June 20,'48 | Newport Bks. |
| 7 | Iliff, Daniel | Private | May 24, 1848 | | | | June 20,'48 | Newport Bks. |
| 8 | Kiser, David | Private | Apr. 15, 1848 | | | | June 20,'48 | Newport Bks. |
| 9 | Lemons, John | Private | Apr. 27, 1848 | | | | June 20,'48 | Newport Bks. |
| 10 | Macatro, Geo. W. | Private | Apr. 28, 1848 | | | | June 20,'48 | Newport Bks. |
| 11 | Miller, Randolph | Private | Apr. 18, 1848 | | | | June 20,'48 | Newport Bks. |
| 12 | Messer, Daniel | Private | May 3, 1848 | | | | June 20,'48 | Newport Bks. |
| 13 | Macginnis, Benj. I. | Private | Apr. 6, 1848 | | | | June 20,'48 | Newport Bks. |
| 14 | Macginnis, David | Private | May 24, 1848 | | | | June 20,'48 | Newport Bks. |
| 15 | Mosely, Samuel | Private | May 19, 1848 | | | | June 20,'48 | Newport Bks. |
| 16 | Norris, Charles | Private | Apr. 6, 1848 | | | | June 20,'48 | Newport Bks. |
| 17 | Osborn, Squire | Private | Apr. 25, 1848 | | | | June 20,'48 | Newport Bks. |
| 18 | Osborn, Nathan | Private | May 15, 1848 | | | | June 20,'48 | Newport Bks. |
| 19 | Ratcliffe, Robert | Private | May 18, 1848 | | | | June 20,'48 | Newport Bks. |
| 20 | Russell, George | Private | May 24, 1848 | | | | June 20,'48 | Newport Bks. |
| 21 | Sullivan, William | Private | May 9, 1848 | | | | June 20,'48 | Newport Bks. |
| 22 | Tasket, Charles | Private | Apr. 28, 1848 | | | | June 20,'48 | Newport Bks. |
| 23 | Willis, Alfred | Private | Apr. 20, 1848 | | | | June 20,'48 | Newport Bks. |

## ROLL OF A DETACHMENT OF AMERICAN

| Name. | Rank. | Joined for Service. | Mustered In. When. | Mustered In. Where. | Period. | Mustered Out. When. | Mustered Out. Where. |
|---|---|---|---|---|---|---|---|
| J. W. Owings | 1st Sergeant | May 21, 1846 | June 9, '46 | Louisville | 1 yr. | Oct. 1, '47 | New Orleans, La. |
| James Springer | Corporal | May 21, 1846 | June 9, '46 | Louisville | 1 yr. | Oct. 1, '47 | New Orleans, La. |
| George Sharp | Corporal | May 21, 1846 | June 9, '46 | Louisville | 1 yr. | Oct. 1, '47 | New Orleans, La. |
| James Kemp | Corporal | May 21, 1846 | June 9, '46 | Louisville | 1 yr. | Oct. 1, '47 | New Orleans, La. |
| Thomas, W. | Farrier | July 4, 1846 | June 9, '46 | Louisville | 1 yr. | Oct. 1, '47 | New Orleans, La. |
| Alexander, A. | Private | May 24, 1846 | June 9, '46 | Louisville | 1 yr. | Oct. 1, '47 | New Orleans, La. |
| Burnett, G. | Private | May 24, 1846 | June 9, '46 | Louisville | 1 yr. | Oct. 1, '47 | New Orleans, La. |
| Koons, W. | Private | May 24, 1846 | June 9, '46 | Louisville | 1 yr. | Oct. 1, '47 | New Orleans, La. |
| Marshall, A. G. | Private | May 24, 1846 | June 9, '46 | Louisville | 1 yr. | Oct. 1, '47 | New Orleans, La. |
| Levan, D. W. | Private | May 24, 1846 | June 9, '46 | Louisville | 1 yr. | Oct. 1, '47 | New Orleans, La. |
| Stollman, J. O. | Private | May 21, 1846 | June 9, '46 | Louisville | 1 yr. | Oct. 1, '47 | New Orleans, La. |
| Vittitoe, James | Private | May 24, 1846 | June 9, '46 | Louisville | 1 yr. | Oct. 1, '47 | New Orleans, La. |
| Augrobrigh, A. | Private | June 9, 1846 | June 9, '46 | Louisville | 1 yr. | Oct. 1, '47 | New Orleans, La. |
| Bryant, C. | Private | June 9, 1846 | June 9, '46 | Louisville | 1 yr. | Oct. 1, '47 | New Orleans, La. |
| Mooney, C. E. | Private | June 9, 1846 | June 9, '46 | Louisville | 1 yr. | Oct. 1, '47 | New Orleans, La. |
| Chapman, B. A. | Private | June 9, 1846 | June 9, '46 | Louisville | 1 yr. | Oct. 1, '47 | New Orleans, La. |
| Jones, D. C. | Private | June 9, 1846 | June 9, '46 | Louisville | 1 yr. | Oct. 1, '47 | New Orleans, La. |
| Ratcliffe, W. D. | Private | June 9, 1846 | June 9, '46 | Louisville | 1 yr. | Oct. 1, '47 | New Orleans, La. |
| Barry, D. | Private | June 9, 1846 | June 9, '46 | Louisville | 1 yr. | Oct. 1, '47 | New Orleans, La. |
| Finch, J. J. | Private | June 9, 1846 | June 9, '46 | Louisville | 1 yr. | Oct. 1, '47 | New Orleans, La. |
| Herring, J. | Bugler | June 9, 1846 | June 9, '46 | Louisville | 1 yr. | Oct. 1, '47 | New Orleans, La. |
| Dougherty, Z. | Private | June 9, 1846 | June 9, '46 | Louisville | 1 yr. | Oct. 1, '47 | New Orleans, La. |
| Woods, H. S. | Private | June 9, 1846 | June 9, '46 | Louisville | 1 yr. | Oct. 1, '47 | New Orleans, La. |
| Wilkinson, A. | Private | June 9, 1846 | June 9, '46 | Louisville | 1 yr. | Oct. 1, '47 | New Orleans, La. |
| Magner, John | Private | June 9, 1846 | June 9, '46 | Louisville | 1 yr. | Oct. 1, '47 | New Orleans, La. |
| Rogers, J. | Private | June 9, 1846 | June 9, '46 | Louisville | 1 yr. | Oct. 1, '47 | New Orleans, La. |
| Myers, B. R. | Private | June 9, 1846 | June 9, '46 | Louisville | 1 yr. | Oct. 1, '47 | New Orleans, La. |
| Kelly, W. T. | Private | June 9, 1846 | June 9, '46 | Louisville | 1 yr. | Oct. 1, '47 | New Orleans, La. |
| Dowell, B. S. | Private | June 9, 1846 | June 9, '46 | Louisville | 1 yr. | Oct. 1, '47 | New Orleans, La. |
| Kennedy, J. | Private | June 9, 1846 | June 9, '46 | Louisville | 1 yr. | Oct. 1, '47 | New Orleans, La. |
| Scott, John | Private | May 21, 1846 | June 9, '46 | Louisville | 1 yr. | Oct. 1, '47 | New Orleans, La. |
| Cason, Simon | 1st Sergeant | June 17, 1846 | July 3, '46 | Washington, Ark. | 1 yr. | Oct. 1, '47 | New Orleans, La. |
| Richmond, James | Farrier | June 17, 1846 | July 3, '46 | Washington, Ark. | 1 yr. | Oct. 1, '47 | New Orleans, La. |
| Crooks, J. | Private | June 17, 1846 | July 3, '46 | Washington, Ark. | 1 yr. | Oct. 1, '47 | New Orleans, La. |
| Nelson, M. | Private | June 17, 1846 | July 3, '46 | Washington, Ark. | 1 yr. | Oct. 1, '47 | New Orleans, La. |
| Edwards, W. L. | Private | June 17, 1846 | July 3, '46 | Washington, Ark. | 1 yr. | Oct. 1, '47 | New Orleans, La. |
| Marshall, A. S. | Private | June 18, 1846 | June 29, '46 | Washington, Ark. | 1 yr. | Oct. 1, '47 | New Orleans, La. |
| Finley, J. | Private | June 18, 1846 | June 29, '46 | Washington, Ark. | 1 yr. | Oct. 1, '47 | New Orleans, La. |
| Martin, E. P. | 2d Sergeant | June 16, 1846 | June 29, '46 | Washington, Ark. | 1 yr. | Oct. 1, '47 | New Orleans, La. |
| Whitten, C. P. | Private | June 16, 1846 | June 29, '46 | Washington, Ark. | 1 yr. | Oct. 1, '47 | New Orleans, La. |
| Mooney, C. S. | Private | June 16, 1846 | July 9, '46 | Washington, Ark. | 1 yr. | Oct. 1, '47 | New Orleans, La. |
| Browers, J. E. | Private | June 16, 1846 | June 9, '46 | Washington, Ark. | 1 yr. | Oct. 1, '47 | New Orleans, La. |
| Speigle, W. R. | Private | June 16, 1846 | June 25, '46 | Washington, Ark. | 1 yr. | Oct. 1, '47 | New Orleans, La. |
| Curtis, J. W. | Private | June 16, 1846 | June 25, '46 | Washington, Ark. | 1 yr. | Oct. 1, '47 | New Orleans, La. |

# THIRD REGIMENT OF KENTUCKY VOLUNTEERS.

REMARKS.

# SOLDIERS LATE PRISONERS IN MEXICO.

Taken prisoner January 27, 1847.

The above remarks are applicable to Springer, Clark and Kemp likewise.

Taken prisoner January 27, 1847.
Taken prisoner January 27, 1847.

The above remarks are applicable to Burnett, Koons, Levan, Marshall, Stollman and Vittitoe.

Taken prisoner January 23, 1847.

The above remarks are applicable to, and including, Kennedy.

Resigned 2d Sergeantship 11th July, 1846; taken prisoner January 23, 1847.

## MEXICAN WAR VETERANS.

### ROLL OF A DETACHMENT OF AMERICAN

| No. of each grade | Name. | Rank. | Joined for Service. | Mustered In. When. | Mustered In. Where. | Period | Mustered Out. When. | Mustered Out. Where. |
|---|---|---|---|---|---|---|---|---|
| | Webb, T. J. | Private | June 16, 1846 | June 25, '46 | Washington, Ark. | 1 yr. | Oct. 1, '47 | New Orleans, La. |
| | Williams, R. | Private | June 16, 1846 | June 25, '46 | Washington, Ark. | 1 yr. | Oct. 1, '47 | New Orleans, La. |
| | Rieves, W. | Private | June 16, 1846 | June 25, '46 | Washington, Ark. | 1 yr. | Oct. 1, '47 | New Orleans, La. |
| | Steele, R. J. | Private | June 16, 1846 | June 25, '46 | Washington, Ark. | 1 yr. | Oct. 1, '47 | New Orleans, La. |
| | Huggins, R. F. | Private | June 16, 1846 | June 25, '46 | Washington, Ark. | 1 yr. | Oct. 1, '47 | New Orleans, La. |
| | Smart, Thomas | Private | June 13, 1846 | July 1, '46 | Washington, Ark. | 1 yr. | Oct. 1, '47 | New Orleans, La. |
| | Jester, Stephen | Private | June 13, 1846 | July 1, '46 | Washington, Ark. | 1 yr. | Oct. 1, '47 | New Orleans, La. |
| | Jester, Joseph | Private | June 13, 1846 | July 1, '46 | Washington, Ark. | 1 yr. | Oct. 1, '47 | New Orleans, La. |
| | Montgomery, W. | Private | June 13, 1846 | July 1, '46 | Washington, Ark. | 1 yr. | Oct. 1, '47 | New Orleans, La. |
| | Stinson, A. | Private | June 13, 1846 | July 1, '46 | Washington, Ark. | 1 yr. | Oct. 1, '47 | New Orleans, La. |
| | Lyons, C. | 2d Sergeant | June 23, 1846 | July 1, '46 | Washington, Ark. | 1 yr. | Oct. 1, '47 | New Orleans, La. |
| | Underwood, Geo. | Private | June 23, 1846 | July 1, '46 | Washington, Ark. | 1 yr. | Oct. 1, '47 | New Orleans, La. |
| | Walker, W. | Private | June 19, 1846 | June 10, '46 | Knoxville, Tenn. | 1 yr. | Oct. 1, '47 | New Orleans, La. |
| | Brake, J. R. | Private | June 22, 1846 | June 28, '46 | Cincinnati, O. | 1 yr. | Oct. 1, '47 | New Orleans, La. |
| | Alpin, Geo. W. | Private | June 22, 1846 | June 28, '46 | Cincinnati, O. | 1 yr. | Oct. 1, '47 | New Orleans, La. |
| | McGloughan, P. | Private | June 22, 1846 | June 28, '46 | Cincinnati, O. | 1 yr. | Oct. 1, '47 | New Orleans, La. |
| | Fleming, J. C. | Private | May 27, 1846 | June 28, '46 | Cincinnati, O. | 1 yr. | Oct. 1, '47 | New Orleans, La. |
| | Follbush, H. | Private | June 1, 1846 | June 1, '46 | Washington, D. C. | 1 yr. | Oct. 1, '47 | New Orleans, La. |
| | Clark, R. C. | Private | July 1, 1846 | July 9, '46 | Columbus, Ga. | 1 yr. | Oct. 1, '47 | New Orleans, La. |
| | Marsh, J. S. | 2d Sergeant | May 17, 1846 | May 17, '46 | Louisville | 1 yr. | Oct. 1, '47 | New Orleans, La. |
| | Stewart, James | Corporal | May 17, 1846 | May 17, '46 | Louisville | 1 yr. | Oct. 1, '47 | New Orleans, La. |
| | Dowing, E. | Private | May 17, 1846 | May 17, '46 | Louisville | 1 yr. | Oct. 1, '47 | New Orleans, La. |
| | Gwynn, H. | Corporal | May 17, 1846 | June 9, '46 | Louisville | 1 yr. | Oct. 1, '47 | New Orleans, La. |
| | Taylor, W. | Private | May 17, 1846 | June 9, '46 | Louisville | 1 yr. | Oct. 1, '47 | New Orleans, La. |
| | Crumone, (?) W. | Private | May 21, 1846 | June 9, '46 | Louisville | 1 yr. | Oct. 1, '47 | New Orleans, La. |
| | Bibb, Chas. A. | Private | May 21, 1846 | June 9, '46 | Louisville | 1 yr. | Oct. 1, '47 | New Orleans, La. |
| | Pinkston, T. | Private | May 17, 1846 | May 17, '46 | Louisville | 1 yr. | Oct. 1, '47 | New Orleans, La. |
| | Groogh, H. | Private | May 17, 1846 | May 17, '46 | Louisville | 1 yr. | Oct. 1, '47 | New Orleans, La. |
| | Traxale, W. | Private | May 17, 1846 | May 17, '46 | Louisville | 1 yr. | Oct. 1, '47 | New Orleans, La. |
| | Wroataman, W. | Private | May 17, 1846 | May 17, '46 | Louisville | 1 yr. | Oct. 1, '47 | New Orleans, La. |
| | Welsh, W. | Private | May 17, 1846 | May 17, '46 | Louisville | 1 yr. | Oct. 1, '47 | New Orleans, La. |
| | Davis, O. | Private | May 17, 1846 | May 17, '46 | Louisville | 1 yr. | Oct. 1, '47 | New Orleans, La. |
| | Warwick, J. | Private | May 17, 1846 | May 17, '46 | Louisville | 1 yr. | Oct. 1, '47 | New Orleans, La. |
| | Fogerty, J. | Private | May 17, 1846 | May 17, '46 | Louisville | 1 yr. | Oct. 1, '47 | New Orleans, La. |
| | Newman, D. | Private | May 17, 1846 | May 17, '46 | Louisville | 1 yr. | Oct. 1, '47 | New Orleans, La. |
| | Jewell, J. | Private | May 17, 1846 | May 17, '46 | Louisville | 1 yr. | Oct. 1, '47 | New Orleans, La. |
| | Barry, L. | Private | May 17, 1846 | May 17, '46 | Louisville | 1 yr. | Oct. 1, '47 | New Orleans, La. |
| | Fairbanks, J. | Private | May 17, 1846 | May 17, '46 | Louisville | 1 yr. | Oct. 1, '47 | New Orleans, La. |
| | Philips, G. A. | Private | May 17, 1846 | May 17, '46 | Louisville | 1 yr. | Oct. 1, '47 | New Orleans, La. |
| | Magness, John | Private | May 17, 1846 | July 3, '46 | Washington, Ark. | 1 yr. | Oct. 1, '47 | New Orleans, La. |
| | Bates, J. G. | Private | May 17, 1846 | June 9, '46 | Louisville | 1 yr. | Oct. 1, '47 | New Orleans, La. |
| | Payne, W. L. | 2d Sergeant | May 17, 1846 | June 9, '46 | Louisville | 1 yr. | Oct. 1, '47 | New Orleans, La. |

## SOLDIERS LATE PRISONERS IN MEXICO—Continued.

| No. of each grade | REMARKS. |
|---|---|
| . . | |
| . . | |
| . . | |
| . . | |
| . . | |
| . . | |
| . . | |
| . . | |
| . . | |
| . . | |
| . . | |
| . . | Taken prisoner 26th February, 1847. |
| . . | The above apply to Fleming. |
| . . | Taken prisoner January 20, 1847. |
| . . | Taken prisoner February 24, 1847. |
| . . | Taken prisoner February 24, 1847. |
| . . | |
| . . | Taken prisoner February 24, 1847, between Canaho and Mareno. |
| . . | |
| . . | |
| . . | |
| . . | |
| . . | Taken prisoner 23d January, 1847. |
| . . | Promoted to 2d Sergeant, at Rio Grande, October 31, 1846; taken prisoner 23d January, 1847. |
| . . | |
| . . | Taken prisoner 23d January, 1847. |
| . . | Taken prisoner 23d January, 1847. |
| . . | Taken prisoner 23d January, 1847; promoted to 2d Sergeant October 31, 1846. |

# A

**Abbott**, John B., 152
   Nelson, 80
   Wm. H., 116
**Abernethy**, Moses F., 156
**Abers**, William, 66
**Able**, Joshua, 162
   Monroe, 14
**Absher**, Granville A., 122
**Ackley**, W. M., 82
**Acton**, Wesley, 112
**Adair**, David T., 54
   Davis L., 116, 136
   Wm., 106
**Adams**, Benjamin, 96
   Eli, 134
   Henry, 126
   James, 166
   John, 132, 166
   Joshua, 150
   Lloyd C., 134
   Milton, 126
   Preston, 126
   Richard M., 26
   Sebastian, 72
   Smith, 46
   Thomas, 154
**Adamson**, Charles, 154
**Adcock**, Joseph, 148
**Adkins**, Benjamin, 140
   Christopher B., 112
   James, 54
**Ahrens**, Frederick, 72
**Akhart**, Alexander, 90
**Akin**, John B., 164
   William E., 36
   Willis, 28
**Akinson**, Appleton, 130
**Albert**, Geo. P., 116
**Albrecht**, John, 66
**Aldridge**, John, 134
**Alexander**, A. J., 70
   A., 174
   Abram S., 12
   Ambrose P., 86
   Benjamin, 80
   George, 20
   Jesse F., 98
   John B., 54
   Thomas, 140
   William H., 102
**Algeier**, Joseph, 72
**Alheim**, Lewis, 72
**Allen**, Arthur R., 146
   Charles, 58

   Cyrus, 162
   George, 32
   George W., 96
   Henry, 30
   J. B., 76
   James, 136
   John, 18, 160
   John H., 44
   William, 96
   William C., 102
**Allender**, James C., 110
   Thomas, 82
**Allison**, James, 160
   William, 158
**Allonder**, James D., 90
**Alpin**, Geo. W., 176
**Alsop**, George, 84
   Leighton, 84
**Alspaugh**, David C., 4
**Alverson**, Mathew M., 100
**Alvin**, Bates, 16
**Ambrose**, Thomas W., 102
   William, 100
**Amer**, John, 32
**Amerine**, David, 20
**Amis**, James F., 158
**Ammerman**, Peter, 40
**Amslie**, Hugh, 70
**Anderson**, Aaron, 166
   Albert G., 50
   George W., 80
   J. N., 12
   James, 100
   Jas. W., 84
   John, 58, 106
   John W., 150
   Lafayette L., 68
   Meredith, 146
   Robert, 26
   Thomas J., 150
**Andrews**, A. M., 14
   Alexander R., 86
**Andrich**, Joseph, 50
**Anton**, Peter, 74
**Apperson**, Richard, 50
   William W., 52
**Applegate**, Elijah, 62
   George, 20
**Arbuckle**, John W., 2
**Argerbright**, Alfred, 22
**Armistead**, John P., 110
**Armstrong**, Benj. F., 138
   G. T., 76
   Geo., 58
   J. Wesley, 20
   Robert, 64

   Thomas, 72
   Thomas J., 36
   William A., 136
   William H., 140
**Arnett**, William W., 140
**Arnold**, Alexander, 2
   Daniel, 30
   E. T., 74
   Elijah C., 48
   Horatio C., 4
   Jackson, 128
   Joshua, 62
   Samuel, 68
**Arthur**, Edward, 112
   Thomas, 116
**Artis**, Robert, 152
**Arvin**, Thomas, 144
**Arweiler**, Jacob, 66
**Asbury**, Henry B., 86
**Ash**, Levi, 124
**Ashburn**, William H., 128
**Ashby**, H. L., 78
   William, 110
**Ashford**, Franklin P., 14
**Ashley**, B. T., 76
   James B., 112
   James P., 52
   Joel, 8
   John R., 54
**Ashmore**, David, 110
   John I., 14
**Ashworth**, Stephen G., 146
**Asper**, J. M., 28
**Astley**, John W., 112
**Atchison**, James, 86, 110
**Atkinson**, Daniel S., 120
   F. M., 82
   Thomas, 40
**Atwell**, John, 116
   Samuel, 120
**Atwood**, John V., 124
**Aubery**, Gabriel, 144
**Aubry**, Jackson, 106
**Augrobrigh**, A., 174
**Aulger**, Riley B., 78
**Austin**, Felix, 58
   J. D., 76
   Walter C., 154
**Awbery**, French, 84
   Will, 84
**Aydelott**, Benjamin, 94
**Aylward**, John, 60

# B

**Babe**, George, 14
**Baber**, Stanley, 150

**Bache**, Franklin, 58
**Bacon**, Henry, 68
   Samuel P., 26
**Bagby**, John W., 84
**Bailes**, Thompson, 4
**Bailey**, Andrew J., 124
   Barnet E., 126
   G. W., 8
   James, 8
   John H., 104
   W. D., 138
   Wm. A., 124
**Bailley**, J. Q. A., 62
**Baird**, Joseph C., 68
**Baker**, Adam, 94
   Benedict, 44
   Benjamin, 16, 110
   Frederick, 134
   Jacob, 124
   James A., 158
   James H., 82
   John A., 140
   John B., 40
   Peter, 22
   Robert M., 56
**Balbs**, John, 88
**Baldwin**, Annis, 18
   David, 94
   John R., 158
   R. N., 160
   William, 56
   Wm. H., 84
**Ball**, Charles W., 130
   Chas. W., 116
   George W., 44
   Richard L., 52
   Thomas, 2
   Thomas P., 108
   Wm. L., 80
**Ballad**, Wm., 150
**Ballance**, James, 90
**Ballard**, James L., 44
   James R., 46
   John T., 122
   Thomas B., 124
**Ballinger**, John, 160
   Joseph, 112
**Balthis**, Isaac, 92
**Banfield**, John, 34, 110
**Banta**, DeWitt C., 106
**Banton**, Daniel, 2
   Mansfield, 54
   Oliver O., 2
**Barbee**, E. L., 28
   Joseph W., 122
   Samuel P., 32

**Barbour**, Edgar D., 130
  W. T., 74
**Barclay**, Hugh A., 16
**Barden**, Louis M., 22
**Barhyat**, Garrett, 64
**Barker**, Abram, 38
  Geo., 100
  Robert H., 166
  Sam'l W., 58
  William, 104
**Barkley**, Samuel S., 22
**Barlay**, James, 22
**Barlow**, Samuel, 2, 56
**Barly**, Timothy, 150
**Barnaby**, Edward, 86
**Barnes**, George O., 20
  Hudson M., 20
  Jackson, 22
  James, 20
  Nathan, 126
  Thomas H., 2, 20
**Barnet**, Theodore, 14
**Barnett**, Charles, 106
  James T. W., 140
  Lee, 130
  Wm., 106
**Barnhill**, Rigdon T., 90
**Barnum**, John W., 82
**Barr**, James, 114
**Barrow**, Napoleon B., 96
**Barry**, D., 174
  David, 22, 68
  L., 176
  Thomas I., 82
**Barth**, Andrew, 62
**Bartlett**, Anthony W., 126
  Elisa T., 32
  Joseph, 80
  Saml. S., 32
  Samuel, 32
  Willis T., 32
**Barton**, George W., 154
  John, 46
  Milton, 164
  Owen, 164
  Samuel, 164
**Basham**, Daniel, 116
  Joel, 144
  Solomell, 144
**Bastian**, John, 46
**Bates**, J. G., 176
  James, 8
  Thomas J., 160
**Batman**, William, 64, 116
**Batsom**, Wesley, 116
**Battail**, Bird W., 150

**Baty**, James, 130
**Bauchamp**, Newell, 80
**Baughn**, James M., 170
**Baumann**, Frederick, 72
  John, 74
**Baumeister**, George, 66
**Baumgaertner**, Joseph, 66
**Bayless**, George W., 80
  William W., 26
**Beakman**, John, 170
**Beall**, Benj. F., 4
**Bean**, John, 12, 94, 124
**Beard**, Ezekiel, 138
  Joseph, 162
  Lowry J., 26
  Oliver P., 26
**Bearnes**, William, 112
**Beasman**, Wm., 40
**Beatey**, Jos., 84
**Beatman**, Thomas, 90
**Beatty**, Addison, 140
  James, 120
**Beaty**, James, 116
**Beaver**, Henry C., 22
  William, 24
**Beck**, James S., 158
  Reddick D., 154
  Samuel T., 96
**Becker**, Louis, 66
**Becket**, Alexander, 154
  Elza, 36
**Beckner**, Sampson C., 52
  William, 86
**Beckwith**, Elisha, 64
**Bedell**, Franklin, 106
  John R., 106
  Wm. P., 106
**Bedford**, Henry P., 96
**Bedou**, Robt. A., 46
**Beecher**, George M., 154
**Beedles**, Robert C., 162
**Bell**, James F., 12
  Jesse, 78
  John W., 24
  Mahlen, 154
  Simeon P., 58
  Thomas A., 120
**Bellis**, Hiram, 100
  William, 100
**Belmont**, Alexander, 170
**Bemer**, Benjamin H., 82
**Benjamin**, George, 24
**Benmie**, William H., 38
**Benner**, D. B. T., 82
**Bennett**, Ben B., 6
  Jas., 84

  John, 62
  John J., 132
  Littleton E., 40
  Oliver P., 120
  Richard, 84
  Robert, 120
  Thomas H., 100
  Wesley, 154
  William, 54
**Benningfield**, John, 100
**Benson**, Jas. C., 68
  Saml. M., 170
**Berkley**, Benjamin, 20
  Henry, 4
**Bermer**, Nicholas, 120
**Bernard**, Richard, 166
**Berrone**, M., 26
**Berry**, E. C., 162
  Edward C., 154
  Enos H., 82, 96
  F. T., 76
  George W., 46
  James M., 62
  John W., 112
  Landon T., 152
  Philip G., 144
  S. O., 26
  Simon, 130
**Bethars**, Pascal M. C., 106
**Bethel**, Christopher, 124
**Bettersworth**, John, 34
**Beymer**, Samuel, 42
**Bibb**, C. A., 74
  Chas. A., 176
  Loyd, 60
  Titus P. A., 126
**Bicknel**, Bolin G., 128
**Bightol**, Joshua, 126
**Biles**, Samuel, 26
**Bills**, Abram, 96
  John, 96
**Birch**, Silas J., 152
  William A., 162
**Bird**, Henry, 62
  Jackson, 146
  W. C., 20
**Birkhead**, Nelson B., 58
**Bishop**, Henry, 28
  Jacob K., 56
  James H., 98
  John, 136
  Joseph, 130
  William L., 134
  Zebalon C., 116
**Bissett**, Thomas F., 124
**Bitterman**, Henry, 26

**Bivens**, Valney H., 106
**Bivins**, John L., 134
**Black**, Calvan, 140
  David, 68
**Blackaby**, Thomas, 4
**Blackburn**, James, 94
**Blackidge**, Woodruff, 140
**Blackster**, Jerry, 36
**Blackwell**, William, 32
**Blaesehard**, James, 34
**Blain**, John, 170
**Blair**, Madison, 150
**Blaize**, William, 90
**Blake**, John, 154
**Bland**, James, 96
  Theodore, 58
**Blankenship**, Noah, 140
**Blanton**, Alexander M., 2
**Blard**, William A., 50
**Blayez**, John, 144
**Blevins**, James, 62
**Blick**, Willis N., 138
**Bligh**, Delos F., 60
**Bloar**, G. W., 70
**Bloodgood**, Samuel, 90
**Blount**, William H., 96
**Blunt**, William, 52
**Board**, William, 36
**Bodine**, Charles, 124
**Bogard**, Benjamin F., 154
**Boggess**, William K., 64
**Boggs**, Edward, 40
  John, 74
**Bohanan**, George, 130
  James W., 130
  Jefferson, 130
  Nathan, 130
**Bohannan**, James, 106
**Boling**, John R., 114
**Bollen**, Daniel, 166
**Bolton**, John L., 132
**Bond**, George W., 136
  Marion, 124
  Waller G., 84
  William, 126
  William F., 34
**Boneville**, Charles, 10
**Bonham**, Archibald D., 18
**Bonnewell**, Elijah, 40
**Bonta**, Harry, 56
**Bookhart**, John, 62
**Boon**, John, 104
**Booth**, Micajah H., 56
  Thomas A., 14
  William E., 112
  Wm., 40

**Bosley**, John S., 46
**Bossart**, Geo. W., 48
**Boswell**, James, 106
   Lewis, 166
**Botts**, Joseph, 52
**Boulton**, John W., 154
**Bowen**, David T., 166
   John W., 130
**Bower**, Christian, 4
   R. F., 60
**Bowlin**, Graham, 158
   John, 158
**Bowman**, J. G., 74
   John L., 36
   William, 26
**Bowyers**, James, 142
**Box**, Zimri, 112
**Boyce**, William, 16
**Boyd**, Alfred, 68
   George G., 130
   Harris, 114
   Jesse T., 10
   John, 104
   Levi F., 10
**Boyden**, Stephen, 78, 120
**Bradford**, Bela C., 84
   Cantrell, 138
   Dozier, 20
   Smith, 86
**Bradley**, Amos K., 136
   Ben. F., 82
   Benjamin F., 84
   Edward L., 136
   John, 90
   Robert W., 86
   Samuel H., 14
**Bradshaw**, David, 104
   Edward, 54
   George W., 80
   John, 54
   Peter G., 36
   William, 104
**Brady**, Henry C., 14
   Philip, 92
**Braisfield**, Randolph, 14
**Brake**, J. R., 176
**Brakebill**, Philip, 20
**Bramlett**, Greenberry, 86
   Marcus, 104
   Wm. P., 106
**Branch**, H. B., 82
**Branden**, Booth, 48
**Brandenburg**, James, 100
**Branham**, Benjamin O., 32
   Bradford, 110
   Joseph, 86

**Brannon**, James W., 166
**Brant**, Jeremiah, 62
**Brashear**, Marshall, 64
**Brashears**, Greenberry, 148
**Bratton**, Richard C., 142
**Brauer**, John, 68
**Braun**, A. J., 4
   Joseph S., 6
**Brawner**, Bazil, 114
   William, 10
**Brea**, Ameal, 32
**Breckinridge**, John C., 82
   Larkin, 36
**Brenan**, Francis M., 22, 56
**Brenhager**, Ansel, 102
**Brevard**, James, 50
**Brewer**, Etna M., 136
**Brewster**, James P., 136
**Bricknell**, Chris. V., 126
**Bridges**, James, 138
   William, 86
**Bridgewater**, Richard F., 38
**Bright**, Warfield, 112
**Brightbill**, Thomas, 62
**Brinsfield**, Littleberry, 130
**Briscoe**, Wm., 106
**Bristow**, James S., 94
   William, 132
**Britenham**, Stephen, 94
**Britten**, William, 60
**Britton**, Thomas, 144
**Broaddus**, G. B. F., 20
**Broadwell**, Silas, 58
**Brock**, John, 112
   Leonard, 166
   Micajah, 162
**Brockway**, Samuel, 52
**Brooking**, Roger K., 52
**Brooks**, John, 100
   John H., 138
**Brotherlin**, Charles, 70, 112
**Browers**, J. E., 174
**Brown**, Alexander D., 70
   Andrew, 14
   Andrew J., 162
   Caswell, 100
   Daniel, 116
   Eli, 104
   Ezekiel, 112
   Geo. Mason, 22
   George, 38, 42
   Green B., 96
   Hugh H., 34
   Isaac, 4

   James, 4, 34
   James T., 116
   Jeremiah, 90
   John, 4, 14
   John A., 64
   John H., 64, 160
   Lindsey B., 82
   Ludwin, 160
   Ludwing, 166
   Peter S., 80
   Peyton, 36
   Richard, 154
   Robert, 16, 158
   Samuel M., 90
   Sanford, 36
   Shadrack D., 30
   Silas F., 10
   Tho, 18
   Thomas, 14, 74
   William, 38, 54, 62, 112, 140
   William S., 130
   Willis, 46
   Wm. D., 42
**Browner**, William C., 112
**Browning**, Wm. T., 108
**Brownlea**, John A., 30
**Bruce**, Brewer, 150
   Eli, 150
   J. C., 20
   Richard P., 2
   William, 150
**Bruitin**, Madison, 136
**Brumfield**, James P., 38
**Bruner**, Henry, 150
   John R., 84
   Thomas J., 42
**Brush**, Jacob, 52
**Bryan**, Abram C., 22
   Albert G., 24
   Enoch, 24
   Thomas, 26
**Bryant**, C., 174
   Carter, 36
   William, 116
**Bryt**, Thomas, 132
**Buchannam**, Ferd'nd A., 126
**Buchholtz**, Archibald, 64
**Buck**, Harry, 18
   Jerome B., 166
   Thomas H., 58
**Buckner**, Bennet B., 142
   Charles M., 28
   Harry T., 122
   Hubard, 24

   Hubart T., 94
   Richard A., 28
   Robert M., 80
   Robt. W., 28
**Buechle**, Peter, 72
**Buil**, Archibald, 130
**Bull**, Jno. Randolph, 58
**Bullen**, Charles W., 80
**Bullion**, John B., 88
**Bullitt**, Cutt, 20
**Bullock**, Charles, 160
   Hardin, 18
**Buly**, John, 30
**Bunch**, Cortney L., 42
**Burbridge**, Benjamin F., 104
**Burch**, James, 146
**Burchell**, Daniel, 42
**Burchill**, Owen, 16
**Burden**, Wm., 100
**Burdett**, Henry, 38
**Burdin**, Benjamin F., 106
**Burger**, Jackson, 140
**Burgess**, Henry, 96
   Timothy, 36
**Burk**, James, 162
**Burke**, Andrew C., 114
   Patrick, 96
**Burkhard**, John, 112
**Burks**, William, 56
**Burmann**, Charles, 74
**Burnett**, Charles T., 122
   G. W., 12
   G., 174
   Robert, 78
   Wesley, 12
**Burns**, Harry J., 56
   James, 50
   John B., 96
   Samuel, 96
   Thomas, 54
**Burrell**, Walter, 62
**Burrett**, George, 64
**Burris**, Albert G., 146
   John B., 146
   William T., 152
**Burriss**, Nelson, 20
**Burton**, Allen B., 132
   Ambrose, 22
   Charles, 10
   Edward, 54
   Enoch G., 54
   George W., 166
   Nathan G., 28
   Theodoric, 42
   William, 48

**Busby**, Napoleon B., 100
**Bush**, Ambrose E., 108
   Joshua B., 96
   William M., 150
   William T., 152
**Busick**, Enok S., 90
**Butler**, A. A., 20
   David H., 52
   J. Russell, 60
   J. R., 80
   James, 146
   Peter, 72
**Butner**, Isaac, 4
**Buttner**, Jesse, 2
**Button**, R. Y., 76
**Butts**, John, 48
**Byerly**, John, 158
**Byers**, Alexander, 88
**Byram**, Jacob S., 10
**Byron**, Alonzo L., 114

## C

**Cabbell**, William, 120
**Cabel**, Jerry, 64
**Cacke**, Thomas, 60
**Cahill**, James, 54
**Cain**, Adam, 120
   James, 158
**Calander**, Abram, 74
**Calbert**, Logan, 128
**Caldwell**, Tarlton, 166
   Thomas L., 58
**Calhoun**, Richard, 124
**Callaghan**, M. B., 26
**Callan**, James, 70
**Callis**, A. C., 74
   O. B., 74
**Calmes**, Albert S., 70
**Calvert**, Cyrus, 8
   Harrison, 124
   Miles, 36
   Spencer M., 138
   William, 166
**Cambron**, John, 162
**Camden**, John, 78
**Cameron**, George, 134
   James, 116
   James A., 134
**Campbell**, Andrew H., 140
   Churchill G., 106
   Daniel P. B., 98
   Ebenezer, 102
   James, 96, 120
   John, 40, 70
   Joseph E., 124
   Morten M., 144

   Thomas L., 26
   Thomas M., 98
   Thomas W., 136
   William M., 100
   Wm. R., 98
**Canada**, John, 114
**Canlin**, Henry N., 114
**Cannon**, Edward G., 58
   John, 138
**Canter**, William C., 100
**Caplinger**, Paul, 128
   Robert, 128
**Carden**, James, 148
**Cardwell**, George N., 28, 54
   John, 34
   Thomas R., 136
**Carey**, Andrew D., 142
   Thomas, 60
**Carl**, Isahil T., 92
**Carlin**, Quincy, 42
**Carlton**, Andrew H., 92
**Carmichael**, David, 116
**Carmicial**, David, 68
**Carner**, Pleasant, 78
**Carnifax**, Jarvis J., 114
**Carpenter**, Simon P., 86
   W. W., 82
   William, 78
**Carrack**, Thomas, 130
**Carrigan**, James M., 140
   John, 140
**Carroll**, Dempsey, 22
**Carson**, John, 120
   John W., 104
**Carter**, Geo. W., 84
   George C., 130
   George W., 26
   Tunstall D., 158
**Cartright**, John F., 52
**Carty**, Henry, 26
**Carver**, Wickliff, 160
**Cary**, Edmond, 88
   James, 88
**Case**, George W., 52
**Casey**, James B., 94
   James H., 142
**Casity**, Alvin, 52
**Cason**, Simon, 174
**Cassiday**, John I., 78
**Cassidy**, James, 90
   James B., 110
   Moses J., 100
**Castellar**, James, 70
**Castigan**, Albert, 104
**Castillo**, Pablo, 164

**Castle**, Augustus B., 42
**Castleman**, Bushrod, 26
   Richard, 154
**Caswell**, Herter A., 116
**Catlett**, Francis, 34
   Jackson, 34
   James H., 136
**Catterson**, Hiram, 4
   Robert W., 94
   Thomas D., 94
   William, 4
   Wm., 96
**Cauman**, Andrew, 144
**Cave**, William D., 122
**Cavel**, William H., 46
**Cavender**, Johnty, 8
**Ceurson**, Steward, 90
**Chadoin**, Austin M., 30
   Isaac C., 28
**Chalfart**, John S., 42
**Chalis**, Andrew, 66
**Chambers**, Alexander, 80
   Frank, 30
   Geo. W., 32
   James C., 6
   James T., 136
   John L., 132
   Patrick H., 32
   Thomas J., 32
**Champion**, Henry, 130
**Chandler**, Anderson, 104
   King S., 138
**Chapline**, Noah Z., 126
**Chapman**, B. A., 174
   Benj. A., 24
   Daniel, 54
**Chappel**, William O., 96
**Charles**, Samuel, 166
**Charlton**, James T., 170
**Cheatham**, John D., 144
**Chenault**, David W., 22
   Wm J., 22
**Child**, Conrad, 116
**Childers**, Elijah, 94
   William H., 122
**Childres**, Henry, 164
**Childs**, James P., 70
**Chiles**, Wm. P., 100
**Chism**, William, 150
**Chowning**, William, 126
**Chrisman**, Abraham, 162
   Charles F., 104
**Chrismore**, Jacob, 132
**Christian**, John C., 140
**Christopher**, John J., 32
   John W., 90

   Thos. S., 90
   Wesley, 34
   Wesley P., 90
**Christy**, William A., 54
**Church**, Andrew J., 90
   Benjamin, 8
**Churchill**, J. J., 12
**Citizen**, George, 62
**Clagett**, Hezedkiah, 58
**Clark**, Christopher F., 100
   Dennis, 64
   John, 162, 170
   John A., 48
   John T., 150
   Joseph, 162
   Joseph S., 88
   Leonard W., 120
   Lewis P., 166
   R. C., 176
   Richard A., 36
   Samuel F., 68
   Thomas, 40, 90
   William H., 162
   Wm. A., 12
**Clarke**, Adam, 68
   James M., 68
   Lafayette W., 58
**Clary**, Alfred, 88
   William P., 88
**Clay**, C. M., 22
   Henry Jr., 28
   Lewis A., 98
**Clem**, Albert G., 152
**Clements**, Charles O., 136
   T. J., 14
**Clemmons**, John, 112
   William, 162
**Clevedence**, Jonathan, 146
**Cleveland**, Geo. W., 144
   John H., 2
**Clever**, Hiram, 148
**Cline**, Alfred, 90
   Levi W., 104
**Clinton**, William, 138
**Clore**, R. B., 74
**Cloud**, John A. W., 78
**Cloyd**, John, 54
   Stephen W., 54
   William, 54
**Clurke**, James W., 50
   Roy S., 50
**Coakley**, Edward, 30
**Cob**, James, 38
**Cochran**, Robert, 8
   Thos. I., 38
**Cockrill**, Robert, 62

**Cofer**, Cyrus W., 30
   Owen, 28
**Coffer**, Jesse, 94
**Coffman**, Eyres A., 162
   Henry, 98
   Peter, 18
**Cohen**, John, 38
**Coke**, John B., 70
   Wilson, 70
**Coldwell**, A. F., 112
**Cole**, Aaron, 102
   Andrew, 106
   Daniel, 50
   George, 158
   Peter R., 156
   Thomas, 88
   William S., 100
**Coleman**, Benjamin, 52
   George M., 50
   James E., 34
   Jesse L., 128
   John, 56
   John C., 12
   Joseph, 158
   Moses, 88
   Samuel, 14
   Signat J., 90
   Skelton, 112
**Collier**, Robert, 2
**Collins**, Bartlett, 134
   Foster, 106
   James R., 162
   Jeptha G., 146
   John, 74, 118
   John L., 32
   William, 44, 90
**Collyer**, Cyrenius W., 140
**Columbus**, Andrew J., 90
   T., 62
**Combs**, John D., 88
**Compton**, Levi F., 90
**Comstock**, Alexander, 112
**Conan**, James E., 36
**Condit**, Stephen R., 92
**Conklin**, H. C., 14
**Conley**, Neil, 130
   Patrick, 38
**Conn**, Joseph S., 136
   Thomas K., 2
   William, 126
**Conner**, Franklin, 124
   George W., 12
   James, 72, 124
   Nathaniel H., 166
   William P., 104
**Connor**, John T., 96

   Moses, 52
**Conover**, Sylvester, 26
**Conquest**, Richard, 166
**Constantine**, Richard, 124
**Conway**, Henry W., 96
**Cook**, Clinton D. W., 8
   G., 14
   George B., 130
   Henry A., 136
   Israel B., 50
   John, 52
   John L., 50
   Joseph, 104
   Joseph P., 136
   Nathanel C., 8
   Robert, 136
   William, 40
**Cookery**, James W., 138
**Cooksey**, William C., 132
**Coons**, Peter E., 106
**Coontz**, J. G. W., 74
**Cooper**, Archibald, 58
   George B., 46
   Thomas, 144
   William H., 126
**Cope**, William D., 104
**Copher**, Jacob, 104
**Coppage**, Charles, 26
**Copper**, Rheuben, 104
**Copperass**, John, 92
**Corbin**, Albert, 94
   John, 50
   Marion, 94
   Randolph B., 52
   Ranolph B., 94
**Corder**, Reuben, 146
**Corey**, John A., 22
**Corley**, James, 110
   John, 144
**Cornelius**, John, 174
   Lorenz D., 174
   Mason, 94
   William, 174
**Corper**, James A., 162
**Cosby**, John D., 142
   William, 110
**Cosgrove**, Geo. C., 40
**Cotter**, Wm., 144
**Courtright**, Wm., 150
**Covington**, Zackariah, 84
**Cowan**, James M., 140
   John M., 36
   Samuel D., 140
**Cox**, Alexander, 16
   Ambrose B., 104
   Champlain, 166

   Chapman, 40
   George, 38
   James A., 52
   James G., 12
   James R., 112
   John H., 28
   John N., 22
   Leander M., 86
   Lorenzo D., 116
   Nathaniel, 144
   Samuel, 64
   Thomas, 58, 142
   William, 42, 146
   William P., 88
**Coyle**, McKenzie, 22
**Crabtree**, James H., 154
**Craddock**, Alexander G., 146
   Jesse J., 146
   John, 106
   Samuel A., 148
   William W., 96
**Craft**, Henry, 68
**Craig**, Geo. W., 82
   Hugh, 48
   James, 120
   John, 36, 104
   John R., 34
   Joseph M., 120
   Samuel, 46
   Silas E., 70
   William, 34
**Crail**, Andrew, 30
**Crain**, James L., 86
   John L., 140
**Craine**, William A., 88
**Crair**, Hiram P., 88
**Crammer**, Washington, 16
**Cranch**, B. T., 76
**Crandell**, Joseph, 78
**Crane**, Aca C., 42
   Hiram P., 110
   James, 38
   John P., 42
   Nelson, 38
   William L., 32
**Craumin**, John, 72
**Craven**, Hiram F., 112
**Cravens**, James L., 136
**Cravin**, George W., 124
**Cravins**, James, 106
**Crawford**, A., 160
   Asa H., 84
   George W., 58
   H. H., 4
   H. T., 160

   John, 54
   Simpson, 100
**Creagh**, Richard, 54
**Creason**, Edward, 64
**Creel**, Charles H., 120
   Chas. H., 116
**Creem**, W. L., 74
**Cregg**, Joseph, 18
**Creighton**, John, 116
**Cress**, Sam'l F., 60
**Crinzer**, John, 88
**Crisler**, Leonard, 94
**Critchlow**, Grafton J., 146
**Crittenden**, Thos. L., 82
**Cromwell**, Wm., 82
**Cronin**, Daniel, 124
**Crook**, John W., 166
   Wiley, 158
**Crooks**, J., 174
**Crouch**, Jonathan, 104
   Levi, 160, 170
   Nathaniel, 24
   Peter, 106
   Robert, 102
**Crow**, David S., 150
   Mortimer C., 132
**Croxton**, William H., 64
**Cruiz**, Theodore, 150
**Crumbaugh**, Henry, 84
**Crummery**, James, 34
**Crumone**, W., 176
**Crump**, David, 148
   Jesse W., 68
   Joshua A., 146
**Cruse**, James B., 134
**Crutcher**, Cortes, 144
   Richard, 146
**Crutchfield**, J. M., 158
**Cryster**, Jacobs, 170
**Culbertson**, David, 150
**Cully**, John L., 148
**Cummings**, Francis M., 34
   Hervey, 26
   James W., 32
   Thomas, 46
   William P., 136
**Cummins**, Worthen, 10
**Cundiff**, Martin V., 140
   Richard, 120
   Stephen, 100
**Cunningham**, Edward, 96
   Isaac L., 154
**Cupps**, Daniel, 106
**Cups**, Jacob, 104
**Curd**, Edward, 154
   John, 154

**Currie**, James, 24
**Curry**, Joseph E., 150
  Mathew, 54
  Robert, 58
  Robert W., 122
  William, 10
**Curtis**, Alexander, 130
  D. Dudley, 150
  David N., 24
  Geo., 18
  J. W., 174
  James J., 150
  Peter, 38
**Cutter**, Geo. W., 40

## D

**Dade**, John, 82
**Dailey**, Wm., 48
**Daily**, John D., 166
**Dalton**, Lewis, 52
**Daly**, Lawrence, 26
**Danforth**, Henry, 18
**Daniel**, George W., 100
  James B., 106
  John M., 102
  William H., 42
**Darkins**, George, 62
**Darneal**, John S., 16
**Dashiell**, Geo. W., 58
**Davenport**, Charles, 158
  Charles F., 46
  Michael A., 46
  Milford E., 150
  Richard, 8
**David**, Franklin, 78
**Davidge**, Robert, 136
**Davidson**, George R., 6
  James B., 32
  James H., 174
  Marion T., 166
  William F., 82
**Daviess**, Thos. D., 38
**Davis**, Aldred P., 136
  Calvin, 90
  Christopher C., 64
  David, 36
  David Allen, 150
  George, 118
  George C., 164, 170
  George W., 126
  Henry H., 136
  James, 30, 70
  Jesse, 96, 122
  Jesse B., 112
  John, 22, 64, 120
  John C., 110
  John G., 34
  John M., 52, 134
  John T., 80
  Joseph, 158
  Joseph D., 112
  Josiah, 112
  Newton, 126
  O., 176
  Samuel, 54, 88, 166
  Silas, 104
  Thomas M., 124
  Thomas R., 34
  Travis H., 34
  Wm., 116
**Davison**, Marion F., 54
**Dawkins**, J. G., 74
**Dawson**, John, 154
**Day**, Elisha, 120
  Joel A., 104
  William, 42
**Dean**, Abial, 94
  Austin E., 60
  Job A., 124
  Newton, 162
  Thomas, 134
**Dear**, Ephraim G., 110
  Jos. C., 110
**Dearing**, Elias R., 66
  George H., 120
**Deaver**, Henry W., 82
**Debonish**, Mathew, 118
**Deck**, Michael, 66
**Deckhard**, Conrad, 68
**DeCoursey**, Samuel B., 22
**Defrance**, Louis, 92
**Degarris**, Wm., 118
**Dehoney**, George W., 120
**Dejarnett**, C. J., 20
**Delance**, Joseph, 106
**Delaney**, Michael, 158
**Delano**, John, 62
**Delisle**, John, 118
**Delph**, Geo. W. M., 26
**Demaree**, Allen, 110
**Dement**, Charles B., 16
**Denham**, Bowen, 20
  James, 22
  Samuel, 140
**Dennis**, George W., 134
  Thomas, 10
**Denormanie**, W. P., 12
**Densford**, John, 76
  William, 80
**Denslow**, John W., 166
**Denweddie**, Jesse, 46
**Derby**, Ira L., 166
**Derickson**, George M., 102
**Derlin**, John, 54
**Detch**, Francis, 80
**Deutsch**, Valentine, 80
**Deutsh**, Georg, 72
**Devall**, Daniel, 160
**Devary**, Benjamin F., 152
**Dever**, Milton, 124
**Devin**, James W., 52
**Devine**, James, 118
**Devitt**, James W., 68
**Devley**, Nicholas, 80
**Devlin**, Peter, 158
**Devore**, John C., 168
**Dewell**, George, 124
  John, 124
**DeWitt**, Collins, 162
**Dews**, Thomas J., 124
**Dick**, David, 76
**Dickenson**, James, 46
  John, 46
**Dickersham**, E., 46
**Dickerson**, Woodson, 42
**Dickson**, John, 154
  Robert, 82
**Diefenbaugh**, Henry, 76
**Digier**, George, 170
**Dillingham**, John T., 66
**Dishler**, Anton, 72
**Dishman**, John, 26
**Ditsler**, John F., 64
**Dively**, James, 48
**Divine**, Andrew, 54
**Dixon**, Coleman, 90
  Darius, 88
  Nooman L., 64
**Doane**, Jesse, 48
**Dobyns**, John, 52
**Dodge**, George S., 90
**Dodson**, Joseph, 66
**Dolan**, James, 62
**Doll**, William, 170
**Donaldson**, John, 16, 88
**Donalson**, Walker R., 104
  William, 88
**Donan**, John, 146
**Donavan**, Chasteen, 166
**Doneghy**, Paul J., 38
**Doolittle**, Charles, 40
**Dorman**, Matthew, 4
**Dorries**, Jeremiah F., 136
**Dorsch**, Joseph, 66
**Doss**, Cyranus W., 112
**Dotson**, James, 38
**Doty**, Samuel, 166
**Double**, Isaac, 64
**Dougherly**, James W., 112
**Dougherty**, George, 16
  John, 48, 64
  Nathan, 78
  William, 44
  Z., 174
  Zachariah, 8
**Douglas**, Wm., 70
**Douglass**, Alexander, 10
  Wm., 90
**Dovan**, Andrew, 166
**Dowell**, B. S., 174
  Benj. S., 18
**Dowing**, E., 176
**Downey**, Hannibal, 54
  William C., 54
**Downing**, Edward, 78
**Doyle**, 12
  Felix, 146
**Dozier**, Charles, 62
**Drain**, John M., 164, 170
**Drake**, Francis S., 100
  John C., 112
**Dramos**, A., 20
**Drinkard**, G. W., 50
  H. M., 50
  J. G., 50
**Driscall**, William N., 166
**Driskell**, Henry, 36
  Thos. L., 36
**Driskin**, Charles, 112
**Duckworth**, James F., 78
  William, 166
**Dudley**, Henry B., 90
  T. Calvert, 12
**Duerr**, Andreas, 66
**Duerson**, William, 74
  William Jr., 58
**Dugan**, Henry, 144
**Duggar**, William, 158
**Duggins**, Daniel, 128
  Hamilton, 2
**Duke**, Wm., 24
**Duman**, James, 42
**Dunagan**, John D., 146
**Dunavan**, Hugh J., 124
**Duncan**, Asa, 56
  Benjamin, 124
  Hankes, 44
  Jepthah, 124
  John, 126, 150
  Jos. S., 4
  Joseph J., 10
  Samuel P., 126
  W. H., 14
  Wm. O., 10

**Dunegin**, Joseph, 158
**Dunham**, Edward, 40
**Dunlap**, Jas., 48
  John, 118
  L. F., 2
**Dunlop**, John M., 50
**Dunn**, Andrew F., 136
  Edward, 118
  James G., 2
  John C., 36
  Joseph, 42
  Matthew, 72
**Dunsil**, Thomas, 114
**Durbins**, George, 118
**Durgeon**, Andrew, 106
**Durham**, Geo. W., 30
  William, 142, 152
**Durman**, Green, 142
**Durrett**, John W., 48
**Duskey**, Wm., 40
**Duvall**, Gabriel, 124
  Theodore C., 84
**Dyer**, James, 124

### E

**Eadens**, Westley, 100
**Eads**, Joel, 100
**Eakin**, Charles W., 162
  William, 110
**Eames**, George W., 118
**Earles**, William, 120
**Early**, Napoleon B., 78
**Easby**, Andrew L., 44
  Josiah, 44
**Easey**, Abraham, 162
**Easley**, Danl., 32
  John, 40
**East**, John, 120
**Eastland**, William W., 158
**Easton**, John, 112
**Eaton**, Chas., 98
**Eaves**, Ambrose, 86
**Ebbs**, John W., 94
**Echols**, Charles D., 52
**Eckfeldt**, G. M., 20
**Eddings**, James W., 16
**Edgerton**, John J., 38
**Edington**, William W., 120
**Edmonson**, Will, 84
**Edmundson**, John W., 166
**Edrington**, Thomas, 170
**Edward**, Archibald, 54
  George W., 32
  Henry, 54
**Edwards**, Bennett, 8
  James F., 46

  Josephus, 46
  Josiah, 46
  Solomon, 114
  W. M. W., 6
  W. L., 174
  William H., 82
**Egan**, Benjamin F., 130
  Mathew, 120
**Egbert**, Joseph, 66
**Eggleston**, Ferdinand, 134
**Eisen**, James C., 136
  John, 72
**Elder**, Jessee T., 140
  John C., 78
  William F., 82
  William J., 150
**Elkin**, William P., 152
**Ellenwood**, William, 138
**Eller**, Michael, 68
**Elleston**, Thomas, 96
**Ellingwood**, J. F., 8
**Elliott**, Abram B., 28
  Charles, 78
  Milford, 140
  Whitfield, 28
**Ellis**, Benjamin E., 16
  Charles C., 24
  James F., 94
  James L. W., 162
  John B., 126
  M., 16
  Richard B., 128
  Richard L., 24
**Ellison**, Paris M., 154
  William R., 114
**Elliston**, Loudon, 16
**Elmore**, Johnson, 30
  Lewis, 30
**Embry**, Henry, 30
**Emerson**, Franklin W., 46
  Rufus S., 150
**Emgelbert**, Grieshaber, 72
**Emison**, John, 84
**Emmison**, Joseph, 84
**Emmons**, St. Clair, 90
**England**, James S., 44
**Englemeier**, Joseph, 66
**Englin**, John M., 114
**Ennis**, James, 106
  William R., 4
**Epperson**, William T., 120
**Escue**, John, 120
**Estelle**, Eli, 26
**Estepp**, James W., 150
**Estice**, William, 128
**Estis**, Clem, 152

  Patrick H., 140
**Eubank**, Harrison, 112
  John, 120
**Evans**, A., 166
  Amos, 48
  Humphrey, 6
  James, 140
  James S., 8
  Jerome, 160
  John, 100
  John L., 124
  John M., 86
  Richard P., 32
  Samuel G., 2
  Silas, 170
  Thomas, 170
  William G., 2
**Ewalt**, Richard, 4
  Wm., 108
**Ewing**, James, 102
  Joseph C., 54
**Exner**, Casper, 64
**Ezell**, Herbert O., 156
  William M., 130

### F

**Fain**, John, 44
**Fairbanks**, Flavius G., 82
  J., 176
**Fairman**, John H., 54
**Falden**, James R., 46
**Falkner**, John C., 22
**Fanlac**, Frederick A., 78
**Fanllin**, Thomas P., 118
**Fanning**, Ed. Barnes, 66
**Faris**, Joseph G., 112
  Thomas C., 140
  Tunstall Q., 140
  Wm. M., 112
**Farlee**, Ansolem, 148
**Farmer**, Harrison, 134
  John, 40, 134
**Farris**, Cyrus, 148
  Jeremiah V., 162
  John H., 46
  John T., 88
**Farse**, James W., 26
**Fatrell**, Wiley, 130
**Fawn**, James R., 136
**Featheringale**, J. T., 76
**Featherston**, Charles R., 32
**Fecklin**, Thomas, 54
**Feeback**, Mathew, 98
**Feldhaus**, Frederick, 72
**Fell**, Treidrich, 68
**Fenton**, David, 18

**Fenwick**, Cornelius M., 162
**Ferguson**, Franklin, 52
  Thomas, 136
  Thomas B., 58, 60
**Ferry**, Charles F., 166
**Fetcher**, John, 170
**Feuley**, William H., 78
**Ficklin**, Charles, 166
  John, 52
**Field**, B. S., 8
  Edmund I., 20
  Ezekiel H., 2
  John, 4
  Logan, 134
  William, 134
**Fieldbush**, Chas. H., 116
**Fig**, James, 64
**Figg**, James, 166
**Finch**, J. J., 174
  John I., 24
**Fincher**, Franklin, 104
**Finley**, J., 174
  Wm., 50
**Finn**, Henry, 90
  Timothy, 70
**Finnes**, J., 12
**Finnie**, William, 86
**Fischer**, Joseph, 66
**Fish**, Wm. E., 106
**Fisher**, Ambrose R., 108
  Erasmus D., 140
  James H., 10
  Joseph, 138
  Victor F., 58
  W. A., 58
**Fishwater**, Edward J., 10
**Fitzgerald**, Smith, 36, 128
**Fitzhenry**, J. M., 78
**Fitzpatrick**, Dennis, 92
  William, 26
**Fitzsimmons**, James, 162
**Fix**, Frederick, 120
**Flanary**, Wm. H., 174
**Flanders**, Oliver P., 124
**Flannery**, George, 82
  George F., 120
**Fleihofer**, Frederick, 66
**Fleming**, David, 12
  J. C., 176
**Fletcher**, Elias, 146
  John, 60
  John C., 120
  Squire, 162
  William R., 52
  Wm. T., 120

**Flinn**, William, 114
**Flood**, Peter G., 50
**Flora**, William, 156
**Florence**, M. D., 12
**Flournoy**, Thomas C., 94
 Thos. C., 40
**Flowers**, George W., 118
 John W., 158
 Roling, 162
**Floyd**, John M., 126
**Fogarty**, John, 72
**Fogerty**, J., 176
**Fogg**, James B., 130
**Fogler**, John, 170
**Foley**, Nicholas, 70
 Patrick, 94
**Follbush**, H., 176
**Fondray**, Washington, 90
**Fondry**, Jefferson, 88
**Foote**, Newton, 126
**Forbes**, William, 2
**Ford**, Benjamin, 106
 Edward D., 44
 Enoch, 34
 Henry E., 130
 Jamees M., 2
 James W., 128
 John P., 128
 Joshua G., 44
 Leander, 32
 Littleberry B., 132
 W. M., 14
**Foreman**, Richard S., 100
**Forman**, Joseph R., 108
**Forquer**, James, 128
**Forson**, John, 90
**Forster**, David, 90
**Forsyth**, Wm., 18
**Foster**, Alonzo, 118
 Charles, 158
 Jackson, 96
 James B., 38
 John W., 84
 Joseph, 166
 Joshua, 88
 Lewis J., 6
**Fowl**, N. W., 106
**Fowle**, Isaac, 108
**Fowler**, Charles H., 10
 J. D., 14
 John B., 10
 William, 88, 146
**Fox**, Allen, 170
 Austin T., 66
 Benjamin S., 138
 Henry, 26
 Hugh, 58
 Jacob, 62
 Thomas, 48
**Foxworthy**, William S., 10
**Foy**, Geo., 106
**Fraley**, Greenberry, 100
 Henry, 100
**Frank**, John, 74
**Franklin**, Benjamin B., 124
 James, 96
**Frast**, John, 16
**Frazier**, Alexander, 114
 Hiram, 42
 Jordan, 36
**Fread**, Henry, 48
**Frederick**, Charles, 62
 Gossman, 72
 Richard, 118
**Fredericks**, Lafayette B., 32
**Freels**, Isaac M., 134
**Freeman**, Finess, 62
 Green C., 140
 Stephen L., 140
 William F., 152
 Wm., 20
**Freeney**, Patrick, 70
**Freer**, Charles W., 136
**Freeranel**, Joseph, 14
**Friar**, Wm., 100
**Frily**, James C., 24
**Frisby**, James, 52
**Frollick**, Frederick, 160
**Frost**, Alexander, 46
**Froste**, Will P., 84
**Fry**, Carey H., 28
 Robert, 156
 Speed S., 36
**Fuchs**, Jacob, 74
**Fugate**, Martin H., 142
 William, 114
**Fulchur**, Robert, 90
**Fulkinson**, Thomas, 146
**Fuller**, Benj. P., 58
 John, 70
**Fullerlove**, Clifton, 102
**Funk**, Wm., 18
**Funkhouser**, Job, 10
**Furgerson**, James, 158
**Furnish**, Garritt, 6

## G

**Gaar**, B. F., 20
 N. H., 20
**Gafhart**, Allen R., 78
**Gaines**, John P., 2
 R. W., 24
 William F., 32
**Gains**, Thomas, 140
**Gaither**, Thomas, 144
**Gaitwood**, Robert, 166
**Gale**, Wallace, 88
**Gales**, Wallace, 110
**Gallager**, John, 24
**Gallagher**, John, 26
**Gallaher**, Charles, 162
**Gallaspie**, Isaac, 106
**Galligher**, William, 54
**Galt**, Andrew J., 34
 W. S., 34
**Gamble**, Jeremiah, 118
**Garard**, Wm., 160
**Gardner**, Arthur, 146
 Patrick H., 146
 Stephen, 40
 West, 150
 Wm. E., 146
**Garison**, John A., 44
**Garner**, Allen, 106
 John G., 100
**Garnett**, Alexander, 118
 Marco T., 56
 Moses R., 112
**Garrard**, Theodore T., 158
 William, 154
**Garrett**, Benjamin, 118
 Bernard H., 158
 William, 38
**Garrison**, Hiram, 96
 Willis H., 22
**Garvey**, Robert, 36
**Garvin**, John L., 146
**Gatton**, James, 68
**Gautier**, Leonard, 134
**Gayle**, B. S., 8
 Richard A., 32
**Gaylord**, Henry M., 24
**Gazlay**, H. M., 74
**Gebbhard**, John, 68
**Gehringer**, Frederick, 66
**Genet**, Charles, 170
**Gentry**, Albert C., 52
**Genverely**, Alfred, 170
**George**, Theophelius, 58
 William, 96
**Gettis**, James, 64
**Gettleman**, George, 64
**Gharam**, George W., 26
**Gibbs**, D. G., 10
 Joshua, 110
 William D., 130
**Gibony**, William, 44
**Gibson**, Achilles K., 128
 Harvey, 38
 J. C., 76
 Joseph, 106
**Gilbert**, Benjamin, 68
 Elijah W., 70
 John, 6
 Nathan, 68
 Wm., 50
**Gilbraith**, Edward, 118
**Gilchrist**, William, 122
**Giles**, James W., 162
 John P., 162
**Gill**, Chiloah, 104
 Richard, 130
**Gillespie**, William C., 14
**Gilliss**, George, 58
**Gillner**, Henry, 16
**Gilmore**, Cyrenius W., 140
 James, 140
**Gilpin**, A. M., 76
 George W., 34
**Ginter**, Jacob, 104
**Githens**, James, 96
**Givens**, George H., 10
**Glacken**, James W., 96
**Glane**, Edward R. M., 10
**Glascock**, Wharton, 166
**Glass**, Andrew, 88
 Henry T., 170
 James, 76, 136
 John, 76
 Samuel E., 86
 Samuel L., 84
 Thomas, 76
 William, 24, 62
 Will R., 86
**Glasscock**, Hall, 162
**Glotsbach**, Sebastian, 72
**Glover**, Dewitt C., 52
 Robert, 106
**Gobin**, Harrison A., 60
**Goe**, William, 100
**Goens**, Kenneday, 114
**Goff**, W. S., 80
**Goggin**, David, 140
**Goldsmith**, Carl, 170
**Gonzales**, Benancio, 164
**Gooch**, Thomas, 48
**Goodard**, John, 90
**Goodler**, Joseph A., 136
**Goodloe**, John Kemp, 16
**Goodman**, Ansel, 28
**Goodpaster**, Abram, 54
**Goodrich**, Dempsey, 132
 William T., 152

**Goodson**, James, 18
**Goodwin**, Milton, 86
**Gordon**, Burgiss P., 16
    Charles, 90
**Gore**, Augustus A., 136
    Charles, 2, 56
    Jonathan R., 110
    Notley D., 154
    William, 54
**Gorman**, Samuel, 88
**Gosney**, Benjamin, 40
**Gossman**, John, 68
**Gotti**, Jacob, 66
**Grable**, Alfred, 80
**Gracie**, Wm., 48
**Grady**, Caleb, 120
    James M., 128
**Graff**, Felix, 58
**Graham**, Alfred, 88
    Archibald, 56
    B. B., 62
    Benjamin F., 4
    Franklin, 4
    John R., 158
    Joseph, 124
    Matthew, 144
    Robert A., 124
**Gramp**, Charles, 74
**Granes**, E. A., 162
**Grant**, Geo. W., 42
    George W., 44
    Jacob, 82
    Moses V., 2, 4
    Noah, 58
    Washington, 120
**Graubb**, John P., 106
**Graves**, Living, 44
    Wm. H., 16
**Gray**, Andrew, 40
    Daniel G., 52
    Ezra W., 142
    Henry, 54
    Robert, 118
**Grebe**, John H., 114
**Green**, Abraham, 40
    Doctor F., 128
    Edward P., 42
    Henry, 144
    Hugh J., 128
    James, 52, 58
    John W., 134
    Joseph, 96
    T. W., 20
    Thomas, 84, 144
    William, 52, 94
    Wilson J., 80

**Greenhouse**, Andrew J., 50
**Greenlee**, James H., 46
**Greenwood**, William, 132
**Gregg**, George, 40
    James C., 6
    Joseph, 40
**Gregory**, Curtis, 96
    George W., 110
    John A., 46
    John W., 136
    Robert, 106
**Grey**, Griffith, 64
    Lafayette W., 154
**Grief**, William H., 74
**Griffery**, Thos. L., 40
**Griffin**, Andrew J., 48
    Daniel, 166
    John, 134
**Griffith**, J. W. D., 76
    James H., 96
**Grigg**, John H., 84
    Michael, 86
**Grinstead**, E. F., 20
**Griswold**, Wiley P., 38
**Groogh**, H., 176
**Grooms**, John T., 2
**Grosh**, Jacob, 58
**Gross**, John T., 90
**Grubb**, Lewis C., 140
**Grubbs**, William, 16
**Grutsch**, Henry, 68
**Grutz**, Richard, 158, 170
**Gudgell**, Thos., 36
**Guess**, William, 20
**Guill**, John M., 84
**Guilliland**, David, 154
**Guillion**, W. O., 76
**Guinan**, John, 58
**Gullett**, Isaac, 158
**Gulp**, John P., 136
**Gunn**, Abraham, 146
    John P., 100
**Gunnell**, Robert, 140
**Guthrie**, David B., 124
    John, 38, 68
    Richard W., 56
**Guy**, Samuel, 40
**Guyan**, H., 74
**Gwartney**, Micajah C., 78
**Gwathmey**, George, 78
**Gwynn**, H., 176
    J. T., 76

# H

**Haas**, Michael, 68
**Hackley**, James A., 98

**Hackney**, John, 94
**Hadermann**, C., 72
**Hadley**, J. S., 160
    William W., 158
**Hagan**, Charles C., 42
    Charles L., 124
    John T., 154
    Joseph F., 126
**Haggard**, Bartlett S., 152
    James, 152
**Haggarty**, John, 162
**Hahn**, Samuel, 118
**Hair**, Nathan G., 78
**Halbert**, George T., 56
**Hale**, James B., 64
    Samuel D., 56
    Willaim, 16
**Hall**, Elijah, 4
    Francis, 108
    Green, 102
    Jesse T., 108
    John T., 170
    Nathaniel G., 48
    Pinckney A., 114
    Sidney, 2
    Squire, 12
    Stephen W., 162
    Tom, 170
    W. J., 8
    William, 46, 150
**Halladay**, Joseph S., 98
    Thos., 100
**Halliday**, James H., 96
    John B., 96
**Halsey**, John J., 22
**Haman**, William, 140
**Hambleton**, Thomas, 170
**Hamblin**, James, 160
**Hamilton**, Edward B., 162
    Ferdinand F., 70
    G. R., 18
    H. P., 76
    Jabez L., 100
    James, 70
    John, 130, 170
    Owen, 102
    Peter, 38
    William, 44, 102
**Hamlin**, James T., 170
**Hammond**, William, 38
**Hammonds**, John H., 132
**Hammons**, James, 100
    John, 100
**Hamon**, Daniel S., 142
**Hamp**, Anderson, 2
**Hampton**, Ambrose W., 32,

    152
    George, 26
    James, 152
    Perry, 108
**Hamptons**, Livingston, 158
**Han**, James, 100
**Hancock**, D., 8
**Hand**, James A., 78
**Handley**, David H., 146
    Michael, 142
    Sanuel C., 146
**Hankla**, George C., 162
**Hanks**, John W., 136
    Joseph, 34
    Richard W., 136
    Samuel, 136
**Hanlin**, Thomas, 98
    Thos., 100
**Hann**, Ferdinand, 64
**Hansford**, Benjamin F., 48
    John Q., 48
**Hanson**, Leonidas, 2
    Roger W., 150
    Thos. J., 18
**Hanttzbaugh**, Beverly, 76
**Happ**, Heinrich, 68
**Harbart**, Obediah B., 134
**Harden**, Joseph, 10
    Owen, 76
    P., 76
**Hardesty**, Edward P., 94
    John F., 94
**Hardin**, B. Rowan, 122
    Harrison, 50
    Jackson W., 120
    James, 4, 40
    Mark R., 142
    Robert, 146
    Thomas, 144
    Thomas P., 80
    William P., 132, 148
**Hardingbrook**, Lewis, 166
**Hardisty**, David A., 124
**Hardy**, Arnold S., 162
    William, 32
    William D., 126
**Hargis**, Samuel, 104
**Hargiss**, Thomas, 140
**Hargrave**, John, 70
**Hargraves**, Hannibal, 42
**Harisly**, Wm., 144
**Harkins**, John, 42
**Harlan**, James, 38
    James M., 168
    Richard D., 6
**Harley**, Moses, 130

**Harlon**, Andrew J., 2
   Giles, 128
**Harlow**, George, 152
   Nathaniel, 128
**Harman**, Bledsoe D., 18
   Blidso, 24
**Harmon**, Thomas R., 114
**Harness**, Anderson, 38
**Harney**, Benjamin, 118
**Harper**, C. H., 58
   George W., 168
   Thomas, 8, 88
   Wm. B., 146
**Harrigan**, John, 70
**Harrington**, A. M., 154
**Harris**, Abel P., 32
   Benjamin F., 22
   Benjamin G., 168
   George W., 48
   James, 158
   James W., 34
   John C., 40, 64
   John L., 140
   Joseph B., 26
   Joseph F., 120
   P. H., 162
   Sanford, 112
**Harrison**, Henry, 64
   Jeremiah, 8
   William D., 134
   Wm. H., 36
**Hart**, James, 12
   Samuel H., 154
   Thomas D., 158
   Wm., 20
**Harter**, Franz, 66
**Hartley**, Hamilton, 124
**Hartmann**, Peter, 118
**Harvey**, Edward, 48
   Jonathan, 20
   Trotter, 44
**Hasher**, William A., 90
**Haslett**, William F., 34
**Hassett**, William, 8
**Hasty**, John, 130
**Hatcher**, Green W., 30
**Hath**, Sanboun, 162
**Hatsell**, David, 80
**Hatten**, James, 144
**Hatton**, Alfred, 152
**Hauck**, Christian, 118
**Haum**, Joseph, 4
**Haumer**, John E., 154
**Hausenburg**, Frederk, 118
**Hauser**, William, 38
**Havenhill**, George, 12

**Hawes**, Samuel, 88
**Hawkins**, Benjamin, 16
   Benjamin H., 154
   Elihuo, 158
   Fielding S., 8
   James, 44
   Reuben A., 32
   Thomas P., 154
   Thomas T., 2, 28, 166
   Wm. A., 16
   Wm. S., 16
**Hawley**, John, 72
**Hayden**, Barnabas, 88
   Isah P., 44
   John R., 32
   Wm. M., 32
**Haydon**, Jessee, 16
   Lafayette, 16
   Thomas E., 124
**Hayes**, James, 144
   Jesse H., 156
**Haynes**, Hardin P., 162
   John, 160, 166
   John P., 124
**Hays**, Charles P., 140
   Isaac, 140
   Patrick F., 46
   Thomas, 6
**Hayworth**, John A., 138
**Hazel**, William, 16
**Hazelett**, Matthew L., 34
**Hazlit**, James, 58
**Head**, William, 76
   William R., 136
**Heady**, William J., 12
**Hearn**, Fleming G., 16
   Franklin, 168
   William, 170
**Hearring**, John A., 162
**Heath**, James H., 130
**Heather**, James H., 144
**Heberson**, John, 120
**Hecock**, Joel, 118
**Heddleson**, John M., 86
**Hedges**, Elias, 144
   John W., 108
**Hedrick**, James, 88
   Rolan T., 88
   William, 98
**Hedspeth**, Wm., 120
**Heffner**, Thos. B., 32
**Heissmann**, Henry, 72
**Hellox**, Harry H., 22
**Helm**, Charles J., 158
   Harry, 28
   Littleton, 154

   Samuel, 16
   Willis, 46
**Help**, Lypold, 20
**Helton**, William, 6
**Helvertine**, Henry, 88
**Helvestine**, John P. J., 90
**Hemmingway**, Silas, 134
**Hen**, Phillipp, 74
**Henderson**, Andrew J., 128
   John L., 70
   Joseph W., 88
   William, 32
**Hendley**, Edmund J. C., 156
**Hendren**, James M., 144
**Hendrick**, Edward H., 146
**Hendricks**, James, 140
   Thomas, 134
**Hendrickson**, Joshua, 116
**Hendron**, Lorenzo D., 22
   Woodson, 56
**Hening**, Robert, 160
**Hennersy**, Patrick, 114
**Henning**, John S., 166
**Henry**, Alexander H., 156
   James, 68
   James R., 108
   James W., 108
   John, 98
   Michael, 72
   R., 60
   Thomas, 30
**Hense**, Charles, 74
**Hensley**, Alexander C., 2
   Lucien, 16
**Hepting**, Paul, 166
**Herd**, John W., 158
**Heritage**, Thomas R., 64
**Herman**, Jacob, 66
   John, 64
**Herndon**, David I., 32
   Henry, 52, 102
   Thomas P., 84
   William, 2
**Herr**, John F., 58
**Herrick**, David, 80
**Herridge**, Tillman T., 156
**Herring**, J., 174
   James, 8
**Herseng**, Benj. F., 84
**Hervey**, James O., 42
**Hess**, Georg, 72
**Hewitt**, DeWitt C., 170
**Hewlett**, James, 34
   Martin, 138
**Hibbard**, Theophilus, 158

**Hick**, Edwin, 114
**Hickey**, Thomas, 70, 118
**Hicks**, Erastus B., 46
   Robert, 70
   Thomas, 68
**Hiette**, George P., 130
   Wesley, 130
**Higgins**, Cornelius, 140
   James F., 92
   James M. B., 108
   John F., 46
**Higgs**, James, 144
**Hightower**, Joshua, 164
**Hilbert**, Michael, 110
**Hilburn**, Edwin, 144
**Hile**, John, 136
**Hilger**, Andreas, 66
**Hill**, Alexander, 158
   David, 160, 170
   Frederick M., 162
   Grandison, 100
   Greenbury, 44
   Henry, 84
   Moses, 100
   Richard, 42
**Hillard**, James, 146
**Hilton**, C. W., 60
**Himer**, Alfred, 50
**Hinds**, Joel, 140
   John W. J., 46
**Hinrich**, Otto, 74
**Hinton**, Joseph, 162
**Hirons**, Robert R., 170
**Hitchins**, Caleb A., 108
**Hite**, A. H., 14
**Hitt**, James K., 128
**Hix**, Henry, 142
**Hoadley**, Benjamin T., 170
**Hobson**, Edward H., 28
**Hocker**, Richard W., 38
**Hockersmith**, Dan J., 58
**Hocket**, Elijah, 162
**Hodge**, Littleberry, 130
**Hodges**, Thomas D., 144
**Hoffman**, Frederick, 34
   John, 66, 126
   Thomas, 72
**Hogan**, Green, 118
   Green M., 46
   James, 152
   John A., 118
   William P., 124
   Zachariah J., 42
**Hogg**, Joseph, 108
**Hogland**, John, 126
**Hohimer**, Benjamin, 164

**Hohmann**, Andreas, 74
**Holder**, Robert, 50
**Holeman**, A. W., 8
   John, 20
**Holland**, G., 20
   Henry, 54
**Holley**, Wesley, 24
**Holliday**, Thomas, 84
**Hollingsworth**, J. R., 134
**Holmes**, Benjamin R., 168
   Jackson, 4
   James, 160, 168
**Holt**, Allen, 132
**Holtsclaw**, William H., 124
**Holtzclaw**, Christopher, 84
   Eli, 84
   Thomas, 84
**Hon**, Simpson, 152
**Hone**, Marshall L., 86
**Honsby**, William R., 30
**Hood**, Jesse, 120
**Hooker**, John, 94
**Hooper**, G. D., 78
**Hoover**, Chas., 98
   George D., 82
**Hopewell**, Erasmus, 126
**Hopkins**, Eldridge, 98
   Francis M., 106
   William, 104
**Horgis**, William, 104
**Horn**, Wiley, 100
**Hornback**, William H., 98
**Horne**, William, 38
**Hornsby**, H. B., 20
**Horr**, John A., 168
**Hoskins**, Gideon, 140
**Houk**, Jasper, 40
**Householder**, Solomon, 154
**Howard**, Aaron, 48
   Benjamin, 104
   Clement, 100
   David, 46
   James, 52
   Joseph, 104
   Louis G., 158
   Montgomery, 102
   R. B., 8
   Robert S., 44
   Samuel, 34
   W. W., 76
   William, 34, 62
**Howe**, Ebenezer B., 62
   James M., 170
**Howell**, Lewis M., 106
   Wm. H., 22

**Howland**, James T., 54
**Hubbard**, Geo. T., 116
   Peter, 100
**Hubel**, Benedick, 72
**Huber**, James H., 58
   Jeremiah, 58
**Hubert**, John, 40
**Huff**, John J., 60
   William P., 54
**Huffman**, Hamilton, 4
   Joel E., 4
   John, 36
   William, 126
**Huggins**, R. F., 176
**Hughes**, A. J., 4
   C. D., 6
   Claburn, 166
   Crawford, 38
   Edward T., 146
   Franklin M., 116
   James M., 98
   John, 62, 84
   John T., 154, 166
   John W., 76, 126
   Leroy C., 106
   Perry A., 108
   Peter R., 132
   Thomas, 46
   William, 90
**Hughey**, Robert, 48
**Hughs**, Joseph H., 68
   Madison M., 100
**Hulett**, Alfred, 108
**Humble**, Harvey, 108
   L. B., 68
**Humphries**, George, 156
   W. H., 12
**Hungate**, Davis, 54
**Hunn**, Dominick, 120
**Hunt**, R., 14
   Robert P., 28
   Silas, 142
   W. H. H., 42
**Hunter**, Abner, 16
   Angress, 154
   James, 138
   James A., 132
   John, 44, 138
**Hupp**, Wm. I., 144
**Hurd**, Joseph, 48
**Hurley**, Wm., 18
**Hursk**, Benjamin F., 130
   George W., 130
**Hurst**, Bolivar, 82
   William, 20
**Hurt**, John S., 52

   Oliver M., 120
   William P., 50
**Huston**, James, 94
   Robert W., 148
   Thomas, 94
**Hutchason**, Oscar F., 28
**Hutchens**, Abner, 26
**Hutcherson**, Benj. M., 120
   James, 108
**Hutchins**, Milton, 78
   Thomas W., 154
**Hutchinson**, Richard, 92
**Hutchison**, James, 4
**Hutchman**, Gillaspie, 174
**Hyatt**, Conradus, 134
**Hyde**, John, 158

## I

**Ieder**, Benjamin, 120
**Igo**, Harison, 24
**Iliff**, Daniel, 174
**Ingram**, John, 104
   William, 104
**Innis**, Isaac, 80
**Ireland**, Thomas, 84
   Thomas C., 126
   Thomas S., 128
**Irvan**, B. B., 166
   Burwell B., 154
**Isbel**, Thomas H., 16
**Ivey**, Jesse, 168

## J

**Jackman**, Joseph, 44
**Jackson**, Columbus, 26
   Edward, 84
   Feries, 20
   George W., 52
   Henry C., 24
   Isaac D., 114
   James, 24
   Jarvis C., 158
   Mathew E., 96
   Thomas, 158
   William, 94
   William O., 162
**Jacobs**, Herod K., 16
**James**, Charles, 102
   D. W., 76
   Decatur, 20
   Falconer, 128
   Richard, 110
   Thomas, 74
   Wil, 18
**Janes**, Greenup, 120
   Preston B., 122

   Wm. D., 120
**Jaquitt**, Isaac, 112
**Jarboe**, Walter S., 144
**Jarvis**, Thompson, 84
**Jasper**, John, 142, 150
   Merrill, 142
   Teral, 150
   Tunstall Q., 140
**Jeaannery**, John, 104
**Jeans**, Beal, 52
   Joseph, 70
**Jeffries**, James, 82
   Thomas A., 148
**Jenger**, Joseph, 66
**Jenkens**, Joseph W., 96
**Jenkins**, Ambrose Y., 124
   Horace, 64, 118
   James, 48
   John D., 64
**Jennings**, William, 2
**Jennison**, James S., 40
   John S., 40
**Jester**, Joseph, 176
   Stephen, 176
**Jeter**, Benjamin, 10
   Henry, 26
   James, 16
   John A., 30
**Jett**, Benjamin F., 168
   Henderson, 76
**Jewell**, J., 176
**Jewet**, Josiah S., 68
**Johartgen**, Mathias, 66
**Johns**, Thomas, 138
**Johnson**, Benjamin W., 90
   Charles, 158
   Clarke, 54
   Clark M., 90
   David, 104
   David F., 168
   H. P., 110
   Henry, 18
   Henry M., 156
   J. W., 18
   James, 12, 36, 80
   James S., 32
   John, 66
   John F., 74
   John H., 116
   John W., 118
   Joseph C., 82
   Nathaniel, 16
   Sidney L., 118
   Thomas F., 138
   William H., 130
   Wm. G., 122

**Johnston**, Hamilton P., 144
   James M., 28
   Thomas, 28
   Thomas M., 28
**Jolly**, Charles, 148
**Jones**, Benjamin, 60
   Charles, 110
   Clement, 26
   D. C., 174
   David C., 24
   David E., 90
   Edward, 118
   Evan, 48
   Frederick, 110
   George, 86, 114
   George W., 104
   Griffith, 128
   Harrison, 82
   Hartsville F., 158
   Harvey, 38
   Jackson A., 154
   James A., 148
   Jesse W., 152
   John A., 10
   John F., 86
   Jonas, 6
   Jonathan, 144
   Joseph I., 138
   Juba M., 6
   Monroe, 138
   Newton, 130
   Robert B., 84
   Robert G., 148
   Shelton, 136
   Stafford, 84
   W. P., 8
   W. E., 60
   Warner E., 28
   Wiley, 114
   William, 88
**Jordan**, Arthur B., 98
   Benjamin, 138
**Jordon**, Wilson J., 32
**Joslin**, Almond, 168
   James, 168
**Jouett**, A. S., 26
   Michael, 92
**Joyner**, William J., 156
   William M., 48
**Judd**, Andrew J., 120
   George W., 122
**Jupin**, James H., 154
**Jurgens**, Frank, 72

# K

**Kaegin**, Ulrich, 68
**Kahill**, Edward S., 52
**Kalfus**, J. W., 76
   William H., 126
**Kaltenback**, Georg, 72
**Kane**, Harry A., 116
   Henry A., 132
**Kauffman**, Richard, 64
**Kavanaugh**, H. W., 22
**Kaye**, George, 60
   Wm. Jr., 58
**Keating**, Timothy, 116
**Keeler**, Joseph C., 168
**Keen**, James W., 98
**Keene**, George W., 4
   Van W., 6
   William R., 42
**Keiger**, James, 90
**Keith**, Nathaniel W., 152
**Keley**, Wm. S., 102
**Keller**, John, 68
   John W., 158
**Kelley**, George M., 128
   James, 170
**Kelly**, David L., 148
   James, 52, 110
   James O., 58
   John H., 22
   Joseph, 154
   Michael, 70
   Robert C., 130
   W. T., 174
   William, 88
   William E., 124
   Wm., 18
**Kelso**, James E., 50
**Kemp**, James, 12, 174
**Kemper**, Samuel, 84
**Kendall**, J. J., 8
   James, 112
   Wm., 18
**Kendrick**, James W., 138
   Joseph L., 94
**Kenedy**, James, 18
**Kennedey**, Berry, 106
**Kennedy**, J., 174
   Robert, 52
   Thomas, 72
   Thomas J., 118
**Kenney**, George M., 108
   James H., 134
   Jeff, 108
**Kens**, James, 138
**Kent**, Alexander, 170
**Kenton**, Eldridge, 98
**Kern**, Florian, 66
**Kerr**, James D., 148
   John, 114
**Ketterer**, Friedrich, 72
**Kettle**, Daniel A., 160
**Key**, Albert M., 148
**Keynon**, William M., 128
**Kilgour**, John, 82
**Killer**, George, 20
**Killinger**, William H., 90
**Kimball**, Amos, 42
   Thomas, 38
**Kimberlin**, John, 134
   William, 134
**Kimbree**, Elijah R., 78
**Kimbrough**, John, 100
   John W., 10
**Kimes**, John, 98
**Kincaid**, Curtis, 102
   Socrates, 102
   William G., 44
**King**, William, 156
   William C., 130
   William P., 128
**Kingcart**, John, 98
**Kinkead**, James M., 14
**Kinkton**, Vinson F., 162
**Kirby**, James, 152
**Kirk**, John, 52
   William G., 52
   Wilson T., 88
**Kirkhai**, Franz, 116
**Kirkham**, Ferdinand, 88
**Kirkpatrick**, Jonathan, 46
   Robert R., 116
**Kirtly**, Cane, 6
**Kiser**, David, 174
**Kleinheintz**, Michael, 66
**Knapp**, Adam, 72
**Knight**, Benjamin, 148
   Granville P., 114
**Knip**, Joel K., 168
**Knott**, Clark, 32
   Samuel, 168
   Timothy C., 162
**Knotts**, James B., 94
**Knowland**, David, 74
   W., 76
**Koons**, R., 12
   W., 174
**Kracht**, Samuel, 118
**Kraft**, Christian, 66
**Krauss**, Christopher, 74
**Krautz**, John, 40
**Kriel**, Andrew, 78
**Kring**, Jos., 50
**Krone**, Benjamin, 138
**Kuh**, William, 66
**Kuhn**, Georg W., 72
**Kyle**, James, 104
   Samuel H., 6

# L

**Labbree**, Wm. D., 116
**Lacey**, Wm. H., 58
**Lacker**, Freidrich, 72
**Lackman**, Griffin L., 132
**Lacomb**, John, 118
**Lacy**, B. D., 102
   Littleton T., 40
   Walter J., 86
**Ladd**, Henry, 138
**Ladyman**, George W., 138
**Lafon**, John W., 8
**Lair**, James, 56
   John G., 140
**Lake**, Joseph, 110
**Lamaster**, Thomas, 128
**Lamb**, Archibald, 138
   James M., 140
   John, 144
   Reuben, 92
   Wiley, 138
**Lamberson**, Joshua, 102
**Lambert**, Geo. W., 144
   Joseph, 66
   Robert B., 138
   William H., 138
**Lampton**, James S., 118
   Joshua L., 80
   William, 68
**Lancaster**, James M., 94
**Lanckart**, Sylvester, 24
**Land**, Hiram, 20
   Thos. H., 22
**Landrain**, William J., 2
**Landrum**, Joel, 162
   John J., 4
**Lane**, Lucien B., 92
   Monroe, 124
   R. N., 76
   William B., 118
**Lang**, Patrick A., 138
**Langley**, William S., 52
**Langston**, Joseph G., 152
**Lanham**, John, 162
   Samuel, 162
**Laprin**, Mitchell, 70
**Lapsley**, Samuel D., 38
**Lard**, Robert, 148
   Thomas G., 148
**Larue**, John H., 28
   Warren J., 124
**Latta**, Robert, 8

**Laughlin**, Alexander, 70
    Mark W., 108
**Launaser**, George, 146
**Law**, John, 128
**Lawless**, James K., 4
    William O., 2
**Lawrence**, B. H., 14
    Gibson, 98
    John, 20
    William, 98
    William S., 152
**Lawson**, Andrew, 92
    George W., 170
    John, 90, 110
    Samuel, 92
**Layten**, James, 36
**Layton**, John G., 62
**Leadenburg**, J. S., 14
**Leahy**, Dennis, 70
**Leake**, Gabriel, 124
**Leathers**, Jefferson, 34
    Larkin, 34
    Mark, 36
**Lebree**, James, 96
**Lecompt**, Francis C., 32
**Lee**, George W., 6
    Henry, 94
    James F., 8
    John, 48
    John B., 90
    Mathew, 94
    Robert S., 50
**Leeper**, George, 46
**Lefferd**, Samuel, 158
**Lefler**, William, 124
**Leftridge**, Harvey, 114
**Leghton**, William, 14
**Lehman**, Jacob, 116
**Lelland**, John A., 154
**Lemaster**, Warren, 2
**Lemon**, Geo. W., 106
**Lemonds**, Nelson, 168
**Lemons**, John, 174
**Lendengen**, Silas, 158
**Lenour**, Hiram, 132
**Lenox**, Moses, 92
**Leohlifer**, Georg, 66
**Leonard**, Samuel C., 8
    William, 26
**Leonhardt**, John, 72
**Leston**, James, 8
**Letcher**, John W., 24
**Levan**, D. W., 12, 174
**Levasay**, James A., 26
    John, 28
**Levering**, Charles W., 58

**Levi**, Andrew J., 10
    David A., 112
**Levinford**, George P., 10
**Lewis**, Charles, 64
    Dozier B., 134
    Edward, 50
    Henry, 138
    John, 80
    John H., 138
    Johnson, 16
    Orin M., 98
    Robert G., 88
    William, 78
    William H., 82
**Lhorton**, Lewis, 78
**Lightell**, John, 50
**Lightfoot**, Goodrich E., 132
**Lighton**, Andrew D., 58
**Ligon**, John B., 154
**Lillard**, David I., 6
    John H., 34
    Jos. S., 4
    William C., 4
    William W., 34
**Lilley**, E. F., 18
**Lilly**, William B., 90
**Lime**, James, 114
    William, 114
**Limebaugh**, Daniel, 118
**Lindsay**, Richard S., 84
    Robert, 98
**Lindsey**, William J., 4
**Lineberry**, B. M., 46
**Linthicum**, Hezekiah, 88
**Lisle**, Valentine, 30
**Lister**, Thomas, 14
**Litason**, Daniel E., 70
**Littell**, John, 28
**Little**, James, 168
**Littlejohn**, Charles, 154
    James W., 98
**Littrell**, William, 66
**Livers**, Henry P., 64
**Livingston**, Wm. J., 110
**Lockite**, James, 14
**Lockwood**, Turman, 42
**Loeffler**, John, 74
**Logan**, David M., 48
    Hugh, 46
    James E., 10
    John A., 82, 110
    Mason, 2
    Oscar D., 128
**Logston**, Dougherty, 168
**Lomon**, Diedrick, 170
**Lon**, William, 152

**Long**, David, 108
    Edward, 86
    Henry C., 30, 58
    James, 28
    James M., 110
    John, 28
    Remus V., 122
    Samuel M., 36
    William, 90
**Longe**, Anthony, 60
**Lore**, Christopher C., 94
    Nathan, 94
**Love**, James M., 124
**Lowe**, John M., 26
**Lowell**, William, 110
**Lowman**, Didrick, 160
**Lowry**, Hugh, 108
    Simpson, 22
    Weedon S., 102
    William C., 42
**Loyall**, John, 28
**Loyd**, John T., 108
**Lucas**, Benjamin, 68
    George W., 130
    Henry, 162
    John, 78, 158
**Luke**, Henry, 58
    Wm. S., 50
    Wm., 144
**Luns**, Anastasio, 156
**Lunsford**, Jesse, 158
    Tarlton, 114
**Lupton**, Cy. C., 82
**Lybarger**, Daniel, 64
**Lyle**, Francis M., 152
**Lynch**, James M. M., 156
    Joshua, 94
**Lynn**, James, 138
    William N., 6
**Lyon**, Matthew M., 138
**Lyons**, C., 176
    Cornelius, 70
    Fletcher, 64
    Leander, 62
    Wm., 98

# M

**McAbee**, John W., 68
**McAlister**, John, 144
    William, 62
**McAtee**, John, 94
**Macatro**, Geo. W., 174
**McAttee**, Ferdinand, 168
**McBath**, John, 110
**McBrayer**, John H., 34
    John M., 36

**McBride**, Isaac, 20
    James, 40
**McCabbins**, James, 30
**McCain**, Wm. H. H., 118
**McCalla**, James P., 16
    William, 30
**McCallister**, Enoch, 16
**McCampbell**, John G., 44
**McCann**, John, 70
**McCanna**, James, 130
**McCarthy**, Patrick, 120
    Wm. P., 12
**McCarty**, Benjamin, 154
    Blair, 110
    Charles, 114
    Edward, 26
    George W., 154
    James, 154
    John D., 156
    Luther, 114
    Thomas, 12
    William H., 154
**McCaslin**, John G., 140
    William H., 138
**McChesney**, Saml. D., 38
    Wm., 12
**McCleary**, Thomas, 72
**McClenden**, Milton R., 78
**McClintock**, Wm. A., 10
**McClung**, Silas, 110
**McClure**, Hosea C., 142
    Moses L., 170
    Solomon, 60
**McComack**, George, 36
**McCombs**, Anderson, 168
**McConnel**, James A., 44
**McConnell**, Wm. A., 150
**McCormac**, William, 38
**McCormack**, Daniel, 64
    John H., 98
**McCormeck**, James T., 60
**McCormick**, James R., 96
    Joseph, 154
**McCoun**, Peter, 98
**McCoy**, Claiborne, 80
    George, 80
    Sanders, 158
**McCracken**, 108
    James, 88
    Marcus W., 26
    Stephen, 94
**McCreery**, Dennis, 132
**McCrorty**, William, 28
**McCullough**, David, 50
**McCurdy**, Robert, 42
**McCure**, David, 104

**McDonald**, A. J., 8
   Edmund H., 116
   George, 72, 168
   Hiram, 110
   James, 144
   John B., 168
   John C., 122
   Robert G., 108
   W. P., 76
   William, 80, 92, 122
**McDonough**, Michael, 12
   Richard, 40
**McDougal**, Wm., 40
**McElroy**, Isaac, 132
   Malaki, 122
**McElvoy**, Benjamin H., 162
**McElwain**, Alexander, 92
**McEver**, David, 100
**McEvoy**, Thomas, 72
**McEwin**, Robert, 72
**Macey**, T. J., 8
**McFarlan**, Wm., 98
**McFarland**, Barthold, 84
   Felix, 98
   James, 140
**McGarrity**, James, 58
**McGaughery**, James, 34
**McGaughey**, William, 36
**McGaw**, Hugh B., 118
**McGeavery**, John, 70
**McGhee**, Joseph, 120
   Meredith, 134
   William J., 136
**McGinley**, Barney, 50
**Macginnis**, Benj. I., 174
   David, 174
**McGinnis**, James C., 140
   Owen, 130
   Patrick, 70
   Thomas, 38
**McGloughan**, P., 176
**McGowan**, Buford, 146
   Henry, 70
**McGran**, Thomas L., 92
**McGrath**, Thomas, 48
**McGrorty**, William, 38
**McGuire**, George, 138
   James, 22
   Nathaniel, 6
   Samuel W., 104
**McGune**, James E., 32
**McHenry**, James, 14
**McHugh**, Samuel, 80
**McIhenney**, Beverley H., 104

**McIlhenney**, Felix, 106
**McIlvain**, William, 52
**McIntire**, Benjamin, 124
**McIntosh**, William E., 92
**McIntyre**, George W., 88
   Hezekiah, 26
**McKamy**, Alexander, 122
**Mackay**, John, 82
**McKeag**, George, 68
   William, 168
**McKee**, J. D., 8
   James H. D., 6
   Samuel F., 2
   William R., 28
**McKegg**, James, 12
**McKinney**, John, 102
   Levi C., 102
   Marion, 148
   Pleasant B., 102
   William M., 140
**Mackison**, Richard, 60
**McKitrick**, Felix, 144
   Fielding, 164
   Joseph C., 144
**McKnight**, Samuel, 154
**McKracken**, James, 110
**McKuney**, James, 102
**McLain**, Theodore, 50
   William, 8
   Wm., 50
**McLaughlin**, John, 40
   Thomas, 70
**McLemore**, Hiram G., 110
**McLilley**, John H., 48
**McLin**, David O., 92
**McMahon**, James, 72
**McMain**, John, 22
**McMannis**, James, 86
**McMichael**, Andrew M., 58
**McMillan**, Joseph, 6
**McMillen**, Hugh, 80
   Jackson, 86
**McMillon**, John C., 22
**McMordie**, Francis, 162
**McMullin**, Daniel, 146
**McMullins**, Daniel, 130
**McMurry**, William, 118
**McMurtry**, Geo. W., 60
**McMurty**, John, 44
**McNamer**, Philip, 134
**McNeill**, John F., 94
**McNute**, George W., 154
**McPherson**, William L., 78
**McPike**, Patrick, 70
**McQuady**, Edmund, 134

**McQueen**, David, 32
   S., 8
**McQuiddy**, Alex. A., 168
**McQuillan**, Andrew, 70
**McQuillen**, Francis, 92
**McQuoin**, Zachariah, 92
**McWhorter**, James B., 164
**Madans**, Sanders, 158
**Madden**, Benedict J., 166
**Maddox**, Andrew J., 144
   Edward, 14
   Edward C., 144
   George C., 110
**Maddy**, Michael, 50
**Magee**, Irwin, 20
   Thos. J., 22
**Magner**, John, 18, 174
**Magness**, John, 176
**Magruder**, Cornelius C., 110
**Mahaff**, William C., 102
**Mahan**, Elijah, 88
**Mahon**, George T., 168
**Mahoney**, James, 26
**Mailey**, Joseph, 64
**Main**, George, 90
**Maischel**, Neuman, 36
**Maitganery**, Minor P., 86
**Maja**, Boon, 14
**Major**, William K., 32
**Makee**, T. T., 12
**Malcom**, Greenburg, 14
**Mallay**, James I., 56
**Maloney**, Edward, 114
   James, 92
**Manley**, Isaac, 104
   William, 104
**Mann**, James B., 54
   Josiah, 54
**Mansfield**, James L., 148
   Washington, 148
**Manson**, William, 14
**Manuel**, Thomas, 46
**Mappin**, Caleb, 52
**Maratea**, Sylvester, 12
**Marbaum**, Heinrich, 74
**Marberry**, William W., 154
**March**, Japtha R., 152
**Marcum**, Joseph, 114
**Markes**, George J., 132
**Markewell**, Alvin, 90
   George W., 88
**Markham**, Jas., 48
   Will, 84
**Marks**, George I., 44

**Markswell**, Elias, 86
**Markwell**, Alvin, 110
**Mars**, Samuel, 8
**Marsh**, A. A., 4
   J. S., 176
   Jos. S., 78
**Marshal**, George W., 126
**Marshall**, A. G., 12, 174
   A. S., 174
   Ben, 12
   Franklin, 124
   George A., 124
   Henry G., 166
   Humphrey, 2
   James M., 134
   Madison, 124
   Silas, 98
   Thomas F., 14
   William, 12, 68, 94, 128
**Martin**, A. J., 6
   Alfred, 132
   Anthony, 72
   Benjamin, 138
   E. P., 174
   George W., 102
   Henry, 114
   Henry H., 156
   James G., 28
   James W., 148
   Jesse G., 18
   Joel, 114
   John, 98, 108, 138
   John O., 28
   Joseph F., 94
   L., 8
   Robert, 44
   Samuel, 34
   Thomas B., 92
   Thos. B., 82
   Will. E., 84
   Willis F., 150
**Marts**, John L., 68
**Marvin**, William F., 44, 68
**Mason**, Anderson G., 126
   Augustus E., 124
   George, 24
   James, 164
   James T., 94
   John F., 94
   William L., 124
**Massey**, John M., 136
**Massie**, James, 60
   James Y., 52
**Masters**, Irvine, 44
   Jackson, 44
**Mathews**, William S., 64

Mathorn, George, 62
Matlock, John, 128
Matney, Thomas J., 122
Matthews, Beverly, 114
    Caleb S., 130
    John S., 58
Mattingly, Richard E., 70
    Sabastian C., 166
    Thomas B., 166
Maury, R. F., 58
    Reuben E., 38
Maxey, Ephraim, 148
    Jeremiah, 150
    Larkin, 150
    W. H., 30
May, Barney, 134
    Coleman C., 138
    Jesse, 2, 142
    Stephen, 12
    William, 124
    Wm. R., 164
Mayer, William D., 118
Mayes, Allen H., 144
Mayfield, Beverly C., 148
    Orill, 146
    Thomas, 146
Mayhall, Hanson S., 32
Mays, Jackson, 28
    Samuel J., 54
Meade, David, 74
Meadows, George W. B., 114
    Reuben, 114
Means, John H., 80
    William C., 118
Mearing, Christopher, 118
Medlicot, Joseph, 70
Meed, Harvey J., 142
Meek, Lee, 92
Meeks, John, 150
    Robert, 150
    William, 150
Megowan, J. T., 86
    James F., 26, 134
    John B., 52
Meissner, John, 74
Melton, George W., 82
    Seth P., 154
Mempel, Adam, 134
Mercer, Henry O., 58
    James T., 58, 168
    John E., 138
    Levi, 76
Merchant, John L., 24
Meredith, John, 16
    Randol, 150

    William, 148
Meriman, John, 144
Merrick, James T., 142
    William G., 94
Merrifield, J. A., 12
Merrill, Micajah, 78
Merritt, James, 64
    Richard, 38
Merryman, Walton, 118
    William, 56
Mershon, Andrew J., 158
    Benjamin F., 2
    James, 4
Messer, Daniel, 174
Metcalf, Francis, 170
    Henry, 4
    Leonidas, 96
    William, 92
Mettan, West A., 136
Meyer, Jacob, 154
Michael, Thomas, 92
Middleton, John, 168
Milam, Ben. G., 6
    F. M., 8
    Moses S., 32
    Thos. J., 32
Miles, Albert, 134
    J. G., 8
    John, 16
Milican, Thomas, 114
Millan, Alexander, 126
    James, 124
Millarey, Daniel, 80
Miller, Christofer, 72
    Elijah, 128
    F. A., 82
    George H., 2
    Henry, 72
    Isaiah, 98
    Jacob, 74
    James F., 2
    James H., 22, 90
    James Q., 134
    John, 4, 98, 124
    John A., 118
    John J., 4
    Joseph, 98
    Milton J., 22
    Randolph, 174
    Thomas, 10
    Washington, 98
    William, 64, 110, 140
    William B., 52
    William C., 154
Milligan, A. M., 14
Million, Squire, 22

Mills, John, 164
    Robert, 60
    Samuel F., 140
Milner, Lafayette, 128
Miner, George G., 118
    L. D., 6
    M. F., 4
    Williams, 18
Minter, Joshua, 62
    Wm. H., 18
Minton, James R., 150
    John, 28
    Jonathan, 150
Mitchell, A. J., 8
    Adison, 152
    Andrew J., 128
    Charles, 118
    James, 138
    James L., 112
    James W., 40
    John, 112
    Strother D., 52
    Thomas E., 92
    W. J., 18
    Warren, 50
Mites, James M., 168
Mize, Henry H., 100
Mobley, Allen, 128
Mocabee, Allen T., 150
Moffat, John, 56
Moffitt, Eri, 82
Mohan, James, 20
Mohundro, John, 132
    William O., 130
Molloy, Pinckney C., 130
Monday, Thomas, 34
Moneymaker, Wilson, 138
Monin, Joseph N., 148
    Rawleigh M., 148
Monohon, Samuel, 164
Monroe, C. E., 14
    James, 30
Montague, Lewis F., 128
    S., 8
Montgomery, Allen S., 38
    Claytor S., 46
    Clifton A., 46
    Frank Z., 120
    George W., 2
    James B., 122
    John, 36, 38
    Jos., 34
    Paul, 144
    Robert, 130
    Squire, 146
    W., 176

Moody, Lewis, 84
Moon, Jas. W., 164
    Robert, 92
    Samuel, 164
Mooney, C. E., 174
    C. S., 174
    Charles E., 24
Moor, John, 166
Moore, Andrew B., 44
    Calvin B., 98
    Charles D., 28
    Collin B., 140
    George W., 124
    Hamilton G., 34
    Harrison, 92
    Henry, 142
    James, 6, 26
    James G. N., 132
    James L., 94
    James W., 168
    Jas., 110
    John, 72, 98, 102, 124
    John A., 80
    John E., 32
    Levi, 30
    Peter, 60
    Richard G. R., 12
    Robert, 76
    Starling, 102
Moppin, Thomas, 24
Mopps, Edward S., 116
Moran, James, 104
Morant, Robert, 130
Morehead, Robert L., 40
Moreland, Daniel M., 46
Morgan, A. G., 26
    Calvin C., 26
    Daniel, 36, 154
    Daniel W., 154
    George, 34
    Gisham, 86
    John, 26, 168
    Joshua, 50
    Milton, 40
    Robert, 98, 114
    Silas, 90
    William, 104, 140
Morh, Frank C., 86
Morrell, Cyrus G., 48
Morris, Daniel B., 62
    Elzy, 30
    James, 144
    Lewis, 98
    Thomas, 30
    William, 84, 90, 110, 170

**Morrison**, Erastus, 136
   Hugh E., 48
   James W., 78
   Joseph, 16, 118
   Robert W., 88
   W., 20
   William, 32
**Morrow**, Alexander, 62
**Morry**, John, 64
**Morse**, Benjamin, 120
   Berry, 130
**Morton**, E. J. H., 6
   John, 16, 108
**Mosby**, L. S., 58
   Thos. J., 78
**Moseby**, William L., 14
**Mosely**, Samuel, 174
**Moss**, Alexander, 34
   James W., 28
   Joel, 156
   John A., 28
   Wm. H., 28
**Mounce**, Greenup R., 142
**Muck**, Humphrey, 102
   Joseph, 102
**Mudd**, George W., 2
   Paul, 144
**Muir**, James, 152
   Jasper W., 124
   John M., 124
**Mulay**, William H., 24
**Mulhall**, Robert, 152
**Mulholland**, Daniel, 70
**Mullen**, Harry, 128
   John, 80
**Muller**, Henry, 78
**Mullin**, Robert, 146
**Mullins**, Samuel, 2, 108
**Mullus**, Richard, 166
**Muncy**, James F., 102
**Munday**, John, 102
**Munpel**, Jacob, 74
**Munson**, Albert, 86
   Samuel, 96
**Munsriur**, Jas., 72
**Murphy**, Bryant Y., 124
   Cornelius, 10
   J., 20
   James C., 18
   John L., 124
   Joseph, 4
   Joseph K., 164
   Joshua, 134
   Kenelian, 164
   Philip, 12
   William, 70

   Wm. T., 106
**Murray**, Daniel, 126
   Jesse M., 148
   Samuel A., 148
   Winfield S., 168
**Murrey**, Thomas, 170
**Murry**, Granville P., 114
**Murs**, William L., 98
**Myers**, B. R., 174
   Benjamin, 98
   D. R., 18
   David, 98
   Geo., 98
   George Jr., 98
   Henry, 114
   Jefferson W. H., 78
   John, 156
   Michael, 94
   Stephen, 118
**Myles**, Stephen G., 112
**Myrick**, Francis, 132
   Joseph A., 6

# N

**Naihart**, Valentin, 66
**Nance**, Jesse, 142
   Reuben L., 116
**Nangle**, Benjamin F., 64
**Napier**, Clabourn, 164
   John, 46
   Levi, 114
   Thomas W., 46
**Nathan**, Levi, 150
**Nave**, Andrew J., 42
**Naylor**, Simeon, 128
**Neal**, James, 82, 100
   John, 98
   William H., 54
**Neale**, Daniel, 84
   James R., 146
   Jas. W., 22
**Nealis**, James, 88
   James L., 88
**Neeley**, Hezekiah F., 34
**Neely**, William W., 158
**Neff**, John, 20
**Neil**, Daniel, 158
   George W., 124
**Nelson**, James O., 120
   Joseph C., 122
   M., 174
   Robert, 152
**Nepp**, Wm., 122
**Nester**, James, 96
**Netherland**, Jos. H., 6
**Nethuby**, John, 92

**Nevill**, Henry D., 146
**Nevin**, Francis, 70
**Newkirk**, J. Y., 18
**Newland**, W. B., 14
**Newman**, D., 176
   Darby, 72
   Nel D., 132
   Richard, 134
   William, 134
**Newton**, Isaac, 148
   W., 8
**Nichols**, John, 134
**Nicholson**, Henry, 84
   Lewis H., 24
**Nickel**, William, 158
**Niel**, Wm. G., 110
**Nieland**, Herman, 68
**Night**, Weston, 150
**Nix**, John, 114
   Joseph D., 114
**Noe**, Felix G., 158
   Nixon, 160
**Noel**, R. P. W., 8
**Noland**, Obid, 102
**Nooe**, Albert K., 44
**Norman**, Henry, 42
   William B., 154
**Norris**, Charles, 174
   Charles M., 128
   George, 160
   William, 104
**North**, Henry B., 6
   Lafayette, 104
**Northern**, Russel H., 144
**Norton**, James, 36
   William J., 94
   Wm. H., 108
**Norvell**, Leonard S., 128
**Nourse**, Charles E., 124
**Nouse**, Michael, 6
**Nuber**, John, 74
**Numan**, James, 108
**Nunnelly**, William B., 142

# O

**Oak**, Frederick, 50
**Oakley**, George, 106
   James B., 104
   Pleasant E., 104
**O'Bannon**, James, 84, 112
**Obannon**, William, 88
**O'Brien**, William, 44, 48
**Oden**, Creason, 152
**Oder**, Thomas W., 10
**Odom**, John George W., 134

**O'Donald**, Michael, 68
**O'Dorherty**, P., 160
**Offutt**, Hezekiah, 84
**Ogden**, Thomas, 98
**Oglesby**, M. W., 74
   R. M., 76
   W. T., 74
**Ohaver**, Thomas, 26
**Oldham**, Allen, 148
   Caleb, 148
   George M., 134
   Thomas, 52
**Oliver**, Amos, 104
   Charles W., 92
   James B., 34
   Richard, 164
   Wm., 50
**Olivers**, Thomas L., 60
**Olmstead**, Freeborn, 128
**O'Neil**, Bryant C., 170
**O'Niel**, John P., 80
**Onslow**, John B., 68
**Orchard**, James, 20
**O'Riley**, D. G., 12
**Orin**, William H., 144
**Ormes**, Nelson, 154
**Ormsby**, Stephen, 58
**Orr**, Charles C., 46
   George R., 132
**Osborn**, Nathan, 174
   Squire, 174
**Osborne**, Charles, 60
   John, 124
**Osburn**, Francis, 144
   Robert J., 158
**O'Sullivan**, Eugene, 118
**Ott**, Columb C., 170
**Overby**, Jno. C., 12
**Overly**, Jacob C., 10
**Overstreet**, Archibald, 38
   Cabel, 38
   J. M., 76
   S. W., 76
   Samuel R., 44
   Samuel W., 134
   W. T., 76
**Overton**, Allen G., 120
**Owen**, John L., 60
   L. D., 60
**Owens**, David D., 142
   George B., 30
   Hamilton N., 120
   Horatio, 2
   William, 138
**Owings**, J. W., 12, 174
   Luther C., 60

Owsley, Benjamin F., 52

# P

Pace, George W. L., 132
  Twitty R., 132
Padder, Richard H., 170
Padgett, Durett, 154
Page, James R., 34
  Thomas C., 44
Painter, Daniel, 10
Palmer, Manley F., 148
  Wilkerson, 36
Pangburn, John, 64, 118
Pankey, James S., 92
Parent, E. T., 8
Parish, Veatchele, 170
Park, Richard W., 86
  Samuel, 160
  Wm., 40
Parke, William, 132
Parker, Cal. C., 168
  Chrisman H., 142
  Mathew, 158
  Rowland S., 32
  William, 4
  William C., 10, 48
  William H., 148, 166
Parks, B. F., 76
  John, 128
  John C., 168
Parnell, John, 94
Parott, Henry, 28
Parr, William H., 54
Parrent, John, 60
Parrish, John N., 154
Parrott, Moses, 124
Parsons, John W., 102
  Thomas W., 102
  William, 64
Passier, Wm., 118
Patrick, Hiram, 46
  Jordan J., 46
Patrum, Francis, 120
Patterson, A. D., 36
  Immanuel, 68
  Isaac, 92
  John, 76, 132
  Joseph R., 26
  Noah S., 10
  Samuel F., 14
  Samuel R., 28
  William, 44
Patton, Jesse H., 150
  Reason, 6
Paxton, Alexander, 46
  James, 36, 48

Payne, Cyrus M., 84
  Hiram, 4
  W. L., 176
  William L., 18
  Wm. P., 122
Peak, Hezekiah, 134
  Jackson, 84
  Jefferson, 4
  Joseph, 6
  Joseph H., 134
  William L., 134
Pearce, Ben Franklin, 8
Peark, Joseph, 118
Pearman, Granville L., 64
Pearson, Alonzo, 60
Peavler, Leonard, 164
Peddicord, James, 152
Pemberton, R. H., 76
Pence, William, 142
Penell, William J., 160
Penn, Nimrod, 128
Pennabaker, C. D., 12
  Thomas, 14
Pennebaker, Chas. D., 122
Pennington, A., 18
  Marcus, 156
Pense, Isaac M., 42
Peouler, Leonard, 56
Percell, William, 54
Percival, William E., 94
Percy, Charles D., 66
Pergram, Robert C., 104
Perkins, George, 36
  Green, 46
  Henry, 106
  Joseph, 20
  Pleasant, 128
  William, 2
  Willis, 122
Perrin, William J., 12
  William W., 32
Perry, Arthur H. W., 154
  Berry, 34
  Daniel, 160
  Miles J., 148
  William, 160
Perteete, Ezekiel, 132
Peter, Armenius, 144
Peters, Harrison, 142
  Jesse, 144
  Walter L., 14
Peterson, Charles, 120
  Joseph, 60
Petit, Harrison, 70
Pettit, Charles B., 84
Petty, Elijah, 96

  James, 36
  Jefferson, 16
  John S., 34
Pfalger, Jacob, 66
Pfister, Heinrich, 66
Phelphs, Edward H., 96
Phelps, James, 130
  Thomas, 146
Philips, G. A., 176
Phillips, Benjamin T., 164
  Gilbert A., 60
  Hiram, 68
  Isaac J., 24
  Jerome, 78
  John R., 60
  William, 156
Philpot, William H., 50
Pickering, Erastus R., 136
Pickett, Austin, 114
Piden, David R., 136
Pierce, George, 104
  James M., 138
  William, 104
Piercy, Henry, 78
Piersall, Hezekiah, 52
  Washington, 52
Pierse, William W., 128
Pifer, Nathan M., 112
Pinkston, T., 176
  Thomas, 60
Piper, Ignatz, 68
Pipper, William O., 88
Pirtle, Samuel S., 134
Pittman, George W., 82
Pitts, Robert G., 146
Platt, Thomas W., 144
Poe, John F., 168
Poindexter, James M., 24
  John A., 154
  L., 16
Poixnett, John S., 76
Pollard, J. C., 76
Pollock, Robert, 50
Polly, Thomas J., 78
Polsgrove, Almus W., 32
  John, 32
Pomeroy, James, 10
Pool, Allen, 136
Poor, Standish F., 60
Pope, John D., 68
  John M., 10
  William A., 98
  William W., 144
  Wm. A., 12
Porch, Henry S., 142
Porter, John, 96

  Joseph, 16
  Samuel W., 64
  William H., 134
Posey, John, 56
Postwood, Dudley, 42
Poteete, Charles, 114
Potter, Wm. H., 42
Pottinger, Samuel, 124
Powel, Stephen, 158
Powell, Anderson, 106
  Ansel D., 100
  Benjamin, 102, 122
  Edley, 122
  Geo. M., 16
  Hilrah, 156
  James, 86
  Jos. W., 50
  Madison, 80
  Thomas R., 24
  William R., 46
Power, Jackson, 104
  John, 168
  John T., 104
  William, 168
Powers, Jacob H., 78
  Samuel L., 96
Prater, Parker B., 110
  Parker V., 88
Prather, James S., 60
Pravitt, William, 20
Preast, James M., 134
Prentis, Nath. S., 24
Presnall, Meshack, 124
Preston, Mordecai, 90
  Otho, 122
  Wm., 116
Prewitt, John N., 38
  Wm. H., 38
Price, Daniel G., 158
  Jackson, 84
  James, 12
  James T., 158
  John, 124
  John C., 128
  John M., 148
  Johnson, 2
  Jonathan, 118
  Noah, 142
  W. H., 8
Prime, William A., 136
Pritchard, James A., 94
Privett, John H., 122
Procter, Francis M., 130
  Rowan P., 132
Proctor, Thomas J., 42
  Wm. G., 60

195

**Prolzman**, E., 26
**Proudfit**, James, 68
**Prouhet**, Alexander, 70
**Pruette**, John, 158
**Pruity**, Joseph B., 138
**Pullin**, Wm. P., 146
**Pumphrey**, Andrew, 142
    Andrew J., 150
**Purdom**, Benjamin F., 48
**Purnell**, Joshua, 48
**Pyth**, Holcomb, 166

# Q

**Queen**, Matthew, 92
**Quertermons**, David B., 64
**Quick**, William, 168
**Quigley**, Patrick, 6
**Quinn**, John, 96
    Robert, 56
**Quinton**, John, 142
**Quissenbury**, Roger T., 150

# R

**Rachford**, Henry, 126
**Radcliff**, William, 24
**Ragen**, Wm., 24
**Ragland**, Hugh, 148
    Nathaniel J. T., 112
**Ragle**, John A., 160
**Raidon**, Geo., 106
**Raily**, John C., 18
**Rainey**, Elihu L., 102
    John W., 148
    Robert, 148
**Rains**, Jerry D., 38
    William, 38
**Raley**, John J., 164
**Ralls**, Daniel, 104
    Eli, 152
**Ralston**, Lewis V., 132
**Ramer**, Lewis, 94
**Ramey**, J. H., 4
    N., 26
**Ramsey**, H. K., 162
**Randall**, Alexander, 38
    James S., 114
**Rankins**, Edmond M., 98
**Ransom**, William S., 96
**Rash**, John, 44
**Rasseau**, David Q., 68
**Ratcliffe**, James, 156
    Reason P., 154
    Robert, 174
    W. D., 174
**Ravanaugh**, Geo. W., 36

**Raveity**, James, 72
**Ray**, Absalom, 164
    Benjamin, 138
    James, 62
    Patrick, 72
    Shelby A., 116, 118
**Raymond**, J. B., 76
**Razor**, Henry, 18
**Read**, Richard D., 80
**Reading**, John B., 18
**Reagan**, William H., 168
**Reames**, Obediah, 68
**Reaves**, William, 154
**Reddish**, John H., 8
**Redfield**, Lyman, 22
**Redman**, John, 52
    Loyd H., 24
    S. G. P., 78
    Thomas, 126
**Redmond**, Washington, 160
**Reed**, A. B., 8
    Elijah, 90
    George W., 34
    James, 162
    James N., 32
    Phelps, 168
    Winkfield, 164
**Reep**, Farmerkey, 160
    Pleasantfield, 160
**Rees**, Lewis M., 48
**Reeves**, George W. L., 132
**Rehbein**, Nicolaus, 74
**Reichert**, Franz, 66
**Reid**, James, 158
    Joseph, 100
    Samuel P., 98
    Tilly W., 60
    William T., 52
**Reigler**, Leonard, 154
**Remme**, John H., 66
**Renboldt**, Henry, 74
**Renfro**, Moses J., 46
    Samuel H., 2
**Renney**, George M., 12
**Renz**, Peter, 66
**Repp**, Farmer K., 168
    Pleaston F., 168
**Resor**, Charles W., 6
    N. B., 6
**Ress**, Conrad, 66
**Reubeling**, Henry, 74
**Reubrecht**, Richard, 72
**Reynolds**, Alexander, 30
    George, 62
    John, 160

    Joseph, 160
    Nicholas S., 46
    Rolly W., 148
    William P., 36
    Wm., 106
**Rham**, Wm., 50
**Rhea**, Horace P., 20
    John, 64
**Rhey**, John, 154
**Rhineland**, John, 40
**Rhodes**, John P., 80
**Rhuark**, Elza, 164
    Wm., 164
**Rice**, George W., 54
    John, 54
    W. M., 76
    William T., 150
    Wm. B., 18
**Richard**, John, 64
**Richards**, James D., 94
    John, 36
    John C., 94
**Richardson**, Daniel, 102
    James, 92, 114
    James E., 156
    John, 24, 62, 94
    Mathew, 52
    Richard, 62, 122, 134
    Robert C., 24
    W., 160
**Richey**, Joseph M., 10
    William B., 10
**Richmon**, Howard, 30
**Richmond**, James, 174
    James H., 134
    Sylvester R., 136
**Rickerson**, John W., 116
**Rickert**, Andreas, 66
**Ricketts**, Benjamin, 98
    John, 88
    Samuel A., 124
**Riddle**, Adam, 102
    William, 58, 72
**Ridgway**, William, 14
**Riesemberger**, Nicolaus, 74
**Rieves**, W., 176
**Rigg**, Samuel, 26
**Riggs**, Caleb F., 152
**Rigney**, Ferdinand, 164
**Riley**, George E., 132
    Jacob, 48
    James, 164
    Owen, 160
    Thomas, 48
**Riney**, Edward G., 164

**Ringo**, James D., 88
    Robert, 88
    Thomas L., 88
    William M., 88
**Rinkeler**, Franz, 66
**Risen**, Josiah, 152
**Ritchey**, John W., 98
    Jos. M., 100
**Ritten**, James, 80
**Roach**, Frederick, 36
    James P., 130
    Philip, 70
**Roan**, F. A., 14
**Roark**, Elzy, 72
    John, 158
    Lewis A., 160
    Saul, 158
**Robards**, Joseph, 80
    Squires S., 60
**Robb**, Joseph, 8
    W. N., 8
**Robbins**, Christopher C., 126
    David D., 130
**Roberson**, Jacob C., 44
**Roberts**, Andrew J., 44
    Francis, 76
    James T., 164
    John P., 130
    John T., 6
    Joseph G., 116
    Lewis, 80
    Merrill, 20
    Montgomery, 142
    Samuel E., 28
    William G., 128
**Robertson**, Arch, 80
    James, 138
    Joseph S., 122
    Louis, 148
    Uriah, 148
    William, 32, 128
**Robeson**, Uriah, 144
**Robinette**, Moses, 64
**Robinson**, Benjamin, 34, 110
    Gabriel, 78
    George, 2
    Harrison K., 104
    Henry, 40
    Hugh L., 160
    Lawrence B., 90
    Marcellus M., 94
    Stephen, 160
    Thornton, 138
    William, 2, 92, 96

Robison, William, 60
Roby, William O., 126
Rock, John B., 88
Rodabaugh, Martin, 42
Rodebaugh, Martin, 40
Rodgers, David P., 10
   Isaac, 18
Roe, Jackson, 88
Rogers, Cyrenius, 92
   David, 16
   Edward C., 54
   Geo. A., 164
   George, 78, 120
   Henry, 164
   Isaac H., 102
   J., 174
   Jason, 58
   John W., 122
   Joseph, 120
   Ransom, 164
   Samuel E., 24
   William, 114, 134
   Wm., 122
Rogerson, John, 68
Rollins, Johnson, 16
Rolston, George J., 148
   John, 148
   William F., 146
Roney, Hercules, 76
   John M., 126
Ronner, Greenberry, 128
   James L., 128
Rooney, James B., 126
Rose, George, 164
   John W., 128
   William S., 12, 154
Rosenburg, Henry, 4
Roshier, George A., 72
Rosing, Anthony W., 74
Ross, David, 10
   Henry, 122
   James, 18, 144
   John, 18, 122
   John W., 62
   Joseph, 78
   Levi, 150
   Ludwell, 108
   Reubin, 54
Rosseau, James A., 142
Rossen, Benjamin, 90
Rossiter, P. P., 16
Roswell, John C., 110
Roundtree, James W., 148
   William, 98
   Wm. H., 148
Rourge, John O., 168

Rousseau, Lawrence, 142
Rouston, Ephraim, 20
Rout, Isham T., 10
Rowham, Daniel C., 118
Rowland, Robert, 102
Rowlin, J. M., 18
Royse, John W., 98
Rucker, Ezekiel, 92
   Wm. C., 122
Ruckstool, John, 18
Ruddle, William H., 94
Rudert, Frederick, 74
Rue, Charles H., 14
Rugg, Charles, 50
Rumsey, Thomas, 16
Runner, Samuel H., 126
Runyon, Daniel, 86
   George W., 26
Rush, David, 74
   William P. D., 132
Russell, Alexander, 168
   George, 38, 174
   James, 72
   Joseph, 122
   Newell, 168
   Robert, 14
   William, 70
   William E., 120
Rutherford, Austin, 62
   John, 168
Ryan, Thomas, 108

# S

Sacre, Edmund, 92
   John, 44
Sadler, Edward, 142
Sage, Jeremiah, 76
   Jesse, 76
St. Clair, Archibald, 118
   Martin, 50
Sale, Elijah D., 128
   Josiah B., 134
Salirro, Clement C., 138
Sammis, Jno. S., 8
Sample, John L., 154
   Thomas H., 108
Samples, Samuel, 164
Samuel, Arthur R., 84
   Wm. L., 106
Samuels, Preston F., 122
Sandbatch, Isaac, 40
Sanderfur, Andrew J., 164
Sanders, James, 128
   John, 8
   Lewis, 6
   Nathaniel L., 6

Taliaferro, 6
   William C., 30
Sandford, Granville, 98
Sandifer, James, 38
   Robert S., 46
Sanford, M. H., 6
   Reuben, 106
   Robert, 6
Sansberry, Giles, 120
Sapers, John, 168
Sappington, James W., 146
Sartain, George F., 2
Sass, Conrad, 66
Satterwhite, Charles, 54
   William M., 128
   William R., 32
Sauer, Henry, 74
Saunders, Benedict J., 118
   Frank, 60
   George W., 44
   John A., 44
Sayre, Adolphus, 6
Scallen, Matthew R., 132
Scandreth, R. M., 6
Scandrett, Thos. B., 6
Scatten, William, 132
Scearce, Albert, 16
   Simeon, 16
Schaefer, Christian, 66
   Thos., 42
Schell, Francis M., 60
Schenck, John W., 88
   Richard, 88
Schenke, William, 66
Schmidt, Michael, 74
   Nicolaus, 74
Schooley, James, 22
Schools, Joseph, 156
Schroader, Lafayette, 156
Schuling, John, 146
Schweitser, Benjamin, 110
Schweitzer, Joseph, 66
Schwenk, Charles, 66
Scott, Columbus M., 138
   Cyrus A., 136
   David, 52
   David R., 18
   James M., 98
   Joab W., 92
   John, 18, 80, 174
   John A., 8
   John B., 164
   Joseph, 2
   Norbourn B., 26
   Samuel, 108
   Thomas W., 58

   William, 138
   William J., 134
Scrugg, William R., 168
Scruggs, Chesley G., 156
Seabough, John, 60
Searcy, Francis M., 20
   John, 16
Sears, Francis, 114
   Peter, 114
Searsey, Beverly, 34
   Geroge, 34
   Thos., 34
Seay, James L., 144
Sebastian, Samuel, 92
Sebree, Muskin, 92
See, John H., 108
Seeman, Cornelius, 66
Seibman, John A., 118
Seifers, James, 126
Sellers, John, 2
Sells, Charles, 140
Semonis, John, 66
Servant, Richard, 38
Sesfield, Stephen, 34
Sessel, Henry, 24
Settles, John, 56
Sexton, James W., 122
   John N., 122
   Preston, 114
Shackelford, James, 48
   John G., 48
   Zackariah, 90
Shackleford, George, 144
   James M., 142
Shade, John, 64
Shaefer, Harrison L., 92
Shaeffer, Christian, 156
Shafar, Hugh S., 62
Shanklin, John B., 126
Shanks, George T., 160
   Thomas, 46
Shannon, Charles, 40
   Geo. M., 8
Sharp, George, 12, 174
   Henry, 108
   Josiah, 70
   William, 56, 108
Sharpe, Ezekiel K., 44
   German B., 80
Sharron, James H., 86
Shaver, Peter A., 168
Shaw, Washington, 140
   William, 24
   William T., 54
Shawhan, John, 10
Shearer, Zachariah, 22

Sheets, James W., 32
　Saml., 32
Sheffield, Richard H., 156
Shelburn, Pascal R., 156
Shelton, Wiley A., 82
Shepherd, Ansel P., 102
　John B., 58, 102
Shepley, Joseph, 140
Sheppard, Charles J., 26
　David, 26
　Isaac, 26
Sherban, Enoch, 156
Sheriaden, Robert, 32
Sheridan, Alexander, 92
Sheriden, James, 64
Sherley, W. M., 14
Sherrin, James, 32
Shield, William, 146
Shields, Jas. L., 48
　John, 92
　Robert, 108
Shifflett, Clifton, 22
　John, 22
Shiplar, John W., 168
　Stephenson, 168
Shipley, Thomas W., 4
Shipman, Samuel, 134
Shipp, David R., 84
Shirley, Ezekiel A., 156
Shlensky, Henry, 74
Shoemate, Wm. H., 78
Shonty, Greenberry, 128
Short, Pelly, 102
　Willaim, 38
Shouse, Leonard, 34
Shrader, Herman, 160
　John A., 12
Shroeder, Conrad, 72
　Frederick, 72
Shryock, Andrew J., 114
Shuck, David, 128
Shuckardt, Francis, 74
Shultz, Henry, 74
　John H., 94
Shurgin, B. H., 52
Sibley, T. S., 76
Sidbottom, Norman, 32
Siegel, Carl, 66
Sigler, George H., 62
Silver, Amos, 50
Silvers, Westley, 142
Silvy, Samuel, 36
Simerall, John T., 82
Simmers, Wm. P., 80
Simmonds, A. M. C., 30
Simmons, Harrison G., 60

Simms, Andrew J., 122
　Otho P., 82, 116
　W. E., 106
　William, 98, 168
　Wm., 80
Simon, James, 58
Simons, Geo., 48
Simpson, Elias W., 144
　Jas., 22
　John F., 80
　John H., 24
　Richard B., 22
　Thomas A., 118
　Winslow C., 120
Sims, G. W., 14
　Joseph C., 148
Singleton, George W., 166
　Philip, 158
Sinithart, John, 144
Siteason, Geo., 70
Skeen, John, 122
Skelton, Hiram W., 16
　John, 28
Skidmore, John, 68
Skillman, Isaac H., 106
Skyler, William, 32
Slack, John B., 30
Slaughter, Edwin R., 126
　John, 168
　P. J., 14
　Philip I., 126
Slepp, George, 24
Sly, Zebedee, 112
Smallwood, W., 160
　Wm., 100
Smart, George W., 96
　Joseph, 98
　Thomas, 176
Smedley, Charles C., 54
Smiley, Grandison, 2
　James J., 2
Smith, Aaron, 168
　Albert G., 128
　Augustus, 68
　Benjamin, 70
　Cyrus, 122
　Edward K., 144
　Francis, 12
　G. Clay, 20
　George W., 122
　Henry, 102
　Horace, 4
　Hugh, 86
　Isaac, 26, 140
　Isham O., 112
　J. C. P., 14

　J. R., 76
　Jabel, 160
　Jackson J., 110
　James, 72
　James M., 158
　James R., 144
　John, 72, 86, 156, 162, 164
　John C., 122
　John I., 30
　John L., 128
　John R., 84
　John W., 30, 86
　Josiah, 138
　Madison M., 64
　Minor T., 152
　Nicholas, 148
　Peter, 148
　Philip, 78, 164
　R. D., 20
　Robert, 148
　Robert C., 122
　Sidney, Sir, 78
　Stephen D., 126
　Thomas J., 116
　V. B., 4
　Wesley, 12
　William, 24, 92, 102
　William L., 42
　Wm. H., 18
　Wm. A., 42
　Wm., 48
　Wm. T., 122
　Zackariah, 114
Smyth, W. H., 78
Snail, James B., 28
Snediger, James, 104
Sneed, Benjamin, 38
　P. D., 76
Snelling, John A., 8
Snider, Geo. W., 24
　George, 52
Snim, Thomas, 90
Snodgrass, Jasper, 12
　Seneca, 142
　William, 10
Snow, Hercules, 42
Snyder, Edley B., 134
　Henry, 160
　James, 94
　James S., 94
　John, 162
　John W., 130
　Peter, 152
　Thomas, 76
　William D., 136

Soerell, John, 126
Sohan, John, 92
Somers, Andrew, 64
　John, 16
Sommer, Julius, 160
Sonsby, Archibald, 98
Sorrell, Augustus, 104
Southerland, Charles, 2
Southern, Simon F., 30
　Stephen, 118
Southworth, George T., 168
Soward, J. J., 8
Sowerby, George, 136
Spalding, James O., 42
　John A., 164
Spaulding, Joseph, 162
Speigle, W. R., 174
Spence, William, 104
Spencer, B. M., 6
　William H., 30
　Wm. H., 16
Spiggle, Will, 84
Spindler, Andy, 80
Spires, Andrew, 108
Spirs, Leopold, 74
Spitznagel, Jacob, 68
Spratt, Andrew G., 46
　Baylor I., 138
　John, 16
Spray, Jefferson, 134
Spriker, Joseph, 56
Springer, Charles P., 54
　James, 174
　S. J., 12
Spurrier, Henry C., 58
　Tevis, 62
Squires, John S., 120
Sraikart, George, 22
Srivers, John P., 84
Stackpole, Edward, 102
Stafford, John, 24, 62
Stagner, Jas. C., 22
Staltman, J. A., 14
Stamper, Geo. R., 156
Stancer, Henry, 78
Stanfield, Joseph, 62
Stanford, Wm. M., 30
Stanley, Harrison, 84
　Robert, 40
　Wm., 40
Stanton, Gabriel, 86
Stapp, W. W., 8
Starbuck, Thaddeus B., 46
Starks, A., 76
Starnes, Robert, 132

**Staten**, Jackson, 106
**Stattman**, William, 42
**Staucer**, Henry, 156
**Steele**, George, 112
    John R., 116
    R. J., 176
    Tillman H., 156
**Steigler**, Jacob, 156
**Stephens**, Alfred P., 98
    John, 82
    Thomas, 64
    William N., 126
**Stephenson**, John, 144
**Steuart**, Charles, 126
**Stevens**, John W., 92
    Walker, 32
    William, 138
**Stevenson**, Andrew M., 16
    Elias E., 132
    John C., 132
    Sam'l G., 60
**Stewart**, B. F., 78
    Benjamin, 118
    Enoch, 128
    George B., 142
    Henry, 98
    James, 78, 176
    John, 128
    Michael, 48
    Milton, 148
    Thomas, 48
**Still**, Adam C., 112
    Wymer, 114
**Stillwell**, John, 122
**Stilly**, Samuel, 10
**Stilwell**, John, 128
**Stiners**, John M., 84
**Stinsar**, James, 104
**Stinson**, A., 176
**Stith**, Abner H., 30
    Thomas, 84
**Stitt**, John W., 80
    William J., 96
**Stivers**, Jeremiah, 20
    John B., 108
    Joseph W., 108
**Stockton**, David R., 110
    Hoblay, 88
    W. C., 8
**Stogsdill**, John, 142
**Stokely**, Jacob, 108
**Stolger**, Marx, 66
**Stollman**, J. O., 174
**Stone**, Berry B., 100
    E. M., 80
    Erastus, 70

    Henry F., 140
    James C., 20
    John T., 132
**Storg**, George J., 66
**Storm**, Ira, 152
**Storms**, James A. B., 22
**Storts**, Charles, 130
    Chas. H., 110
**Stotsworth**, John, 160
**Stotts**, George W., 122
    John, 122
**Stowers**, David L., 12
**Stoy**, David C., 60
**Strader**, George W., 30
**Strang**, Thomas, 146
**Stratton**, D. P. H., 76
    Peter A., 156
**Strawn**, Edward J., 92
**Stringer**, Charles, 142
    Cyremus W., 142
    William, 46
**Stringfellow**, Chris F., 156
**Strong**, John, 102
**Stroph**, Jos., 48
**Stroud**, Saml. M. D., 38
**Struthmann**, Henry, 68
**Stuard**, Ranson, 160
**Stuart**, John W., 152
**Stubbs**, Robert J., 84
**Stuck**, Matthias, 38
**Stump**, Frederick C., 130
**Stumpf**, John, 68
**Stumpfs**, John, 112
**Sturgeon**, Willis, 148
**Sublett**, Jerred, 136
**Suddeth**, James W., 38
**Suddith**, W. H., 8
**Sudduth**, James E., 126
**Sudlow**, William, 76
**Suel**, James, 2
**Suggeth**, Samuel, 86
**Suiter**, Johnson M., 86
**Sullavan**, John R., 84
**Sullinger**, James, 128
**Sullivan**, James, 70, 112
    Josiah, 114
    Lasser, 114
    Patrick, 16
    William, 88, 116, 174
    Wm., 80
**Summers**, James G., 98
    Milton, 94
    Samuel C., 30
    T. T., 80
**Sumner**, George, 16
**Sumpter**, Andrew J., 164

**Sumrall**, John T., 88
**Surber**, Galen C., 142
**Surratt**, William P., 132
**Suter**, Andrew T., 154
**Sutherland**, Frederick, 152
    Geo. S., 150
    James, 152
**Suttles**, Andrew J., 160
    Willis, 116
**Sutton**, Alexander, 164
    Armsted, 164
    John, 30
    Nicholas, 88
    Wm., 48
**Swails**, William A., 130
**Swan**, Commodore, 78
    Thomas, 38
**Swartz**, Philip, 108
**Sweany**, Thomas A., 30
**Sweeny**, Joseph J., 64
**Sweet**, Samuel, 86
**Swenk**, Alexander, 24
**Swigert**, John, 6
**Swinea**, Stephen, 150
**Swinney**, D. G., 80
    Daniel B. F., 142
    Edmund, 62
    Jos., 80
**Switser**, John, 44
**Sydnor**, Anthony, 30
**Syres**, John, 34
    Joseph, 34
    Thomas, 34

# T

**Tacket**, Charles, 174
**Tagan**, Joseph, 128
**Tague**, Jacob, 170
**Talbot**, Horatio, 108
**Talbott**, John, 126
    Lyttleton, 126
    Presley, 116
**Tally**, Reubin, 56
**Tanner**, Benjamin, 132
    Benjamin F., 134
    William D., 132
**Tarter**, Alvadas, 142
    Caleb, 142
    James, 150
**Tate**, George W., 152
**Taulbee**, Wm. H., 90
**Taylor**, Creed, 156
    Geo. W., 156
    George A., 76
    Harrison M., 22
    Henry, 34

    J. W., 76
    Jackson M., 24
    James D., 32, 88
    James M., 24, 28
    James T., 106
    James W., 60
    Jarvis, 142
    Jas., 164
    Jesse, 160
    John, 34
    John H., 50
    John R., 42
    John W., 110
    Levi, 30
    Lewis, 60
    R. Wolfe, 74
    Robert, 18
    Thomas H., 82, 112
    W. J., 76
    W., 176
**Tayman**, Elisha G., 142
**Teasley**, Presley D., 110
    Wm., 110
**Teater**, Stephen F., 4
**Tegner**, John W., 132
**Temple**, Philip G., 42
**Templeman**, Wm., 106
**Tempy**, Christopher, 26
**Terrell**, James W., 122
    Paul W., 156
**Terrill**, Henry B., 2
    Uriah, 62
**Terry**, John T., 108
    Michael, 118
**Thacker**, Arthur, 36
    James, 142
**Thatcher**, John P., 112
**Thawsen**, John, 86
**Theobald**, G. P., 10
**Theobold**, Griffin, 86
**Thomas**, Alexander, 40
    Benedict, 164
    George W., 156
    Henry C., 100
    James, 130
    John, 136
    Joseph, 48
    Jourdan, 108
    Robert F., 52
    Ruban, 144
    Samuel, 152
    W., 174
    William, 26
    William A., 166
    Wm. H., 12
    Wm. M., 42

**Thomasson**, Allen, 110
**Thompson**, Alexander, 118
  C. B., 14
  David, 156
  Elijah, 164
  Geo. H., 164
  George R., 94
  Green B., 164
  Hilory M., 164
  James, 110, 164
  James A., 60
  James M., 110
  Jas. H., 164
  Jeroam A., 144
  John, 46, 160
  John H., 108
  John T., 44
  John W., 134
  Joseph, 108, 118
  McCalla, 10
  Manlius V., 82
  Philip B., 54
  Rufus L., 132
  Thomas, 68
  Thomas A., 104
  William, 70, 144, 152
  Wm. H., 110
  Wm. A., 110
  Wm. F., 110
**Thomson**, Lewis P., 84
**Thoreau**, Eva, 54
**Thorn**, John, 6
**Thornhill**, Henry, 144
**Thornton**, George, 16
  James, 16
  James B., 2
  Jos. J., 92
  Joseph, 24
**Thorpe**, James H., 170
**Threldkell**, Alvey C., 34
**Thurman**, John J., 112
**Thwaits**, Ezekiel, 26
  William, 26
**Tibon**, Theodore, 68
**Tilden**, William M., 80
**Tilford**, Edward A., 28
  Joseph, 14
  Robert B., 126
**Tilhart**, Philip, 62
**Tillett**, William, 102
**Tilley**, James B., 112
**Tincher**, Franklin, 104
**Tindle**, John, 34
**Tirk**, John, 158
**Titman**, Henry, 48
**Tod**, Samuel B., 158

**Todd**, David H., 92
  John, 60
  Samuel, 122
  Thomas, 110
  Thomas J., 28, 34
  William, 122
**Todlock**, James B., 168
**Tolbert**, Presly, 64
**Tolly**, William, 30
**Tome**, Jacob, 156
**Tomlin**, William N., 92
**Tomlinson**, John A., 52
**Tompkins**, John W., 36
  Robt. W., 58
**Toombs**, Jefferson, 126
**Toppass**, James, 18
**Tormy**, Thomas, 86
**Torrence**, W. M. G., 18
**Towles**, David T., 30
**Townsend**, Eli, 144
  Westley, 102
**Townson**, William, 144
**Trabue**, Robert P., 116, 120
**Tracey**, James, 132
**Tranch**, John N., 170
**Travis**, Charles, 134
**Traxale**, W., 176
**Traylor**, Greenbury, 88
**Treadway**, Elisha B., 100
**Tredway**, Edward E., 52
  Moses X., 52
**Treloar**, John, 80
**Trigg**, Ben, 14
**Trimble**, John, 12
**Triplett**, Benjamin F., 94
  F. F. C., 74
  Leroy, 62
**Trotter**, Charles L., 138
**Trough**, Peter, 38
**Trout**, Daniel B., 130
**Troxler**, Wm., 74
**True**, Claban H., 108
  Elijah, 108
**Truill**, John L., 112
**Truman**, James W., 168
**Trumbo**, Jacob F., 102
**Tucker**, George B., 62
  Isacher, 78
  Nelson B., 134
  Weston, 76
**Tuder**, Thomas H., 22
**Tuells**, Charles, 62
**Tuggles**, William, 56
**Tull**, Frederick, 30
  Lewis, 32

**Tullis**, Thomas, 168
**Tully**, Joshua C., 98
**Turk**, William C., 120
**Turnbull**, Henry, 106
**Turner**, George, 4
  Henry T., 30
  Milton, 118
  Thomas, 2
  William, 48
**Turney**, William, 56
**Turpin**, Smith, 102
  William F., 142
  William S., 140
**Turry**, W. H., 160
**Tuthill**, Charles, 40
**Tutt**, William, 44
  William R., 150
**Tuttle**, James A., 152
  John, 114
  Preston M. C., 96
**Twyman**, Allen H., 152
  Geo. R., 68
  William, 56
**Tyler**, Thomas A., 110
**Tyson**, John, 170

## U

**Udell**, Henry E., 92
**Ulrich**, John, 66
**Umstedholt**, John P., 88
**Underwood**, Eli, 30
  Geo., 176
**Updike**, Major, 32
**Utterback**, B., 8
  Benj., 108
**Utz**, George M., 94

## V

**Vail**, Jacob G., 80
**Vallandingham**, Geo., 86
**Vandergrift**, John, 160
**Vanderpool**, Isaac W., 102
  Jacob W., 100
**Vandiver**, John S., 42
**VanEvery**, Martin, 6
**Vanfleet**, John, 164
**Vanflute**, Henry, 38
**Vanhook**, John M., 10
  William H., 10
**Vanmetre**, William P., 122
**Vanse**, Peter, 76
**Varble**, Wm., 78
**Vardemon**, William, 48
**Varmoy**, William, 38
**Vaughan**, Fielding, 30
  John L., 30

**Vaughn**, Andrew J., 56
  Edmond, 36
  Edward M., 28
  Edward W., 2
  James R., 110
  Thomas, 4
**Vaught**, Stephen, 142
**Veach**, Andrew J., 112
**Veatch**, Absalom, 168
**Venable**, Joseph W., 112
**Verhines**, James, 132
**Vest**, Willis, 46
**Vetter**, John, 64
**Vettitoe**, James, 14
**Vice**, Isaac, 106
**Vickers**, Jackson, 168
**Vigus**, William T., 122
**Vinzant**, Jacob, 160
**Violett**, F. T., 6
**Vittitoe**, James, 174
  Samuel, 64
**Vogel**, Georg, 68
**Volz**, Joseph, 66
**Vories**, A. H., 6

## W

**Waddington**, Davis M., 138
  John B., 136
**Waddle**, Jacob, 148
**Wade**, Benjamin, 30
  David P., 48
  John E., 86
  Wm. P., 38
**Wait**, John, 28
**Wakeman**, W. H., 14
**Walden**, Joseph, 40
**Walker**, Alexander, 118
  David, 40
  Elzey C., 122
  George H., 52
  Jesse, 156
  John, 52, 56, 96
  John I., 6
  Silas G., 138
  W., 176
  William T., 86
**Wall**, John T., 10
**Wallace**, David, 44
  Edward, 38
  G. W., 18
  Samuel, 16, 30
  William, 52, 168
**Waller**, Amos J., 134
  James H., 10, 106
  Jesse J., 46

Walls, Armistead, 100
　Jesse, 48
　John, 46
Walt, Rufus, 78
Walter, Francis E., 10
Walters, Walter B., 148
Walton, Caleb, 56
　John W., 80
Ward, Campbell, 122
　Granville, 128
　Hugh, 78
　Joseph, 48, 134
　Lafayette, 42
　Legran R., 126
　Matthew, 156
　Pleasant P., 138
　Wm. F., 116
Ware, Jas. M., 48
　Nicholas, 18
Warford, George, 36
　James H., 10
　Nathaniel, 36
　Wm., 36
Warmeck, James A., 64
Warren, Alexander, 142
　Banson, 4
　C. Greenhalch, 22
　Charles, 112
　Henry C., 132
　Jael, 62
　Joseph, 34
Warrington, Urich, 42
Warwick, J., 176
Washburn, Isaac P., 132
Washington, W. L., 70
Waterbery, Abitha, 64
Waterfield, Tholbert, 64
Waters, Garland, 94
　Joseph, 168
　Thomas, 96
Watkins, Benjamin, 156
　Burrell, 98
　John, 18, 108
　Noah M., 136
　Samuel, 98
　Wm., 98
Watsnider, Ellison, 68
Watson, H., 76
　Henry, 122
　John, 60
　John W., 36, 76
　Riley W., 102
　Thomas J., 134
　Warren, 122
　Wm., 100
Watts, John, 94

　Jordan, 102
　Oscar F., 20
　William H., 56
Waugh, Thomas, 96
Way, Elias, 108
Wayman, Noble R., 96
Wayne, David, 110
Weaver, John, 118
Webb, Benjamin, 148
　James, 38, 110
　T. J., 176
　Thomas, 32
Webber, Simpson, 76
Weber, Peter, 66
Webster, Leslie C., 150
Weddle, Daniel, 142
Weedon, John, 134
Weeks, Jerome, 42
Wegnell, Samuel, 40
Weibel, Peter, 74
Weigart, A. B., 26
　Thomas, 24
　William, 26
Weighart, Andrew, 108
　Lorran, 108
Weiner, Peter, 52
Welch, James C., 18
　Sanford, 78
　William E., 88
Welker, Daniel, 138
Welkins, Henry, 108
Weller, David R., 126
　W. L., 78
Wellington, John, 48
Wells, Alfred, 104
　Baswell, 86
　Calvin, 114
　David, 148
　James, 114, 156
　John M., 142
　Julius C., 156
　Milton H., 68
　Mordecai, 88
　Oliver P., 104
　Richard, 64, 104, 118
　William, 62, 108
Welsh, Edgar, 148
　John, 64
　Thomas, 40
　W., 176
Werk, David, 42
　Griffith Jacob, 18
Werner, Anton, 66
Werst, George W., 42
West, Balser B., 140
Westbrook, Thomas H.,

　136
Westerfield, John A., 112
Wetherill, Richard, 168
Wheat, John P., 30
　William, 122
Wheatley, Elam, 168
　Mark, 140
　Richard, 144
Wheatly, John, 28, 56
Wheeler, Henry D., 98
　John H., 76
Whetmeyer, Jacob, 82
Whip, James W., 36
Whitaker, Julius, 94
　Walter C., 110
White, Albert, 14
　Alpheus, 42
　Aquilla, 102
　Benjamin, 138
　Edward P., 52
　Fielding W., 152
　Franklin, 22
　Hugh L., 158
　James, 38, 44, 132
　John, 10, 34
　Johnson, 90
　Joseph, 12
　Joshua, 140
　L. B., 58
　Levi, 78, 116
　Matthew C., 92
　Nathan, 16
　Nicholas A., 18
　Richard, 144
　Robert, 4, 80
　Thomas, 24
　William, 78, 146
　Zachariah, 14
Whitecraft, John E., 98
Whitefield, Edward, 164
Whitehead, William, 8, 40
Whiteley, Burr H., 128
　Joseph, 126
Whitesides, Wm. B., 164
Whitfield, James W., 164
Whitley, W. J., 160
Whitney, Richard P., 26
Whitten, C. P., 174
Whittington, Richard, 138
Whittle, John, 164
Whitton, Robert, 156
Wicker, David, 156
Wickersham, E., 28
Wickham, Robert, 42
Wickliffe, Charles, 154
　Charles A., 146

Wicks, Nathaniel, 92
Wiest, Friedrich, 74
Wiggins, James, 62
Wigginton, E. G., 60
　Elijah, 86
Wilbank, Edwin, 160
Wilburn, Francis G., 156
　Miles W., 156
Wilcox, George, 166
　John, 62
　Morrison D., 136
　Stephen T., 80
Wild, John, 66
Wiley, James, 138
　Robert M., 86
Wilhelm, Jacob, 148
Wilhoite, A. N., 76
Wilker, Daniel, 74
Wilkers, Parks, 62
Wilkerson, A., 8
　James, 52
　Stith, 164
　Thomas J., 22
　Turpin, 50
　Wyatt, 22
Wilkey, James, 80
Wilkinson, A., 174
Willard, George W., 60
Willett, Robert A., 126
William, John, 110
Williams, A., 76
　Alford, 22
　Alonzo, 60
　Bennet, 94
　Drury B., 104
　E. B., 28
　Edward, 64
　Ellison, 168
　Franklin, 18
　George, 44, 138
　George B., 142
　George W., 96, 156
　Henry, 10, 152
　James, 10, 32, 124, 160
　John, 30, 50, 96, 116,
　　128, 134, 146,
　　150, 168
　Joseph, 88, 108, 148
　L. C., 76
　Milton, 86
　Morrison, 156
　O. G., 76
　Peter, 50
　R., 176
　Reuben, 46
　Shadrack, 22

201

**Williams**, (cont.) Sydney M., 56
  W. M., 12
  W. W., 82
  William, 58, 100, 138
  William A., 152
  William C., 78
  William J., 92
  Zedekiah H., 52
**Williamson**, Alexander, 50
  E. G., 156
  John J., 112
  P. O. J., 4
  W., 8
  Wm., 50
**Willis**, Alfred, 174
  Edmond C., 44
  James H., 44
  John A., 42
  William T., 44
**Willock**, James, 30
  John, 30
**Willoughby**, Lewis, 100
  Malin, 54
**Wills**, Peter C., 30
**Willson**, Edward, 96
  Samuel, 94
  Stephen, 96
**Wilmot**, Samuel T., 24
**Wilson**, Benjamin, 142
  Edward, 48
  Eli C., 88, 110
  Franklin B., 22
  George H., 10
  Harrison, 128
  J., 8
  James, 40
  James A., 118
  Jas., 22
  John, 44
  John E., 148
  John T., 164
  Jonathan C., 12
  Lewis M., 108
  Michael C., 10
  Robert C., 132
  Thos., 90
  Washington, 148
  William, 168
  William A., 30
  Wm. S., 28
  Wm. W., 50
**Winbourne**, Andrew J., 128
**Winlock**, Robert S., 30
**Winningham**, Duffin, 92

**Winright**, John, 168
**Winsett**, Calvin, 124
**Winston**, Thos. M., 166
**Winter**, John C., 42
**Wise**, Charles, 130
  Charley, 112
  George, 110, 156
  Henderson, 36
**Wisecarver**, John, 26
**Wisely**, Robert, 62
**Withers**, Horace, 38
  Joseph H., 56
  William T., 54
**Witherspoon**, John L., 148
**Withington**, Samuel, 64
**Witt**, John D., 50
  John N., 94
  Wm. E., 100
**Woldridge**, Greenberry, 92
**Wolf**, Geo. W., 6
  Henry, 32
  William H., 6
**Wolfe**, Hervey, 86
**Womack**, John, 20
**Wood**, Allen, 78
  Allison M., 114
  Archibald, 16
  Burril, 108
  Isaiah, 40
  John, 86
  Peter, 18
  W. S., 8
  William L., 114
**Woodal**, John, 142
**Woodall**, William, 46
**Wooden**, William, 148
**Woodfin**, John, 156
**Wooding**, Samuel H., 28
**Woodruff**, Hiram, 156
  James, 24
  Jessee, 22
  Wm. E., 116
**Woods**, H. S., 174
  John B., 102
  Peyton, 50
  R. E., 14
  Thomas C., 56
  W. H., 14
  William, 18, 46
**Woodson**, Thomas D., 146
**Woodward**, Harvey, 146
**Woodworth**, Jas. O., 48
**Woodyard**, Henry W., 10
**Woolfalk**, E. H. T., 60
**Woolford**, Franklin L., 46
**Woolsey**, Richard, 150

**Worford**, John, 46
**Work**, David P., 6
**Worrel**, John, 152
**Worthen**, Osker B., 12
**Wray**, John G., 156
**Wright**, Calvin A., 104
  George, 80
  Harrison, 144
  Henry W., 22
  James, 152
  John G., 56
  John W., 170
  Malcolm, 70
  R. R., 18
  Robert, 128
  Thomas, 6, 104
  Washington, 134
  William, 126, 152
  William F., 126
**Wroataman**, W., 176
**Wrotmann**, Wm., 74
**Wyman**, Lewis, 108
**Wynne**, Thomas, 82
**Wysner**, Hiram, 160

## Y

**Yales**, Elijah, 164
**Yarbor**, Jackson, 24
**Yarbough**, Alfred, 104
**Yarbrough**, Harrison, 104
  Jackson, 104
**Yates**, James G., 148
  Oliver, 4
  Thompson, 4
  William, 164
**Yeck**, Wm., 118
**Yeiser**, James G., 38
**Yelton**, Isaac, 40
**Yewell**, John, 134
**Yilhart**, George, 18
**Youell**, Pinckney P., 94
**Young**, Alfred, 24, 114
  Franklin, 138
  Hezekiah, 160
  Hugh A., 102
  James, 108, 146
  James H., 144
  James T., 102, 106
  John, 164
  John J., 6
  Lewis, 82
  Mason, 54
  Matthew, 146
  Merriat, 34
  Nathan, 50
  Richard, 114

  Samuel, 114
  William, 86

## Z

**Zane**, Richard, 42
**Zeller**, John, 66
**Zimmerman**, 36
  Dillard, 88
  Jos., 160
**Zink**, John H., 160